LIBRARY OF NEW TESTAMENT STUDIES

302

formerly the Journal for the Study of the New Testament Supplement series

Editor
Mark Goodacre

The Message of Acts in Codex Bezae

A Comparison with the Alexandrian Tradition

VOLUME 2
Acts 6.1–12.25:
From Judaea and Samaria to the Church in Antioch

Josep Rius-Camps and
Jenny Read-Heimerdinger

t&t clark

NEW YORK • LONDON

Published by T&T Clark

A Continuum imprint

The Tower Building, 11 York Road, London SE1 7NX

80 Maiden Lane, Suite 704, New York, NY 10038

www.tandtclark.com

ISBN 0-567-04012-7 (hardback)

British Library Cataloguing-in-Publication Data
A catalogue record for this book is available from the British Library

Printed on acid-free paper in Great Britain by
Antony Rowe Ltd, Chippenham, Wiltshire

CONTENTS

PREFACE

This is the second volume of a four-part work comparing the message of Acts as it has been transmitted by Codex Bezae with that of the Alexandrian manuscripts, principally Codex Vaticanus. The first volume dealt with Acts 1.1–5.42, the chapters relating to the church in Jerusalem. We continue by looking at 6.1–12.25 which cover the early spread of the Gospel outside Jerusalem up to the founding of the church in Antioch. The approach adopted is the same as in the first volume – we treat the MSS as documents standing in their own right, and in examining every variant reading between them we not only compare the texts but, more especially, analyse the difference the readings make to the message conveyed by the texts. A difficulty arises in the present volume that will occur again in the final one, that of the pages missing from Codex Bezae. The text affected here spans nearly two chapters which contain two important narratives, both the baptism of the Ethiopian eunuch and also the conversion of Saul. For those verses we have only been able to compare the Vaticanus text with sporadic readings that differ from it in other witnesses, notably early versions. This point, along with a summary of other aspects of our approach, is discussed in the *General Introduction* to the present volume.

A number of readers of Volume 1 have asked for the complete Greek text of Codex Bezae to be provided. Unfortunately, restrictions on length make that impossible but we are preparing a separate edition of Acts that sets out in parallel columns the Greek texts of Codex Vaticanus and Codex Bezae, alongside the Latin text of Codex Bezae and an English translation. Meanwhile, F.H. Scrivener's edition of Codex Bezae is readily available.

A Small Research Grant was made available from the British Academy to Jenny Read-Heimerdinger specifically for the investigation of the context of early Judaism in Bezan readings of Acts 6–12, which is acknowledged with gratitude. We would also like to thank warmly Enric Muñarch for his expertise and assistance in preparing our work for publication, and the editorial staff at T&T Clark International for their invaluable help in preparing the final draft.

Josep Rius-Camps and Jenny Read-Heimerdinger

Bib	*Biblica*
CBQ	*Catholic Biblical Quarterly*
ExpT	*Expository Times*
FN	*Filología Neotestamentaria*
JBL	*Journal of Biblical Studies*
JSNT	*Journal for the Study of the New Testament*
JSNTSup	*Journal for the Study of the New Testament: Supplement Series*
JSOTSup	*Journal for the Study of the Old Testament: Supplement Series*
JTS	*Journal of Theological Studies*
NTS	*New Testament Studies*
RB	*Revue Biblique*
RCatT	*Revista Catalana de Teologia*
Rev. Sc. ph. th.	*Revue des Sciences philosophiques et théologiques*
SBL	*Society of Biblical Literature*
SE	*Studia Evangelica*
SNTS	*Studiorum Novi Testamenti Societas*
ZNW	*Zeitschrift für die neutestamentliche Wissenschaft*

ABBREVIATIONS OF REFERENCE WORKS

ABD — D.N. Freedman (ed.), *Anchor Bible Dictionary* (6 vols; New York: Doubleday, 1992).

Atlas of the Bible — J. Pritchard (ed.), *Atlas of the Bible* (London: HarperCollins, 2nd edn, 1989).

B-A-G — W. Bauer, *A Greek English Lexicon of the New Testament and Other Early Christian Literature* (ed. and trans. W.F. Arndt and F.W. Gingrich; Chicago: Chicago University Press, 1957).

B-D-B — F. Brown, S. Driver and C. Briggs, *Hebrew and English Lexicon* (Peabody, MA: Hendrickson Publishers Inc., repr. 2003).

B-D-R   F. Blass, A. Debrunner and F. Rehkopf, *Grammatik des neutestamentlichen Griechisch* (Göttingen: Vandenhoeck & Ruprecht, 15th edn, 1979).

Dictionary of Judaism
               J. Neusner, and W.S. Green (eds), *Dictionary of Judaism in the Biblical Period 450 BCE to 600 CE* (New York: Macmillan Reference Library, 1996).

Enc. Jud.   C. Roth (ed.), *Encyclopaedia Judaica* (16 vols; 3rd edn; Jerusalem: Ketev Publishing House, 1974).

EWNT   H. Balz and G. Schneider (eds), *Exegetisches Wörterbuch zum Neuen Testament* (Stuttgart: Verlag W. Kohlhammer GmbH, 1981.

IGNTP   The American and British Committees of the International Greek New Testament Project (eds), *The Gospel According to St. Luke*. Part I, Chapters 1–12; Part II, Chapters 13–28 (Oxford: Clarendon Press, 1984, 1987).

Jew. Enc.   I. Singer (ed.), *The Jewish Encyclopaedia* (12 vols; New York: KTAV Publishing House, 1901).

Jewish Study Bible
               A. Berlin and M.Z. Brettler (eds), *The Jewish Study Bible* (Jewish Publication Society; TANAKH Translation; Oxford: Oxford University Press, 2004).

Jewish Symbols
               E.R. Goodenough *Jewish Symbols in the Greco-Roman Period* (13 vols; New York: Pantheon Books, 1953–65).

L-S-J   H.G. Liddell, R.J. Scott and H.S. Jones, *A Greek-English Lexicon: A New Edition* (Oxford: Clarendon Press, 1940).

N-A^{27} B. Aland, K. Aland *et al.* (eds), *Novum Testamentum Graece* (Stuttgart: Deutsche Bibelgesellschaft, 27th edn, 1993).

UBS^4 B. Aland, K. Aland *et al.* (eds), *The Greek New Testament* (Stuttgart: Deutsche Bibelgesellschaft/United Bible Societies, 4th edn, 1993).

TEXT-CRITICAL SIGNS AND ABBREVIATIONS

In addition to the conventional signs and abbreviations adopted by N-A^{27}, the following are used:

cj.   conjectured reading
lac.   lacuna
MS, MSS   manuscript, manuscripts
vl, vll   variant reading, variant readings

After a manuscript letter or number, in superscript:

*	original hand
p.m.	first hand
s.m.	second hand
2, c	corrector
B, C, D…	capital letter assigned to successive correctors of D05, or to manuscripts of vg or sy
ms, mss	one or several manuscripts only

Principal manuscripts cited

ℵ01	Codex Sinaiticus
B03	Codex Vaticanus
D05	Codex Bezae: Greek pages
d05	Codex Bezae: Latin pages

In the first volume of the *The Message of Acts*, the reasons for comparing the narrative of Codex Bezae with that of the more familiar Alexandrian tradition were set out in the *General Introduction*,[1] along with an explanation of the basic tools and methods employed. For a full presentation, these pages should be consulted but for ease of reference a summary of the salient points is provided here, which also provides the opportunity for making some refinements to the earlier discussion. Two articles published in French that present the approach adopted in our work and the interpretative principles on which it is based may also be consulted.[2]

I. *Codex Bezae*

From a linguistic, literary and theological point of view, the Bezan text represents a version of Luke's writings that stands in its own right as a coherent and cohesive work. When it is read in this way, the interrelationship between the Gospel and Acts is evident, with theological concerns guiding the narrative more than historical or biographical ones. Furthermore, it also becomes apparent that the narrator is viewing the incidents he relates and the characters that participate in them from within the context of first-century Judaism, and is adopting a typically Jewish approach to theological debate. There is frequent evidence of a first-hand familiarity with the Jewish world in which the events unfold that is considerably less visible in the manuscripts of the Alexandrian tradition (AT). Our conclusion is that the Bezan text was written at a time when there were still people who had known Jesus and the first generations of his disciples, and who knew the difficulties they faced within Judaism; and that the AT arose from a revision of that writing, made in order to adapt the narrative of Acts for a Christian audience who were less familiar with the Jewish setting.

It has been becoming more common in recent years for work on Acts in its familiar Alexandrian form to be open to a range of interpretations, so that it is a less straightforward matter now than previously to affirm what the message of

---

1. J. Rius-Camps and J. Read-Heimerdinger, *The Message of Acts in Codex Bezae: A Comparison with the Alexandrian Tradition*, I . *Acts 1.1–5.42: Jerusalem* (JSNTSup, 257; London: T&T Clark International, 2004), pp. 1–44.

2. J. Read-Heimerdinger, 'Les Actes des Apôtres dans le Codex de Bèze: leur intérêt et leur valeur', in *Saint Luc, évangéliste et historien* (*Dossiers d'Archéologie* 279 [2002–3]), pp. 44–55; J. Rius-Camps, 'Une lecture différente de l'œuvre de Luc', in *idem*, pp. 56–63.

the AT actually is. In consequence, we endeavour to limit our comments on the AT to the less contentious points, concentrating on its differences with the Bezan text.

II. *Luke's Two-Volume Work*

In agreement with most scholars, we believe that the Gospel of Luke and the Acts of the Apostles are both the work of Luke; more specifically, though, we consider them to be two volumes of the same work that share a common purpose. On this understanding, the frequent echoes in Acts of the vocabulary, structure, characters and themes of the Gospel are not simply evidence of the same author's quirks of style or his preoccupations but are deliberate allusions to the Gospel that are designed to comment on the characters and events of the Acts narrative. The intention of the narrator is to present in the Gospel the sayings and deeds of Jesus as a model, against whom his disciples in Acts are measured as they strive to imitate the master and live out his teachings in their communities. The parallels between the two volumes are thus not always positive: they illustrate the difficulties experienced by the apostles, including Paul, in grasping the radical nature of Jesus' teaching and applying it to the traditional teachings and inter-pretations of the Jewish Scriptures with which they had so far been familiar.

III. *A Jewish Perspective*

The events narrated in Acts are set in the context of first-century Judaism, and in the text of Codex Bezae they are viewed through Jewish eyes, from within that context. The Bezan narrator situates the incidents he relates within the history of Israel, seeking out incidents in the Torah that they could be seen as re-enacting; likewise, he assimilates his characters with paradigmatic characters from the past. In this way, his work stands as a prophetic statement about the real meaning of the incidents that took place in the early Church. These are viewed as standing in the line of Jewish history and are interpreted in the context of earlier prophetic traditions, not just where prophecies are fulfilled but where they are turned upside down as well. It is in this latter respect that Luke in the Bezan text is, himself, most prophetic – when he interprets the Jewish hostility with which the disciples were confronted as the reversal of scriptural promises, to the extent that Israel is no longer a privileged people but an equal with all other nations. Despite the ready conclusion that such an attack on the Jews is the work of a Gentile Christian who altered the text so as to intensify the hostility of the Jews reported in Acts,[3] the way the crisis situations are addressed in the Bezan text is, in fact,

---

3.   This is, in a nutshell, the view proposed by E.J. Epp, *The Theological Tendency of Codex Bezae Cantabrigiensis in Acts* (Cambridge: Cambridge University Press, 1966), and adopted by many commentators. The two main difficulties with Epp's examination are that a) it does not examine the text of Codex Bezae systematically but only those passages that seem relevant to the theme of the theological tendency, and b) it supposes that hostility towards Jewish people or practices must express a Gentile point of view. The first problem is dealt with by considering the Bezan text as a

typically Jewish. It is not unlike the procedures adopted by Jesus or the prophets of the Jewish Scriptures themselves, who are at times virulent in their criticism of the Jews: they are forceful and direct in their attacks precisely because they have an insider's understanding of the Jewish people and care intensely about what happens to them, and are much more likely to be effective than an outsider in speaking to their own people. It is our contention that this insider understanding and concern is reflected in the narrative of the Bezan text of Luke-Acts, and is the basis for the relationship between Luke and Theophilus.

Underlying the message of the Bezan text is a basic principle concerning the Jewish understanding of life in Israel, namely that all of history is contained in the Torah: the work of the contemporary historian, in this case Luke, consists in bringing to light the ancient models that lie behind present events and that give them coherence and meaning. If his audience were Jewish, Luke could suppose that the biblical stories were already known and that it was sufficient to make isolated references to the model for the allusion to be clear. While he could do this by explicit quotation, it was more frequent in early Jewish literature to slip in a simple word or phrase from the text he had in mind as a means to identify it. Such words or phrases, taken from the scriptural form of the story as well as from later traditional forms, served as keys to the biblical paradigm.[4] These abound in the Bezan text of Acts and are discussed in the *Commentary* as they are detected, with the realization that a better knowledge of first-century Judaism would allow many more to be brought to light.

IV. *Theophilus*

In view of the strongly Jewish perspective of Acts in Codex Bezae, it is most probable that Theophilus was a sophisticated Jewish person with an intense interest in what he had witnessed taking place among the Jesus-believers. The High Priest of this name, third son of Annas and brother-in-law of Caiaphas (Jn 18.13), appointed by Agrippa I to serve between 37 and 41 CE, could have been that person.[5] As a Hellenistic Jew who had had close contact with the people and events of the early Church, it is plausible that he should have had questions about

---

whole text, standing in its own right; the second is corrected by taking into account the numerous and subtle references to Jewish teachings and traditions that are made from a Jewish perspective.

4. On oral tradition, see B. Barc, 'Le texte de la Torah a-t-il été récrit?', in M. Tardieu (ed.), *Les règles de l'interprétation* (Paris: Cerf, 1987), pp. 69–88; see also M. Fishbane, *Biblical Interpretation in Ancient Israel* (Oxford: Clarendon Press, 1987), pp. 281–91, where he discusses in some detail the interconnectedness of biblical texts in Jewish exegesis and sets out useful guidelines for recognizing intended exegetical links. J.L. Kugel presents detailed information on how scriptural traditions developed in different ways, see *Traditions of the Bible. A Guide to the Bible as it was at the Start of the Common Era* (Cambridge, MA.: Harvard University Press, 1998).

5. The case for Theophilus being the High Priest has been made by R. Anderson, 'À la recherche de Théophile', in *Saint Luc, évangéliste et historien* (*Dossiers d'Archéologie* 279 [2002–3]), pp. 64–71; see also R. Puigdollers i Noblom, 'Els grans sacerdots jueus des de l'època d'Herodes el Gran fins a la guerra jueva', *RCatT* 30 (2005), pp. 49–89 (67–69).

what he had seen and heard and that Luke should write to inform him about everything from a Jewish point of view. It is, meanwhile, also possible that the addressee of the AT was a Roman officer of high standing or some other eminent Gentile, but whether or not it was him that Luke wrote for is another question.

V. *Character Development*
An interpretative key for understanding Luke's purpose is the recognition that as the narrator he does not agree with everything his characters do or say. His attitude is not one of unmitigated approval. This is clear enough for the non-Christian characters, but it is also true of his 'heroes', including the apostles and even Paul. He is critical of them, especially in the early days when they were struggling to grasp the full extent of Jesus' teachings and to move away from the traditional Jewish teachings and expectations with which they had grown up. This critical presentation of the characters is more apparent in the Bezan text (though it can be glimpsed in the AT once it is known to be there) which, coupled with the way the narrator looks at his story with Jewish eyes, suggests that Bezan text dates from a time when the apostles had not yet become idealized and when it was still relevant to portray their struggle to change their mentality.

VI. *The Speeches*
One important consequence of the narrator's critical attitude to his protagonists is that the speeches of the believers, even the apostles and Paul, are not intended to represent the narrator's thought. Instead, they are a narrative device to express the thoughts and mentality of a given character at a certain point in time and, since even the followers of Jesus do not understand all of the master's teaching immediately or perfectly, there are inevitably contradictions between speeches of different speakers, or even the same speaker. The failure to recognize Luke's intention of presenting the divergent positions of the early Church leaders or of portraying their growth towards a mature understanding, is perhaps the chief reason why scholars come to such contrasting conclusions concerning Luke, for example on his view of Israel or even his own religious background.

VII. *Jerusalem*
Another interpretative key is the spelling of Jerusalem, which varies between the Hebrew-derived form Ἰερουσαλήμ, Ierousalem, and the Hellenistic form, Ἱερο-σόλυμα, Hierosoluma. In the Bezan text there is a regular pattern accord-ing to which Ierousalem is the term used when Luke refers to the holy city with the Temple and the associated religious authority, while Hierosoluma is a neutral term designating the city as a geographical location. The spelling of Jerusalem is thus a tool the narrator uses to evaluate the degree of spiritual attachment his characters experience to the traditional views and attitudes of Judaism. From Acts 6 onwards, he also uses it to distinguish between distinct communities of disciples living in Jerusalem and to highlight the conflicts existing between them.

VIII. *The Word of God/Word of the Lord*
A further device that operates in a similar way to the dual spelling of Jerusalem is the alternation of 'the word of God' (ὁ λόγος τοῦ θεοῦ) and 'the word of the Lord' (ὁ λόγος τοῦ κυρίου). These two phrases are not synonymous, at least not in the Bezan text: each has a discrete significance that allows the narrator to evaluate the progress of his characters. The 'word of God' is the earlier of the two phrases, the only 'word' proclaimed by Jesus in the Gospel (Lk. 5.1; 8.11, 15 D05; 8.21; 11.28), where it refers to familiar Jewish teaching but with the new focus of the kingdom of God (4.43) and pronounced with authority (4.32). In Acts, it is likewise the only term used up to Acts 6.7, to refer to the preaching of the apostles as the interpretation of the Scriptures about the Messiah – explaining how Jesus had fulfilled the ancient prophecies in terms of the people of Israel to whom they were originally spoken but without going beyond them to communicate the radically new teaching that he was equally for people outside Israel. That is expressed by 'the word of the Lord', Jesus' unique message which began to be spread once the seven Hellenist leaders had been appointed (6.7) with first, Stephen boldly imitating Jesus in challenging the attitude of the Jews to the Temple and the Law, and secondly, Philip taking the message of Jesus outside Jerusalem for the first time.

These devices Luke uses to express what he thinks of a person or situation could be thought of as a code that allows the narrator to express his opinion without intruding directly into the story. It is important, however, to see that it is not a code designed to conceal the author's meaning and thereby to restrict the accessibility of his text to an initiated few; rather, it is a code that opens up the sense of his text and gives it a dimension that is readily accessible to anyone who was familiar with methods of Jewish exegesis in the first century.

IX. *The Structure*
When the structure of Acts is compared with the rhetorical and poetical structures known in classical and biblical literature, it becomes apparent that the whole work, from the level of the book overall down to the level of individual sentences, is constructed to form a hierarchy of finely balanced patterns. At each level, a carefully planned framework organizes the narrative in arrangements that are frequently concentric or symmetrical, with the centre of the structure being the point that the narrator wants to highlight as the focus of that part of the story (not always the expected one!).[6] Although linguistic markers serve to indicate strong connections between them. The table below displays the structure identified for the second part of Acts (6.1–12.25), following the text of Codex Bezae where variant readings affect the structure.

---

6.   Two works of particular interest for an analysis of the structure are S. Bar-Efrat, *Narrative Art in the Bible* (Sheffield: Sheffield Academic Press, 1989; repr. T&T Clark International, 2004); J.W. Welch, *Chiasmus in Antiquity* (Hildesheim: Gerstenberg, 1981).

TABLE OF STRUCTURAL ANALYSIS

Part II

Sections	Sequences	Sub-sequences	Episodes	Scenes	Elements
I 6.1–8.1a	A 6.1-7				a b c / d \ c' b' a'
	A' 6.8–8.1a		A'-*A* 6.8-15		a b c ‖ c' b' a'
			A'-*B* 7.1-54		a / b \ a'
			A'-*A'* 7.55–8.1a		a b c ‖ c' b' a'
II 8.1b–11.26	A 8.1b-3				a b ‖ b' a'
	B 8.4–11.18	BA 8.4-40	BA-*A* 8.4-13		Intro. a–e ‖ a'–e'
			BA-*B* 8.14-24		a b c ‖ c' b' a'
			BA-*A'* 8.25-40		Intro. a–h ‖ h'–a'
		BB 9.1-30	BB-*A* 9.1-9		a–f ‖ f'–a'
			BB-*B* 9.10-19a		a b c d e ‖ e' d' c' b' a'
			BB-*A'* 9.19b-30	BB-*A'A* 9.19b-22	a b ‖ b' a'
				BB-*A'B* 9.23-25	a b ‖ b' a'
				BB-*A'A'* 9.26-30	a b c / d \ c' b' a'
		BA' 9.31–11.18	BA'-*A* 9.31-43	BA'-*AA* 9.31-35	Intro. a b / c \ b' a'
				BA'-*AA'* 9.36-43	a–f ‖ f'–a'

			BA'-BA 10.1-8	a b $\parallel$ b' a'
		BA'-B 10.1–11.1	BA'-BB 10.9-16	a b c d $\parallel$ d' c' b' a'
			BA'-BB' 10.17-23a	a b c $\parallel$ c' b' a'
			BA'-BA' 10.23b–11.1	a–g / h $\setminus$ g'–a'
		BA'-A' 11.2-18		Intro. a / b $\setminus$ a'
	A' 11.19-26b	A'-A 11.19-21		a b c
		A'-B 11.22-24		a b c
		A'-A' 11.25-26b		a b c
	Col. 11.26c			
III 11.27-30				a$_1$ a$_2$ / b$_1$ b$_2$ $\setminus$ a'$_1$ a'$_2$
IV 12.1-25	A 12.1-4			a b / c $\setminus$ b' a'
	B 12.5-17			a–m $\parallel$ a'–m'
	A' 12.18-23			a–e $\parallel$ e'–a'
	Col. 12.24-25			a $\parallel$ a'

X. *English Translation*

The aim of the English translation is to reflect the shades of meaning of the Greek text as closely as possible, especially where there are variant readings. This sometimes results in English that is less than stylish but in this case elegance has been sacrificed for the sake of communicating the differences in the Greek text.

XI. *The Critical Apparatus*

The critical apparatus displays the variant readings of Codex Vaticanus (B03) and Codex Bezae (D05), and lists the witnesses that support each of them. The readings of Codex Sinaiticus (ℵ01) are also displayed where they differ from those of Codex Vaticanus because of the importance of this MS as a witness to the AT. The abbreviations used to refer to MSS are those used by the Nestle-Aland 27th edition of the Greek New Testament. For versions and Church Fathers not cited by N-A[27], the abbreviations of Boismard and Lamouille's edition of Acts[7] have been adopted. In the discussion of readings in the *Critical Apparatus*, as in the *Commentary* proper, uncial MSS are referred to by their number and letter, but in the list of readings uncial MSS are cited by their letter alone in order to prevent the apparatus from becoming overcrowded.

In identifying the support for Codex Vaticanus and Codex Bezae respectively, the principal tools have been, as previously, the *Horizontal Line Synopsis* by Swanson[8] and the critical apparatus of Boismard and Lamouille, with note taken of errors and omissions. For the Old Latin version, use has been made of the database prepared by the Vetus Latina Institut in Beuron.[9] In the case of the folios missing from Codex Bezae (8.29b–10.14b, Greek ; 8.20b–10.4, Latin), Codex Vaticanus has been compared with other witnesses that from time to time attest a variant text, referred to as the 'Western' text. Since none vary as extensively or as consistently as does Codex Bezae, the nature of the comparison is somewhat different and the commentary, particularly on the conversion of Saul, has to work from the partial clues that have survived in other witnesses in an attempt to retrieve aspects of the Jewish context of the original narrative.

XII. *General Overview of the Second Volume*

The second part of the book of Acts narrates the growth of the Church and the spread of the gospel message beyond the confines of Jerusalem. The acceptance

---

7.   M.-É. Boismard and A. Lamouille, *Le texte occidental des Actes des Apôtres: Reconstitution et réhabilitation.* I. *Introduction et textes*; II. *Apparat Critique* (Paris: Éditions Recherche sur les Civilisations, 1984).

8.   R. Swanson, *New Testament Greek Manuscripts: Variant Readings Arranged in Horizontal Lines against Codex Vaticanus. The Acts of the Apostles* (Sheffield: Sheffield Academic Press, 1998).

9.   R. Gryson (dir. Vetus Latina Institut, Beuron), *Vetus Latina Database* (Brepols: Turnhout, 2002).

of Jesus by the Samaritans, the eunuch and the Gentiles in turn, is confirmed by the gift of the Holy Spirit to them. A division among the believers, merely hinted at in the first part of the book, becomes more openly apparent as the narrator's criticism of the apostles continues and a separate group of disciples emerges, the Hellenists. The principal issue on which disagreement turns is the continuation of Israel as the privileged people of God, with all that that implies – the importance of Jerusalem and the Temple, the significance of the twelve apostles, the fulfilment of the scriptural promises concerning the end times, the conditions for the entry of Gentiles into the people of God. The matter comes to a head in Acts 12 with Peter's final realization that God is bringing his people out of the old religious order and that the traditional expectations have been superseded.

The dominant theme of Acts 6–12 is the establishing of the church of Antioch as an assembly of believers in Jesus who are distinct from the Jerusalem church. The account of its formation is related in four steps:

I	6.1–8.1a	Constitution of the Hellenist group
II	8.1b–11.26	Gestation of the Church outside Jerusalem
III	11.27-30	Public manifestation of the Antioch church to Jerusalem
IV	12.1-23	Persecution/separation of the Church from Israel
Colophon	12.24-25	

These steps correspond to the four stages in the formation of the Jerusalem church narrated in Acts 1–5:[10]

I	1.15-26	Reconstitution of the 'Twelve'
II	2.1-47	Gestation of the Jerusalem church
III	3.1–4.35	Public manifestation of the Church to Israel
IV	4.36–5.42	Persecution/separation of the Church from the Temple
Colophon	6.7	

The final section (IV) of each part is brought to a close with a colophon summarizing the growth and expansion of the Church; in the case of the church in Jerusalem, the colophon is held over until the narrative relating the emergence of the Hellenists is under way so as to create an overlap between the two parts. It may be noticed that the length of the corresponding sections varies in each case: the first part focusing on the Jerusalem church devotes the longest section to the issue of the persecution of the Jesus-believers by the religious authorities in Jerusalem and its eventual separation from the Temple; in the second part dealing with the church in Antioch, it is necessary to give more space to the emergence of the Hellenists as a distinct group of believers but, in contrast, the public manifestation of the Antioch church to Jerusalem is exemplified in a single incident that is only briefly narrated in four verses.

---

10. We have re-defined here the description of the various stages given in the first volume (*The Message of Acts,* I, pp. 31–32) in order to bring out more clearly the similarities that may be observed between the development of the two churches.

These two parts of Acts, spanning the first 12 chapters of Acts, form a unit relating the emergence of the different communities of disciples; another, distinct, unit is formed by the remaining chapters 13–28 which relate the outcome of the mission entrusted by the Holy Spirit to Barnabas and Saul as members of the Antioch church.

I. The Emergence of the Hellenists
6.1–8.1a

General Overview

The Hellenist, Greek-speaking Jews, have already been introduced into the narrative, though in an indirect fashion, in the person of Barnabas. In Codex Bezae, his name is mentioned as early a Acts 1.23 where he appears as Peter's first choice to replace Judas as one of the Twelve. His rejection by the disciples who elect in preference the alternative candidate, Matthias, echoes the rejection by Jacob's sons of their brother Joseph, whose name Barnabas bears as his real name (cf. 4.36). The assimilation of Barnabas in the Bezan text with Joseph the hero of Diaspora Judaism[1] underlines his role as a representative of the Hellenists and lets the audience know that the narrator approves of the group he represents. That he was rejected in favour of Matthias is a first hint in the Bezan text that his Hellenist origin may somehow have been a problem for the Jews from Palestine, the 'Hebrews', from whom the narrator distances himself.

Barnabas' Hellenistic, and Jewish, origin was confirmed in 4.36 where he is described as being 'from Cyprus, a Levite by birth' (D05; 'a Levite, a Cypriot by birth', B03). In the brief mention of him in 4.36-37, Barnabas is presented as a model of generosity and wholehearted acceptance of the practices characterizing the new Jesus-believing community, in contrast with Ananias and Sapphira (5.1-11) who, standing for the more reluctant Jews of Israel, hesitate to give themselves over entirely to the new movement. A strong suggestion of tension between the two groups of believers was thus created in this sequence but nothing more is made of it until Acts 6.

It is only then, when the Hellenist issue has been brought to the fore, that the narrative dealing with the church in Jerusalem is truly brought to a close, the summary statement of 6.7 serving as a kind of colophon concluding the story of the Jerusalem community.

No sooner have the leaders of the Hellenist disciples been elected than they are attacked by other Hellenist Jews. The reasons for their opposition are explored in *Excursus* 1.

---

1. See *The Message of Acts,* I, pp. 129–31.

Structure and Themes
The first section of this second part of Acts is made up of two sequences:

> [A]   6.1-7   The election of the seven Hellenist leaders
> [A']   6.8–8.1a   Stephen's prophetic witness

In the opening verses [A], the scene is set for the introduction of the Hellenist disciples as an identifiable group of believers who are invited to elect their own leaders. The first-named among them is Stephen; he becomes the central character of the second sequence [A'] which is largely taken up with his speech to the Sanhedrin. He is presented as an exemplary model of wisdom and prophetic inspiration. He attracts the hostility of his own circle of Hellenistic Jews who bring him to trial before the Jerusalem authorities, but his response to their attack is guided from beginning to end by the Holy Spirit. Section I concludes with his death by stoning and a note on Saul.

[A] 6.1-7 *The Election of the Seven Hellenist Leaders*

Overview

The appointment of men specifically to look after the interests of the Hellenists is prompted by a quarrel over a perceived injustice in the daily distribution of goods (cf. 4.35).[2] The arrangement was suggested by the apostles who intended them to have a purely administrative function but, as will be seen in the following sequence, the Holy Spirit had other ideas.

Structure and Themes
The theme of the leadership of the apostles follows on in this sequence from the previous section (5.12-42), although the particular reference to their administration of the daily distribution of goods is picked up from 4.35 (cf. 2.45, esp. D05 which reads καθημέραν). Luke's use of the label 'the Twelve' further activates the notion, not alluded to since 1.26 D05, that the apostles saw themselves as representing the twelve tribes of Israel. It is in this capacity that they take action in this sequence but, as already indicated in the Bezan text of Acts 1, their self-understanding is erroneous in the context of the changes that have taken place since the death of Judas.[3] As the story unfolds in the next sequence, the narrator will allow it to become clearer that their authority and power is neither supreme nor unique. This is the last time that the 'Twelve' will be mentioned in Luke's two-volume work, suggesting that they themselves finally came to terms with the fact that the plan for them to represent the patri-

---

2.   The dispute among the Jesus-believers apparently corresponds to a more general social problem: in the time of Agrippa I, the Greeks reproached the Jews for only looking after their own poor and Gamaliel I, as head of the Sanhedrin, passed the decree that the Jews had to look after foreigners in the same way as their own (Abécassis and Nataf, *Mystique juive,* cols. 318–20).

3.   See *The Message of Acts,* I, pp. 116–36.

archs of Israel had been abandoned. The reference to the distribution of goods among the believers is also made for the last time in Acts.

This sequence opens with the setting out of a problem in the Jerusalem church [a]; there follows a proposal to solve the problem [b] which is received positively [c]. The carrying out of the apostles' plan forms the central element [d], with the results leading from it [c′–b′]. A conclusion summarizing the effect of the solution on the church in Jerusalem [a′] closes the sequence:

[a]	6.1	The dissatisfaction among the growing number of disciples
[b]	6.2-4	The apostles' proposed solution
[c]	6.5a	The approval of all the disciples
[d]	6.5b	The election of seven Hellenist leaders
[c′]	6.6a	They present themselves to the apostles
[b′]	6.6b	The apostles' ratification of the Seven
[a′]	6.7	The growth of the Church in Ierousalem

Although a new part of the book begins in these verses, there is some overlap with the earlier part from which themes spill over. By making, as it were, a final comment on earlier topics, Luke uses these verses to bring the chapters on the Jerusalem church to a conclusion while at the same time introducing new ideas and themes into his narrative that will carry the plot forward.

Translation

	Codex Bezae D05	Codex Vaticanus B03
[a]	**6.1** It was in those days, when the disciples were increasing, that there was a murmuring of the Hellenists against the Hebrews because their widows were overlooked in the daily service, the service that was administered by the Hebrews.	**6.1** In those days, when the disciples were increasing, there was a murmuring of the Hellenists against the Hebrews because their widows were overlooked in the daily service.
[b]	**2** The Twelve called together the multitude of the disciples and said to them: 'We are not happy to leave the word of God to serve tables. So what is to be done, brethren? **3** Search out from among yourselves seven men of good reputation, full of the Spirit and wisdom whom we shall appoint for the particular need. **4** We, though, shall be persevering in prayer and the service of the word.'	**2** The Twelve called together the multitude of the disciples and said: 'It is not satisfactory that we should leave the word of God to serve tables. **3** Search out, brethren, seven men among you of good reputation, full of the Spirit and wisdom whom we shall appoint for this need. **4** We, though, shall persevere in prayer and the service of the word.'
[c]	**5a** And this proposal met with the approval of the whole multitude of the disciples;	**5a** And the proposal met with the approval of the whole multitude;
[d]	**5b** and they chose Stephen, a man full of faith and the Holy Spirit, and Philip and Prochorus and Nicor and Timon and Parmenas and Nicolaus a proselyte from Antioch.	**5b** and they chose Stephen, a man full of faith and the Holy Spirit, and Philip and Prochorus and Nicanor and Timon and Parmenas and Nicolaus a proselyte from Antioch,
[c′]	**6a** These men stood before the apostles.	**6a** whom they set before the apostles
[b′]	**6b** They prayed and laid hands on them.	**6b** and prayed and laid hands on them.

[a']   7 And the word of the Lord was fruitful   7 And the word of God was fruitful and
         and the number of disciples in Ierousalem   the number of disciples in Ierousalem was
         was multiplied greatly and, more-over, a   multiplied greatly and, moreover, a great
         great crowd of priests obeyed the faith.   crowd of priests obeyed the faith.

Critical Apparatus

6.1 Ἐν δὲ ταῖς ἡμέραις ταύταις Β 𝔓⁷⁴ ℵ A C* *rell*, *In diebus autem istis* d | Ἐν δὲ
τ. ἡμ. ἐκείναις C² 945. 1245. 2147. 2495 ‖ Ἐν δὲ ταύταις ταῖς ἡμέραις D gig
geo.

The position of the demonstrative following the noun it qualifies (B03) is the
usual position in Acts and indicates that the connection between the present event
and the previous scene is a loose one; by placing it before the noun (D05), the
narrator ties the two events more closely together, situating the growth of the
Church and the grumbling of the Hellenists within the same time frame as the
conflict between the apostles and the Jewish religious authorities (Read-
Heimerdinger, *The Bezan Text*, pp. 106, 113–14). The choice of ταύταις by both
B03 and D05, rather than ἐκείναις read by some Greek MSS, confirms that the
time of the previous scene is in focus and still important (Levinsohn, 'Towards a
Unified Linguistic Description of οὗτος and ἐκεῖνος' [SBL Seminar Papers 2003,
ed. K.H. Richards, Atlanta: Scholars Press, 2003]).

(ἐν τῇ διακονίᾳ) τῇ (καθημερινῇ) Β ℵ Dᶠ *rell* ‖ *om.* D*.

The presence in B03 of the article before the adjective καθημερινῇ describing
the service is a way of distinguishing it from other possible services (cf. τῇ
διακονίᾳ τοῦ λόγου, v. 4). D05 omits the article since it qualifies the service with
an additional phrase (see below).

(αἱ χῆραι αὐτῶν) ἐν τῇ διακονίᾳ τῶν Ἑβραίων D* d h mae ‖ *om.* Β 𝔓⁸·⁷⁴ ℵ Dˢ·ᵐ·
rell.

The presence or absence of the descriptive phrase operates in combination
with the previous variant (see above). B03 limits the description of the service to
'daily' whereas D05 amplifies the description by relating it to the 'Hebrews'.
This seems to mean the apostles, who have been responsible for the 'daily'
distribution of goods since 2.45 (καθημέραν D05) and who, as the 'Twelve' (6.2)
respond to the Hellenists' complaints. The first introduction in the earlier part of
this verse of the term 'Hebrews', without any further explanation, assumes that
the name was understood by the audience; its repetition by D05 has the effect of
sharpening the focus of the dispute, setting it in terms of a Hellenist/Hebrew
conflict.

6.2 (προσκαλεσάμενοι) δέ Β 𝔓⁸·⁷⁴ ℵ Dᴬ *rell* | *itaque* (= οὖν) d ‖ *om.* D* saᵐˢ
boᵐˢˢ.

In place of the usual connective δέ (as in B03) to introduce a new development in the story, D05 begins the next sentence without any linking word. The

asyndeton creates a hiatus that causes the sudden re-appearance of the 'Twelve' to be highlighted (Read-Heimerdinger, *The Bezan Text*, p. 248). The name is unexpected, having not been used since 1.26 D05 (and since 2.14 B03 by implication) but it is the key to understanding the politics of the episode. d05's *itaque* introduces a notion of consequence not expressed by δέ.

εἶπαν B 𝔓⁷⁴ A C 1175 | εἶπον ℵ *rell* || εἶπον πρὸς αὐτούς D d h syᵖ sa mae boᵐˢˢ; Cyp.

The aorist endings vary between weak (B03) and strong (D05), but the more significant variant is the spelling out of the addressees of the apostles' words in the Bezan text. Generally, when the addressee is not specified in the book of Acts, it is because it is clear from the immediately preceding context who is being spoken to (Read-Heimerdinger, *The Bezan Text*, pp. 181–82). In the AT, the apostles seem to address the 'multitude of the disciples' whom they have just called together, though at various points in the following verses it would make better sense if their words were directed only to the Hellenists. In the Bezan text, a series of variant readings makes it clear that this was indeed the case. The spelling out of the addressees in this verse, unnecessary if the whole group of disciples was meant, is the first of the series (see also the first three variants of 6.3, and the second of 6.5), with the pronoun αὐτούς referring back to the last mention of the Hellenists in v. 1 (αἱ χῆραι αὐτῶν).

(Οὐκ ἀρεστόν ἐστιν) ἡμᾶς B 𝔓⁸·⁷⁴ ℵ *rell* || ἡμῖν D d C gig h p.

B03 considers the pronoun to be the subject of the infinitive διακονεῖν, causing the introductory verb to be impersonal: 'It is not satisfactory that we should…' The verb takes on a personal force in D05: 'We are not happy to…', causing the apostles' reaction to reflect their own feeling rather than an implicit code of conduct.

6.3 τί οὖν ἐστίν, ἀδελφοί; D d h p mae; (Marc) || *om.* B 𝔓⁸ ℵ *rell*.

This variant functions in combination with the following one. The interpersonal tone of the speech is apparent in the reading of D05 (as elsewhere, cf. 2.37 D05; 5.8 D05; 21.22 D05) which has the apostles ask the assembled disciples a rhetorical question before going on to tell them how to solve the problem (Read-Heimerdinger, *The Bezan Text*, p. 229).

ἐπισκέψασθε (-ώμεθα B) δέ, ἀδελφοί B ℵ w saᵐˢˢ | ἐπ. οὖν, ἀδ. C E P H Ψ 049. 056. 1739 𝔐 lat sy bo; Orˡᵃᵗ Didˡᵃᵗ Chr | ἐπ. δή A | ἐπ. οὖν 33, *prospicite itaque* d | ἐπ. δὲ οὖν, ἀδ. 1175 || ἐπισκέψασθε D h p saᵐˢ mae; (Marc) | ἐπ., ἀδ. 𝔓⁷⁴ saᵐˢˢ arm aeth geo.

B03 not only does not draw the assembly into the discussion (cf. comments on the above variant) but in addition has the apostles take action without involving the rest of the Church. The asyndeton in D05 corresponds to the question just asked (see above, and cf. 5.28).

ἄνδρας ἐξ ὑμῶν B 𝔓^{8.74} ℵ *rell* || ἐξ ὑμῶν αὐτῶν ἄνδρας D, *ex vobis viros* d h p t mae; (Marc).

The partitive ἐξ ὑμῶν is associated in B03 with the direct object ἄνδρας ('men among you'), but in D05 is more closely connected with the imperative and is reinforced with the emphatic pronoun ('Search out from among yourselves'). The emphasis on the second person operates in combination with the additional pronoun in the introduction to the speech (πρὸς αὐτούς, 6.2) as a reference to the Hellenists who are being addressed by the apostles.

(ἐπὶ τῆς χρείας) ταύτης B 𝔓^{74} ℵ A C D^{C?} *rell, in negotio hoc* d || αὐτῆς D*.

The demonstrative adjective (more strictly speaking a pronoun – see Moule, *Idiom-Book*, p. 93) is used in B03 and is placed post-noun in its usual non-emphatic position to refer to a noun whose identity is readily deduced from the context (Read-Heimerdinger, *The Bezan Text*, p. 103). The use of the personal pronoun (D05) is, by its very meaning, emphatic; its position post-noun causes the noun to be in focus and has the effect of restricting the scope of the appointment of the Seven to 'the particular need', that is the table service. The apostles are careful, in the Bezan text, to limit the responsibility they will confer on the Hellenists.

6.4 προσκαρτερήσομεν B 𝔓^{8.74} ℵ *rell* || ἐσόμεθα ... προσκαρτεροῦντες D (*sumus ... perseveramus* d lat sy^{hmg}).

The periphrastic construction of D05 underlines the intention of the apostles to pursue their activities of prayer and service of the word.

6.5 (ὁ λόγος) οὗτος D d h (gig t) sy^p sa mae aeth || *om.* B 𝔓^{74} ℵ *rell.*

According to D05, what the hearers approved of was the apostles' proposal, which is in focus at the end of their speech (lit.: 'this word'); it is the speech more generally (lit.: 'the word') that was approved of according to B03.

(παντὸς τοῦ πλήθους) τῶν μαθητῶν D d h mae || *om.* B 𝔓^{8.74} ℵ *rell.*

While it is unnecessary to clarify that the assembled hearers were disciples, the phrase in D05 echoes the introduction to the speech (τὸ πλῆθος τῶν μαθητῶν, v. 2) and so insists that the apostles spoke to the Hellenists (πρὸς αὐτούς, v. 2) in the hearing and with the approval of all the disciples.

πλήρη B C² 056^c. 226*. 323. 440. 547. 927. 945. 1241. 1270*. 1611. 1739. 1891. 2492. 2495 || -ης D 𝔓^{74} ℵ A C* E H P Ψ 049. 056*. 1. 33. 69. 88. 104. 226^c. 330. 614. 1175. 1241. 1243. 1270^c. 1505. 1828. 1854. 2147. 2412 *pm.*

The declined form of the adjective (B03) is usual and is in line with the declined form used with reference to Stephen at 6.3, 8; 7.55 (as elsewhere in Acts: 9.36; 11.24; 13.10; 19.28). The non-declined form (D05) is not used on any other occasion by either B03 or D05, though some MSS read it at 6.3, for example.

Νικάνορα Β ℵ *rell, Nicanorem* d ‖ Νίκορα D.

Nicanor was a common name among Jews, though it appears only to be known outside Palestine in the first century CE. It was, for example, Nicanor who had given money for the lavish gates between the Court of Women and the Court of Men in Herod's Temple. Nicora may be associated with the root of the Greek verb νικάω ('conquer') or its corresponding noun νῖκος, but no occurrence of the name in contemporary writings is recorded.

6.6 οὓς ἔστησαν Β ℵ *rell, quos statuerunt* d h ‖ οὗτοι ἐστάθησαν D p sy^p.

The subject of the third person plural active verb in B03 can be presumed to be the same as that of the previous verb (ἐξελέξαντο), that is the disciples; they had chosen the Seven who continue to be expressed as the object of the verb. D05 begins a new sentence in which the Seven are brought into focus as the subject of the intransitive verb (1 aor. pass., see B-A-G, ἵστημι, II, 1, b; Zerwick, *Biblical Greek*, § 231); having been chosen by the disciples, they now act autonomously. The asyndeton in D05 further accords prominence to the Seven (Read-Heimerdinger, *The Bezan Text*, pp. 246–50, where the reference to 6.6 D05 should be added to the list of additional Bezan readings of asyndeton in narrative).

καὶ προσευξάμενοι Β ℵ *rell, cumque orassent* d ‖ οἵτινες πρ. D.

Attention then switches back in D05 to the apostles, setting up a contrast between the two groups: οὗτοι … οἵτινες. In B03, there is some ambiguity about the identity of the subject of the participle, and therefore of the main verb (ἐπέθηκαν) following: either it is the disciples who were the subject of the previous main verbs (see previous variant), or there is change of subject to the apostles. The solution preferred depends on who is understood to have laid hands on the Seven (see Barrett, I, pp. 315–16).

6.7 (ὁ λόγος) τοῦ θεοῦ Β 𝔓^74 ℵ A C P 049. 056. 1. 33. 36. 69. 88. 104. 181. 307. 323. 330. 440. 453. 547. 610. 618. 927. 945. 1409. 1505. 1646. 1678. 1739. 1828. 1837. 1854. 1891. 2147. 2344^vid. 2492. 2495 ar dem gig vg^ww.st sy^p co arm ‖ τ. κυρίου D d E Ψ 614. 1611. 2412 *pc* it vg^cl sy^h; Or^lat Chr.

This is the first of variant readings concerning the phrase ὁ λόγος τοῦ θεοῦ / κυρίου in which the divine name varies (cf. 12.24; 13.5, 48; 16.32; see Read-Heimerdinger, *The Bezan Text*, pp. 297–310). In the B03 text of Acts generally, a clear distinction between the two phrases is not made; here, the same expression is used as that spoken by the apostles in their words to the assembled disciples (6.2), and ὁ λόγος τοῦ κυρίου is not used until 8.25. The Bezan text of Acts, on the other hand, differentiates between the 'word of God' which refers to the interpretation of the Scriptures to explain their teachings about the Messiah and the 'word of the Lord' which is a specific reference to the message of, or concerning, Jesus (*General Introduction*, § VIII). ὁ λόγος τοῦ κυρίου is found here for the first time in D05, a device used by the narrator to imply that through the activity of the Hellenist leaders, Jesus' distinctive message became more widely known or influential, for the previous preaching of the apostles had been restricted to explanations about Jesus as Messiah that were set in the context of the Jewish Scriptures.

(ὄχλος) τῶν ἱερέων B D 𝔓⁴⁵·⁷⁴ ℵ² *rell* ‖ τ. Ἰουδαίων ℵ* 330. 440. 1243. 1270. 2495 syᵖ.

As all the adherents to the community were Jews at this time, the reading of ℵ01* would appear to reflect a later, Gentile perspective and avoids testifying that priests joined the Jesus-believers.

Commentary

[a] 6.1 *The Dissatisfaction among the Growing Number of Disciples*
6.1 The new section is linked to the previous material by being set within the same span of time.[4] The word order of the Bezan text makes the time link a particularly strong one by placing the demonstrative before the noun, an indication that not only is the action of the two sections situated within the same period of time but furthermore there is a close relationship between the earlier action and the new development about to be narrated. In other words, the growth of the Jesus-believing community and the dissatisfaction of the Hellenists with the Hebrews had something to do with the earlier incident involving the apostles. Certainly, the fact that the apostles had not been detained by the authorities or, worse, been put to death, and the liberty they took to preach and teach daily in the Temple and in private houses (5.41-42), were favourable circumstances for encouraging others to join the believers.

But the cause of the discord is also to be found in the previous account of the conflict between the apostles and the Jerusalem authorities. The result of the opposition of the latter to anything connected with Jesus was the emergence of the apostles as the spiritual leaders of the Jerusalem community of Jewish Jesus-believers in place of the traditional rulers.[5] The new situation gave a prominence to the apostles that may well have led them to make much of their identity as Jews born in the land of Israel and speaking Aramaic, that is, 'Hebrews' as opposed to 'Hellenists' who, largely from the Diaspora, were Greek-speaking (see *Excursus* 1). That the two terms 'Hellenists' and 'Hebrews' could be introduced without any explanation to identify distinct groups among the Jesus-believers is an indication that the distinction was well established among the Jews in Jerusalem, that it was a feature of Jewish communities generally and not just the disciples of Jesus.

---

4.   Levinsohn (*Textual Connections*, pp. 44–50; 61–62) argues that the basis on which a new development in narrative is related to previous material can be identified by its position at the front of the sentence, before the verb. Time is one basis among others (place or theme) that is used in narrative text to link episodes together. Cf. B-D-R, § 291, n. 5.

5.   See *The Message of Acts*, I, pp. 272–81.

The choice of the label 'the Twelve' in the next verse would, indeed, suggest that Luke wishes to convey that the apostles' role as the new leaders of Israel was uppermost among their concerns at this point (see on 6.2 below). The careful repetition by the Bezan text of the term 'the Hebrews' to define those responsible for the daily service adds weight to the supposition that the apostles (for it is they who had taken on the administration of the charity funds, 4.35, 37) were insisting on their Hebrew identity, and underlines the fact that it was precisely tension between Hellenists and Hebrews that characterized the discontent.

The discord between the two groups of believers is shocking in the context of the growing community where it threatens the ideals of unity and harmony that have so prominently featured in the narrator's summaries so far (2.41-47; 4.32-35). It comes to the fore in this scene on account of the Hellenist widows who are being overlooked in the daily distribution (cf. the qualification of the distribution as 'daily' in 2.45 D05) managed, as Codex Bezae insists, by the Hebrews under the supervision of the apostles who are therefore ultimately the ones responsible for the situation.[6] The grumbling of the Hellenists is directed towards the Hebrews though not expressed openly, so it would seem, to the apostles themselves.[7]

The sudden mention of widows at this point in the narrative needs to be considered against the earlier appearances of widows in Luke's two-volume work, in particular those whom Jesus encounters or speaks about (the widow of Zarephath, Lk. 4.25-26; the widow of Nain, 7.11-17; the persistent widow, 18.1-8; the poor widow, 21.1-4), all of whom are to some extent women in need, dependent on charitable support.[8] Each one is mentioned either to show Jesus' support of her, or his criticism of those who fail to fulfil their obligations towards her (cf. his warning about 'the scribes … who devour widows' houses', 20.46-47). Widows in Jewish tradition were, of course, representatives of the most destitute and needy members of society for whom the Law made explicit pro-

6. Cf. T. Stamford, 'The Neglected Widows: Were they Stinted or Snubbed? An Examination of the Literary Evidence' (paper presented to the British New Testament Conference, 2001).

7. The noun γογγυσμός is used here with the preposition πρός + accusative, just as in Lk. 5.30 where the Pharisees and scribes 'murmured towards' (ἐγόγγυζον πρός) the disciples with a complaint concerning Jesus: on both occasions, the complaint is voiced but not directly to the person responsible. The complaint is more actively communicated than those places in the Gospels where γογγυσμός is used alone (Jn 7.12; cf. 1 Cor. 10.10; Phil. 2.14; 1 Pet. 4.9) or γογγύζω with the preposition περί (Jn 6.41, 43, 61; 7.32). In the LXX, grumblings are made against (κατά) Moses and Aaron (Exod. 16.2-12; Num. 17.20, 25; cf. Mt. 20.11) but addressed to (ἐπί + dat.) God (Exod. 16.7, 8, 9, 12).

8. The first widow who appears in the Gospel, Anna (Lk. 2.36-38), stands apart from the others because of her role in the infancy narrative as distinct from the account of Jesus' ministry. Although she is linked, in a profound way, to the other widows of the Gospel, the complexities of the links are such that they cannot be discussed here. The continuity of treatment of the widows in Luke's work and the way that the narrator uses them to comment (positively or negatively) on the conduct of his protagonists is admirably discussed by F.S. Spencer, 'Neglected Widows in Acts 6.1-7', *CBQ* 56 (1994), pp. 715–33.

vision through the obligations of care that fell on the rest of the Israelites, a practical outworking of God's own special care of widows.[9] The Jewish prophets, representatives of Yahweh, frequently refer to care of the widows among other marginalized sections of society, as evidence of Israel's obedience and faithfulness to God and its absence as indicative of an attitude of rejection of God.

In the Jewish context of the early Church, in other words, looking after the widows was not an incidental concern but one that was at the very heart of putting adherence to Jesus into practice. The narrator's decision to deal with the omission of the Hebrews to fulfil equitably their responsibility towards the widows in the community is not his way of quickly skimming over a dispute that arose among the early disciples[10] but, on the contrary, constitutes criticism of the apostles of the strongest kind. Only when Peter responds positively to the death of the widow Tabitha in Joppa, with so many signs of his growing obedience to the message of Jesus (see *Commentary*, 9.36-43), is Luke's series of widow characters finally brought to a close.[11]

In view of these negative connotations of the Hebrews' neglect of the Hellenist widows, Luke is unlikely to be using the term 'murmuring' in a derogatory sense,[12] meaning to say that the complaint was unjustified or to be disapproved of. There are, nonetheless, striking parallels between this incident and the murmuring of the Israelites ('Hebrews') in the wilderness, for which the Greek noun used in Acts 6 (γογγυσμός), or the associated verb (γογγύζω), are used. The occurrences cluster firstly around Exodus 16–17, when the people lacked food (Exod. 16.2-12) or water (Exod. 17.1-7); the second occasion of their grumbling is condemned (Exod. 17.7, cf. Ps. 94.7-10 LXX). Another cluster of references occurs in Numbers 11; 14; 16–17, describing the increasingly desperate complaints of the Israelites about the dangerous conditions as they cross the desert; these murmurings are met with anger expressed by Yahweh, or Moses on his behalf, because they represent rebellion against God. The onset of God's anger is mentioned in Num. 11.10 when the people loudly protest about the lack of variety in the food he has provided them with. When Moses himself takes issue with Yahweh for having left him alone to manage the Israelites, the solution the Lord proposes is to appoint 70 elders to share his responsibility and, to that end, the prophetic spirit (11.16-25). The people are nevertheless subsequently punished for their murmuring when God, in his anger, sends a plague on them as they are filling themselves with the over-abundance of quails he has provided for them to eat (11.31-34).

---

9. Exod. 22.22; Deut. 10.18; 14.29; 24.17, 19-21; 26.12-13; 27.19; cf. Pss. 68.5; 146.9.

10. Barrett refers to the unjust treatment of the Hellenist widows as 'a minor deficiency in administration' (I, p. 303)! Cf. Spencer 'Neglected Widows', pp. 715–16.

11. See Spencer, 'Neglected Widows', pp. 731–33.

12. The noun γογγυσμός is only found here in Luke; elsewhere in the New Testament, it has a negative sense (Jn 7.12; Phil. 2.14; 1 Pet. 4.9). The verb γογγύζω occurs at Mt. 20.11; Lk. 5.30; Jn 6.41, 43, 61; 7.32; 1 Cor. 10.10 (× 2).

The most obvious similarity between Numbers 11 and Acts 6 is the action taken by the apostles as they propose to elect a group of seven well-respected men to take over some of their responsibilities. Since, as has been noted above, Luke as narrator does not signal any criticism of the Hellenists but, on the contrary, suggests that it was the Hebrews who were at fault, it may be that the apostles' action implies that it is *they* who view the situation as reflecting the situation faced by Moses in the wilderness.[13] Any parallel with Numbers 11 arises, in other words, because they see themselves as standing in some sense for Moses, responsible for and ruling over the people of Israel. It does not, however, convey Luke's own evaluation of the Hellenists' complaint. It will be seen in examining the contents of the apostles' speech below that their view of the role they see themselves as fulfilling is not approved of by Luke.

[b] 6.2-4 *The Apostles' Proposed Solution*
6.2 The mention of 'the Twelve' is abrupt and quite unexpected. The apostles have not been referred to by this title in the AT of Acts, except by implication in the mention of 'the Eleven' at 1.26 AT and 2.14 AT. In the Bezan text of 1.26, 'the Twelve' was used as a name describing the apostles as a body representative of the twelve tribes of Israel in line with its use in the Gospel (Lk. 6.13; 8.1; 9.1, 12; 18.31; cf. 22.28-30, esp. D05). The narrator has made clear, however, that the number had lost its literal value following the death of Judas whose 'estate' was left vacant, with his replacement appointed to take over his work but not his unique place among the Twelve chosen by Jesus, as Peter explains (1.20). In the Bezan text, Matthias disappears from view once he is appointed, an inevitable consequence of the fact that Jesus had not intended Judas to be replaced[14] and that the disciples had undertaken his election of their own accord. That is why, in 2.14 D05, Peter is mentioned alongside the 'ten' other apostles and not the Eleven as in the AT. So 'Twelve' is a number that is no longer a literal reality according to the Bezan narrative, but rather a symbolic title designating the apostles as leaders representing the twelve tribes of Israel.

That the narrator should choose to refer to the apostles as the Twelve at this point, therefore, is highly significant, being a reference to their own self-understanding as the new leaders of Israel. His choice of title does not mean that he agrees with their opinion of themselves; on the contrary, Luke has already made it plain in the opening scenes of Acts that Israel has lost its place as the privileged people of God and that Jesus' message is that all people are accepted by God on an equal basis. The use of the 'Twelve' at this point furthermore anticipates the emergence of the 'Seven' as a counter-group, as will be seen in the next verse.

In their capacity as leaders, then, the apostles take on the task of resolving the conflict that has arisen, addressing the meeting they have called of all the dis-

---

13. Cf. Exod. 18.13-27 (and Deut. 1.9-18) where Moses appointed judges to assist him in the easier cases of dispute.
14. See *The Message of Acts,* I, pp. 71–74.

ciples. It is important for the understanding of the subsequent actions to clarify to whom the various verbs that follow refer and to establish who is meant at each step of the account. The problem arises for English readers because Greek uses different means from English to specify the subject of verbs and to keep track of participants. In 6.1, it is the Hellenists throughout who are in focus. With the introduction of 'the multitude of the disciples' in v. 2, it looks as if they have been absorbed into the mixed congregation made up of Hebrews and Hellenists and that all the third person plural verbs describing the actions that result from the apostles' speech relate to this mixed congregation. However, in the Bezan form of the text it is clear that the apostles' speech is directed solely towards the Hellenists, and it is they who act in accordance with the advice given. The first indication is given by the third person pronoun in the Bezan introduction to the speech: '[they] said to them…'. If the apostles addressed the multitude they had called, there is no need to specify to whom they spoke. It seems that this is how the AT, which does not specify the addressees, has understood the situation (see *Critical Apparatus*). The reference to 'them' in Codex Bezae is thus a means to maintain the Hellenists in focus, picking up the pronoun from the last mention of them in v. 1 ([αἱ χῆραι] αὐτῶν, 'their [widows]'). Although in English translation the Bezan pronoun does nothing to clarify the addressees, in Greek it serves to remove the ambiguity. Further Bezan readings within the speech will confirm that the apostles direct their words to the Hellenists, in the hearing of all the disciples.

They state at the outset that they do not want to take time from their proclamation of the word to look after administrative affairs. The word is qualified as 'the word of God' (ὁ λόγος τοῦ θεοῦ) which has rather specific connotations in Luke's work, especially in the Bezan text.[15] In contrast with 'the word of the Lord' (ὁ λόγος τοῦ κυρίου) which will be used in 6.7 D05, it does not designate the message of Jesus so much as the interpretation of the Scriptures about the Messiah (see *General Introduction,* § VIII).

The opposition that the apostles set before their audience, between serving the word (cf. 'the service of the word', 6.4) and serving tables, is not one that sits easily with the teaching of Jesus in the Gospel on the value of practical service or, indeed, with his own example.[16] It says something about the mentality of the apostles that they consider the tasks of prayer and preaching to be more properly theirs.[17] Whereas the AT implies an accepted code of practice (sanctioned, perhaps they mean, by divine will), the Bezan wording rather reflects the apostles' own feelings. Whatever their wording, the importance of these tasks is no excuse for the partiality that has been shown, not even in view of the increasing amount of work that doubtless fell to the apostles as the number of disciples grew.

---

15. Read-Heimerdinger, *The Bezan Text*, pp. 297–310, esp. 302.

16. See esp. Lk. 22.14-27; cf. 12.37.

17. Spencer is a rare commentator prepared to envisage that Luke implies criticism of the apostles: 'While the Twelve show genuine concern for helping the deprived widows, their reluctance to become personally involved in table-service suggests that they still have not fully accepted Jesus' holistic model of ministry' (*Acts*, p. 67).

6.3-4 As frequently happens, the relationships between characters are more strongly delineated in Codex Bezae as the apostles put to the Hellenists a rhetorical question. That it is the Hellenists in particular who are addressed, and not the whole of the disciples, is evident from the response they give to their own question as they instruct them to find seven men 'from among yourselves' to take on the duties of table service – the emphasis would be unecessary if the apostles were addressing the entire assembly, which is what is indeed suggested by the absence of emphasis in the AT.

It remains unclear, nevertheless, whether the appointed Hellenists are to have responsibility for the distribution to all those in need in the community or just the Hellenists. It may seem odd that all of the seven men should be Hellenists (cf. the names in 6.5 below) if they are to look after the Hebrew disciples as well, and yet at the same time this arrangement could be thought, according to the apostles' way of thinking, to reflect accurately the relative strengths and importance of the two groups, with the Hebrews (represented by the apostles) taking the role of spiritual leaders of the whole group and the Hellenists (represented by the Seven) assuming responsibility for their material welfare.

The strategy proposed by the apostles was not in itself a new one, for there is evidence that the practice of having seven men in charge of administrative tasks was employed widely in Jewish cities.[18] These administrators, for all that they needed to possess outstanding qualities to be chosen for the positions and even though they were invested with considerable authority, nevertheless they were subordinate to the central Jewish authorities. This fact may help to explain the relationship the apostles envisaged between themselves and the men whom they would appoint. For indeed, despite their stipulation that the Seven should have excellent qualifications in order to carry out their work, certain aspects of the apostles' proposal reveal that their position will be a subordinate one. For one thing, although they will all be Hellenists and selected by their own people, it will be the apostles who actually install them in their responsibilities. Furthermore, in requiring that the Seven should be filled with the Spirit it is not without significance that the apostles do not include the adjective 'holy'. In Luke's writings (more especially in the Bezan text of the Gospel and Acts), the adjective 'holy' qualifying the Spirit of God is a reference to prophetic activity in the sense of communicating a message from God, as it was already in the Aramaic versions of the Jewish Scriptures.[19] The apostles apparently do not intend the Hellenist workers to undertake more than the daily distribution. They will be the ones who will be carrying on the spiritual work, as they indicate in v. 4 with an insistence on the firmness of their intention in the Bezan text.[20]

---

18. Safrai and Stern, I, p. 414. They cite Josephus (*War* II, 568-71): 'As rulers, let each city have seven men long exercised in virtue and in the pursuit of justice.'

19. Read-Heimerdinger, *The Bezan Text*, pp. 145–72. Some MSS (A C* E Ψ, as well as most minuscules and several early versions) include the adjective ἅγιον but not ℵ01, B03 or D05.

20. The parallels between the apostles' plan and the parable of the faithful steward told by Jesus (Lk. 12.42-48) also suggest that the Seven were meant to be a group under their authority. The

The solution adopted by the apostles of having a second group of seven men to take on part of the leadership of the Jesus-believing community reflects the pattern in the Gospel of the twelve apostles and the 'seventy (seventy-two) others'[21] whom Jesus sent out ahead of him on his journey up to Jerusalem, announcing the kingdom of God to the towns he was about to visit (Lk. 10.1-24). The travelling ministry of this large group chosen by Jesus will eventually be parallelled by the activity of the seven Hellenists but it is not envisaged by the apostles when they appoint them. The clear division in the type of work they allocate to the Hellenists on the one hand, and reserve for themselves on the other, may well reflect a traditional view among Jews of Israel that they were superior to Jews from the Diaspora (see *Excursus* 1). It will be the power of God himself working through the Hellenists (beginning in 6.8) that turns this distinction on its head and establishes the Seven as a recognizable group serving in prophecy and preaching, and that continues to be identified as such long after the last mention of the Twelve in 6.2 (cf. 21.8). They will testify in deed and word to Jesus (6.8-10; 7.2-53, 55-56: Stephen; 8.5, 12, 35, 40; 21.8: Philip), and will be joined by other Hellenists in proclaiming the good news about him (8.4, [cf. 5.42, where εὐαγγελίζομαι is used first in Acts]; 11.19-20). Indeed, it will be the Hellenists who play a leading role in taking the gospel beyond the confines of Judaea and later Israel, and they who thereby initiate the fulfillment of Jesus' last command (cf. 1.8).

[c] 6.5a *The Approval of All the Disciples*
6.5a The first part of the reaction to the apostles' proposal refers to the whole community, with the Bezan text repeating exactly the phrase from v. 2 in order to make this clear. All the disciples, then, were happy with the plan; the verb echoes the negative declaration of the apostles with which they opened their speech (οὐκ ἀρεστόν ἐστιν ἡμῖν D05 / ἡμᾶς B03..., 'we are not happy to...' D05 / 'It is not satisfactory that we should...' B03, v. 2), but this time in the affirmative (καὶ ἤρεσεν ὁ λόγος [οὗτος], 'the [this, D05] proposal met with the approval...'). Whether or not the Hellenists were to look after the daily distribution to all the needy in the community or just the Hellenists, the solution was approved of by the Hebrews as well as the Hellenists themselves.

[d] 6.5b *The Election of the Seven Hellenist Leaders*
6.5b In relating the action that is taken, the narrative maintains the Hellenists as the subject, those who were addressed by the apostles (see on vv. 2-4 above). It is

---

'faithful and wise steward' (ὁ πιστὸς οἰκονόμος ὁ φρόνιμος) is 'set up' (καταστήσει) by his master over his household to 'give' (διδόναι) them their share of food at the proper time; similarly, the Seven are to be full of wisdom (σοφίας) and Stephen will be said to be full of faith (πίστεως, 6.5), they will be appointed by the apostles (καταστήσομεν) to give out (cf. 4.35, διεδίδετο) the shared proceeds of the community's wealth to any who had need (cf. 2.45; 4.35).

21. 'Seventy' is read by ℵ A C L W Θ Ξ Ψ *f*[1.13] 𝔐 f q sy[p. h] bo; Ir[lat] Cl Or; 'seventy-two' by 𝔓[75] B D 0181 *pc* lat sy[s.c] sa bo[ms]; Ad.

they who act upon the apostles' command to choose seven men from among their own people, the seven names all being Greek rather than Semitic. They are each presented separately in turn (unlike the list of the Eleven in 1.13 [cf. Lk. 6.14-16] where the names are grouped in pairs and a final threesome), with the first and the last names the only ones with any kind of qualifying information. Stephen is accorded the position at the head of the list in anticipation of the leading role he will play among the Hellenists until he is killed. His name itself means 'a crown', and mention is made of his special qualities that go beyond the apostles' requirements for the candidates: he is full of faith, and not just the Spirit but the Holy Spirit. The adjective used to describe the fulness (πλήρης, in accordance with the instruction of v. 3) is one that expresses a permanent state as opposed to a temporary filling for a specific purpose and limited duration (expressed by the verb πίμπλημι).[22] From the narrator's first comments on Stephen, he makes it known that his qualities exceed the expectations, and even the requirements, of the apostles. Far from the group of the Seven disintegrating after Stephen's death, as does the group of Twelve following the death of Judas, it will remain intact as if 'crowned' by his martyrdom. Philip, the next named of the list, will take over from Stephen the role of representing the group in the narrative of Acts (8.5-40; 21.8).

The final person, Nicolaus, is described as a proselyte, a characteristic that is expressed by his name (Νικό-λαος, 'he who conquers the people'), of which the very meaning is a reminder that the people of Israel (referred to by Luke as ὁ λαός) no longer hold a superior position. His origin in Antioch is the first discreet mention of this city which will play such an important part in the story of Acts (cf. 11.19-26). It is typical of Luke's narrative art to use a mere passing mention in order to bring a crucial element into his story for the first time (cf., e.g., Barnabas, 1.23 D05; Saul/Paul, 7.58; 8.1). The presence of a proselyte among the seven Hellenists is telling of the readiness of the Hellenists disciples to consider a proselyte on a par with those born Jewish. This is the first indication in Acts of an openness among the disciples to people from outside Israel, and it does not originate with the apostles. That such details are not accidental in Luke's writing is confirmed by the leading role the Seven will take – despite being elected for a limited, administrative, task – in moving the gospel message out of Judaea from Acts 8 onwards.

[c′] 6.6a *They Present Themselves to the Apostles*
6.6a In the AT, the subject of the verbs through vv. 5-6 could be the entire group of the disciples: 'they chose … they set before the apostles … they prayed … they laid hands on them', assuming that when the apostles said 'we shall appoint' (v. 3) they intended their addressees to be included; alternatively, if the apostles meant that they themselves would undertake the appointment, then the subject of the last two verbs must be taken as switching to refer to them. The wording of the

22. See *The Message of Acts,* I, pp. 150–51.

Bezan text avoids any ambiguity, since it is the men who present themselves to the apostles who, in turn, pray and lay hands on them. It should be noted that in either case, the designation 'the Twelve' is no longer used. Viewed through the eyes of the Hellenists (or possibly the believers in general in the AT), the apostles are not seen as representatives of Israel (cf. v. 2) but in their more dynamic capacity of envoys (the meaning of ἀπόστολοι) of Jesus.

[b'] 6.6b *The Apostles' Ratification of the Seven*
6.6b The actions of praying and laying on of hands are found together on three other occasions in Acts, each time in different circumstances: for the Samaritans to receive the Holy Spirit (8.15-17), for Barnabas and Saul in preparation for their work (13.3) and for the healing of Publius' father (28.8).[23] Elsewhere in the Gospel and Acts, hands are laid on people without prayer being mentioned explicitly, for healing (Lk. 4.40; 13.13; Acts 9.12, 17) and/or for receiving the Holy Spirit (Acts 9.17; 19.6). The apostles' purpose here would be to ratify the election of the Seven and to communicate their blessing as well as God's own for their work (possibly analogous with the commissioning of Joshua by Moses [Num. 27.18-23] whereby Moses invested his successor with some of his authority [27.20]).

[a'] 6.7 *The Growth of the Church in Ierousalem*
6.7 The closing comment of this sequence brings to a conclusion not only the incident concerning the conflict between the Hellenists and the Hebrews but also the first part of the book of Acts dealing with the founding of the Church, which at this stage is the Church generally as well as the local church in Ierousalem. The Greek word καί used by Luke to link his final statement with the preceding narrative introduces the spread of the word and the growth in the Church without any further ado, as part of the appointment of the seven Hellenist leaders rather than as a separate development.[24] That is, the flourishing of the Church is linked directly by Luke to the arrival of the Hellenist leaders on the scene. This will be borne out by subsequent events as the gospel is taken out of Judaea by the Hellenists following the martyrdom of their most prominent member, Stephen.

The expression used to describe the word in the AT, 'the word of God', is the same as that used by the apostles in their speech to the disciples (6.2, cf. v. 4). It was noted in the *Commentary* above (on 6.2) that 'the word of God' is equivalent

---

23. Apart from at 8.15-17, it is not possible to determine whether the prayer precedes or accompanies the act of laying on hands. At both 13.3. and 28.8, although the prayer is expressed by an aorist participle, this cannot be taken as an indication of anteriority (Zerwick, *Biblical Greek*, §§ 261, 262). In the case of the seven Hellenists, both the aorist participle προσευξάμενοι and the aorist verb ἐπέθηκαν could express actions that are viewed globally.

24. The connective καί is used to link the appointment of the Seven with the growth of the Jerusalem church, indicating that the two are closely connected. If Luke had wanted to present the growth in the church as a new or independent development, the expected conjunction would be δέ (Levinsohn, *Textual Connections*, pp. 83–85).

in Luke's writing to the Jewish Scriptures; these are the vehicle of God's communication with people, and the preaching of the 'word of God' involves the interpretation of the scriptural message concerning the Messiah. The repetition in positive terms of the apostles' phrase by the AT narrator in his concluding sentence constitutes his endorsement of their proposal to serve the word and not tables.

The narrator in the Bezan text, however, makes a more negative comment on the apostles by abandoning their expression to replace it, for the first time in his writings, with the new phrase 'the word of the Lord' which specifically designates the message of Jesus (see *Commentary*, 6.2). It is not that Luke criticizes the apostles wholesale, but that he draws attention to the weaknesses in their plan because of its limitations and to the way that these limitations were overruled by God. Already in presenting the qualities of the seven men put forward from among the Hellenist disciples, he described Stephen as being full of the Holy Spirit, and not just the Spirit as required by the apostles (see on 6.5 above). Now, in bringing the episode to a close, he announces that rather than simply the 'word of God' being proclaimed, the 'word of the Lord' grew through the appointment of the Hellenist leaders. The singularity of the message of Jesus compared with the message that was being preached from the Scriptures was its universal application: the Hellenists will be instrumental in causing this dimension of Jesus' teaching to be understood within Jerusalem itself, and to spread beyond the city (cf. 8.25;11.20).

Overall, then, Luke endorses the plan of the apostles to establish a body of Hellenists to assist them but at the same time indicates how the Hellenists themselves were even more effective than the apostles anticipated. The consequence of the leading role taken on by the Hellenists will be, in the end, not so much to unite the believers in one global Church as set the scene for the beginning of a new, separate church identified initially with Hierosoluma (cf. 8.1b). It is too early to speak of a distinct Hellenistic community at this stage but at 8.1b its existence is implied, and by Acts 12 a division among the disciples in the city of Jerusalem will be alluded to (by Peter, 12.17) and will be increasingly apparent throughout the ministry of Paul.

Meanwhile, one particular aspect of the Church's growth is singled out (with τε) as being of special significance, namely the great number of priests who joined the believers. In combination with the Hebrew-derived spelling of Jerusalem, Ἰερουσαλήμ, this detail reveals that belief in Jesus was having no little effect on the Jewish institution (see *General Introduction*, § VII).

Excursus 1

The Hellenists

The Hellenists, Ἑλληνισταί, in Acts are named only twice: at 6.1 and 9.29 (D05 lac.). On both occasions, the people so called live in Jerusalem and are Jews: at 6.1 the name is applied to Jesus-believers who as yet did not include Gentiles;

and at 9.29, they are opponents of Saul who objected to the name of Jesus. A third mention occurs at 11.20 B03 where it is applied to Gentiles (cf. Ἕλληνας D05; εὐαγγελιστάς ℵ01, see *Critical Apparatus, ad loc.*), in accordance with the later attestation of the word.[25]

There is a consensus of opinion among historians that the verb from which the label Hellenist is derived, ἑλληνίζω, means to 'speak Greek' but beyond this, commentators frequently express difficulty in identifying who Luke means by the 'Hellenists'.[26] That the obscurity, however, is a problem for interpreters and not for Luke is evident when account is taken of the socio-religious context of Jerusalem in which the narrative of Acts takes place, namely that of first-century Judaism. Within that setting, even though the term as such was apparently not used by writers of the time, the Hellenists correspond to Jews who originate from the Diaspora, whether living in the Diaspora or in the land of Israel. The situation Luke describes as existing between the Hellenist and Hebrew Jesus-believers (6.1-6), between the Jesus-believing Hellenists and the Hellenists who opposed the name of Jesus (6.9-14; 9.28-30), between the Jesus-believing Hellenists and other Jews (7.54–8.1; 11.19) or the Gentiles (11.20), all make sense when viewed from a Jewish perspective.

It is dangerous to reduce the complex relationships among first-century Jews to general notions, as many historians point out. On the other hand, there are some basic facts that can clarify the status of the Hellenists,[27] and the picture Luke paints in Acts can itself contribute to a better understanding.

Jerusalem for all Jews was the centre of the world, the capital of the Jewish people, the place of the Temple and the Sanhedrin with its religious authority. Those who lived in the land of Israel had the natural advantage of access to Jerusalem and all that it signified. In the first century, however, the majority of Jews lived outside Israel. While maintaining their attachment to the land, they were inevitably influenced by the language and practices of non-Jewish society, and enjoyed a certain degree of freedom and social contact with regard to their Gentile neighbours not experienced in Israel.[28] And often, it must be said, not tolerated by the authorities in Israel either. The influence of Gentile, and especially, Greek ways on Jewish life was not a new problem in the first century, since it had been the basis of the Maccabaean wars in the two centuries BCE, but

---

25. The historical attestation of Ἑλληνισταί is presented in Cadbury, *Notes*, pp. 59–74.

26. See Barrett, I, pp. 309, 470; cf. Metzger, *Commentary*, p. 342.

27. For detailed information about Palestinian and Diaspora Judaism, the volumes of Safrai and Stern are most valuable, esp. I, chs. 3, 4, 7. See also J.M.G. Barclay, *Jews in the Mediterranean Diaspora: From Alexander to Trajan (323 BCE – 117CE)* (Edinburgh: T&T Clark, 1996); J.J. Collins, *Jewish Identity in the Hellenistic Diaspora* (Grand Rapids: Eerdmans, 2nd edn, 2000); M. Simon and A. Benoit, *Le Judaisme et le Christianisme antique d'Antiochus à Constantin* (Nouvelle Clio, l'histoire et ses problèmes, 10; Paris: PUF, 1968), esp. pp. 69–76.

28. The degree of syncretism among Jews in the Diaspora should not be over-emphasized; for a discussion, see the contributions to J.A. Overman and R.S. MacLennan (eds), *Diaspora Jews and Judaism* (Atlanta: Scholars Press, 1992).

it was made all the more complicated by the presence of the Roman army of occupation in Israel. It was natural that in the struggle to maintain the purity of the Jewish religion and guard against foreign contamination at all costs, those Jews who were natives of Israel, who understood the Scriptures in Hebrew and who could perform the sacrifices and other acts of worship in the Temple, should regard themselves as superior to the Jews in the Diaspora whom they would look down upon.

Despite some measure of independence enjoyed by the synagogues outside Israel, the Jews of the Diaspora were nevertheless subjected to inspection and control by the Jerusalem authorities, for example by the monthly sending of envoys, distinguished 'apostles' whose duty it was to supervise life in the Jewish communities.[29] Among other things, they would check that the regulations of the Torah were being followed and that no foreign teachings or practices were being followed. It is probably in this context that Saul was given authority to arrest Jesus-believing Jews in Damascus.[30]

As a result of this supervision from Jerusalem, which was a reminder of their inferior status, it would be inevitable that Diaspora Jews should either be resentful of the interference in their lives or, as happened with many, that they should do all they could to satisfy the authorities and to prove that even though they were not from Israel they were still faithful and honourable Jews. Some Jews from the Diaspora who had initially come as visitors to Jerusalem often stayed there because of their belief in the holiness of the city and of the homeland. Thus there existed synagogues of various groups and nationalities within the city (cf. Acts 6.9), whose members may have engaged in the study of the Torah or joined the movements that fought to protect Israel from foreign domination. It is important to remember, too, that the families of the High Priests in the first century CE were from Babylon or Alexandria.

These aspects of the Jewish situation in the first century provide a context for the different groups of Jews that appear in Acts, among believers and non-believers, and make sense of the Hellenists as Jews from the Diaspora who had to defend themselves in view of the superior attitudes of the Jews from Israel. In the case of Stephen, the leader of the Hellenist Jesus-believers, it was precisely Diaspora Jews in Jerusalem who attacked him. Their motive in doing so could well have been to avoid giving the impression that there was any laxity or compromise in terms of the Law within their communities and so avoid disapproval or, worse, punishment. The Diaspora Jews had to work hard to convince the Jews of Israel and especially the Jerusalem authorities that they were pure and Law-abiding. They would, therefore, be alarmed by any of their members who proclaimed teachings about the Messiah and the Temple contrary to the

---

29. See Safrai and Stern, pp. 204–207, but cf. Barclay, *Jews in the Mediterranean Diaspora*, p. 420, who disputes the dating of this information.

30. Cf. Acts 28.21, where the Jews in Rome informed Paul that, contrary to expectation, they had not received letters about him from Judaea.

Jewish core beliefs and would be quick to deal with any who risked giving them a bad reputation.[31] So once Stephen was dealt with, they went on to persecute other Hellenist Jesus-believers and drive them out of Jerusalem (8.1a; 9.29-30).

Among the Jesus-believers themselves, distinctions are also apparent in Acts between the Diaspora Jews, the Hellenists, and the 'Hebrews', Ἑβραῖοι, those of Israel, represented initially by the apostles and later by James, the brother of Jesus.[32] The original disciples of Jesus were all from Galilee, and although they had separated from the Temple authorities when the latter refused to hear any mention of the name of Jesus (4.23-31), they none the less remained attached to Ierousalem as the centre of Judaism and the focus of the Church (cf. 8.1b D05, 14 D05) for some time. Their attitude towards the Hellenists, whom they entrusted with material tasks without envisaging for one moment that they would be engaged in spiritual activity (6.2-4, esp. D05), suggests that they considered them to be of a lower order. Furthermore, as leaders of the Ierousalem church, the apostles continued to seek to supervise the churches outside Judaea (cf. 8.14; 11.3, 22; 15.1-34, esp. D05), an attitude that mirrors the practice among the Jews described above.[33]

Luke makes clear, in the Bezan text of Acts at least, his own attitude to the two groups, presenting the Hellenists as closer to understanding the message of Jesus than the apostles, and quicker in overcoming the obstacles to extending the Church to include Gentiles. Stephen is chosen by Luke to represent the Hellenist point of view. Although the apostles had already separated from the Temple, he is the first to openly declare his opposition to the importance accorded to it by the Jews (7.2-53). It is only once the Hellenist leaders are appointed that the gospel begins to be preached outside Jerusalem (by Philip in Samaria and to an Ethiopian eunuch [8.5-40]; by some from Cyprus and Cyrene in Antioch [11.20]). Their detachment from the Jewish religious views concerning Israel (represented by the term Ierousalem) is affirmed by Luke in his use of the term Hierosoluma at 8.1b when he applies it for the first time to believers who were persecuted following the killing of Stephen.

---

31. In Gal. 6.12-16, Paul speaks of those Jewish disciples in Galatia who want to circumcise the Gentile believers in order to cut a good figure so as not to be persecuted for their belief in Jesus. Again, the greatest threat to the Jewish believers would be from their fellow Jews in Galatia, who would be fierce in their opposition to Jews who could spoil their good reputation with the central authorities in Jerusalem.

32. That a division existed among the early believers is denied by, e.g., C.C. Hill, *Hellenists and Hebrews: Reappraising Division within the Earliest Church* (Minneapolis: Augsburg, 1992). The outcome of Hill's approach is a testimony to the bewildering number of possible and contradictory interpretations that may be given to Acts 6 and 7 when the narrative is not read within the context of first-century Judaism and when it is not recognized that Luke does not endorse everything he puts into the mouths of the apostles.

33. The control that the apostles and James sought to exercise from Jerusalem over the churches outside Judaea is likely to reflect an existing Jewish situation even if the evidence for the control of the Diaspora Jews by Jerusalem authorities is only found in rabbinic sources (cf. Safrai and Stern, I, pp. 204–207).

Barnabas is another Hellenist, a Levite from Cyprus, whom Luke portrays as a positive model in contrast to those who remain attached to Jewish traditions, initially Ananias and Sapphira (4.36–5.11) but later Paul, too, when he refused to accept John-Mark, the Hellenist 'minister of the word', as an assistant on the second journey (15.36-40).[34]

Paul himself presents at first sight a contradiction for, though born in Tarsus (Acts 21.39; 22.3; cf. 9.11, 30; 11.25), he refers to himself as a 'Hebrew' (Phil. 3.5; 2 Cor. 11.22), and takes considerable care to underline his upbringing and education in Jerusalem (Acts 22.3; 26.4), describing himself as an Israelite, Ἰσραηλίτης (Rom. 11.1; 2 Cor. 11.22) and knowing the importance of speaking Hebrew, Ἑβραΐς (Acts 21.40; 22.2; 26.14). Paul's insistence on the quality of his credentials is explicable in the Jewish context outlined here: because of the low esteem in which Diaspora Jews were held, he had to work all the harder to prove his worth to other Jews and appealed to the formative years he had spent in Jerusalem in order to outweigh the disadvantages of his birth.[35] It is correct, therefore, to refer to Paul as a Hellenist[36] (Jesus had no qualms in identifying him by his place of birth, cf. 9.11) even though Paul himself seems to have preferred to ignore his place of origin and displayed a Jewish nationalistic fervour that was more characteristic of the Jews of Israel than of the Diaspora.

[A'] 6.8–8.1a *Stephen's Prophetic Witness*

General Overview

Corresponding to the appointment of the seven Hellenist leaders and the conflict among the Jesus-believers that prompted it, is the testimony, by his deeds, his words and his death, of the first-named of the chosen men, Stephen. That such drama should occur over one of the men whom the apostles thought they were appointing simply to take over an administrative task must

---

34. See J. Rius-Camps, 'Qui és Joan, l'anomenat "Marc"?', *RCatT* 5 (1980), pp. 297–329, on the identity of John-Mark as the author of the second Gospel.

35. It is possible to envisage that Paul was a member of the Zealots who aggressively fought to preserve Israel as a people faithfully upholding the Law, free from the domination and the contamination of the Gentiles and ready for Israel's restoration in the end-times. This would account for his readiness to endorse the killing of Stephen and his pursuit of the Jesus-believers in Damascus. For discussion of Paul's possible Zealot associations, see J. Taylor, 'Why Did Paul Persecute the Church?', in G.N. Stanton and G.G. Stroumsa (eds), *Tolerance and Intolerance in Early Judaism and Christianity* (Cambridge: Cambridge University Press, 1998), pp. 99–120; cf. N.T. Wright, *What Saint Paul Really Said: Was Paul of Tarsus the Real Founder of Christianity?* (Oxford: Lion, 1997), pp. 25–38.

36. Paul's attitudes to people in the Diaspora, both Jews and Gentiles, and the ease with which he travelled around the various countries are consistent with those of a Jew who had personal experience of life outside Israel; see M.E. Thrall, 'Paul of Tarsus: a Hellenistic Jew', in R. Pope (ed.), *Honouring the Past and Shaping the Future: Religious and Biblical Studies in Wales* (Leominster: Gracewing, 2003), pp. 97–111, for evidence of Hellenistic culture in his writings.

have been entirely unexpected from the apostles' point of view. It allows Luke, however, to show the prominent part played by the Hellenist believers and the profound effect they had not just among the disciples but also among the Jewish people and the authorities in Jerusalem. Initially, it is Stephen who will act as their spokesman, bringing to completion testimony to Jesus in the holy city (cf. 1.8). He will stand as an example of faithfulness, wisdom and holiness for the rest of the book of Acts. Similarities with the trial and killing of Jesus reinforce the innocence of Stephen and the injustice of his opponents.[37] At the same time, aspects of the attack on Stephen are taken up in the arrest and trial of Paul where they serve as a foil to show up the latter's weaknesses.

Structure and Themes

The bulk of this sequence is taken up by Stephen's speech to the Sanhedrin which stands at the centre of the sequence [A'-B], framed by the two brief episodes either side – the accusations leading up to his arrest beforehand [A'-A] and his death by stoning following [A'-A'] – mirroring each other to some extent:

[A'-A]	6.8-15	Stephen is accused of blasphemy
[A'-B]	7.1-54	Stephen before the Sanhedrin
[A'-A']	7.55–8.1a	The stoning of Stephen

The opening frame prepares the atmosphere for the intense hostility worked out in the closing frame. In each case, there is a heavenly vision, which is placed just before and just after the hearing in the Sanhedrin, in such a way that they reflect each other and leave the reader in no doubt as to God's approval of Stephen. Though the result of the trial is Stephen's death, his innocence is affirmed.

[A'-A] 6.8-15 *Stephen is Accused of Blasphemy*

Overview

The preparatory scene leading up to Stephen's trial contains striking echoes of the incident involving Naboth and Jezebel in the first (third, LXX) book of Kings (1 Kgs 21.8-13).[38] Naboth stands as an example of a truly honourable

---

37. For a detailed comparison of the trial of Jesus and that of Stephen, see Rius-Camps, *Comentari*, II, pp. 133–38; cf. Witherington, *Commentary*, p. 253.

38. The parallels have been discussed in some detail by T.L. Brodie, 'The Accusing and Stoning of Naboth (1 Kgs 21:8-13) as One Component of the Stephen Text (Acts 6:9-14; 7:58a)', *CBQ* 45 (1983), pp. 417–32. This is but one example among the many that Brodie has identified of the allusions to the Elijah–Elisha narratives in Luke's work (see p. 420, n. 13). A most interesting link between Stephen and Naboth is the term 'freedmen' in both passages, though it is in the Latin form in Luke's narrative (ἐκ τῆς συναγωγῆς τῆς λεγομένης Λιβερτίνων, Acts 6.9; οἱ ἐλεύθεροι οἱ κατοικοῦντες ἐν τῇ πόλει, 3 Kgdms 20.11 LXX). By virtue of its unexpected occurrence in the context (see *Com-*

man who was stoned to death because he refused to dishonour his family by handing over his vineyard to the king, Ahab. Ahab's wife Jezebel, in contrast, who set up the plot to bring shame on Naboth and have him killed, is presented as the epitome of wickedness and is punished by God with the most horrible of deaths when she is eaten by dogs (2 Kgs 9.30-37). The principal parallel between Naboth and Stephen is the manner of their deaths by stoning, but the parallel is only meaningful because in both cases they were accused on false grounds by witnesses set up by their opponents specially for the purpose of bringing them into disrepute. There are important dissimilarities between the two incidents – notably the motive of Jezebel to obtain land for the king is not shared by the Hellenist Jews who wish rather to protect themselves from incurring the displeasure of the religious authorities. Yet the underlying ressemblance between the two plots allows comparisons to be drawn between the protagonists: not just Naboth and Stephen, but more importantly between Jezebel and the Hellenists, and between Ahab and the Sanhedrin. Those who schemed to bring about the death of a good man are equally responsible for presenting lying witnesses; and those who accepted their scheming, both representatives of Israel either as king or as supreme court, fail to maintain justice on behalf of the people.[39] The effect of the parallel is to express an implicit evaluation of the opponents of Stephen in the strongest possible terms.

Structure and Themes

The first of the framing narratives builds up through a crescendo to a climax of hostility on the part of certain Jews who, like Stephen, are also Hellenists. Their opposition to Stephen initially takes the form of disagreement with him, but leads on to their suborning other men to accuse him of blasphemy. Things then take on a different colour when they drag him before the formal court, the Sanhedrin, where they set up false witnesses to testify against him. In contrast with this progressive assault, the final picture of Stephen in this sequence will be one in which he appears to his judges as an angel in the middle of the earthly court, an image that expresses his innocence:

[a]	6.8	Stephen works signs and wonders
[b]	6.9-10	The disagreement of certain Hellenists: first attack
[c]	6.11-12a	Men are suborned to accuse Stephen: second attack
[c']	6.12b	Stephen is brought to the Sanhedrin
[b']	6.13-14	False witnesses are set up: third attack
[a']	6.15	The Sanhedrin see Stephen with the face of an angel

mentary on 6.9), it may be viewed as one of the possible pegs on which the connection between the two stories hangs.

39. See 1 Kgs 21.22, where Elijah speaks to Ahab on behalf of the Lord: 'you have made Israel to sin'.

Translation

Codex Bezae D05	Codex Vaticanus B03
[a]	**6.8** Stephen, full of grace and power did great signs and wonders among the people in the name of the Lord Jesus Christ.	**6.8** Stephen, full of grace and power did great signs and wonders among the people.
[b]	**9** Some members of the synagogue of the Freedmen, as it was known, both Cyrenians and Alexandrians, and some people from Cilicia, rose up and disputed with Stephen, **10** and these men were unable to withstand the wisdom which was in him or the Holy Spirit with which he spoke because they were proven wrong by him with all his boldness.	**9** Some members of the synagogue of the Freedmen, as it was known, both Cyrenians and Alexandrians, and some people from Cilicia and Asia, rose up and disputed with Stephen, **10** and they were unable to withstand the wisdom or the Spirit with which he spoke.
[c]	**11** So since they were powerless to face the truth, they then suborned men to say, 'We have heard him speaking words of blasphemy against Moses and God', **12a** and they went on to stir up the people, and the elders and the scribes.	**11** Then they suborned men to say, 'We have heard him speak blasphemous words against Moses and God', **12a** and they went on to stir up the people, and the elders and the scribes.
[c']	**12b** They came on him by surprise and seized him and led him to the Sanhedrin;	**12b** They came on him by surprise and seized him and led him to the Sanhedrin,
[b']	**13** and they set up false witnesses against him who said, 'This man here never ceases to say things against the holy place and the Law. **14** Indeed, we have heard him saying that this Jesus, the Nazorene, will destroy this place and change the customs that Moses gave to us.'	**13** and, in addition, they set up false witnesses who said, 'This man here never ceases to say things against this holy place and the Law. **14** Indeed, we have heard him saying that this Jesus, the Nazorene, will destroy this place and change the customs that Moses gave to us.'
[a']	**15** (But all those seated in the Sanhedrin gazed at him and they saw his face like the face of an angel that was standing in the middle of them.)	**15** And gazing at him, all those sitting in the Sanhedrin saw his face like the face of an angel.

Critical Apparatus

6.8 διὰ τοῦ ὀνόματος (+ τοῦ E 33. 88. 104. 614. 927. 1837. 2344. 2412) κυρίου Ἰησοῦ Χριστοῦ D d (E) 5. 33. 88. 104. 431. 453. 614. 876. 927. 1611. 1837. 2344. 2412 *pc* it (sy^h**) sa mae; Aug || *om.* B 𝔓^8.45.74 ℵ *rell*.

The phrase read by D05 picks up the terms used in the apostles' prayer after their release from the Sanhedrin when they asked God to work miracles through Jesus (4.30). The resultant clause echoes the earlier one: σημεῖα καὶ τέρατα γίνεσθαι διὰ τοῦ ὀνόματος τοῦ ἁγίου παιδός σου Ἰησοῦ, 4.30 // τέρατα καὶ σημεῖα μεγάλα ἐν τῷ λαῷ διὰ τοῦ ὀνόματος κυρίου Ἰησοῦ Χριστοῦ, 6.8.

6.9 (τῶν ἐκ τῆς συναγωγῆς) τῆς λεγομένης B D d 𝔓^74 049. 056. 88 *rell* || τῶν λεγομένων ℵ A 0175. 33. 181. 326. 927. 1270. 1837. 1898. 2344. 2495 *pc* gig g^2 sa mae; Chr.

ℵ01 defines the members of the synagogue as 'Freedmen', unlike both B03 and D05 which define the synagogue itself as being 'of the Freedmen'.

(τῶν ἀπὸ Κιλικίας) καὶ Ἀσίας Β 𝔓⁸·⁴⁵·⁷⁴ ℵ Dᴮ *rell* ‖ *om.* D* d A *l*60.

It is possible that the second place of the pair has been omitted through homoioteleuton (Delebecque, *Les deux Actes*, p. 52), especially since the letters ΙΑΣ occur three times in the two names: ΚΙΛΙΚΙΑΣΚΑΙΑΣΙΑΣ.

6.10 καὶ (οὐκ ἴσχυον) Β 𝔓⁸·⁷⁴ ℵ *rell* ‖ οἵτινες D d h t mae.

The relative pronoun of D05 maintains the Jewish opponents of Stephen in focus, and is the first of a series of readings that reinforces the contrast between Stephen and his attackers (see the following *vll* of this verse).

(τῇ σοφίᾳ) τῇ οὔσῃ ἐν αὐτῷ D d E h mae ‖ *om.* B 𝔓⁸·⁴⁵·⁷⁴ ℵ *rell*.

D05 presents Stephen as full of wisdom, and not just speaking with it as in B03, in accordance with the requirements for the Hellenist leaders stated by the apostles (cf. 6.3).

(τῷ πνεύματι) τῷ ἁγίῳ D d E gig h p t g² vgᵐˢ mae aeth ‖ *om.* B 𝔓⁸·⁴⁵·⁷⁴ ℵ *rell*.

The mention of the Spirit also echoes the apostles' conditions (see above) but the inclusion of the adjective 'holy' in D05 repeats the contrast made in 6.5 between their limited requirement for the Seven to be full of the Spirit and the reality that the chosen men were full of the Holy Spirit (see *Commentary*, 6.3, 5).

διὰ τὸ ἐλέγχεσθαι αὐτοὺς ἐπ (ὑπ' Dᴮ E) αὐτοῦ μετὰ πάσης παρρησίας D d (E e) h t w y vg bhm tpl syʰᵐᵍ mae; Ephr ‖ *om.* B 𝔓⁷⁴ ℵ *rell*.

The verb ἐλέγχω in D05 has the meaning of 'be convicted' or 'proven wrong'. Since the preposition Luke regularly uses to introduce passive verbs in the D05 text is ὑπό (as in Dᴮ), the preposition ἐπί of the original hand in this verse suggests that rather than the arguments of his attackers being intentionally disproved by Stephen, they are exposed as being wrong by what he says, given that he speaks with πάσης παρρησίας. It was seen at the occurrence of this phrase at 4.29 (cf. 4.31; see *Commentary*, *ad loc.*), that the 'boldness' in question has to do with the daring and radical nature of the interpretation of Scripture which, in Stephen's account, has the effect of showing up the wrong reasoning of his opponents.

The reference by D05 to πάσης παρρησίας recalls the apostles' prayer (μετὰ πάσης παρρησίας λαλεῖν τὸν λόγον σου, 4.29 [following the emphatic word order of D05, see Read-Heimerdinger, *The Bezan Text*, p. 98]) in the same way as the mention of signs and wonders at 6.8 (see above). A contrast is set up between the apostles' partial fulfilment of the prayer (μετὰ παρρησίας, 4.31) and Stephen's perfect fulfilment.

6.11 μὴ δυνάμενοι οὖν ἀντοφθαλμεῖν τῇ ἀληθείᾳ D d (E e) h t w vg^{mss} bhm tpl sy^{hmg} (mae); Ephr || *om.* B 𝔓^{74} ℵ *rell.*

D05 introduces the subsequent action (τότε) of Stephen's opponents, that of secretly setting up men to speak against him, with a clause spelling out the reason for it: they were unable to face up to the truth. The clause recalls the promise of Jesus to the apostles that when they were brought before kings and governors he would give them speech and wisdom which their enemies would be unable to resist (Lk. 21.15; cf. Acts 6.10). The verb ἀντοφθαλμεῖν is found in Wis. 12.14 in a passage that was already evoked in 5.39 D05 (see *The Message of Acts,* I, p. 354).

βλάσφημα B 𝔓^{8.74} ℵ² *rell, blasphema* d || -μίας D ℵ* 614. 2412 lat sy.

B03 reads the neuter plural adjective in place of the more forceful singular noun.

6.12 ἐπιστάντες (συνήρπασαν) B D 𝔓^{8.74} ℵ² *rell* || *om.* ℵ*.

ℵ01* is alone in omitting the circumstantial participle.

6.13 ἔστησάν τε B 𝔓^{8.74} ℵ *rell* | ἔστ. δέ H 33. 2147. 2344 || καὶ ἔστ. D d gig h t g² vg.

The MSS view the development of the narrative over the next sentences differently. τε in B03 comes at the end of a series of clauses linked by καί, giving thereby a special importance to the setting up false witnesses, which is the action that leads on to the next significant event, the questioning of Stephen by the High Priest (7.1, introduced with δέ; see Levinsohn, *Textual Connections,* pp. 130–31). Since the false witnesses have already been introduced (cf. 6.11), they are not a new element in the story at this point and δέ is not called for. D05, for its part, considers all the actions of the Jewish opponents as preparatory for the interrogation of the High Priest (the δέ clause of 6.15 stands as a parenthetical comment rather than a principal event of the narrative).

κατὰ αὐτοῦ (λέγοντας | -τες ℵ 0175) D d (h z) mae (aeth) || *om.* B 𝔓^{74} ℵ *rell.*

D05 spells out that the false witnesses were set up against Stephen, information that is implicit in the B03 text. It is possible that κατὰ αὐτοῦ qualifies the participle (cf. Mk 14.56-57, where in place of ἐψευδομαρτύρουν κατ' αὐτοῦ, D05 twice reads: ἐψευδομαρτύρουν ἔλεγον κατ' αὐτοῦ).

λαλῶν ῥήματα B 𝔓^{8vid.45vid.74} ℵ C 0175. 323. 945. 1175*. 1739 *al* lat sy sa bo; GrNy || ῥήμ. λαλ. D d A h g² | ῥήμ. βλάσφημα λαλ. E H* P Ψ 049. 056. (33. 614 *pc*) 𝔐 (t w vg^{mss}) mae.

The word order of D05 emphasizes the 'words' spoken by Stephen, recalling the previous accusation of v. 11, λαλοῦντος ῥήματα βλάσφημα (-μίας D05).

(τοῦ ἁγίου) τούτου B (𝔓⁸) C 33. 36. 69. 323. 945. 1739 *al* h p t vg^{mss} sy co; GrNy || *om.* D d 𝔓^{74} ℵ A E H P Ψ 049. 056. 066. 0175 𝔐 lat arm aeth.

The demonstrative adjective is not necessary for 'the holy place' to be clearly understood by Jews as a familiar phrase referring to the Temple; non-Jews, on the other hand, may feel the need for clarification. Metzger suggests (*Commentary*, p. 298) that the inclusion of τούτου could cause the phrase to mean the place where the Sanhedrin was gathered and that it was dropped to avoid the inappropriate application to the Sanhedrin meeting place of a reference more suited to the Temple. That explanation raises the question of why Luke would portray Jews misusing such a standard and well-established phrase in the first place.

6.14 τὰ ἔθνη B* 1854*. 2147. 2412* ‖ τ. ἔθη D Bᶜ𝔓⁷⁴ ℵ *rell.*

The confusion between ἔθνη and ἔθη also occurs at 16.21 where D05 reads ἔθνη for ἔθη.

6.15 καὶ ἀτενίσαντες εἰς (– ℵ* 1837.1854*) αὐτόν B 𝔓⁴⁵·⁷⁴ ℵ² Dᴮ *rell, et intuiti in eum* d ‖ καὶ ἠτένιζον δὲ αὐτῷ D* (saᵐˢˢ mae).

B03 uses καί to introduce a parenthetical series of comments (in so far as they are not part of the main story line) about what the council members saw as they looked (aorist participle) at Stephen, closely linking the appearance of Stephen with the accusations of the false witnesses. D05 also uses καί but with the imperfect, possibly with an adverbial function suggesting that even as the Sanhedrin were looking at him while the charges were being made, his appearance was changed. δέ is then the connecting word in D05, being the more usual conjunction in Acts to introduce background information that is relevant to what follows, as it is here (see Levinsohn, *Textual Connections*, p. 91).

The choice between the dative pronoun (D05) and the prepositional phrase (B03) may be compared to the two ways used in Acts to express the addressee of speech, that is, either with the dative of the noun/pronoun or πρός + accusative. The former tends to be used when the relationship between speaker and addressee has already been established, or is not significant to the story or to maintain a certain distance between them; the preposition, in contrast, underlines the relationship between the participants and is used especially at the outset of a dialogue. When the usual pattern is disrupted, attention is drawn to the relationship (Read-Heimerdinger, *The Bezan Text*, pp. 176–78). A similar distinction is possibly expressed by the alternative structures following other verbs of expressing interaction, as the two successive occurrences of ἀτενίζω at 3.4-5 in D05 suggest (3.4 D05: ἀτένισον εἰς ἡμᾶς; 3.5 D05: ὁ δὲ ἀτενίσας αὐτοῖς; cf. 7.55). In that case, B03's use of the prepositional phrase here can be accounted for on the grounds that a relationship between the Sanhedrin and Stephen is mentioned for the first time. The use of the dative pronoun by D05 stands out as unusual and keeps Stephen and the Sanhedrin at a distance from each other, as if the authorities stare at him as a person removed from them and without engaging with him in any way.

οἱ καθεζόμενοι B 𝔓⁷⁴ ℵ *rell* ‖ οἱ καθήμενοι D Ψ 255. 431. 614. 913. 1518. 1611. 2138. 2344. 2412.

The same variation, between the present participles of καθέζομαι and κάθημαι, arises at 3.10 in the description of the lame man where, however, B03 reads the latter and D05 the former. Whereas οἱ καθεζόμενοι conveys the present aspect, referring to the onlookers of the council in their capacity as Sanhedrin members at that moment ('those sitting'), οἱ καθήμενοι has a perfective sense and refers to the established status of the authorities ('those seated').

καὶ (εἶδον) D d sa^mss mae ‖ *om.* B 𝔓⁷⁴ ℵ *rell.*

There is no need for a connective in B03 since the previous verb was a participle and not a conjugated verb as in D05 (see the first variant of this verse).

(ἀγγέλου) ἑστῶτος ἐν μέσῳ αὐτῶν D d h t mae; Ephr ‖ *om.* B 𝔓⁷⁴ ℵ *rell.*

D05 provides the detail that the angel, whose face Stephen's resembled, was standing in the middle of the council, the position taken up by the witness for the defence in a Jewish court (E. Bammel, 'Erwägungen zur Eschatologie Jesu', *SE* 3 [1964], pp. 3–32), in contrast to the seated position of the council members who serve as judges.

Commentary

[a] 6.8 *Stephen Works Signs and Wonders*
Following the introduction of the Seven, Luke focuses attention on the first-named of the list who had been introduced as 'a man full of faith and the Holy Spirit' (6.5).

6.8 For the third time (cf. 6.3, 5), Luke applies the term 'full of' to Stephen, this time referring to his grace and power which are both, by their very nature, of divine origin. The gift of grace is a mark of God's favour with a person, frequently mentioned by Luke[40] and in particular at various points in the spread of the gospel (cf. 11.2 D05; 13.43; 14.3, 26; 15.40; 18.27; 20.32). Power, too, is given by God, sometimes in combination with grace, to reinforce the message preached by means of various 'signs and wonders' (Lk. 24.49; Acts 1.8; 2.22; 3.12; 4.7, 33). The combination of grace and power was already noted in the account of the apostles' activity in the first stage of the formation of the Jesus-believing community (4.33), and by echoing that account in his presentation of Stephen the narrator establishes a favourable comparison with them.

The phrase 'signs and wonders' is a fixed expression used more in Acts than in all the rest of the New Testament put together.[41] It entails far more than simply

---

40. χάρις is used in the sense of divine favour at Lk. 1.30; 2.40; 4.22; Acts 4.33; 7.10; 11.2 D05; 13.43, 26; 14.3; 15.11, 40; 18.27; 20.24, 32. It is also found, usually in a human context, with the sense of 'esteem' at Lk. 2.52; Acts 2.47; 7.10. John is the only other gospel writer to use χάρις (× 4).

41. Mt. × 1; Mk × 1; Jn × 1; Acts × 9; Paul × 4.

working miracles, as the example of Stephen demonstrates. 'Signs and wonders' are a recollection of the activities of Moses as he led the Israelites to freedom – performed in Egypt, as they left Egypt and throughout the wilderness.[42] The parallel between Moses and the apostles, both leading the people of God to freedom from oppression, was noted with reference to 5.12-40[43] and the parallel is being extended here to Stephen. The earlier reference to the apostles' working of signs and wonders at 5.12 corresponds to their prayer after their release from the Sanhedrin (4.30), and now the prayer is being seen to be answered through Stephen likewise. The allusion to the apostolic prayer is especially strong in the Bezan text where the explicit qualification 'through the name of the Lord Jesus Christ' echoes the request made in the prayer: 'through the name of your holy servant Jesus'.[44]

It is important to be clear about Stephen's identity at this point, for the picture that is created by the narrator prepares for the attack on him that follows. He is a Jew, living in Jerusalem and his activity is carried out among the people of Israel, fellow-Jews. He is one of the Jews who believe in Jesus; under the direction of the apostles, their leaders, the group has dissociated itself from the authority of the Temple. He is a Hellenistic Jew and because of that is, in some sense, regarded as inferior by the Jews of the land of Israel (see *Excursus* 1); yet he has a power and authority hitherto exercised only by the apostles. He may well have belonged to a synagogue of Hellenistic Jews, since such can be surmised to have existed from the next verse; in any case, his Hellenistic origin was a recognizable and distinguishing feature of his identity since it was a requirement that all of the Seven be chosen from among the Hellenists (6.3 D05).

[b] 6.9-10 *The Disagreement of Certain Hellenists: First Attack*
6.9 When the apostles had performed signs and wonders among the people (5.12; cf. 3.1-10), it was the Jewish authorities in Jerusalem who had opposed them and brought them to trial before the Sanhedrin. In accordance with the advice of the Pharisee Gamaliel, however, they had not detained them in prison, much less gone ahead with their plan (D05; wish, AT) to kill them. Once they had released them, under strict orders not to mention the name of Jesus (5.40), they did not, as far as the account of Acts tells us, intervene again directly to prevent them from teaching about Jesus (cf. 5.41-42).

---

42. Exod. 7.3; Wis. 19.8b. *Targ. Ps.-J. Exod.* 15.11 amplifies the Hebrew text to describe the Lord 'doing signs and wonders for your people, the house of Israel'.

43. See also J. Read-Heimerdinger, 'The Re-Enactment of the History of Israel: Exodus Traditions in the Bezan Text of Acts', in R. Pope (ed.), *Remembering the Past and Shaping the Future*, (Leominster: Gracewing, 2003), pp. 81–96 (82–88).

44. σημεῖα καὶ τέρατα γίνεσθαι διὰ τοῦ ὀνόματος τοῦ ἁγίου παιδός σου ᾽ Ιησοῦ, 4.30, the apostles' prayer // διὰ ... τῶν χειρῶν τῶν ἀποστόλων ἐγίνετο σημεῖα καὶ τέρατα πολλὰ ἐν τῷ λαῷ, 5.12, the apostles // τέρατα καὶ σημεῖα μεγάλα ἐν τῷ λαῷ διὰ τοῦ ὀνόματος κυρίου Ἰησοῦ Χριστοῦ, 6.8 D05, Stephen.

It is, therefore, significant that the opposition to Stephen comes from another quarter, not the Jerusalem authorities but other Hellenist Jews living in Jerusalem. Originally from various countries in the Diaspora, these people had settled in the religious capital and had established meeting places – synagogues[45]– for themselves. The synagogue here is said to be of the Freedmen, Jewish slaves whose master had given them their freedom.[46] It is possible to interpret the Greek as meaning that the Freedmen were made up of Cyrenians and Alexandrians or, alternatively, that they constituted three separate groups. The people from Cilicia (and Asia according to the AT) are probably not members of this synagogue but form an independent gathering.[47] They would, of course, have included Saul (cf. 7.58) – it is typical of Luke's art to make the first allusion to a person who will later become an important character in the narrative as a discreet or, as here, implicit reference (cf. Barnabas, 1.23 D05; John-Mark, 12.12). However many groups are represented, the point is that all those who oppose Stephen are identifiable as Jews originating from the Diaspora. It is they, and not the Temple authorities, who take objection to Stephen's public activities among the Jewish people.

The reason for their hostility, and eventually their killing of Stephen, is to be deduced from the religious context of the first century when Jews of the Diaspora have to prove their worth to the Jerusalem authorities by showing their commitment to the Law (see *Excursus* 1). It was obviously clear to Luke's intended audience since he provides no explanation as to why objections to Stephen should have been made so ferociously by Jews who were of the same background.

Luke's portrayal of the Hellenists who became disciples of Jesus includes their greater freedom with respect to the Gentiles (cf. Acts 8.1b; 11.19-20), as may be expected of Diaspora Jews. It is, in consequence, entirely plausible that these Jesus-believers caused other Hellenists, those who were striving to prove to the Jerusalem authorities that they were upholding in total faithfulness all of the

---

45. This is one of the earliest references to synagogues in Palestine, although they had been well established in the Diaspora for at least three centuries previously. The only other evidence of a synagogue in Jerusalem is an inscription by Theodotus who was a priest (so prior to 70 CE), a leader (ἀρχισυνάγωγος) and founder of a synagogue for foreigners in the city (see P.V.M. Flesher, 'Prolegomenon to a Theory of Early Synagogue Development', in A.J. Avery-Peck and J. Neusner [eds], *Judaism in Late Antiquity*. Part 3, *Where We Stand: Issues and Debates in Ancient Judaism*. IV, *The Special Problem of the Synagogue* [Leiden: Brill, 2001], pp. 121–53). The absence of any reference to prayer among the activities listed as taking place in the synagogue suggests that the Temple was still used for that purpose.

46. The use of λεγομένος is characteristic of Luke to introduce a foreign word or explain a name, cf. Passover, Lk. 22.1; Gate Beautiful, Acts 3.2; Tabitha, 9.36. The Latin term translates the Greek ἐλεύθεροι, a word that arises in the story of Naboth's vineyard on which the current narrative appears to draw (cf. the *Overview* to this episode).

47. The interpretation that Luke is speaking of two independent groups, the members of a synagogue and the people from Cilicia (and Asia, AT) is made on the basis of the sentence structure: τινὲς τῶν ἐκ ... καὶ τῶν ἀπό. For suggestions of alternative groupings, see Bruce, *Text*, p. 156; Barrett, I, pp. 323–34.

Jewish principles and practices, no little alarm. In order to protect themselves from accusations of the Jerusalem leaders, they would therefore wish to dissociate themselves from the believers and express their disagreement in the strongest possible terms. The desire of the Hellenists to maintain a good standing among the Jerusalem Jews explains why they did away with the one among them who, from their point of view, had the potential to damage their reputation before the Jewish leaders.

6.10 Their first tactic was to engage in dispute with Stephen but his wisdom was such that they were not strong enough to destroy his arguments or counter the power of the Holy Spirit (cf. 6.5). The explicit mention of the adjective 'holy' by the Bezan text is due to no mere scribal fondness for the adjective nor is it simply the reflection of a theological tendency.[48] Its purpose is to underline the prophetic nature of Stephen's speech which transmitted not his own thoughts but those of God. Within the scheme of the narrative, it demonstrates how faithfully Stephen puts into practice the teaching of Jesus to his disciples that they were to rely on the Holy Spirit to answer their accusers.[49]

This is the first time that Jesus' commands and promises with respect to the defence of his disciples have been enacted as he intended. It should be especially noted that the verb 'to defend oneself' (ἀπολογηθῆναι) is absent from the account of Stephen's trial: he says nothing in his own defence but allows the Holy Spirit to speak through him. The full significance of this will become apparent in the various stages of the trial of Paul who, in contrast to Stephen, does have recourse to self-defence (ἀπολογέομαι × 5; ἀπολογία × 2) and receives no help from the Holy Spirit.[50]

The errors of the arguments of Stephen's attackers were exposed by him, according to the reading of Codex Bezae – that is, by the radical nature of what he said (see *Critical Apparatus*). When examining the significance of 'boldness' in Luke's vocabulary at the earlier occurrences of the word (4.13; cf. 2.29; 4.29, 31), it was seen that the daring was not so much in the attitude of the speakers as in the contents of their speaking, specifically in the interpretation of Scripture.

---

48. Cf. Metzger, *Commentary*, pp. 297–98. Read-Heimerdinger (*The Bezan Text*, pp. 145–72) examines Luke's usage of the adjective ἅγιον in referring to the Spirit of God and concludes that, contrary to the popular claim, Codex Bezae does not have a preference for including the adjective.

49. Lk. 12.11-12: 'When they bring you to synagogues and rulers and authorities, do not think beforehand how or what you are to defend yourselves (ἀπολογήσησθε) or say, for the Holy Spirit will teach you at the time what should be said'; 21.14-15: 'Be quite decided not to work out in advance how to defend yourselves (ἀπολογηθῆναι), for I will give you a mouth and a wisdom that they will not be able to withstand' (or 'contradict', omit D05). The Bezan text of Acts takes up three of the terms used by Jesus, as Stephen's accusers from the synagogue are said to be unable to 'withstand' (ἀντιστῆναι) the 'wisdom' (σοφία) in him or the 'Holy Spirit' (τὸ πνεῦμα τὸ ἅγιον) with which he spoke (cf. στόμα, 'mouth', Lk. 21.15).

50. For a presentation of the negative aspects of Paul's trial, see J. Rius-Camps, 'The Gradual Awakening of Paul's Awareness of his Mission to the Gentiles', in T. Nicklas and M. Tilly (eds), *Apostelgeschichte als Kirchengeschichte. Text, Traditionen und antike Auslegungen* (BZNW, 122: Berlin-New York: Walter de Gruyter, 2003), pp. 281–96.

The apostles had prayed to speak the word 'with all boldness' (4.29), a request that was seen to receive only a partial fulfilment in the following events ('with boldness', 4.31). It is Stephen who will be bold enough as to give a thoroughly radical exposition of the Scriptures concerning the Messiah.

[c] 6.11-12a *Men are Suborned to Accuse Stephen: Second Attack*
6.11 The next stage in the Hellenists' attack is secretly[51] to get other men to make accusations against Stephen. The Bezan text specifies that it was because they were powerless to stand face to face (ἀντοφθαλμεῖν, cf. 27.15) with the truth that they took further action to bring Stephen down. The charges to be made were that Stephen had been heard[52] reviling Moses and God. Moses represents the Torah, as is made explicit twice in the next series of accusations (6.13, 14); blasphemy against God consists in speech against the Temple, again made clear in the words of the second set of accusers. According to the terms of the Torah itself (see Num. 15.30-31), despising the word of God and breaking his commandments constitutes blasphemy, punishable with rejection from the people of Israel.

6.12a The effect of the accusations is to cause agitation among the people as well as the Jewish authorities. The people have already been on the scene as witnesses to the signs and wonders performed by Stephen (6.8). For the first time in Acts, they will be part of the opposition to the Jesus-believers. The elders and the scribes, in contrast, have so far been absent from this incident but were, on the other hand, responsible for the earlier opposition to the activities of the apostles, having been mentioned by their office (4.5, cf. 4.23) and, implicitly, as members of the Sanhedrin (5.21). This body, responsible for the government of all matters of Jewish life, was characterized by the diverse factions within it, principally the Pharisees and the Sadducees. The scribes were important representatives of the Pharisees as highly-regarded interpreters of the Jewish Law and exercised considerable influence within the Sanhedrin. The Sadducees included the priests (and the High Priest) who played a prominent role in the trial of the apostles (5.17-40). Another identifiable group were the 'elders' (cf. 4.5: 'the rulers, the elders and the scribes') who were leading nobles or wealthy men.[53] It is noticeable that the Sadducees are not the ones who initiate the proceedings against Stephen although many of them, including the High Priest (cf. 7.1), will participate as members of the Sanhedrin which is likely to have

51. The verb ὑποβάλλω has a negative sense, suggesting that underhand means were used (B-A-G); it was a 'put up job'.

52. The perfect ἀκηκόαμεν presents the charge as a state of affairs, not a one-off event. Stephen is accused of repeating his teaching, not of a single occurrence (see also pres. part. λαλοῦντος, and cf. 6.13-14).

53. Safrai and Stern (I, pp. 383–400) discuss the identity of the various groups that belonged to the Sanhedrin and evaluate the evidence for its function. Cf. E.M. Smallwood, *The Jews under Roman Rule: From Pompey to Diocletian* (Leiden: E.J. Brill, 1976), pp. 32, 147–50; M. Grant, *The Jews in the Roman World* (London: Weidenfeld and Nicolson, 1973), pp. 92–93.

required all its members to be present for charges as serious as the ones brought in this instance.

[c′] 6.12b *Stephen is Brought to the Sanhedrin*

6.12b The involvement of the elders and scribes may well have been necessary for obtaining a hearing with the Sanhedrin. The driving force is still, nonetheless, the group of Hellenist opponents introduced at the beginning of the scene (v. 9). It is they who surprise Stephen and take him by force to the place where the Sanhedrin met. Although the exact location is disputed, it is possible that at this date, the meeting place for the council was in the Herodian extension to the Temple, in the semi-circular apse at the end of the Royal Portico.[54] If this was the case, the room was open for spectators to view the proceedings and Stephen's speech would have been heard by a great many more than the 71 members of the council, as the detail of Luke's account implies.

[b′] 6.13-14 *False Witnesses are Set up: Third Attack*

6.13 The Hellenist opponents move on to a third step in their attack on Stephen by setting up false witnesses to testify against him before the Sanhedrin. The setting has moved from the original context of the synagogue, through the public arena and, finally, to that of the supreme Jewish court.

The charges against Stephen are similar to those laid by the earlier accusers (v. 11), which is not surprising given that both groups were put together by the Hellenist opponents. The tone is immediately disrespectful, 'this man here' (οὗτος), and he is said to have been talking for some time[55] against the Temple, using the standard Jewish expression 'the holy place', and the Law. The latter two elements correspond to those of the previous accusation (Moses and God, with the Temple being the 'house of God') but are more specific and are also in the reverse order. No doubt the precision carries more weight before the council, for whom the Temple was of prime concern.

6.14 Evidence for the charges once more depends on what the witnesses have heard (cf. v. 11) Stephen saying, namely that it is 'this Jesus, the Nazorene' (the mocking demonstrative οὗτος repeated from the first statement and revealing their own thoughts) who will destroy the place where they are gathered (implied by 'this', an indication that the Sanhedrin did indeed meet within the Temple building) and alter the practices laid down in the Mosaic Law, which could be a reference to both written and oral regulations. The description of Jesus as 'the Nazorene' denoting his messiahship is appropriate

---

54. A. Garrard (*The Splendour of the Temple* [Eye, Suffolk: Moat Farm Publications, 1997], pp. 39–41, 44) cites rabbinic evidence (e.g. *Sanh.* 4.3). Josephus provides the conflicting information that the Sanhedrin met in the *Xystus*, a building in the city (see J. González Echegaray, *Arqueología y evangelios* [Estella, Navarra: Verbo Divino, 2nd edn, 1999], pp. 215–16).

55. Cf. ἀκηκόαμεν, 6.11, repeated in the second statement in 6.14.

in this context where the nationalistic connotations of 'the Nazarene', would be out of place.[56]

The accusation that Jesus would destroy the Temple takes up the saying attributed to Jesus in Mark's Gospel, also by false witnesses and also during his appearance before the Sanhedrin (Mk 14.57-58; cf. Mt. 26.61, but without parallel in Luke).[57] The reference to the Mosaic customs could mean that Stephen spoke about Jesus' attitude and practice concerning the Sabbath, or the laws of purity. However, the truth or falsehood of the accusers claims can only be assessed once Stephen's speech has been examined.

It is important to note that the Temple was a relatively new construction, still unfinished at this time. The rebuilding of Jerusalem had been started by Herod the Great, and even though the Temple was only finished in 64 CE, already people came from all over to admire its magnificence.[58]

[a'] 6.15 *The Sanhedrin See Stephen with the Face of an Angel*
6.15 The preparation for Stephen's speech is concluded with a comment, par-enthetical in Codex Bezae, describing how Stephen appeared to the members of the Sanhedrin like an angel. The verb ἀτενίζω Luke uses to speak of their gazing at him is the one he typically selects to mean a deliberate and careful scrutiny. According to the Bezan text, they were watching him even as the charges were being made, a meaning that is less clear in the AT. It is specifically his face that takes on the appearance of an angel, but Codex Bezae goes further by qualifying the angel as one standing among them. An angel is a representative from God, speaking or acting on his behalf. That the Sanhedrin saw Stephen in this guise indicates that they were confronted with his innocence even before he uttered a word. His standing position is typical of that of the defence in Jewish judicial practice, contrasting with the seated position of the council. The charges brought against him, in other words, have not had the desired effect; the opponents of the Jesus-believers are no match for a witness who has been empowered by God.

---

56. Ναζωραῖος is used exclusively in Acts (cf. 2.22; 3.6; 4.10; 6.14; 9.5 WT; 22.8; 24.5; 26.9) where the context is always messianic; the alternative form Ναζαρηνός is found in Luke's Gospel, usually with variant readings (Lk. 4.34; 18.37 D05; 24.19 ℵ01/B03), as a term that is more of a geographical designation. See J. Rius-Camps, '"Nazareno" y "Nazoreo", con especial atención al Códice Bezae', in R. Pierri (ed.), *Grammatica Intellectio Scripturae: Saggi filologici di Greco biblico* (forthcoming).

57. There are number of elements in Mark's Gospel that Luke reserves for the second volume of his work and uses for his own purpose. Certain differences exist between the saying attributed to Jesus in Mark and in the testimony against Stephen in Acts: a) instead of ἠκούσαμεν (aor.) αὐτοῦ (Jesus) λέγοντος ὅτι, Acts reads ἀκηκόαμεν (perf.) αὐτοῦ (Stephen) λέγοντος ὅτι; b) Jesus' words are not cited in the first person, ἐγὼ καταλύσω, but in the third, Ἰησοῦς ... καταλύσει; c) the designation of the Temple as τὸν ναὸν τοῦτον is replaced by the traditional phrase τὸν τόπον τοῦτον, Luke reserving ὁ ναός to refer to the inner sanctuary (Lk. 1.9, 21; 23.45); d) the reference to the Temple being rebuilt in three days is omitted (Mk 14.58; 15.29; Mt. 26.61; Jn 2.19, 20).

58. Both Tacitus and Pliny refer to the splendour of the rebuilt Jerusalem, see S. Perowne, *The Life and Times of Herod the Great* (London: Arrow Books, 1960), p. 159.

[A'-B] 7.1-54 *Stephen before the Sanhedrin*

Overview

Stephen's appearance before the Sanhedrin, where he responds at length to the charges brought against him, is a key episode in the book of Acts and, indeed, in the history of the early Church. Although the speech does not proceed in the style of a logical argument, and despite some disagreement among scholars over the exact intention of some of his pronouncements, the main thrust of his message with regard both to Moses and the Temple is sufficiently clear for the speech to stand as a statement of belief of the early followers of Jesus. Difficulties arise, however, when this statement is set against not only the practice of the Jesus-believers such as is recorded in the earlier chapters of Acts but also some of the activities and speeches of the disciples (not least Paul) in later chapters. When different episodes and characters are compared, it is evident that there are some contradictions that cannot easily be reconciled. The result is that, as far as Stephen's speech is concerned, attempts are often made to discard some of the material as later (Lukan) interpolations, for example, or to impose an inter-pretation that will force the speech to fit with the rest of the book of Acts.

Underlying such scholarly activity is the assumption that first, all the leaders in Acts held the same theological beliefs and adopted the same practices with regard to worship; and secondly, that Luke endorsed their supposed uniform creed and practice. However, these assumptions are based not on fact but on a traditional reading of the book of Acts, one, moreover, that depends on the Alexandrian text. In the Bezan text, in contrast, the distinction between the narrator's point of view and that of some of his protagonists is clearer, as are also differences of opinion among the early Church leaders. Luke's evaluation of the various characters is signalled by a variety of devices indicating either his approval or his criticism: a comparison with the teaching or behaviour of Jesus in the Gospel, and the witness of the Holy Spirit[59] are both examples of central importance (see *General Introduction,* § VI).

The picture of the early Church in the Bezan text of Acts is one not of harmony, much less of uniformity, but of divergence and disagreement. That aspect of the message of Acts can be detected in the Alexandrian text, too, even if it is harder to recognize because some of the negative comments are absent and the critical perspective is toned down. So when, in the opening sequence of the section (6.1-7), Luke relates one particular instance of discord that set the Hellenists in conflict with the Hebrews, it need be no surprise that Stephen expresses ideas that do not reflect the position adopted so far by the apostles.

---

59. The importance accorded by Luke to the role of the Holy Spirit in signalling approval has been recognized by J. Hur, *A Dynamic Reading of the Holy Spirit in Luke-Acts* (JSNTSup, 211; Sheffield: Sheffield Academic Press, 2001).

Structure and Themes

The speech of Stephen delivered to the Sanhedrin takes up the bulk of this episode ([b] 7.2-53), framed by an introductory invitation from the High Priest to answer the charges against him ([a] 7.1) and a concluding description of the immediate response ([a′] 7.54). The structure of the speech itself is analysed in the preliminary *Commentary* on 7.2-53 below:

[a]	7.1	The High Priest invites Stephen to answer charges
[b]	7.2-53	Stephen's speech to the Sanhedrin
[a′]	7.54	The response of the Sanhedrin

Translation

	Codex Bezae D05	*Codex Vaticanus B03*
[a]	**7.1** The High Priest said to Stephen, 'Is this really so?'	**7.1** The High Priest said, 'Are these things so?'
[b] [αα]	**2** He said, 'Brethren and fathers, listen: The God of glory appeared to our father Abraham when he was in Mesopotamia before he lived in Haran, **3** and he said to him, "Go away from your land and your family and go into whichever land I show you".	**2** He said, 'Brethren and fathers, listen: The God of glory appeared to our father Abraham when he was in Mesopotamia before he lived in Haran, **3** and he said to him, "Go out of your land and your family and go into whichever land I show you".
[αβ]	**4a** Then Abraham went out of the land of the Chaldees and did indeed live in Haran.	**4a** Then he went out of the land of the Chaldees and lived in Haran.
[αγ]	**4b** And God was there after his father died, and he removed him into this land in which you now dwell and our fathers who were before us. **5** And he did not give him any inheritance in it, not even a foot's length, but promised to give it to him in possession and to his seed though he did not have a child.	**4b** And, after his father died, God removed him from there into this land in which you now dwell. **5** And he did not give him any inheritance in it, not even a foot's length, and promised to give it to him in possession and to his seed though he did not have a child.
[αδ]	**6** God spoke to him to this effect, that his seed would be sojourners in a land belonging to others and that they would enslave them and ill-treat them for 400 years. **7** "And the nation that they serve, I shall judge", says God. "And after this, they will come out and will worship me in this place."	**6** God spoke to this effect, that his seed would be sojourners in a land belonging to others and that they would enslave them and ill-treat them for 400 years. **7** "And the nation that they serve, I shall judge", says God. "And after this, they will come out and will worship me in this place."
[αδ′]	**8a** And he gave him a covenant of circumcision.	**8a** And he gave him a covenant of circumcision.
[αγ′]	**8b** And so Abraham fathered Isaac and he circumcised him on the eighth day, and Isaac fathered Jacob and Jacob the twelve patriarchs.	**8b** And so Abraham fathered Isaac and he circumcised him on the eighth day, and Isaac fathered Jacob and Jacob the twelve patriarchs.
[αβ′]	**9a** And the patriarchs became jealous of Joseph and sold him into Egypt.	**9a** And the patriarchs became jealous of Joseph and sold him into Egypt.
[αα′]	**9b** And God was with him **10** and he rescued him from all of his afflictions	**9b** And God was with him **10** and he rescued him from all of his afflictions

and gave him grace and wisdom before Pharaoh the king of Egypt, and he appointed him governor over Egypt and over all his household.

[βα] **11** A famine came over the whole of Egypt and Canaan, and great affliction, and our fathers could not find food.

[ββ] **12** When, therefore, Jacob heard that there was corn in Egypt, he sent out our fathers a first time;

[βγ] **13** and on the second occasion, Joseph was recognized by his brothers and Joseph's race became apparent to Pharaoh.

[βγ'] **14** Joseph sent and called Jacob, his father, and all his family, seventy-five souls.

[ββ'] **15** Jacob went down to Egypt and he died, both he and our fathers;

[βα'] **16** and they were taken back to Shechen and were put in the tomb which Abraham had bought for a sum of silver from the sons of Hamor, the father of Shechem.

[γα] **17** As the time of the promise that God had promised to Abraham drew near, the people grew strong and multiplied in Egypt **18** until there arose another king who did not remember Joseph;

[γβ] **19** and dealing shrewdly with our race, he ill-treated the fathers by making them expose their newborn infants so that they would not be kept alive.

[γγ] **20a** At this time, Moses was born and he was well-pleasing to God;

[γγ'] **20b** he was reared for three months in his father's house.

[γβ'] **21** Then, when he was exposed beside the river, the daughter of Pharaoh picked him up – she reared him as her son.

[γα'] **22** And Moses was instructed in all the wisdom of the Egyptians and was powerful in his words and deeds.

[δα] **23** When he was approaching the age of 40, there came to him the idea of going to visit his brethren, the sons of Israel.

[δβ] **24** When he saw that a certain man from his race was being harmed, he started defending him and he carried out justice for the man who was being mistreated by striking the Egyptian, and he hid him in the sand.

and gave him grace and wisdom before Pharaoh the king of Egypt, and he appointed him governor over Egypt and over all his household.

11 A famine came to the whole of Egypt and Canaan, and great affliction, and our fathers could not find food.

12 When Jacob heard that there was corn in Egypt, he sent out our fathers a first time;

13 and on the second occasion, Joseph let himself be made known to his brothers and Joseph's race became apparent to Pharaoh.

14 Joseph sent and called Jacob, his father, and all his family, seventy-five souls.

15 And Jacob went down and he died, he and our fathers;

16 and they were transported to Shechem and were put in the tomb which Abraham had bought for a sum of silver from the sons of Hamor, in Shechem.

17 As the time of the promise that God had spoken to Abraham drew near, the people grew strong and multiplied in Egypt **18** until there arose another king over Egypt who had not known Joseph.

19 He, dealing shrewdly with our race, ill-treated our fathers by making them expose their newborn infants so that they would not be kept alive.

20a At this time, Moses was born and he was well-pleasing to God;

20b he was reared for three months in the father's house.

21 Then, when he was exposed, the daughter of Pharaoh picked him up and reared him as her own son.

22 And Moses was instructed with all the wisdom of the Egyptians; he was poweful in his words and deeds.

23 When he was approaching 40 years old, there came to him the idea of going to visit his brethren, the sons of Israel.

24 When he saw that a certain man was being harmed, he defended him and he carried out justice for the man who was being mistreated by striking the Egyptian.

[δγ] **25a** He supposed that his brethren understood that God was giving salvation through his hand.

25a He supposed that the brethren understood that God was giving salvation through his hand.

[δδ] **25b** But they did not understand.

25b But they did not understand.

[δγ′] **26** The next day, he again appeared to them while they were fighting and saw them doing wrong and he tried to get them to come to terms saying, "What are you doing, brethren? Why are you doing wrong to each other?"

26 The next day, he again appeared to them and he tried to get them to come to terms saying, "Men, you are brothers. Why are you wronging each other?"

[δβ′] **27** But the man who was wronging his neighbour pushed him aside and said, **28** "Who appointed you as a ruler and a judge over us? Do you perhaps want to kill me the way you killed the Egyptian yesterday?"

27 But the man who was wronging his neighbour pushed him aside and said, **28** "Who appointed you as a ruler and a judge over us? Do you perhaps want to kill me the way you killed the Egyptian yesterday?"

[δα′] **29** And so it was that Moses became a fugitive on account of this word, and became a sojourner in the land of Midian where he had two sons.

29 Moses fled on account of this word and became a sojourner in the land of Midian where he had two sons.

[γ′α] **30** And after this, when he was 40 years older, the angel of the Lord appeared to him in the desert of Mt Sinai in a flame of fire in a thorn bush.

30 And when 40 years had passed, an angel appeared to him in the desert of Mt Sinai in a flame of fire in a thorn bush.

[γ′β] **31a** When Moses saw it, he was amazed at the vision;

31a When Moses saw it, he marvelled at the vision.

[γ′γ] **31b** and as he was moving nearer so that he could take a closer look, the Lord spoke to him saying, **32a** "I am the God of your fathers, the God of Abraham and the God of Isaac and the God of Jacob".

31b As he was moving nearer to look more closely, the voice of the Lord came, **32a** "I am the God of your fathers, the God of Abraham and Isaac and Jacob".

[γ′δ] **32b** But since Moses began to tremble, he did not dare look more closely;

32b But since Moses began to tremble, he did not dare look more closely.

[γ′ε] **33** and a voice came to him, "Take off the sandals from your feet, for the place where you are standing is holy ground. **34** I am here because I have indeed seen the ill-treatment of the people in Egypt and I have heard their suffering and I have come down to rescue them; and now, come, I will send you to Egypt."

33 The Lord said to him, "Take off your sandals from your feet, for the place upon which you are standing is holy ground. **34** Surely I have seen the ill-treatment of my people in Egypt and I have heard their suffering and I have come down to rescue them; and now, come, I will send you to Egypt."

[γ′δ′] **35** This Moses whom they denied saying, "Who appointed you as a ruler and a judge over us?", this man God sent as a ruler and a deliverer by means of an angel who appeared to him in the bush.

35 This Moses whom they denied saying, "Who appointed you as a ruler and a judge?", this man God sent as both a ruler and a deliverer by means of an angel who appeared to him in the bush.

[γ′γ′] **36** This man led them out, the one who did wonders and signs in the land of Egypt and in the Red Sea and in the desert for 40 years.

36 This man led them out, doing wonders and signs in Egypt and in the Red Sea and in the desert for 40 years.

[γ′β′]

37 This is Moses, the one who said to the sons of Israel, "God will raise up a prophet from among your brethren like me; listen to him".

37 This is Moses, the one who said to the sons of Israel, "God will raise up a prophet from among your brethren like me".

[γ′α′]

38 This is the one who was in the assembly in the desert as a mediator between the angel, while he was speaking to him on Mt Sinai, and our fathers; who received living words to give to us, 39 and whom our fathers did not want to obey, but instead they pushed him aside and turned back in their hearts to Egypt, 40 saying to Aaron, "Make gods for us which will go before us; for this Moses, who led us out of the land of Egypt, we do not know what has become of him".

38 This is the one who was in the assembly in the desert as a mediator between the angel, who spoke to him on Mt Sinai, and our fathers; who chose living words to give to you 39 and whom our fathers did not want to obey, but instead they pushed him aside and turned in their hearts to Egypt, 40 saying to Aaron, "Make gods for us which will go before us; for this Moses, who led us out of the land of Egypt, we do not know what happened to him".

[β′α]

41 They made a calf in those days, and they started to render sacrifice to the idol for themselves and to rejoice in the works of their hands.

41 They made a calf in those days, and they brought a sacrifice to the idol and started to rejoice in the works of their hands.

[β′β]

42 So God turned his back and gave them over to worship the host of heaven, just as it is written in the book of the Prophets, "You failed to bring me offerings and sacrifices for 40 years in the desert, did you not, O house of Israel? 43 And you took up the tent of Moloch and the star of the god Rempham, the models you made so you could worship them; and I will remove you to the regions of Babylon."

42 So God turned his back and gave them over to worship the host of heaven, just as it is written in the book of the Prophets, "You failed to bring me offerings and sacrifices for 40 years in the desert, did you not, O house of Israel? 43 And you took up the tent of Moloch and the star of the god Rompham, the models you made so you could worship them; and I will remove you beyond Babylon."

[β′γ]

44 Our fathers had the tent of testimony at their disposal in the desert, in accordance with what he commanded in speaking to Moses, to make it according to the imperfect representation of the things he saw.

44 Our fathers had the tent of testimony in the desert, in accordance with what the one speaking to Moses commanded, to make it according to the model that he had seen.

[β′δ]

45 Our fathers received it in turn with Joshua, and did indeed bring it in when they came into possession of the nations whom God put out before our fathers, and this continued until the days of David.

45 Our fathers received it in turn with Joshua, and did indeed bring it in when they came into possession of the nations whom God put out before our fathers, and this continued until the days of David.

[β′γ′]

46 He found favour with God and asked to find a tent for the house of Jacob.

46 He found favour with God and asked to find a tent for the house of Jacob.

[β′β′]

47 Solomon, however, built a house for him.

47 Solomon, however, built a house for him.

[β′α′]

48 The Most High, however, does not live in things made with hands, as the prophet says, 49 "Heaven is my throne, the earth is the footstool of my feet.

48 But the Most High most certainly does not live in things made with hands, just as the prophet says, 49 "Heaven is my throne, and the earth is the footstool

	What kind of a house will you build for me?", says the Lord, "or what kind of place is the place of my rest? **50** Did not my hand make all these things?"	of my feet. What kind of a house will you build for me?", says the Lord, "or what is the place of my rest? **50** Did not my hand make all these things?"
[α′α]	**51** You stiff-necked and uncircumcised in hearts and ears, you always oppose the Holy Spirit, exactly like the fathers, *your* fathers.	**51** You stiff-necked and uncircumcised in hearts and ears, you always oppose the Holy Spirit, you yourselves just like your fathers.
[α′β]	**52a** Which of the prophets did those men not persecute? and they killed them when they were proclaiming in advance the coming of the Righteous One.	**52a** Which of the prophets did your fathers not persecute? and they killed those who proclaimed in advance the coming of the Righteous One.
[α′α′]	**52b** His betrayers and murderers you have now become, **53** you who received the Law as delivered by angels and did not keep it.'	**52b** His betrayers and murderers you have now become, **53** you who received the Law as delivered by angels and did not keep it.'
[a′]	**54** When they heard him, they were enraged and began to grind their teeth against him.	**54** As they listened to him, they were enraged and began to grind their teeth against him.

Critical Apparatus

7.1 (ὁ ἀρχιερεὺς) τῷ Στεφάνῳ D d E it ^{vgCDΘTW} (sy^p) mae || *om.* B 𝔓^{74} ℵ *rell.*

There are other occasions in Acts when D05 (× 3) or B03 (× 18) leave the addressee of speech unspecified, usually because the person can be deduced from the context, as it can here (Read-Heimerdinger, *The Bezan Text*, pp. 180–82). The effect of naming Stephen is to create a formal opening for the trial proceedings and to underline the seriousness of the occasion on which Stephen will pronounce a key discourse. The use of the dative rather than πρός + accusative further confers a note of formality on the High Priest's interrogation of Stephen.

Εἰ B 𝔓^{74vid} ℵ A C 36. 323. 945. 1175*. 1646. 1739. 1891 *pc* || Εἰ ἄρα D E H P S Ψ 049. 056. 33 𝔐 sy^h.

ἄρα reinforces the question in D05 (cf. 5.8 D05; 8.22; 17.27).

ταῦτα B 𝔓$^{45.74}$ ℵ *rell, haec* d || τοῦτο D.

The singular pronoun refers more specifically to the declaration Stephen is supposed to have made of Jesus' intentions with regard to the Temple and the Law. The plural of B03 refers to the accusations generally.

7.3 (ἔξελθε) ἐκ (τῆς γῆς σου) B 𝔓^{74} ℵ D^H *rell* || ἀπό D*.

B03 follows the LXX of Gen. 12.1 being quoted here. Both prepositions express the idea of separation from a place, and over time ἀπό tended to supplant ἐκ. Of the two MSS, D05 is usually more conservative in this respect in Acts overall, as is the text common to the two traditions which uses ἐκ when it is a question of 'extracting oneself' from a place rather than simply leaving it (Read-Heimerdinger, *The Bezan Text*, pp. 189–90). This can be seen in the following verse where, in response to God's command, Abraham 'gets out of' (ἐκ, without *vl*) the land belonging to the Chaldeans.

Both B03 and D05, but not ℵ01, omit the second preposition ἐκ before τῆς συγγενείας, another departure from the LXX text.

7.4 (τότε)ʹΑβραάμ D d syᵖ mae; Aug || *om.* B 𝔓⁷⁴ ℵ *rell.*

D05 repeats the name of the character whose story is being told here which, while unnecessary for following the narrative, maintains him clearly in focus. The repetition of πρὸς αὐτόν at 7.6 D05 (see below) has a similar effect.

καὶ (κατῴκησεν) D* d || *om.* B 𝔓⁷⁴ ℵ Dˢ·ᵐ· *rell.*

D05 reads καί before a main verb that follows a participle on up to 20 occasions (at some places, the text of the MS is not clear; see Read-Heimerdinger, *The Bezan Text*, pp. 206–10). An examination of all the occurrences suggests that it is not simply a quirk of style on the part of the scribe but is used deliberately to draw attention to the action of the main verb. In this instance, the previous mention of Abraham's living in Haran is picked up from 7.3 where the narrator was careful to insist that Abraham moved to Haran only after he had received the command from God (contrary to Gen. 11.31–12.1, 4; but cf. Gen. 15.7; Neh. 9.7). The thrust of the sentence in v. 4 is that when Abraham left the land of the Chaldeans, then (τότε) he did indeed (καί) live in Haran.

κἀκεῖθεν B 𝔓⁷⁴ ℵ Dᴮ *rell* || κἀκεῖ ἦν D* d.

According to B03, God (as implied subject) moved Abraham from Haran to Israel after the death of his father. D05 indicates that Abraham stayed in Haran after the death of his father and (see next *vl*) God moved him to Israel at some unspecified time later. Some Old Latin MSS (including gig p) read at the end of 7.2 that his father had died *before* Abraham lived in Haran. This is in contradiction of Gen. 11.27-32 (*pace* Metzger, *Commentary*, p. 300).

The Greek of D05 may not, in fact, be intended to express a literal meaning, for the words (καὶ) ἐκεῖ ἦν reflect a play on words that frequently occurs in the Hebrew Bible in order to hide the unutterable name of the divine: 1) the consonants שׁם represent the word 'name' or 'there', according to the vocalization, and 2) יהוה, the consonants for the name of God, also represent the third person of the verb 'to be'. In consequence, the phrase ἐκεῖ ἦν is found in the LXX as a translation of the Hebrew device to express the name, and presence, of God. This is the phrase used by D05, expressing the presence of God with Abraham in Haran. It is then all the clearer that he is the underlying subject of the next verb, μετῴκησεν.

καὶ (μετῴκισεν) D* d a; Ir^lat || *om.* B 𝔓^74 ℵ D^s.m. *rell.*

See above *vl.* The conjunction is unnecessary in B03 since it does not start a new sentence at this point.

(κατοικεῖτε) καὶ οἱ πατέρες ἡμῶν οἱ πρὸ ἡμῶν D d | κ. οἱ πατ. ὑμῶν πρὸ ὑμῶν (E) 876. 913. 1611. 1765. 2138 sy^h** (mae; Aug) || *om.* B 𝔓^74 ℵ *rell.*

The additional words of D05, in the first person plural, contrast with the verb immediately preceding them, κατοικεῖτε, which is second person. Stephen apparently does not view himself as an inhabitant of Israel (see *Commentary*) but does acknowledge his common Jewish ancestry.

7.5 καὶ (ἐπηγγείλατο) B 𝔓^74 ℵ *rell* || ἀλλ᾽ D d b c dem gig r vg^mss sa mae aeth; Ir^lat.

ἀλλά of D05 expresses more forcefully than connective καί the fact that instead of Abraham himself receiving any part in Israel, God made a promise to give it to his descendants.

7.6 (ἐλάλησεν ... ὁ θεὸς) πρὸς αὐτόν D d; Ir^lat || *om.* B 𝔓^74 ℵ *rell.*

It is typical of the careful narrative construction evident in the D05 text to specify the addressee in order to maintain the character clearly in focus (cf. Ἀβραάμ, 7.4 D05). The introduction to the citation of God's promise to Abraham thus echoes the introduction to his command (cf. 7.3). The omission of the addressee in B03 reflects more accurately the fact that the final part of the promise cited by Stephen was not spoken to Abraham (cf. Exod. 3.12).

(δουλώσουσιν) αὐτό B 𝔓^74vid ℵ *rell* | αὐτῷ 𝔓^33 6. 33. 88. 181*. 255. 383. 467. 618. 915. 945. 1175. 1245. 1837. 1891. 2147. 2344. 2495* *pc* | *om.* 1646; Ir^lat || αὐτούς D d 1270 lat sa bo^mss.

The neuter singular of B03 (read also at Gen. 15.13 LXX by A02) refers to τὸ σπέρμα, the masculine plural of D05 to the people implied by it (as in the other MSS of Gen. 15.13 LXX).

7.7 (ᾧ ἄν) δουλεύσωσιν B 𝔓^33 ℵ E H P Ψ 049. 056. 33. 1739 𝔐, *servierint* d; LXX || -σουσιν D 𝔓^74 A C 618 *pc*; Ir^lat vid.

Here, it is B03 that has the LXX reading of Gen 15.14, with the subjunctive in accordance with classical usage; D05 reads the future which became an acceptable alternative in Hellenistic Greek (Zerwick, *Biblical Greek*, §§ 340–41).

ὁ θεὸς εἶπεν B 𝔓^33vid.74 ℵ A C 1175 *pc* || εἶπεν ὁ θ. D E H P S Ψ 049. 056. 33. 383. 614. 1739 𝔐 latt sy | *dicit dominus* d gig p vg; Ir^lat.

B03 confers emphasis on ὁ θεός by placing the noun before the verb, directly following the words spoken by God, thus underlining the change from indirect to direct speech for the final clause of the promise.

7.8 τὸν Ἰσαὰκ ... Ἰσαάκ Β^C 𝔓^{33·74} ℵ *rell* || τ. Ἰσὰκ ... ὁ Ἰσάκ Β* D.

The genealogy cited by Stephen may be compared with the genealogy of Jesus provided by Matthew 1.2-16 where the article is regularly included at the naming of the son, but omitted at the second naming of the character as the father of the next generation. Thus, 1.2 reads: Ἀβραὰμ ἐγέννησεν τὸν Ἰσαάκ, Ἰσαὰκ δὲ ἐγέννησεν τὸν Ἰακώβ, Ἰακὼβ δὲ ἐγέννησεν τὸν Ἰούδαν καὶ τοὺς ἀδελφοὺς αὐτοῦ (N-A^{27}, D05 lac.). The omission of the article would appear to have the function of bringing the son into focus as the father of the next generation for it is in this capacity that he acquires his importance in a genealogy. The same is true of the brief list provided by Stephen. The difference in the case of Isaac, however, is that special information concerning his circumcision is mentioned immediately after his introduction as a son, which has the effect of bringing him into focus already before he is named as a father, and it may be for this reason that D05 does not see a need to omit the article in order to signal his importance because it has already been established.

7.10 (ἔδωκεν) αὐτῷ χάριν Β ℵ *rell, ei gratiam* d | χάριν 𝔓^{74} A || χ. αὐτῷ D.

B03 links χάριν and σοφίας together with καί, placing them on an equal footing; by separating them with the pronoun αὐτῷ, D05 confers special emphasis on the first noun of the pair.

7.11 ἐφ᾽ ὅλην τὴν Αἴγυπτον Β 𝔓^{45.74} ℵ A C Ψ 88. 618. 1175 | ἐφ᾽ ὅλην τὴν γῆν A-του E H P 049. 056. 33^{vid}. (945. 1505. 1739) 𝔐 a d gig p vg^{mss} sy^h aeth || ἐφ᾽ ὅλης τῆς A-του D* | ἐφ᾽ ὅλης τῆς γῆς A-του D^B.

The difference in case after ἐπί, with B03 reading the accusative and D05 the genitive, has an effect on the exact sense of the preposition. While the accusative suggests that the famine *extended* over all of Egypt and Canaan, the genitive indicates rather that it was *established* there (Delebecque, *Actes*, p. 54).

7.12 (ἀκούσας) δέ Β 𝔓^{74} ℵ *rell, vero* d || οὖν D gig.

δέ has the effect of switching attention to Jacob's involvement in looking for sustenance during the time of famine. The interest in D05, on the other hand, is to explain how Jacob comes to be in Egypt, using οὖν to maintain the focus on the country which is the dominant theme throughout the larger part of Stephen's speech (see Read-Heimerdinger, *The Bezan Text*, pp. 229–30).

(σιτία) εἰς Αἴγυπτον Β 𝔓^{74} ℵ A C E 453. 1175 *pc* || ἐν A-τῳ D d H P Ψ 049. 056. 33^{vid}. 383. 614. 1739 𝔐 gig vg.

The preposition ἐν, read here by D05 as also Gen. 42.2 LXX, was used in classical Greek to indicate location. It was supplanted over time by εἰς, read by B03, losing the sense of movement it had earlier carried. D05 is typically more conservative in this respect (Read-Heimerdinger, *The Bezan Text*, pp. 192–97).

7.13 ἐν (τῷ δευτέρῳ) B 𝔓⁷⁴ ℵ *rell, in* d ‖ ἐπί D.

The prepositions ἐν and ἐπί (followed by the dative) are found as alternatives at other places in the MSS of Acts (cf. 2.38; 3.11). Since, however, this is the only occurrence of the variation within an expression of time, it is not possible to establish what, if any, difference in meaning is implied (see Read-Heimerdinger, *The Bezan Text*, pp. 199–200).

ἐγνωρίσθη B A p vg ‖ ἀνεγ- D, *recognitus est* d 𝔓⁷⁴ ℵ C E H P Ψ 049. 056. 1739 𝔐 gig.

Metzger (*Commentary*, p. 301) cites evidence for the same *vl* in Gen. 45.1 LXX where the story is first told. His conclusion, that the compound would have been altered to the simple form of the verb so as to avoid giving the impression that Joseph had already been recognized on his first visit, is not necessarily correct since the compound verb may simply mean 'recognize'.

(φανερὸν) ἐγένετο B 𝔓⁷⁴ ℵ *rell* ‖ ἐγενήθη D.

The middle and the passive voices of γίνομαι are practically equivalent, but the aorist of D05 confers a certain solemn tone, being found frequently in the LXX (Winer, *Grammar*, p. 760, n. 2). B03 follows Gen. 45.3 LXX.

τῷ (Φαραώ) B D *rell* ‖ om. 𝔓⁷⁴ ℵ 1175. 1243. 1891.

Where the article is retained, Pharaoh is assumed to have already been introduced on the scene (cf. 7.10, anarthrous). The omission of the article can be explained by the fact that he has not been mentioned in the present context (Heimerdinger and Levinsohn, 'The Use of the Article', p. 25).

(τὸ γένος) Ἰωσήφ B 𝔓³³ C 88. 90. 915 *pc* | αὐτοῦ 𝔓⁷⁴ ℵ A E 181. 1895 vg ‖ τοῦ Ἰω. D 𝔓⁴⁵ H P Ψ 049. 056. 33ᵛⁱᵈ. 1739 𝔐.

The name of Joseph is mentioned here for the third time since his introduction at 7.9 and is about to appear for a fourth time in the following clause (7.14); it is mentioned for the final time in Stephen's speech at 7.18. At the first mention, the name is arthrous (no *vl*) which is highly unusual for Acts (see Heimerdinger and Levinsohn, 'The Use of the Article'), but it maintains the pattern established in the genealogy so far – namely, of the name of the descendant being introduced with the article each time (see on v. 8 above). Even though the pattern is being disrupted, since the patriarchs are not the father of Joseph and he is mentioned because they are jealous of him, it is the patriarchs who are still in focus as their brother is named.

At the second mention (7.13), the article is omitted (again no *vl*), this time because Joseph is re-introduced into the story as a salient participant, quite distinct from his brothers. When, though, his name is mentioned again in the next clause, his presence is established in the incident and the article can be retained. To omit it, on the other hand, as B03 does, could be a way to contrast Pharaoh and Joseph. The third person pronoun (א01) would appear to be used at this point because it was not felt necessary to repeat the name so soon after a previous mention.

The anarthrous reference in the next new sentence, v. 14, arises because Joseph takes over as the new protagonist. By the final mention of his name at v. 18, he is no longer an active participant and the reference is therefore arthrous.

7.14 (τὴν συγγένειαν) αὐτοῦ D d E Ψ 88. 104. 323. 618. 927. 945. 1245. 1270. 1739. 1891 gig p vg sy sa || *om.* B 𝔓³³·⁷⁴ א *rell.*

There is ambiguity with the pronoun in D05 as to whether 'all the family' are that of Joseph or of Jacob. The size of the family (75 souls) suggests that it is Jacob's family that is meant, which concords with the LXX (Gen. 46.27) and is how the Old Latin understands it (*cognationem eius*, cf. *patrem suum*). Omitting the pronoun does not remove the ambiguity altogether but it avoids the potentially misleading parallel: τὸν πατέρα αὐτοῦ // πᾶσαν τὴν συγγένειαν αὐτοῦ.

ἐν ψυχαῖς ἑβδομήκοντα πέντε B 𝔓³³·⁷⁴ א *rell* || ἐν .ο. καὶ .ε. ψυχ. D d H Ψ 69. 88. 323. 614. 1270. 1611. 1837. 2412. 2495 gig p sy; Hier.

B03 follows the word order of Gen. 46.27 LXX.

7.15 κατέβη δέ B 049. 056. 33 𝔐 | καὶ κατ. 𝔓³³·⁷⁴ א A C E P 36. 88. 945. 1175. 1243. 1646. 1739 *al* vg || κατ. D d Ψ *pc* gig p syʰ mae; Hier.

The absence of connective, coupled with the anarthrous mention of the name of Jacob, draws attention to the sentence in a powerful way. It shows how the new sentence parallels the previous one, Jacob going down to Egypt in response to Joseph's call (Read-Heimerdinger, *The Bezan Text*, p. 250). The importance of the sentence becomes apparent in the next *vl* of D05 (see below). δέ in B03 presents Jacob's move to Egypt as the next development in the story, which it undoubtedly can be considered to be, but without drawing special attention to it. καί, in contrast, treats this next step in the narrative as associated with the previous one.

('Ιακώβ) εἰς Αἴγυπτον D d 𝔓⁴⁵ᵛⁱᵈ·⁷⁴ א *rell* || *om.* B.

The information that Jacob went down *to Egypt* (Gen. 46.3, 4 LXX; Deut. 26.5 LXX) is strictly unnecessary but it is a crucial step for the focus Stephen is giving to his account of the history of Israel. B03 is alone in omitting the detail. It is typical of D05 to include redundant information in order to give emphasis to a point of importance. In this case, Egypt is the central theme of Stephen's speech and is underlined as such by the repeated mention of the name even when it is unnecessary. The absence of connective in D05 (see *vl* above), together with the anarthrous mention of Jacob by name, function in combination with the detail εἰς Αἴγυπτον to indicate the central significance of the sentence for Stephen's argument.

αὐτός τε (καί) D d ‖ αὐτός B 𝔓³³·⁷⁴ ℵ *rell.*

The reinforced conjunction, τε καί, creates a clear distinction between Jacob and 'our fathers', the latter being regarded more negatively throughout Stephen's account.

7.16 (καὶ) μετετέθησαν B 𝔓³³·⁷⁴ ℵ *rell* ‖ μετήχθησαν D, *translati sunt* d.

Whereas B03 speaks of the bodies being 'put in another place' (μετα-τίθημι), D05 has them uses a verb that has a more forceful sense of direction (μετάγω).

εἰς Συχέμ B 𝔓⁷⁴ ℵ *rell, in Sychem* d ‖ εἰς Σ-ν D.— (Ἐμμὼρ) ἐν Σ-μ B 𝔓³³ ℵ* C 36. 88. 181. 307. 323. 453. 610. 945. 1175. 1678. 1739. 1891 *al* co arm ‖ τοῦ Σ. D 𝔓⁷⁴ H P S Ψ 049. 056. 33. 614. 𝔐 it vg mae (aeth); Chr Hier ‖ τοῦ ἐν Σ. ℵ² A E 1409 *pc* e vgᵐˢˢ syʰ; Bedaᵍʳ ᵐˢˢ ᵃᶜᶜ· ᵗᵒ ‖ *et Sychem* d ‖ *om.* syᵖ.

In Gen. 33.19, the LXX speaks of Jacob purchasing a field from Ἐμμὼρ πατρὸς Συχέμ (cf. Josh. 24.32) which is the spelling followed here by D05 for the name of the person. D05 distinguishes between the name of the person and that of the town, Συχέν. B03 takes both references to be to the town, using the same spelling each time as well as a preposition indicating place.

The order of words in D05 appears to mean that Shechem was the father of Hamor, the contrary of the Genesis passage. If it intends to convey the original sense, that Hamor was the father of Shechem, it looks as if πατρός has dropped out or is to be understood, but the order of the father before the son is strange. B03's reading avoids the difficulty, as do the other readings including that of d05.

7.17 (τῆς ἐπαγγελίας ἧς) ὡμολόγησεν B 𝔓⁷⁴ ℵ A C 36*. 453. 610. 945. 1175. 1678 *pc* it vg syʰᵐᵍ saᵍʳ aeth | ὤμοσεν H P S Ψ 049. 056. 614. 1739 𝔐 gig sy⁽ᵖ⁾·ʰ fay bo; Chr ‖ ἐπηγγείλατο D, *pollicitus est* d 𝔓⁴⁵ E e p vgᵐˢˢ syᵖ·ʰᵐᵍ mae aeth; Bedaᵍʳ ᵐˢˢ ᵃᶜᶜ· ᵗᵒ.

B03 offers an alternative to the Hebraism of D05 which reads the verb with its cognate noun ἐπαγγελία. ὤμοσεν is another alternative.

7.18 (βασιλεὺς ἕτερος) ἐπ᾽ Αἴγυπτον B 𝔓³³ᵛⁱᵈ·⁷⁴ ℵ A C Ψ 36. 88. 104. 181. 242. 307. 323. 453. 467. 522. 610. 876. 915. 945. 1175. 1409. 1505. 1678. 1739. 1765. 1838. 1891. 1898. 2298 *pc* (it vg) vgᵐˢˢ syᵖ·ʰᵐᵍ co arm ‖ *om.* D d 𝔓⁴⁵ᵛⁱᵈ E H P 049. 056. 614 𝔐 e gig p syʰ; Chr.

The detail included by B03 corresponds to the LXX text of Exod. 1.8a. Its omission in D05 can be accounted for by the mention of Egypt at the end of the previous clause which is itself a modification of Exod. 1.7 LXX.

(ὃς) οὐκ ᾔδει τὸν Ἰωσήφ B 𝔓⁷⁴ ℵ *rell* ‖ οὐκ ἐμνήσθη τοῦ Ἰ. D, *non meminisset ipsius Ioseph* d E gig p; Chr.

Again, B03 follows Exod. 1.8b LXX while D05 words the text differently.

7.19 οὗτος (κατασοφισάμενος) B 𝔓⁴⁵·⁷⁴ ℵ *rell* ‖ καί D syᵖ | *om.* d.

The demonstrative pronoun in B03 switches attention away from ὁ λαός (cf. v. 17) to the character of the new Pharaoh; the simple conjunction in D05 keeps Pharaoh in the background and allows the focus to be kept on the Jewish participants: ὁ λαός ... τοῦ Ἰωσὴφ ... τὸ γένος ἡμῶν ... τοὺς πατέρας ... τὰ βρέφη αὐτῶν.

(τοῦ ποιεῖν) τὰ βρέφη ἔκθετα αὐτῶν B 𝔓⁷⁴ ℵ A C (81. 1175). 1241 *pc* ‖ ἔκθ. τ. βρ. αὐ. D, *exponi infantes* d 𝔓⁴⁵ E H P S Ψ 049. 056*. 33. 1739 𝔐 p.

By the position of τὰ βρέφη before the participle and its separation from the pronominal adjective αὐτῶν, B03 places emphasis on 'the newborn infants'. D05 has a neutral word order.

7.20 (τοῦ πατρὸς) αὐτοῦ D d E 36. 88. 104. 188. 257. 323. 383. 431. 440. 453. 522. 614. 913. 915. 927. 1108. 1175. 1270. 1518. 1611. 1765. 1837. 1838. 1898. 2138. 2298. 2344. 2412 gig p vg syᵖ·ʰ sa mae aeth; QvD Theoph | μου ℵ* ‖ *om.* B 𝔓⁷⁴ ℵ² *rell.*

D05 frequently spells out the pronoun implicit in the B03 text.

7.21 (αὐτοῦ) παρὰ τὸν ποταμόν D d (E) 88. 915 a w tpl vgᵐˢˢ syʰ** mae ‖ *om.* B 𝔓⁷⁴ ℵ *rell.*

The detail specifying where the baby was exposed concords with the words in Exod. 2.3 LXX where it is stated that the basket was placed among the reeds παρὰ τὸν ποταμόν.

καὶ (ἀνεθρέψατο) B 𝔓⁷⁴ ℵ Dᴮ/ᴰ *rell, et* d ‖ *om.* D*.

There is another instance of asyndeton in D05 where B03 uses a regular conjunction as a link with the next sentence. Asyndeton causes the link with the previous sentence to be reinforced at the same time as moving the story on to a new idea (Read-Heimerdinger, *The Bezan Text*, p. 250; cf. *vl* below).

(ἀνεθρέψατο) αὐτὸν ἑαυτῇ εἰς (– B) υἱόν B 𝔓⁷⁴ ℵ Dᶜ *rell* ‖ αὐτῇ εἰς υἱόν D*, *vice filii ... sibi* d Ψ 431. 547. 614. 1611. 2412.

The absence of object pronoun in D05 further strengthens the link with the previous sentence because the pronoun αὐτόν found there serves both of the main verbs (ἀνείλατο αὐτὸν ... ἀνεθρέψατο).

7.22 πάσῃ σοφίᾳ B Dˢ·ᵐ· Ψ 33. 1739 𝔐, *omni sapientia* d vg; Or Eus Did | ἐν π. σοφ. 𝔓⁷⁴ᵛⁱᵈ ℵ A C E 2344 gig p; Thret ‖ πᾶσαν τὴν σοφίαν D*; Cl Chr.

The dative (B03), or the preposition ἐν + dative (ℵ01), is used after παιδεύω to define the *means* of training, especially without the article; the accusative (D05), on the other hand, identifies the *content* of what Moses was taught (Winer, *Grammar*, p. 284, n. 2; see also Delebecque, *Les deux Actes*, p. 247; but cf. Barrett, I, p. 355, 'the dative ... specifies the field in which he was trained').

ἦν δέ Β ℵ *rell* ‖ ἦν τε D, *eratque* d E.

D05 closely links (τε) the strength of Moses' speech and action with his education, unlike B03 which makes a clearer distinction (δέ) between the two.

7.23 (ἐπληροῦτο) αὐτῷ τεσσερακονταετὴς χρόνος Β 𝔓⁷⁴ ℵ *rell, ei quadraginta annorum tempus* d ‖ .μ. ἐτὴς αὐ. χρ. D.

In both texts, the adjectival number 40 is highlighted by being placed before the noun χρόνος. D05 further highlights the number by placing the indirect pronoun between the adjective and the noun (Read-Heimerdinger, *The Bezan Text*, p. 95). At the two further references to 40 year periods in Stephen's speech (7.30, 36), the phrase ἔτη τεσσεράκοντα is used with the usual order of noun–number.

(τοὺς ἀδελφοὺς αὐτοῦ) υἱοὺς 'Ισραήλ Β ‖ τοὺς υἱ. 'Ισρ. D 𝔓⁷⁴ ℵ *rell*.

It is possible that B03 has omitted the article through homoioteleuton (ΑΥΤΟΥ[ΤΟΥΣ]ΥΙΟΥΣ). If not, then the terms of the apposition have been reversed by the omission of the second article, so that instead of reading 'visit his brethren, the sons of Israel' (Exod. 2.11a LXX), B03 reads 'visits the sons of Israel, his brethren'.

7.24 (ἀδικούμενον) ἐκ τοῦ γένους D (+ αὐτοῦ E), *de genere suo* d gig syᵖ·ʰ** mae aeth ‖ *om*. Β 𝔓⁷⁴ ℵ *rell*.

D05 makes it clear that the man being mis-treated was an Israelite, paraphrasing Exod. 2.11 LXX: τινὰ ῾Εβραῖον τῶν ἑαυτοῦ ἀδελφῶν τῶν υἱῶν 'Ισραήλ. In the B03 text, any ambiguity that is possible initially is cleared up as the story unfolds.

ἠμύνατο Β 𝔓⁷⁴ ℵ Dᴮ? *rell* ‖ -νετο D* 1270.

B03 uses the aorist, D05 the imperfect with an ingressive sense which is rare: 'he started defending...'.

(πατάξας τὸν Αἰγύπτιον) καὶ ἔκρυψεν αὐτὸν ἐν τῇ ἄμμῳ D d w fay aeth ‖ *om*. Β 𝔓⁷⁴ ℵ *rell*.

Although both texts cite the first part of Exod. 2.12b LXX, B03 does not finish the verse whereas D05 does.

7.25 ἐνόμιζεν Β 𝔓⁷⁴ ℵ *rell, arbitrabatur* d | -σεν Ψ ‖ -ζον D 33.

The reading of D05 is nonsense, since neither the third person plural nor the first singular have any meaning here.

(τοὺς ἀδελφοὺς) αὐτοῦ D d A E Ψ 33. 1739 𝔐 p vgᵐˢˢ sy ‖ *om*. Β 𝔓⁷⁴ ℵ C 6 *pc* gig vg.

D05 insists that it is *his* brethren whom Moses understands, for the third time underlining Moses' relationship with 'the sons of Israel' (cf. v. 23: τοὺς υἱοὺς 'Ισραήλ; v. 24: ἐκ τοῦ γένους).

οὐ (συνῆκαν) B 𝔓⁷⁴ ℵ Dᴬ *rell* d ‖ *om.* D*.

The omission of the article is a copyist's error, corrected by a later scribe.

7.26 τῇ τε (ἐπιούσῃ ἡμέρᾳ) B 𝔓⁷⁴ ℵ A C Dᴮ H *al* | τῇ δέ E P Ψ 88. 2344 p vg syᵖ ‖ τότε D* d.

The original hand of D05 appears to have read TOTE for THTE. Not only is the article before ἐπιούσῃ ἡμέρᾳ necessary, but τότε is not used by Luke to introduce an event in the middle of a sequence; τε, on the other hand, expresses the close connection between Moses' attempt to defend one of his brethren and his intervention the following day in a quarrel between two of his brethren (Read-Heimerdinger, *The Bezan Text*, pp. 218–19).

μαχομένοις B 𝔓⁷⁴ ℵ Dᴮ *rell, litigantibus* d ‖ μαχόμενος D*.

Another copyist's error, corrected by Dᴮ. The succession of errors in D05 testifies to a lack of attention in these verses on the part of the first copyist of the MS.

καὶ εἶδεν αὐτοὺς ἀδικοῦντας D* d ‖ *om.* B 𝔓⁷⁴ ℵ Dˢ·ᵐ· *rell.*

This explicit statement of what Moses saw uses the same verb (ἀδικέω) that was used in the description of the previous incident when Moses saw one of the Israelites being 'wronged' by an Egyptian (ἀδικούμενον, v. 24). The active verb will occur again at the end of the verse (ἀδικεῖτε) and once more in the next verse (ἀδικῶν). All four uses of the active verb to refer to the Israelites hurting each other echo its occurrence in the passive referring to an Israelite being harmed by an Egyptian, demonstrating that it was not just Egyptians who harmed the Israelites. It may be the frequent repetition of the verb in such a short span of text that has caused its elimination here in B03.

Ἄνδρες, ἀδελφοί ἐστε B 𝔓⁷⁴ ℵ *rell* | Ἄν. ἀδ. ἐ. ὑμεῖς C P 049. 1. 33. 88. 330. 1175. 1243. 1828. 2147. 2344 ‖ Τί ποιεῖτε, ἄν. ἀδ.; D d.

B03 has Moses appeal to the fighting men on the grounds that they are brethren (cf. Gamaliel to the Sanhedrin, 5.38 D05). In D05, however, he addresses the men as brethren, asking them what they are doing (cf. 2.37; 6.3 D05; 14.15).

ἀλλήλους B 𝔓⁷⁴ ℵ Dˢ·ᵐ· *rell* | -λοις 049 ‖ εἰς -λους D*.

ἀδικέω can be used transitively (B03) or intransitively (D05), with similar meanings of 'do wrong', but the transitive use has perhaps a more physical and personal sense (as opposed to moral or legal sense; see B-A-G, ἀδικέω, 1., cf. 2.).

7.27 εἰπών B 𝔓⁷⁴ ℵ *rell* ‖ εἴπας D.

B03 uses the second aorist of λέγω (cf. 1.9 B03; 7.60; 20.36 B03), D05 the first (cf. 7.37; 20.36 D05; 22.24; 24.22; 27.35). See B-D-R, § 81.1.

ἐφ᾽ ἡμῶν B 𝔓⁷⁴ ℵ A C H P Ψ 049. 056. 28. 33. 69ᶜ. 81. 1175. 1241 | ἐφ᾽ ἡμᾶς D E 1. 69*. 88. 323. 614. 945. 1505. 1611. 1739. 1891. 2344. 2412. 2492. 2495.

For καθίστημι ἐπί + genitive, see Mt. 2.45; 25.21, 23; Lk. 12.42 B03; Acts 6.3; 7.35 D05 (B-D-R, § 243.3, n. 5); for the construction with the accusative, see Lk. 12.14, 42 D05; Acts 7.10 (B-D-R, § 233.2, n. 3). B03 has the same construction as Exod. 2.14 LXX. The meaning would appear not to change (Delebecque, *Les deux Actes*, p. 56).

7.29 ἔφυγεν δέ B 𝔓⁷⁴ ℵ Dᴴ *rell* ‖ οὕτως καὶ ἐφυγάδευσεν D*, *atque ita profugit* d (E) gig p mae.

φεύγω (B03) expresses the basic sense of 'flee'; φυγαδεύω (D05) has the more complex meaning of 'become a fugitive' when it is used intransitively as here. (Only if it were being used transitively would the case of be an error for the accusative, cf. Delebecque, *Les deux Actes*, p. 57; Metzger [*Commentary*, p. 304] notes that it chiefly occurs intransitively in the LXX.)

7.30 Καί B 𝔓⁷⁴ ℵ *rell* ‖ Καὶ μετὰ ταῦτα D, *Et post haec et* (– dˢ·ᵐ·) d*.

In introducing the fourth point of the promise to Abraham, D05 picks up the time reference from Stephen's summary of the promise at 7.7: καὶ μετὰ ταῦτα ἐξελεύσονται. B03 begins the new period with a simple καί and a genitive absolute clause to express time. d05 offers a conflation of the D05 and B03 readings ('A translation of the D text has been tacked onto the front of d's rendering of the majority rendering', Parker, *Codex Bezae*, p. 234).

πληρωθέντων ἐτῶν τεσσεράκοντα B 𝔓⁷⁴ ℵ Dᴮ *rell, inpletis annis quadriginta* d ‖ πλησθέντων αὐτῷ ἔτη .μ. D*.

πίμπλημι (D05) is used in the same sense as πληρόω (B03) at Lk. 1.20 D05, 23, 57; 2.6, 21, 22; 21.22; 24.44 D05. The dative of interest αὐτῷ, while being excellent Greek, is peculiar to Luke in the New Testament (Delebecque, *Les deux Actes*, p. 57). ἔτη .μ. (D05) does not agree with the genitive absolute, probably through scribal error under the influence of the more usual expression ἔτη .υ. (7.6), ἔτη .μ. (7.36, 42).

(ἄγγελος) κυρίου D d E H P Ψ 049. 056. 33. 69. 81. 88. 323. 614. 945. 1241. 1243. 1611. 1739. 1828. 1891. 2147. 2344. 2492. 2495 p q w sy mae boᵐˢ arm aeth; Exod. 3.2 LXX ‖ *om.* B 𝔓⁷⁴ ℵ A C 81. 1175 *pc* gig vg sa bo.

D05 follows Exod. 3.2 LXX in specifying 'angel of the Lord'. B03 in general tends to avoid the use of κύριος to refer to Yahweh, reserving the title to refer to Jesus where possible (Read-Heimerdinger, *The Bezan Text*, pp. 289–90).

7.31 ἐθαύμασεν B C Ψ (33). 326. 1175 *pc* ‖ -ζεν D d 𝔓⁷⁴ ℵ E H P 049. 1739 𝔐.

Whereas B03 records the fact that Moses marvelled (aor.), D05 describes his state of mind (imperf.).

προσερχομένου δὲ αὐτοῦ Β 𝔓⁷⁴ ℵ *rell* ‖ καὶ πρ. αὐτοῦ D, *cumque ipse accederet* d gig vg syᵖ.

The conjunction δέ marks a new development in B03; καί, on the other hand, fits with the previous verb in the imperfect in D05 (see above), viewing Moses' action of approaching the burning bush as closely linked to his wonderment.

<κ>αὶ (κατανοῆσαι) D d ‖ *om.* Β 𝔓⁷⁴ ℵ *rell.*

καί in D05 could be adverbial, functioning in the same way as adverbial καί between a participle and a conjugated verb, namely to intensify the drama of the scene as Moses goes to look more closely at the burning bush (see Read-Heimerdinger, *The Bezan Text*, pp. 208–10). The infinitive κατανοῆσαι that follows καί is of particular importance in Stephen's account, being repeated at 7.32 where it is said that he 'dared not look closely'. In the Exodus account (Exod. 3.3-4a), some importance is accorded to Moses' decision to take a closer look at the burning bush, for his thinking is recorded: εἶπεν δὲ Μωυσῆς· Παρελθὼν ὄψομαι τὸ ὅραμα τὸ μέγα τοῦτο, τί ὅτι οὐ κατακαίεται ὁ βάτος. ὡς δὲ εἶδεν κύριος ὅτι προσάγει ἰδεῖν...

ἐγένετο φωνὴ κυρίου Β 𝔓⁷⁴ ℵ *rell* ‖ ὁ κύριος εἶπεν αὐτῷ λέγων D d (syᵖ).

These two speech introducers occur (with slight variations) in both texts but in a different order. The second one is found in the first clause of 7.33 (see below). In the Exodus account (Exod. 3.1-10), the Lord's declaration of his identity and his command to Moses to take off his sandals are given in the reverse order to that reported by Stephen. Neither is introduced with a formula including 'the voice', but the declaration of the Lord's identity is prefaced in the LXX with καὶ εἶπεν αὐτῷ, which is closer to the D05 reading here than the B03 one. This may be taken as further evidence that D05 is following the LXX more closely than is B03.

7.32 Ἰσαάκ (Ἰσάκ C) Β 𝔓⁷⁴ ℵ A C Ψ 36. 81. 614. 1175. 1611. 2412 *al* w vgᵐˢˢ sy saᵐˢˢ ‖ θεὸς Ἰσάκ D, *deus Isac* d | ὁ θ. Ἰσαάκ E H P 049. 056. 33. 1739 𝔐 lat co.— Ἰακώβ Β 𝔓⁷⁴ ℵ A C Ψ 36. 81. 614. 1175. 1611. 2412 *al* w vgᵐˢˢ sy saᵐˢˢ ‖ θεὸς Ἰ. D d | ὁ θ. Ἰ. E H P 049. 056. 33. 1739 𝔐 lat co.

D05 repeats the word θεός before each of the patriarchs, as do most MSS of Exod. 3.6 LXX. B03 reads it only before the first name in the list, Abraham, in agreement with certain MSS of the LXX (cf. Metzger, *Commentary*, pp. 348–49).

7.33 εἶπεν δὲ αὐτῷ ὁ κύριος Β 𝔓⁴⁵ᵛⁱᵈ·⁷⁴ ℵ *rell* ‖ καὶ ἐγένετο φωνὴ πρὸς αὐτόν D d.

The order of the two clauses introducing speech is reversed in the respective MSS, with the alternative being read at 7.31 (see above).

(τὸ ὑπόδημα) σου τῶν ποδῶν B | σου ἐκ τ. ποδ. σου C* ‖ τ. ποδ. σου D d 𝔓⁷⁴ ℵ *rell* | ἐκ τ. ποδ. σου C¹ E 33. 323. 927. 945. 1270. 1739. 1891.

B03 qualifies the sandal with the possessive article rather than the feet; D05 follows the order read by Exod. 3.5 LXX. Both texts, however, omit ἐκ read by the LXX.

(τόπος) ἐφ᾽ ᾧ B 𝔓⁷⁴ ℵ A C Dᴮ Ψ 81. 88. 2344 | ἐν ᾧ E H P 049. 056. 1. 33. 69. 323. 614. 945. 1175. 1245. 1505. 1611. 1739. 1891. 2412. 2492. 2495, *in quo* d ‖ οὗ D*.

B03 intensifies the preposition read by Exod. 3.5 LXX, accentuating the notion that the ground is separate from Moses. D05 simply refers to the place, 'where'.

7.34 ἰδὼν εἶδον B 𝔓⁷⁴ ℵ Dˢ·ᵐ· *rell* ‖ καὶ ἰδ. γὰρ εἶδ. D*, *intuitus enim vidi* d.

B03 cites the LXX text of Exod. 3.7b where the words open a new part of the conversation between Moses and God: εἶπεν δὲ κύριος πρὸς Μωυσῆν· Ἰδὼν εἶδον... In Stephen's speech, however, these words follow on directly from the instruction to Moses to take off his shoes. The result is that there is no connective between the two sentences, but this is not inappropriate following a command (Read-Heimerdinger, *The Bezan Text*, pp. 250–51). The D05 reading appears to have combined Exod. 3.7b with the next clause, οἶδα γάρ (3.7c), which repeats the idea that God has seen his people's suffering (*The Bezan Text*, pp. 241–42). γάρ in the LXX translates the Hebrew כִּי which is an emphatic particle confirming what has just been said. In bringing the two clauses together, D05 uses both καί and γάρ as intensifying particles; γάρ could perhaps also have the function of introducing the reason why God encourages Moses to take off his shoes (B-A-G, γάρ, 1, e).

(τοῦ λαοῦ) μου B 𝔓⁷⁴ ℵ Dᴱ *rell* ‖ *om.* D* d.

B03 follows Exod. 3.7 LXX; the omission in D05 could reflect Stephen's understanding of God distancing himself to some extent from his people.

(τοῦ στεναγμοῦ) αὐτοῦ B D d *pc* syᵖ ‖ αὐτῶν 𝔓⁷⁴ ℵ A C E Ψ 33. 1739 𝔐 syʰ.

Both B03 and D05 read the singular pronoun to refer to the people collectively, whereas the other witnesses follow Exod. 3.7 LXX.

ἤκουσα B 𝔓⁷⁴ ℵ *rell* ‖ ἀκήκοα D 1175 *pc*.

D05 has the perfect, following Exod. 3.7 LXX, referring to the whole state of affairs that is implied by Yahweh's hearing his people's suffering; the aorist of B03 refers rather to the hearing as a completed event (Porter, *Idioms*, pp. 21–22).

7.35 (δικαστὴν) ἐφ᾽ ἡμῶν D, *super nos* d ℵ C Ψ 36. 81. 440. 1175. 1245. 1837 *pc* co ‖ ἐφ᾽ ἡμᾶς E 33. 88. 323. 458. 945. 1505. 1739. 2344; Chr ‖ *om.* B 𝔓⁴⁵·⁷⁴ A H P 049. 056. 1. 6. 69. 104. 330. 614. 1241. 1611. 2492. 2495 *pm* vg.

As Stephen repeats the words spoken against Moses, already cited at 7.27, he includes the prepositional phrase used in the first reference, whereas B03 omits it. At 7.27, B03 reads ἐφ’ ἡμῶν in line with Exod. 2.14 LXX, while D05 reads the accusative (without change of meaning, see above on 7.27). Here, D05 has the genitive.

καὶ (ἄρχοντα) B D d ℵ² E Ψ 36. 81. 323. 614. 1175. 2412. 2344 *al* sy^h ‖ *om.* 𝔓^45.74 ℵ* A C H P 049. 056. 33. 1739 𝔐 lat sy^p.

The omission in ℵ01* could be due to the influence of the parallel in 7.27 and 7.35a. B03/D05 emphasise that not only was Moses 'a ruler and a judge' but God had sent him as both a ruler and a deliverer.

7.36 ὁ (ποιήσας) D* 1243 ‖ *om.* B 𝔓^74 ℵ D^s.m. *rell, cum fecisset* d.

In correlation with the pronoun οὗτος which runs throughout vv. 35-38 as a reference to Moses, D05 has Stephen use an articular participle three times: ὁ ποιήσας … ὁ εἴπας … ὁ γενόμενος (7.36a, 37a, 38a). The omission of the article undoes the pattern. The article before the participle is not necessary from a grammatical point of view; what it does is to keep the focus on Moses as a person who performed actions that are well-known about him.

ἐν τῇ Αἰγύπτῳ B C 36. 69. 453 *pc, in Aegypto* d sa | ἐν γῇ Α-τῳ ℵ A E H P 049. 056. 33^vid 𝔐 lat ‖ ἐν γῇ Α-του D 𝔓^74 Ψ 547. 614. 945. 1611. 1739. 1891. 2412 gig p vg sy.

The B03 reading may be a corruption of the second one listed here, which is found in Exod. 7.3 LXX. The article is read in none of the other references to Egypt in Stephen's speech; γῇ, however, is also read at 7.40.

7.37 ὁ (Μωϋσῆς) B ℵ A C E P Ψ 049. 33. 69. 81. 104. 226. 618. 640. 1241. 1245. 1270. 1837. 2147 ‖ *om.* D 𝔓^74 H 049. 1. 88. 323. 330. 383. 614. 945. 1175. 1505. 1611. 1739. 1891. 2344. 2412. 2492. 2495.

The absence of the article before the name of Moses draws attention to it (Heimerdinger and Levinsohn, 'The Use of the Article', p. 23).

(ἐκ τῶν ἀδελφῶν ὑμῶν [– ὑμῶν ℵ]) ὡς ἐμέ B 𝔓^74 ℵ D^s.m. *rell* ‖ ὡσεὶ ἐμέ D*.

ὡς of B03 is read by Deut. 18.15 LXX from which Stephen cites (see also next *vl*). ὡσεί is often found as a variant to ὡς in Luke's writing. See Read-Heimerdinger, 'Luke's Use of ὡς and ὡσεί: Comparison and Correspondence as a Means to Convey His Message', in R. Pierri (ed.), *Grammatica Intellectio Scripturae: Saggi filologici di Greco biblico* (forthcoming).

αὐτοῦ ἀκούεσθε D*, *ipsum audietis* d | αὐτοῦ -σεσθε C D^A/p.m.? E 33. 88. 323. 440. 547. 927. 945. 614. (1175). 1241. 1611. 1739. (1837). 1891. 2412 gig vg^cl.ww sy mae bo ‖ *om.* B 𝔓^45vid ℵ A D^s.m. H P Ψ 049. 056. 69 𝔐 vg^st sa.

B03 does not cite the final part of Moses' prophecy found in Deut. 18.15 LXX.

7.38 τοῦ λαλοῦντος B 𝔓⁴⁵·⁷⁴ ℵ Dᶠ rell, *qui loquebatur* d ‖ λαλ. D* 1828.

The article with the participial adjective is not necessary although its use here is justified. It is normally only used 'where reference is made to some relation which is already known, or which is especially worthy of remark' (Winer, *Grammar*, p. 167). That the angel spoke to Moses is, of course, a well-known fact; on the other hand, omitting the article turns attention to the speaking rather than the angel.

ὅς ἐξελέξατο B (ὡς ἐξ. 1243) ‖ ὅς ἐδέξατο D 𝔓⁴⁵·⁷⁴ ℵ rell, *qui accipit* d.

B03 is alone in reading 'chose', possibly in error unless there is a reference to some unknown tradition.

(δοῦναι) ὑμῖν B 𝔓⁷⁴ ℵ 36. 453. 547. 927. 2492. 2495 *al* p co; Irˡᵃᵗ ‖ ἡμῖν D d A C E H P Ψ 049. 056. 33. 1739 𝔐 lat sy.

Confusion between the first and second person plural pronouns is a frequent occurrence. The second person (B03) is not appropriate here where Stephen is speaking of the history of all Jews and twice makes reference to 'our fathers' in the preceding and following clauses.

7.39 ᾧ (οὐκ ἠθέλησαν) B 𝔓⁷⁴ ℵ rell, *cui* d ‖ ὅτι D.

Causal ὅτι for a relative pronoun occurs elsewhere in the New Testament (Zerwick, *Biblical Greek*, § 424). Cf. Mk 4.41, where D05 omits αὐτῷ at the end of the ὅτι clause.

ἐστράφησαν B 𝔓⁷⁴ ℵ rell ‖ ἀπ- D, *conversi sunt* d 69 *pc*.

The compound verb of D05, combined with the next *vl*, expresses more clearly the idea of an inner return to Egypt. The same verb is used in Num. 14.3 LXX which is apparently being alluded to by Stephen at this point.

ἐν ταῖς καρδίαις αὐτῶν B 𝔓⁴⁵ᵛⁱᵈ ℵ A C 453. 1175 *pc* sa | ταῖς καρδ. αὐ. 𝔓⁷⁴ E 81. 323. 945. 1739 *al* syᵖ sa | τῇ καρδίᾳ αὐ. P Ψ 049. 056. 33. 69. 104. 614. 1245. 1505. 1611. (2344). 2412. 2492. 2495 syʰ; Irˡᵃᵗ ‖ ταῖς καρδίαις D, *cordibus* d; (Or).

The dative of means in D05 is expressed in B03 by the preposition ἐν.

7.40 ἐγένετο B 𝔓⁷⁴ ℵ A C 36. 945. 1175. 1505. 1739. 1891 *pc*, *contegerit* d ‖ γέγονεν D E H P Ψ 049. 056. 33 𝔐; Cyr.

D05 retains the perfect read by Exod. 32.1, 23 LXX but B03 reads the aorist.

7.41 ἀνήγαγον (θυσίαν) B 𝔓⁷⁴ ℵ Dᴬ rell ‖ ἀπήγοντο D* (ἀπηγάγοντο Dᵖ·ᵐ·?, *obtulerunt* d).

The verb of B03 (ἀνάγω) is the usual one to describe the offering of sacrifices (B-A-G, ἀνάγω, 2); the aorist corresponds to the aorist of ἐμοσχοποίησαν which relates the making of the calf. ἀπάγω used by D05 generally means to 'lead away' (cf. Lk. 13.15, of the animal led to water on the Sabbath), a sense that seems out of place here, which may well have prompted the correction of Corrector A (cf. Parker, *Codex Bezae*, p. 130). The verb has the alternative meaning, however, of 'render what one owes' (L-S-J, ἀπάγω, III) with the middle voice, as here, underlining the self-interest of the sacrifice. The imperfect tense of the original reading in D05 corresponds to the imperfect used to describe the merry-making (εὐφραίνοντο): the Israelites, having made a calf, started a practice of sacrificing to it and rejoicing in what they had made.

7.42 (ἐν βίβλῳ) τῶν προφητῶν B 𝔓⁷⁴ ℵ *rell* ‖ προφ. D 1646.

In referring to biblical books, Luke uses elsewhere an expression without the article, cf. Lk. 3.4: ἐν βίβλῳ λόγων Ἡσαΐου; 20.42 B03: ἐν βίβλῳ ψαλμῶν; Acts 1.20: ἐν βίβλῳ ψαλμῶν. Only once does an expression occur with the article, where the article is repeated, Lk. 20.42 D05: ἐν τῇ βίβλῳ τῶν ψαλμῶν. The reference here is to the roll of the Twelve Prophets, where the article is not necessary in so far as the title is a fixed expression (Heimerdinger and Levinsohn, 'The Use of the Article', pp. 29–30).

7.43 (τοῦ θεοῦ) ὑμῶν 𝔓⁷⁴ ℵ A C E Ψ 33. (614. 1505). 1739 𝔐 h p vg syʰ mae bo; Cyr ‖ *om.* B D d 36. 453 *pc* gig syᵖ sa; Irˡᵃᵗ Or.

The second person pronoun is included in Amos 5.26 LXX; its omission by both B03 and D05 is one of the several differences in Stephen's use of it.

Ῥομφά(ν ℵ*) B ℵ*; Or ‖ Ῥεμφάμ D, *Rempham* d (-αν 323. 945. 1739 *pm* lat; Irˡᵃᵗ | -φφάν 1241. 2495 | -φά 81. 1505) | Ῥεφά 104 *pc* | Ῥαιφάν 𝔓⁷⁴ ℵ² A 453. 1175 *pc* sy | Ῥεφάν C E Ψ 33. 36. 383 *pm* sy sa.

The name of this god is absent from the Hebrew text of Amos 5.26; the form read in the LXX has the same vowel ε as the D05 spelling, but both D05 and B03 have included an additional μ in the first syllable.

ἐπέκεινα (Βαβυλῶνος) B 𝔓⁷⁴ ℵ Dᴰ *rell* ‖ ἐπὶ <τὰ μέ>ρη D*, *in illas partes* d gig (e p).

The construction of B03 is that of Amos 5.27 LXX, so Stephen's rendering of Amos agrees with it except that the destination of exile becomes 'beyond Babylon' instead of 'beyond Damascus'. The modification to the Amos text transmitted by D05 has the effect of bringing the meaning more into line with the original prophecy, 'the regions of Babylon' being 'beyond Damascus', while at the same time representing Mesopotamia from where the people of Israel were said to have originated.

7.44 ἦν τοῖς πατράσιν ἡμῶν (– ἡμῶν 𝔓⁷⁴ 33. 326 *pc*) B 𝔓⁷⁴ ℵ A C Dˢ·ᵐ·/ᴰ H P 049. 056. 1. 33. 69. 326. 330. 440. 547. 1270. 1646. 1837. 2344. 2495 ‖ ἦν ἐν τ. πατέρεσιν ἡμῶν D*, *erat penes patres nostros* d E Ψ 88. 323. 614. 927. 945. 1611. 1739. 1891. 2412.

εἶναι + dative in B03 is a turn of phrase that underlines the object possessed (Wallace, *Greek Grammar*, pp. 149–50; cf. B-D-R, § 189.1). In the construction that places the preposition ἐν before the noun in the dative (εἶναι + ἐν + dative, D05), the subject is not so much possessed as at the disposition of the person (Mayser II, 2, 395, 41: 'Bei Personen bedeutet ἐν τινι [cf. ἐπί τινι] im allgemeinen "in der Hand, Macht, Gewalt, zur Verfügung jemandes" [= penes]'; cf. Zerwick, *Biblical Greek*, §§ 116–17). The dative form of the noun πατήρ is sometimes seen to vary in the plural, though evidence concerning dating or location is lacking (on the disappearance of unaccented vowels after liquid consonants, see Moulton and Howard, §§ 30, 33).

ὁ (λαλῶν) B 𝔓⁷⁴ ℵ *rell* || *om.* D 1828*. 2412.

The article may have been omitted by D05 through haplography; on the other hand, the subject of the main verb διετάξατο may be understood as God (cf. v. 42) without needing to make explicit the subject by means of the article before the participle.

(κατὰ) τὸν τύπον B 𝔓⁷⁴ ℵ Dᴰ *rell, iuxta figuram* d || τὸ πα<ράτ>υπον D*.— ὃν ἑωράκει B 𝔓⁷⁴ ℵ A C P 056. 1. 33. 69. 81. 88. 323. 614. 1241. 1243. 1245. 1505. 1611. 2412 gig | ὃν ἑώρακεν E H Ψ 049. 104. 330. 945. 1175. 1646. 1739. 1891. 2492. 2495 d h || <ὧ>ν (ὃν D*) ἑόρακεν Dᶜʲ.

According to B03, Moses made the tent of witness following the pattern God had shown him when he was on the mountain with Joshua (Exodus 25, cf. especially v. 40). The pluperfect of the verb ὁράω (extremely rare and the only occurrence in the New Testament against 34 × perf.) suggests that the vision Moses was given of the Tabernacle had already been acquired once work on it began. The form of the verb in D05, with O instead of Ω, is also pluperfect (B-A-G, ὁράω). There is a significant difference, however, in the word read by D05 for the 'pattern': παράτυπον is an adjective used as a noun, not found elsewhere in Greek (Delebecque, *Les deux Actes*, p. 59; but cf. Scrivener, *Bezae Codex*, p. 442, '*anne potius* παρατυπον? cf. Stephani, *Thesaur., qui Schol. in Aristoph. Acharn.* 516 *citat*'). It means a 'counterfeit' (L-S-J), that is an imperfect reproduction or an illusory representation rather than a faithful model. If it is indeed the word intended by D05, the following relative pronoun should be a genitive (ὅν for neut. pl. ὧν, the confusion of vowels in D05 not uncommon): 'the imperfect reproduction of the things he saw' (cf. a similar genitive pronoun at Lk. 9.36). Cf. παράδειγμα, Exod. 25.9 LXX.

7.45 μετὰ Ἰησοῦ B 𝔓⁷⁴ ℵ Dˢ·ᵐ· *rell* || μ. Ἰ-ν D*, *cum Iesum*.

The accusative case following μετά can have a temporal meaning, 'during the time of' (Bailly, μετά, B, III, 1). The accusative in d05, incorrect in Latin, suggests this case was read in the Greek exemplar.

(τῶν πατέρων) ἡμῶν B 𝔓⁷⁴ ℵ *rell, nostrorum* d ‖ ὑμῶν D.

Since D05 reads the first person pronoun throughout this episode (cf. vv. 38, 39, 44, 45a), the second person here is to be explained as yet another example of the frequent confusion between the two pronouns due to itacism.

7.46 (ᾐτήσατο) εὑρεῖν σκήνωμα B 𝔓⁷⁴ ℵ *rell* ‖ σκ. εὑρ. D, *tabernaculum invenire* d h.

By placing the noun σκήνωμα before the verb, D05 gives it emphasis.

7.48 ἀλλ᾽ οὐχ (+ ὡς 𝔓⁷⁴) ὁ ὕψιστος ἐν χειροποιήτοις κατοικεῖ B 𝔓⁷⁴ ℵ *rell* ‖ ὁ δὲ ὕψ. οὐ κατ. ἐν χειρ. D, *sed ipse altissimus inhabitavit in manufactis* d h (syᵖ); Tert.

The emphasis in B03 is on the fact that the Most High does not dwell in places made with hands, whereas D05 draws a contrast between Solomon on the one hand, and the Most High on the other.

καθώς B 𝔓⁷⁴ ℵ *rell* ‖ ὡς D | ὡς καί E.

B03 reinforces the testimony of Scripture with the adverb καθώς. With ὡς, D05 considers that the saying of the prophet is directly applicable to the circumstances (Solomon's building of the Temple) that he is referring to.

7.49 μοι (θρόνος) B ℵ A C E H P Ψ 049. 056. 1. 33. 69. 81. 88. 614. 945. 1175. 1241. 1611. 1739. 2412. 2492 | μου 𝔓⁷⁴ ‖ μού ἐστιν D*, *est meus* d e p syᵖ | μοί ἐστιν Dᴴ.

The variation between the dative and genitive pronouns is found in the LXX MSS of Isa. 66.1 which Stephen cites.

καὶ ἡ γῆ B h vg ‖ ἡ δὲ γῆ D, *terra vero* d 𝔓⁷⁴ ℵ *rell*.

Once again, the variation in conjunctions is found in the LXX MSS of Isa. 66.1.

τίς (τόπος) B 𝔓⁷⁴ ℵ *rell, quis locus* d ‖ ποῖος D.

D05 follows Isa. 66.1 LXX. The repetition of ποῖος establishes a clear link between the two rhetorical questions: 'what house?' ‖ 'what place?'

(μού) ἐστιν D d Ψ 33. 927. 1646. 2344 p² vg syʰ ‖ *om.* B 𝔓⁷⁴ ℵ *rell*.

Here, it is B03 that agrees with the Isaiah citation; the verb is not indispensable, no more than at 7.49 D05 (see above).

7.50 ταῦτα πάντα B ℵ Ψ 049. 33. 81. 323. 614. 945. 1175. 1241. 1505. 1739 *pm*, *haec omnia* d lat ‖ π. ταῦτα D 𝔓⁷⁴ A C E P 056. 69. 2147 *pm* p; Or.

D05 reproduces Isa. 66.2 LXX, while the word order of B03 places particular emphasis on the demonstrative.

7.51 (ἀπερίτμητοι) καρδίας B ‖ καρδίαις D d 𝔓⁷⁴ A C *pc* p vg; Cyrᵖᵗ | ταῖς καρδίαις ὑμῶν ℵ (Ψ) 945. 1175. (1611. 1646). 1739. 1891 *pc* | τῇ καρδίᾳ E H P 049. 056. 614 𝔐 it vgᵐˢˢ syᵖ sa; Eus Aug Lcf GrNy Cyrᵖᵗ.

The difference between the accusative (of respect, B03) and the dative (of location, D05) does not alter the sense, no more than do the other variants.

ὡς Β 𝔓⁷⁴ ℵ *rell* ‖ καθώς D.— (οἱ πατέρες) ὑμῶν καὶ ὑμεῖς Β 𝔓⁷⁴ ℵ *rell, et vos* d‖ καὶ ὑμῶν D* | ὑμῶν Dˢ·ᵐ· gig h.

Here, it is D05 that reinforces the comparison (cf. v. 48), insisting on the similarity between the ancestors of Israel and the present leaders not only by the stronger adverb but also by the emphatic καί.

7.52 οἱ πατέρες ὑμῶν Β 𝔓⁷⁴ ℵ Dᶠ *rell* ‖ ἐκεῖνοι D*, *illi* d (h t).

Instead of repeating the phrase 'your fathers', D05 uses the disrespectful demonstrative. The choice of ἐκεῖνος rather than οὗτος is in keeping with the fact that it is not the ancestors who are now in focus but the prophets (Levinsohn, 'Towards a Unified Linguistic Description of οὗτος and ἐκεῖνος').

(ἀπέκτειναν) τοὺς προκαταγγείλαντας Β 𝔓⁷⁴ ℵ *rell, eos qui praenuntiaverunt* d ‖ αὐτοὺς τ. -γέλλοντας D gig p; Aug.

Where B03 reads the articular participle in the aorist, keeping the subject ('your fathers') in focus, D05 highlights the object, the prophets, with the accusative pronoun and the present participle in apposition to it. There is thus a closer association between the killing of the prophets and their foretelling of the Messiah.

τῆς (ἐλεύσεως) Β 𝔓⁷⁴ ℵ Dᶜ *rell* ‖ *om.* D*.

The omission of the article in D05 is a means to draw attention to the object of the prophesying, the coming (of the Messiah), since it is introduced here as a completely new topic.

7.54 ἀκούοντες δὲ ταῦτα Β 𝔓⁷⁴ ℵ *rell* ‖ -σαντες δὲ αὐτοῦ D (*audientes autem eum* d, ταῦτα h 1837; Luc).

The present participle of B03 suggests that the reaction of Stephen's audience began even as he was speaking. According to D05, on the other hand, Stephen had finished speaking before the reaction made itself apparent.

(καὶ ἔβρυχόν) τε D* ‖ *om.* Β 𝔓⁷⁴ ℵ Dˢ·ᵐ· *rell*.

The construction καί ... τε as a simple connective is extremely rare but is found in D05 at 2.3; 4.4; 8.13; 10.27. τε in such instances highlights the second action.

Commentary

[a] 7.1 *The High Priest Invites Stephen to Answer the Charges*
7.1 The High Priest speaks as the president of the Sanhedrin. Since the exact date of the incident cannot be determined, it is not possible to be sure who the High Priest at

the time was. The choice can probably be narrowed down to two: either Caiaphas, Annas' son-in-law, who had presided over Jesus' trial and remained in office until 37 CE; or Theophilus, Annas' third son, who took over the high priesthood in 37 following his brother Jonathan's two-month period in office (cf. 4.6 D05). Clearly, if the High Priest was Theophilus, who may be identified as the addressee of Luke's work (see *General Introduction*, § IV), this whole episode is of especial significance for him. However, the similarity between the question the High Priest asks here of Stephen and that asked by Caiaphas of Jesus (cf. Mk 14.60-61) perhaps indicates that it is the same person who is involved on each occasion.

The tone of the question put to Stephen is less harsh than the demand recorded in Luke's Gospel (Lk. 22.67) of the priests and the scribes of the Council to know if Jesus is the Christ, where the phrasing of the AT is particularly aggressive: Εἰ σὺ εἶ ὁ Χριστός, εἰπὸν ἡμῖν (AT) / Σὺ εἶ ὁ Χριστός; (D05). It corresponds more closely to the parallel account in Mark's Gospel where Caiaphas, on hearing the false witnesses accuse Jesus of intending to tear down the 'Temple made with hands', asks the initial question: Οὐκ ἀποκρίνη οὐδὲν τί οὗτοί σου καταμαρτυροῦσιν; (Mk 14.60); only when Jesus does not answer does he go on to ask: Σὺ εἶ ὁ Χριστὸς ὁ υἱὸς τοῦ εὐλογητοῦ; (14.61). Luke would appear once again (as with the accusations of the false witnesses) to have held over Markan material concerning Jesus to his second volume, where he applies it to the disciples.

The effect of this displacing is twofold. On the one hand, it establishes the similarities between the two trials of Jesus and Stephen and sets up a positive parallel between the master and his disciple. On the other hand, it allows Stephen to give the High Priest the answer that Jesus would have given – in Luke's view – concerning the Temple building. For Luke had made evident Jesus' criticism of the Temple in describing him as entering it at the end of his journey to confront Jerusalem (Ἰερουσαλήμ, Lk. 9.51) without mentioning explicitly his entry into the city (19.41, 45; cf. Mk 11.15).[60] The apostolic community has by now separated itself from the authorities of the Temple, the building itself having been shaken as a sign of its disintegration of its power and importance (see 4.31). At this point, Stephen will take the bold step of spelling out to the High Priest the community's position with regard to the Temple.

[b] 7.2-53 *Stephen's Speech to the Sanhedrin*
As with the apostolic speeches in Luke's work, Stephen's speech is to be viewed as a means the narrator uses to convey the essence of what Stephen would have said (see *General Introduction*, § VI). In that sense, it is Luke's construction but

---

60. At Mk 11.11, Jesus is first reported to have entered city and then the Temple: Καὶ εἰσῆλθεν εἰς Ἰεροσόλυμα εἰς τὸ ἱερόν, and again at 11.15: Καὶ ἔρχονται εἰς Ἰεροσόλυμα. Καὶ εἰσελθὼν εἰς τὸ ἱερὸν ἤρξατο ἐκβάλλειν... In the D05 text, the distinction between city and Temple is more marked: Καὶ εἰσελθὼν εἰς Ἰεροσόλυμα καὶ εἰς τὸ ἱερὸν (11.11) ... Καὶ εἰσελθὼν εἰς Ἰεροσόλυμα καὶ ὅτε ἦν ἐν τῷ ἱερῷ ἤρξατο ἐκβάλλειν... (11.15).

that is not to say that he invented the speech simply to serve his own purpose. It is entirely possible that Stephen delivered a speech of this nature, which Luke recreates and places at this point in order to spell out the thinking of the Hellenists among the followers of Jesus and to lay down a standard with which to compare the attitudes and actions of other disciples, both before and after Stephen. It should be noted in particular that Stephen's speech is not a defence. Unlike the speeches of Paul at the time of his trial, the word 'apology' is never used (see *Commentary*, 6.10), and God's presence with Stephen through the Holy Spirit is assured.

As a summary of Stephen's response to the accusations concerning the Law and Moses, it can be said that he does not criticize the Law as such. What he brings out over and over again, is that Moses was sent by God, chosen by him to transmit God's commands to Israel and to bring them out of slavery; the problem was not with Moses but with the rebellious response of the people of Israel to Moses as leader and deliverer.

His criticism of the Temple is much more direct, as he equates it with the making of the idol of the golden calf by the people of Israel with the connivance of Aaron. No attempt need be made to reconcile Stephen's fundamental criticism of the Temple with the practice of the Jesus-believers observed so far, of attending the Temple for prayer (cf. Lk. 24.53; Acts 3.1-8, esp. D05). It is an essential aim of Luke's narrative to show that the believers, in particular the apostles, did not understand the scope of Jesus' teaching all at once but only gradually came to see the radical nature of it. There has already been some detachment from the Temple authorities and the beginning of a recognition by the apostles that they had to separate themselves from the Temple (cf. 4.31-35). That the Hellenists (represented in the earlier chapters by Barnabas, cf. 1.23 D05; 4.36) were more open to change is part of Luke's message and it is not surprising that it is the leader of the Hellenist disciples who takes the initiative in spelling out why the Temple had to be abandoned.[61] In time, the apostles will follow his lead in accepting that the Temple, and Ierousalem, were no longer intended to be the focus of God's presence though Peter, for example, will not grasp the full extent of that truth until his release from prison in Acts 12; Paul will still attach significance to the Temple, and especially to Jerusalem as the religious centre, until he begins his journey to Rome (21.20-29).[62]

Much of the time, the source for Stephen's scriptural references is the LXX to which the Bezan text conforms more closely than the AT.[63] However, Stephen

61. The division among the Jesus-believers over the Temple is clearly identified by J.D.G. Dunn, *The Partings of the Ways Between Christianity and Judaism and their Significance for the Character of Christianity* (London: SCM Press, 1991, repr. 1996), see esp. pp. 57–64.

62. For the development in Paul's thinking with regard to the Temple and Jerusalem, see Rius-Camps, 'Gradual Awakening'.

63. It is nevertheless an exaggeration to say that, at places of *vll*, the AT only once agrees with the LXX against D05 (Metzger [citing Ropes], *Commentary*, pp. 299–300; see *Critical Apparatus* for many instances).

does not only base his account on the Jewish Scriptures but also draws on traditional Jewish teaching and legend. A rich variety of traditions grew up around the scriptural stories, often as a means to explain difficulties contained within them or to make explicit the hidden connections between two or more of them. Many of these additional stories were not written down until the rabbinic period so their origin is generally difficult to date, and their appearance in the New Testament is therefore a valuable means for confirming at least a pre-rabbinic origin. The existence of the traditional material, of which only part is known today in any case, means that there is no reason to suppose that, where Stephen's account of the history of Israel differs from the MT or LXX, Luke either made up versions of events to suit his purpose or made mistakes. Not only that, but the traces of traditional elements in Stephen's speech are an indication of its authenticity in so far as they are appropriate both to Stephen as a first-century Hellenistic Jew and to his audience, the Sanhedrin.[64] Later Christians would have been more likely to stick to the scriptural version of the history of Israel, even had they been aware of diverging Jewish interpretations.

Stephen's theme throughout the bulk of his speech is the presence of God with his people wherever they were. So he traces their journeyings, from Chaldea in Mesopotamia, through Haran to Canaan, and thence to Egypt which he deals with at considerable length; then through the wilderness until they finally arrive for good in Israel. A fundamental claim that emerges throughout all the wanderings is that God was with them at all times, except when they turned away from him (7.39-43).[65]

The speech itself is divided into three parts with an opening *Prologue* [α] 7.2-10, followed by an *Exposition* in five elements [β γ / δ \ γ′ β′] 7.11-50, and a final *Invective* [α′] 7.51-53 which occupies the place of the more usual parenesis. In the prologue Stephen takes his hearers to the beginning of the history of Israel and the story of Abraham. He cites the promise given by God to Abraham for the benefit of his descendants and then, in the body of the speech, takes up the five distinct elements of the promise in turn:

[β]	7.11-16	Sojourners in a foreign land
[γ]	7.17-22	Enslavement
[δ]	7.23-29	God's judgment on Egypt
[γ′]	7.30-40	Exodus
[β′]	7.41-50	Worship of God in Israel

It is the promise with its separate aspects that can be seen as providing the structure for the speech. The divisions that are thus created cut across the boundaries that are indicated by the introduction of successive characters (Abraham, Joseph,

---

64. Contra J. Kilgallen, *The Stephen Speech: A Literary and Redactional Study of Acts 7.2-53* (Rome: Biblical Institute Press, 1976), p. 97.

65. The emphasis of the first part of the speech has been well summarized by Dunn: 'the presence of God in Israel's history had not been restricted to one land or building' (*The Partings of the Ways*, p. 65).

Moses) whose function is to give a chronological support to the framework set up by the promise rather than provide essential structure of the speech.[66]

Having worked through the separate elements of the promise to Abraham, Stephen goes on in his invective ([α'] 7.51-53) to launch his attack on his hearers as he assesses their condition in the light of his account of the history of Israel. It is this that sparks off the reaction within the Sanhedrin ([a'] 7.54) and leads to their stoning of him in the following episode ([A'-A'] 7.55–8.1a).

[α] 7.2-10 *Prologue*
Following an opening greeting, there are eight elements in the prologue, leading up to the promise to Abraham in vv. 6-7 and devolving from the sign of the covenant in v. 8a: αα αβ αγ αδ ‖ αδ' αγ' αβ' αα'. Stephen presents the promise as the framework for all the subsequent history of the Jewish people.

7.2a The opening address of Stephen's speech is deliberately imitated by Luke when he writes Paul's first speech of defence but with the significant difference that, unlike Paul, Stephen makes no mention of his defence (cf. 22.1). These are the only two occasions in Acts when 'fathers' is included with 'brethren' in the address of a speech to a Jewish audience, whether it be made up of Jewish believers in Jesus (1.16; 2.37; 13.15; 15.7, 13) or the people of Israel in general (2.29 [cf. v. 22]; 13.26 [cf. v. 16], 38; 23.1b [cf. v. 1a], 6; 28.17b [cf. v. 17a]).[67] A further indication that Stephen in no way intends to use his speech to make his defence is that he does not ask the Sanhedrin to listen to him (the pronoun 'me' [μου] is absent, cf. James, 15.13; and Paul, 22.1; 26.3).

[αα] 7.2b-3 *God's Order to Abraham*
7.2b Stephen begins with a reminder of the appearance of the 'God of glory' to Abraham (as opposed to an angel in the case of Moses, cf. 7.30, 35; and also vv. 38, 44, 53). Abraham is qualified as 'our father' meaning 'our ancestor' and used only here in the singular, with a positive connotation. In contrast, the plural 'our fathers' will have a negative force when Stephen uses the term shortly as an equivalent to 'the patriarchs' or their descendants (οἱ πατριάρχαι, 7.9 = οἱ πατέρες ἡμῶν, vv. 11, 12, 15, [19], 38, 39, 45a, 45b), who were jealous, uncomprehending, disobedient, rebellious and murderers (cf. vv. 8, 9, 12, 15, 38, 39).

Stephen is careful to underline that the revelation to Abraham took place in Mesopotamia, the 'land of the Chaldees', *before* he lived in Haran. This information contradicts the first scriptural account of God's appearance to Abraham (Gen. 11.31–12.1, 4), but since the book of Genesis itself later refers to Abraham being

---

66. Unlike many commentators who regard Stephen's speech as a loose (and defective) collection of sources, Kilgallen discerns the links between the units and identifies the tight thematic unity of the speech overall; he further describes the way in which the five points of the promise are taken up in turn in the course of the speech as a 'rough outline' (*The Stephen Speech*, pp. 41–42).

67. The observation made by Haenchen (*Commentary*, p. 229), that the formula 'brethren and fathers' is typically Greek, is hardly valid for Paul's speech which is made in Hebrew (cf. 21.40; 22.2).

called out from 'Ur of the Chaldees' (Gen. 15.7; cf. Neh. 9.7), as do other Jewish writers,[68] it can hardly be called an invention or error on Luke's (or Stephen's) part. The result of underlining Abraham's original dwelling as his place of departure is to show that from the very beginning his departure from his country was in perfect obedience to the divine command.

7.3 Stephen's citation from Gen. 12.1 is close to the LXX text (see *Critical Apparatus*) though with notable modifications. First, 'from the house of your father' is omitted since Abraham does not in fact leave his father's house until after his death, as Stephen stresses in 7.4. Secondly, 'and come (to the land I will show you)' is added, with the effect of heightening the contrast between leaving a familiar land and following the direction of God to enter a new one. The contrast is further strengthened by the close association of 'your land and your family' in the opening line of the quotation, where the preposition ('from' or 'out of') is not repeated as it is in the LXX.

[αβ] 7.4a *Abraham's Obedience*
7.4a Abraham's immediate response to the command (τότε) was to leave his country of origin and to settle temporarily in Haran, another region of Meso-potamia closer to Canaan.[69] Once there, he waited for God's intervention to take him on to the new country chosen for him. The Bezan text maintains Abraham clearly in focus by repeating his name, and stresses that he did indeed live in Haran for a time, as mentioned in 7.3 and in accordance with the first account of God's revelation to him at Gen. 12.1.

[αγ] 7.4b-5 *God Brings Abraham into the Promised Land*
7.4b The Greek expression used by Codex Bezae, καὶ ἐκεῖ ἦν in its uncontracted form, is used frequently in the LXX to represent a play on words that is already present in the Hebrew text as a means to conceal the name of God (see *Critical Apparatus*).[70] The clause, in consequence, rather than referring to Abraham, alludes to the presence of God with Abraham after his father died. This play on words would, of course, have been meaningless to an audience unfamiliar with the techniques employed in the Jewish Scriptures for hiding the name of God, which could account for its absence in the Alexandrian text.

The information that Abraham left Haran after the death of his father does not agree with part of the Genesis account which seems to contain contradictions (Gen. 11.26: Abraham's father, Terah, was 70 when Abraham was born; 11.32:

---

68. Philo, *Abr.* 62–67; Josephus, *Ant.* I, 154–57.

69. The same verb that is used in God's order, 7.3 (ἔξελθε), is repeated to demonstrate how faithfully Abraham obeyed the command, 7.4 (ἐξελθών).

70. In 1 Sam. 19.3, for example, the sentence 'I will stand next to my father in the field where you are', reads in Hebrew as '…in the field which you there'; in Greek, this is rendered as ἐν ἀγρῷ οὗ ἐὰν ᾖς ἐκεῖ (Lucian has οὗ ἐὰν ᾖς σὺ ἐκεῖ). ἐκεῖ translates the Hebrew שם which, according to the pointing, can also mean 'name'. Furthermore, ᾖς as the third person of the verb 'to be' corresponds to the consonants of the Tetragram, made even clearer by the Lucianic text.

he was 205 when he died in Haran; 12.4: Abraham was only 75 when he left
Haran, which means his father was only 145 and had not yet died). There is,
however, at least one extant version of the Torah, the Samaritan Pentateuch, that
cites Terah's age at death as 145.[71] Here, as elsewhere, Stephen appears to know
a version of the stories he is relating other than that transmitted by the presently
available MSS of the LXX, or indeed the Hebrew MSS.

Whatever the chronology, the point made by Stephen is that Abraham's move
to Canaan was again not at his own initiative but directly dependent on God's
action. The country is not in fact named at this point but is described in a circum-
locution as the place where Stephen's audience live just as, the Bezan text adds,
their fathers before them. Interestingly, Stephen does not include himself as a
resident of Israel ('you live'), an indication, perhaps, that as a Hellenist, Israel
was not his permanent place of dwelling; at the same time, he does include
himself in referring in the Bezan text to the ancestors of those now living in
Israel ('our fathers'; the AT seems not to have identified this distinction). In
reconstructing Abraham's journey from his departure from Mesopotamia to his
arrival in Israel, from the giving of the promise to its fulfilment, Stephen has told
the story in such a way as to select those aspects that bring out his complete
obedience to God.[72] This feature is significant for the point he will make throughout his speech about the disobedience of Abraham's descendants.

7.5 The detail that God did not give to Abraham any part ('inheritance ... not
even a foot's length') of the land of Canaan concords with the use in the Genesis
account of the term 'sojourner' (πάροικος, Gen. 17.8; 23.4 LXX). Against it is set
God's promise (ἀλλὰ [D05, καὶ AT] ἐπηγγείλατο) that it would be given to him
through his descendants. The fact that Abraham had no children at the time (by
his wife Sarah, cf. Gen. 16.1) is further evidence of the divine control over all
these events and the part played by Abraham's faith in the word of God despite
the all too apparent absence of favourable circumstances.

[αδ] 7.6-7 *The Five-Fold Promise*
The promise is now spelt out with each of its five points, claiming to repeat the
words spoken by God (ἐλάλησεν δὲ οὕτως), to Abraham according to Codex
Bezae though in fact they are a combination of words spoken to Abraham and an
adaptation of a later promise given to Moses[73] (numbers in brackets refer to the
corresponding elements of the promise as quoted by Stephen):

---

71. Bruce, *Text*, p. 162, n. 1. Other Jewish traditions, on the other hand, make much of the fact
that Abraham was willing to trust God sufficiently to leave his elderly father behind when he left
Haran (see L. Ginzberg, *The Legends of the Jews* [7 vols; Philadelphia: The Jewish Publication
Society of America, 11th edn, 1982], I, pp. 217–18).

72. Abraham's perfect trust in God is the dominant characteristic of Jewish legends concerning
his early life (Ginzberg, *The Legends of the Jews*, I, pp. 198–225).

73. The two promises were doubtless already associated in Jewish tradition. For example, when
Abraham received the promise from God (Gen. 15.12), he was in a deep sleep during which he saw
the revelation on Sinai (see Ginzberg, *The Legends of the Jews*, I, p. 236).

> Know for sure that (1) your seed will be sojourners in a land that is not theirs (2) and they will enslave them, and ill-treat and humiliate them for 400 years; (3) but I will bring judgment on the nation that they serve and (4) afterward they will come out... (Gen. 15.13-14; cf. Exod. 2.22).
> When you have brought my people out of Egypt, (5) you will worship God on this mountain (Exod. 3.12).

7.6 Apart from the conflation of the two texts, there are some differences in the actual wording. Concerning the first aspect of the promise, Stephen expresses the idea of 'a land that is not theirs' more forcefully with 'a land belonging to others'. As for the second, in both the Genesis and the Acts accounts, the word 'seed' is singular in Greek (as in the Hebrew of Genesis); the corresponding pronoun in the following clause is plural in the LXX (again following the Hebrew), presumably viewing 'the seed' as numerous people, but the AT of Acts (not Codex Bezae) reads the singular, viewing the people collectively.[74] Both texts of Acts omit the statement 'and will humiliate them', which is not read by the Hebrew text nor the Targum either.[75] The duration of 400 years means that the enslavement will last through several generations (40 × 10).[76]

7.7 The final three aspects of the promise are given authenticity and particular emphasis by the parenthesis 'God says' which is added to the Genesis text. Points three and four reproduce the account of Gen. 15.14, with the exception of a final phrase that Stephen omits: 'they will come out *here with great riches*'.[77]

The adverb of place 'here' (ὧδε, Gen. 15.14 LXX) is held over to the final point of the promise and expressed by 'in this place'. This last point, however, is no longer taken from words addressed to Abraham but rather is a paraphrase of words originally addressed to Moses at the point when, the oppression of the Israelites by the Egyptians having become unbearable, God 'remembered his covenant with Abraham (and Isaac and Jacob)' (Exod. 2.23-24). To Moses, who was then the leader of the Jews in Egypt, he restated his promise to lead his people out of Egypt so they could worship him 'on this mountain' (Exod. 3.12). The reference is to Mt Horeb but because Stephen has applied the whole of the promise to Abraham, he adapts the location to 'this place' (ἐν τῷ τόπῳ τούτῳ) meaning Canaan, the place where Abraham was when God spoke with him. The choice of term is no doubt

---

74. On the singular and plural interpretation of the seed, see M. Wilcox, 'The Promise of the "Seed" in the New Testament and the Targumim', *JSNT* 5 (1979), pp. 275–93 (esp. 276–77 on Gen. 15.13).

75. M. Harl, *La Genèse*, in *idem* (ed.), *La Bible d'Alexandrie*, I (Paris: Cerf, 1986), p. 165.

76. At Exod. 12.21, the Israelites leave Egypt after 430 years, which is reconciled with Gen. 15.12 in the LXX by including in the duration the 30 years spent previously in Canaan (Harl, *La Genèse*, p. 165). See *Commentary*, 7.19 below.

77. In the book of Exodus, the Israelites are said three times to have taken great riches from the Egyptians when they left the land (cf. Exod. 3.21-22; 11.2; 12.35-36). The idea seems to have posed a problem at least for some, for 12.36 LXX speaks of the precious goods being 'lent', an interpretation also found in rabbinic exegesis (D. Daube, *The Exodus Pattern in the Bible* [London: Faber and Faber, 1963], pp. 56–57). Other traditions are at pains to explain that it was the Egyptians who forced the goods on the Israelites (Ginzberg, *The Legends of the Jews*, II, pp. 371–72 and nn. 232, 233).

deliberate, for 'the place' had become precisely a fixed expression to designate the Temple, that used by Stephen's accusers in listing the charges against him (6.13, 14). At this stage, by establishing that God first envisaged the land of Israel as the 'place' where his people would worship him, Stephen is setting out the facts in such a way as to prepare for the con-clusion of his diatribe when he will argue against the rightness of the Temple as the 'place'.

The five points of the promise provide the framework for the body of Stephen's speech after the prologue, each aspect being developed in turn as noted in the introductory discussion to the speech, above.

The setting for the first four topics is Egypt, and even for the final topic of worship the starting point is the desert (cf. 7.44) which the Israelites crossed on their departure from Egypt. The association between God's promise to Abraham and Israel's time in the land of Egypt is made explicit in the book of Exodus (Exod. 2.24), but the links are developed in complex ways in other scriptures (for example, the writings of Ezekiel) and throughout Jewish tradition.[78] That Stephen should take the separate aspects of the promise as the framework for his review of the history of Israel should not, therefore, be thought of as something new, and especially not as a literary convention on the part of Luke.

[αδ'] 7.8a *Circumcision*
7.8a Corresponding to the promise of God to give the land of Canaan to Abraham's descendants, reiterated when he had been living there for some time (Gen. 17.1-8), is the covenant of circumcision to be kept by his people (Gen. 17.9-14). Circumcision was not an unknown practice in the Ancient Near East, but the distinguishing feature of the Jewish ritual was that it was to be carried out on the eighth day of a boy's life rather than at puberty.

[αγ'] 7.8b *Abraham's Descendants*
7.8b The particular facts that Stephen selects from the scriptural account of the history of Israel are an indication of his purpose in re-telling the story. He does not spend time narrating the events relating to Abraham as an individual but rather is interested in his role as the first ancestor of Israel, 'our father', the first in a line of positive characters whom he sets against another line of negative characters. Isaac and Jacob are important links in the former but, perhaps surprisingly, the twelve patriarchs (οἱ δώδεκα πατριάρχαι) are not portrayed favourably. When they are first mentioned, it is as the sons of Jacob but then, as the term 'the patriarchs' is repeated at the head of the next clause, v. 9a (as if the genealogy were being continued), the unexpected word 'jealous' (ζηλώσαντες, cf. Gen. 37.11 LXX) appears in an ironic interruption to the pattern set up so far. This is the first negative point in a long list of instances of infidelity and opposition to the plan of God.

---

78. The links between the promise to Abraham and the Exodus in Jewish tradition are discussed by R. Le Déaut, *La nuit pascale* (Rome: Biblical Institute Press, 1963), pp. 144–47.

[αβ'] 7.9a *The Patriarchs Sell Joseph*

7.9a The patriarchs were jealous of one among them, Joseph, so that instead of the twelve continuing the line of salvation, it is Joseph who is singled out and who enables the promises God made to Abraham to be fulfilled. The patriarchs as the heads of the twelve tribes of Israel are thereafter ignored in Stephen's story, which moves on at this point to focus on the incidents of the following period spent by the Jews in Egypt. Egypt becomes a theme of central importance to Stephen's discourse, no doubt reflecting an understanding of Jewish history from a Hellenistic point of view. Indeed, Joseph was the great hero of Hellenistic Judaism, the perfect example of fidelity and purity who maintained a holy and upright life even though in exile among foreigners (cf. Joseph Barnabas, 1.23 D05; 4.36).[79]

Stephen summarizes the Genesis story of the jealousy of Joseph's brothers in the single statement, that they sold him (ἀπέδοντο, cf. Gen. 37.28; 45.4 LXX) into Egypt.

[αα'] 7.9b-10 *God Rescues Joseph*

7.9b-10 In Egypt, God acted to counter the betrayal of Joseph by his brothers by being 'with him' (Gen. 39.2-3, 21, 23 LXX),[80] and turning the evil intentions of Jacob's sons to good for his people (cf. 50.19-20). He therefore rescued him (ἐξείλατο), where the middle voice in the Greek suggests the personal interest of God in the deed.[81] Not only did he rescue him from all his afflictions (ἐκ πασῶν θλίψεων αὐτοῦ, cf. 42.21 LXX) but he gave him 'favour (χάρις) and wisdom'. The account of Acts combines Gen. 39.21 ('he gave him favour before the head of the prison guard') with 41.46 ('before Pharaoh king of Egypt'), adding the quality of wisdom to the scriptural account. Contained in this description are words that cause Stephen, persecuted by his own brethren, to be identified with Joseph: not only does the term 'affliction' anticipate the 'affliction' that will follow the death of Stephen (θλῖψις, Acts 8.1 D05; 11.19); but Stephen, too, is full of 'favour' (χάρις [translated as 'grace']) and wisdom (cf. 6.3, 8, 10). He is also 'full of the Holy Spirit' (6.3, 5) and had appeared with the face of an angel (6.15), corresponding to the presence of God with Joseph.

Finally, God (who is still to be understood as the subject) set Joseph up as governor over the country of Egypt as well as over the royal household (a combination of Gen. 39.4-5, 'he appointed him over his household' and 41.43, 'he appointed him over the whole of the land of Egypt'). In a similar way, Stephen and the other six Hellenists had been 'appointed over' the administration of the goods of the Jesus-believing community (Acts 6.3).

The parallels between Stephen and Joseph do not, of course, eclipse the parallels that also exist between Stephen and Jesus. But in the present context, it

79. See *The Message of Acts*, I, pp. 129–31, 298–300.
80. The same phrase is used by Peter of Jesus, Acts 10.35.
81. Zerwick and Grosvenor (*Analysis*, p. 370): 'Aor[2] mid. (ἐξ)αιρέω *take out*; mid. *rescue* ([ἐξείλ]ατο for -ετο § 489)'.

is the similarity between the circumstances of Joseph and Stephen, both of them persecuted by their brothers while being themselves models of virtue and godliness, that is important.

[β–β′] 7.11-50 *Exposition: Expansion of the Promise*
The five distinct elements of the Promise are now developed in turn (see preliminary *Commentary* on 7.2-53, above).

[β] 7.11-16 *Sojourners in a Foreign Land*
Stephen develops the first point of God's promise to Abraham which he stated in 7.6-7. There are six elements within it: βα ββ βγ ‖ βγ′ ββ′ βα′.

[βα] 7.11 *The Famine*
7.11 Stephen continues to select from the scriptural story those elements that serve his purpose. His concern at this point is to explain how the people of Israel came to be in Egypt, which is the essential component of the first four aspects of God's promise (see on 7.10 above). The famine is described in Gen. 41.53-57 as being all over the earth, with the country of Canaan specifically mentioned (42.5). The theme of affliction continues (θλῖψις, cf. Joseph, 7.10).

For the first time, Stephen uses the expression 'our fathers' as equivalent to 'the patriarchs' (7.9), meaning the sons of Jacob but not Jacob himself (cf. 7.12, 15 where they are referred to separately). As at 7.9 where they were first introduced, there is a negative implication in this second mention: in the comment that they did not have enough food to eat is the underlying idea that God had withdrawn his blessing from them. Furthermore, their lack of food is referred to by the term χορτάσματα which, in the Genesis account, is used twice (Gen. 42.27; 43.24 LXX), each time to speak of 'fodder' for the asses. Throughout Genesis 41–44, the LXX uses βρώματα to mean human sustenance (e.g. 42.2, 10). It is possible that Stephen is being deliberately ironic in his choice of vocabulary.[82]

[ββ] 7.12 *Jacob Sends his Sons to Egypt*
7.12 Stephen condenses the story of the visit of Joseph's brothers to Egypt into one sentence. In the Genesis account, they are not presented in a good light, with Jacob having to take the initiative in sending them there and they themselves understanding, when they are made to go back for Benjamin, that they are being paid back for their past ill-treatment of Joseph. Although Stephen says nothing of this (knowing that the entire story is familiar to his audience), the critical

---

82. Against this suggestion, it may be pointed out that the cognate verb χορτάζω is used in Ps. 36.19 LXX to speak of God providing an abundance of food for his people, and in Lk. 9.17 of the 5,000 being filled to satisfaction with the bread and fish that Jesus miraculously multiplied (cf. E. Richard, 'The Polemical Character of the Joseph Episode in Acts 7', *JBL* 98 [1979], pp. 255–67 [260–62]). Nonetheless, the noun χόρτασμα always means animals' food in the LXX and secular literature (B-A-G, χόρτασμα); it is not used elsewhere in the New Testament.

overtones that are fundamental to the scriptural account would inevitably be heard in his brief summary.

With the connecting word 'therefore', the Bezan text keeps the attention on Egypt in this new development of the story, using the famine to explain how the Jewish people came to be there, rather than switching attention back to Jacob (see *Critical Apparatus*).

[βγ] 7.13 *Joseph's Identity is Revealed*
7.13 Without detailing the circumstances of the second journey (Gen. 43.11-15), Stephen focuses on the moment when Joseph's identity became known, both to his brothers (cf. Gen. 45.1)[83] and Pharaoh (45.2). This is the second time Stephen has spoken of this Pharaoh (cf. 7.10) who appears only in a positive light since he has treated Joseph well.

[βγ'] 7.14 *Joseph Sends for his Father*
7.14 As Joseph takes the initiative in calling for his father and his family (by which is probably meant Jacob's, cf. Gen. 46.27), it becomes clear that he is the next in the line of Abraham's descendants through whom the promise is passed on. The number of family members is given as 75 by the LXX (cf. Exod. 1.5 LXX) although other witnesses read 70.[84]

[ββ'] 7.15 *Death of Jacob and his Sons*
7.15 With the arrival of Jacob and his family in Egypt, the first part of the promise is accomplished. Once they are there, both Jacob, on the one hand, and 'our fathers' (cf. vv. 11, 12 above) on the other, have fulfilled their function and Stephen moves the story on with the account of their deaths and removal back to Canaan.

[βα'] 7.16 *Burial in Shechem*
7.16 In Stephen's account of the burial of Jacob and his sons, the patriarchs, two stories from Genesis are conflated. It is unlikely that Stephen, or Luke, was responsible for inventing a new account but more probable that an established, if not universal, tradition was drawn upon. It is obvious from the extant Jewish literature that traditions did develop that modified the scriptural account of the history of Israel, often in an attempt to reconcile conflicting information within it or to bring them into line with later events and circumstances.

According to Genesis (23.3-20), Abraham bought from Ephron the Hittite a cave in a field near Hebron, where Abraham, Sarah, Isaac, Rebecca, Leah and also Jacob were buried (49.31; 50.13); Jacob, for his part, bought a field in

---

83. The D05 text follows the LXX closely: Ἰωσὴφ ... ἀνεγνωρίζετο τοῖς ἀδελφοῖς αὐτοῦ (Genesis); ἀνεγνωρίσθη Ἰωσὴφ τοῖς ἀδελφοῖς αὐτοῦ (Acts).

84. The MT reads 70 at both Gen. 46.27 and Exod. 1.5; cf. Deut. 10.22, MT and LXX. Josephus follows the Hebrew count (*Ant.* II, 176; VI, 89); Philo knows both numbers and attempts to harmonize them by means of allegorization (*Migr. Abr.* 199).

Shechem (33.19; Josh. 24.32; 'Shechen', D05, see *Critical Apparatus*), from Hamor, the father of Shechem, and that was where Joseph was buried (Josh. 24.32).[85] There is no canonical tradition concerning the burial place of Jacob's other sons but according to *Jub.* 46.9 and Josephus (*War* IV, 532; *Ant.* II, 198–99), they were buried in Hebron. Since Shechem was the holy city for the Samaritans, the statement that all of Jacob's family were buried at Shechem could be viewed as inflammatory, made as it is to the Sanhedrin in Jerusalem who did not accept the validity of the Samaritan holy place.

[γ] 7.17-22 *Enslavement*
Having explained how the Israelites came to be in Egypt, Stephen moves on to expand on the second point of God's promise to Abraham (cf. 7.6-7), their enslavement in a foreign land. It consists of six elements, with the character of Moses making a first appearance at the centre of the structure: γα γβ γγ ‖ γγ′ γβ′ γα′. On either side of the central elements, stands a reference to Pharaoh's attempt to deal with the increasing Jewish population by exposing the male infants.

[γα] 7.17-18 *Increase in the People of Israel*
7.17 A new time clause[86] signals the start of Stephen's development of the second aspect of God's promise to Abraham, with an overt reminder of it (cf. 7.5).[87] As if in anticipation of the people of Israel being enslaved in the country where they were living as sojourners, their presence became stronger as their numbers increased. The same expression 'grew strong and multiplied' (ηὔξησεν ... καὶ ἐπληθύνθη) is used of 'the word of God/Lord' (ηὔξανεν καὶ ἐπληθύνετο, Acts 6.7; 12.24). Its use here with reference to the Jewish people occurs already (in the plural) in the Exodus account on which Stephen is drawing: 'The descendants of Israel were strengthened and multiplied (ηὐξήθησαν καὶ ἐπληθύνθησαν); they increased and grew exceedingly strong, so that the land was filled with them' (Exod. 1.7 LXX; cf. Gen. 1.28). 'The people' (ὁ λαός) is a technical term that Luke uses consistently to refer to the people of Israel.

7.18 Stephen presents the growth in the Jewish presence in Egypt as interrupted by the arrival of a new pharaoh on the scene, one who did not know Joseph, as Exod. 1.8 relates; or, as the Bezan text puts it, did not remember him, possibly implying that he did not understand what he had been about.[88]

---

85. Barrett (I, p. 351) has two errors on this verse: for Josh. 13.32 read Josh. 24.32; and for 'Joseph was buried in Hebron' read 'Joseph was buried in Shechem'.

86. As an adverb of time, καθώς is extremely rare (Zerwick and Grosvenor, *Analysis*, p. 371). More than simply indicating time, it explains the context of the increase in the population of the Jewish people in Egypt.

87 The wording of Codex Bezae ('the promise that God had promised') has the effect of drawing particular attention to Stephen's earlier mention.

88. Luke uses this verb (μιμνήσκομαι) elsewhere with the sense of 'understand' a saying or a fact that was known but not comprehended until some later time: Lk. 24.6, 8; Acts 11.16; cf. Mt. 26.75; Jn 2.17, 22; 12.16.

[γβ] 7.19 *Pharaoh's Plan*

7.19 According to the Exodus account, the new pharaoh was alarmed that the Egyptians could be overpowered by the Israelites and consequently devised a plan to prevent them increasing any further. The verb used in Exod. 1.10 and repeated by Stephen (κατασοφίζομαι, translated here as 'dealt shrewdly') has the sense of evil intent but also trickery.[89] In fact, the original plan was to make the Israelites work on various building and agricultural projects in difficult conditions with harsh masters overseeing them, in other words as their slaves (κατε-δουλοῦντο αὐτούς, Exod. 1.14), which Stephen had cited as part of the promise to Abraham (δουλώσουσιν αὐτό/αὐτούς, 7.7). It was when that plan did not have the effect of reducing their numbers (quite the contrary, since they went on increasing, Exod. 1.12) that Pharaoh gave orders, first that the Egyptian midwives should kill all the baby boys and secondly, since his orders were not carried out effectively, that the male babies were to be thrown into the Nile so that they would not survive.[90] This is part of the 'ill-treatment' of which Stephen spoke in his outline of the promise (κακώσουσιν, 7.6), a word that is used in Exodus (ἵνα κακώσωσιν αὐτούς) and that he repeats now (ἐκάκωσεν).

The duration of the enslavement in Egypt was given in the outline of the promise as '400 years' (7.6), echoing Gen. 15.13. From both the Exodus account and Stephen's summary here, it is far from apparent that the ill-treatment of the Israelites extended over such a lengthy period. And yet, though there is some discrepancy among the various versions of the story as to just what the 400 years included,[91] all nevertheless insist that the time spent in Egypt lasted for a considerable length of time, 400 years representing 10 generations. Two of these are accounted for in the lifetime of Moses, who was said to be 80 years old when he led the Israelites out of Egypt.

[γγ] 7.20a *The Birth of Moses*

7.20a At the centre of this episode is the birth of Moses, which took place during this period that Stephen has been describing.[92] The adjective used to describe

---

89. B-A-G, κατασοφίζομαι.

90. μὴ ζῳογονεῖσθαι, passive infinitive in Acts 7.19. The verb is used in the active in Exod. 1.17, 18, 22 with reference to the babies that were allowed to live. In the passive, it has the sense of 'survive', the equivalent of the middle περιποιοῦμαι (Exod. 1.16; cf. Lk. 17.33: ὃς ἐὰν ζητήσῃ τὴν ψυχὴν αὐτοῦ περιποιήσασθαι ἀπολέσει αὐτήν, where D05 reads θελήσῃ ζῳογονῆσαι for ζητήσῃ ... περιποιήσασθαι).

91. According to Exod. 12.40 MT, the whole stay in Egypt lasted 430 years, so 30 years are assigned to the good years when Joseph was governor. In the LXX, however, as well as the Samaritan Pentateuch and Gal. 3.17, the time spent in Canaan before Egypt is also included in the 430 years, which means that the good years under Joseph are interpreted as belonging to the 400 years. This, though, is specifically excluded from the way the years are counted at Gen. 15.13 LXX and in Stephen's summary, Acts 7.6. For further variations on the counting of the years spent in Egypt, see Le Déaut, *La nuit pascale*, p. 101, n. 87; pp. 149–50.

92. The time indication given at the beginning of v. 20 does not introduce a new period of time, such as is signalled at 7.11, 17, 23, 30, but rather moves from the general situation to focus on a

Moses as being 'well-pleasing' to God has the first meaning of 'beautiful'.[93] It is possible to interpret 'to God' as a Hebraic idiom expressing the superlative degree of Moses' attractiveness.[94] It was this that led his mother to conceal him according to Exod. 2.2, with no mention of his father.

[γγ'] 7.20b *Moses' First Three Months*
7.20b Stephen's account introduces a new element into the story with the reference to 'the father's house', with Codex Bezae removing any ambiguity as to whose father is meant with the pronoun 'his'.

[γβ'] 7.21 *Moses' Upbringing*
7.21 The details of the Exodus account continue to be taken as known as Stephen rapidly summarizes the abandonment of Moses in the Nile (spelt out by the Bezan text, cf. Exod. 2.3), the finding of him by Pharaoh's daughter (2.5),[95] and the rearing of him as her own child (2.10). Stephen omits any reference to Moses' sister (2.4, 7-8) or his mother (2.7-9) who was responsible for his early upbringing, focusing instead on the role played by Pharaoh's family in adopting him.

The story of Moses runs parallel to that of Joseph, both of them abandoned by their blood family and taken into Pharaoh's household, Joseph as 'governor' and Moses as 'son'. The Egyptian Pharaoh again has a positive role in the unfolding of Israel's history; it is not accidental that Stephen avoids naming him in the negative reference to him in Acts 7.18-19, or even employing the term 'Pharaoh' to paraphrase the reference to 'the king' of Egypt (Exod. 1.8, cf. Acts 7.18).

[γα'] 7.22 *Moses' Education*
7.22 The steps of Moses' birth, upbringing and education are now completed, following a pattern that Paul will repeat with respect to himself (Acts 22.3). As with Joseph, there is once again a reference to wisdom. Joseph was said to have received his wisdom as a gift from God (7.10), just as he received from God 'favour' in the sight of Pharaoh. In the case of Moses, the divine role is less obvious for the wisdom is that of the Egyptians; according to the AT, he is instructed by means of their wisdom, but in the Bezan text he is actually taught their wisdom (see *Critical Apparatus*). He also has considerable power, in his words and his actions.[96]

---

specific case. Verse 20 is not, therefore, to be viewed as the start of a new episode (cf. N-A[27], which writes Ἐν with a capital letter).

93. B-A-G, ἀστεῖον.

94. Zerwick, *Biblical Greek*, § 56; Zerwick and Grosvenor, *Analysis*, p. 371: ' "even to (in the judgment of) God"; in Hebr. idiom, *in the highest degree, extremely*, Jon 3:3'.

95. The sense of ἀνείλατο αὐτόν, 'she picked him up', repeats Exod. 2.5, ἀνείλατο αὐτήν, 'she picked it up', referring to the basket.

96. The disciples who met Jesus on the road to 'Emmaus' ('Oulammaous', D05) commented that he was 'a prophet powerful in work and deed, δυνατὸς ἐν ἔργῳ καὶ λόγῳ (λόγῳ καὶ ἔργῳ D05, adopting the same order as Stephen has here), before God and all the people' (Lk. 24.19).

The parallels between Stephen's presentation of Joseph and Moses are sufficient to establish that a deliberate comparison is being made, and the nature of
the parallels is such that the comparison is somewhat unfavourable towards Moses:

1. God was with Joseph (v. 9b: καὶ ἦν ὁ θεὸς μετ' αὐτοῦ) // Moses was 'well-
    pleasing' to God (v. 20: καὶ ἦν ἀστεῖος τῷ θεῷ).
2. Joseph was sold to Egypt because of his brothers' jealousy (v. 9a) //
    Moses was abandoned by his parents because of the king of Egypt's
    scheming (v. 21a).
3. God rescued (ἐξείλατο) Joseph from all his afflictions (v. 10a) //
    Pharaoh's daughter picked up (ἀνείλατο) Moses from the water (v. 21b).
4. Joseph was appointed governor of Egypt (v. 10c) // Moses was brought
    up as the son of Pharaoh's daughter (v. 21c).
5. God gave to Joseph wisdom (v. 10b: σοφίαν) // Moses was instructed in
    the wisdom of the Egyptians (v. 22a: πάσῃ σοφίᾳ / πάσην τὴν σοφίαν).

The purpose of the parallel presentation of the two characters is two-fold:
first, Joseph is established as the superior leader of the two, representing the
standard against which future leaders of Israel may be evaluated; secondly, the
alignment of Stephen with Joseph[97] rather than with Moses endows him with a
particular strength that arms him against the charge of his opponents – that he
had spoken against Moses – and undergirds the answer he will give to their
accusation.

[δ] 7.23-29 *God's Judgment on Egypt*
The third step in Stephen's account of the history of Israel is linked to the third
aspect of the promise to Abraham, God's judgment (7.7). The judgment is carried
out initially by Moses in a symbolic action, but in a way that is not entirely satisfactory and that brings fresh problems to Moses. God himself will judge Egypt
when he brings his people out of the land of slavery, a deliverance that results
from the enforcement of his judgment on the slave masters.[98]

The internal structure of the episode is concentric, with three elements either
side of a central one: δα δβ δγ / δδ \ δγ′ δβ′ δα′. Focus is thus given to the stark
declaration in [δδ] 7.25b that, contrary to expectation, the Israelites did not
understand the role God had given to Moses for their salvation. At the beginning
of the episode, Moses is viewed in the context of Israel, in contrast to the end
where he has become a sojourner in the desert.

[δα] 7.23 *Moses Visits his Brethren*
7.23 The start of the next step in Stephen's account is marked, as are the others,
with an indication of a new time: as Moses was approaching 40. According to

---

97. Richard ('The Polemical Character', p. 265) concludes, 'In fact, Joseph is a forerunner of
Stephen himself'.

98. Daube (*Exodus Pattern*, pp. 35–38) highlights the close association of God's judgment with his
promise of deliverance in Exodus, which makes of the exodus a legal process whereby judgment is
executed on Egypt and justice rendered to Israel.

Deut. 34.7, Moses was 120 when he died; the division of his life into three equal periods of 40 years appears to be traditional as it is found in at least one rabbinic writing.[99] The maximum life-span decreed by God in Gen 6.3 was 120 years. Moses' first 40 years were spent in the royal household, where he was immersed in Egyptian ways (Exod. 2.2-10; cf. Acts 7.21-22); the next 40 were spent in Midian living as an exile (Exod. 2.15-22; cf. Acts 7.23-29); during the final 40, following the vision at Mt Horeb (Exod. 3.1–4.17; cf. Acts 7.30-34 [Mt Sinai]), he led the Israelites through the desert (Exod. 13.17-22; Deut. 34.1-7; cf. Acts 7.36).

The expression translated as 'there came to him the idea' is literally 'there came upon his heart' (ἀνέβη ἐπὶ τὴν καρδίαν αὐτοῦ), an expression found in the LXX (4 Kgdms 12.5; Isa. 65.16; Jer. 3.16; 39.35; 51.21; Ezek. 38.10) where the heart (as in Hebrew) is the seat of the intelligence and not the emotions (cf. Lk. 24.38).

The idea of Moses visiting his brethren is derived from Exod. 2.11 LXX: 'when Moses was grown up, he went out towards his brethren the sons of Israel' ('he went out to his people', MT). The word for 'visit' (ἐπισκέπτομαι) expresses the purpose as being to bring help.[100]

[δβ] 7.24 *Moses' Intervention to Bring Justice*
7.24 The incident in which Moses killed an Egyptian fighting with an Israelite is recorded in Exod. 2.11b-12, but Stephen adds two important details in saying that Moses 'defended/started to defend (ἠμύνατο/-ετο) and carried out justice (ἐποίη-σεν ἐκδίκησιν)' for the man being wronged. In this way, Moses becomes the one who 'judges' Egypt, the two men representing Israel and Egypt and Moses acting to punish the oppression of his people. The judgment of God in Exodus consists in the ten plagues leading up to the final liberation of the Israelites from Egypt, but Stephen says not a word about them. When God announces the final plague in Exod. 12.12, it is there that he uses words that are used here of Moses: 'I will pass through the land of Egypt that night and I will strike (πατάξω) all the first-born in the land of Egypt ... and on all the gods of Egypt I will carry out justice (ποιήσω τὴν ἐκδίκησιν).' Not only is the idea of executing judgment transferred to Moses, but also the same verb used for 'strike' in the last plague is used of Moses hitting the Egyptian (7.24, πατάξας). The effect of transferring judgment from God to Moses not only removes the blame for the oppression of the Israelites from Pharaoh, it also prepares the way for the rejection of Moses by the people of Israel.

Further expressions that Stephen applies to the gesture of Moses are found in the central section of the Exodus narrative:

99. *Sifre* § 357; 150a. The threefold division of Moses' life is also a theme found in some Patristic writings, see A. Le Boulluec and P. Sandevoir, *L'Exode*, in M. Harl (ed.), *La Bible d'Alexandrie*. II (Paris: Cerf, 1989), p. 83.
100. Zerwick and Grosvenor, *Analysis,* p. 372. The verb is especially used by Luke in the New Testament: out of 11 occurrences seven are in Luke's writings (Lk. × 3; Acts × 4).

1. Visit (ἐπισκέψασθαι), cf. Exod. 3.16; 4.31; 13.19.
2. The sons of Israel (τοὺς υἱοὺς ᾿Ισραήλ), cf. Exodus *passim.*
3. Carry out justice (ἐποίησεν ἐκδίκησιν), cf. Exod. 12.12 (7.4).
4. Strike the Egyptian dead (πατάξας τὸν Αἰγύπτιον), cf. Exod. 2.12; 3.20 (pl.); 12.23 (pl.), 27 (pl.).

However, it is not yet said that Moses was acting on behalf of God or that he had been sent by him to free his people from slavery; on the contrary, it looks for the moment as if the initiative came from Moses.

[δγ] 7.25a *Moses is God's Instrument for Salvation*
7.25a The reasoning behind Moses' action becomes clearer in Stephen's explanatory comment which reveals that Moses knew already at this stage that he was the instrument God was using to save his people from the oppression of the Egyptians – not just a quarrel between individuals but ill-treatment on a much larger scale since he speaks of God giving them 'salvation' (δίδωσιν σωτηρίαν αὐτοῖς).[101] What is not clear is how Moses knew this or on what the grounds he might presume that the Israelites would understand it.

[δδ] 7.25b *The Israelites do not Understand Moses' Role*
7.25b That the Israelites did not understand is the great obstacle to the plan of salvation, expressed appropriately in the briefest of sentences: 'But they did not understand.'[102] The presentation of the story of salvation in this way, as Moses' intervention in the quarrel between an individual Israelite and an Egyptian, views the intervention of God in Israel's history not as a national event on a spectacular scale, such as is the dramatic night-time escape with the angel of death in Exodus, but rather as localized action through the person of Moses. Stephen focuses on the unfavourable reaction of the Israelites to Moses' attempts at imposing justice in order to bring out the hostility of the Jews to God's plan for salvation, even at this early stage. There is a certain irony in the fact that Stephen tells this story to an audience who are accusing him of blaspheming against Moses: he demonstrates that Israel's rejection of Moses was a problem from the beginning.

[δγ′] 7.26 *Moses' Second Intervention*
7.26 That the intervention of Moses in the attack of an Israelite by an Egyptian was no minor incident but was to serve as a model for Moses' role in the salvation of Israel, is confirmed in the next event that is closely tied to the previous one: firstly, by the connective τε which expresses a close link with the previous sentence and which could be translated by 'furthermore' or 'moreover';

---

101. The present tense is used, representing the tense of Moses' words to himself (Zerwick, *Biblical Greek*, § 347). Moses' awareness of himself as God's instrument for salvation applies to the present incident, not some event in the future.

102. The wording of the negative statement, οὐ συνῆκαν, corresponds to the wording of Moses' assumption συνιέναι (v. 25a). The verb occurs many times in Luke: Lk. 2.50; 8.10; 18.34; 24.45; Acts 28.26, 27.

and secondly, by the expression of time, 'the next day'. The original narrative of Exod. 2.13 makes it clear that the two men fighting on this second occasion were both Hebrews.

The verb used to describe Moses' appearing to them (ὤφθη) always refers elsewhere in Luke to the manifestation of a divine presence.[103] Stephen already used it to describe the appearance of God to Abraham (7.2). The Israelites, then, had ample opportunity to recognize that Moses was acting on behalf of God, just as the Hellenists had had opportunity to observe that Stephen was favoured by God (6.15, see *Commentary* above). Even so, they rejected him.

The parallel between the two fighting scenes is brought out explicitly in Codex Bezae by the detail 'he saw them doing wrong', using the same verb (ἀδικέω)[104] as has already been used in v. 24 (see *Critical Apparatus*). At the first occurrence, in the passive, it described an Israelite being harmed by an Egyptian, but now it is applied in the active to people of Moses' own race; Moses himself will use it in his question 'Why are you wronging/doing wrong to each other?', and it will occur once more in v. 27 to refer to one of the two men. The implication of the parallels is that just as they are oppressed by the Egyptians, so the Israelites harm each other even though they are brethren of the same race. The term 'brethren' is used three times in this central part of Stephen's speech (vv. 23, 25, 26), equivalent to 'the sons of Israel' (v. 23). For Stephen's own audience, there is the message that they, too, are doing wrong to one of their own people.

[δβ'] 7.27-28 *The Rejection of Moses*

7.27-28 For a second time, Moses' attempt to bring peace is rejected, this time by the two men he was seeking to reconcile. This view of the way God's plan for salvation was received is somewhat different from the traditional view, which presents the Egyptians as the evil-doers and the Israelites as the innocent party. Compared with the Exodus account where the response to Moses is simply introduced with 'He answered' (Exod. 2.14), the guilty party in Stephen's account is described more fully: 'The man who was wronging his neighbour...', taking up the word neighbour (ὁ πλησίος) from Exod. 2.13, and using the verb that has been running through this account (ἀδικέω) for the third time (fourth in Codex Bezae). Furthermore, this man pushed Moses away, for which Stephen uses the verb that is a technical term in Luke's writing to express the rejection of God by Israel, ἀπωθέω.[105] Not only is Moses confronted with the Israelites' lack

103. The angel of the Lord: Lk. 1.11; 22.43; Acts 7.30, 35; Moses and Elijah at the transfiguration: Lk. 9.31; the resurrected Jesus: Lk. 24.34; Acts 9.17; 13.31; 26.16a, 16b; the tongues of fire at Pentecost: Acts 2.3; a vision in the night: 16.9.

104. ἀδικέω has been rendered in the translation of this passage as 'do wrong' or simply 'wrong'. The verb in Greek contains the idea of injustice, or unrighteousness contrasting with the ideal of the perfect person who is δίκαιος, 'righteous', or 'just'.

105. For the technical sense of ἀπωθέω, cf. 7.39 and 13.46 where it is the equivalent of 'denying' God; cf. further examples at Lk. 22.34, 57, 61; Acts 3.13, 14.

of understanding that he is God's chosen instrument for salvation but worse, with his rejection by those among the people who play the part of the aggressor. The two rhetorical questions he addresses to the wrong-doer are found in Exod. 2.14 LXX, with the answer to the first, 'Who appointed you as a ruler and a judge over us?', already suggested in Acts 7.25: contrary to the man's expectation, it is God who had entrusted him with these roles.

[δα´] 7.29 *Moses Flees to Midian*

7.29 In Exodus, Moses flees because Pharaoh was wanting to kill Moses when he heard about the killing of the Egyptian (Exod. 2.14b, 15). In Stephen's account, there is another slight but telling change, for here it is the words of the Israelite that cause Moses to flee. The motive is clearly made evident in the Bezan text: 'And so it was…' (οὕτως καί); the verb in Codex Bezae (ἐφυγάδευσεν) also goes further than to say simply that he fled (ἔφυγεν), by insisting on his fugitive status.

Moses' situation once more resembles that of Joseph in that he, too, has now been rejected by his brethren and is forced to live in a foreign land, to be a 'sojourner' (cf. 7.6). The story is told in Exod. 2.15b-22, where the name of his eldest son is precisely the Hebrew for 'sojourner' (Moses' second son is not mentioned until 18.3-4).

[γ´] 7.30-40 *Exodus*

Stephen continues with the story of Moses by developing the fourth aspect of the promise made to Abraham (7.6-7), namely that after Abraham's descendants have been enslaved in a foreign land for 400 years and that land has been judged by God, the people will leave it. His deliverance of his people from Egypt is, in itself, an execution of his judgment on the land since it constituted a punishment for the slave masters (see *Commentary*, 7.23-29).

In the book of Exodus, the departure of the Israelites from Egypt is described in some detail, especially the plagues that were sent by God to punish the Egyptians, culminating in the last plague of the killing of the first-born (Exodus 3–12). It was already noted in the previous section that Stephen does not mention the plagues, presenting instead Moses' killing of an individual Egyptian as the symbolic enactment of God's judgment on the country. In a similar disregard for the focus of the original account, Stephen will avoid referring to the Passover but will concentrate on Moses' leadership of the Israelites showing how he was the one God chose to be responsible for bringing them out of Egypt but whom the people did not accept.

The scene falls into two distinct and structurally balanced parts with four elements in each of them, and a central element that is the crux of the scene: γ´α γ´β γ´γ γ´δ / γ´ε \ γ´δ´ γ´γ´ γ´β´ γ´α´. The first part describes in detail God's appearance to Moses in the burning bush while he was in the desert (7.30-32), and the second then selects aspects of his relationship with the people of Israel (7.35-40). At the centre (7.33-34) stand God's instructions to Moses.

[γ'α] 7.30 *The Burning Bush*
7.30 A new temporal clause signals the start of a new scene in Stephen's speech. The phrase of the Bezan text, 'And after this', echoes the corresponding element of Stephen's summary of the promise ('And after this they will come out', καὶ μετὰ ταῦτα ἐξελεύσονται, cf. 7,6). Moses is by now 80 years old, two-thirds of his life having been lived. This tallies with the traditional division of Moses' life into three equal periods of 40 years each (see *Commentary*, 7.23).

The angel who appears to Moses is none other than the angel of the Lord, who represents God himself in the Hebrew Bible. This becomes clear when the one speaking from the bush reveals himself as God. Exod. 3.2 specifies the 'angel of the Lord', as read here by Codex Bezae.

Stephen places the appearance of the angel of the Lord to Moses in the desert of Sinai. In the Exodus account, Moses is said to have been looking after his father-in-law's sheep in Midian when he went 'beyond the desert' to Mt Horeb (qualified in the Hebrew by 'the mountain of God'). Horeb is the name by which Mt Sinai is sometimes known, though there is much debate as to its location. The significance of Stephen's choice of the name Sinai rather than Horeb lies in the assimilation, common in Judaism, between Mt Sinai and Mt Zion. By placing God's revelation to Moses at Sinai, where God declares 'the place' (ὁ τόπος) to be 'holy ground' (cf. 7.33), Stephen shows how the exclusive claim for Jerusalem to be the 'holy place' (cf. 6.13) is contradicted by Scripture.[106]

[γ'β] 7.31a *Moses Marvels*
7.31a The wonder of the bush, which blazed without burning away, is not spelled out in the Exodus account (Exod. 3.1-6), though it is implied in the comment 'the bush was burning yet it was not consumed' (3.2). Stephen links the amazement of Moses with his desire to see just what was happening.

[γ'γ] 7.31b-32a *God Reveals Himself*
7.31b In the Exodus account, Moses speaks aloud at this point: 'I will go alongside it and see this great sight, to find out why the bush is not burnt' (3.3). The point is repeated in indirect speech: 'When the Lord saw that he was coming nearer to see...' (3.4a). Moses' wonderment and curiosity is underlined in the Bezan text by highlighting the verb 'look closely'.[107]

The order of the declarations that come from the bush according to the Exodus account (3.5, 6) is inverted in Acts, with God first revealing his identity and then proclaiming the land holy. Codex Bezae attributes the first utterance to 'the

106. On the assimilation of Sinai and Zion, see Le Déaut, *La nuit pascale*, p. 162, n. 77. Commentators miss the theological point when they assume that Stephen, or Luke, simply said the first name they thought of (see, e.g., Barrett, I, p. 360: 'Sinai was the name that came to mind').

107. The verb κατανοέω has the sense of 'observe' or 'consider' with clarity, and can apply equally to perception with the mind as with the senses (Zerwick and Grosvenor, *Analysis*, p. 372, 'to ascertain what it was').

Lord' and the second to 'a voice', whereas the AT has 'the voice' first and 'the Lord' second; in Exodus 3 LXX, 'the Lord' first calls Moses by his name (3.4a); thereafter, he is simply understood to be the speaker who continues to address Moses (3.4b, 6) until the title 'Lord' is repeated (3.7).[108]

7.32a For Stephen's account, the most important utterance in the Exodus story of these events is the revelation of the divine presence. This revelation to Moses became the cornerstone of the Jewish understanding of the nature of God, for it is to him that he declares, in a play on the letters of the divine name in Hebrew, 'I am who I am' (Exod. 3.14).[109] Thus, in the first declaration of his identity, he says, 'I am (ἐγώ εἰμι) the God of your father, the God of Abraham and the God of Isaac and the God of Jacob' (3.6 LXX). Stephen, however, who is not concerned here to insist on the nature of God but rather on his relationship with Moses and his ancestors, omits the verb 'am' and alters 'your father' to the plural 'your fathers' so as to echo the phrase that he has used throughout his speech to refer to the patriarchs (Acts 7.4 D05, 11, 12, 15; cf. v. 19 D05 where the possessive is omitted because the 'fathers' in question are not the patriarchs). Here, the phrase refers to the three founders of Israel, Abraham, Isaac and Jacob, whom Stephen presents as being the ones through whom salvation is transmitted; it is handed on through Joseph and not the Twelve, and is about to pass to Moses.

[γ'δ] 7.32b *Moses' Fear*
7.32b Moses had initially made a move to look more closely (κατανοῆσαι) at the burning bush (cf. 7.31). Once he hears the Lord speak, he is so overcome (lit. 'he became trembling')[110] that he no longer dares approach to have a better look (κατανοῆσαι). In the Exodus passage, Moses is said to be afraid to fix his eyes on God who was speaking to him (κατεμβλέψαι, Exod. 3.6b). Stephen, in contrast, presents Moses as afraid to continue to get nearer to the burning bush. The subsequent command of the Lord, which Stephen has displaced from before the revelation of God's identity, takes on a different significance in this new context.

[γ'ε] 7.33-34 *God's Instructions to Moses*
7.33 The exact meaning of the Lord's command to Moses, in the original context of Exodus, to take off his sandals, has been much debated, not least among the early Church Fathers.[111] Whatever its precise intention, it was given as Moses was about to step closer to the place from the Lord had addressed him: 'Do not come near; take off the sandals from your feet, for the place on which you are

---

108. In the subsequent conversation that is not reported in Acts, κύριος is found throughout, e.g. 4.2, 4, 6.

109. The play is on the consonants of the name YHWH which means 'he/it is'. See Le Boulluec and Sandevoir, *L'Exode*, p. 92.

110. The same expression ἔντρομος γενόμενος recurs in Acts 16.29 AT (ἔντρ. ὑπάρχων D05).

111. For details, see Le Boulluec and Sandevoir, *L'Exode*, pp. 89–90.

standing is holy ground' (Exod. 3.5). According to Stephen, however, Moses is instructed to remove his shoes at the point when he feared to move nearer. The order therefore becomes an encouragement to overcome his fear in the presence of God. Since he is standing on holy ground, he should remove his shoes; this will enable him to 'take careful notice' and understand what it is that God will tell him. The declaration that the ground of Mt Sinai, the 'place' (ὁ τόπος) where Moses is standing, is holy, is a challenge to Stephen's accusers who restrict the designation of 'holy' to the Temple in Jerusalem, the 'place' par excellence.

7.34 The Lord's words that follow explain why he encourages Moses to approach; Codex Bezae makes the connection explicit with the word 'for' (γάρ, see *Critical Apparatus*) – God wants to talk with Moses because he has seen the suffering of the people in Egypt. Stephen's text follows Exod. 3.7-8, 10 but with omissions that are significant, for they reinforce the relatively positive portrayal of the Egyptians that has been observed earlier in his speech. Thus, after saying he has heard the suffering (τοῦ στεναγμοῦ) of the people (Exod. 3.7 LXX has 'groan', τῆς κραυγῆς), he does not include 'because of the taskmasters'; he does not say he will rescue them 'out of the hand of the Egyptians' (3.8a); he does not repeat that he has heard their cry and seen 'the oppression with which the Egyptians oppress them' (3.9); finally, he reduces the statement of Exodus LXX, 'I will send you to Pharaoh the king of Egypt and you will lead my people the sons of Israel out of Egypt', to simply 'I will send you to Egypt'. The effect of these modifications is to shift the focus in the book of Exodus on the evil of Pharaoh and the Egyptians to Moses and the people of Israel.

[γ'δ'] 7.35 Moses: The People's Rejection and God's Call
7.35 Stephen switches from detailing God's call of Moses to lead the Israelites out of Egypt to selecting aspects of the people's response to Moses. The switch is abrupt (there is no connecting word which is highly unusual in Acts)[112] but it does not indicate a new section since the theme is still the Exodus and continues to be so until the notion of worship is introduced in 7.41. Throughout vv. 35-40, Moses is referred to with the demonstrative, 'this man' (οὗτος). In v. 35, a contrast is drawn between the rejection of Moses by the Israelites, exemplified by the reaction of the man harming his fellow-Israelite when Moses intervened (cf. vv. 26-28), and the choosing of him by God to lead his people out of slavery.

Those who rejected Moses are not actually specified but are simply referred to with the plural verb, 'they denied' (ἠρνήσαντο). Significantly, the same verb, or its compound (ἀπαρνέομαι) is used of the denial of Jesus by Peter, first (Lk. 22.34, 57, 61), then by the people of Israel before Pilate (Acts 3.13, 14 AT; cf. Lk. 23.13-23). A parallel between Moses and Jesus is thereby signalled, with the refusal of the people to listen to Moses anticipating the rejection of Jesus by the people. This is important for Stephen whose purpose is to demonstrate to his

---

112. See Read-Heimerdinger, *The Bezan Text*, pp. 246–53.

listeners how, despite their apparent reverence of Moses, they are mistreating Jesus in the same way as their ancestors mistreated Moses.

Moses was rejected as 'ruler and judge' by the people; God sent him as '(both, B03/D05) ruler and deliverer'. The word used for 'deliverer' (λυτρωτής) is associated with the verb 'to redeem' (λυτρόομαι), in the sense of 'set free', often from slavery. The notion of the payment of a ransom is sometimes involved (e.g. for the release of slaves or prisoners) but more generally it is a matter of a rescue that is difficult to carry out for some reason without payment as such being involved, and that would seem to be the meaning here. It is also a verb used of Jesus, where the idea of a ransom may be implied (Lk. 24.21; cf. Isa. 44.22-24; 1 Macc. 4.11). It occurs at Exod. 6.6 LXX: 'I will redeem (λυτρώσομαι) you with an outstretched arm'.

[γ′γ′] 7.36 *Moses Leads the People out of Egypt*

7.36 A concise summary of how the deliverance took place takes up the verb used throughout the book of Exodus in LXX to describe how God 'brought out' (ἐξήγαγεν) his people from Egypt, and applies it here to the whole journey from Egypt to Canaan. Stephen's description highlights the working of 'wonders and signs' which are associated not just with Egypt where the 10 plagues were performed (Exod. 7.3; 11.9-10), but also with the Red Sea and the desert. In Jewish tradition, the scriptural account of Moses' power to perform miracles was considerably enhanced, especially at the Red Sea.[113] The third mention here of a 40 year period, encompassing the exodus from beginning to end, is an indirect reference to the death of Moses at the age of 120 before the people of Israel entered the Promised Land (cf. Deut. 31.2).

[γ′β′] 7.37 *A Prophet Like Moses*

7.37 Stephen recalls a specific declaration Moses spoke to the people of Israel as they were about to pass over into Canaan. Since he would not enter with them into the Promised Land, he left them detailed and clear instructions, insisting on the need for their absolute obedience (Deuteronomy 1–30) and reminding them of the consequences of both their faithfulness and their rebellion. Among all the promises God had made to his people in the wilderness, Moses recalls that at Mt Horeb (in the desert of Sinai, Exod. 19.1-2) God had undertaken to speak to them through a prophet because it was too terrible a thing for them to hear his voice directly (Deut. 18.15-16; cf. Exod. 20.19). As he himself will no longer be with them, he urges them to pay heed to the one who will replace him. For the second time in Acts, the promise of a prophet like Moses is applied to the Messiah rather than Moses' immediate successor (cf. Peter's speech to the people of Jerusalem,

---

113. *Targ. Ps.-J. Exod.* 15.11 amplifies the Hebrew text when it speaks of the Lord 'performing signs and wonders for your people, the house of Israel' at the Red Sea; cf. P. Enns, *Exodus Retold: Ancient Exegesis of the Departure from Egypt in Wis 10:15-21 and 19:1-9* (Harvard Semitic Museum Monographs, 57; Atlanta: Scholars Press, 1997), pp. 128–30.

3.22-23). Already in Luke's Gospel, the promise is associated with Jesus at the scene of the transfiguration when the words 'listen to him' are applied to Jesus as distinct from both Moses and Elijah (Lk. 9.35). The AT omits these words from Stephen's recollection of God's promise to raise up a prophet like Moses, but the inclusion of them in Codex Bezae makes quite clear to his audience that the failure to heed the Messiah, whom they are well aware Stephen identifies as Jesus, has dire consequences. Stephen is indirectly showing that the accusation that he speaks against Moses is false as far as he is concerned, and that it is those who refuse to accept Jesus who are guilty of rejecting Moses.

[γ´α´] 7.38-40 *The Israelites' Rebellion against Moses*
7.38 In the original context of Sinai, God had given a solemn warning that the people must listen to his voice (communicated through his chosen prophet) and on no account make other gods for themselves (Exod. 20.21-24). Following the same pattern, Stephen goes on to remind his audience how, although Moses received commandments from God for the people so that they would have life, they refused to obey. The mention of the 'assembly' is a direct evocation of the day when the Law was given to Moses,[114] with the Torah represented by the term 'living words' (λόγια ζῶντα), in line with its traditional designation as 'the tree of life'.[115]

The presence of the angel as an intermediary between God and the people of Israel has already been mentioned twice in Stephen's speech (cf. 7.30, 35), although in the scriptural account only at God's first appearance to Moses in the burning bush is an angel mentioned (cf. Exod. 3.2). The tradition of the Law being delivered through angels seems to have developed outside the Hebrew Bible. The presence of angels at the giving of the Law is alluded to in Deut. 33.2 LXX which speaks of the angels that accompanied God at his right hand when he came to Mt Sinai.[116] They are more clearly implicated in the book of *Jubilees* (*Jub.* 1.27; 2.1; cf. Gal. 3.19).

According to one strand of tradition, an angel was required because of the sinfulness of the people who could not come into direct communication with God.[117] Here, not only does the angel cause God's voice to be heard indirectly,

---

114. ἐν τῇ ἐκκλησίᾳ, cf. Deut. 4.10; 9.10; 18.16. The same word has already been used in Codex Bezae to describe the 'assembly' of those who follow Jesus as the 'church' (Acts 2.47 D05).

115. 'As I shall breathe the breath of life into the nostrils of man, so will I do for Israel – I will give the Torah unto him, the tree of life' (cited by Ginzberg, *The Legends of the Jews*, I, p. 51; see also Kugel, *Traditions of the Bible*, pp. 614–15, 627). Cf. Deut. 32.47.

116. The presence of angels in Deut. 33.2 LXX may be derived from the mention in the previous clause of the 'myriads of holy ones', rendered by the targums as 'myriads of holy angels' (Le Boulluec and Sandevoir, *L'Exode*, p. 344).

117. Evidence that the presence of an angel in place of the Lord himself was seen as a punishment is found in Exod. 33.2-4, where the people were grieved when he undertook to send an angel to lead them into the Promised Land instead of leading them there himself (see Daube, *Exodus Pattern*, pp. 40–41; and see *The Message of Acts,* I, p. 330).

but the presence of Moses himself removes God's voice further still from the people. The literal expression used by Stephen is that he was 'with the angel' and 'with our fathers', suggesting his role as intermediary. Underlying all of this is the comparison with Jesus who, like Moses according to Stephen's claims, has given words of life for the people. In the Bezan text, Stephen fully identifies with the people he is talking to, as could be expected, but in the AT he distances himself in a way that is at odds with his inclusion in the first person pronoun when he speaks of the Jewish ancestors as 'our fathers'.

7.39-40 For the second time in Stephen's account of Moses the people of Israel are presented as rejecting him (cf. 7.26-27). Not only do they refuse to listen to him, but they hanker after their life as it was when they were slaves in Egypt. In consequence, they ask Aaron, Moses' brother and mouthpiece (cf. Exod. 4.14-16), to make gods for them.

In the original context, the reason the people of Israel asked Aaron to make them gods is that they were tired of waiting for Moses to come down from talking with God on Sinai (Exod. 32.1); Aaron later explains to Moses that it is because their hearts are 'set on evil' that they would not wait for him (32.22). In the scriptural account, their turning back to Egypt occurred when the spies who had gone ahead to see what awaited them in the Promised Land came back with frightening reports of the inhabitants whom they were not strong enough to overpower (Num. 13.25–14.3).

The rejection of Moses is clear in the contemptuous reference to him as 'this Moses', as Stephen quotes from Exod. 32.2, 23. This verse concludes Stephen's account of the hostile treatment of Moses, God's chosen prophet, by the people of Israel whom he was sent to bring out of slavery. Without defending himself against the accusation that he has blasphemed against Moses (Acts 6.11, 13-14), he presents Moses in the most positive of ways while demonstrating how, right from the beginning, the first people to whom he was sent refused to listen to him or to obey the commandments that God spoke through him for the benefit of the people. This has been the focus of the sections dealing with the sojourn of Israel in Egypt and their release from slavery – not the mistreatment of them by the Egyptians or the stubbornness and cruelty of Pharaoh, but the Israelites' refusal of God's help.

[β'] 7.41-50 *Worship of God in Israel*
Stephen arrives at the final aspect of the promise given to Abraham (cf. 7.7), which brings him to the culminating point of his account of the history of Israel, the question of worship of God. In a rapid survey of the years from the wanderings of the Israelites in the desert to the times of Solomon, he traces the development of the people's worship up to the building of the Temple in Israel. His aim will be to demonstrate that the Temple is not, and never could be, an appropriate place for God to dwell, that it was not what God himself had prescribed. He will draw on various texts of the Scriptures, interpreting them in such a way as to give authority to his denunciation of the Temple as a place for God to be contained. In doing so, he was not alone for there were various groups (among

whom the community at Qumran) who did not agree with worship in the Temple as it was being carried out.

There are seven elements in the development: β′α β′β β′γ / β′δ \ β′γ′ β′β′ β′α′. The first part up to 7.44 relates to Israel in the wilderness; the entry into the Promised Land up to the days of David is described in the centre (7.45) and thereafter, the theme is the worship of God in the land of Israel.

[β′α] 7.41 *The Making of the Calf-Idol*

7.41 A fresh expression of time, 'in those days', marks the start of this last point, as it has marked the previous points, and establishes the setting as the beginning of the years spent by the Israelites in the desert. Stephen thus continues the story of the people's rebellion against Moses, describing how they made an idol and with what consequences.

The story is situated in Exodus at the moment the people are waiting for Moses to come down from Mt Sinai, as noted at the end of the previous scene (7.40). In the scriptural account, it is Aaron who is responsible for devising the scheme to make a golden calf from the gold earrings worn by the Israelites and who initiated the worship of it (Exod. 32.2-5). The people, nonetheless, join in only too readily: 'they offered burnt offerings and brought peace offerings; and the people sat down to eat and drink, and rose up to play' (32.6). Stephen's version is a paraphrase rather than a citation of the Exodus account; in particular, he places the responsibility squarely on the people, and gives the impression not of a one-off event but of an on-going celebration that was repeated over a period of time.[118]

The relation between the making of the golden-calf and the present situation of the people of Israel will become more and more apparent as Stephen continues his exposition. For the time being, he prepares the ground by introducing the idea of rejoicing in things 'made with hands' (ἐν τοῖς ἔργοις τῶν χειρῶν αὐτῶν; cf. ἐν χειροποιήτοις, 7.48).

[β′β] 7.42-43 *The Consequences of the Idol Worship*

In the Exodus story, the making of the golden calf had the immediate consequence of arousing God's wrath to the extent that he intended to destroy the people of Israel (Exod. 32.7-10); Moses, after pleading on behalf of the people and reminding God of his promise to Abraham to give him many descendants and bring them into the Promised Land (32.11-13, 31-32), was able to avert God's anger (32.14, 34a). The consequences of the idolatry nevertheless persisted, in that God sent an angel with them into Canaan instead of going in with

---

118. The repeated action is indicated by the verbs in the imperfect which contrast with the more punctual action expressed by the aorist. The AT has the first two verbs ('made a calf', 'offered') in the aorist (ἐμοσχοποίησαν, ἀνήγαγον), followed by 'rejoicing' in the imperfect (εὐφραίνοντο). The Bezan text, however, has only the first verb in the aorist, thus heightening the impression of repeated worship over a period of time (see *Critical Apparatus*).

them himself (32.34a; 33.1-3), to the great distress of the people (33.4-6; see *Commentary,* 7.38). It is in this context that God rebukes the people for being 'stiff-necked' (σκληροτράχηλος, 33.3, 5; 34.9 LXX; cf. 32.9 MT), an expression that Stephen will take up in his invective (Acts 7.51).

Despite Moses' success in assuaging God's anger for the time being, the problems created by the idolatry of the people are not resolved, for the scene concludes with threatening overtones of future punishment hanging in the air (Exod. 32.33-34; 33.3), which are only partially dispelled by the fresh disclosure he makes to Moses of his glory together with the new conditions of the covenant (33.12–34.28).

7.42-43 Stephen makes an explicit connection between Israel's sin of idolatry and the punishment described by Amos (Amos 5.25-27), following the LXX text which interprets the prophecy as accomplished during the years in the wilderness: not only did the people of Israel not obey the requirements laid down by God for the offering of sacrifices but, in addition, they gave themselves over to worshipping celestial bodies, or rather the models of them that they themselves had made. Stephen interprets the worship of the star-gods as a punishment inflicted on the people by God because of their disobedience: he 'turned' (in the sense that he turned away from his people) and 'gave them over' to the cult of the heavenly bodies. This particular punishment is not mentioned in Exodus but the Amos passage may well have been linked to Exodus 32 in the Jewish lectionary tradition because of the reference to the sacrifice in the desert in both places.[119] Furthermore, another connection is created by the mention of the 'tent' of Moloch, which contrasts with the tent of testimony that God had been describing to Moses when he was delayed on Mt Sinai, and about which Stephen is about to speak. Yet another link is the reference to the 'models' (τύπους), which again contrast with the tabernacle model Moses was to transmit to the people (cf. τύπον, 7.44 AT; παράτυπον D05).

Amos warns of a future dispersion 'beyond Damascus' as a chastisement for Israel's idolatry (Amos 5.27). The context of his prophecy was the Assyrian invasion of the northern kingdom of Israel in the latter half of the eighth century BCE. The removal of the Jews living there to distant parts of the Assyrian Empire was prophesied by Amos, and by other prophets of the northern kingdom, as a punishment for idolatry and rebellion against God. Stephen takes up the idea of exile, speaking either of a destination 'beyond Babylon' (AT), or 'the regions of Babylon' (D05) which are, in fact, 'beyond Damascus'. Though he does not develop the possibility of dispersion explicitly, the idea remains as a threat throughout the rest of his speech since his aim is to demonstrate that the people of Israel of his time are in a position equally idolatrous to that of their ancestors in the desert. Just as the earlier punishment was held over from the time of Moses

---

119. In addition to the similarity of theme, the presence of the word 'star' in both texts may have served as a peg to link the two: Exod. 32.13, 'the stars of heaven (τὰ ἄστρα τοῦ οὐρανοῦ)' // Amos 5.26, 'your star-god (τὸ ἄστρον τοῦ θεοῦ ὑμῶν)'; cf. Acts 7.42: τῇ στρατιᾷ τοῦ οὐρανοῦ.

until the time of the fall of the northern kingdom (according to Amos), so the punishment of the Temple worshippers can be said to be held over from the time of Solomon (cf. 7.47) to a future date in 70 CE when the Temple will be destroyed and the inhabitants of Jerusalem dispersed. So, in one sense, Stephen's reference to Amos is a parenthesis in the chronology of his exposition of the history of Israel; and yet, at the same time, it will serve as a prophetic glimpse of the future, showing that worshipping things made by hand is not acceptable to God and requires drastic punishment.

[β′γ] 7.44 *The Tent of Testimony*

7.44 Stephen picks up the chronological thread from 7.41, returning to God's revelation to Moses in the desert (cf. v. 38). While the people of Israel were busy making the golden calf and offering it sacrifices, God was showing to Moses the design of the 'tent of testimony' (Exodus 25–31) – the same word 'tent' (σκηνή) is used by Amos referring to the 'tent of Moloch', cf. Acts 7.43. The instructions for the construction of the tent were extremely detailed and testify to the use of the finest and most valuable materials in order to produce a 'tabernacle' (an alternative translation of the Greek σκηνή) of superlative craftsmanship and beauty. It was to be made in exact accordance with the vision of it God showed to Moses (Exod. 25.9; 27.9). At its heart, was the 'ark' containing the 'testimony', that is the tablets on which were written the covenant (25.10-16; 40.20), where God would speak with Moses (25.22; 30.6). There was to be an altar where daily sacrifices of burnt offerings were to be made to God (27.1-8; 29.38-41), at the door in front of the tabernacle (29.10-12, 42); and a second altar for the burning of incense was inside, in front of the veil that concealed the ark (30.1-10). Aaron, the Levite (4.14), was to be richly dressed as the High Priest, and his sons were to serve as priests under him (Exodus 28), in charge of making the offerings and ministering to God on behalf of the people of Israel. God himself would stand at the door of the tent for his people when burnt offerings were made (29.42-43 LXX) – where the Hebrew says that he will 'meet' (נֹעַדְתִּי) them, the Greek avoids this verb by saying he would 'give commandments' to them (τάξομαι, 29.43; cf. also the expression 'the tent of meeting' in Hebrew [אֹהֶל מוֹעֵד] which is replaced in the Greek by 'the tent of testimony' [ἡ σκηνὴ τοῦ μαρτυρίου, first occurrence at 27.21]).[120] In a similar manner, the LXX is careful to avoid saying that God would thus 'dwell' among the people of Israel (שָׁכַנְתִּי, 29.45, 46 MT), reading in Greek the verb 'be invoked' in its place (ἐπικληθήσομαι, ἐπικληθῆναι). Indeed, the tabernacle according to the LXX was intended as 'a sanctuary so that I may appear among you' (ὀφθήσομαι, 25.8 LXX) but according to the MT 'so that I may dwell among you'. The Greek text of Exodus appears to have

---

120. Le Boulluec and Sandevoir suggest that the middle of τάσσω is to be interpreted as meaning 'give orders' (*L'Exode*, p. 303, on 25.43); they further note that all instances of 'meeting' in these chapters of Exodus are replaced with verbs of revelation (cf. on 25.42).

gone to some lengths to ensure that the tabernacle could not in any way be understood as the place where God lived.[121]

These differences between the Greek and Hebrew texts may well indicate the existence of a wider debate among diverse Jewish factions concerning the nature of God's relationship with the tabernacle and later the Temple, a debate that Stephen is responding to throughout this section of his speech. It must always be borne in mind that Stephen is speaking in a Jewish context and that he has at his disposal a complex collection of arguments and teachings on which to draw. He makes use of these in order to arrive at his point about Jesus, as he brings the debate to a conclusion.

The wording chosen by Codex Bezae to indicate that the tabernacle was modelled on that which Moses was given to see, suggests that the finished work was an imperfect execution rather than a faithful representation of the instructions. By this account, the earthly reality was never a perfect copy of what Moses was shown, the word 'imperfect representation' (παράτυπον) serving as a pointer to the fact that divine reality cannot be genuinely reproduced on the earth.

[β'δ] 7.45 *The Entry into the Promised Land*

7.45 The tabernacle was made in the desert in accordance with Moses' vision and brought into the Promised Land under the leadership of Joshua, where it lasted until the time of David. With this statement Stephen now brings the story of the people of God into Israel, the final destination of God's promise to Abraham in which 'this place' was originally a reference to the Promised Land and not restricted to the Temple (see *Commentary*, 7.7).

The ancestors, 'our fathers', are referred to repeatedly, emphasizing the continuity of the story. Once again, it is God who was responsible for giving the land to his people, he himself who removed the nations living in Canaan when they entered there. Up to this point, the account is favourable, with the presence of the tabernacle no cause for criticism.

[β'γ'] 7.46 *David's Proposal for a Meeting Place for Israel*

7.46 With David a shift begins to be felt, but at first David is described approvingly as having 'found favour' with God, a possible reference to the occasion when David was fleeing from his son Absalom, taking the ark of the tabernacle with him; once outside Jerusalem, he ordered the priest to take the ark back, declaring that if he 'found favour' (εὕρω χάριν) with God, he would be brought back to Jerusalem by God to see the ark and its beauty (τὴν εὐπρέπειαν αὐτῆς, 2 Kdgms 15.25 LXX; MT reads 'his dwelling', נָוֵהוּ, in place of beauty; cf. on 7.44 above).

The idea that he sought to construct some kind of new building derives from Ps. 131.5 LXX, but once more there are difficulties with the notion of a dwelling being built for God and consequent variation in the wording of the Psalm is

---

121. The intention may have been not to limit God to a particular place, or alternatively to reserve the Temple for his 'dwelling place' (Le Boulluec and Sandevoir, *L'Exode*, p. 252).

evident from a comparison of the LXX text, the Hebrew text and the text of Acts. The Psalm overall deals with the theme of God's 'dwelling place' in Zion (Ps. 131.13-14). According to the MT, v. 5 recalls David's pledge to find a 'place for Yahweh, a tent for the Mighty One of Jacob'. In the LXX, this is rendered fairly literally as τόπον τῷ κυρίῳ, σκήνωμα τῷ θεῷ Ἰακώβ, with the word for 'a place' the term that became a way of referring to the Temple (cf. 6.13; 7.7), and 'God' representing 'the Mighty One'. The word translated as 'tent' is a compound of the word used for the tabernacle (cf. Acts 7.44).

In Stephen's speech, it is the second phrase of the Psalm that is cited, with the variation 'house of Jacob' in place of 'God of Jacob' (according to both Codex Bezae and the AT but not all MSS agree, see *Critical Apparatus*). Stephen's rendering thus avoids any suggestion at all that David attempted to confine God to a building, not even a tent, since it was intended for the people of Israel and not God himself.

In the scriptural narrative concerning David, however, there is indeed an account of his wanting to build a house of cedar wood for God, because he felt it was wrong for the ark to be in a tent when he himself had a solid house (2 Sam. [= 2 Kgdms LXX] 7.1-3). Through the prophet Nathan, God refused most emphatically to accept a permanent dwelling place, saying that since the days of the wilderness 'I have not dwelt in a house … but I have been moving about in a tent' (7.6). In contrast, God promises that he will create a place for his people and cause them to have a fixed dwelling (7.10); he will likewise give David a son whose kingdom he will establish (7.12). The son in turn will 'build a house for my (God's) name' (7.13). In the Hebrew text, God refers to the family he will give to David as his 'house', which he will make for him (7.11 MT), the same word בית serving for the 'building' at 7.13. Curiously, 7.11 LXX is rendered as 'you (David) will build a house (οἶκος) for him (God)' (but cf. 7.27 MT and LXX). In the event, it is David's son Solomon who builds a 'house of cedar wood' for God, which is the Temple (1 Kgs [= 3 Kgdms LXX] 5.3-5; cf. Acts 7.47).

It is evident from the variations between the Hebrew and the Greek texts of this story that there were problems over David's building of a house for God in the material sense. These problems can be sensed as undercurrents to the arguments Stephen puts forward, with his statement that David intended only to build a tent for the house of Jacob (that word οἶκος again) meant as a favourable comment on his actions. In accordance with God's refusal to be confined to a house, David did not build one for him.

[β′β′] 7.47 *Solomon's Temple*
7.47 The single statement contained in this verse expresses a multitude of implicit undertones of arguments, over whether Solomon was right or not to build the Temple and what he intended it to represent, arguments that must have been familiar to Stephen's audience, the Sanhedrin (and the audience of the Bezan text, bearing in mind that his principal addressee was none less than a former High Priest of the Temple [see *General Introduction,* § IV]). The diffi-

culty for the reader of Acts today is that most of the underlying debate, with its own inner logic and language, is inaccessible and we have to deduce what we can from the surface language.

Thus, Stephen declares that what David did not do, his son Solomon carried out. Playing on the word 'house', he changes the meaning of οἶκος from referring to the 'people (of Jacob)' to signify a building. Solomon built a house (cf. 1 Kgs 5–8), and although there is at this point in Stephen's words some ambiguity concerning for whom he built it (Stephen says simply αὐτῷ, which can mean either for the people of Jacob [cf. previous sentence] or for God [cf. last reference, v. 46]), in Solomon's dedication of the Temple it is clear that he has built it for God (1 Kgs 8.15-21): the expression used is 'for his name' (cf. 2 Sam. 7.13) where 'the name' is the perfect representation of God. Yet even in the dedication of the Temple, he recognizes that God cannot live on earth but has his dwelling place in heaven (1 Kgs 8.27-30). Solomon is, therefore, perhaps not held to blame by Stephen for the way the Temple came to be mis-used as he will go on to describe.

[β′α′] 7.48-50 *The Inappropriateness of the Temple*

7.48-50 Whatever Solomon intended with the building of the Temple, it is clear from Stephen's denunciation that follows that it was used inappropriately because it was claimed to be the place where God lived. He cites Isa. 66.1, with its echoes of both God's refusal to allow David to build him a house (2 Sam. 7.5-6) and Solomon's awareness of the incongruity of the Temple (1 Kgs 8.27-30), each based on the fact that God did not dwell in a house. The word-order of the AT focuses on the issue of God not living in a place made with hands, whereas the Bezan text at this point brings God, as the 'Most High', into focus (see *Critical Apparatus*). In the Bezan wording especially, it is possible to understand Stephen as meaning that although Solomon built a house for him, God does not dwell in buildings (as Solomon himself had acknowledged).

The problem of 'things made with hands' is an issue raised by the Isaiah passage which allows Stephen to return to the theme he had introduced in his account of the making of the calf-idol, the worship of 'things made with hands'. The golden calf was worshipped because it was said of it 'These are your gods, O Israel, who brought you up out of the land of Egypt' (Exod. 32.4). In a similar way, the concept of the Temple caused God to be imprisoned within it, and the building became itself an object of worship because it contained God within it.[122]

Thus, the final part of God's promise to Abraham is presented by Stephen as not fulfilled, not because of any failure on God's part but because the people did not obey his commands, given to Moses as long ago as in the wilderness (cf. 7.44). God had intended his people to worship him in Israel ('in this place', cf.

---

122. The Greek word 'made with hands' (χειροποίητος) is that used precisely to define an idol in the LXX (see, e.g., Lev. 26.1, 30; Isa. 2.18; 10.11; 16.12; 19.1; 21.9; 31.7; 46.6). The effect on a Jewish audience on hearing the Temple described with such a term is brought out by Dunn, *Partings of the Ways*, pp. 66–67.

7.7), and to that end drove out the Gentiles with their idolatrous practices so that the Israelites would not be contaminated by them (cf. Exod. 34.11-17). They, however, have limited their worship to the Temple, which they (but not God) regard as the 'place' par excellence, and in so doing have created an idol.[123]

Stephen's line of attack on the Temple concentrates on its idolatrous nature. It is worth noting that the Temple was a relatively new construction at the time of Stephen's trial. The rebuilding of Jerusalem had been started by Herod the Great, but the Temple was finished finally only in 64 CE. Elsewhere in his writings, Luke indicates other aspects of the problems associated with it;[124] all are different symptoms of the Temple's shortcomings and failure as a place of worship; they are all backed up by Jesus' own declaration, pronounced when some were admiring the beauty of the building: 'These things that you see, the days will come when there will be left here no stone upon another that will not be broken down' (Lk. 21.6). So far, the saying of Jesus recorded by Mark, that 'I will destroy this Temple made with hands, and in three days I will build (raise up, D05) another not made with hands' (Mk. 14.58, cf. 13.1 D05), has not been transmitted by Luke. It is left to his faithful disciple to pass on the teaching that Jesus himself described the Temple as being 'made with hands'.

[α'] 7.51-53 *Invective*
The wrongness of the Temple as a place in which God is confined reflects directly on the Jewish authorities who have made of the Temple an institution in which worship of God is controlled and regulated. The Sanhedrin, who represent the leaders of the people of Israel, are therefore addressed by Stephen in terms that reveal their rebellious condition. He has prepared for his attack from the beginning when he presented the sons of Jacob, the 'patriarchs', as opposed to God's chosen representative, Joseph, who was to be an instrument for carrying forward his promise to Abraham; the attack is further anticipated in the repeated occurrence of the term 'our fathers' who refused to accept Moses, also chosen by God, and who rebelled against him.

The conclusion to Stephen's speech has three elements to it: α'α / α'β \ α'α'.

---

123. Luke frequently uses the term 'place' symbolically in his two volumes to indicate an activity that has been wrongly confined to the Temple, or an activity that shows up a failing of the Temple: 'a place of prayer' (Lk. 11.1); the place where the man in need of help lay on the road to Jericho and where the Levite passed him by (10.32); the place of salvation for those excluded from Israel (19.5 AT, 9-10); the place opposite the Temple (22.40; cf. 19.29-30, the Mt of Olives confronts Mt Zion); the place called 'The Skull' (23.33; cf. Mk 15.22; Jn 19.17); the place that is shaken as the apostles detach themselves from the Temple authority (Acts 4.31); the other place where Peter goes when he makes his final exodus from the Temple (12.17).

124. E.g., the use that had been made of it for commerce and extortion, cf. Lk. 19.45-46; the separation between the people and God represented by the veil, cf. Lk. 23.45 (46 D05); the power exercised by the religious authorities, cf. Acts 4.31-35.

[α´α] 7.51 *Resistance to the Holy Spirit*

7.51 Stephen takes up now the charge of rebelliousness that was brought by God himself against the Israelites when they made the golden calf, picking up the motif of idolatry from 7.41-43. With the figurative expression 'stiff-necked' (σκληροτράχηλοι), he attacks the Jewish authorities who have been called to judge him; he adds to his attack a familiar expression from the Prophets, that they are 'uncircumcised in their hearts' and not only that but in their 'ears', too[125] – they neither understand nor even listen to the voice of God. The invective recalls Jesus' words at the end of the parable about Lazarus and Abraham: 'If they do not hear Moses and the prophets, neither will they be convinced if someone should rise from the dead' (Lk. 16.31).

In the reference to Isaiah Stephen has just made, he reproduces the words God gave to Isaiah to speak to the people of Israel. In so far as the Jewish leaders, those who were responsible for all that the Temple involved, have not listened to the prophet's message (Isaiah goes on to say that God will pay attention rather to those who are 'humble and quiet and tremble at my words' [Isa. 66.2b]), they have rejected the Holy Spirit who inspired the prophets and spoke through them to communicate God's word.[126] The contents of Stephen's speech, selected to highlight the disobedience of the people of Israel and their refusal to accept God's instruments for salvation, demonstrates how they are no different in this respect from their ancestors – 'your fathers', with Stephen distancing himself for the first time (he has used 'our fathers' eight times before) from his Jewish heritage. They had been jealous of Joseph (7.9), had not understood God's plan (7.25), had pushed Moses aside (7.27) and had been disobedient (7.39). The last act had the greatest consequences, for they had refused to accept the 'living words' that Moses had received for Israel. It led directly to their making of the calf-idol; and in a comparable manner, the Jews of a later generation had refused the words of God spoken through Isaiah and had made an idol of the Temple.

[α´β] 7.52a *The Killing of the Prophets in the Past*

7.52a Stephen continues his theme of the rejection of the prophets by taking up a denunciation that Jesus made of the Jews' hostility against their own prophets: first, speaking to the lawyers, those in charge of interpreting the Jewish Law (Lk.

---

125. The first occurrence of 'uncircumcised in heart' (ἀπερίτμητοι καρδίαις) is found in Lev. 26.41, with reference to the rebellion of the people of Israel against God's commandments; it is later used by Jeremiah (Jer. 9.25-26) who assimilates the rebellious people of Israel with the (literally) uncircumcised nations; and Ezekiel (Ezek. 44.7, 9) who uses the expression of Gentiles in the Temple. Jeremiah also speaks of the people of Israel who cannot understand God's message as having ears that are uncircumcised (ἀπερίτμητα τὰ ὦτα αὐτῶν, Jer. 6.10).

126. The term 'Holy Spirit' is rarely found in the Jewish Scriptures where Spirit is usually read on its own without the adjective (Read-Heimerdinger, *The Bezan Text*, pp. 153–56). However, in the Targum to Isaiah the adjective is added to the mention of the Spirit at four places where the prophetic force of the passage is underlined (*Targ. Isa.* 40.13a; 42.1b; 44.3b; 59.21).

11.47-51; cf. 6.23); and later, addressing Jerusalem as the personification of the Jewish religious institution ('Ιηρουσαλήμ, Lk.13.33-34). In applying it to his own audience, he is doing no more than repeating a long-standing accusation,[127] bringing out the aspect of the prophetic message that announced the coming of the Messiah. The term that he uses for the 'coming' (ή ἔλευσις) is found nowhere else in the New Testament, except twice in Codex Bezae at Lk. 21.7 and 23.42 where it refers to the second coming, and is spoken by the disciples and the thief on the cross respectively. Stephen, in contrast, applies it to the 'coming of the Righteous One' which has already taken place. The figure of the suffering righteous man appears in the book of Wisdom (Wis. 2.12-20; 5.1-7) and is presented by Stephen as the Messiah (cf. Acts 3.14), identified as Jesus as he continues his invective against the present leaders.

[α'α'] 7.52b-53 *The Rejection of the Prophets in the Present*
7.52b-53 Reference has already been made twice by Peter to the responsibility of the Jews for the death of the Messiah (3.13-15; cf. 4.27-28; Lk. 23.13-23). Luke has a special interest in two negative expressions which he used in his first volume of the disciples of Jesus and applies in his second to the people of Israel: the first refers to the act of denial of Jesus by Peter (ἀπαρνέομαι, Lk. 22.34, 57, 61; cf. Acts 3.13, 14 [of Jesus]; 7.35 [of Moses]), and the second to the act of betrayal of Jesus by Judas Iscariot (παραδίδωμι, Lk. 22.4, 6, 21, 22, 48; cf. Acts 3.13) who thus became a traitor (προδότης, Lk. 6.16; cf. Acts 7.52). The culmination of this denunciation is Stephen's description of the Jewish leaders as 'murderers' (φονεῖς), the very people who had asked Pilate to give them a 'murderer' in place of Jesus (φονέα, Acts 3.14; cf. Lk. 23.18-19).

Stephen has one more attack to make, one final severe reproach concerning the Law which he mentions now for the first time in his speech. He had alluded to it indirectly at 7.38, when he spoke of it in positive terms as the 'living words' that Moses gave to the Jewish people. Already there, however, a problem was hinted at by the mention of the angel who acted as an intermediary between God and the people, a reminder that God did not speak directly because of the people's sinfulness (see *Commentary*, 7.38 above); indeed, their hostility to the Law was immediately apparent: 'our fathers did not wish to be obedient' (v. 39). The same situation exists among Stephen's judges: they (no less than their fathers) received the Law by means of angelic ordinances and they have not kept it.

Looking back over Stephen's speech overall it is striking that he did not, in answer to the accusations against him, try to defend himself nor, indeed, did he answer the charges directly. His response was to show the Jewish authorities their own rebelliousness, and this he did by referring to the Jewish Scriptures

---

127. It is unwarranted to accuse Stephen of 'exaggeration', however 'pardonable', for apparently making untrue statements that cannot be backed up by Scripture (cf. Barrett, I, p. 376). That Jesus denounced the Jewish authorities in exactly the same terms as Stephen is evidence of a tradition that was sufficiently secure for it to be invoked without creating any kind of overstatement.

(including familiar traditions associated with them) without once citing any new or specific teachings of Jesus or even mentioning him by name. The Jewish leaders thus stand condemned, according to Stephen, by the Law itself and the prophets who spoke on God's behalf.

[a'] 7.54 *The Response of the Sanhedrin*
According to the overall structure of the section, in which Stephen's speech is the central element, the introduction of the High Priest, who invites Stephen to answer the charges brought against him, is counter-balanced by the reaction of the members of the Sanhedrin who are filled with rage by what he says. This element concludes the speech sequence and anticipates the final sequence that relates the consequences of the Sanhedrin meeting.

7.54 The members of the Sanhedrin, whose function was to judge Stephen, had seen 'his face like that of an angel (standing in the middle of them', D05) (6.15), and knew, therefore, that he was a messenger of God. This vision not-withstanding, Stephen's words have so offended them that they are enraged by him. According to the AT, their fury has been growing as they have been listening to his invective against them, leaving open the question as to whether or not he had finished saying what he intended. The wording of the Bezan text assumes that he had reached the end of his speech and that it was at that point that his hearers became incensed with anger.

Luke uses two strong expressions to paint a violent picture of their fury: the first speaks of their inner reaction, literally 'they were cut through in their hearts';[128] the second portrays the outward manifestation, as they 'ground their teeth against him', an expression representing their extreme hostility.[129] A comparison of the reaction of the Sanhedrin to Stephen with their reaction at the last confrontation with the apostles (5.40) reveals a marked increase in hostility.

[A'-A'] 7.55–8.1a *The Stoning of Stephen*

Overview

Section I of this second part of the book of Acts concludes with the outcome of Stephen's appearance before the supreme council. His denunciation of their hypocrisy and rebelliousness is given further force by the violence of their reaction, which ends in their stoning of him. The ending proper of the story of Stephen is not, however, his death but the consent that Saul gave to his killing.

---

128. Luke is alone in using the verb διαπρίω, always in the passive and each time with reference to the members of the Sanhedrin: at 5.33, as a reaction to the apostles' refusal to obey them, and here. The active means (literally) to 'saw right the way through', and in the passive seems to have the figurative meaning of being 'cut up with rage' (cf. B-A-G, διαπρίω).

129. The verb βρύχω is used only here in the New Testament but cf. LXX Job 16.9; Pss. 34.16; 36.12 where the same construction of ἐπί + accusative is found. A similar expression with the noun (ὁ βρυγμὸς τῶν ὀδόντων) is found in Lk. 13.28; cf. Mt. 8.12; 13.42, 50; 22.13; 24.51; 25.30.

The start of a new section at 8.1b is indicated by the presence of a time expression ('On that day…') which Luke typically employs to introduce a new section of his work.

Structure and Themes

The trial does not achieve the aim intended by Stephen's opponents since not only is his guilt not established by the Sanhedrin but God's approval of him is made plain to the council members. Thus, the closing frame opens with Stephen's vision of Jesus standing in judgment in heaven, corresponding to the vision of Stephen which was seen by the Sanhedrin in the opening frame of this section (cf. 6.15). The vision given now to Stephen confirms his innocence but the response of his attackers is to intensify their opposition, culminating in his stoning.

There is a strong contrast between the stoning of Stephen and the presentation of him as a man full of faith, wisdom and the Holy Spirit in the sequence in which he was introduced (cf. 6.1-7) and in the following one, which preceded his speech (cf. 6.8-15). Both of these have shown the falseness of the accusation brought against him, and will show now the flagrant injustice of his killing.

In these concluding verses, a new character, Saul, is introduced for the first time who will in time become God's chosen instrument to take the message of Jesus to the Gentiles. There will be several occasions when Saul/Paul is compared retrospectively with Stephen to show up his weakness and the struggles he had in order to reach perfect acceptance of the mission Jesus wanted him to accomplish. It is entirely fitting that he should be brought into the story at this point as the main instigator of Stephen's killing. Saul, like Stephen, is a Hellenist but has been actively engaged in fighting to protect the purity of Israel and will experience immense difficulties in coming to terms with Jesus' teaching – not only before his encounter with Jesus on the Damascus road, as is traditionally understood and as is perhaps intended to be understood by the AT, but especially after his 'conversion' which, far from bringing about an instantaneous change, was to continue over many years until he arrived in Rome.[130]

There are six elements in this final episode, corresponding to the six elements in the first episode [A'-A] 6.8-15: they start with Stephen's vision [a], work through the stages of his stoning [b–b'] and conclude with the presentation of Saul as a counter-example to Stephen [a']; Saul is introduced at the centre of the structure [c], balanced by Stephen's prayer of forgiveness [c']:

[a]	7.55-56	Stephen's vision of Jesus
[b]	7.57-58a	The attack of the Jews
[c]	7.58b-59	Introduction of Saul

---

130. Rius-Camps ('Gradual Awakening', pp. 281–96) traces the major landmarks along the road of Saul/Paul's acceptance of Jesus' message. The journey is described in greater detail in *El camino de Pablo a la misión de los paganos. Comentario lingüístico y exegético a Hch 13–28* (Madrid: Cristiandad, 1984).

[c′]	7.60a	Stephen's last words
[b′]	7.60b	Stephen's death
[a′]	8.1a	Saul's consent

Translation

Codex Bezae D05

[a] **7.55** But he, being full of the Holy Spirit, gazed into heaven and saw the glory of God and Jesus the Lord at the right hand of God, standing, **56** and he said, 'Behold! I see the heavens opened and the Son of Man standing on the right, at the right hand of God.'

[b] **57** They, however, shouted with a loud voice and closed their ears and with one accord rushed on him, **58a** and they took him outside the city and they started to stone him;

[c] **58b** and the witnesses laid aside their cloaks at the feet of a certain young man called Saul **59** and they were stoning Stephen as he was praying and saying, 'Lord Jesus, receive my spirit'.

[c′] **60a** Kneeling down, he gave a loud shout saying, 'Lord, do not hold *this* sin against them'.

[b′] **60b** And having said this, he fell asleep.

[a′] **8.1a** Saul was consenting to his execution.

Codex Vaticanus B03

7.55 But he, being full of the Holy Spirit, gazed into heaven and saw the glory of God and Jesus standing at the right hand of God **56** and he said, 'Behold! I see the heavens opened and the Son of Man standing on the right, at the right hand of God.'

57 They, however, shouted with a loud voice and closed their ears and with one accord rushed on him, **58a** and they took him outside the city and they started the stoning;

58b and the witnesses laid aside their own cloaks at the feet of a young man called Saul **59** and they were stoning Stephen as he was praying and saying, 'Lord Jesus, receive my spirit.

60a Then kneeling down, he cried with a loud voice, 'Lord, do not hold *this* sin against them'.

60b And having said this, he fell asleep.

8.1a Saul was consenting to his execution.

Critical Apparatus

7.55 (Ἰησοῦν) τὸν κύριον D d h p (sa^mss) mae || *om.* B 𝔓^74 ℵ *rell*.

D05 has a clear allusion to Ps. 109.1 LXX (cf. Lk. 20.42; Acts 2.34), placing in close parallel Jesus as τὸν κύριον ἐκ δεξιῶν τοῦ θεοῦ ἑστῶτα and, in the following verse, as τὸν υἱὸν τοῦ ἀνθρώπου ἐκ δεξιῶν ἑστῶτα τοῦ θεοῦ (see next *vl* for word order). It is possible that B03 has sought to avoid the conflict between Jesus' divine nature as Lord and his semi-divine nature as Son of Man; the same concern to avoid identifying the κύριος with the man Jesus is apparent elsewhere in the AT (Read-Heimerdinger, *The Bezan Text*, pp. 290, 293).

ἑστῶτα ἐκ δεξιῶν τοῦ θεοῦ B 𝔓^74 ℵ *rell* || ἐκ δεξ. τ. θ. ἑστ. D, *ad dexteram dei stantem* d h.

The word order of D05 emphasizes 'at the right hand of God' and reinforces the parallel noted above.

7.56 διηνοιγμένους B ℵ A C 81. 88. 323. 945. 1175. 1739. 1891 *pc* || ἀνεῳγ- (ἠνεῳγ- D* E) D, *apertos* d 𝔓^74 E H P Ψ 049. 056. 33 𝔐.

When referring to the opening of heaven as the expression of a spiritual experience, D05 always uses the verb ἀνοίγω: ἠνοιγμένους (σχιζο- B03), Mk 1.10; ἀνοιχθῆναι (ἀνεῳχ- B03), Lk. 3.21; ἠνεῳγμένους (διηνοιγ- B03), Acts 7.56. There are three further occurrences of the verb with the same sense at places where D05 is missing: ἠνεῴχθησαν, Mt. 3.16; ἀνεῳγότα, Jn 1.51; ἀνεῳγμένον, Acts 10.11. Although the difference between the two verbs is very slight from a lexical point of view (Delebecque, *Les deux Actes*, p. 60), from a theological point of view the consistent use of the verb ἀνοίγω causes it to become a technical term to indicate the openness of a person to receive an understanding from God.

7.58 (ἐλιθοβόλουν) αὐτόν D d h p sy sa ‖ *om.* B ℵ *rell.*

It may be that by omitting the pronoun at this first mention of the stoning, the B03 text gets round the difficulty of an apparent repetition of the stoning, conveying first the impression of a general statement before going on to describe the actual event in 7.59.

(τὰ ἱμάτια) ἑαυτῶν B *pc* ‖ αὐτῶν D, *sua* d ℵ A C E 81. 323. 614. 945. 1175. 1241. 1611. 1739. 1891. 2412. 2344 *al* | *om.* H P Ψ 049. 056. 1. 69 𝔐 gig.

D05 reads the weak form of the reflexive pronoun.

7.59 (νεανίου) τινός D, (*adulescentes* [*-is* d^(s.m.)]) *cuiusdam* d gig p (t vg^(ms)) sy^p ‖ *om.* B ℵ *rell.*

It is typical of Luke to use the indefinite adjective τις when introducing a character who will serve as a representative of a group of people. In this case, Saul represents the fanatical group of Hellenistic Jews who persecuted the Jesus-believers. In B03, with the omission of the representative marker, Saul is simply an individual in his own right.

7.60 θεὶς δέ B 𝔓^74 ℵ D^A *rell, cumque posuisset* d gig ‖ θείς D* 614. 2412.

By continuing the narrative after the direct speech without any connecting word, D05 confers particular emphasis on Stephen's action.

(ἔκραξεν) φωνῇ μεγάλῃ B 𝔓^74 ℵ^2 D^(s.m.) *rell, voce magna* d ‖ φωνὴν μεγάλην D* | *om.* ℵ*.— λέγων D d 88 gig p vg sy^p; Spec ‖ *om.* B 𝔓^74 ℵ *rell.*

The use of the accusative by D05 is unlikely to be a copyist's error (*pace* Delebecque, *Les deux Actes*, p. 60). The proximity of the expression in the dative at 7.57, and the use of the participle λέγων (see below), suggests that the accusative should be taken as intentional, with the sense 'he gave a loud cry, saying…'. This is, nonetheless, the only occurrence in the New Testament of κράζω with φωνὴν μεγάλην in the accusative.

ταύτην τὴν ἁμαρτίαν B D 𝔓^(45vid) A C ‖ τὴν ἁμ. ταύτην 𝔓^74 ℵ E H P Ψ 049. 056. 33. 1739 𝔐, *peccatum hoc* d; Ir^(lat) Or.

By placing the demonstrative before the noun, both B03 and D05 cause the meaning to be 'this sin in particular' (Read-Heimerdinger, *The Bezan Text*, p. 109). The word order of ℵ01 does not confer any special emphasis on the demonstrative.

Commentary

[a] 7.55-56 *Stephen's Vision of Jesus*

7.55 When the apostles appeared before the Sanhedrin (5.27-40), and were about to be sentenced to death (5.33), it turned out that they had an able defender in the person of Gamaliel the Pharisee. In the case of Stephen, in contrast, none of the Sanhedrin members speaks in his defence and it is Jesus himself, the Messiah whom the Jewish leaders betrayed and killed, who appears to him in a vision of heaven. Jesus allows Stephen to see him standing at the right hand of God, proof that he has been correct in his belief in Jesus as the Messiah who has been received by God beside his throne in heaven. Codex Bezae identifies him as 'the Lord' (τὸν κύριον), providing (from a Jewish point of view) a striking juxtaposition of God, known by the name of Yahweh which is translated into Greek in the LXX as κύριος, and Jesus who is now also called κύριος. The AT, here and elsewhere in Acts, avoids drawing attention to the divinity of Jesus at the same time as his humanity (see *Critical Apparatus*).

To see the glory of God is a supreme mark of God's favour towards a person, reminiscent of the example of Moses whose face shone after he had been talking with God on Mt Sinai (Exod. 34.29-35). The earliest example in the Scriptures of one who saw God's glory was Isaac at the time that Abraham was about to sacrifice him, according to certain traditions.[131]

The importance of Jesus' 'standing' at the right hand of God is underlined in Codex Bezae, as it is in both texts of the words attributed to Stephen (cf. v. 56). The significance of his position is, however, not easy to determine as there is little in Jewish tradition that throws light on the question.[132] It is possible to interpret it as evidence that Jesus had adopted the position of a witness for the defence, as opposed to the seated position of an accuser that Jesus is described in the Gospel (Lk. 22.69) as adopting.[133] The distinction is discussed further with reference to 7.56 below.

The contrast between the rage of the Sanhedrin and Stephen's serenity at this point could not be greater. Luke has already described Stephen as 'full of' (πλή-

---

131. Le Déaut (*La nuit pascale*, pp. 140–41) cites the targums of Genesis 22.14 as referring to the revelation given to Isaac of the glory of the 'Shekinah' of God.

132. Barrett, I, pp. 384–85 enumerates the theories that have been posited to account for Jesus' standing position. Most concur in seeing it as a pose adopted to welcome Stephen or intercede on his behalf.

133. See E. Bammel, 'Erwägungen zur Eschatologie Jesu', who compares *1 En.* 49.2 with *1 En.* 12.3; 15.1; 90.14ff; *T.Abr.* XII.

ρης) the Spirit and wisdom (6.3, cf. v. 10), faith and the Holy Spirit (6.5), grace and power (6.8), and now the Holy Spirit alone: all these facets of his character contribute to the portrayal of him as the perfect example of the model disciple of the master, a comparison that is reinforced by a series of underlying parallels between Stephen and Jesus (see *General Overview* to this sequence).

Stephen's vision is related in terms remarkably similar to those Luke used to describe how the Sanhedrin members saw him when he was brought before them (Bezan variants in italics): 'all those seated (καθεζόμενοι/*καθήμενοι*) in the Sanhedrin gazed at (ἀτενίσαντες/*ἠτένιζον*) him and they saw (εἶδον) his face like the face of an angel (ὡσεὶ πρόσωπον ἀγγέλου) *that was standing (ἑστῶτος) in the middle (ἐν μέσῳ) of them*' (6.15) // 'he ... gazed into (ἀτενίσας εἰς) heaven and saw (εἶδεν) the glory of God (δόξαν θεοῦ) and Jesus *the Lord* at the right hand (ἐκ δεξιῶν) of God, standing (ἑστῶτα)' (7.55). It is no happy coincidence that these two visions are found in corresponding positions either side of Stephen's speech [*Aa* // *A'*a]: the structure of the sequence serves to highlight the contrast between the council of the Sanhedrin which sat in order to judge Stephen, even after they had been presented with a vision of him that could only signify God's approval of him and therefore his innocence, and the person of Jesus approving him from heaven at the right hand of God, this same Jesus whom the Sanhedrin had condemned to death.

7.56 This verse takes up in direct speech what Luke has reported in the previous statement but it is more than a simple repetition. It echoes the words of Jesus which he pronounced concerning himself when he was before the Sanhedrin at his own trial: 'From now on, the Son of Man shall be seated at the right hand of the power of God.'[134] There, Jesus was presenting himself to the Sanhedrin as taking up the role of accuser, seated (καθήμενος) in heaven. In Acts, for the first and only time in Luke's work, the words 'Son of Man' are not spoken by Jesus[135] but by Stephen for whom the Son of Man does not appear as an accuser but as a defender (see on 7.55 above). In drawing the attention of his earthly judges to what he sees ('Behold!') he demonstrates to them that they have no cause to condemn him, otherwise he would not be able to see the heavens opened and the vision of the throne of God. As with Jesus, for whom the heavens were opened at his baptism (Lk. 3.21-23), the vision is a sign of God's grace with him. It is striking that Stephen does not appeal to the Temple but to the heavens as the throne of God, nor to the Messiah but to the Son of Man as his defender.

---

134. Jesus' words spoken at his trial according to Luke are found in the same context in Mark's Gospel (Mk 14.62) and Matthew's (Mt. 26.64) but in both those gospels Jesus continues with the declaration that he will be seen 'coming with the clouds of heaven' as a reference to his coming again. Luke holds back this element of the declaration and only alludes to it indirectly in the promise of Moses and Elijah at the ascension. On the other hand, at Lk. 21.27 the reference to Jesus' second coming is as clear as in the other gospels (cf. Mt. 24.30; Mk 13.26).

135. Cf. John's Gospel (Jn 12.34), where the Jewish crowd use the expression as they question Jesus about what he has just said concerning his 'lifting up' from the earth.

[b] 7.57-58a *The Attack of the Jews*
It is suggested that the opponents of Stephen are no longer limited to the Sanhedrin from this point, although it is only because their actions go outside the
bounds of legitimate procedure that that conclusion is drawn.[136] Since, however,
Luke presents the whole trial as irregular, the illegitimacy of the killing of
Stephen does not necessarily mean that the people take over the Sanhedrin
proceedings; it is even doubtful whether such a step were possible. At the most,
those who attack him at this point could include his accusers, the Hellenists or
the false witnesses speaking on their behalf.

   7.57-58a The fury of the Sanhedrin resembles the reaction of the council to the
parallel declaration concerning the Son of Man made by Jesus according to the
Synoptic Gospels (see on 7.55 above), but only as recorded by Matthew and Mark
where his words are interpreted as blasphemy (Mt. 26.65; Mk 14.63-64; cf. Acts
6.11, 13) and provoke the sentence of death (Mt. 26.66; Mk 14.64). Despite the
divine signs of Stephen's innocence, and even though his speech has not given
evidence of blasphemy against Moses, the Law, the Temple or God, the Jewish
leaders could hardly have missed the signs that revealed their own guilt. In
consequence, they are so outraged that they refuse to listen further and, without
even stopping to proclaim a sentence, they take him outside the city for stoning.
   It was essential for any kind of execution to take place outside the city limits.[137]
At this point, it is more likely that a wider crowd of ordinary people is involved.

[c] 7.58b-59 *Introduction of Saul*
7.58b Even though the attack on Stephen may have become a public affair, Luke
is careful to record a detail that shows that the stoning was authorized by the
Sanhedrin. He mentions the witnesses whose presence indicates an official legal
procedure rather than a mob lynching. It is not clear exactly how Luke understood the stoning to have taken place. According to what is known from Jewish
records of this method of execution,[138] two witnesses would take the condemned
person outside the town where he would be stripped of his clothing; the first
witness would then throw him down from a height at least twice that of a man
after which, if he still lived, the second witness would drop a block of stone on
his chest; only if he continued to live after that would all the people be involved
in stoning him to death. Luke, in fact, does not describe the detail of the stoning;
his purpose is rather to draw attention to the young man, Saul, at whose feet the
witnesses deposited their cloaks.[139]

---

136. Barrett (I, p. 385) draws attention to the reading of the Old Latin h, which specifies the
'people' as the subject of the verbs in 7.57.
   137. See Lev. 24.14, 23; Num. 15.35; Deut. 17.5.
   138. See *Sanh.* 6.1-4 which interprets the passages in the Torah listed in the previous note.
   139. The garments that the witnesses removed were their outer cloaks (τὰ ἱμάτια). For what
purpose they would have taken them off is a question that cannot be answered from the available
evidence, but there is no more reason to suppose that 'Luke shows his ignorance of the proper
procedure by which stoning as a legally imposed punishment … was carried out' (Barrett, I, p, 380)

Luke chooses this somewhat indirect way (Saul's feet are mentioned even before his name!) to introduce into his narrative the character who will become the main protagonist of over half the book (chapters 13–28). Yet for all that the introduction is oblique, it is accorded the greatest of attention by being placed between the repeated statements, 'they stoned him/Stephen' (cf. v. 59). Far form being a careless fusion of sources, the repetition functions as a deliberate technique to underline in the strongest possible way the role played by the young Saul. It is possible to see in him the person who would have acted as the herald to announce, on behalf of the Sanhedrin, the name of the accused and his crime (see *Commentary* on 8.1a below). Even without reading into the scene as much as that, it is important to recognize that Luke has used in his presentation of Saul an expression that he has repeated in key scenes previously to indicate the authority and power of a person. In saying that the witnesses laid their cloaks 'at the feet' (παρὰ τοὺς πόδας) of Saul, he is taking up the expression already used of the apostles (4.35, 37 D05; 5.2) to refer to their positions of authority over the Jesus-believing community. In the case of Saul, it is known that at some point he received authority from the High Priests to persecute the Jesus-believers (cf. 9.1-2; 22.5; 26.10, 12). The fact that those involved in the stoning of Stephen were already acting in a way that acknowledged his authority would indicate that even at this stage he had been invested with power to act on behalf of the Temple rulers. Their gesture, beyond its literal meaning, stands as a symbol of the recognition of the role accorded to Saul as the representative of the wave of persecution that will follow the stoning of Stephen (8.1b). The Bezan text signals the fact that Saul is a representative of an event, and not just a person in his own right, with the indefinite adjective 'a certain young man' (νεανίου τινός).[140]

7.59 The repetition of the statement 'they stoned him/Stephen' (ἐλιθοβόλουν, each time in the imperfect) could be seen simply as a picking up of the narrative after a parenthetical insertion about the witnesses. Rather more could be going on, however. Up to the mention of the witnesses, the stoning of Stephen is related as an impromptu reaction on the part of the Jewish authorities, in which the people may well have joined once he was taken outside the city. With the introduction of the witnesses, though, and the allusion to Saul's authority (insinuated again at 8.1a), the events take on a more legal aspect, and at its second mention the procedure of stoning continues in a more formal guise.

While the stoning continues, Stephen is heard to repeatedly address Jesus ('Lord Jesus') whom he has seen standing beside the throne of God in heaven and to whom he now entrusts his spirit. The words echo the last words pro-

---

than to acknowledge that our own current knowledge of the historical situation is liable to be very patchy.

140. See *The Message of Acts*, I, pp. 210–11, on the use of the indefinite adjective τις as a marker of representativity in Luke's writings.

nounced by Jesus himself at his crucifixion ('Father, I place my spirit into your hands', Lk. 23.46a).

[c´] 7.60a *Stephen's Last Words*

7.60a Stephen's last recorded gesture is one of prayer, expressed first of all with the typically Lukan expression θεὶς τὰ γόνατα, 'placing the knees', to denote prayer.[141] In striking contrast to the great cry of anger with which the Sanhedrin had responded to his vision of Jesus in heaven (cf. 7.57), Stephen utters a cry of pardon for his persecutors. His prayer is addressed to the 'Lord', reiterating the address of his previous words spoken to the 'Lord Jesus'. A parallel to Stephen's prayer is found in Jesus' words on the cross according to some MSS of Luke's Gospel, where he is said to have prayed for the forgiveness of his killers ('Father, forgive them for they do not know what they are doing', Lk. 23.34a, but not the first hand of either D05 or B03),[142] except that in his case these words were spoken before his handing over of his spirit to God whereas they are Stephen's last words. In both cases, the final words are uttered with a 'loud cry'.[143]

[b´] 7.60b *Stephen's Death*

7.60b As he brings his account of Stephen to a close, Luke echoes the sentence used to conclude his account of Jesus' death ('And having said this, he died', Lk. 23.46b). The verb used of Jesus (ἐξέπνευσεν, literally, 'he expired') corresponds to his last words when he placed his spirit (πνεῦμα) in the hands of God. The difference in the case of Stephen is that his death does not follow directly on from his handing of his spirit to Jesus, and is described as a 'sleep' (ἐκοιμήθη), a word that is used elsewhere in the New Testament to speak of the death of Christians but the idea was already present in Judaism (cf. 13.36 with reference to David) and, indeed, in other cultures.[144]

[a´] 8.1a *Saul's Consent*

8.1a When Luke reports that Saul 'was consenting' to Stephen's death, he means rather more than he was simply passively approving it. The unusual periphrastic form of the verb (ἦν συνευδοκῶν) underlines the force and significance of his agreement. When Paul gives his own account of the part he played in the killing

---

141. τιθέναι τὰ γόνατα is a Latinism (*genua ponere*; B-D-R, § 5.4); it is only found, apart from at Mk 15.19 (of the Roman soldiers), in Luke where it always occurs in a context of prayer (and generally followed by προσεύχομαι): Lk. 22.41; Acts 9.40; 20.36; 21.5.

142. The words ὁ δὲ Ἰησοῦς ἔλεγεν· Πάτερ, ἄφες αὐτοῖς, οὐ γὰρ οἴδασιν τί ποιοῦσιν are read by ℵ*[2] (A) D[L] L Ψ 0250 *f*[1.(13)] 33 𝔐 lat sy[c.p.h] (bo[pt]); (Ir[lat]), but are omitted by 𝔓[75] ℵ[1] B D* W Θ 070. 579. 1241 *pc* a sy[s] sa bo[pt]. See Metzger, *Commentary*, p. 154 for the reasons why the words are not accepted as original in the current editions.

143. Lk. 23.46a has φωνήσας φωνῇ μεγάλῃ, whereas Acts 7.60 reads ἔκραξεν φωνῇ μεγάλῃ as in Mt. 27.50.

144. Barrett, I, p. 388.

of Stephen in his defence speeches later in Acts (cf. 22.20; 26.10b),[145] it is clear that he was not only a consenting witness but was actively responsible for the Sanhedrin's decision to stone Stephen to death. This may imply that he was a member of the Sanhedrin or, at the very least, that he had an influential role to play (cf. 26.10b: 'when they were executed I cast my vote against them').[146] He will appeal to the fierceness of his persecution of the Jesus-believers as an argument against Jesus' command to him to leave Jerusalem after he comes to believe in Jesus himself (22.17-21),[147] apparently on the grounds that the news of his change of heart would serve as effective testimony to the Jews there.

The comment referring to Saul establishes a further and final comparison between the trial of Stephen and that of Jesus, for in the Gospel, Luke introduces the good and righteous character of Joseph of Arimathea, a member of the Sanhedrin, with precisely the opposite comment: 'he was not consenting' to their part in the killing of Jesus (οὐκ ἦν συγκατατεθειμένος B03 / -τιθέμενος D05, Lk. 23.51).

---

145. In Paul's own accounts, he uses the cognate verb ἀναίρω of the noun ἀναίρεσις which is used only here in the New Testament.

146. Cf. Barrett, II, p. 1155 on the various inferences to be drawn from 26.10.

147. Cf. the use of the periphrastic again: αὐτὸς ἤμην ... συνευδοκῶν, 22.20.

II. REMOVING THE OBSTACLES
8.1b–11.26

General Overview

The death of Stephen opens the way for the expansion of the Church outside Jerusalem. His testimony to the misuse of the Temple and the disregard for the Law by the Jews stands as a programmatic statement of the ideological position of the Hellenist disciples at the same time as provoking a wholesale persecution of those who adopted this position. They are represented by the church in Hierosoluma, a term applied to believers for the first time at the opening of this section,[1] and one that will increasingly be used throughout the rest of Acts to distinguish between the Jesus-believers who were free from the religious aspirations of Israel and those who remained attached to them and, therefore, to Ierousalem (see *General Introduction*, § VII).

The dispersion of the Hellenists from Jerusalem leads directly to the progressive spread of the message of Jesus to a series of people who were traditionally despised or even excluded from Israel: first, the Samaritans; secondly, a eunuch; thirdly, a Gentile sympathizer with Judaism; and finally, in Antioch, Gentiles generally. In order to arrive at the ultimate goal of a Church that was independent of the nationalistically-minded disciples who make up the church in Ierousalem, various changes need to take place to correct the understanding of those who will lead the expansion of the Church outside Ierousalem. These are achieved by the direct intervention of God: modifying the approach of Philip (leader of the Hellenists) who depended on charismatic manifestations and accepted superficial conversions without checking beneath the surface; showing Saul (the future apostle to the Gentiles) that the believers he was persecuting were right in their claims that the Messiah had come in the person of Jesus; and convincing Peter (leader of the apostles) that the time for the Gentiles to be fully accepted by God on an equal footing with the Jews had already arrived.

Thus, the section concludes with a glimpse of the church in Antioch that at last consists of Jews and Gentiles in line with the intention of Jesus.

---

1. Cf. the previous use of Hierosoluma by Jesus in Acts 1.4 (see *The Message of Acts*, I, p. 66–69).

Structure and Themes
The second section of this part of Acts is made up of three sequences:

[A]	8.1b-3	The dispersion of the Hellenists
[B]	8.4–11.18	Three key characters
[BA]	8.4-40	Philip
[BB]	9.1-30	Saul
[BA']	9.31–11.18	Peter
[A']	11.19-26b	Jews and Gentiles in Antioch
Colophon	11.26c	A 'Christian' identity

The first and the last sequences form a continuous narrative about the expansion of the Church, with the middle sequence forming an important digression focusing on three major participants. The last sequence picks up the story from the first, and develops it to a conclusion. The central sequence is made up of three sub-sequences: these are embedded within the story of the Church and present the obstacles, real and potential, to the carrying out of Jesus' instructions to the apostles (1.8), showing how far and in what way the problems were overcome by divine intervention.

[A] 8.1b-3 *The Dispersion of the Hellenists*

Overview

The opening verses of Section II of the Acts narrative take up the story of the Jesus-believers who had last appeared in the narrative before the sequence involving Stephen, at 6.7. This first, brief sequence [A] is extremely dense in the amount of the new information that it transmits, some of it expressed in condensed form by means of verbal tags such as the spellings of names, or opposing statements set side by side. The narrator makes use of these techniques to convey his evaluation of the characters and events and to set the scene for the detailed stories of Philip, Saul and Peter that will follow in the second sequence [B].

Structure and Themes
The narrative concentrates on the persecution to which the believers were subjected [a] // [a'], relating to it the dispersion of the believers [b], and also the death of Stephen [b']:

[a]	8.1b	The persecution of the church in Hierosoluma
[b]	8.1c	The dispersion of the believers
[b']	8.2	The burial of Stephen
[a']	8.3	Saul's role as persecutor

The structural division follows the text of Codex Bezae and Codex Vaticanus, for in other MSS (e.g. Codex Sinaiticus, see *Critical Apparatus*) [a] and [b] are closely connected and form part of the same element.

A large number of varied characters appear in the space of a few sentences: the church in Hierosoluma, 'everyone', the apostles, Stephen, devout men, Saul, men and women in the Church. They are all viewed in turn from the point of view of the narrator; except for the 'devout men', they will all reappear and play a more or less prominent role in the narrative. Saul, in particular, will become the main character of the book of Acts after chapter 13.

Translation

Codex Bezae D05		*Codex Vaticanus B03*
[a]	**8.1b** On that day, great persecution and oppression arose against the church that was in Hierosoluma.	**8.1b** On that day, great persecution arose against the church that was in Hierosoluma.
[b]	**1c** Everyone was scattered throughout the regions of Judaea and of Samaria, with the exception of the apostles who remained in Ierousalem.	**1c** Everyone was scattered throughout the regions of Judaea and Samaria, with the exception of the apostles.
[b']	**2** Devout men carried out Stephen's burial and also made great lamentation over him.	**2** Devout men, though, carried out Stephen's burial and made great lamentation over him.
[a']	**3** As for Saul, he was trying to destroy the church as he went into house after house; dragging off both men and women, he had them put in prison.	**3** Saul, on the other hand, was trying to destroy the church as he went into house after house; dragging off both men and women, he had them put in prison.

Critical Apparatus

8.1b (διωγμὸς μέγας) καὶ θλῖψις D, *et tribulatio* d (h sa^mss mae invert the word order) ‖ *om.* B 𝔓⁷⁴ ℵ *rell*.

A similar variant is found in 13.50 where D05 reads θλῖψιν μεγάλην καὶ διωγμόν, a reading supported by d05, but where B03 reads simply διωγμόν. The dual construction is also found in Mt. 13.21; Mk 4.17 D05 (cf., e.g., Mt. 24.9, 21, 29; Mk 13.19, 24 where θλῖψις is used alone to denote trouble arising out of persecution); MSS other than D05 read θλίψεως ἢ διωγμοῦ at Mk 4.17. The word θλῖψις reappears on its own with reference to the persecution arising after Stephen's death at 11.19.

πάντες δὲ (διεσπάρησαν) B D 𝔓⁷⁴ *rell* | πάν. τε A (t); Aug | καὶ πάν. ℵ² 33. 323. 440. 927. 1270. 1837. 2344 | πάν. γάρ 226, *omnes enim* d | πάν. ℵ*.

Both B03 and D05, with the connective δέ, view the dispersion of the believers as a development that is separate from the persecution. τε in A02 links the two closely, as if the dispersion represents the height of the persecution. The absence of connective in ℵ01 intensifies the link even further, assimilating the dispersion with the persecution. On the force of the different connectives, see Read-Heimerdinger, *The Bezan Text*, pp. 204–206; on asyndeton, pp. 246–48.

(κατὰ τὰς χώρας) τῆς Ἰουδαίας καὶ Σαμαρείας B 𝔓⁷⁴ ℵ Dᶜ *rell* ‖ Ἰ. κ. Σ. D*.

The single article before the pair of nouns in B03 has the effect of presenting them as a unit, and a unit that is familiar or expected (Heimerdinger and Levinsohn, 'The Use of the Article', p. 29). Indeed, the narrator's reference to Judaea and Samaria picks up the mention of the regions from 1.8 where Jesus gives the apostles his command to witness in 'Ierousalem, and Judaea and Samaria, and the ends of the earth'. There, in both B03 and D05, a single article is used for the two names (πάσῃ τῇ Ἰουδαίᾳ καὶ Σαμαρείᾳ); but B03 furthermore identifies the pair as a block by marking it off from the previous name, Ierousalem, with the repetition of the preposition (ἐν τε Ἰερουσαλὴμ καὶ ἐν πάσῃ τῇ Ἰουδαίᾳ καὶ Σαμαρείᾳ; see *Critical Apparatus*, 1.8). The effect in 1.8 B03 is that Jesus' command is associated with three distinct areas moving progressively away from Ierousalem (Ierousalem / Judaea and Samaria / the ends of the earth); and by picking up the reference to 'Judaea and Samaria' as an identifiable unit here at 8.1, B03 gives a signal that the narrative is moving on to the anticipated second stage.

At 1.8 D05, in contrast, the two regions of Judaea and Samaria were grouped with Ierousalem by the use of a single preposition for all three names (further unified by τε ... καὶ ... καί), so that a two-fold (not a three-fold) division of territories for the apostles' witnessing activity was created: 'in Ierousalem, and Judaea and Samaria / the ends of the earth'. When at 8.1, therefore, the narrative moves the action into the next geographical area, coherence does not require D05 to maintain Judaea and Samaria as a unit. The absence of an article before either of the names allows them to be viewed independently of each other, in anticipation of the separate journeys of Peter in Judaea (9.32-35, Lydda; 9.36-42, Joppa) and that of Philip in Samaria (cf. 8.5, a city of Samaria).

(πλὴν τῶν ἀποστόλων) οἳ ἔμειναν ἐν Ἰερουσαλήμ D* d 1175 it saᵐˢˢ mae aeth; Aug BarSalibi ‖ *om.* B 𝔓⁷⁴ ℵ Dˢ·ᵐ· *rell*.

According to both texts, the apostles were not affected by the dispersion that followed, or was part of, the persecution of the church in Hierosoluma (8.1b). D05 adds a further comment on the apostles, saying that they remained in Ierousalem with the spelling of Jerusalem that D05 uses to represent the Jewish religious institution (see *General Introduction*, § VII). The outcome of using the two forms of the name in close proximity in 8.1 D05 is that the apostles are seen as remaining attached to the old religious order, keeping themselves protected from the persecution that affected the assembly (ἐκκλησία) of disciples in the town of Hierosoluma. The association of the apostles with Ierousalem has already been reinforced in the Bezan text with the mention of the name at 2.42 (not B03), as it will be again at 8.14 D05. B03 avoids any hint of a division among the believers by neither connecting the apostles specifically with Ierousalem nor thereby distinguishing them from other believers in the city.

8.2 συνεκόμισαν δὲ (... καὶ ἐποίησαν) B 𝔓⁷⁴ ℵ *rell* | συνεκόμισάν τε Dᴱ E 917. 1646. 1828. 1874, *comportaverunt quae* (-*que* dˢ·ᵐ) d* ‖ συγκομίσαντες D*.

The use of δέ with a finite verb in B03 implies a negative contrast between the devout men who grieved over Stephen's death and took care of his body, and those responsible for the persecution of the believers (8.1b). A further, neutral, contrast is established between those who were forced to flee because of the persecution (8.1c) and these pious people who took it upon themselves to bury Stephen.

An even more forceful contrast is made by the structure of D05: 1) the absence of a connective conveys a sense of strong dissimilarity with what has gone before; 2) the detail in 8.1 D05 that the apostles had stayed in Ierousalem causes them to be the element with which the devout men are being contrasted – they did what the apostles could have done but did not; 3) the use of a participle leads to a construction typical of the Bezan text: participle + adverbial καί + finite verb, which has the effect of drawing attention to the main action, the great mourning made over Stephen which is set against the 'great persecution and oppression' of 8.1b (Read-Heimerdinger, *The Bezan Text*, pp. 206–10).

8.3 Σαῦλος δέ B 𝔓⁷⁴ ℵ *rell* ‖ ὁ δὲ Σ. D

With the omission of the article, B03 creates a contrast between Saul and the devout men, which is possible because of the attenuated contrast implied between the devout men and the participants in the preceding clauses (see above). In D05, however, where a strong contrast was made between the devout men and all the various participants of the previous clauses, Saul is not brought back into the story by way of contrast but as a character already established on stage and the article is therefore retained (cf. 7.58; 8.1a).

Commentary

[a] 8.1b *The Persecution of the Church in Hierosoluma*
8.1b The mention of persecution is not entirely unexpected, since the opposition manifested against Stephen, the leader of the Hellenists, has been the topic of the previous sequence (6.8–8.1a). To introduce the new sequence (and section), Luke uses a time expression in a peculiarly emphatic way,[2] which has the effect of highlighting the connection between the new event and the previous one because they take place within the same time frame. At the same time, the emphatic phrasing underlines the significance of the new event for the development of the story, as the persecution forces an important shift of direction to take place in the activities of the Church.

---

2. The fore-fronted position of the demonstrative (ἐν ἐκείνῃ τῇ ἡμέρᾳ) draws attention to the word, for it is not its usual position in a time phrase (Read-Heimerdinger, *The Bezan Text*, pp. 103–105, esp. 104).

The attacks to which Stephen had been subjected now affect other believers, and for the first time in Luke's work the word 'persecution' (διωγμός) is used of an actual happening, echoing the warnings of Jesus in the Gospel (cf. διώξουσιν, Lk. 11.49 [ἐκ- D05]; 21.12). It is the witness borne by Stephen, before the people (6.8) and before the Sanhedrin (6.12–7.58), that has unleashed the more general opposition, described by Codex Bezae with the additional word 'oppression' (θλῖψις), a word that will be picked up when the narrative is resumed at 11.19.

It was noted (*Commentary*, 6.1-7) that the Hellenists represented a body of believers in Jesus who were to some extent independent from the apostles: despite the apostles' intention in appointing administrators from among the Hellenists, which was to have a group of men to take over practical duties from them, the leader of these chosen Hellenists was soon seen to do rather more than 'serve tables' (6.2). He was filled with the Holy Spirit (6.5b), as well as faith (6.5a), grace and power (6.8a); and he performed miracles through the name of Jesus Christ (6.8b). The favour he had with God was manifested publicly on two occasions, at the beginning (6.15) and the end (7.55-56) of his trial by the Sanhedrin.

Stephen's Hellenist origin, and the emergence of a group of believers who are in some way separate from the apostles, is indicated by the spelling of the name of the city, Hierosoluma. In the Bezan form of the text of Luke's work, this Hellenistic form of the name (Ἱεροσόλυμα) operates in opposition to the Hebrew-derived spelling (Ἱερουσαλήμ, Ierousalem), the former referring to the city as a neutral place and the latter used to denote the spiritual centre of Judaism, the location of the Temple and the seat of authority (see *General Introduction*, § VII). This is only the second time that Hierosoluma has been named in Acts, the other occasion being the very first mention of Jerusalem in Acts, made by Jesus when he commanded his apostles not to leave the city (1.4;[3] cf. Lk. 24.49, καθίσατε ἐν τῇ πόλει). If they had followed his instructions, they would have gone back to Hierosoluma after he had left them and, once they had received the power of the Holy Spirit, they would have begun their witnessing activity in Ierousalem (Jesus himself had led his disciples 'out of' Ierousalem, Lk. 24.50, cf. 24.33). The apostles, however, did not carry out his orders but followed their own understanding by returning to Ierousalem (Lk. 24.52; Acts 1.12), the familiar Jewish institution where they continued to worship in the Temple even after they had received the Spirit (cf. Lk. 24.53; Acts 2.46; 3.1).

To conclude from the different names for Jerusalem that the author is carelessly sticking together stories from different sources is to ignore the skilful techniques Luke deliberately uses to create his narrative. He is not simply a compiler of traditions and accounts, putting together what he has gleaned

---

3. See *The Message of Acts*, I, pp. 67–68.

from divergent sources and combining them with what he has observed or heard himself, in order to create a narrative that fulfils some historical purpose. He uses his role as narrator to evaluate what he is relating, and to comment on his characters and their actions.

From Acts 1 until now, all the references to Jerusalem have been to the holy city. Although the apostles have separated themselves from the Temple authorities and have established distinct communities of Jesus-believers under their leadership, the narrator signals by the continued use of Ierousalem (cf. the last mention at 6.7) an ongoing association between the Jesus-believers and Ierousalem as the religious centre. The Bezan text had underlined the continuing attachment of the apostles to the traditional Jewish way of thinking by an additional reference to Ierousalem at 2.42 D05. Now, for the first time, a shift is taking place, brought about by the witness and death of Stephen. The persecution that follows from his death affects the church in Hierosoluma. The significance of the spelling becomes apparent in the last part of the verse, when those affected by persecution are seen not to include the apostles who, Codex Bezae once again insists, remain in Ierousalem (see 8.1c below).

The 'church' has been mentioned before, the first time at 2.47 in Codex Bezae where the Jesus-believers were characterized by their unity as they adhered to the apostles 'in Ierousalem' (2.42). The AT omits not only the reference to Ierousalem but also to the church in 2.42. The next reference to the 'church' at 5.11 is therefore the first for the AT: the Jesus-believers are again characterized by their unity at this point when, having started to organize themselves independently from the Temple, they witness the fatal consequences of dividing one's allegiance between the traditions of Judaism and the teaching of Jesus.[4] They are led by the apostles whose focus of activity continues to be the Temple (spelt out in 5.12 D05). At this stage, they constitute the only church, they are the Church in general. With the emergence of the Hellenists as a recognizable group with their own leaders, among whom Stephen has spoken clearly against the institution of the Temple (see *Commentary*, 7.1-53; *Excursus* 1) and severely criticized its authorities, it becomes apparent that these disciples of Jesus for the first time (cf. 6.7) now constitute a separate 'church' (ἐκκλησία) among the believers. They, unlike the apostles, have fulfilled Jesus' orders to be in Hierosoluma; and the outcome of their faithfulness is persecution and oppression.

[b] 8.1c *The Dispersion of the Believers*
8.1c The result of the persecution of those believers who were faithful to Jesus' plan is that they were forced to leave the city boundaries and go to

---

4. The story of Ananias and Sapphira is interpreted, on the basis of the Bezan text, as a metaphor for the consequences of clinging to the old ways of thinking at the same time as attempting to embrace the new. For detailed discussion of this reading, see *The Message of Acts*, I, pp. 301–308; *Excursus* 6, pp. 311–14.

Judaea and Samaria, the places that followed Ierousalem in Jesus' command
to the apostles. In this way, it is the Hellenists who are initially responsible for
the progress of the gospel witness, and not the apostles at all.

Why the Jewish authorities did not pursue their opposition to the apostles
when they disobeyed the ban on speaking about the name of Jesus (cf. 5.40,
42), or to what extent Gamaliel continued to have an influence on their behalf,
are questions that are not directly answered. Theophilus, as High Priest, would
have been well aware of the internal situation. Whatever the reasons, the
apostles clearly did not attract the fierceness of the hostility with which the
Hellenists were opposed. Thus, not only were they not driven out of the city
but furthermore, according to the detail provided by Codex Bezae, they were
even able to stay 'in Ierousalem'. The implication is that the message they
were preaching was not as disturbing to other Jews as that announced by the
Hellenists.

[b'] 8.2 *The Burial of Stephen*
8.2 Evidence for the distance separating the apostles from the Hellenists is
seen in their lack of involvement in the aftermath of Stephen's stoning. For
it was not the apostles who took care of his burial or who publicly lamented
his death even though they, much more than the Hellenist believers, would
have had opportunity to do so, still living in Jerusalem as they were. In the
event, it was 'devout men' who had the courage to demonstrate their opposition to the killing of Stephen by dealing openly and appropriately with his
body after his death. In the Bezan text, the wording draws attention to the
actions of these men and sets them in the context of the previous verse:
since the disciples generally were dispersed and since the apostles were
remaining attached to the Jewish institution, Stephen's body was taken care
of by 'devout men'.

The term 'devout' (εὐλαβής) is the only one by which the men are identified. They have a clear symbolic value, not only because they act as a foil to
show up the weakness of the apostles but also because they establish a parallel
with the death of Jesus by their action in burying and making open lamentation of Stephen. The respect with which they treated the body of Stephen is
comparable to that shown by Joseph of Arimathea to Jesus. Although a member of the Sanhedrin, he had not been in agreement with the Jews' plan to get
rid of Jesus (cf. Mk 15.43; Mt. 27.57; Jn 19.38); he is described by Luke as 'a
good and righteous man' (Lk. 23.50) and asks for the body of Jesus in order to
make a proper burial of him (23.53). A second parallel element exists in the
expression used by Luke to denote the men's lamentation in Acts: κοπετός
literally means 'mourning by beating (κόπτω) the breast'[5] and recalls the
crowds who had come to watch the execution of Jesus: 'beating their breasts

---

5. Zerwick and Grosvenor, *Analysis*, p. 375.

(and foreheads, D05), they turned away' (τύπτοντες τὰ στήθη ὑπέστρεψον [καὶ τὰ μέτωπα ὑπέστρεφαν, D05], Lk. 23.48).

The adjective 'devout' (εὐλαβής) provides further points of comparison that help to identify the symbolic importance of these men. It is a Greek term used only by Luke in the New Testament, there being three other occurrences. It is used first of Simeon in the infancy narrative of Luke's Gospel (Lk. 2.25, not ℵ01) who is presented in similar terms to those used to describe Joseph of Arimathea (both were righteous [δίκαιος], both were living in expectation of some future hope for Israel [Simeon: 'the consolation of Israel'; Joseph of Arimathea, 'the kingdom of God']). The next occurrence of εὐλαβής is in Acts 2.5 where it describes the men from all over the world who were in Jerusalem at the time of the outpouring of the Holy Spirit and who responded positively to Peter's message.[6] Finally, the adjective is used by Paul of Ananias, the highly respected Jew in Damascus who was chosen by God to reveal to Paul God's will for him (Acts 22.12: Ἀνανίας δέ τις, ἀνὴρ εὐλαβὴς κατὰ τὸν νόμον). In all three places, εὐλαβής refers to people who carry out God's will and who have a clear view of his plan.

[a'] 8.3 *Saul's Role as Persecutor*
8.3 Saul is mentioned for the third time in the space of a very short span of narrative (cf. 7.58; 8.1a). In the AT, he is contrasted with the devout men of the previous verse (see *Critical Apparatus*), whose actions of pious care and respect for Stephen are the contrary of Saul's ill-treatment of the Church. In the Bezan text, where a different contrast had already been established between the devout men and the two sets of believers in the previous clause (those who were scattered and the apostles; see *Critical Apparatus*), Saul is brought back into the narrative with a backward glance, as it were, at the earlier references to him. The account of his persecution of the Church generally will be taken up again after the episode concerning Philip, in such a way that the attacks on the believers are seen to be the context in which the spread of the gospel takes place.

Saul is described here as entering the houses in the city of Hierosoluma (cf. 8.1b) where there were disciples, perhaps where the local church met (cf. 2.46), and using a measure of force and violence to have believers taken off to prison. The prison would have been in the Temple under the Jewish Temple guard, where Peter and John (4.3-21) and later all the apostles (5.18-40) were detained, rather than a secular prison under Roman guard. That both men and women were dealt with in this way is a fact the narrator repeats when he takes up the account of Saul's persecution in 9.2.

Saul's violent opposition to the Jesus-believers is a measure of the strength of his own beliefs, and is in contrast to the more tolerant attitude for which

---

6. See *The Message of Acts*, I, pp. 153–55, 158–61.

Gamaliel, his teacher and leader of the Hillel school of Pharisees, was known. A highly respected and influential member of the Sanhedrin, Gamaliel had been responsible for the protection of the apostles when the Sanhedrin had been wanting to kill them.[7] Saul, as Paul, will inform the hearers of Acts that he was taught in Ierousalem by this same Gamaliel (cf. 22.3), but his own behaviour is more in line with the strict teachings of the opposing school of Shammai (see *Excursus* 1).

[B] 8.4–11.18 *Three Key Characters*

General Overview

As was pointed out in the *Critical Apparatus*, the pages containing the Greek text of Acts 8.29b–10.14a (fol. 447b–454b) are missing from Codex Bezae, though the Latin page of 10.4-14a (fol. 455a) is extant. Consequently, for the verses represented by this lacuna, witnesses that sometimes share Bezan readings in other parts of Acts have been consulted in order to identify readings that differ from the AT. These MSS are collectively referred to with the conventional label of the 'Western Text' (WT). Since no other text varies as consistently from the AT as Codex Bezae, a reconstruction of the Bezan text cannot be attempted for the missing verses and, in consequence, detailed comparison with the AT is not possible. The comparative aspect of the commentary will be necessarily limited to some observations about variants in the MSS consulted and their implications for the interpretation of Acts.

At 8.4, the story of persecution is interrupted, to be taken up again at 11.19. The diversion focuses on three characters who, for quite different reasons, were confronted with difficulties that were resolved by divine intervention. The series of incidents reflects Luke's purpose to demonstrate the profound changes that had to take place in the people who were to take the message of Jesus beyond the confines of Judaism in order for them to carry out their task. It is too easy to assume that being chosen as God's instrument was sufficient qualification; that is to treat the people as unreal, as stereotypes who do not correspond to reality. On the contrary, as Luke shows in these three sub-sequences, Philip, Saul and Peter each had to undergo a profound experience of being re-modelled in which their understanding, thinking, and attitudes were changed, from conforming to a Jewish mentality and expectations to being brought into line with Jesus' teaching. That is true of Philip and Peter just as it is of Saul. Only when these changes have taken place can the narrative thread be taken up again in 11.19, using similar terms or equivalent ones to those used at 8.4.

---

7. See *The Message of Acts*, I, pp. 350–55.

Structure and Themes

The sequence falls into three sub-sequences, each one centred on a different character:

[BA]	8.4-40	Philip
[BB]	9.1-30	Saul
[BA']	9.31–11.18	Peter

Saul has been introduced into the narrative with clear identifying traits in 7.58b; 8.1a, 3; Philip is known from the list of the Seven appointed from among the Hellenists (6.5), while Peter is the most familiar figure of the three. The association of the latter with the other two underlines the fact that he, too, needed to be guided and corrected in order to reach an accurate understanding of Jesus' teaching. For indeed, each sub-sequence tells the story of an obstacle, great or small, in the character's understanding to the divine plan for the spread of the message about Jesus. A similar pattern is found in all three: 1) the character's is presented as behaving in some way erroneously; 2) the events that bring about a change, either directly or indirectly, take place; 3) the character is presented as acting correctly.

In each case, one or more characters serve to show up the protagonist's errors or faults in the opening verses: Philip – Simon Magus; Saul – Jesus; Peter – Aeneas / Tabitha / Simon the Tanner. A further group of characters in the central verses functions as a positive contrast to the protagonist: Philip – Peter and John; Saul – Ananias; Peter – Cornelius. Finally, in order to present evidence for the change that the main characters undergo, a new character is introduced in the closing episode of the sub-sequence: Philip – the Ethiopian eunuch; Saul – Barnabas; Peter – the circumcised brethren of the Ierousalem church.

The first and the last sub-sequences (Philip and Peter) tell the story of the spread of the gospel message to people hitherto excluded from the people of God, to the Samaritans followed by a eunuch in the first one, then finally on to Gentiles in the last. In between, comes the account of the conversion of Saul who was chosen by Jesus to announce the good news about him to 'Gentiles and kings and the sons of Israel' (9.15). His story forms the core of the sequence, since it is his persecution of the believers that prompts them to leave Jerusalem, with the other two stories taking their meaning and purpose from the central one. All three sub-sequences are essential components in the founding of the new churches: in Samaria, in Caesarea and, ultimately, in Antioch.

[BA] 8.4-40 *Philip*

General Overview

Philip is already known to the hearers of Acts from the first mention of his name among the seven Hellenists, being the second one named following Stephen (cf. 6.3). The story of his activity constitutes the first report in Acts of evangelization outside Judaea. The significance of Samaria is that there was long-standing reciprocal hostility between the Jews whose centre of worship was the Temple in Jerusalem and those whose Temple was on Mt Gerizim. In Jesus' order to the apostles before he left them, Samaria is the next region named after Jerusalem and Judaea where they are to be witnesses to him. With Philip's arrival in Samaria, there is a clear progression in the movement of the gospel away from the Jewish centre in Ierousalem to regions regarded by the Jews with considerable disapproval or even outright animosity.

Structure and Themes
Luke uses Philip's story to illustrate how lack of discernment was a problem to the successful spread of the gospel message.

There are three episodes in the sub-sequence:

[BA-*A*]	8.4-13	Philip in Samaria, and Simon
[BA-*B*]	8.14-24	Peter and John in Samaria, and Simon
[BA-*A′*]	8.25-40	Philip and the Ethiopian eunuch

Philip's apparent success in Samaria is presented with particular reference to Simon, popularly known as Simon Magus. When Peter and John come to Samaria, however, the reaction of Simon shows that Philip's activity had been carried out without discernment: he failed to check the reality or the depth of the conversions before baptizing and for this reason the Holy Spirit was not given. The apostles, in contrast, demonstrate clear discernment as illustrated by the case of Simon Magus, and the Samaritans receive the Holy Spirit through their ministry. Philip learnt his lesson from what he witnessed in Samaria so that his proclamation of the gospel to the Ethiopian eunuch in the final scene results in an unqualified success, including the gift of the Holy Spirit following baptism according to many manuscripts. Some of these manuscripts, as well as others (see *Critical Apparatus*), include the verification Philip made of the eunuch's faith before baptizing him, underlining the importance of this key element that was omitted from his preaching in Samaria.

The theme of money runs through the central and final episodes of the subsequence.

[BA-*A*] 8.4-13 *Philip in Samaria, and Simon*

Overview

The opening episode of the sub-sequence sets the scene by showing Philip in action in Samaria and the reception given to him by the local people.

Structure and Themes
Although Philip's message is received warmly and is accompanied by miraculous signs, the narrator leaves clues from the start that his manner of preaching

will cause problems to surface. Simon the magician will be the character that brings the problems to light.

There are two parallel accounts in these verses, with the second imitating the first quite closely: Luke relates first, the effect of Philip's preaching among the Samaritans generally, and secondly, his impact on Simon in particular. The elements that make up the episode follow a two-part pattern in which, after a brief introduction, the role of Philip [a–e] is contrasted with that of Simon Magus [a′–e′]:

Intro.	8.4	The dispersion of the disciples
[a]	8.5	Philip preaches the Messiah in Samaria
[b]	8.6a	The crowds pay attention to Philip
[c]	8.6b	They are won over by him
[d]	8.7a	Deliverances
[e]	8.7b-8	Healings and joy
[a′]	8.9	Simon in Samaria
[b′]	8.10	The Great Power of God
[c′]	8.11	The crowds pay attention to Simon
[d′]	8.12	They transfer allegiance to Philip
[e′]	8.13	Simon joins Philip, amazed by the miracles

Translation

	Codex Bezae D05	Codex Vaticanus B03
Intro.	**8.4** Now those who had been scattered travelled about announcing the good news of the word.	**8.4** Now those who had been scattered travelled about announcing the good news of the word.
[a]	**5** Philip went down to a city of Samaria and began preaching to them the Messiah.	**5** Philip went down to the city of Samaria and began preaching to them the Messiah.
[b]	**6a** As the crowds were accustomed to listen to anything, so they paid eager attention to the things Philip was saying.	**6a** The crowds paid eager attention to the things Philip was saying
[c]	**6b** They were won over as they listened and saw the signs he was doing.	**6b** as they all listened together and saw the signs he was doing.
[d]	**7a** For from many of those who had unclean spirits, they were coming out, shouting with a loud voice.	**7a** For out of many of those who had unclean spirits, they were coming out, shouting with a loud voice;
[e]	**7b** Many paralysed people who were lame were being healed, **8** and great joy arose in that city.	**7b** and many paralysed and lame people were healed. **8** So there arose great joy in that city.
[a′]	**9** A certain man named Simon, who was already in the city practising magic, astonished the people of Samaria saying that he himself was someone great.	**9** A certain man named Simon was already practising magic in the city and astonishing the people of Samaria, saying that he himself was someone great.
[b′]	**10** Everyone paid him eager attention, from the smallest to the greatest, saying, 'This man is the power of God called the Great Power'.	**10** Everyone paid him eager attention, from the smallest to the greatest, saying, 'This man is the power of God called the Great Power'.

[c']   11 They eagerly paid attention to him   11 They eagerly paid attention to him
              because he had astonished them for some   because he had astonished them for
              time by his sorceries.   some time by his sorceries.
[d']   12 But when they believed Philip as he   12 But when they believed Philip as he
              preached about the kingdom of God and   preached about the kingdom of God and
              the name of Jesus Christ, they were   the name of Jesus Christ, they were
              baptized, both men and women.   baptized, both men and women.
[e']   13 Simon himself believed and indeed,   13 Simon himself believed and, having
              having been baptized, followed Philip   been baptized, followed Philip continu-
              continually and, seeing signs and great   ally and, seeing signs and great miracles
              miracles happening, he was astonished.   happening, he was astonished.

Critical Apparatus

8.4 διῆλθον B D 𝔓⁷⁴ ℵ² *rell* | δι. κατὰ πόλεις καὶ κώμας g² w p (sa mae); Aug |
adnuntiabant d | ἦλθον ℵ*.

In the readings of the versions an attempt to give a goal to the verb διῆλθον
can be observed; ℵ01* gets round the problem in a different way by using the
simple verb which does not require a goal. The use of the verb διέρχομαι in an
absolute sense is rare (though it occurs again at 10.38); when the story of the
dispersion is picked up at 11.19, διῆλθον is repeated with the direction specified this time (ἕως Φοινίκης καὶ Κύπρου καὶ ᾽Αντιοχείας).

8.5 εἰς τὴν πόλιν B 𝔓⁷⁴ ℵ A 69. 1175. 2344 *pc* ‖ εἰς πόλ. D C E Ψ 049. 056. 33
𝔐 co.

B03's reference to 'the city of Samaria' sounds as if it means 'the city
called Samaria', although in the time of Augustus, when Samaria was rebuilt
by Herod the Great, it had been renamed Sebaste. The absence of the article
makes D05's reference to Samaria apply to the region and the city is not
named, as if it were typical of any city in the country. The construction of D05
may be compared to two other places where a city is mentioned in the Gospels, though with the difference that the city is given a name: first, at Lk. 1.26,
Gabriel is sent 'to a city of Galilee (Judaea, ℵ01) called Nazareth', εἰς πόλιν
τῆς Γαλιλαίας ᾗ ὄνομα Ναζαρέθ (εἰς πόλιν Γαλιλαίαν, D05); secondly, at Jn
4.5, Jesus is said to arrive 'at a city of Samaria called Sychar', εἰς πόλιν τῆς
Σαμαρείας (*om.* ℵ01, probably through haplography) λεγομένην Συχάρ. Cf.
Lk. 9.52, εἰς πόλιν (κώμην B03 D05) Σαμαριτῶν.

8.6 προσεῖχον δὲ οἱ ὄχλοι B 𝔓⁷⁴ ℵ A C Dᶜ 81. 88. 226. 323. 618. 945. 1175.
1739. 1891. 2344 (d) | πρ. τε οἱ ὄχ. E H P Ψ 049. 056. 33. 69. 614. 1241.
1245. 1611. 2412. 2492. 2495 *al* ‖ ὡς δὲ ἤκουον πᾶν, οἱ ὄχ. προσεῖχον D* (syᵖ
mae).

The reading of D05 should be considered in conjunction with the verb in
the second part of the verse (see below). It is possible to take πᾶν as a neuter
singular, signifying 'anything' (L-S-J; *pace* Delebecque, *Les deux Actes*, p. 62),

and to understand Luke as meaning that the Samaritans were in the habit of listening to anything whatsoever, without discrimination. In accordance with their custom, they started listening eagerly to what Philip was saying. B03 eliminates the clause and thereby removes any negative reflection on the Samaritans. d05 produces a conflation: *intendebant autem* (= B03) *omnis* (! = D05) *turbae*.

(ὑπὸ) τοῦ Φιλίππου B 𝔓⁷⁴ ℵ *rell* ‖ Φ. D Ψ 88. 330. 945. 1243. 1739. 1891 *pc*.

Since this is not the first mention of Philip in this episode, the absence of the article in D05 is unusual. The explanation that it is omitted because the name arises in a phrase in which there is a preceding articular noun (τοῖς λεγομένοις ὑπὸ Φιλίππου) is unsatisfactory since on some (but not all) comparable occasions, the article is retained by D05: cf. 13.45; 15.12; 16.14. The more likely reason for the omission of the article is that the story is being seen through the eyes of the Samaritans who, from their point of view, encounter Philip for the first time (Read-Heimerdinger, *The Bezan Text*, pp. 139–41).

ὁμοθυμαδόν B 𝔓⁷⁴ ℵ Dᶜ *rell, unanimo* d ‖ ἐ<πε>ίθουτ<ο> D* syᵖ.

The reconstruction of the verb in D05 is based on the visible letters in the MS: 'on distingue encore nettement le *epsilon* initial, le *iota*, le *thèta* et, après *on*, le *tau*' (Boismard and Lamouille, II, pp. 55–56). By virtue of the asyndetic link, this clause reads as an expansion of the previous one in D05.

8.7 πολλοὶ (γὰρ τῶν ἐχόντων) B 𝔓⁷⁴ ℵ A E 81. 88. 1175 | πολλῶν H P Ψ 049. 056. 1. 33 𝔐 bo; Chr ‖ <παρὰ> πολλοῖς D*, *a multis* d.

The *nominativus pendens* of B03 constitutes a loose construction since the subject of the verb is the neuter plural πνεύματα. In D05, the dative is clear but there is doubt over the initial preposition. Boismard and Lamouille (II, p. 353, n. 45) propose ἀπό following Wetstein, saying that the first and the last letters can be seen, which clashes with the dative of the pronoun. Scrivener (*Bezae Codex*, p. 442) suggests παρά which concords with the dative, and there is room in the MS for four letters at the beginning of the line.

πολλοὶ δὲ παραλελυμένοι καὶ χωλοὶ ἐθεραπεύθησαν B 𝔓⁷⁴ ℵ A C H P 049. 056. 1. 81. 88. 104. 330. 440. 945. 1175. 1241. 1245. 1739. 1891. 2147. 2492. 2495 *al* | πολ. δὲ καὶ παρ. κ. χωλ. ἐθεραπεύθησαν (-εύοντο 33. 2344) E Ψ 33. 614. 1611. 2344. 2412 ‖ πολ. δὲ παρ. (+ καὶ Dᴮ) χωλ. ἐθεραπεύοντο D*, *multi enim paralysin passi clodi curabantur* d (69).

B03 distinguishes between the paralysed and the lame, and views their healing as a completed, or overall, event with the aorist; D05* speaks of the 'paralysed lame', and uses the imperfect tense to express their healing, in line with the series of imperfect verbs in the preceding clauses.

8.8 ἐγένετο δὲ πολλὴ χαρά B 𝔓74 ℵ A C 81. 1175 | ἐγ. δὲ χαρὰ μεγάλη 88. 945. 1739. 1891 | καὶ ἐγ. χαρὰ μεγάλη E H P Ψ 049. 056. 1. 33. 69. 323. 614c. 927. 1245. 1505. 1611. 2344. (2412). 2492. 2495 || χαρά τε μεγάλη ἐγ. D (d).

The construction of B03 is not found elsewhere in Luke's work, χαρὰ μεγάλη being the usual expression (Lk. 2.10; 24.52 [not B03]; Acts 15.3). The position of the phrase at the head of the sentence in D05 underlines its importance, with the connective τε presenting the joy as being the dominating effect of Philip's activity (cf. Levinsohn, *Textual Connections*, pp. 121–23).

8.9 προϋπῆρχεν … μαγεύων καὶ ἐξιστάνων B 𝔓74 ℵ A C P 81. 1175 (d) | προϋπῆρχεν … μαγ. κ. ἐξίστων DB E H P Ψ 049. 056. 1. 33. 69. 88. 614. 945. 1241. 1245. 1611. 1739. 2344. 2412. 2492. 2495 *pler* || προϋπάρχων … μαγ. ἐξίστανεν D*vid.

The verb προϋπάρχω is used to compose a periphrastic form of the verb with the function of indicating a state of affairs that had already existed for some time. B03 reads an imperfect with the participles μαγεύων and ἐξιστάνων depending on it (cf. Lk. 23.12 B03). D05, on the other hand, reads the present participles προϋπάρχων and μαγεύων, followed by ἐξίστανε which represents a form of the imperfect of ἐξίστημι, constructed on ἐξιστάνω (see B-A-G, ἐξίστημι). Delebecque citing Blass, gives ἐξίστανεν (*Les deux Actes,* p. 63); Wetstein suggests 'ἐξέστανε *p.m.*' (Scrivener, *Bezae Codex*, p. 442). In the MS, the letters ΕΞΕ… can be read, indicating that the original form was ΕΞΕΙΣΤΑΝΕ[Ν].

8.13 ἦν προσκαρτερῶν B 𝔓74 ℵ Ds.m. *rell* || ἦν καὶ πρ. D*, *et adhaerebat* d.

The periphrastic construction underlines the fact of Simon's attachment to Philip, which is doubly emphasized by the insertion of the adverbial καί in D05.

Commentary

Introduction 8.4 *The Dispersion of the Disciples*

8.4 The context for the story about Philip is set by the opening clause which picks up the thread of the persecution and dispersion of the church in Hierosoluma first mentioned in 8.1b. The Greek conjunction that is used to continue the story (μὲν οὖν) is used typically by Luke to introduce two events arising from the previous narrative, the second often being the more important or specific (introduced with δέ).[8] In this instance, he first explains what became

8. Levinsohn, *Textual Connections*, pp. 137–50; Read-Heimerdinger, *The Bezan Text*, pp. 237–40.

of the believers who were scattered, and then goes on to tell the story of one person in particular, Philip.

Having been forced to move away from the city, the believers announced the good news (lit. 'evangelized') of the word as they travelled. Apart from Mt. 11.5, Luke is the only evangelist to use the term 'evangelize' (εὐαγγελίζομαι).[9] The content of the word is not specified, though it will be seen in the case of Philip to relate to 'the kingdom of God and the name of Jesus Christ' (8.12).

[a] 8.5 *Philip Preaches the Messiah in Samaria*

8.5 Philip is singled out as one of the people who had to leave Hierosoluma because of the persecution.[10] To some extent, this account of his initial preaching activity, its weak and its strong points, should be taken as an example of the Hellenists' experience in general. Philip was apparently well known as one of the Seven (even after they became six on Stephen's death) and as an evangelist, later living in Caesarea with his four daughters who were prophets (cf. 21.8-9). He is seen here 'going down'[11] to Samaria, according to the AT to the capital city (εἰς τὴν πόλιν; see *Critical Apparatus*) but it is more likely that Luke means the city to stand for any town in Samaria (εἰς πόλιν, D05; cf. the 'people of Samaria', 8.9; 'Samaria', 8.14). The important detail is that the location is Samaria, a region utterly despised by the Jews because the people were of mixed race (cf. Lk. 17.18, ἀλλογενής) and because they rejected the Jerusalem Temple.[12] A highly significant step forward is thus taken, as the message of Jesus is announced for the first time to people who had been totally rejected by the Jews. And it is a step taken by a Hellenist, not an apostle.

The description of Philip's preaching as being 'the Messiah' concords with the evidence for Samaritan expectations of a future prophetic figure who,

9. More than half of the New Testament occurrences of the verb εὐαγγελίζομαι are in Luke's writings (Lk. × 10; Acts × 15 [17, D05]); 21 of them are in Paul's letters.

10. F.S. Spencer, *The Portrait of Philip in Acts: A Study of Roles and Relations* (Sheffield: JSOT Press, 1992), is a comprehensive and valuable study of Philip, looking at his contribution to the narrative overall.

11. The verb κατέρχομαι, used only by Luke apart from Jas 3.15 (Lk. × 2; Acts × 13 [+ 2 D05]), is distinct from καταβαίνω in Luke's work (Lk. × 13; Acts × 19 [+ 3 D05]): the latter has a metaphorical sense, often referring specifically to departure from Ierousalem, the holy city, whereas the former is a neutral term with a purely geographical meaning.

12. The origin of the Samaritans as a separate sect is dated to the Maccabaean period, see F. Dexinger, 'Samaritan Eschatology', in A.D. Crown (ed.), *The Samaritans* (Tübingen: J.C.B. Mohr [Paul Siebeck], 1989, pp. 266–92), p. 271; F. Schmidt, *How the Temple Thinks. Identity and Social Cohesion in Ancient Judaism* (E.T.: J.E. Crowley; The Biblical Seminar 78; Sheffield: Sheffield Academic Press, 2001), pp. 116–29. Josephus writes that 'the Jews … declare that they are sojourners who come from other countries' (*Ant.* IX, 288–91). In the Jewish haggadic tradition, it is recorded that the Samaritans were excommunicated by the Jews and forbidden to have any contact with them.

although he is not referred to as the 'Messiah' as such in the Samaritan literature, broadly resembles in his characteristics the Messiah of the Jews. He is the Taheb, the 'prophet like Moses' of Deut. 18.15-22, who represents God returning to his people after the time of absence,[13] and who will rule as their king. An important difference is that he is closely associated with Mt Gerizim where the Samaritans had built their own Temple, destroyed in 108 BCE by John Hyrcanus, and with the ancient capital of Samaria, Shechem. It appears from Josephus[14] that at this time the Taheb was actively awaited. Philip must have been sufficiently aware of the Samaritan expectations to be able to adapt his message in such a way that those who heard him welcomed it (cf. 8.6, 12).

An important factor in the timing of the evangelization of the Samaritans, according to the narrative scheme of Acts, is that Stephen had by then denounced the Jerusalem Temple as the place which God required for the people's worship of him. The final split between the Samaritans and the other Jews in the second century BCE had occurred precisely over the place of worship, with the Samaritans refusing to accept the Jerusalem Temple even though their own on Mt Gerizim had been destroyed.[15] Since those followers of Jesus who shared Stephen's ideas on the Temple were free from the Jewish view of Jerusalem as the unique 'holy place', Philip would have been able to sympathize with the Samaritans' opposition to the Temple there and would have preached a message that allowed for God to be worshipped in any place.

[b] 8.6a *The Crowds Pay Attention to Philip*
8.6a The readiness of the Samaritans to listen to Philip is explained by a comment in the Bezan text that they were in the habit of listening to anything (πᾶν; cf. 17.21).

[c] 8.6b *They are Won Over by Him*
8.6b The Samaritans' acceptance of Philip's words contrasts with the reception given to the envoys sent out by Jesus to Samaria, to go ahead of him and prepare for him when he was on his way from Galilee to Ierousalem (Lk. 9.51-56).[16] On that occasion, the Samaritans had not accepted him, 'because

---

13. The root of the word Taheb has been identified as שוב, meaning 'turn back, return' (Dexinger, 'Samaritan Eschatology', p. 268; 275–76); it may refer to the return of either God or Moses.

14. Josephus, *Ant.* XVIII, 85–87.

15. Schmidt, *How the Temple Thinks*, pp. 121–29.

16. The following similarities between Lk. 9.51-56 and Acts 8 may be observed: 1) Lk. 9.52, 56: a village of the Samaritans // Acts 8.5: a/the city of Samaria; 2) Lk. 9.54: the incomprehension of the apostles (James and John) // Acts 8.14: Peter and John; 3) Lk. 9.60, 62; 10.9, 11: the kingdom of God // Acts 8.12: the kingdom of God; 4) Lk. 10.1: the sending of 70/72 others // Acts 6.5: Philip, one of the Seven; 5) Lk. 10.17: the casting out of spirits/miracles // Acts 8.6-7, 13: signs/great miracles/unclean spirits; 6) Lk. 10.16: he who listens to you // Acts 8.6a D05: they

his face was set towards Ierousalem' (9.53, in contrast to v. 51) which is presumably what the envoys announced. It can be supposed, therefore, that an essential part of Philip's message is that Ierousalem no longer has a privileged place in the kingdom of God, since Jesus had been going there to make his exodus from it (cf. Lk. 9.31). Philip himself was not attached to it, even if the apostles were (cf. Acts 8.1c D05). Certainly, if he spoke along the same lines as Stephen, the leader of the Hellenists, had done, with his opposition to the sitting of a fixed Temple in Ierousalem, there was every reason for his reasoning to appeal to the Samaritans.

As much as his words, it was the miraculous signs that drew the attention of the Samaritans and, according to Codex Bezae, won them over.

[d] 8.7a *Deliverances*

8.7a The chief sign that attracted the attention of the Samaritans, or indeed won them over as the Bezan text has it, was the release of people from unclean spirits. This, too, was an integral part of the activity of the Seventy whom Jesus sent out ahead of him in the Gospel, after the failure of the original envoys to win over the Samaritans (cf. Lk. 10.17-20). This is the first time in Acts that mention is made of people who 'had' unclean spirits. At the earlier mention of unclean spirits in the context of the apostles' healing activity in Ierousalem (5.16), the people were said to be 'tormented' by the spirits rather than 'having' them as here.[17] It should be noted that not all those with unclean spirits were freed but nevertheless a large number.

[e] 8.7b-8 *Healings and Joy*

8.7b-8 In contrast, Luke says of a second group of Samaritans who were paralyzed that many were healed of their lameness but without suggesting that there were others who were not. The Bezan text sets this group in close parallel with the first by continuing to use the imperfect tense as in the previous sentences.

The coupling of healing and deliverance from unclean spirits recalls the activity of the apostles prior to their second arrest. There, too, the people were impressed by the miracles they witnessed and became believers in Jesus (5.12-16). At the same time, there are some important differences: the apostles were based in Ierousalem (5.16, especially D05) not Samaria, and were carried along by events rather than initiating them as Philip appears to have done; on the other hand, the apostles were dealing with all manner of illnesses, not just lameness as here. Both the possession by unclean spirits and the paralysis may

---

used to listen to anything; 8.6b: they listened to Philip; 7) Lk. 10.17: they returned with joy // Acts 8.8: there was great joy.

17. At 5.16, the verb ὀχλέω was used, a *hapax legomenon*. Here, Luke uses the verb ἔχω (cf. Lk. 4.33; 8.27; 13.11; Acts 16.16; 19.13), where the active has the same passive sense it has in modern languages, 'be possessed by'.

be considered to be symbolic symptoms of inner diseases that affected the Samaritans because of their religious condition. On the one hand, there is evidence of fanaticism, as people were 'possessed' by their nationalistic fervour and zeal for the Samaritan religion – the reaction to Simon in the following verses will exemplify this trait; on the other, they could be viewed as paralysed by their beliefs and traditions which immobilised them in a system that kept them from an active spiritual life.

8.8 The deliverances and healings resulted in great joy, which the Bezan text highlights by placing the phrase at the start of the sentence; this text also associates the joy closely with the healings. Joy is not, in itself, necessarily a positive sign in Luke's writings: it may be merely transitory, as it was for those in the parable who eagerly accepted the word (Lk. 8.13); it may result from hearing good news (Lk. 1.14; 2.10; 15.7, 10; 24.41; Acts 12.14; 15.3) or from fulfilling a mission (Acts 13.52); it may, in context, be inappropriate as was the case for the Seventy who rejoiced at their power over demons (Lk. 10.17, 20) or for the apostles who returned to worship in the Temple after the departure of Jesus (Lk. 24.52-53). It is only in the development of the story that it will become clear if the joy is warranted. In this instance, the enthusiastic response of the Samaritans to Philip will result not only in joy but also in belief and baptism (Acts 8.12).

[a′] 8.9 *Simon in Samaria*

8.9 A new character, Simon, is presented both as a representative of the Samaritans ('a certain man') and a real person in his own right ('named Simon'). As he is brought on stage, a second account is begun which runs in parallel to the account of the Samaritans in general. The nature of the second account is such that it builds two sets of comparisons, activated simply by the juxtaposition of the successive stories: the first between Simon and Philip in their public activity, and the second, between Simon and the rest of the believing Samaritans in their response to Philip.

The comparison with Philip depends on the following elements:

1. Both were active in the same city, but Simon had been there for some time already before Philip arrived.
2. Both were doing extraordinary deeds, but Simon performed them by means of magic in contrast to the divine power that worked through Philip (cf. 6.3, 'full of the Spirit and wisdom').
3. Both had a powerful effect on the people of Samaria; in each case, it is said that the people paid them eager attention.
4. Both spoke of a Messiah, though Simon proclaimed himself to be the one Philip announced as Jesus.

This last point requires further exploration. That the principal goal of Philip's preaching was the proclamation of the Messiah is clear from the statement that introduces his activity (8.5). In the case of Simon, a euphemistic expression is used to express the fact that he proclaimed himself to be the Messiah, the word Messiah itself being reserved by Luke for Jesus. The expression is 'someone great', found as a messianic designation when Gamaliel refers to Theudas in the Bezan text of 5.36: he said 'he was himself someone great' (AT omits 'great'). A similar construction is used in the Sanhedrin's accusation of Jesus, that he said 'he was himself Christ a king' (Lk. 23.2).[18]

[b'] 8.10 *The Great Power of God*
8.10 The impact of Simon on the population of Samaria is reported to have been overwhelming, to the extent that the entire nation had become his followers. The narrative is intensely emphatic, with the words of the Samaritans themselves repeating Simon's own claims about himself, that he was the Great Power of God.

[c'] 8.11 *The Crowds Pay Attention to Simon*
8.11 The narrative continues to heavily underline what has already been said in the two previous verses, insisting that the people were a) following Simon because b) he had been active for a long time already and c) had astonished them with his magic. The same verb, 'paid eager attention', is repeated, a clear echo of its use when speaking of Philip (8.6).[19]

[d'] 8.12 *They Transfer Allegiance to Philip*
8.12 Having established the similarities between Simon and Philip, the parallel between Simon and the other Samaritans is drawn, first of all recording how the Samaritans signalled publicly their change of allegiance from Simon to Philip by taking the step of baptism. The earlier comments about the Samaritans' reaction to Philip should be recalled (cf. 8.6-8). According to the Bezan text, the Samaritans were in the habit of listening to anything and everything; this is what inclined them to pay attention to Philip as he spoke about the Messiah, and they were persuaded by what he said because of the supernatural happenings that they witnessed. The AT plays down the effect of Philip somewhat, omitting any comment on the Samaritans' predisposition to be attracted by public speakers (cf. 8.6a) and also omitting to say that they were persuaded by Philip (cf. v. 6b). Now, both texts agree in recording that as Philip preached about the kingdom of God and the name of Jesus Christ, the Samaritans believed him – it is to him that they gave allegiance, not Jesus (cf. Simon, 8.13).[20]

---

18. Compare 5.36: λέγων εἶναί τινα (μέγαν D05) ἑαυτόν, with 8.9: λέγων εἶναί τινα ἑαυτὸν μέγαν and Lk. 23.2: λέγοντα ἑαυτὸν Χριστὸν βασιλέα εἶναι.

19. What is said of Philip (according to Codex Bezae): προσεῖχον/ἐπείθοντο (8.6), and of Simon: ᾧ προσεῖχον / προσεῖχον δὲ αὐτῷ (8.10-11), may be compared with what is said of Theudas: ᾧ προσεκλίθη / πάντες ὅσοι ἐπείθοντο αὐτῷ (5.36) and of Judas the Galilean: ἀπέστησεν λαὸν (+ πολὺν D05) ὀπίσω αὐτοῦ / καὶ πάντες (– D05) ὅσοι ἐπείθοντο αὐτῷ (5.37).

20. When the verb πιστεύω is used with the dative of the person (Lk. 1.20; 20.5; Acts 8.12; 16.34; 18.8 B03; 24.14; 26.27; 27.25), the meaning is simply that the person is believed, but

[e′] 8.13 *Simon Joins Philip, Amazed by the Miracles*

8.13 The first part of Philip's story concludes with the apparent conversion of Simon Magus – 'apparent' because it will be seen in the following episode that Simon has not been persuaded to believe in Jesus but rather has been impressed by external manifestations of faith.

Simon is compared directly with the other Samaritans, as he is described as believing and being baptized in the same way as them.[21] Not only that, but he starts following Philip in a persistent way.[22] The significant feature[23] of his interest in Philip, however, was his astonishment at the signs and 'great miracles' he performed. Several elements are picked up here from earlier in the story. First, the adjective 'great' was used four times (of the joy of the Samaritans, v. 8; of Simon, v. 9; of the Samaritans, v. 10a; of Simon's power, v. 10b). Secondly, where 'great' referred to Simon's power, the same word was used in the singular (δύναμις)[24] as that which refers here in the plural to Philip's miracles. Thirdly, Simon's capacity to astonish the Samaritans was carefully noted (ἐξιστάνων AT / ἐξίστανεν D05, v. 9; ἐξεστακέναι, v. 11), just as now he himself is astonished by Philip's performance. The two-fold comparison between Simon and the Samaritans, and between Simon and Philip, thus continues with the latter coming to the fore in what follows.

As Simon has followed the general movement of the Samaritans in giving his allegiance to Philip, Philip has accepted him and has been responsible for baptizing him. In view of the rapid transfer of allegiance of the Samaritans from Simon to Philip, with the use of comparable terms to describe the activity of both as well as to relate the reaction manifested to each of them, it is legitimate to wonder how far either the Samaritans or Simon had really understood the message of Jesus. It was pointed out with reference to 8.12 that the Samaritans 'believed Philip'; likewise, Simon attaches himself 'to Philip'. There is no doubt that they were all impressed by Philip's miracles, and it seems that this was the main ground for their change of allegiance. Philip's message is, nonetheless, described in positive terms, for he preached 'about

---

without signifying a personal trust in the person, which is expressed by πιστεύω + εἰς (Acts 10.43; 14.23; 18.8 D05; 19.4) or ἐπί + accusative (Lk. 24.25; Acts 9.42; 11.17; 16.31; 22.19).

21. The sequence ἐπίστευσεν … βαπτισθείς corresponds exactly to the plural construction of 8.12: ἐπίστευσαν … ἐβαπτίζοντο.

22. The periphrastic construction ἦν προσκαρτερῶν emphasizes Simon's continual presence beside Philip (Zerwick, *Biblical Greek*, § 360: '*he continued to stay beside*'). In the Bezan text, his persistence is further underlined by the adverbial καί before the present participle.

23. The particle τε, especially when it precedes the last element in a description, may introduce an idea that is of special importance for the events that follow (Levinsohn, *Textual Connections*, pp. 132–36: 'τε gives prominence to this sentence, over against the previous sentence, which is of a more general or preliminary nature' [136]).

24. The term δύναμις can designate the ability or power – physical, moral or spiritual – to do something and therefore, by extension, the miraculous actions that are the manifestation of that power.

the kingdom of God and the name of Jesus Christ'; nor is there any reason to doubt Philip's good faith in accepting their change of heart as sincere and moving on to baptize them. What will become apparent in the subsequent events is a certain lack of discernment on his part.

[BA-*B*] 8.14-24 *Peter and John in Samaria, and Simon*

Overview

The sub-sequence concerning Philip moves on in this episode with the introduction of the two leading representatives of the apostles, Peter and John. According to Codex Bezae, they will come from Ierousalem but, after witnessing the work of God among the Samaritans, will return to Hierosoluma – in other words, no longer firmly attached to traditional Jewish beliefs and teaching which have been overturned by the intervention of the Holy Spirit. Peter and John will be instrumental in allowing Philip to discover his mistake in accepting too readily and uncritically the enthusiastic response of the Samaritans, represented by Simon the magician. The note on which the action in Samaria ends is not entirely positive for Peter will declare Simon's unhealthy interest in the Holy Spirit to be a sign of unrighteousness.

The meeting of Peter and John with Philip in Samaria will prepare for the final episode of the sub-sequence concerning Philip, in which he will be successful in taking the gospel for the first time to an uncircumcised person.

Structure and Themes

The first half of this episode relates the visit of Peter and John to the area where Philip had been evangelizing and baptizing. The second half takes up the story of Simon and his reaction to the giving of the Holy Spirit which he witnesses. The structure mirrors that of the first episode of the sub-sequence in that the role of the apostles [a–c] is set against that of the magician [c′–a′], just as the role of Philip was set against that of Simon Magus, except that here the arrangement of elements is reversed in the second half of the pattern:

[a]	8.14	Peter and John in Samaria
[b]	8.15-16	Prayer for the Holy Spirit
[c]	8.17	The Samaritans receive the Holy Spirit
[c′]	8.18-19	Simon's request
[b′]	8.20-23	Peter's reply
[a′]	8.24	Simon's plea

Translation

Codex Bezae D05

[a]   **8.14** When the apostles in Ierousalem heard that Samaria had received the

Codex Vaticanus B03

8.14 When the apostles in Hierosoluma heard that Samaria had received the word of God, they sent Peter and John to them.

[b] **15** They went down and prayed for them so that they might receive the Holy Spirit. (**16** It had not yet fallen upon any of them – they had only been baptized in the name of the Lord Jesus Christ.)

[c] **17** Then they began to lay hands on them and they received the Holy Spirit.

[c′] **18** When Simon saw that through the laying on of the apostles' hands the Holy Spirit was given, he offered them money, pleading as he said, **19** 'Give this authority to me as well, so that whoever I, too, lay my hands on might receive the Holy Spirit'.

[b′] **20** Peter said to him, 'May you and money perish, because you thought you could get the gift of God through money. **21** There is no part or share in this matter for you; your heart is not right before God. **22** So repent of this wickedness of yours and pray to the Lord in the hope that the intent of your heart will then be forgiven. **23** For I perceive that you are in the gall of bitterness and the bond of unrighteousness.'

[a′] **24** Simon answered and said to them, 'I beg you to pray yourselves to God for me so that none of these bad things that you have spoken to me might happen to me', and he did not cease weeping.

word of God, they sent Peter and John to them.

15 They went down and prayed for them so that they might receive the Holy Spirit. (**16** It had not yet fallen on any of them – they had only been baptized in the name of the Lord Jesus.)

17 Then they began to lay hands on them and they received the Holy Spirit.

18 When Simon saw that through the laying on of the apostles' hands the Spirit was given, he offered them money as he said, **19** 'Give this authority to me as well, so that whoever I lay my hands on might receive the Holy Spirit'.

20 Peter said to him, 'May your money perish with you, because you thought you could get the gift of God through money. **21** There is no part or share in this matter for you, for your heart is not right before God. **22** So repent of this wickedness of yours and pray to the Lord in the hope that, then, you will be forgiven the intent of your heart. **23** For I see that you are in the gall of bitterness and the bond of unrighteousness.'

24 Simon answered and said, 'Pray yourselves to the Lord on my behalf so that nothing of what you have said might happen to me'.

Critical Apparatus

8.14 Ἱεροσολύμοις B 𝔓[74] ℵ *rell* || Ἱερουσαλήμ D d.

These variants must be considered against the mention of Jerusalem in 8.1 where, in both texts, the church was referred to as being in Hierosoluma (v. 1b). D05 then had a second contrasting reference to Ierousalem (v. 1c) where the apostles were said to have remained. B03 takes up the earlier Hellenistic spelling which, if done deliberately, causes the apostles to be seen as having distanced themselves from the Jewish institution since this is the first time in Acts that they are associated with the Hellenistic form of the name. D05's reading is consistent with the earlier comment in 8.1c whereby the apostles continue to be represented as still attached to the Jewish religious institution. According to this text, their separation will not take place until later when the links they create with Samaria (cf. 8.15 and 8.25) make it impossible to continue in favour with Ierousalem.

8.16 ἐπ᾽ οὐδενί B ℵ D^{D?} *rell* ‖ ἐπὶ οὐδένα D* d.

There is a slight difference in meaning between the dative of B03, 'on' (answering the question 'where?') and the accusative of D05 'upon' (answering the question 'to where?'). Within the New Testament, the construction ἐπιπίπτω ἐπί + accusative is found at Jn 13.25 *vl*; Lk. 1.12; 15.20; Acts 10.44 (ἔπεσεν D05); 11.15 (ἔπεσεν D05); 19.17 (ἔπεσεν D05); 20.37; Rom. 15.3; Rev. 11.11; ἐπί + dative, apart from here at Acts 8.16 B03, is only found at 19.6 D05; 20.10 D05; ἐπιπίπτω is followed by the dative alone at Mk 3.10; Acts 20.10 B03.

κυρίου Ἰησοῦ B 𝔓⁷⁴ ℵ *rell* ‖ κυ. Ἰ. Χριστοῦ D d vg^{mss} mae aeth.

D05 always uses the full name and title of Jesus in a baptismal context (cf. Read-Heimerdinger, *The Bezan Text*, pp. 266, 271).

8.17 ἐπετίθεσαν (-θοσαν B) B 𝔓⁷⁴ ℵ A (C) D^A 81. 323. 440. 945. 1175. 1739. 1891 *al* ‖ -θουν D* 𝔓⁴⁵ E H L P Ψ 049. 056 𝔐.

The variants are different forms of the imperfect of the same verb (cf. 3.2; 4.35: Zerwick and Grosvenor, *Analysis*, p. 357; Zerwick, *Biblical Greek*, § 488). The versions cannot be appealed to in support of either text (*pace* Boismard and Lamouille, II, p. 57).

8.18 τὸ πνεῦμα B ℵ sa mae; ConstAp ‖ τ. πν. τὸ ἅγιον D d 𝔓⁴⁵·⁷⁴ A C E H L P Ψ 049. 056. 33. 1739 𝔐 latt sy bo aeth; Bas Chr.

The references to the Holy Spirit in 8.15, 17, 19 are in the form πνεῦμα ἅγιον which is the form normally used in Acts for the gift of the Spirit to believers (Read-Heimerdinger, *The Bezan Text*, pp. 160–63). B03 simply takes up this earlier reference by repeating the noun without qualification. D05, however, now views the situation from the point of view of Simon Magus and adopts the form used to refer to the Holy Spirit when the notion of holiness is being spelt out (*The Bezan Text*, pp. 163–64; 167–68). Much has been made of the inclusion of the adjective ἅγιον by D05 in this verse as a supposed example of a typical 'fondness' for the full expression in the Bezan text; an exhaustive analysis of the forms of the expression used in Codex Bezae to refer to the Holy Spirit does not, however, confirm a preference for the use of ἅγιον with πνεῦμα (*The Bezan Text*, pp. 146; 149–51).

8.19 λέγων B 𝔓⁷⁴ ℵ *rell* ‖ παρακαλῶν καὶ λέγ. D d gig p mae.

The request in D05 is more explicit and more insistent that in B03: cf. 2.40; 16.9, 15, 39 D05.

(ἐπιθῶ) κἀγώ D d (p; CAp) ‖ *om.* B 𝔓⁷⁴ ℵ *rell*.

κἀγώ in D05 corresponds to κἀμοί in the main clause, and is an indirect anaphoric reference to the apostles, mentioned in 8.17a, 18a. B03 possibly considers it superfluous to insist so much on Simon Magus' hope of emulating the apostles.

8.20 Τὸ ἀργύριόν σου B 𝔓⁷⁴ ℵ Dᴰ *rell* || ᾿Αργ. D*, d lac.

The anaphoric article together with the possessive adjective in B03 causes Peter's denunciation of money to refer to the money Simon has just offered the apostles (χρήματα, v. 18). D05, in contrast, treats money in general as a problem.

8.21 ἡ γὰρ καρδία B 𝔓⁷⁴ᵛⁱᵈ ℵ Dᶜ *rell* || ἡ καρ. D* 522 saᵐˢ, d lac.

The absence of connective in D05 serves to tie the second sentence closely to the first as an expansion or a comment on it and strengthens the connection (cf. Delebecque, *Les deux Actes*, p. 239). γὰρ in B03 makes the connection explicit.

8.22 (ἀφεθήσεταί) σοι B ℵ *rell* || σου D, d lac.

The dative pronoun in B03 is associated with the preceding verb, 'will be forgiven'. The possessive pronoun in D05, on the other hand, qualifies the noun ἡ ἐπίνοια which, coming after the pronoun, is thus underlined (Levinsohn, *Discourse Features*, pp. 75–76).

8.23 εἰς γὰρ χολὴν πικρίας καὶ σύνδεσμον ἀδικίας ὁρῶ σε ὄντα B 𝔓⁷⁴ ℵ Dᴮ *rell* || ἐν γ. πικρ. χολῇ καὶ συνδέσμῳ ἀδ. θεωρῶ σε ὄντα D*, d lac.

The variants in this clause affect, first, the initial preposition and the associated case of the nouns they govern; then secondly, the word order of the first pair of nouns; and finally, the verb. Whereas with ἐν in D05, Peter views Simon as already in the undesirable state he describes, it is possible that with εἰς in B03 he sees him as heading towards that state; that said, B03 tends to use εἰς with a static force equivalent to the meaning of ἐν (Read-Heimerdinger, *The Bezan Text*, pp. 192–95). The phrase χολὴν πικρίας translates a Hebrew idiom in which the noun in the genitive has an adjectival force ('bitter gall', Zerwick and Grosvenor, *Analysis*, p. 376). The construction occurs elsewhere in the New Testament, usually with the genitive noun in second place which is the Hebrew word order, as is seen here in the second pair of nouns (cf., e.g., Lk. 4.22; 16.9; Acts 9.15). By disrupting the word order pattern here, D05 sets up a chiastic structure with the second pair of nouns (genitive–dative // dative–genitive), which reinforces Peter's description of Simon's desperate state. As for the verb, finally, θεωρῶ in D05 conveys more readily the sense of inner perception than does ὁρῶ.

8.24 εἶπεν B 𝔓⁷⁴ ℵ *rell* || εἶ. πρὸς αὐτούς D mae, d lac.

A prepositional phrase that makes explicit the addressee after a verb of speaking is typically used to insist on the relationship between the speaker and hearer, and is considerably more common in the text of D05 than in B03 (Read-Heimerdinger, *The Bezan Text*, pp. 176–82). It concords with the D05 reading of παρακαλῶ (see next *vl*) and also the detail at the end of the verse in D05 describing Simon's distress.

Δεήθητε Β 𝔓⁷⁴ ℵ *rell* ‖ Παρακαλῶ· δεήθετε D 614. 1611. 2412 *pc* gig r sy^h** mae.

The insistence of Simon Magus echoes not only the earlier narrative description (cf. 8.19 D05) but, in a more distant past, the pleading of Simon Peter during the incident of the miraculous catch of fish when he begs Jesus to leave him – though there, too, only in D05 (Lk. 5.8 D05).

ὑπὲρ ἐμοῦ Β 𝔓⁷⁴ ℵ D^B *rell* ‖ περὶ ἐμοῦ D* 88. 1175 *pc*, d lac.

There is a slight difference in Simon's request: 'pray for me' (B03) or 'pray about me' (D05).

(πρὸς τὸν) κύριον Β 𝔓⁷⁴ ℵ *rell* ‖ θεόν D 33. 69. 431. 547. 614. 913. 927. 1108. 1245. 1505. 1611. 1828^c. 2138. 2147. 2298. 2344. 2412. 2495 *pc* c dem p vg^mss sy^p.h mae, d lac.

This is one among many variant readings concerning θεός and κύριος. In D05, the 'Lord' is never used by people of non-Jewish origin, and rarely with reference to them. Peter's use of κύριος at 8.22 is therefore exceptional if it refers to Yahweh (τοῦ θεοῦ, v. 21), though not if he means Jesus (Read-Heimerdinger, *The Bezan Text*, p. 286).

(μηδὲν ἐπέλθῃ) ἐπ᾽ ἐμὲ ὧν εἰρήκατε Β 𝔓⁷⁴ ℵ *rell* ‖ μοι τούτων τῶν κακῶν ὧν εἰρήκατέ μοι D (E vg^ms mae; Chr), d lac.

Simon's plea to Peter and John is formulated in more concrete and personal terms in D05.

ὃς πολλὰ κλαίων οὐ διελίμπανεν D* sy^hmg mae, d lac. ‖ *om.* Β 𝔓⁷⁴ ℵ D^s.m. *rell*.

The only other occurrences of διαλιμπάνω in the New Testament are at Lk. 7.45 and Acts 17.13 D05, the latter with a construction very similar to the one read here (pres. part. + negative + imperf.). There would seem to be an intended allusion to Peter's distress after his denial of Jesus (Lk. 22.62, ἔκλαυσεν πικρῶς), which B03 avoids. The parallel between the two Simons may well have been effaced because of the role Simon Magus soon acquired among the Church Fathers as the leader of Gnosticism. Although Metzger (*Commentary*, p. 359) and Bruce (*Text*, p. 188) both find the clause reads awkwardly, the use of ὅς in place of οὗτος to add further information concerning a character is common in the New Testament (cf. B-D-R, § 293.3c).

Commentary

[a] 8.14 *Peter and John in Samaria*

8.14 The narrative switches briefly away from Samaria, back to Jerusalem and to the apostles. Once again in the Bezan text, the spelling of the city is an important means whereby the narrator continues to signal his evaluation of the apostles' mentality. They were last mentioned in Codex Bezae as being in Ierousalem (8.1c), representing their attachment to the Jewish institution in contrast with the freedom of another group of disciples who, being in Hierosoluma (8.1b), were persecuted and forced to leave the area. The separation of the apostles from Ierousalem will occur through the incidents in Samaria, as indicated by the use of Hierosoluma at 8.25. In the Bezan text, this will be the first time that Hierosoluma is used in association with the apostles who, despite their discovery of the gulf between the ideology of the Jewish authorities and the plan of God (4.24-30), nevertheless had continued in their belief in the unique status of Ierousalem. They had also witnessed the shaking of the Temple on that earlier occasion (4.31),[25] yet apparently still struggle with detaching themselves completely from the traditional understanding and expectations concerning the 'holy place'. For that separation to be achieved, the intervention of God in Samaria will be decisive. It is necessary, in other words, for Peter and John to witness God himself acting in favour of the Samaritans before they can accept the changes that Jesus has brought about with respect to what they have hitherto believed to be fundamental principles of Jewish faithfulness to God.

The apostles in Ierousalem or, more neutrally according to the AT, in Hierosoluma, have heard about what had been going on in Samaria, and that the people had 'received the word of God' (ὁ λόγος τοῦ θεοῦ). The use of the term 'the word of God' should be carefully noted here standing, as it does, in contrast to the parallel expression 'the word of the Lord' (ὁ λόγος τοῦ κυρίου) which is found at 6.7. As was explained with reference to 6.7, and to 6.2 earlier, the two phrases function, in the Bezan text, as a pair of alternatives that express distinct notions. According to the pattern that is evident in the Bezan text, ὁ λόγος τοῦ θεοῦ represents the general notion of God communicating with people or a general message about religious principles (cf., e.g., Lk. 8.11, 15 D05, 21; 11.28), in contrast to ὁ λόγος τοῦ κυρίου which refers to the teaching of or about Jesus. Both expressions are used to speak about the 'word' being transmitted to various people or groups who are said to 'receive' it. The Jews are deemed to be already in possession of the word of God, either because they have been given the Torah or because God has long communicated with them in other ways. It is only Samaritans or Gentiles who have to be given the word of God, and it is only once they have received it that the word of the Lord can be spoken to them. Receiving the word of God is a one-off event that is effective for a people in general, as reflected in the choice of the perfect tense.[26] That is why it is said later (8.25) when Peter and

---

25. See *The Message of Acts*, I, pp. 273–81.

26. The perfect δέδεκται expresses a permanent change in state, which is precisely what is implied in the receiving of the word of God, a change from being 'outside' the people of God to

John evangelized many villages in Samaria, that they spoke the 'word of the Lord', a message about Jesus in particular. Luke, in other words, makes a deliberate choice between the two expressions in order to reflect the particular situation or mentality. This dual usage is quite clear in Codex Bezae, though it is scarcely evident in the AT.

The present situation is viewed, first of all, from the point of view of the apostles in Ierousalem who regard the Samaritans as outside the people of God and therefore needing to receive his word. The word order of the Greek sentence juxtaposes the two nouns, Samaria/the word of God, and so highlights the unusual nature of their association.[27] From a Jewish point of view, this is a crucial development, and it is no accident that it is placed on a par with the reception of the word of God by the Gentiles later in Acts (cf. 11.1). The news of the response of the Samaritans to Philip is, therefore, quite unexpected as far as the apostles are concerned. Luke has a device that he uses to express the fact that those who learn of a happening had no prior awareness of or involvement in the events leading up to it – he simply says that they 'heard', omitting any mention of the how they learnt the news.[28] The use of the verb here serves as a comment on the apostles who had, according to the Bezan text, taken refuge in Ierousalem. If they had been alert to the command of Jesus to go beyond Ierousalem with their witness to him, they could have been expected to be taking a more supportive interest in the Hellenists' activity in Samaria.

Nonetheless, at the point at which they do hear about it, they are sufficiently open to accepting the news to send two of their representatives to the Samaritans. Peter and John have already appeared together as representatives of the apostles, in preparing the Passover preparation (Lk. 22.8); in attending the Temple for prayer (Acts 3.1, 3); in speaking to the people about the healing of the lame man (3.11–4.2); and in testifying about Jesus to the Sanhedrin (4.13, 19).

[b] 8.15-16 *Prayer for the Holy Spirit*
8.15 For the first time since they had returned to Ierousalem after Jesus' departure (cf. 1.12), members of the apostolic group leave the holy city which Luke expresses with the verb typical of leaving Ierousalem in a metaphorical sense, 'go down', καταβαίνω (cf. 8.5). In going among the Samaritans, Peter and John exposed themselves to the criticism of other Jews, notably the leaders, who refused contact with the Samaritans (see above on 8.14).

---

being inside. Comparison may be made with 11.1, where the apostles, among others, hear that the Gentiles 'received the word of God', using the aorist ἐδέξαντο (sing., D05).

27. The Greek reads ὅτι δέδεκται ἡ Σαμάρεια τὸν λόγον τοῦ θεοῦ.

28. The aorist of the verb of hearing is generally used: Lk. 1.58; 4.23; 7.3; 9.7; 21.9; Acts 7.12; 8.14; 9.13, 38; 11.1, 22; 15.24; 23.16; 28.15. Twice, the tense is present: Lk. 16.2; 23.8; and once future: Acts 21.22.

When Peter and John arrived in Samaria, they prayed specifically for the Samaritans to receive the Holy Spirit.[29] According to the explanation that follows, this had not yet happened because they had only been baptized in the name of Jesus. Consequently, it may be deduced that they lacked the experience of the manifestation of the Holy Spirit, such as was seen in earlier incidents relating the effect of the Holy Spirit on the personal and community life of believers: speaking in other languages, praising God (2.4, 11); speaking the word of God with boldness (4.31). It is not so much that an event has not taken place as that an inner experience, one that brings about a permanent change and external manifestations, is missing.[30] The Samaritans have believed what Philip had been preaching about the kingdom and Jesus and have indicated their acceptance of his message by water baptism, but they have not as yet had a personal experience of the power of God.

8.16 It is often supposed that the reason the Samaritans had not received the Holy Spirit when Philip baptized them is because he was only qualified to baptize with water – being, as is said, a mere deacon. This interpretation is, however, anachronistic, for not only does the book of Acts not use the term 'deacon' but Philip is presented as one of the seven Hellenists who was full of the Spirit and wisdom (6.3), and nowhere is it suggested that the apostles were the exclusive channel of the Holy Spirit. Furthermore, according to the text of 8.39 read by many manuscripts (see *Critical Apparatus*), the Ethiopian eunuch does receive the Holy Spirit as he emerges from the water following his baptism carried out by Philip.

A series of markers left by the narrator in the text indicate that, in fact, the reason that the Samaritans had not received the Holy Spirit has nothing to do with Philip's status but everything to do with the condition of the Samaritans themselves. The markers are verbal allusions to the parable of the soils in Luke's Gospel (Lk. 8.4-15), in particular to the rocky type of soil. The following parallels can be noticed:

1. The dominant theme is the word of God (τὸν λόγον τοῦ θεοῦ):
   Lk. 8.11 (esp. D05: ὁ τοῦ θεοῦ), 15 D05;   Acts 8.14; cf. v. 4
   cf. τὸν λόγον, vv. 12, 13[31]

2. The core of the message is the kingdom of God:
   Lk. 8.10, τὰ μυστήρια τῆς   Acts 8.12, περὶ τῆς βασιλείας τοῦ
   βασιλείας τοῦ θεοῦ   θεοῦ

3. There is an insistence on the act of listening:
   Lk. 8.13, ὅταν ἀκούσωσιν, referring to   Acts 8.6, ἐν τῷ ἀκούειν (esp. D05,

---

29. The preposition ὅπως after προσεύχομαι is exceptional in the New Testament, ἵνα being more usual. In Luke's writing, however, ὅπως is often found after verbs of petition: δέομαι (Lk. 10.2; Acts 8.24); ἐρωτάω (Lk. 7.3; 11.37 [not D05]; 16.28; Acts 23.20); αἰτέω (Acts 9.2; 25.3).

30. Note that the tense of the verbs 'fallen' and 'baptized' is the perfect in each case, denoting a state rather than an action or event.

31. Matthew refers to the 'word of the kingdom' (13.19; cf. 'the word', 13.20, 21, 22 [× 2], 23), while Mark simply refers to 'the word' (4.14, 15 [× 2], 16, 17, 18, 19).

	those on rocky ground; cf. vv. 14, 15	'as they listened to anything', ὡς δὲ ἤκουον πᾶν)
4.	The message is well-received: Lk. 8.13a, δέχονται τὸν λόγον[32]	Acts 8.14, δέδεκται
5.	It is associated with joy: Lk. 8.13b, μετὰ χαρᾶς	Acts 8.8, πολλὴ χαρά (D05: χαρά τε μεγάλη)
6.	The people believe: Lk. 8.13d, οἱ πρὸς καιρὸν πιστεύουσιν	Acts 8.12, ἐπίστευσαν τῷ Φιλίππῳ, cf. v. 13
7.	Yet there is a problem with growth: Lk. 8.6, the plant had no moisture, διὰ τὸ μὴ ἔχειν ἰκμάδα; 13c, the people have no root, ῥίζαν οὐκ ἔχουσιν	Acts 8.16, the fruits of the Spirit are not in evidence, οὐδέπω γὰρ ἦν ἐπ᾽ οὐδενὶ (οὐδένα D05) αὐτῶν ἐπιπεπτωκός

The force of the allusions to the parable of the soils is that the Samaritans are portrayed as responding superficially with much enthusiasm, but there is a lack of depth to their belief. This picture fits with Luke's description of the Samaritans as greatly impressed by Simon's miracle working, and his account of their easy change of allegiance from Simon to the newcomer, Philip, when they saw the power he was wielding. So, once they were won over by Philip's exorcisms and healings, they accepted the truth of his preaching (cf. 8.14) and on that basis were baptized by Philip with water (8.12). It was the superficial nature of their commitment, however, that meant that they did not have an inner experience of the personal presence and activity of the Spirit.

[c] 8.17 *The Samaritans Receive the Holy Spirit*

8.17 The use of the conjunction τότε ('then') indicates that Peter and John act in response to the situation that they find in order to resolve it.[33] Unlike those represented by the rocky soil in Jesus' parable, the Samaritans will not 'fall away' but will have the opportunity to put down deeper roots. So, having prayed for the Samaritans to receive the Holy Spirit, the apostles placed their hands on them which resulted in their prayers being answered (καὶ ἐλάμβανον, cf. ὅπως λάβωσιν, 8.15). The form of the expression used here to refer to the Holy Spirit, as in the previous mention at v. 15, is typical of the form used in Luke's writings when it is a question of the Holy Spirit being 'received' in a general way, that is, not for a particular purpose.[34] The act of laying on hands

---

32. Matthew (13.20) and Mark (4.16) have the verb λαμβάνω; in altering it to δέχομαι in his rendering of the parable, Luke anticipates the enactment of the second element of the parable in Samaria.

33. Read-Heimerdinger, *The Bezan Text*, pp. 211–25.

34. In Luke's work, four expressions are used to refer to the Spirit: τὸ πνεῦμα, πνεῦμα ἅγιον, τὸ πνεῦμα τὸ ἅγιον, and τὸ ἅγιον πνεῦμα. Each of them has a distinct connotation, with the form found here in Acts 8.15, 17, πνεῦμα ἅγιον, being the one always used in speaking of being filled or baptized with the Holy Spirit, or receiving the Holy Spirit. It refers to the Spirit as God's

is not some magic ritual but has the effect of personalizing the prayer and directing it to individual believers; it ensures an individual response rather than a mass movement. The continued use of the imperfect tenses (ἐπετίθουν D05 / ἐπετίθεσαν AT ... ἐλάμβανον) conveys the idea of this taking some time rather than being a sudden event. From this point onwards, with the personal and community experience of the Holy Spirit, the church among the Samaritans can be said to have been fully formed, just as it had been already among the Jewish believers (2.4-21; 4.31) and will be among the Gentiles (cf. 10.44-47; 11.15-17).

[c'] 8.18-19 *Simon's Request*
8.18-19 A negative counterpart to the previous verses now arises as the spotlight falls once more on Simon, already singled out in vv. 9-13, where a number of negative features of Simon's attachment to Philip were observed.

Simon is impressed by the effects of the apostles' action that he witnesses – not in himself, however, but in other people, which implies that hands had not been laid on Simon himself.[35] That he had not received the Spirit is confirmed by his offer of money to buy the power, for detachment from material possessions was seen to be precisely a mark of the believers who had received the Spirit in Jerusalem (cf. 4.37; Lk. 18.24). While he had been content to attach himself to Philip and marvel at his miracles, he sees clearly that the workings of the Holy Spirit that result from the apostles' laying on of hands is something greater. The insistence with which he approaches the apostles in order to obtain their 'authority' is stronger in the Bezan text.

This passage has given rise to the term 'simony', referring to the buying or selling of sacred things with money. The original incident concerning Simon, however, involves a more profound opposition between God and money and the values belonging to each (cf. Lk. 16.13).

[b'] 8.20-23 *Peter's Reply*
8.20-23 Peter is the one who responds to Simon, though speaking on behalf of John, too, as is made clear when Simon replies to them in the plural (8.24 [+ πρὸς αὐτούς D05]; and cf. a similar situation involving Peter and John with the lame man, 3.4, 6). Peter reacts with considerable force to Simon's request to purchase the gift of God, effectively pronouncing a curse and consigning

---

means of self-revelation in a general way rather than for a specific action or purpose. Although there are a number of variant readings (between the AT and D05) involving the form of expression referring to the Holy Spirit, only one variant reading arises over this particular form. For more details, see Read-Heimerdinger, *The Bezan Text*, pp. 145–72, esp. 160–62.

35. Simon's position of observer, as he compared no doubt the manifestations of the Holy Spirit with what he has previously known of spiritual power, accounts for the form of expression in the Bezan text, τὸ πνεῦμα τὸ ἅγιον, which underlines the quality of holiness (see *Critical Apparatus*).

him and his money to damnation.[36] The strength of Peter's words recalls his denunciation of Ananias and Sapphira when they, too, showed a wrong attitude to money, though in a different way to Simon (5.3-4, 8-9). On both occasions, Peter discerns, on the basis of their concern with money, the true nature of their spiritual state. In the case of Simon, he sees that he has no place in the new community that is being created by the activity of the Holy Spirit.[37] The terms he uses are typical expressions denoting membership of the people of God among Jews, for to have a 'part or share' is found in the Jewish Scriptures referring to the distribution of the land of Israel among the twelve tribes (Deut. 12.12; 14.27, 29; cf. Wis. 2.9).[38] A further echo of the Scriptures is heard in the judgment 'your heart is not right with God' which may be compared with Ps. 77.37 LXX.

Peter offers Simon the possibility of escaping from his situation, and from the proclamation of his curse (v. 20), by urging him to repent and pray to the Lord. By 'the Lord' Peter could mean either Yahweh or Jesus. In the Bezan text, 'Lord' is never used of or by a non-Jewish person; it is possible that Peter considers Simon as sharing a common Jewish ancestry and therefore appeals to his knowledge of Yahweh through the Scriptures and tradition. It is interesting that in the Bezan text Simon himself avoids using the term 'Lord' but replaces it with 'God' when he responds to Peter (8.24 D05), suggesting that he himself is uncomfortable with it. The contrast between the term chosen by each speaker is stronger, and more meaningful, if Peter intends to refer to Jesus with whom Simon does not have a personal relationship, therefore preferring the term 'God' when he himself speaks of prayer.[39]

The description Peter gives of Simon's state recalls the use of the scriptural expression at Deut. 29.18 and Lam. 3.15. The context of the first mention is especially relevant, referring as it does to the people who, because their hearts are torn between serving Yahweh and serving idols, bear fruit that is 'poisonous and bitter'. The inevitable disaster anticipated by this double life is not just a personal one (Deut. 29.20-21) but will affect the whole nation (Deut. 29.19b, 22-28). The discernment that Peter exercises enables him to accurately perceive what lies behind Simon's allegiance to Jesus, a characteristic already evident in his dealings with Ananias and Sapphira, as mentioned above. But unlike on the earlier occasion, and unlike in the underlying Deu-

---

36. The optative εἴη expresses Peter's reaction in the strongest way possible, coupled with the noun ἀπώλεια which is the opposite of salvation (cf. Lk. 15.4, 6, 8, 9, 24, 32).

37. The expression ἐν τῷ λόγῳ τούτῳ is to be understood not as referring to the 'word' but in the more general sense of 'matter'. But cf. Barrett, I, pp. 414–15 for opinions to the contrary.

38. The expression in the LXX is οὐκ ἔστιν + dative + μερὶς οὐδὲ κλῆρος.

39. The indirectness of prayer in Simon's understanding is further suggested by the prepositional construction after the verb: δεήθητε ... πρὸς τὸν θεόν, which contrasts with the construction used by Peter: δεήθητι τοῦ κυρίου.

teronomy parallel, this time Peter has offered Simon the chance to be par-
doned.[40]

[a'] 8.24 *Simon's Plea*

8.24 Simon seizes on the possibility of pardon as he pleads with Peter and
John to pray for him ('on his behalf', AT). There is a fair amount of variation
between the two texts at this point, with the Bezan text consistently portraying
Simon's pleas as insistent and his distress as marked, in comparison with
which the AT presents a more banal account. To start with, the mere spelling
out in Codex Bezae of the addressees of Simon's words, 'he said to them' is
an indication given by the narrator that Simon is trying to create a personal
relationship with them (both Peter and John) as he speaks to them (cf. v. 19
where the addressees are not mentioned).[41] The notion of a relationship is
reinforced in the Bezan text by the personal pronoun 'to me' at the end of his
plea. The verb 'I beg' (παρακαλῶ D05), the same as at v. 19 D05, translated
there by 'pleading') expresses Simon's sense of urgency as he acknowledges
the seriousness of his situation, as does his definition of the warnings they
have pronouned (plural, εἰρήκατε) as 'these bad things'. Although Peter had
urged him to 'pray to the Lord' (see on v. 22 above), Simon steps back from
entering into prayer himself: not only does he ask the apostles to pray for him,
but in the Bezan text he uses the term 'God' which avoids the personal relationship of trust implicit in prayer to the 'Lord'. Finally, his distress is conveyed by his copious weeping.

This last element in the Bezan account of Simon's change of heart is
far from being a colourful detail. Another character in Luke's work had,
on an earlier occasion, 'wept bitterly', none other than Simon Peter after
denying Jesus three times (ἔκλαυσεν πικρῶς, Lk. 22.62). The association
of both weeping and bitterness in the story of one who bears the same
name sets up a parallel between the two characters – which is a reminder
of the weakness of Peter in the text of Codex Bezae, where Peter continues
to struggle with fully accepting Jesus and his message until his release
from prison in chapter 12 (see *Excursus* 5). The tradition that Simon was
the founder of Gnosticism, which was being propagated by the middle of
the second century, could well have provided a reason for the AT to avoid

---

40. The use of the term ἐπίνοια, 'intent', becomes part of the legend later surrounding Simon
according to which he was the father of Gnosticism, accompanied by Helena who represented the
'First Intuition', πρώτη ἔννοια (Justin, *1 Apol.* 26), also referred to as ἐπίνοια (Hippolytus,
Refutatio 6.19).

41. A detailed examination of the ways Luke introduces speeches shows that when πρός +
accusative is used after a verb of speaking, a relationship between the speaker and the addressee is
being established; the dative of the addressee (noun or pronoun) indicates, on the contrary, that
the relationship has already been secured or that there is a distance between the two parties. The
absence of addressee occurs for a number of reasons, often because it is clear from the context (as
in this case) who is being spoken to. See Read-Heimerdinger, *The Bezan Text*, pp. 176–82.

any hint of comparison here with Simon Peter. In fact, nothing is known for certain concerning Simon of Samaria: all that is conveyed by Luke's account is that he is on the right path towards becoming a disciple by the end of the story.

[BA-*A'*] 8.25-40 *Philip and the Ethiopian Eunuch*

Overview

Although the account of the conversion of the Ethiopian eunuch reads as a story complete in itself, it only takes on its full meaning when it is heard against the background of the earlier incidents involving Philip in Samaria. There, he had preached the message about Jesus and the kingdom of God, but failed to exercise proper discernment about the spiritual state of the Samaritans in general, and of Simon in particular. However, in his encounter with the Ethiopian eunuch it will become evident that he applies the lessons he has observed in Samaria to the new situation.

This concluding episode in the sub-sequence concerning Philip represents a crucial development in the spread of the gospel, as for the first time a Jesus-believer is presented as explaining the message about Jesus to a person who is unable to be circumcised. It is to be noted that, as with the Samaritans, it was not one of the apostles who carried out this critical step but one of the seven Hellenist leaders.

Structure and Themes

The structural analysis follows the longer text which includes v. 37 and a δέ clause in v. 39 (see *Critical Apparatus*). After a preliminary sentence to introduce the episode, the focus of the narrative shifts to the Ethiopian eunuch, though it is Philip's movements that provide the main framework [a–b || b'– a']. At the centre of the structure [h || h'] is the eunuch's question to Philip concerning the meaning of the passage of Isaiah he was reading and Philip's explanation in response:

Intro.	8.25a	The return from Samaria
[a]	8.26	The angel of the Lord directs Philip to the Gaza road
[b]	8.27a	Philip obeys
[c]	8.27b-28	The Ethiopian eunuch
[d]	8.29	The Spirit orders Philip to join the eunuch
[e]	8.30	Philip hears him reading from Isaiah
[f]	8.31	The eunuch request Philip
[g]	8.32-33	Isaiah 53.7-8
[h]	8.34	The eunuch's question about the passage
[h']	8.35	Philip's explanation about Jesus
[g']	8.36	The eunuch requests baptism
[f']	8.37a	Philip's condition
[e']	8.37b	The eunuch's declaration of faith
[d']	8.38	The eunuch's baptism

[c']	8.39a	The eunuch receives the Holy Spirit
[b']	8.39b	The angel of the Lord takes up Philip
[a']	8.40	Philip in Caesarea

Translation

	Codex Bezae D05	*Codex Vaticanus B03*
Intro.	**8.25** Now when they had borne witness and spoken the word of the Lord, they set off back to Hierosoluma. They announced the gospel to many villages of the Samaritans.	**8.25** Now when they had borne witness and spoken the word of the Lord, they set off back to Hierosoluma, announcing moreover the gospel to many villages of the Samaritans.
[a]	**26** But the angel of the Lord spoke to Philip saying, 'Get up, go down towards the south on the road that goes down from Ierousalem to Gaza, which is a desert'.	**26** But the angel of the Lord spoke to Philip saying, 'Get up and start going down towards the south on the road that goes down from Ierousalem to Gaza, which is a desert'.
[b]	**27a** And he got up and went.	**27a** And he got up and went.
[c]	**27b** And behold!, an Ethiopian man, a eunuch, a court ruler of a certain Queen Candace of Ethiopia who was in charge over all his treasure, had gone with the intention of worshipping Ierousalem, **28** and he was on his way back, seated on the chariot reading the prophet Isaiah.	**27b** And there, there was an Ethiopian man, a eunuch, a court ruler of Queen Candace of Ethiopia who was in charge over all her treasure, and who had gone with the intention of worshipping in Ierousalem. **28** He was on his way back and was seated on his chariot and reading the prophet Isaiah.
[d]	**29** The Spirit said to Philip,	**29** The Spirit said to Philip,
'Western' Text		*Codex Vaticanus*
	'Go on and join this chariot'.	'Go on and join this chariot'.
[e]	**30** So Philip went and heard him reading the prophet Isaiah and he said, 'Do you really understand what you are reading?'	**30** So Philip ran and heard him reading Isaiah the prophet and he said, 'Do you really understand what you are reading?'
[f]	**31** He said, 'However can I, unless someone guides me?' and he begged Philip to come up and sit with him.	**31** He said, 'However can I, unless someone guides me?' and he begged Philip to come up and sit with him.
[g]	**32** The passage of Scripture he was reading was this: 'As a sheep is led to slaughter, or a lamb before its shearer is dumb, so he opens not his mouth. **33** In the humiliation, justice was taken away from him. Who can describe his descendants? For his life is taken up from the earth.'	**32** The passage of Scripture he was reading was this: 'As a sheep is led to slaughter, or a lamb before its shearer is dumb, so he opens not his mouth. **33** In his humiliation, justice was taken away from him. Who can describe his descendants? For his life is taken up from the earth.'
[h]	**34** The eunuch said to Philip, 'I beg you, concerning whom does the prophet say this? About himself or about some other person?'	**34** The eunuch said to Philip, 'I beg you, concerning whom does the prophet say this? About himself or about some other person?'
[h']	**35** Philip opened his mouth and, beginning with this Scripture, announced to him the good news about Jesus.	**35** Philip opened his mouth and, beginning with this Scripture, announced to him the good news about Jesus.

[g′]	**36** As they went on down the way, they came to some water, and the eunuch said, 'Look! here is water. What is to prevent me being baptized?'
[f′]	**37a** He said to him, 'If you believe with all your heart, it is permissible'.
[e′]	**37b** He answered, 'I believe that the Son of God is Jesus, the Messiah'.
[d′]	**38** And he ordered the chariot to stop and they both went down into the water, Philip and the eunuch, and he baptized him.
[c′]	**39a** When they came up out of the water, the Holy Spirit fell on the eunuch.
[b′]	**39b** The angel of the Lord snatched Philip away from him and the eunuch did not see him any more, for he was going on his way, rejoicing.
[a′]	**40** Philip was found at Azotus, and he travelled on and announced the good news in all the towns until he came to Caesarea.

36 As they went on down the way, they came to some water, and the eunuch said, 'Look! here is water. What is to prevent me being baptized?'

38 And he ordered the chariot to stop and they both went down into the water, Philip and the eunuch, and he baptized him.

39 When they came up out of the water, the Spirit of the Lord snatched Philip away and the eunuch did not see him any more, for he was going on his way, rejoicing.

40 Philip was found at Azotus, and he travelled on and announced the good news in all the towns until he came to Caesarea.

Critical Apparatus

8.25 πολλάς τε (κώμας) B 𝔓⁷⁴ ℵ *rell* ‖ πολλὰς δέ D sa bo, d lac.

This clause follows a clause introduced by μὲν οὖν (8.25a) whose function is to bring an incident to a close at the same time as providing a transition between two incidents; μὲν οὖν normally anticipates a δέ clause that is the second part of the transition or the start of the new incident (Levinsohn, *Textual Connections*, pp. 137–50: 'The sentence featuring μέν provides the transition to the new incident, and presents the general background for it. Δέ then introduces the incident proper' [146]). In this instance, the δέ clause corresponding to μέν is found in 8.26 with the introduction of the angel of the Lord who speaks to Philip. The present clause, describing the evangelization of Samaritan villages by the apostles, provides background information: in B03 where it is introduced with τε, it is viewed as part and parcel of their return to Jerusalem, whereas with δέ in D05 it is more of the status of a clarification. (A similar variant of δέ/τε following a μὲν οὖν clause is found at 5.41-42 where B03 again joins the two activities of the apostles with τε and leaves the δέ clause to the start of the new section of the book at 6.1. D05, on the other hand, presents the second action of the apostles [their teaching in the Temple] as the correlation [δέ] of their joyful release from the Sanhedrin.)

8.26 ἀνάστηθι καὶ πορεύου B 𝔓⁷⁴ ℵ *rell* | ἀνάστηθι καὶ πορεύθητι C 181. 257. 2401 *pc* ‖ ἀναστὰς πορεύθητι D 𝔓⁵⁰, d lac.

The expressions of B03 and D05 are practically equivalent, with the emphasis in the former on the start of the movement (aor. imper. followed by pres. imper.) and in the latter on the act of going and the urgency of it (aor. part. followed by aor. imper.). The pattern of D05 is echoed in the fulfilment of the command, 8.27. Though πορεύθητι may be rare, it is found again in the order of Jesus to Ananias (cf. Zerwick and Grosvenor, *Analysis*, Acts 9.11, p. 379).

8.27 βασιλίσσης (Αἰθιόπων) B 𝔓⁵⁰ ℵ A C Dˢ·ᵐ· E 81. 88. 1175 *pc* | τῆς βας. L H P Ψ 049. 056. 33 𝔐 | βας. τινός D* (t), d lac.

The tone of B03 is, as often, purely narrative. Candace is the queen of the Ethiopians. D05, with Luke's typical marker of representativity, τις, introduces her as a representative of foreigners far-removed from Israel.

γάζης αὐτῆς B 𝔓⁷⁴ ℵ Dᴮ *rell* || γάζ. αὐτοῦ D*, d lac.

Delebecque comments (*Les deux Actes*, p. 64): 'par négligence, le copiste de D écrit αὐτοῦ pour αὐτῆς'. This would be undoubtedly true were it not that the word γάζης could have a symbolic meaning by virtue of its assimilation with the name of the town, Γάζαν (v. 26). The sense suggested is that the 'treasure' that the eunuch is in charge of is in some way his own.

ὃς ἐληλύθει B 𝔓⁵⁰ ℵ² C² Dᴮ E H P (Ψ) 049. 056. (33) 𝔐 (it) || ἐληλύθει D* 𝔓⁷⁴ᵛⁱᵈ ℵ* A C* 915. 1505 a p vg syᵖ co, d lac.; Oecum.

With the relative pronoun, B03 minimizes the force of the verb, by giving it a subordinate role: καὶ ἰδού ... ὃς ἐληλύθει. In contrast, D05 gives it its full force because it is the main verb after καὶ ἰδού.

εἰς Ἰερουσαλήμ B 𝔓⁷⁴ ℵ *rell* | ἐν Ἰ. Dᴮ L 1175 || Ἰερ. D*, d lac.

D05 considers Ierousalem to be the object of worship. This synecdoche, if intentional, is an ironic comment on the status of Ierousalem as the holy city. According to Parker (*Codex Bezae*, p. 149), 'Dᴮ has supplied the wrong preposition, agreeing by chance with L'; however, according to the pattern of prepositions εἰς/ἐν followed by D05, it is quite normal for ἐν, as in D05ᴮ, to be used in order to focus on an activity that went on in a place (worship) despite a main verb of movement that requires εἰς (Read-Heimerdinger, *The Bezan Text*, pp. 192–97).

8.28 ἦν δέ (ὑποστρέφων) B C 431. 614. 913. 1108. 1175. 1611. 2138. 2412 e p || ἦν τε D ℵ *rell*, d lac.— καὶ καθήμενος ἐπὶ τοῦ ἅρματος αὐτοῦ B 𝔓⁷⁴ ℵ Dᴮ *rell* || καθ. ἐπὶ τ. ἅρμ. D* syᵖ, d lac.; Cass.— καὶ ἀνεγίνωσκεν B 𝔓⁵⁰ ℵ² C E H L P Ψ 049. 056. 614 𝔐 | ἀνεγ. 𝔓⁷⁴ ℵ* (A) 33. 88. 323. 547. 945. 1175. 1270. 1505. 1739. 1837. 1891. 2344. 2495 *al* r || ἀναγινώσκων D lat sa mae, d lac.; Cass.

By virtue of these three variants, D05 produces a sentence that ties the activity of the eunuch closely to his return from Ierousalem, beginning with τε to indicate the close relationship between the two main actions: ἐληλύθει (in the pluperfect) … ἦν τε ὑποστρέφων καθήμενος … ἀναγινώσκων. Not so in B03, which moves on to a new development in the story with the return journey, and then separates out the different activities: ἦν δὲ ὑποστρέφων καὶ καθήμενος … καὶ ἀνεγίνωσκεν. The participle ἀναγινώσκων in D05 closely links his reading of the Scriptures to his visit to Ierousalem.

[Eight folios of Codex Bezae are missing from 8.29b to 10.14b for the Greek text, and from 8.20b to 10.4 for the Latin. Readings for comparison with B03 have to be taken, therefore, from other witnesses that from time to time attest a variant text, either Greek or, more often, the early versions. They will be referred to as the 'Western text' (WT). None, however, vary so consistently or extensively as does Codex Bezae. The uncial E08 cannot be used as a constant basis for comparison since its Greek text is most likely to be a retroversion of the Greek underlying its Latin text, which has the place of honour on the left hand page. The most notable 'Western' MS is the Middle Egyptian Codex Glazier (mae, also known as G⁶⁷) which often, though not always, has the support of the Old Latin Codex Floriacensis (h). The procedure followed for the missing pages of D05 is quite different from the practice we have rigorously followed elsewhere of comparing individual MSS; it is far from satisfactory but unavoidable in the absence of a single MS that consistently attests a variant text.]

8.30 προσδραμών B 𝔓⁷⁴ ℵ *rell* ‖ προσελθών 𝔓⁵⁰ 181. 460 syᵖ sa mae.
  While B03 indicates that Philip hurried to carry out the angel's order, the WT shows his compliance by taking up the verb of the command (Πρόσελθε … προσελθών).

(ἀναγινώσκοντος) Ἡσαΐαν τὸν προφήτην B 𝔓⁷⁴ ℵ 33. 88. 945. 1175. 1646. 1739. 1891 ‖ τ. προφ. Ἡ. E H L P Ψ 049. 056. 614 𝔐.
  B03 inverts the word order used in the previous mention of the eunuch's reading of Isaiah (cf. 8.28), unlike the WT which maintains the same order. Elsewhere, when Luke places the name of the prophet first the reference is to the actual words spoken (Isaiah: Lk. 3.4; Acts 28.27; cf. however, Acts 2.16 B03) or to the prophet himself (Elisha: Lk. 4.27), but not the book (Lk. 4.17).

8.31 ὁδηγήσει B* 𝔓⁵⁰ ℵ C E L 1. 6. 69. 88. 330. 614. 1175. 2344. 2412 *al* ‖ -ση 𝔓⁷⁴ A B² H L P Ψ 049. 056. 1739 𝔐.
  B03 uses the future in place of the subjunctive (cf. Zerwick, *Biblical Greek*, §§ 340–44; Zerwick and Grosvenor, *Analysis*, p. 377). At 2.37 and 4.16, B03 reads the subjunctive against the future of D05.

8.32 κείροντος B P 33. 1739 𝔐 ‖ -ραντος 𝔓⁵⁰ᵛⁱᵈ·⁷⁴ ℵ A C E L Ψ 049. 056. 36. 69. 88. 323. 330. 614. 1175. 1243. 1505. 1611. 2344. 2412. 2495 *al*.

Both forms, κείρων and κείρας, are known (B-A-G, κείρω) with the same variant found in the Greek MSS of Isa. 53.7 from where the citation is taken.

8.33 (Ἐν τῇ ταπεινώσει) αὐτοῦ C E Ψ 𝔐̣ sy ‖ *om.* B 𝔓⁷⁴ ℵ A 1739 *pc* lat; Ir^lat.

The insertion of the pronoun may have been intended to clarify the meaning of a sentence that is difficult in Greek as well as Hebrew; cf. Ireneus, *Adv. Haer.,* IV, 23.1.

8.37 εἶπεν δὲ αὐτῷ (– 1869)· Εἰ πιστεύεις ἐξ ὅλης τῆς (– 36. 180. 307. 453. 610. 1642. 1877ᶜ) καρδίας σου (– 323), ἔξεστιν. ἀποκριθεὶς δὲ (κ. ἀπ. 1642. 1877ᶜ | ἀπ. τε 1780) (+ εὐνοῦχος 88^cmg. 1851. 2805) εἶπεν (+ αὐτῷ 88^cmg 1851. 2805)· Πιστεύω τὸν υἱὸν τοῦ θεοῦ εἶναι (+ τὸν 4^cmg. 429ᶜ. 455. 628^cvid. 1642. 1869. 1877ᶜ)Ἰησοῦν Χριστόν (Χρ. Ἰ. 4^cmg): 4^cmg. 36. 88^cmg. 94. 103. 180. 307. 323. 385. 429*. 453. 455. 464. 606. 607. 610. 628^cvid. 630. 641. 876. 913. 945. 1501. 1509. 1607. 1610. 1642. 1739. 1751. 1765. 1780. 1830. 1832. 1839. 1851. 1855. 1869. 1877ᶜ. 1891. 1892ᶜ. 2200. 2298. 2494. 2805 it vg^cl sy^h** mae aeth^ms; Ir Tert Cyp Ambrst Pac Ambr Aug Theoph PsOec ChrAq | εἶπεν δὲ αὐτῷ ὁ Φίλιππος·Ἐὰν πιστεύεις ἐξ ὅλης τῆς καρδίας σου, σωθήσει. ἀποκριθεὶς δὲ εἶπεν· Πιστ. εἰς τὸν Χρ. τὸν υἱὸν τ. θ. E 1884 ‖ *om.* B 𝔓^45.74 ℵ A C H L P Ψ 049. 056. 0142. 4*. 33^vid. 88*. 206ˢ. 221*. 452*. 628*. 808*. 1877*. 1892*. 2544* *rell* vg^ww sy^p.h sa bo aeth; Chr Theoph.

K. Aland ('Der neutestamentliche Text in der vorkonstantinischen Epoche', in E. Romero-Pose [ed.], *PLEROMA. Salus carnis* [Santiago de Compostela: Publicaciones Compostellanum, 1990], pp. 53–79 [66–70]) sets out the eight forms in which this verse is found in the 64 MSS he consulted, all of them minuscules except for E08 (whose singular Greek form is due to its being a retroversion of its Latin text). The reading of Ireneus (*Adv. Haer.*, III, 12.8) represents the text in its simplest form: *Credo filium dei esse Iesum,* as does the Greek fragment of the Catena of Ireneus: Πιστεύω τὸν υἱὸν τοῦ θεοῦ εἶναι Ἰησοῦν Χριστόν (cf. *Adv. Haer.*, IV, 23.2). Ir^lat, together with b dem vg^mss, omit Χριστόν. Despite the weight of evidence against the reading, the witnesses that include it are a mixed collection without the usual profile of the WT readings (see analysis in J. Read-Heimerdinger, 'La foi de l'eunuque éthiopien: le problème textuel de Actes 8:37', *Études Théologiques et Religieuses* 4 [1988], pp. 521–28). The significance of the reading is discussed in detail in the *Commentary*.

8.39 πνεῦμα κυρίου ἥρπασεν τὸν Φίλιππον B 𝔓^45vid.74vid ℵ *rell* ‖ πν. ἅγιον ἐπέπεσεν ἐπὶ τὸν εὐνοῦχον, ἄγγελος δὲ κυ. ἥρπ. τ. Φ. A 36. 323. 453. 467. 876. 913. 945. 1739. 1765. 1891. 2298 *pc* l p w vg^ms sy^h** mae geo arm; Ephr Hier Aug Cass.

The reading of B03 has echoes of the scene when Elijah was taken up: 'It may be the Spirit of the Lord has caught him up (ἦρεν)' (LXX 4 Kgdms 2.16: cf. 3 Kgdms 18.12). This may have been deliberate, or it may have been an error caused by a scribe accidentally jumping from πνεῦμα to κυρίου in the following clause. There could equally have been a theological reason for wanting to avoid the suggestion that the Holy Spirit could fall on someone without the presence of the apostles. See M. Black, 'The Holy Spirit in the Western Text of Acts', in E.J. Epp and G.D. Fee (eds), *New Testament Textual Criticism* [Oxford: Clarendon, 1981]), pp. 166–67: 'the shorter text could … have arisen by scribal parablepsis … The omission of the Holy Spirit clause is more readily explained than its insertion, for, as Menoud ('The Western Text and the Theology of Acts', *SNTS Bulletin* 2 [1951], pp. 19–32 [30]) has convincingly argued, its inclusion contradicts the narrative a few verses earlier, which implies that the Spirit came only through the hands of the apostles.' The arguments are considered more fully in the *Commentary*.

(τὸν Φίλιππον) ἀπ᾽ αὐτοῦ p y sy^hmg mae; Aug^b || *om.* B ℵ *rell.*

Several of the witnesses to the longer text (cf. previous *vl*) also specify that Philip was taken away from the eunuch, using a construction found in the LXX at Deut. 28.31; Job 24.9; Bar. 4.26, where it has a certain connotation of violence.

(ἐπορεύετο γὰρ) αὐτοῦ τὴν ὁδόν B | τ. ὁδ. sa; Ir^lat || τ. ὁδ. αὐτοῦ 𝔓^74 ℵ *rell.*

B03 is alone in drawing attention to the noun by pre-positioning the non-emphatic possessive adjective (cf. v. 22 above). The intention is possibly to suggest the metaphorical meaning of 'the Way', the path of the Jewish Jesus-believers (cf. 9.2). A similar effect is achieved by the omission of the pronoun altogether in some versions.

Commentary

Introduction 8.25 *The Return from Samaria*
8.25 The start of the new episode is signalled by the connective μὲν οὖν, which Luke uses as he moves on from one episode to another to introduce an event arising from the previous episode, which in turn is then followed by a second event signalled with the connective δέ (see *Critical Apparatus*).[42] On the face of it, this first event, the return to Hierosoluma, is mentioned simply as a concluding statement to round off the Samaria episode. If attention is paid to the language, however, Luke can be seen to be making a comment of considerable significance.

The apostles (and it is likely that the narrator means Philip, too) begin to return from Samaria after having successfully borne witness to Jesus there in accordance with his command (cf. 1.8). The fulfilment of Jesus' order is

---

42. Commentaries attach 8.25 to the previous episode but although a sentence connected by μὲν οὖν is transitional (see Barrett, I, p. 418), the fact that it anticipates the new episode and a second incident connected with δέ, means that it more properly belongs to the new episode rather than the previous one. Cf. Acts 8.4; 9.31; 11.2 D05, 19; 12.5.

implied by the choice of the expression the 'word of the Lord'. This is the first time that this particular phrase occurs in Acts, except in Codex Bezae where it was found at 6.7 with reference to the spread of the gospel after the election of the seven Hellenists. Otherwise, the expression chosen has always been the 'word of God', and it has always been used with reference to the activity of the apostles. As was noted before (see *Critical Apparatus* and *Commentary* on 6.7), in Codex Bezae Luke makes use of the alternative forms to distinguish between the message or revelation of God in a general sense (as already contained in the Jewish Scriptures, for example), and the specific teaching of, or about, Jesus. That distinction will not be maintained in the AT, but in all the earlier references to the 'word' in both the Bezan text and the AT it is the case that the apostles have been solely concerned with the 'word of God' (cf. 4.31; 6.2; 8.14). Their teaching has been focused on Jesus as the Messiah who fulfilled the Scriptures, as they explained and interpreted them in such a way as to justify their belief in him as the one promised by God to bring salvation to the Jews and restoration to Israel. Now, for the first time, Luke notes that they had spoken to the Samaritans the message of Jesus, the 'word of the Lord' – no longer confining the benefits of the Messiah to those who were faithful to worship in the Temple in Ierousalem but extending their proclamation of his teaching to people who had hitherto been regarded as beyond the pale, even to the point of expecting God to confirm his acceptance of the Samaritans by sending the gift of the Holy Spirit.

Such a step was of the greatest significance for the people of Samaria, for whom the principal cause of conflict with other Jews had been the insistence on the Ierousalem Temple as the only acceptable place for worship. At last, what the apostles have experienced in Ierousalem from the hands of the Temple authorities, and what they have heard from Stephen, has apparently made them realize how both Ierousalem and the Temple have lost their unique importance in the message of Jesus so that neither is any longer an issue of discord. A confirmation of their progress in their understanding of Jesus' message is immediately given by the narrator as he reports that they returned to 'Hierosoluma'. Just as the apostles had been attached to the 'word of God' until their visit to Samaria, so, too, they had been firmly settled in Ierousalem, the holy city (cf. 8.1c D05, 14 D05).

By his choice of wording – both the 'word of the Lord' and Hierosoluma – the narrator makes a statement of the highest importance, namely that a major shift has taken place in the progress of the apostles, represented by Peter and John, towards aligning themselves with Jesus. The consequences of the positive steps taken by Peter and John are that they make their way back with Philip to Hierosoluma, not in haste but, putting into action their new awareness of the equal status of the Samaritans, by taking time to announce the good news in many of their villages as they go. The importance of Jews and Samaritans talking to each other must not be underestimated – the conflict

between the two peoples that had existed for centuries has finally been overcome by Jews who believe in Jesus as the Messiah.

[a] 8.26 *The Angel of the Lord Directs Philip to the Gaza Road*
8.26 The narrator, having brought to a satisfying conclusion the interlude
involving Peter and John, now turns his attention back to Philip. For although
Philip, as a Hellenist, has already enabled the spread of the 'word of the Lord'
(see *Commentary*, 6.7) and has been associated with Hierosoluma rather than
Ierousalem (see 8.1b), yet his work in Samaria resulted neither in the gift of
the Holy Spirit nor in the exposure of Simon's insincerity. As was noted
above (on 8.15-16), the acceptance by the Samaritans of Philip's preaching
had been a mass response, with a superficiality that Philip had failed to discern or challenge. The encounter the angel of the Lord leads him to in the final
episode of the chapter will ensure that the lesson enacted for him by the
apostles, as he observed them laying hands on each Samaritan individually in
turn, has been learnt.

The formula referring to the angel, ἄγγελος κυρίου, is that used in the
LXX to translate the frequent mention of the divine representative who, as
is generally understood in the Jewish Scriptures, is none other than God
himself. This is the second time in Acts that he intervenes directly in
events, the first occasion being to release the apostles from the Temple
prison. The order given to Philip ('Get up') may reflect something of his
discouragement at the outcome of his own evangelization in Samaria;[43]
certainly, he is given a new task that causes him to set out in a fresh
direction. The instructions are carefully precise: he is to head south (the
opposite direction to Samaria which was in the north) and join the road
leading away from Ierousalem, in the sense of the holy city, towards the
town of Gaza, one of the five coastal towns of the Philistines. The name of
the destination is no accident: the meaning of the word in Greek, γάζα, is
'treasure' or 'treasury', but it had been a desert since its destruction
around 100 BCE. Like other encounters with the divine (cf. John the
Baptist, Lk. 3.2; the lost sheep, 15.34), this one will also take place in the
wilderness, far from the ancient holy city of the Jews.[44]

[b] 8.27a *Philip Obeys*
8.27a Philip fulfils the angel's command in perfect obedience, the terms of the
order being repeated to describe his response (especially according to the
wording of Codex Bezae, see *Critical Apparatus*). His willingness to under-

---

43. The verb ἀνίστημι may have a literal, physical meaning, but it is also used to indicate the
beginning of decisive action in a metaphorical sense (cf. 9.18, Saul; 10.13, 20, Peter).

44. The parallels between the eunuch and the lost sheep in particular are discussed in J. Rius-
Camps, *De Jerusalén a Antioquía: Génesis de la iglesia cristiana. Comentario lingüístico y exegético a Hch 1–12* (Córdoba: El Almendro, 1989), pp. 276–50.

take a task that was not only incomprehensible but also potentially dangerous conveys a highly positive evaluation of Philip's disposition.[45]

[c] 8.27b-28 *The Ethiopian Eunuch*

8.27b The new character of the Ethiopian eunuch is brought onto the scene with the formula 'And behold!' (καὶ ἰδού), so common in the Jewish Scriptures. Its purpose is not simply to draw the audience's attention to a dramatic development in the story but above all to present a scene through the eyes of the participant already on stage.[46] In other words, we discover the man on the Jerusalem–Gaza road as if we were there with Philip. The narrator then fills in some background information:

1. The man is Ethiopian. His origin in Africa (modern-day Sudan) situates him as coming from the furthest regions of the earth (cf. Ps. 68.32; Zeph. 3.10). He is nevertheless a Jew, for Luke introduces Gentiles into the narrative only at 10.1 with Cornelius.[47]

2. He is a eunuch (sometimes translated in English as 'chamberlain') – the practice of removing the genitals of court officials in the Orient was common. The purpose would appear to be to prevent any possible competition for the attentions of the women kept by the court; the result, in any case, was that the man could have no hope of descendants.

3. He held the position of 'court ruler', in charge of all the monarch's 'treasure' or 'treasury', for which the word is γάζα, the same word as the place which lay at the end of the road he was travelling on (Gaza, cf. v. 26), thus making plain the metaphorical meaning of the direction of his journey. According to Plutarch, the guardians of the royal treasure were customarily eunuchs,[48] a fact echoed in references in the Jewish Scriptures.[49]

4. The name of the ruling queen was Candace, a hereditary title rather than a personal name, whose country is named for a second time as

---

45. Various elements of the angel's instructions in Acts 8 are reminiscent of the parable of the Good Samaritan (Lk. 10.30-37): the road (ἐν τῇ ὁδῷ ἐκείνῃ, v. 31; ὁδεύων, v. 33) going down (κατέβαινεν, v. 30; καταβαίνων, v. 31 D05) from Ierousalem (ἀπὸ Ἰερουσαλήμ, v. 30), the assistance of the Samaritan (Σαμαρίτης ... τις, v. 33), the order to go (Πορεύου, v. 37), and do likewise. Other indications will be noted as the story progresses. The result is that Philip is aligned with the character presented by Jesus as a supreme example of one who, despite his inferior status (see *Excursus* 1), fully accomplishes the Law and is destined to have eternal life (Lk. 10.25-28). See also the notes on 8.29, 30 below.

46. 'In many cases, where we find the word "behold" (hinneh) the narrator shows us a certain detail from the point of view of one of the characters ... the narrator explicitly informs us that what is being described is what one of the characters is seeing at that moment, even though it has been proved to us that the narrator actually knew this beforehand or knows more than that character discerns at moment' (S. Bar-Efrat, *Narrative Art in the Bible* [Sheffield: Sheffield Academic Press, 1989; repr. T&T Clark International, 2004], pp. 35–36).

47. Luke presents the Jesus-believers' openness to the universal nature of the Messiah as a gradual progression, advancing step by step (see *General Overview* to Section II).

48. Plutarch, *Demetrius* 25.5: ἐπιεικῶς γὰρ εἰώθεσαν εὐνούχους ἔχειν γαζοφύλακας.

49. 2 Kgs 23.11 refers to the keeper of the Temple treasury, Nathan-Melech, as a eunuch.

Ethiopia as a way of underlining the importance of the origin of the eunuch. The Bezan text designates her with a Lukan device, βασιλίσσης τινός, 'a certain queen', as a representative of the rulers of Ethiopia and so standing for the 'daughter of my dispersed ones' who would bring offerings in the last days to God (Zeph. 3.10 MT).

8.27c-28 The description of the eunuch continues with an account of his movements:

1. He had gone to Ierousalem with the intention of worshipping. The pluperfect verb followed by the future participle indicates an action that belongs to the past, and implies that the intention was frustrated in some way.
2. The focus of the account is on the fact that the eunuch was on his way back from Ierousalem, again consigning his visit to the past.[50] He was sitting on his chariot, a circumstantial detail that will serve to move on the story as the action develops but also will act as a 'peg' on which to hang a scriptural paradigm (see 8.38).
3. He was reading the prophet Isaiah – the picture is one of him holding a papyrus scroll in Greek, from which he was reading aloud.

Various facts are implicit in the narrator's presentation of the man Philip met, facts that would have been readily obvious to a Jewish audience but that people without an awareness of Jewish principles and teaching may well have failed to deduce:

1. The man is a Jew from the Diaspora who had undertaken a long pilgrimage to worship in Ierousalem; he had furthermore acquired, at no little expense, a scroll of the prophet Isaiah.
2. His inability to be circumcised would cause him to be despised and viewed as an outcast (cf. Lev. 21.16-23; Deut. 23.2).
3. His journey to Jerusalem suggests he had heard something about the Messiah that gave him hope that things had changed and that he had a 'future in the sacred community'[51] after all. But his disappointment means that he found no-one in Ierousalem (not even the apostles! cf. 8.1c D05) who explained to him the good news about Jesus.
4. Eunuchs are given a special mention in the prophecies of Isaiah concerning the messianic age, and it is no accident that Luke presents him as having chosen the scroll of Isaiah to read:
   'To the eunuchs who keep my sabbaths, who choose the things that please me and hold fast my covenant ... I will give them an everlasting name which shall not be cut off; [together with foreigners who join themselves to the Lord] these I will bring to my holy mountain and make them joyful in my house of prayer...' (Isa. 56.3-7).

---

50. The periphrastic verb, ἦν ... ὑποστρέφων, draws special attention to the eunuch's action of returning home.
51. *Jewish Study Bible,* Isa. 56.3-6.

[d] 8.29 *The Spirit Orders Philip to Join the Eunuch*
[From the middle of this verse to 10.14b, the Greek text of Codex Bezae is missing (see *Critical Apparatus*).]

8.29 It is now no longer the angel of the Lord but the Spirit who speaks to Philip. It is characteristic of Luke's usage not to include the adjective 'holy' when the Spirit gives guidance to a believer.[52] The Spirit is to be distinguished from the angel of the Lord who gave Philip the initial order to head in the direction of the Gaza road: in that instance, Philip was commanded to take a new direction contrary to that which he was already embarked upon, circumstances in which the Spirit is never found to act in Luke's writings. Now that Philip is committed to the Lord's plan, however, the Spirit intervenes to give specific guidance, instructing him to go up to the chariot and join it.[53]

[e] 8.30 *Philip Hears Him Reading from Isaiah*
8.30 Philip's response is as prompt as his obedience to the angel, as he runs up to the chariot.[54] Naming the book of Isaiah for a second time, the narrator relates how Philip hears the eunuch reading aloud and asks whether he understands what he is reading. The three-fold repetition of the verb 'read' (ἀναγινώσκω) in this account (cf. 8.28, 30a, 30b)[55] highlights the play on words in the Greek of Philip's enquiry, for ἀναγινώσκω is a compound of the verb 'understand' (γινώσκω).[56]

[f] 8.31 *The Eunuch's Request to Philip*
8.31 The eunuch himself acknowledges his need of a guide to explain the sense of what he is reading and, recognizing that Philip is that person, he invites him to sit with him in the chariot, so accomplishing the Spirit's intention for Philip (cf. 8.29).

[g] 8.32-33 *Isaiah 53.7-8*
8.32-33 The citation from Isa. 53.7-8 prepares for the central elements of this episode. The verb 'read' is repeated for a fourth time, a reflection of the fact that the Scriptures were read faithfully over and over again and were well known, and yet their meaning was not grasped. The passage was a key extract

---

52. Read-Heimerdinger, *The Bezan Text*, pp. 158–60; see also on 8.18, *Critical Apparatus*.

53. Echoes of the parable of the Good Samaritan can be heard once again: the Samaritan 'went up' to (προσελθών) the injured man (Lk. 10.34), and thus became (lit.) 'close' (πλησίον) to him (i.e. he became his 'neighbour', 10.36).

54. The verb προστρέχω is not read by some witnesses (see *Critical Apparatus*). The ones that do, provide the only occasion on which Luke uses the verb; significantly, it is otherwise found in Mark's Gospel (Mk 10.17) in the passage that Luke uses as a basis for his parable of the Good Samaritan.

55. ἀναγινώσκω is yet another term taken from the parable of the Good Samaritan and which Luke adds to the material borrowed from Mark (Lk. 10.26, cf. Mk 10.17-19).

56. The Vulgate reproduces the play on words: *intellegis quae legis?*

from the second part of Isaiah which speaks of the humiliation of the messianic figure prophesied by the author. The eunuch's preoccupation with the passage recalls the puzzlement of the disciples on the road to Emmaus (Codex Bezae reads Oulammaous)[57] as they struggled to understand how their hopes that Jesus was the redeemer of Israel could have come to nothing with his crucifixion. On his visit to Ierousalem, the eunuch has no doubt come across discussion about exactly the issue that Isaiah appears to anticipate.

The citation makes certain modifications to the text as it appears in the LXX or Hebrew text with two parallel sets of four lines each. In Luke's text, the opening line of the first set and the closing line of the second have been omitted (in italics):

> *Though oppressed and afflicted he did not open his mouth.*
>   Like a sheep that is led to the slaughter
>   or like a lamb that is dumb before its shearer,
>   so he does not open his mouth.
> In his humiliation, justice was taken away from him;
>   As for his descendants, who will speak of them?
>   For his life is taken from the earth.
> *He was led to death for the sins of my people.*

The omission of the opening line can be accounted for by its repetition in line 4; that of the last line is more noteworthy, leaving out as it does (intentionally?) the idea of Jesus' death being a vicarious one.

[h] 8.34 *The Eunuch's Question about the Passage*
8.34 The eunuch's question forms the climax of the first half [h–a] of this episode and reflects a real debate for which evidence exists, as to whether Isaiah was speaking of his own suffering as was contended by Hellenistic Jews, or the Messiah as the Palestinian Jews claimed.[58] Within the development of the narrative, the question naturally prepares the way for Philip to introduce the topic of Jesus.[59]

[h'] 8.35 *Philip's Explanation about Jesus*
8.35 The description of Philip's response represents the first element of the second half [h'–a'] of this episode and gives full weight to the solemnity of the moment – unlike the sheep of the quotation, he opens his mouth to declare the good news about Jesus. This is not simply some opportunistic preaching to

---

57. For an interpretation of the significance of the name, see J. Read-Heimerdinger and J. Rius-Camps, 'Emmaous or Oulammaous? Luke's Use of the Jewish Scriptures in the Text of Luke 24 in Codex Bezae', *RCatT* 27 (2002), pp. 23–42.

58. Cf. *EWNT*, III, pp. 12–14.

59. The eunuch's question is yet another echo of the pericope in the Gospel containing the parable of the Good Samaritan, for in a similar fashion in Luke 10 the lawyer's question, 'Who is my neighbour?' (10.29) prepares the way for Jesus to tell the parable.

someone who happened to ask the right questions; on the contrary, it is a moment that fits perfectly into the divine plan such as Luke has been carefully setting out in the preceding narrative, and one that he has prepared for meticulously in the 'clues' he has been dropping about the significance of the eunuch (see on 8.27-28 above). For, at this moment, in Philip's proclamation of Jesus, the Ethiopian eunuch's fate is turned upside down. Despite his exemplary piety, seen in his journey to Ierousalem and in his eagerness to know and understand the Scriptures, he is a eunuch whose mutilated physical condition prevents him from fully participating in the Jewish people. That is all about to change.

The good news about Jesus is that the old regulations and prohibitions no longer apply, as will become apparent in the following verses. Since the scroll of Isaiah was to hand, it is entirely plausible that Philip went on ('starting from this Scripture') to consider Isaiah 56 where he could point to the promises that eunuchs were given free access to worshipping God on the same basis as other Jews (see Isa. 56.3-7, cited above in discussing Acts 8.28). In the original context of Isaiah, it is in the Temple ('my house') that this worship is seen as taking place ('my house shall become a house of prayer'). By this stage in Luke's story, however, it has been made abundantly plain that the Temple is no more to be considered to be the privileged place for worship.

It is noteworthy that Philip is not said to preach 'the Messiah' to the eunuch as he had done in Samaria (cf. 8.5); rather he announced Jesus, the man who only recently had fulfilled the prophecy of Isaiah as the servant of God, the one who had been rejected, humiliated and killed in Ierousalem by the people he had come to save.

[g'] 8.36 *The Eunuch Requests Baptism*

8.36 The conversation unfolds as the eunuch and Philip continue to travel along the road away from Ierousalem (cf. v. 26).[60] The point of departure is given a metaphorical significance by the example set by Jesus whose own departure ('exodus') from Ierousalem was spoken about in the transfiguration scene (Lk. 9.31). The example serves as a motif underlying many of the journeys in Acts, as has already been seen with the apostles (cf. 1.4, 12; and 8.1, 14, 25 above) and will re-occur most insistently in the case of Paul.[61]

---

60. The detail that it is a 'downward' journey away from the holy city is reinforced by the preposition κατά.

61. For a summary of the journeying motif with respect to Paul and Ierousalem, see Rius-Camps, 'The Gradual Awakening of Paul's Awareness of his Mission to the Gentiles', in T.N. Nicklas and M. Tilly (eds), *Apostelgeschichte als Kirchengeschichte. Text, Traditionen und antike Auslegungen* (BZNW, 122; Berlin: Walter de Gruyter, 2003), pp. 281–96.

As they travel, they come across water.[62] The eunuch then has another question for Philip which is full of meaning: 'What is to prevent me being baptized?' This is no rhetorical question that occurs to the eunuch because they happen to pass some water and he thinks they may as well make use of it. From what Luke has said about this man, the hearers of the story know that he had wanted to be accepted as one who worshipped the true God but he had been prevented from being accepted by the community of Israel because he cannot be circumcised. Now, though, Philip has explained to him about Jesus and the eunuch has understood the teaching well, including the news that his physical condition no longer bars him from belonging fully to the people of God. So he asks the question that would be asked on the day that a convert to Judaism stood beside the water ready to be baptized, 'What is to prevent him being baptized?'[63] Hitherto, the answer the eunuch would have heard would have been, 'His inability to be circumcised'.

On this occasion, according to the MSS that do not read v. 37, there is no answer so that the question is indeed a rhetorical one, nothing more than a suggestion that they go ahead with baptism. According to a diverse range of witnesses (see *Critical Apparatus*), however, Philip does give an answer, one that is, as the eunuch anticipates, somewhat different from what he would have received before.

[f′] 8.37a *Philip's Condition*
8.37a The condition for baptism stated by Philip is striking for its simplicity, requiring only belief 'with all your heart'.[64] On these grounds, baptism is permissible, ἔξεστιν. The word used is the legal term found in the pronouncements and questionings of the Pharisees when they challenge Jesus: the prohibition laid down by the Law no longer exists on the basis of the new conditions established by Jesus for entering the people of God.

[e′] 8.37b *The Eunuch's Declaration of Faith*
8.37b The object of belief must have been clear enough to the eunuch for Philip not to have to spell it out; certainly, it is quite clear from the eunuch's

---

62. In much the same way as Philip and the eunuch come across water, the Good Samaritan comes across the man who is lying wounded in the road. In neither instance were the travellers looking for anything but circumstances bring them into contact with an element that brings the story to its climax.

63. Peter will use the same expression when describing the gift of the Holy Spirit to the Gentile household of Cornelius in Caesarea – he could not understand how the Spirit could be given to uncircumcised Gentiles, but since God saw fit to send the Spirit, how could he, Peter, have prevented him? ἐγὼ τίς ἤμην δυνατὸς κωλῦσαι τὸν θεόν; (11.17).

64. The condition that Philip lays down is strikingly similar to the summary of the Law given by the lawyer in Luke's Gospel who enquires of Jesus about how to inherit eternal life, prompting the parable of the Good Samaritan: 'You shall love the Lord your God with all your heart...' (Lk. 10.27).

response that he understands what Philip has in mind. The actual wording varies from one document to another but the earliest form seems to have been a recognition that the Son of God was Jesus, and that he was the Messiah. Commentators who examine this verse generally suppose that Philip's response to the eunuch and the subsequent declaration of faith were inserted into the primitive text by later scribes in order to bring the text into line with Christian liturgical practice, on the grounds that a baptism without a confession of faith was unthinkable. There are two principal objections to this view:

1. The verse is found in witnesses as early as the latter half of the second century CE, but the earliest evidence for baptismal confessions of faith dates from after the fourth century. In the writings of the second and third centuries (Justin, Tertullian, Hippolytus, Cyprian, Irenaeus), one finds not declarations of faith but interrogations of the type, 'Do you believe in Jesus Christ' and the response, 'Yes, I believe'. It was the baptizer, not the baptizand, who asked questions and the candidate answered them briefly without making an actual statement himself. When such a statement was made, it was before the day of baptism, at the end of catechism.

2. The contents of the eunuch's statement of faith differ from the baptismal or credal formulas found either in the New Testament or in the early Church Fathers where the focus is on declaring Jesus as Lord (see, for example, Acts 11.17; 16.31; cf. 9.42; 18.8). The focus of the eunuch's declaration is the identity of the Son of God.[65]

The wording of the declaration is out of place in an established Church context, but wholly in place in a Jewish context. The term 'Son of God' is noticeable for its absence in Luke's writings, for it is never used in the teaching of Jesus nor the apostles. On the one occasion that it is found elsewhere in Acts, it is attributed to Paul who proclaimed in the synagogues in Damascus that Jesus was 'the Son of God' (9.20). The identity of Jesus as the Son of God is again stated implicitly by Paul in the synagogue in Antioch of Pisidia (13.33) where he identifies Jesus as the one meant by Ps. 2.7: 'You are my son, today I have begotten you.' These same words are heard, according to the Bezan text (and the early Latin witnesses) of Lk. 3.22, at the baptism of Jesus. Identifying the Son of God as Jesus, and assimilating him with the Messiah, was a peculiarly Jewish concern which would have had limited meaning to a Gentile audience.[66]

By laying down a condition for the baptism of the eunuch, Philip verifies the nature and firmness of the faith of the one asking for baptism, making sure

---

65. The presence of the article before τὸν υἱὸν τοῦ θεοῦ causes 'the Son of God' to be the subject, with ᾽Ιησοῦν Χριστόν functioning as the complement; see J. Callow, 'Constituent Order in Copula Clauses: A Partial Study', in D. Black and S.H. Levinsohn (eds), *Linguistics and New Testament Interpretation* (Nashville, TN: Broadman Press, 1992), pp. 68–89. In other words, the eunuch is concerned not to identify Jesus, but to declare his belief in who the Son of God is.

66. See G. Vermes, *Jesus the Jew* (London: SCM, 1973), p. 195; see also *Commentary*, 9.20.

this time that he will not repeat the mistake he made in Samaria of accepting a superficial belief or, even, an attachment to his own person rather than to Jesus (see on 8.5-24 above).

[d'] 8.38 *The Eunuch's Baptism*

8.38 Accepting the declaration of the eunuch's faith, Philip stops the chariot beside the water and, as the narrator underlines, both he and the eunuch go down into it. It is as if Philip shares fully in the eunuch's experience of baptism, having himself come to the realization of the immense change that was taking place. For the very first time, he is performing an act that recognizes a person as belonging to the people of God without demanding circumcision. This is totally new; new for the Church, certainly, where, even though legal boundaries have been pushed back to allow in, first, the ritually impure (the lame man, 3.1-10) and then the Samaritans (8.5-24), the question for circumcision had not yet arisen. But far more dramatically, this is new for Israel. Circumcision has been the defining feature of belonging and participating fully in God's chosen people since its earliest beginnings in the time of Abraham. Now, on the simple basis of belief in Jesus as the Son of God and the Messiah, circumcision has been done away with – in the case of the Jewish eunuch, at least; it will take many struggles and disputes before the change is accepted as applying even to Gentiles. That is a story that will be told in the subsequent chapters concerning Peter. For the time being, the road that the eunuch was travelling along away from Ierousalem has indeed led to 'Gaza', a 'treasure' of incalculable worth (cf. 8.26, 27 above).

The insistence in this verse on the joint action of Philip and the eunuch (ἀμφότεροι) combines with the repetition of another motif, the chariot (τὸ ἅρμα, cf. vv. 28, 29, 38) to evoke another parallel from Scripture, the story of the Elijah and Elisha at the moment of Elijah's departure (4 Kgdms 2.1-18). In that incident, too, the two characters had acted together as they went through the waters of the Jordan (2.6, καὶ ἐπορεύθησαν ἀμφότεροι; 2.7, καὶ ἀμφότεροι ἔστησαν; 2.8, καὶ διέβησαν ἀμφότεροι), until finally, they were separated by a chariot of fire (ἰδοὺ ἅρμα πυρός, 2.11). Echoes of the parallel will continue to sound in the end of the story of Philip and the eunuch.

[c'] 8.39a *The Eunuch Receives the Holy Spirit*

8.39a It is the reading of the AT that maintains the parallel in a more straight-forward way. Just as it was supposed when Elijah disappeared and Elisha returned alone to Jericho that the Spirit of the Lord had caught him up (4 Kgdms 2.16, ἦρεν αὐτὸν πνεῦμα κυρίου; cf. 3 Kgdms 18.12), so, too, the Spirit of the Lord snatches away Philip (πνεῦμα κυρίου ἥρπασεν τὸν Φίλιππον); the eunuch sees him no more (καὶ οὐκ εἶδεν αὐτὸν οὐκέτι), recalling how Elisha likewise saw Elijah no more (καὶ οὐκ εἶδεν αὐτὸν ἔτι, 4 Kgdms 2.12) and was even unwilling to have people look for him (2.16-18).

Other MSS, many of which also include 8.37, modify the paradigm at this point so that the Holy Spirit falls on the eunuch and it is the angel of the Lord who takes Philip away from him. It is typical of Luke's work as narrator, in setting up parallels between the incidents in his story and incidents from the Jewish Scriptures, to modify certain details in such a way as to bring out some development of the story that is new compared with the earlier event. What has changed in this case is that whereas Elisha was said to have received the spirit of Elijah (4 Kgdms 2.15; cf. 'a double share', 2.9-10), the eunuch received the Holy Spirit. The Spirit 'fell on him' in the same way that the Spirit will be said to fall on Cornelius and his household when Peter is explaining the gospel to them (Acts 10.44; cf. 11.15) or on the Ephesians when Paul laid hands on them (19.6 D05). The same expression was used in the negative of the Samaritans on whom the Spirit had *not* fallen when Philip evangelized them (8.16). The effect of the comment is twofold: on the one hand, it makes clear that Philip's teaching has been effective this time, that the eunuch's faith is sincere and profound; on the other hand, it serves as confirmation that God has accepted the eunuch as a member of the community of his people without circumcision. This is confirmation that only God could give, that is more powerful than any theological arguments or pleadings, as Peter will later acknowledge when he witnesses the same thing happening with Gentile believers, saying that he could not have prevented (κωλῦσαι, cf. τί κωλύει; 8.37) God from giving his Spirit (11.17).[67]

[b′] 8.39b *The Angel of the Lord Takes Up Philip*

8.39b The angel of the Lord, meanwhile, who had originally given Philip the order to go down onto the Gaza road, now takes him away from the eunuch, so entrusting the latter to the Spirit. That the eunuch is capable of continuing on his own is seen in the comment that he was rejoicing as he went on his way. The prophecy of Isaiah noted earlier regarding the entry of eunuchs and foreigners into the house of God (Is. 56.3-8; cf. on 8.28 above) also concludes with a promise of joy: 'I will make them joyful in my house of prayer.'[68]

---

67. The Bezan text (with support from some versions, see *Critical Apparatus*, 10.17) makes quite clear what it is that Peter understands God to have done, adding as the object of κωλῦσαι, τοῦ μὴ δοῦναι αὐτοῖς πνεῦμα ἅγιον πιστεύσασιν ἐπ' αὐτῷ.

68. In his reconstruction of the liturgical cycles of synagogue readings, J. Mann (*The Bible as Read and Preached in the Old Synagogue*, I [New York: KTAV, 1971], pp. 420–22) suggested that the Passover reading of Exod. 12.43–13.1 was grouped with the passage from the Prophets of Isa. 56.3-8, and that the theme of the accompanying homily, based on Prov. 14.10 ('The heart knows its own bitterness, and no stranger shares its joy'), was that of joy.

[a'] 8.40 *Philip in Caesarea*

8.40 Philip has accomplished his task as far as the eunuch is concerned and is taken by the angel (or the Spirit, AT) of the Lord to Azotus. Another difference with Elijah is apparent, in that 'they did not find' Elijah (4 Kgdms 2.18) for he had completed all his work, whereas there is still work for Philip elsewhere and so he 'was found' in Azotus. From there, he made his way up the coast to Caesarea, announcing the gospel as he went to the cities along the way. The account is similar to that of the evangelization of the Samaritan villages (see 8.25) which, in its own way, was recorded as a positive development, but here there is an important difference in that the coastal towns were predominantly Gentile. As for Caesarea, it was a city founded by Herod the Great in honour of Augustus Caesar for a Gentile population, though there was also a Jewish community there.[69] Philip will settle there and a community of believers will develop with a strongly prophetic character (cf. 21.8-9); furthermore, the Roman centurion living there, Cornelius, will be the first Gentile to receive the Holy Spirit.

[BB] 9.1-30 *Saul*

General Overview

Saul is the second character of the three who are presented in successive sub-sequences in Acts 8.1b–11.18 (see *General Overview* to this sequence [B]), the story of his conversion occupying the central place in the series.

Like the story of Philip in the previous sub-sequence [BA] 8.4-40, that of Saul/Paul will also involve a learning process but one that will result in a much more extensive change and that will have dramatic consequences. At this stage in the narrative, Luke allows his audience to know only that Jesus intended Saul to bear his name 'before the Gentiles, and kings, and also the sons of Israel' (cf. 9.15), as a general statement entrusting to Saul the role of 'name-bearer' rather than the specific mission that he was asked to undertake. It is only later that Paul will reveal, when he is more ready and more able to comply, that Jesus commanded him to take the gospel principally to the Gentiles (22.21; cf. Gal. 2.7). Once Luke's audience know this, it becomes clear in retrospect that Saul's responsibility was to ensure the spread of the gospel out of Judaea to people previously excluded from the people of God, a notion already introduced in Philip's evangelization of the Ethiopian eunuch who could not fully participate in Israel because he could not be circumcised (8.14-26). Indeed, the call of Saul as apostle to the Gentiles contains the seed of the ultimate fulfilment of Jesus' command to the apostles before his ascension to testify to him to the ends of the earth. It is only the seed, however, and

---

69. M. Goodman, *The Ruling Class of Judaea. The Origins of the Jewish Revolt against Rome AD 66-70* (Cambridge: Cambridge University Press, 1987), p. 3.

while it germinates Peter will be the first, unwittingly and despite his profound resistance, who is used by God to announce the gospel to non-Jews and
to witness the gift of the Holy Spirit to them. Peter's story will form the third
sub-sequence of the present series ([BA'] 9.31–11.18).

Structure and Themes
The sub-sequence opens in Jerusalem, with the name of Saul and the theme of
persecution making a link back to the first mention of his name (7.58; 8.1a, 3).
The setting then transfers to Damascus where a new character, Ananias, is
introduced and where Saul stays with the disciples after his baptism, preaching in
the synagogues. However, on account of the persecution that arises against him
within the synagogues, Saul has to flee to Ierousalem where Barnabas re-appears
(cf. 4.36) to introduce Saul to the apostles, but it is not long before he also has to
leave there amidst continued hostility and return to his home town of Tarsus.

The theme of opposition on the part of Hellenist Jews towards the followers of Jesus from among their own people continues throughout the sub-
sequence, this time directed at Saul himself. It is to be noted that Saul begins
his preaching activity immediately after his own baptism and that his message
is directed at a Jewish audience.

The sub-sequence falls clearly into three episodes, [*A*], [*B*] and [*A'*], with
the central one describing the mission entrusted by Jesus to Saul. The final
episode is made up of three smaller scenes, [*A'A* / *A'B* \ *A'A'*]:

[BB-*A*]	9.1-9	Saul's encounter with Jesus
[BB-*B*]	9.10-19a	Ananias
[BB-*A'*]	9.19b-30	Saul among the disciples
[*A'A*]	9.19b-22	Saul in Damascus
[*A'B*]	9.23-25	The plot of the Jews
[*A'A'*]	9.26-30	Saul in Ierousalem

[BB-*A*] 9.1-9 *Saul's Encounter with Jesus*

Overview

In the first episode, the leading role Saul will play in the book of Acts is
anticipated by the dramatic story of his encounter with Jesus. Saul, as Paul,
will give his own account of his encounter with Jesus on two further occasions
during his speeches of defence (to the Jews in Ierousalem, 22.4-21; to Agrippa
in Caesarea, 26.9-18). A comparison of the three accounts reveals similarities
as well as differences; rather than suppose an inept narrator who clumsily put
together elements from various sources without taking care to ensure consistency,[70] it is more valuable to notice how the contradictions become
meaningful when the separate accounts are seen as reflecting the different

---

70. See Barrett, I, pp. 439–45, for a discussion of the reasons advanced for variety among the
three accounts.

circumstances of their telling. Some comparison between the account in the present chapter will be made with Paul's later accounts but a detailed comparison will be reserved for the *Commentary* on Acts 22 and 26 when the particular circumstances can be discussed.

Structure and Themes

As the theme of persecution is picked up from 8.3, Saul's attacks on the Jesus-believers are for the first time directed outside Jerusalem, towards the disciples who had had to flee from Hierosoluma (8.3, cf. 11.19). The authority for the persecution is nevertheless given by the High Priest in Ierousalem and it is to there that the arrested believers are to be brought. It is within this context that Jesus appears to Saul.

The structure of the episode naturally follows the course of events which are presented in greater detail in the 'Western' text (WT).[71] The first part deals with Saul's plans of persecution which are interrupted by the appearance of Jesus; the second part presents Saul's actions that are a consequence of that encounter with the turning point being, according to the WT, Saul's question about what he should do and Jesus' command in response:

[a]	9.1-2	Saul's intended persecution
[b]	9.3	A light from heaven, near Damascus
[c]	9.4	Saul falls to the ground and hears a voice
[d]	9.5a	Saul questions the speaker
[e]	9.5b	Jesus makes himself known
[f]	9.6a	Saul asks what he should do
[f′]	9.6b	Jesus' command
[e′]	9.7	Saul's companions
[d′]	9.8a	Saul asks them for help
[c′]	9.8b	They help him up from the ground
[b′]	9.8c	They take him into Damascus
[a′]	9.9	Saul's punishment

Translation

'Western' Text	Codex Vaticanus B03
[a]	
9.1 Saul, still breathing threats and murder against the disciples of the Lord, went to the High Priest **2** and asked for letters from him to the synagogues in Damascus, so that if he found anyone from this 'Way', whether men or women, he could arrest them and bring them to Ierousalem.	**9.1** Saul, because he was breathing threats and murder against the disciples of the Lord, went to the High Priest **2** and asked for letters from him to the synagogues in Damascus, so that if he found anyone who belonged to the 'Way', whether men or women, he could arrest them and bring them to Ierousalem.

---

71. 'Western' text (WT) is the label commonly used to refer to the witnesses whose chief characteristic in common is their disagreement with the Alexandrian tradition (see *Critical Apparatus*, 8.29).

[b]	**3** In the course of his journey, he had reached the point where he was getting near to Damascus when suddenly there flashed around him a light from heaven.	**3** In the course of his journey, he had reached the point where he was getting near to Damascus when suddenly around him there flashed a light out of heaven.
[c]	**4** And he fell to the ground, in great bewilderment, and heard a voice saying, 'Saul, Saul, why do you persecute me? It hurts you to kick against the goads.'	**4** And he fell to the ground and heard a voice saying, 'Saul, Saul, why do you persecute me?'
[d]	**5a** He said, 'Who are you, lord?'	**5a** He said, 'Who are you, lord?'
[e]	**5b** The Lord said, 'I am Jesus the Nazorean whom you are persecuting'.	**5b** and he said, 'I am Jesus whom you are persecuting;
[f]	**6a** He, trembling and terrified at what had happened to him, said, 'Lord, what do you want me to do?'	
[f']	**6b** And the Lord said, 'Get up and go into the city and it will be told to you what you must do'.	**6** but get up and go into the city and it will be told to you what you must do'.
[e']	**7** The men who were travelling with him had been standing speechless, hearing the voice but seeing no-one whom he was talking to.	**7** The men who were travelling with him had been standing speechless, hearing the voice but seeing no-one.
[d']	**8a** But he said to them, 'Lift me up from the ground';	**8a** Saul got up from the ground.
[c']	**8b** and when they had raised him, although his eyes were open he saw nothing.	**8b** Although his eyes were open he saw nothing.
[b']	**8c** They took him by the hand and led him to Damascus;	**8c** They took him by the hand and led him to Damascus;
[a']	**9** and thus he remained for three days seeing nothing, and he neither ate nor drank.	**9** and for three days he could not see, and he neither ate nor drank.

Critical Apparatus

[Since the Greek pages of Codex Bezae are missing from 8.29–10.14 and the Latin ones from 8.20b–10.4, we have noted in the *Critical Apparatus* the variants of other witnesses that differ from the Alexandrian text, but at no time consider that a single text, equivalent in its uniformity to the Alexandrian one, can be reconstructed from these readings. The differences among the so-called 'Western' witnesses are considerable, and it is almost certain that there were readings of Codex Bezae that are represented by none of them and that cannot therefore be retrieved.]

9.1 ὅτι ἐμπνέων B* | ἐμπ. ℵ* *pc* co ‖ ἔτι ἐμπ. 𝔓⁷⁴ ℵ² A C *rell*.

B03 is alone in explicitly attributing Saul's request for letters from the High Priest to his violent intentions against the disciples. Most other MSS link this incident back to the last mention of Saul's persecution of the disciples at

8.3, with the adverb 'still'. The first hand of א01, however, connects the mention of Saul's hostility to nothing either before or after.

παρ᾽ αὐτοῦ ἐπιστολάς B 𝔓⁷⁴ A C *rell* ‖ ἐπ. παρ᾽ αὐ. א.

All MSS except א01 highlight the role of the High Priest by placing the prepositional phrase before the noun (ἐπιστολάς) that depends on it.

9.2 τῆς ὁδοῦ ὄντας B C E H L P Ψ 049. 056. 614 𝔐 | τ. ὁδ. 33. 522. 547*. 1175. 1891 *pc*; Theoph | ὄντας τ. ὁδ. 𝔓⁷⁴ א A 81. 88. 181. 242. 323. 453. 467. 915. 945. 1646. 1739. 1891. 2298 *pc* ‖ τ. ὁδ. ταύτης 104. 181. 1838 lat sy^{p.h} aeth; Aug.

The use of the demonstrative 'this' confers a note of disdain on the reference to the 'Way', causing Saul's request to be viewed through his own eyes (cf. 22.4) as he mentions the movement of the Jesus-believers by the term by which they were becoming known (cf. 8.39; 18.26 D05; 19.9, 23; 24.14, 22).

9.3 ἐξαίφνης τε αὐτὸν περιέστραψεν φῶς B 𝔓⁷⁴ א (A) C 36. (69). 81. 181. 242. 453. 522. 945. 1646. 1175. 1739. 1891. 2298 vg^D | καὶ ἐξ. περιέστ. αὐτὸν φ. 𝔓^{45vid} E H L P Ψ 049. 056. 1. 104. 226. 330. 440. 547. 614. 618. 927. 1241. 1243. 1245. 1270. 1505. 1611. 1828. 1837. 2147. 2344. 2412. 1492. 2495.

With the connective τε and the word order that places the object pronoun before the verb, Saul is maintained in focus as the narrator introduces the new topic of the light. The alternative reading has the effect, in contrast, of directing attention to the light.

ἐκ (τοῦ οὐρανοῦ) B 𝔓⁷⁴ א A C L 36. 81. 88. 181. 242. 255. 323. 453. 467. 522. 876. 945. 1175. 1505. 1646. 1739. 1765. 1891. 2298. 2495; Chr ‖ ἀπό 𝔓⁴⁵ E H P Ψ 049. 056. 1. 33. 69. 104. 226. 330. 440. 547. 614. 618. 927. 1241. 1243. 1245. 1270. 1611. 1828. 1837. 1854. 2147. 2344. 2412. 1492.

Most of the witnesses that maintained attention on Saul when the light was introduced (see variant above) also describe the light as emanating 'out of' (ἐκ) heaven, which is the usual preposition in Acts in relation to something coming from heaven (cf. 2.2; 11.5, 9; Read-Heimerdinger, *The Bezan Text*, p. 192). The preposition ἐκ is also found in Saul/Paul's own account of his experience at 22.6, though again with the *vl* ἀπό, notably in D05.

9.4 (ἐπὶ τὴν γῆν) *cum magna mentis alienatione* (h) p t mae; Amb (*dum stupefactus stabat* Ephr^{kc}) (retroversion: ἐκστάσει μεγάλῃ: cf. Mk 5.42) ‖ *om.* B 𝔓⁷⁴ א *rell*.

Witnesses of the 'Western' text comment on Saul's state of mind as he falls to the ground. Such observations of the psychological state of characters is characteristic of the extant text of D05 (see on 9.6 below).

Σαοὺλ Σαούλ B ℵ A C E* *rell* ‖ Σαῦλε Σαῦλε E² 917 lat sa mae; Ir.

The Greek form of Saul's name, read by some witnesses, is also found in the Bezan text of Paul's own account of his conversion at 22.7; cf. 22.13 d05. See 9.17 below for the same variant.

(διώκεις) σκληρόν σοι πρὸς κέντρα λακτίζειν E 431 e vg^AcM sy^p.h** mae aeth^pt; Chr Jer Aug ‖ *om.* B 𝔓⁷⁴ ℵ *rell.*

The majority of the versions, as well as E08 and occasional minuscules, attest the inclusion of a proverbial saying in this first account of Jesus' appearance to Saul, though some leave it to the end of 9.5 (see below). The majority of Greek MSS, in contrast, mention it only in the last account spoken by Saul/Paul himself, at 26.14. A comment in sy^hmg notes that the Greek does not have this phrase here but at 26.14 (Boismard and Lamouille, II, p. 62).

9.5 (κύριε) ὁ δέ B 𝔓⁴⁵·⁷⁴ A C 1175. 1646. 1739. 1891 | ὁ δὲ εἶπεν ℵ 81. 614. 927. 945. 1241. 2412 ‖ ὁ δὲ κύριος πρὸς αὐτόν E Ψ 323. 440 p vg^Θ | ὁ δὲ κύριος εἶπεν H L P 049. 056 𝔐 h sa mae.

Whilst there is no doubt about the identity of the speaker in the AT, some MSS spell out that it is the Lord who answers Saul.

Ἰησοῦς B 𝔓⁷⁴ ℵ *rell* ‖ Ἰ. ὁ Ναζωραῖος A C E 104. 467. 917. 1838 *pc* it vg^ΘMSU sy^p.h** bo^pt aeth; EusEm Aug Hil Amb | Ἰ. Χριστός Ir^lat.

The qualification of Jesus as the 'Nazorean' (on Luke's use of Ναζωραῖος, see *The Message of Acts,* I, p. 184, n. 28 and Acts 22.8) contributes to establishing a parallel between this passage and the episode concerning the blind man on the road to Jericho in Luke's Gospel (cf. Lk. 18.37 B03 [Ναζαρηνός D05], spoken by the blind man).

9.5-6 σκληρόν σοι πρὸς κέντρα λακτίζειν 69^c. 629 ar b c gig h l p r t dem vg^CT aeth^pt; Lcf Ephr QvD Ambr Theoph ‖ *om.* B 𝔓⁷⁴ ℵ *rell.*— ἀλλά B 𝔓⁷⁴ ℵ *rell* ‖ τρέμων τε καὶ θαμβῶν 69^c, *et tremens ac stupens* vg^codd (*ille autem tremens et pavens* p) sy^h** mae, *qui tremens, timore plenus* h; Aug Hil (Ephr).

The inclusion in 'Western' witnesses of a description of Saul's inner state was noted above (9.4).

9.6 *in isto sibi facto* (retroversion: ἐπὶ τῷ γεγενημένῳ) h p t vg^codd sy^h** mae; Hil Ephr ‖ *om.* B 𝔓⁷⁴ ℵ *rell.*

A similar phrase is found at 3.10 referring to the healing of the lame man.

εἶπεν· Κύριε, τί με θέλεις ποιῆσαι; 69^c, *dixit: Domine, quid me vis facere?* h p t vg^codd sy^h** mae; Aug Hil Ambr Ephr ‖ *om.* B 𝔓⁷⁴ ℵ *rell.*

Saul's question to the Lord is found in his own account of the incident at 22.10 though in a different form. This, together with the additional information about Saul's state of mind, suggests that the mention of it here is not simply harmonization: 'une harmonisation faite par un scribe est peu vraisemblable' (Boismard and Lamouille, II, p. 63). It is typical of the AT to omit descriptions of the apostle's psychological reactions (cf. Acts 11.2 D05; 16.7 D05; 19.1 D05; 20.3 D05). The wording of the AT, ἀλλά (ἀνάστηθι), is found in the parallel account of 26.16 which could suggest that it is a harmonization, although the construction ἀλλά + imperative is Lukan (cf. 1.8; B-D-R, § 448.3).

καὶ ὁ κύριος πρὸς αὐτόν 69ᶜ, *et dominus ad eum* it vgᶜˡ syʰ** mae aeth ‖ *om.* B 𝔓⁷⁴ℵ *rell.*

Those MSS that include Saul's question above continue the narrative with a fresh mention of the Lord as speaker.

9.7 θεωροῦντες B 𝔓⁷⁴ ℵ² *rell* | ὁρῶντες ℵ* ‖ *videbant, cum loqueretur* h, *qui loqueretur* p w tepl, *cum quo loqueretur* gig l mae (retroversion: θεωροῦντες λαλοῦντα).

Some of the versions make clear that it was the one with whom Saul was talking, or the one talking (p), that his companions did not see. In Saul's own account in 22.9, he comments that they saw the light but 'did not hear the voice of the one speaking to me'. Again, as in 9.6, the difference between the two passages suggests that this is not a case of scribal harmonization despite apparent similarities. It is possible to understand the comment in this verse that the companions heard the voice as meaning Saul's voice, which explains the observation that they did not see anyone he was talking to.

9.8 ἠγέρθη δὲ ὁ (*om.* B 𝔓⁷⁴ ℵ A C E 81. 1175. 1646) Σαῦλος ἀπὸ τῆς γῆς B 𝔓⁷⁴ ℵ *rell* ‖ *sed ait ad eos: Levate me de terra. Et cum levassent illum* (retroversion: ὁ δὲ εἶπεν πρὸς αὐτούς· Ἐγείρατέ με ἀπὸ τῆς γῆς. καὶ ὡς ἤγειρον αὐτόν) h (p w) vgᵐˢˢ mae.

In the early versions, Saul himself asks his companions to help him up which they do. In the Greek MSS, it is not specified who lifted him up from the ground – though this could suggest a divine passive, ἠγέρθη often is used with an active meaning (cf. Zerwick, *Biblical Greek*, § 231: 'it may simply mean "arose"').

9.9 καὶ ἦν B 𝔓⁷⁴ ℵ *rell* ‖ *et sic mansit* (retroversion: καὶ οὕτως ἔμεινεν) h; (Ephrᵏ).

The durative notion of the periphrastic imperfect in Greek (ἦν ... μὴ βλέπων) is expressed by the verb *maneo* in the Latin of h.

μὴ (βλέπων) B 𝔓⁷⁴ℵ *rell* ‖ *nihil* (μηδέν) h p.

The pronoun 'nothing' insists on the previous comment that Saul 'saw nothing' by repeating it (cf. 9.8).

Commentary

[a] 9.1-2 *Saul's Intended Persecution*
The account of Saul's campaign against those who believed in Jesus is picked up again now from 7.58; 8.1, in the context of the dispersion of the believers from Hierosoluma and the consequent spread of the gospel message. His activity is typical of the members of the Jewish nationalist movements that fought in the first century CE to preserve the purity of Israel (see *Excursus* 1).

9.1 As Saul is brought back onto centre stage, his name is prefaced with the article, an indication that he has never been entirely off stage since the last mention of his name (8.3).[72] In other words, the earlier introduction of him into the narrative already established him at that point as one of the protagonists. Just as he was last seen persecuting the disciples of Jesus, so he is reintroduced pursuing the same aim ('still', ἔτι, according to all the Greek MSS except Codex Vaticanus), though this time his intention of having the believers killed is made explicit.[73]

His intention is to seek out Jesus-believers among Jews outside Israel for which he required the authority of the High Priest in Ierousalem. The date, which can be ascertained approximately from the date of Saul's conversion, was around 37 CE but as it cannot be established more exactly it is not possible to know who would have been the High Priest in question: Caiaphas was replaced by his brother-in-law, Jonathan son of Annas in 37 but only held power for 3 months before Annas' next son took over. This was Theophilus who, given the Jewish perspective of the Bezan text, could well have been the person to whom Luke addressed his work (see *General Introduction*, § IV). Theophilus was High Priest until Agrippa I, after being appointed king of Judaea in 41, installed a member of another high-priestly family in his place. But whether or not Theophilus was actually occupying the position of High Priest at the time of Saul's persecution, he would have been well aware of the events of this time and Luke writes, too, knowing what he knew.

9.2 Saul goes to the High Priest to ask for letters for the synagogues in Damascus. The disciples, being Jews, would be found in the synagogues, both those who had fled from the persecution in Hierosoluma as well as those who were natives of Damascus, and this was precisely the problem. If the Jesus-believers had broken away and formed an independent movement, separate from Judaism, Saul would have had no cause to pursue them nor would the High Priest have had authority over them. For the time being, however, the disciples of Jesus continue to be a group within Judaism. Apart from anything, the ongoing presence of the apostles 'in Ierousalem' (cf. 8.1 D05) ensures that

---

72. Heimerdinger and Levinsohn, 'The Use of the Article', pp. 20–22, 25.
73. 'Threats and slaughter' could be taken as a hendiadys meaning 'threats of slaughter', suggesting that Saul only threatened to kill the people he was arresting without carrying out his threat; see Barrett, I, p. 445.

this is so. Their group has acquired the label of the 'Way' which would appear from the WT to be a name they themselves adopted, for Saul uses it in mockery, 'this "Way"' (see *Critical Apparatus*).[74]

The same insistence on the persecution of both men and women as at 8.3 is noted. It will be seen again at 22.4. The believers are to be brought as prisoners to Ierousalem, the centre of Jewish authority, which underlines that even though the Temple authorities may have suspended their attacks on the apostles, they had by no means abandoned their desire to stamp out the Jesus movement.

[b] 9.3 *A Light from Heaven, near Damascus*
9.3 The setting changes to the road leading from Jerusalem (in both its geographical and religious [cf. 9.2] sense) to Damascus, with the exact location carefully specified as being close to the Syrian capital. Saul, that is, is on the point of reaching his goal when he is stopped in his tracks by a light that suddenly appears from out of the sky.[75] The abruptness of the appearance of the light and its brightness as it shone around Saul is presented as a powerful and invasive force against which he is quite unable to resist. This is no gentle awakening but a violent and alarming experience, corresponding to the degree to which Saul's purpose was contrary to the truth of God.

[c] 9.4 *Saul Falls to the Ground and Hears a Voice*
9.4 Saul's immediate reaction is to fall to the ground, setting up a contrast between the light shining from above and Saul falling to the earth below. His prostrate position illustrates his helplessness to either resist or collaborate with the supernatural power of the light. The WT describes Saul's reaction as one of 'great bewilderment', the kind of comment that is typical of the interest shown elsewhere by the Bezan text in the inner feelings and thoughts of characters in the narrative.[76]

---

74. The term 'the Way' was used by the narrator for the first time in Acts at the end of the previous episode when it was said of the eunuch that 'he went on his way rejoicing' after being baptized. It will be used by the narrator later, again in the context of opposition (Jewish, 19.9; 24.22; and Greek, 19.23), as well as in Paul's own account of his conversion (22.4 – where ταύτην τὴν ὁδόν is not disrespectful but, with the adjective before the noun, simply has the force of a demonstrative) and in his defence speech to Felix (24.14). The group of believers collectively known as 'the Way' appear to have also been referred to as 'the sect of the Nazoreans' (24.5) and to be specifically Jewish Jesus-believers (see M.C. De Boer, 'The Nazoreans: Living at the Boundary of Judaism and Christianity', in G.N. Stanton and G.G. Stroumsa [eds], *Tolerance and Intolerance in Early Judaism and Christianity* [Cambridge: Cambridge University Press, 1998], pp. 239–62 [244]).

75. The connective τε closely connects the proximity of Saul to Damascus and the appearance of the light. A similarly close connection is made by Paul at 22.6 by the use of present participles, πορευομένῳ and ἐγγίζοντι.

76. Cf., e.g., 11.2 D05; 19.1 D05. In his *Commentary on Acts*, Ephrem offers an insight into Saul's reaction to the voice of Jesus, saying he 'fainted in his mind, and thought: I for sake of the

There are a certain number of similarities in this account, especially in its 'Western' form, with the story recorded in 2 Maccabees of Heliodorus who, in the early part of the second century BCE, was sent by the king of Asia, Seleucid IV, to Jerusalem with the task of transferring the treasure from the Temple to the royal treasury. As he approached the treasury with his men, intending to make an inventory, he was confronted with a terrifying vision sent by God and which left him blind and helpless. He was only saved from death by the High Priest who interceded on his behalf with prayers to God. Following his recovery, Heliodorus testified to the greatness of the divine power he had encountered and acknowledged the protection of God over his Temple. The numerous parallels contain some striking verbal similarities and it is probable that Luke intended to place Saul's conversion on a par with this earlier occasion which was so significant for the history of Israel (see *Excursus* 2.1).

The indirect allusions to the story of Heliodorus are not the only echoes to the Scriptures that can be heard in the Acts story of Saul. More important still are the similarities with the story of Saul, the king of Israel. Especially relevant for the present episode is the account in 1 Samuel 28 of his visit to the medium of Endor in order to consult the spirit of Samuel (see *Excursus* 2.2).

In Luke's account of Saul's experience, the light is accompanied by a voice, as is common in manifestations of the divine.[77] According to Saul/Paul's own account (26.14), he was addressed in 'Hebrew' which could mean Aramaic as the spoken language of the Jewish people in Israel but it may also be a reference to what was regarded by Jews as the divine language because it was the language of the Torah. That would not exclude Jesus addressing Saul with the Greek form of his name as a reminder of his origin in Tarsus, in the Diaspora (cf. 9.11; see *Excursus* 1).

The identification made by Jesus between himself and the disciples whom Saul was persecuting recalls the comment made by him to the Seventy (Seventy-Two, D05) disciples in Luke's Gospel: 'The one who rejects you rejects me' (Lk. 10.16), a saying that has no exact parallel in the other Gospels. Within the scheme of Luke's work, the Seventy(-Two) represent the precursors of the Hellenist disciples whom Saul was persecuting.

Lord of heaven do persecute, can it be that I persecute him who dwells in heaven? Next he asks: … Who art thou, Lord, who in the heavens art persecuted?' (F. Conybeare, 'The Commentary of Ephrem on Acts', in Ropes, *Text*, pp. 373–453 [411]). I. Czachesz, who draws attention to Ephrem's comments on the conversion of Paul, suggests that information relayed by Ephrem and the apocryphal Acts of Paul may have been derived from the text of Codex Bezae, now lost ('The Acts of Paul and the Western Text of Luke's Acts: Paul between Canon and Apocrypha', in J. N. Bremer [ed.], *The Apocryphal Acts of Paul and Thecla* [Kampen: Kok Pharos, 1996], pp. 106–25 [111, 125]).

77. Cf. Lk 3.21-22; 9.29-31, 35; Acts 10.3-6; 10.11-12, 13-16; 10.30, 31-32; 11.5-6, 7-10; 12.7-8; 16.9.

[d] 9.5a *Saul Questions the Speaker*
This verse contains the first words spoken by Saul, and is mirrored in the WT by 9.8a [d'] with his last words in this episode which are not recorded in the AT. Again in the WT, Saul's first question to Jesus opens a dialogue between the two speakers which takes the form of questions and answers; in the AT, where 9.6a is absent, Saul asks only this initial question.

9.5a Though Saul would recognize the situation as a supernatural occurrence, his question 'Who are you?' reflects his lack of belief at this stage in the resurrection of Jesus, whose appearance would therefore leave him totally bewildered (cf. 9.4 WT). The Greek word κύριος, 'lord', is the same for a human or divine master and so could perhaps be translated as 'sir' here since Saul does not yet recognize the voice as being that of Jesus. On the other hand, the supernatural nature of the experience would demonstrate to him that it belonged to no earthly being and the translation 'lord' has been preferred to indicate the respect that recognition would engender, but without a capital letter to avoid the confusion with 'Lord' as a designation for Jesus.

[e] 9.5b *Jesus Makes Himself Known*
9.5b Jesus' presentation of himself relates to the knowledge Saul already had of him. The inclusion in the WT of 'the Nazorean' is a reference to Jesus' identity as the Messiah.[78] The form of the title Jesus is reported to use (in Hebrew, according to Paul, 26.14) should be noted, for the alternative form, ὁ Ναζαρηνός, is found only in the Gospels where it denotes more the place of origin of Jesus than his messianic status. Jesus defines himself for a second time as the object of Saul's persecution.

[f] 9.6a *Saul Asks What He Should Do*
9.6a This element is absent from the AT, one of a number of observations that are not reported by the AT. The comment in some MSS that Saul was 'trembling and terrified' corresponds to the first description found in certain of the

---

78. The title ὁ Ναζωραῖος designates the Messiah, and was a term that appears to have been already current among Jews before it was applied to Jesus. In that context, its origin was probably the messianic prophecy of Isaiah who describes the Messiah as a 'shoot' (נֵצֶר, netser) from the root of Jesse (Isa. 11.1; cf. 11.10); it would seem from Mt. 2.23 (and Lk. 2.51 D05) that Isaiah's prophecy had been developed so that the Messiah became known as the one who would be called ὁ Ναζωραῖος (perhaps derived from the Hebrew נָצֹר, natsor, 'he is protected/observed', see Barrett I, p. 140; cf. H. Kuhli, 'Ναζωραῖος', *EWNT*, II, cols. 1117-21). The linking of this designation with Jesus' hometown of Nazareth was not without a certain irony since the disdain among Jews for Galilee in general (cf. Jn 7.41-42, 52) and Nazareth in particular (cf. 1.46) would certainly not cause them to expect the Messiah to come from there (cf. 7.42). The followers of Jesus at some point became known as οἱ Ναζωραῖοι (Acts 24.5), a name already adopted by the Mandaeans, a Jewish sect that existed probably before the first century CE. The topic is explored by J. Rius-Camps, '"Nazareno" y "Nazoreo", con especial atención al Códice Bezae', in R. Pierri (ed.), *Grammatica Intellectio Scripturae, Saggi filologici di Greco biblico* (forthcoming).

same MSS of his 'great bewilderment' (see 9.4, and *Critical Apparatus*). The picture painted is a far cry from the traditional image of the apostle Paul as a strong and courageous hero. It is also a more realistic one if one takes into account, first, Saul's fanatical belief that he was being obedient to the demands of the Jewish Scriptures in persecuting those whom he perceived as having abandoned the Jewish Law (see *Excursus* 1) and, second, in contradiction to this conviction, his growing realization in this scene that Jesus had indeed been resurrected and that the Jesus-believers were therefore right to proclaim him as Lord.[79] Saul's acceptance of the identity of Jesus is unquestioning, as shown by his immediate submission to his will.

[f'] 9.6b *Jesus' Command*

9.6b Instead of God's purpose for Saul being revealed at once, that will follow some three days later (cf. 9.9), after a period of physical distress.[80] In Greek, a double impersonal expression is used: λαληθήσεται, 'it will be told to you' and ὅ τί σε δεῖ ποιεῖν, 'what it is necessary for you to do' (translated as 'what you must do'). The latter verb δεῖ is a verb form that Luke uses typically to denote the divine plan. In this instance, it corresponds to nothing less than the purpose of God for Saul to be his 'chosen instrument' (cf. 9.15).

[e'] 9.7 *Saul's Companions*

9.7 Attention now turns to the people who had accompanied Saul and who are mentioned for the first time in the story. While the dialogue between Saul and Jesus was going on, they had been standing there, not knowing what to say nor being able to speak.[81] The narrator's explanation that they 'heard a voice' is ambiguous since it could refer to the voice of Saul or of Jesus. In Paul's account in 22.9 he states clearly that the men with him 'did not hear the voice of the one talking with me', and in 26.14 implies as much when he says 'When we had all fallen to the ground, I heard a voice...'. Unless Luke is contradicting Paul's version, it is entirely possible to understand that the voice the men heard was that of Saul, especially with the reading of the WT which

---

79. Ephrem comments that Saul's fear would have arisen from his realization that he should be heavily punished since Jesus, whose disciples he had been persecuting, was in heaven (Conybeare, 'The Commentary of Ephrem on Acts', pp. 411–12).

80. The apparent contradiction with Paul's own account in 26.16-18, where he says that Jesus revealed to him there and then on the Damascus road what his mission was to be, can be explained by the fact that here in chapter 9 it is Luke as narrator who describes the sequence of events and who has an interest in explaining in detail the successive steps of Saul's experience.

81. εἱστήκεισαν ἐνεοί. In the pluperfect, ἵστημι has an intransitive sense and could be interpreted as a simple imperfect ('they were standing'), corresponding to the past tense of the perfect which normally expresses the present tense (Zerwick and Grosvenor, *Analysis*, p. 379). However, since the reference is to the men's reaction during the time that Jesus and Saul have been talking, there is a true sense of pluperfect here, especially in the WT where Saul interrupts their shocked reaction with his order to them to help him up (cf. 1.10, παρειστήκεισαν).

specifies that they did not see anyone (with whom he was) talking (see *Critical Apparatus*).[82]

[d´] 9.8a *Saul Asks Them for Help*
9.8a The AT, somewhat disjointedly, switches attention back to Saul[83] and reports that he got up, using a passive verb which often, however, has an active sense. The WT enters into more detail, presenting the interaction between Saul and his companions and making clear that Saul asks them to help him up. The picture of Saul's helplessness and his dependence on his companions is thus reinforced.

[c´] 9.8b *They Help Him Up from the Ground*
9.8b The WT goes on to specify that the companions complied with his request for assistance, with the result that it is they who enable Saul to obey the command of Jesus to 'get up' (as will also be the case with the second order, to 'go into the city'). It is at that point he discovered that he could not see. The AT continues to be more concise and to omit continued reference to the companions.

A series of parallels between the vision of Saul and that of Stephen establishes a contrast between the two.[84] Saul had played a significant role in the stoning of Stephen (cf. 8.1a) and had been no doubt present when Stephen, full of the Holy Spirit, saw 'the heavens opened and the Son of Man standing at the right hand of God' (7.56). He would have heard, too, Stephen praying for forgiveness for his persecutors. Saul now, in turn, has a revelation of Jesus and the effect of the parallel is to contrast the two experiences in such a way

82. It should be observed that in 9.4, the accusative is used of Saul hearing the voice: ἤκουσεν φωνήν, which could be interpreted as meaning that he heard the words, in contrast to 9.7 where the genitive is used: ἀκούοντες τῆς φωνῆς, indicating that the companions only heard the sound of the voice (see Moulton, I, p. 66).

83. The switch of focus is indicated by the absence of the article before Σαῦλος (Heimerdinger and Levinsohn, 'The Use of the Article', pp. 25–26).

84. The following parallels between the visions of Stephen (7.55-56) and Saul (9.3-6) may be observed. They both: 1) experience a revelation of, or from, heaven: Stephen gazes into heaven (εἰς τὸν οὐρανόν, 7.55) and sees the divine glory; Saul is surrounded by a flash of light from heaven (ἐκ τοῦ οὐρανοῦ, 9.3); 2) fall to the ground: Stephen falls to his knees and prays for his persecutors, among them Saul, to be forgiven (7.60–8.1a); Saul falls under the effect of the light (9.4); 3) encounter Jesus: Stephen sees Jesus standing at the right hand of God and calls on him as Lord (κύριε Ἰησοῦ, 7.59, 60); Saul hears only his voice and does not know his identity ('Who are you, lord [κύριε]?', 9.4) until Jesus reveals it (9.5).

Three further verbal parallels can be identified: 4) the verb 'stand', ἵστημι, is used of Jesus whom Stephen sees standing at the right hand of God (7.55), and of Saul's companions who 'had been standing speechless' (9.7) during his encounter with Jesus; 5) the verb 'see', θεωρέω, is used of Stephen who sees the heavens opened (7.56), and of Saul's companions who saw no-one (9.7); 6) finally, the verb 'open', ἀνοίγω, is used of the heavens which Stephen saw opened (7.56), and of Saul who could not see even when his eyes were opened (9.8).

that Saul's conversion experience appears as the first fruit of Stephen's prayer for forgiveness.

[b'] 9.8c *They Take Him into Damascus*

9.8c Contrary to all his plans, Saul is led helpless by his companions into the city he had been intending to enter aggressively with threats of death against the disciples of Jesus. Stripped of all power and authority, he is guided by the hand, dependant on his companions to carry out Jesus' command to 'go into the city' (cf. 9.6b).

It appears, from the instructions given to Ananias about where to find Saul in Damascus, that he was taken to the house of 'Judah' in the street called 'Straight'. The symbolic significance of these names will be explored when they occur in 9.11.

[a'] 9.9 *Saul's Punishment*

9.9 The three days that Saul spent waiting in Damascus are a duration that represents completeness, a period that enables Saul to leave the past behind and start on a new life. The idea of a total break with his past life is suggested as much by the unfolding of events in the narrative as by the echo of the three days spent by Jesus in the tomb. His blindness can be interpreted, on the one hand, as a punishment for his persecution (cf. Heliodorus, 2 Macc. 3.27 [*Excursus* 2.1]; Elymas ['Ετοιμᾶς D05] the magician, Acts 13.11). At the same time, his physical condition is a metaphor for his spiritual blindness to the truth concerning Jesus, which the Damascus disciple Ananias will be sent to make clear.

Fasting was a practice commonly associated with repentance which, although no explicit mention is made of Saul's thoughts and feelings at this point, is implied by the fact that he abandoned his attack on the disciples after his encounter with Jesus; a change in attitude towards Jesus is more clearly evident in the WT where his willingness to obey is spelt out (9.6a, 'Lord, what do you want me to do?').

[BB-*B*] 9.10-19a *Ananias*

Overview

At the centre of the narration concerning Saul, which is itself at the centre of a series of three stories concerning prominent disciples (Philip, 8.1-26, and Peter, 9.31–11.18, being the other two), there occurs the account of the first steps of Saul's conversion. The step taken by Saul at this point marks his acceptance of Jesus as Messiah and his general calling to represent the name of Jesus. There is no mention yet, though, of his particular calling to take the gospel to the Gentiles. Saul will only be seen to fully understand and accept that mission when he finally arrives in Rome in chapter 28, following a long and difficult struggle to come to terms with the radical change brought by Jesus to the traditional Jewish expectations concerning the status of the Jews in the messianic age. This present incident, therefore, should be understood in the context of the rest of the book which makes it clear that what is recorded in chapter 9 does not mark a definitive, once and for all experience that suddenly transforms Saul from Jew to Christian but rather is the first step in the process of becoming a faithful disciple of Jesus.

Structure and Themes

A new character is introduced, bearing the same name as the representative of the traditional Jewish believers who, along with his wife, deceived the apostles by holding back some of the proceeds of the sale of his land (5.1-11). This Ananias is, in contrast, an entirely positive character for, being himself a disciple of Jesus, he is entrusted with explaining to Saul God's purpose for him and will be responsible for enlightening him concerning Jesus, symbolized by the recovery of his sight.

The encounter between Ananias and Saul has elements of similarity with the encounter between Philip and the eunuch, and also with the encounter between Peter and Cornelius in the following sequence [A′] in chapter 10. All three entail a meeting directed by Jesus which is the means for the leader (or future leader in the case of Saul) to take steps forward in their understanding of the message of Jesus. Strongest similarities exist, perhaps, between Saul and Peter, for both are prepared for the encounter by means of a vision that is related to the person who will serve as the channel for God's revelation.

The episode is arranged in a symmetrical pattern, with elements [a–e] presenting Jesus' command to Ananias to meet Saul and elements [e′–a′] describing how he undertook Jesus' command. The conjunction δέ opens the episode and the following five elements are also linked with δέ because they consist of a series of speech exchanges between Jesus and Ananias for which Luke typically uses δέ. Once, however, Ananias begins to carry out Jesus' instructions (his response is signalled in the WT with τότε, see *Critical Apparatus*), the actions follow as a series of steps without any difficulty or anything new being introduced and they are therefore linked with καί:

[a]	9.10a	Jesus calls Ananias
[b]	9.10b	Ananias responds
[c]	9.11-12	Jesus' command
[d]	9.13-14	Ananias' objection
[e]	9.15-16	Jesus' explanation
[e′]	9.17a	Ananias goes into the house
[d′]	9.17b	Ananias lays hands on Saul
[c′]	9.18a	Saul recovers his sight
[b′]	9.18b	Saul is baptized
[a′]	9.19a	Saul is strengthened

Translation

'Western' Text	Codex Vaticanus B03
[a] **9.10a** There was a certain disciple in Damascus called Ananias and the Lord said to him in a vision, 'Ananias'.	**9.10a** There was a certain disciple in Damascus called Ananias and the Lord said to him in a vision, 'Ananias'.
[b] **10b** He said, 'Here am I, Lord'.	**10b** He said, 'Here am I, Lord'.
[c] **11** The Lord said to him, 'Get up and go to the street called Straight and look in the house of Judah for Saul called the man from Tarsus; for behold, he is praying **12** and he has seen a man named Ananias coming in and placing a hand on him so that he could see again'.	**11** The Lord said to him, 'Get up, go to the street called Straight and look in the house of Judah for Saul called the man from Tarsus; for behold, he is praying **12** and he has seen in a vision a man named Ananias coming in and laying his hands on him so that he could see again'.
[d] **13** Ananias replied, 'Lord, I have heard from many people about this man, the evil things that he has done to your holy ones in Ierousalem; **14** and here he has authority from the High Priests to arrest all those who call on your name'.	**13** Ananias replied, 'Lord, I have heard from many people about this man, the evil things that he has done to your holy ones in Ierousalem; **14** and here he has authority from the High Priests to arrest all those who call on your name'.
[e] **15** But the Lord said to him, 'Go on, because this person is my chosen vessel to bear my name before the Gentiles and even their kings, and also the sons of Israel. **16** I will show him what he must suffer for the sake of my name.'	**15** But the Lord said to him, 'Go on, because this person is my chosen vessel to bear my name before the Gentiles and even kings, and also sons of Israel. **16** I will show him what he must suffer for the sake of my name.'
[e'] **17a** So Ananias got up and set off;	**17a** Ananias set off
[d'] **17b** and he went into the house and having laid his hands on him said, 'Brother Saul, the Lord has sent me, Jesus who appeared to you on the way which you were pursuing, so that you may see again and be filled with the Holy Spirit';	**17b** and went into the house and having laid his hands on him said, 'Brother Saul, the Lord has sent me, Jesus who appeared to you on the way which you were pursuing, so that you may see again and be filled with the Holy Spirit';
[c'] **18a** and straightaway there fell from his eyes something like scales and he could immediately see again;	**18a** and straightaway there fell from his very eyes something like scales and he could see again;
[b'] **18b** and he got up and was baptized;	**18b** and he got up and was baptized,
[a'] **19a** and after taking food, he gained strength.	**19a** and after taking food, he was strengthened.

Critical Apparatus

9.11 Ἀνάστα B *pc* ‖ Ἀναστάς 𝔓⁷⁴ ℵ *rell*.

In B03, two commands are given to Ananias, both in the aorist, whereas most other MSS give the first verb as an aorist participle.

9.12 ἄνδρα ἐν ὁράματι B C 1175 bo^ms | ἐν ὁρ. ἄν. E H L P 049. 056. 0142. 33. 1739 𝔐 ar e sy^{p.h} mae; Chr | ἐν ὁρ. Ψ 88* *pc* ‖ ἄνδρα 𝔓⁷⁴ ℵ A 81. 629. 1646. 1877* *pc* lat sa bo aeth^{pt}.

The absence of the mention of the vision in ℵ01 among others avoids stating the obvious but does not alter the sense. h omits the whole of 9.12.

τὰς χεῖρας Β ℵ² E 88. 1646 *pc* ‖ χεῖρας 𝔓^74vid ℵ* A C 81. 945. 1505. 1739. 1891. 2495 *pc*: cf. 19.6 | χεῖρα Η L Ρ Ψ 049. 056. 33 𝔐 it vg^mss sy.

The reading of B03, in the plural with the article, resembles the wording of 9.17 which describes how Ananias accomplishes the command he is given here. It is also found in accounts of the laying on of hands to accompany prayer at 8.17, 18, 19 (Peter and John in Samaria), and finally at 19.6 (Paul in Ephesus) where, however, the article is omitted in a variant reading of 𝔓^74 ℵ A B D *al.* The absence of the article may indicate that the phrase 'lay on hands' is being used as a fixed expression and that when the article is included the action is being carried out more deliberately than as an expected gesture accompanying prayer; in this case, the equivalent could be the use of the possessive in English. Thus, in Jesus' command the action is part and parcel of praying for Saul but when Ananias actually carries out the order his separate movements are spelt out in detail. The singular χεῖρα without the article is unusual and not found elsewhere in a description of prayer.

9.13 ἤκουσα Β 𝔓^74 ℵ A C E 36. 81. 88. 453. 1175. 1646 *pc* ‖ ἀκήκοα Η L Ρ Ψ 049. 056. 1739 𝔐.

The aorist ἤκουσα focuses on the fact that Ananias heard about Saul sometime in the past, rather than on his present knowledge as the perfect does. In English translation, however, the perfect is the only acceptable past tense to use in this instance.

9.15 τῶν ἐθνῶν ... βασιλέων υἱῶν (τε Ἰσραήλ) Β C* 1245 *pc* | ἐθ. ... βασ. υἱῶν 𝔓^74 ℵ A C² E H L Ρ Ψ 049. 056. 33. 1739 𝔐 ‖ τῶν ἐθ. ... τῶν βασ. τῶν υἱῶν (retroversion) mae.

The inclusion of the article before the first member of the group of three has the effect of repeating a known phrase associated with Saul/Paul as the apostle 'to the Gentiles'. The mention of 'kings and sons of Israel' suggests, however, that the phrase is not being used here as the familiar expression associated with Saul/Paul. In mae, all three groups mentioned are arthrous: 'the Gentiles and also the (= their?) kings and the sons of Israel'.

9.17 ἀπῆλθεν δὲ Ἀνανίας Β 𝔓^45.74 ℵ *rell* ‖ τότε ἐγερθεὶς Ἀ. ἀπ. 614. 1611. 2412 *pc* (h) p (sy^p) mae.

With the connective τότε, the response of Ananias is presented as a result of the insistent persuasion of Jesus (cf. Read-Heimerdinger, *The Bezan Text*, pp. 212–13): when he hears his explanation, he responds by getting up and carrying out his commands.

Σαούλ B 𝔓⁴⁵·⁷⁴ℵ *rell* || Σαῦλε E h mae.

The same variant is found in Jesus' address to Saul in 9.4. The Aramaic form of the name would be the more expected form between Aramaic speakers, but it contrasts with the use of the Greek form by Jesus in 9.11 (cf. 22.7 D05, where Jesus addresses Saul by the Greek form of his name, and 22.13 d05 where Ananias addresses him by the same Greek form).

9.18 αὐτοῦ ἀπὸ τῶν ὀφθαλμῶν B 𝔓⁴⁵ᵛⁱᵈ A 69. 1175 *pc* || ἀπὸ τ. ὀφθ. αὐτοῦ 𝔓⁷⁴ ℵ C E H L P Ψ 049. 056. 33ᵛⁱᵈ. 1739 𝔐.

The attestation of both these readings is Alexandrian but the word order of ℵ01 differs from that of B03.

ἀνέβλεψέν τε B 𝔓⁷⁴ A H P Ψ 049. 056. 1. 69. 81. 226*. 330. 547. 618. 1243. 1245. 1505. 1646. 1828. 1854. 2147. 2495 | ἀν. δέ ℵ C* 2492 | καὶ ἀν. 𝔓⁴⁵ || ἀν. τε παραχρῆμα (C²) E L 33. 88. (104). 226ᶜ. 323. 440. 614. 927. 945. 1175. 1241. 1270. 1611. 1739. 1837. 1891. 2344. 2412 *pm* (h) p syᵖ sa mae aeth; Chr.

The inclusion of the adverb παραχρῆμα in the WT, repeating the idea already expressed by εὐθέως at the beginning of the verse, insists on the immediacy of the effect of Ananias' prayer.

9.19a ἐνισχύθη B (𝔓⁴⁵) C* 323. 945. 1175. 1611. 1739. (1891) *pc, confortatus est* h || ἐνίσχυσεν 𝔓⁷⁴ ℵ A C² E H L P Ψ 049. 056. 33 𝔐 mae.

The difference in the readings is between the passive ('was strengthened') and the active ('gained strength').

Commentary

[a] 9. 10a *Jesus Calls Ananias*
The first two elements form an introduction to the episode, bringing a new character on stage and establishing a dialogue between him and Jesus.

9.10a Ananias is a representative character, indicated by the adjective τις, which Luke typically uses to present a character who acts not so much as an individual as a representative of a type (cf. 8.9, 27 D05). In this case, being a member of the Jesus-believing Jewish community in Damascus, he acts on their behalf. Jesus is said to have spoken to him 'in a vision', though it is what Ananias hears rather than what he sees that is recorded.

[b] 9.10b *Ananias Responds*
9.10b As much in Jesus' call as in Ananias' response there is an echo of the call of Samuel (1 Sam. 3.4-8) but with the difference that whereas Samuel did not recognize the voice of God and had to be called four times, Ananias responds immediately and recognizes the one calling him as 'Lord'. It would

seem from the succession of visions that Luke relates in Acts that the early disciples were familiar with this kind of direct communication with the divine.

[c] 9.11-12 *Jesus' Command*

9.11 The instructions given to Ananias by Jesus resemble those given to Philip when he was instructed to go and meet the Ethiopian eunuch (8.26). Ananias is to get up and go, without further ado (πορεύθητι),[85] to the street called Straight (Εὐθεῖαν). This is a street that still exists in Damascus,[86] but in Luke's account the name has a metaphorical as well as a historical value, referring to the 'straight paths' of John the Baptist's prophetic cries in the wilderness. Quoting the words of Isaiah, he had called the Jewish people to repentance, exhorting them to 'make the ways of the Lord straight (εὐθείας)' or again, 'make the crooked paths straight (εὐθείας)' (Lk. 3.4-5, and par., cf. Isa. 40.3-4). An allusion to the prophecy of Isaiah here is made clear by the parallel passage in Acts in which Saul reproaches the Jewish magician, Elymas ('Ετοιμᾶς D05) called Bar-Jesus, for 'making crooked the straight paths of the Lord' before warning him of his impending blindness (Acts 13.9-11). Saul, in other words, has been taken to a household that is faithfully following God.

The name of the householder is given as Judah,[87] who may well have been a real person but in view of the significance of the street where his house was situated his name also has the force of representing a Jewish community, one that is being faithful to God. It is not, though, a household of believers since Ananias has to be sent from elsewhere in the city to communicate the message of Jesus to Saul; rather it would appear to be a community of Jews who had followed the commands of John the Baptist to repent and be ready for the Messiah.[88] They are to be distinguished from other Jews who would not have given Saul a sympathetic welcome in view of his experience of the risen Jesus. Ananias is to look for a man called Saul who was known as being from Tarsus. His name is pronounced here in its Greek form (in contrast to the Aramaic form with which Jesus addressed him according to some MSS, cf. 9.4, and see *Critical Apparatus*). The

85. Zerwick and Grosvenor, *Analysis*, p. 379: 'Aor. impv. of this verb rare, implying ? "without delay".'

86. The 'street called Straight' is a main thoroughfare, known today as *Derb el-Mustaqîm*, which formerly had porticos on either side and gates at the end (K. Lake and H.J. Cadbury, *English Translation and Commentary*, in Foakes-Jackson and Lake (eds), *Beginnings of Christianity*, IV, p. 102).

87. The Greek Ἰούδα could be translated 'Judas' in English, but as it is the same name in Greek that is used for the patriarch (and, indeed, the apostle Judas) this is the form of the name that has been used here to show the similarity and the play on names that is possible in Greek.

88. Similar groups of Jews who had adhered to the teachings of John the Baptist (19.1-7) or who are noted as being devout (8.2) are identified in the narrative of Acts. It is clear that not all Jews shared Saul's opposition to the Jesus-believers even though they did not believe themselves.

mention of his place of origin defines him as a Jew from the Diaspora, a fact not explicitly stated in earlier references to him although to a contemporary reader of Acts it would no doubt have been apparent from his role as persecutor of the Hellenistic disciples that he was himself a Diaspora Jew (see *Excursus* 1). The directions given to Ananias for finding Saul will be echoed in the parallel story of Cornelius who is directed to the house where Peter was lodging in 10.3-6.

9.12 Saul is to be found praying, having seen in a vision Ananias performing actions which must have seemed to Ananias, as he heard Jesus relating them, astonishing: he went into the house and laid hands on Saul so he could see again. It is not clear if Saul already knew Ananias or if his identity was only revealed in the vision; he later describes him as 'a devout man according to the Law and by the testimony of all the Jews' (22.12).

'Laying on hands' is a gesture of blessing, accompanying prayer of a personal nature for the person concerned (cf. 8.14). The term 'see again' (ἀνα-βλέπω) is used by Luke in his Gospel as a sign of the coming of the Messiah in an apparent allusion to Isa. 42.18 (cf. 61.1 LXX), when Jesus himself cites the prophecy as evidence of his identity (Lk. 7.22). It is also used in a metaphorical sense to express spiritual 'sight' in the healing of the blind beggar on the road to Jericho whom Jesus causes to 'see again' (18.41, 42, 43): here the beggar was a symbol of the Twelve who were unable to 'see' what Jesus was telling them about his death (18.31-34) but the recovery of their sight is anticipated by the miraculous healing of the blind man by Jesus.[89] In the same way, Saul's blindness is a sign of his lack of spiritual understanding, despite his high status within Judaism and his fanatical zeal for the Law, and he needs divine healing in order to comprehend the true nature of Jesus.

[d] 9.13-14 *Ananias' Objection*
The narrator makes use of this dialogue between Ananias and Jesus first, to reiterate what has already been stated twice about the intensity of Saul's opposition to the Jesus-believers and, secondly, to present for the first time a statement of the mission given to Saul by Jesus (see 9.15-16 below).

9.13-14 The initial reaction of Ananias is not necessarily to challenge the veracity of the vision nor to refuse to carry out Jesus' command but rather to express his puzzlement, for what he has heard about Saul does not concord with the vision: Saul is known to be a fierce persecutor of the followers of Jesus in Ierousalem and to have come to Damascus to arrest the disciples there.

---

89. The metaphorical meaning of 'see spiritually' is close to the other literal meaning of the verb ἀναβλέπω, 'look up', which Luke always uses with reference to 'looking up to heaven' (Lk. 9.16; 19.5; 21.1). In Acts 22.13 where Saul/Paul himself tells the story of Ananias, the verb is ambiguous, meaning either 'look up (at Ananias)' or 'see again'.

The reference to Saul as 'this man' (τοῦ ἀνδρὸς τούτου) contrasts with the designation of the disciples in Jerusalem as 'your saints' (τοῖς ἁγίοις σου), the first application in Acts to believers of this term that was used in the Jewish Scriptures for what was set aside for God – such as people (e.g. a prophet, cf. Acts 3.21; 4.27, 30) or places (cf. 7.33). The spelling in the extant MSS for Jerusalem is the Hebrew-derived form (Ἰερουσαλήμ) which conflicts with the information given by the narrator in 8.1-2 that it was the believers in Hierosoluma (Ἱεροσόλυμα, see *Commentary, ad loc.*) who were affected by the persecution. Since most MSS do not maintain the distinction between the two forms of the name with the same regularity as the Bezan text (see *General Introduction*, § VII), here missing, the Hebrew-derived spelling may be a scribal or editorial choice. If it is the reading Luke intended, it would reflect the attitude of the Jews, including the disciples, in Damascus who continued to view Jerusalem as the religious centre. That Ananias is later spoken of by Saul/Paul as 'a devout man according to the Law' (22.12) confirms this impression.

Saul's activities have obviously been much talked about among the Jesus-believers: on the one hand, news has been brought about his attacks in Jerusalem, possibly by Hellenist believers who had been forced to flee (cf. 8.3); and on the other, his business in Damascus is common knowledge – why, then, Ananias may well wonder, can Saul not see and why should Ananias be the one to go and pray for him?

[e] 9.15-16 *Jesus' Explanation*

9.15 Jesus repeats his command even more insistently than the first time, but answers Ananias' implicit questions about what he has told him concerning Saul by explaining his own intervention in choosing Saul for a particular mission.

First, Saul is a 'chosen instrument'[90] belonging to Jesus, an expression with a positive connotation.[91] Secondly, his task is to bear the name of Jesus, information that counters Ananias' fears based on what he has heard of Saul's attacks on those who 'call on your name'. The Greek verb βαστάζω has the same metaphorical meaning as the English 'bear', with the implication of something to be endured (cf. 15.10), as Jesus' final comment will indicate.

---

90. The demonstrative here is a nominative pronoun (οὗτος), without the negative tone of Ananias' phrase 'this man' (τοῦ ἀνδρὸς τούτου). The Greek expression σκεῦος ἐκλογῆς consisting of noun + genitive reflects a common Hebraic construction which, being unnecessary in Greek (cf. Zerwick, *Biblical Greek*, § 40), illustrates the extent to which the election of Saul by God to carry out a mission belongs to a Jewish framework of theological concepts. Comparison may be made with King Saul who was known as 'the elect of God' (L. Ginzberg, *Legends of the Jews* [7 vols; Philadelphia: The Jewish Publication Society of America, 11th edn, 1982], IV, p. 72).

91. Literally, 'he is a chosen instrument *for me* (μοι)' using the dative of the personal pronoun: 'Where εἶναι with dative forms part of the predicate it usually carries the idea of credit (or discredit) in the person's eyes' (Turner, *Syntax*, p. 329).

Careful note should be made of Jesus' portrayal of Saul's task here: he is not defining the particular mission of Saul as apostle to the Gentiles but rather describing a general situation, with the result that the meaning of 'bear my name' is not so much 'to witness' as to 'bear the weight of'. The word 'name' (ὄνομα) echoes the use of the same term in the Jewish Scriptures (םש in Hebrew) as an oblique reverential reference to God as well, of course, as to the orders given to the apostles by the Sanhedrin not so long ago to do nothing in 'this name' (4.17; cf. 4.18, 30; 5.28). Finally, Saul is to bear the name of Jesus before Gentiles, kings and Jews. ἔθνη means both the 'nations' and the 'Gentiles' but the inclusion in the list of the 'sons of Israel' suggests that it is the religious sense that is intended here. For the time being, the specific nature of Saul's mission is not spelt out. As the mention of 'the kings' between the two peoples indicates, he will be used by Jesus to uphold his name before everyone, including kings of foreign powers (cf. 22.15: 'you will be a witness for him to all men').

9.16 In the climate of hostility to Jesus, 'bearing' his name was inevitably a task involving risk and hardship. Jesus continues to reassure Ananias by further making clear his personal involvement with Saul: he himself will take care of revealing to Saul the sufferings that await him. From being the one who persecuted those who 'call on the name' of Jesus (9.14), Saul will become one who is persecuted for the same reason.

[e'] 9.17a *Ananias Goes into the House*
9.17a As a result of Jesus' explanations, Ananias now obeys his commands without further ado and acts out the details of Saul's vision. By relating not only how Ananias fulfilled Jesus' orders but also replicated the vision given to Saul, the narrator demonstrates how the events in this passage are fully planned and directed by God. Even so, the willingness of the human agents to accept the divine plan is a *sine qua non* of its execution, as will be seen in later incidents in Acts where the plan of God is frustrated by disciples who insist on their own plan, notably Saul himself.

[d'] 9.17b *Ananias Lays Hands on Saul*
9,17b Once at the house where Saul was staying, Ananias having laid his hands on him speaks to him directly, with the Jewish greeting 'Brother Saul',[92] which is a clue to the Jewish mentality of Ananias and the rooting of this meeting in Jewish tradition (cf. 22.14: 'The God of our fathers appointed you...'). He announces that the Lord has sent him, immediately assimilating

92. The term 'brother' is used typically in addressing fellow Jews (cf. 2.29; 3.17; 6.3; 7.2; 13.26, 38; 22.1; 23.1, 5, 6; 28.17) which may have prompted the Aramaic spelling here (Σαουλ = לואש) although E h mae use the Greek form. The Aramaic form is the only one found in the LXX; Luke alone among biblical writers uses the Greek form Σαῦλος, cf. 9.1, 4 WT, 11, 17 WT; 22.7 D05, 13 d05.

the divine title with the person of Jesus which, while quite startling from a Jewish point of view, would be comprehensible to Saul since he had experienced the divine presence of the risen Jesus on the road to Damascus. Ananias' reference to 'the way which you were pursuing' is emphasized in the Greek, and the whole clause can have a double meaning: literally, it refers to the road Saul was pursuing to reach Damascus; metaphorically, it can be understood as meaning the 'Way' of the Jesus-believers (cf. 9.2) which Saul was pursuing (in the sense of 'persecuting').[93]

Ananias clarifies the purpose of his visit as being for Saul to recover his sight and be filled with the Holy Spirit, juxtaposing the two aspects – physical and spiritual – implied by the Greek verb ἀναβλέπω (see on 9.12 above). Although Jesus has already mentioned the role played by Ananias in the recovery of his sight, as seen by Saul in a vision (cf. 9.12), this is the first mention of the Holy Spirit in relation to Saul. It did not form part of Saul's vision of Ananias nor, indeed, will it be made explicit as a consequence of Ananias' prayer for him (see 9.18a below).

[c′] 9.18a *Saul Recovers His Sight*
The episode is brought to a conclusion in the final three elements as the intention of Jesus in sending Ananias to Saul is fulfilled.

9.18a It is striking that the first part of Ananias' purpose in visiting Saul, so that he 'may see again', is related in graphic detail and as an instantaneous result, whereas no mention is made of his being 'filled with the Holy Spirit'. Though it may be reading too much into the absence of any manifestation of the Holy Spirit in response to Ananias' visit, the fact that Luke does not give any indication about how this aspect of Jesus' command was fulfilled is probably quite intentional.[94] His silence about the Holy Spirit at the beginning of Saul's life as a disciple of Jesus is in keeping with the resistance Saul/Paul will show towards the Holy Spirit in the later chapters of the narrative and the absence of the Holy Spirit from the trial scenes. As Saul/Paul continues in his missionary activity, his relationship with the Holy Spirit will be seen to be far from straightforward, and on repeated occasions he will resist the guidance given by the Spirit until he finally reaches Rome where he announces the good news to the Gen-

---

93. ἔρχομαι + dative in the clause ἐν τῇ ὁδῷ ᾗ ἔρχου could be considered to be a 'dative of disadvantage' (Turner, *Syntax*, p. 238; cf. B-D-R, § 192), meaning that Saul was 'coming against the Way' (cf. Mt. 21.5; Rev. 2.5, 16).

94. The narrator's technique of passing over facts in silence when there is some problem with them was seen, for example, in the replacement of the twelfth apostle. No mention at all is made of the fact that Jesus did not elect a replacement for Judas before his ascension; instead, his lack of action is made all the more evident by Luke's underlining of a) Jesus' responsibility for choosing the original Twelve (1.2 D05), and b) Peter's initiative in organizing the election of a replacement. See *The Message of Acts*, I, pp. 107–39.

tiles 'in all boldness and without any obstacle' (28.31).[95] In fact, the first mention of Saul being filled with the Holy Spirit will be when, having aroused the interest of Sergius Paulus in the good news at the beginning of his mission in Cyprus (13.9), he changes his name to the Gentile name 'Paul' and opposes the Jewish magician Elymas (Ἐτοιμᾶς D05) by causing him to be blind for a time.[96] In other words, it is possible that Luke's silence concerning Saul being filled with the Spirit at the outset of his conversion is to be interpreted in the light of his later resistance, not as a sign that he did not receive the Spirit at this point but that there was something unsatisfactory about his being filled in accordance with what Jesus intended.

For the time being, a decisive change nevertheless takes place in Saul's attitude towards Jesus, instantly as some MSS stress (see *Critical Apparatus*), as his sight is restored when 'scales' fall from his eyes, an image found in the apocryphal book of Tobit (*Tob.* 11.12).

[b'] 9.18b *Saul is Baptized*

9.18b Once he can see again, Saul becomes an active participant[97] and goes on to be baptized. Saul's own account spells out the meaning of this baptism: 'wash away your sins, calling on his name' (22.16). It is, in other words, an outward witness to an inner experience of accepting the Lordship of Jesus and acknowledging his power to forgive his sins, which would, of course, include his persecution of Jesus and his people.

[a'] 9.19a *Saul is Strengthened*

9.19a Saul then goes on to eat and recover his physical strength. The parallels in this comment with the conclusion to king Saul's visit to the medium at Endor are striking (see *Excursus* 2.2).

[BB-A'] 9.19b-30 *Saul among the Disciples*

Overview

This third episode in the story of Saul contrasts with the first, the persecutor becoming the object of persecution in his turn. The action is set at first in Damascus but then moves to Jerusalem as Saul goes back to his point of departure when he is forced to flee from the Syrian capital. When that also

---

95. For a fuller discussion of Paul's resistance to the Holy Spirit, see Rius-Camps, 'Gradual Awakening'.

96. There are strong and deliberate parallels between Saul's blindness and the blindness of Elymas/Etoimas the magician (13.6-11); these will be discussed in detail in *The Message of Acts*, III, *ad loc.*

97. The active participle ἀναστάς, 'having got up', contrasts with Saul's attitude of helplessness in 9.8 where, according to the MSS, it is the companions who help Saul up (ἤγειρον αὐτόν); see *Critical Apparatus*.

becomes too dangerous, he goes back to his home city of Tarsus and will remain there until Barnabas goes to fetch him to Antioch (11.25-26).

The chronology of these events is difficult to fix with certainty, not least because Paul mentions a time lapse of 3 years between his conversion (or his stay in Damascus) and his first visit to Jerusalem (Gal. 1.18a), which is not apparent from the Acts account though it is not impossible by any means. In speaking of his first visit, Paul will specify that it lasted only 15 days (1.18b), which concords with the problems Luke says he encountered in Jerusalem; but also that he only saw Cephas (Peter) and James (1.18a, 19), which is more difficult to reconcile with the Acts account where the apostles as a whole are mentioned.

Structure and Themes

The theme of persecution that dominated the first episode (9.1-9) is taken up again in this episode, with Saul being on the receiving end this time. The opponents are the Hellenist Jews, both in Damascus and in Jerusalem.

There are three separate scenes in this episode dealing with the period following Saul's conversion. He initially spends time in Damascus but has to flee from there when the Jews plot against him. He escapes to Jerusalem but eventually has to flee from there, too, when confronted by the hostility of the Hellenistic Jews:

[*A'A*]		9.19b-22	Saul in Damascus
	[a]	9.19b	Saul with the disciples
	[b]	9.20	Saul in the synagogues
	[b']	9.21	The amazement of the hearers
	[a']	9.22	Saul's perseverance
[*A'B*]		9.23-25	The plot of the Jews
	[a]	9.23	Preparation of the plot
	[b]	9.24a	Saul learns of the plot
	[b']	9.24b	The watch on the gates
	[a']	9.25	Saul's escape
[*A'A'*]		9.26-30	Saul in Ierousalem
	[a]	9.26a	Saul's arrival in Ierousalem
	[b]	9.26b	The fear of the disciples
	[c]	9.27a	Barnabas' support
	[d]	9.27b	Saul's report of his conversion
	[c']	9.28-29a	Saul's activity with the apostles
	[b']	9.29b	The hostility of the Hellenists
	[a']	9.30	Saul's escape to Tarsus

Translation

'Western' Text	Codex Vaticanus B03
[*A*a] **9.19b** He was with the disciples in Damascus for a considerable number of days;	**9.19b** He was with the disciples in Damascus for some days;
[b] **20** and he proclaimed Jesus with boldness as he went into the synagogues of the Jews, that this was the Son of God, the Messiah.	**20** and he immediately began to proclaim Jesus in the synagogues, that this was the Son of God.

[b′]   **21** All the people were amazed on hearing him and said, 'Isn't this the man who decimated the people who call on this name in Ierousalem? And hadn't he come here for this purpose, to bind them and take them to the High Priests?'

[a′]   **22** But Saul became all the more powerful in the word and confounded the Jews who lived in Damascus by demonstrating that the Messiah was Jesus, in whom God was well pleased.

[Ba]   **23** When a considerable number of days had passed, the Jews plotted together to kill him.

[b]   **24a** Their plot, however, became known to Saul.

[b′]   **24b** But they were keeping a close watch even on the gates, day and night, so that they might kill him.

[a′]   **25** But the brethren took him at night and lowered him through the wall, letting him down in a basket.

[A′a]   **26** When he arrived in Ierousalem, he tried to join the disciples;

[b]   **26b** and they were all afraid of him, not trusting that he was a disciple.

[c]   **27a** But Barnabas took an interest and introduced him to the apostles;

[d]   **27b** and he explained to them how he had seen the Lord on the road and that he had spoken to him and how in Damascus he had boldly spoken publicly in the name of Jesus.

[c′]   **28** And with them he went in and out in Ierousalem, boldly speaking publicly in the name of the Lord, **29a** and in addition he spoke and disputed with the Hellenists.

[b′]   **29b** They, however, set about trying to kill him.

[a′]   **30** When the brethren found out, they took him down to Caesarea by night and sent him off to Tarsus.

21 All the people were amazed on hearing him and said, 'Isn't this the man who decimated the people who call on this name in Ierousalem? And hadn't he come here for this purpose, to bind them and take them to the High Priests?'

22 But Saul became all the more powerful and confounded the Jews who lived in Damascus by demonstrating that the Messiah was Jesus.

23 When a considerable number of days had passed, the Jews plotted together to kill him.

24a Their plot, however, became known to Saul.

24b But they were keeping a close watch even on the gates, day and night, so that they might kill him.

25 But his disciples took him at night and through the wall lowered him, letting him down in a basket.

26 When he arrived in Ierousalem, he tried to join the disciples;

26b and they were all afraid of him, not trusting that he was a disciple.

27 But Barnabas took an interest and introduced him to the apostles;

27b and he explained to them how he had seen the Lord on the road and that he had spoken to him and how in Damascus he had boldly spoken publicly in the name of Jesus.

28 And with them he went in and out in Ierousalem, boldly speaking publicly in the name of the Lord, **29a** and in addition he spoke and disputed with the Hellenists.

29b They, however, set about trying to kill him.

30 When the brethren found out, they took him down to Caesarea and sent him off to Tarsus.

Critical Apparatus

9.19b (ἡμέρας) τινάς B 𝔓⁷⁴ ℵ *rell* ‖ ἱκανάς 𝔓⁴⁵, *pllurimos* h mae.

The adjective ἱκανάς conveys the impression of a longer period of time than τινάς, and coincides with the repeated reference at 9.23 to the time Saul spent in Damascus.

9.20 (καὶ) εὐθέως B 𝔓⁷⁴ ℵ *rell* ‖ *om.* h mae aeth.— εἰσελθών a b c h p q w vg^mss mae sy^p sa mae; Spec ‖ *om.* B 𝔓⁷⁴ ℵ *rell*.— ἐν ταῖς συναγωγαῖς B 𝔓⁷⁴ ℵ *rell* ‖ εἰς τὰς συναγωγὰς τῶν Ἰουδαίων h (p w sy^p sa) mae; Spec. — ἐκήρυσσεν B 𝔓⁷⁴ ℵ *rell*; Ir ‖ ἐκήρυξεν E e gig h mae.— μετὰ (+ πάσης h; Ir) παρρησίας h l mae; Ir Spec ‖ *om.* B 𝔓⁴⁵·⁷⁴ ℵ *rell*.— (ὅτι οὗτός ἐστιν) ὁ υἱὸς τοῦ θεοῦ B 𝔓⁷⁴ ℵ *rell* ‖ ὁ Χριστὸς ὁ υἱ. τ. θ. 441 h l t sa; Spec Theoph | ὁ υἱ. τ. θ. ὁ Χρ. mae; Ir.

According to 'Western' witnesses, Luke uses for the first time the expression 'the synagogue of the Jews' (cf. 13.5; 14.1: 17.1, 10), combined with the idea of 'movement into' rather than 'in', to show that Saul has distanced himself from his fellow-Jews. The imperfect of B03 indicates the onset of Saul's action of preaching as soon as (εὐθέως) he stayed with the disciples. The aorist of the WT means much the same but views the two actions globally. In addition, Luke uses the expression 'with (all) boldness' that was used in earlier chapters to evaluate the freedom with which the apostles preached the message of Jesus (cf. 4.13, 29, 31); the more attenuated comment in mae, however, suggests that Saul's preaching was not yet totally free. What Saul proclaimed is limited in B03 to Jesus being the Son of God, while the WT couples this term with that of the Messiah – both terms carry the article in the Greek witnesses because they are in apposition.

9.22 (ἐνεδυναμοῦτο) ἐν (– C) τῷ λόγῳ C E *pc* h l p (mae) ‖ *om.* B 𝔓⁴⁵·⁷⁴ ℵ *rell*.

The 'Western' reading is a rare use in Acts of ὁ λόγος on its own, without the qualification of either τοῦ θεοῦ or τοῦ κυρίου. The reference would seem to be to the contents of Saul's preaching in a general sense, rather than the specific message of Jesus which Saul/Paul is not presented in Acts as announcing until 13.5 D05; 15.35 B03 (see Read-Heimerdinger, *The Bezan Text*, pp. 297–310).

(Χριστός) + *in quo deus bene sensit* (retroversion: ἐν ᾧ ὁ θεὸς εὐδόκησεν) gig (h) l p mae ‖ *om.* B 𝔓⁷⁴ℵ *rell*.

The explanation that the additional words are a 'scribal gloss derived from either Mt 3.17 or Lk 3.22' (Metzger, *Commentary*, p. 321) is unsatisfactory, for the Gospel context is the baptism of Jesus and scribes would not typically add in words from another context (a point made by Lake and Cadbury, *Translation and Commentary*, p. 105, cited by Metzger, *ibid.*). Furthermore, the D05 reading of Lk. 3.22 does not have these words but a citation from Ps. 2.7. If the words are Luke's, however, it is entirely possible that, having omitted them from his reporting of Mark's baptism scene (Mk 1.11) according to the Bezan text of Lk. 3.22, he then introduces them into the first accounts of proclamation to the Jews that the Son of God and the Messiah was Jesus (cf. 9.20; see *Commentary*, 8.37).

9.25 οἱ μαθηταὶ αὐτοῦ (αὐτόν 69. 81*) B 𝔓⁷⁴ ℵ A C 6. 81ᶜ. 88. 1175. 1646 *pc* vgˢᵗ·ʷʷ; Dion | αὐτὸν οἱ μαθ. E H L P Ψ 056. 33ᵛⁱᵈ. 1739 𝔐 a c gig l p vgᶜˡ syᵖ·ʰ sa bo || 'the brethren' (οἱ ἀδελφοί) mae.

The idea that Saul already had disciples in Damascus is anachronistic.

9.30 (εἰς Καισάρειαν) διὰ νυκτός E (614. 1611. 2412 *pc*) p (gig vgᵐˢˢ) syᵖ·ʰ** sa mae || *om.* B 𝔓⁷⁴ ℵ *rell.*

The considerable attestation to the time detail among the early versions would be a reason to consider its authenticity here. On the other hand, the fact that διὰ νυκτός is found in two different places within the Greek MSS (before and after the name of the town) suggests that it was inserted later, perhaps to mirror the account of Saul's escape from Damascus (cf. 9.25).

Commentary

[BB-*A´A*] 9.19b-22 *Saul in Damascus*

[a] 9.19b *Saul with the Disciples*
9.19b Following his baptism, Saul spent some time in Damascus (whether a longer or shorter time varies according to the MSS). He stayed not with the Jews whose house he had gone to when he first arrived and where Ananias had come to see him (cf. 9.11) but with the Jesus-believers.

[b] 9.20 *Saul in the Synagogues*
9.20 While he was with the disciples he lost no time in going to the synagogues and teaching the Jews of Damascus about Jesus. The plural 'synagogues' indicates a large number of Jews in the city, among whom would be the Jesus-believers who at this date continued to meet with other Jews. It was, of course, in these synagogues that Saul had gone to track down the Jesus-believers to take them as prisoners to Ierousalem. The reversal in his attitude towards them must have been a powerful incentive to listen to him. The qualification of the synagogues as 'of the Jews' in certain MSS (see *Critical Apparatus*) shows the distance Saul had put between himself and his fellow-Jews, especially combined with the idea of his going 'into them'.

The fact that the name of Jesus is preceded with the article in Greek is an indication that the people he was talking to already knew of him.[98] What is new is that Saul proclaims him as the Son of God and, according to the WT, the Messiah. The only other occasion in Acts when Jesus is declared to be the Son of God is when the Ethiopian eunuch declares his belief that Jesus is the Son of God following his conversation with Philip (8.37). As was noted there, the expression was used by Jews in a special sense as a term referring to

---

98. τὸν Ἰησοῦν; see Heimerdinger and Levinsohn, 'The Use of the Article', pp. 22–23.

the Messiah,[99] by virtue of the messianic application of Ps. 2.7: 'You are my son, today I have begotten you'. Saul/Paul will make the connection between Jesus (the Messiah, D05) and the quotation from the Psalms in his speech to the synagogue in Antioch of Pisidia (13.33). For both the eunuch and Saul, the truth they discovered concerning Jesus was that he was the beloved Son of God, anointed by him to rule as Messiah.

The WT qualifies Saul's manner of preaching as 'with (all) boldness'. This is a phrase that first appeared in the prayer of the apostles when they were released from prison (4.29). An analysis of the occurrences of the word 'boldness' in the context of Acts suggests that the word is used in the dual sense of courage and frankness, 'daring' in that the speaker spoke in the face of opposition and at the same time delivered startlingly new teachings.[100] The narrator's comment following the apostles' prayer indicates that their boldness at that point was not complete ('they started to speak the word of God with boldness' and not 'with all boldness' as they had requested). In the case of Saul, since Luke does not present him as preaching the message of Jesus in all its freedom until the end of the book (cf. 28.31), the reading 'with boldness' is probably the one to be accepted here.

[b'] 9.21 *The Amazement of the Hearers*

9.21 Those who heard Saul in the synagogues could have been both believing and unbelieving Jews, 'all' of them, although it is chiefly the reaction of the latter which is in focus at this point (see following verse). Their stupefaction at seeing Saul in his changed state is similar to the reaction of the people to Jesus in the synagogue of Nazareth (Lk. 4.22) where the same kind of question ('Isn't this the son of Joseph?') was asked. In Damascus, there are in fact two questions, corresponding to the two objections raised by Ananias in response to Jesus (9.13-14): a) Saul is known to have savagely attacked[101] the disciples in Jerusalem; b) his visit to Damascus had been[102] for the purpose of

---

99. Although in biblical writings the term 'Son of God' was not specifically applied to the Messiah, the meaning seems to have become a designation for the Messiah in post-biblical Judaism (see *Commentary*, 8.37b). Vermes observes that while 'Son of God' was not used as an independent term as an equivalent for 'Messiah', the two were sometimes used together: 'Whereas every Jew was called "son of God", the title came to be given preferably to the just man, and in a very special sense, to the most righteous of all just men, the Messiah, the Son of David' (*Jesus the Jew*, p. 195). The use in the New Testament (by Matthew and John and in the Letter to the Hebrews) of the term 'Son of God' to designate the Messiah, without this application being introduced as something new or innovative, suggests that the development had already taken place at least in some Jewish circles before the Messiah appeared.

100. See *The Message of Acts*, I, pp. 261–62, esp. n. 46.

101. Saul/Paul uses the same verb πορθέω, 'destroy, annihilate', twice in his letter to the Galatians (1.13, 23).

102. The pluperfect participle ἐληλύθει has the effect of expressing an unfulfilled intention, as in the case of the eunuch at 8.27-28.

arresting the believers and taking them back to the Ierousalem authorities. The fact that far from persecuting them he has now become one of them must have been not only perplexing but also quite shocking to Jews who were as opposed as he had been to Jesus-believers.

[a′] 9.22 *Saul's Perseverance*

9.22 The implicit hostility in the response of the Jews causes Saul to intensify his preaching as he argued against them. The chief concern of his teaching was to prove that the Messiah, the one longed for by the Jews, was Jesus.[103] This is the equivalent of the summary of his proclamation in the synagogues in 9.20. In both cases, his aim is to take two known entities, Jesus and the expected Messiah/Son of God, and to show that they are one and the same. The term 'Messiah' is amplified in several versions with the typical messianic definition, he 'in whom God was well-pleased' (see *Critical Apparatus*). The phrase had already been associated with Jesus in the words attributed to God at his baptism (Mk 1.11; cf. Mt. 3.17; Lk. 3.22 but not D05) and the transfiguration (Mt. 17.5; Lk. 9.35 D05); by reiterating them here in the context of the Damascus synagogues, the narrator situates in a Jewish framework Saul's demonstration of how the longed-for ideal has been fulfilled in the person of Jesus.[104]

[BB-*A′B*] 9.23-25 *The Plot of the Jews*

[a] 9.23 *Preparation of the Plot*

9.23 The plot of the Jews to kill Saul was not hatched immediately but only after he had been preaching in Damascus for some time. This will be the first

---

103. Which element of the clause is the subject is ambiguous at both 9.20 and 9.22. There is grammatical uncertainty among linguists as to what allows the subject to be distinguished from the complement in copula clauses containing two nouns (with a verb such as εἰμί or γίνομαι); see, e.g., Porter, *Idioms*, pp. 109–10. Often, it is the article before one of the two nouns that allows that element to be identified as the subject (known) and the anarthrous noun as the complement (new information) (e.g. καὶ θεὸς ἦν ὁ λόγος, Jn 1.1). This seems to be the case in the declaration made by the Ethiopian eunuch, Πιστεύω τὸν υἱὸν τοῦ θεοῦ εἶναι Ἰησοῦν Χριστόν (8.37, see *Commentary*). However, when the subject is a demonstrative, it seems that the complement can be articular (e.g. οὐχ οὗτός ἐστιν ὁ τέκτον;, Mk 6.3). The reason for this may be that in this case two known elements are being identified as one and the same rather than new information being given about one of them. The order of nouns does not, in any case, help to determine the subject since word order in copula clauses varies considerably (see Callow, 'Constituent Order in Copula Clauses', pp. 68–89).

104. The recognition of the phrase 'my Son "in whom I am well-pleased"' as a messianic designation derives from such references in the Jewish Scriptures as 2 Sam. 2.20 (David referring to himself); Isa. 42.1 (God referring to his 'servant'). In Hebrew, the verb רצה is read in both instances, whereas the LXX reads the verb εὐδοκέω at 2 Kgdms 2.20 (as in the Gospel references to the baptism and transfiguration) and προσδέχομαι at Isa. 40.1 (where the 'servant' is identified as Jacob/Israel in the LXX).

of a series of repeated attempts on the life of Saul/Paul by his fellow Jews; they will continue, in fact, as long as he persists in teaching about Jesus in the synagogues. From one point of view, this persistence looks heroic and is generally interpreted in such a way; from the point of view of the narrator of Codex Bezae, however, it is stubbornness on Saul's part to insist on going to the Jews when, as the reader of Acts will learn in due course, Jesus had ordered him to go to the Gentiles (cf. 22.21 [esp. D05]; Gal. 1.16). Unfortunately, as Codex Bezae is missing in chapter 9 no more can be said on the matter for the time being.

The plot to kill[105] Saul in Damascus is mentioned by Saul/Paul himself in 2 Cor. 11.32. According to the chronology he provides in Gal. 1.17, it would have arisen some two or three[106] years after his conversion experience, when he had returned to Damascus following a visit to Arabia, the purpose of which is not stated. According to 2 Corinthians, the person who wanted to seize him was the governor of the Nabataean King Aretas of Arabia who apparently held some kind of power within Damascus; from the telling of the story by Luke, it was the Jews who were behind the plot, which is by no means impossible by virtue of collusion between the Jews of Damascus and the Nabataean governor.

[b] 9.24a *Saul Learns of the Plot*

9.24a It is probable that Saul gets to hear about the plot[107] from Jews who were sympathetic to him, as will happen on future occasions, too (cf. 20.3; 23.16).

[b'] 9.24b *The Watch on the Gates*

9.24b As a result of Saul's knowledge of the plot, the Jews take particular care to have the walls of the city guarded. The watch kept on the walls is confirmed by the information Saul/Paul gives in 2 Cor. 11.32 ('the governor under King Aretas guarded the city of Damascus in order to seize me') where there is no mention of the Jews but only the foreign powers in Damascus. Since Saul/Paul provides no motive for the attempt to seize him (and implicitly do away with him), it would seem that he has chosen instead to name

---

105. The verb ἀναιρέω is used particularly by Luke in the New Testament, and with great frequency: with reference to Jesus (Lk. 22.2; Acts 2.23; 10.39; 13.28); the men crucified with him (Lk. 23.32); the apostles (Acts 5.33); James (12.2); Stephen (22.20 [cf. 8.1]; 26.10); other characters (5.36, Theudas; 7.28a, an Israelite, 28b, an Egyptian); and most frequently to Saul/Paul (9.23, 24, 29; 21.36 D05; 23.15, 21, 27; 25.3).

106. τρία may be reckoned inclusively (Bruce, *Text*, p. 205); cf. the 'three days' between Jesus' death and resurrection.

107. The word ἐπιβουλή, 'plot', is always used of Saul/Paul (cf. 20.3, 19; 23.30) to refer to plots against him by Jews; συστροφή, 'conspiracy', is also found at 23.12, although this word elsewhere means 'commotion' (19.40); finally, ἐνέδρα, to mean more specifically an 'ambush', is found at 23.16; 25.3, cf. 23.21.

only the political powers that had the ability to force a capture. Luke's interest, on the other hand, is to draw attention to the danger Saul put his life in by preaching in the synagogues.

[a′] 9.25 *Saul's Escape*
9.25 It is the details of Saul's escape through the walls of Damascus in a basket in the account of both 2 Corinthians and Acts that confirm that the two accounts refer to the same incident. Saul/Paul will allude to it as an example of his weakness; although in the context of his letter to the Corinthians it is not clear in what way his escape from Damascus 'showed his weakness' (2 Cor. 11.30), his comment suggests that it is all the more justified to interpret Luke's account as a criticism of his preaching in the synagogues since it led to the threat of death.

[BB-*A′A′*] 9.26-30 *Saul in Ierousalem*

[a] 9.26a *Saul's Arrival in Ierousalem*
9.26a If the spelling Ἰερουσαλήμ, Ierousalem, is intentional,[108] Saul is said to go from Damascus back to the religious centre of Judaism.

[b] 9.26b *The Fear of the Disciples*
9.26b Once there, his attempt to join the disciples met with fear on their part. It is not clear whether a precise group of disciples is meant: those in Ierousalem, that is the disciples who had remained attached to the Jewish religious system, or the Jesus-believers in general. To recap the situation as it has been presented so far in the narrative of Acts: When the Hellenist disciples in Hierosoluma (Ἱεροσόλυμα) were scattered by the persecution following Stephen's death (8.1), the apostles had stayed behind, in Ierousalem according to the Bezan text. They were not alone, however, since in time James will also be found there (12.17) and indeed, he will become the leader of the disciples who adhered most strictly to the Jewish Law (cf. 21.18-25). And two of the apostles, Peter and John, are presented in 8.25 as having begun to move forward in their attitude to traditional Jewish ways of thinking when, following the gift of the Holy Spirit to the Samaritans, they return to Hierosoluma instead of Ierousalem. The presence of Barnabas (see 9.27) in the city suggests that some Hellenists had either managed to stay or had returned by now, but his positive support of Saul indicates that he was not part of the group that Saul tried to meet with initially and who were afraid of him.

---

108. The absence in this chapter of the Bezan text makes it impossible to be sure how the spelling of Jerusalem in these passages fits with the narrative intention. The AT does not seem to maintain a pattern systematically in the same way as does the Bezan text (see *General Introduction*, § VII).

The particular circumstances that gave rise to the disciples' fear are not explained. In fact, there is a fair amount of background activity, known from Saul/Paul's letter to the Galatians (Gal. 1.15-24), that is not mentioned at all here by Luke. It is possible to suppose that Luke did not know the details of what went on in these early years of Saul's life as a disciple but it is equally possible that he did not need to explain the circumstances in detail, either because he knew that his reader was familiar with them already (entirely plausible in the case of Theophilus the High Priest) or was sufficiently close to the events to be able to read the situation correctly from his own experience. The main cause of the disciples' mistrust would, in any case, presumably be their difficulty in believing the reality of the radical change in Saul, from being a leading persecutor to being on the side of the persecuted.

[c] 9.27a *Barnabas' Support*
9.27a Barnabas has already been introduced in his role as 'encourager' which the apostles recognized in 4.36 (and in 1.23 D05 where his function as 'son of encouragement' was implied by the use of the name given to him by the apostles). Here, he continues to exercise his gift in the support he lends to Saul. The one who was intending to lead (ἀγάγῃ) the arrested disciples to Ierousalem is now led in his turn by Barnabas (ἤγαγεν) to the apostles (Saul/Paul insists that he only saw Peter [Cephas] and James [Gal. 1.18-19]).

[d] 9.27b *Saul's Report of his Conversion*
9.27b Once with them, Saul[109] explains to the apostles what had happened, summarizing his experience on the road to Damascus as seeing and hearing the Lord, which resulted in his bold proclamation of Jesus in Damascus. Barnabas will continue to act as support for Saul when he later goes to fetch him from Tarsus to introduce him to the Antioch church (11.25-26a).

[c'] 9.28-29a *Saul's Activity with the Apostles*
9.28 The result of the explanation of Saul's experience in Damascus was that the apostles were reassured, to the extent that he joined them.[110] His

---

109. Since the subject of the second verb διηγήσατο, 'he explained', is not specified and the connective καί links it to the previous verb ἤγαγεν, 'he led', it could be understood that the same subject for both verbs is intended, meaning that Barnabas acted as Saul's advocate. However, the following clause is also connected with καί with a clear change of subject from Barnabas to Saul. It is perhaps more to be expected that Saul should relate his experience than that Barnabas should do so for him. The Middle Egyptian MS mae, which often agrees with Codex Bezae in its extant chapters, spells out that the subject of this sentence is 'Saul'.

110. The Greek is ambiguous at this point: either the verb ἦν can be taken to mean that Saul 'was with them', and the three present participles that follow (εἰσπορευόμενος, ἐκπορευό–

activity as part of their group is described in terms similar to the description of the presence of Jesus with the disciples in 1.21: 'he went in and out among us'.[111] The same expression is found in the Jewish Scriptures of David who led the Israelites in their military campaigns, 'going out and coming in' to fight with their enemies (1 Sam. 18.13, 16). Consequently, more than meaning simply that Saul went about his daily business, the use of the expression here could have the sense that Saul and the apostles would go to meet with the people and the authorities in Ierousalem where they would speak boldly in the name of Jesus, and afterwards return to their own place. This activity would be carried out in part at least in the Temple where, like the apostles in the earlier days, they would be able to teach in the public porticoes (cf. 3.11; 5.20-21, 25, 42).[112]

Although no length of time is actually stated here, according to Gal.1.18 Saul stayed only two weeks in Jerusalem.

9.29a His audience was not restricted to local, Aramaic-speaking Jews but extended to the Hellenists, the Greek speakers in the city. Saul, of course, was no stranger to them since, being from Tarsus himself, he would have previously been one of their number.

[b′] 9.29b *The Hostility of the Hellenists*

9.29b It was the Hellenist Jews with the young Saul as their delegate (cf. 7.58) who had already led the opposition to Stephen (cf. 6.9-14) when he had worked miracles and spoken in the power of the Holy Spirit (6.8-10). They now oppose Saul in his turn and attempt to kill him just as the Jews of Damascus had tried to do. It is notable that in contrast to the account of the Hellenists' dispute with Stephen, whom they were not able to resist (6.10), no such comment is made of their discussions with Saul. While it is true that Saul spoke openly and boldly, there is no indication from the narrator that he was doing what God wanted him to do in spending time in Ierousalem, arguing with Jews. We will learn later from Saul/Paul himself that Jesus instructed him to get out of Ierousalem because 'I am sending you to the Gentiles' (Σπεῦσον, καὶ ἔξελθε ἐν τάχει ἐξ Ἰερουσαλὴμ ... ὅτι ἐγὼ εἰς ἔθνη μακρὰν ἐξαποστέλλω σε [fut. AT], 22.18, 21 D05).

μενος, παρρησιαζόμενος) describe his activity while he was part of their group; or, ἦν + participle is periphrastic and the sentence means that Saul was doing each of these activities with the apostles.

111.   In 1.21, the prepositional phrase ἐφ' ἡμᾶς is used to link Jesus' activity of 'going in and out' to the group of disciples. In view of the use of the verbal expression to describe David's leadership of Israel in their military campaigns (1 Sam 18.13, 16), it is possible to understand the preposition ἐπί as expressing the sense of Jesus' leadership over his disciples.

112.   Of the nine occurrences in the New Testament, the verb παρρησιάζομαι is used 7 times in Acts, and elsewhere it is always used of public preaching: 9.27 (synagogues of Damascus); 13.46 (synagogue/city, cf. 13.14, 44); 14.3 (synagogue, cf. 14.1); 18.26 (synagogue); 19.8 (synagogue); 26.26 (audience hall, cf. 25.23).

[a'] 9.30 *Saul's Escape to Tarsus*

9.30 For the second time, Saul needs help to escape from Jewish opponents. As in Damascus, his fellow-disciples assist him to leave the city, though without having recourse to such dramatic means this time, and take him down to Caesarea on the coast from where he was sent off (presumably in a ship) to Tarsus. In his letter to the Galatians (Gal. 2.1), Saul/Paul will say that he did not return to Jerusalem for 14 years: the next visit recorded in Acts was when he was sent with Barnabas to take the gift from the Antioch church in *c*.44 CE (11.30; 12.25).

Excursus 2

Parallels in the Jewish Scriptures with the Conversion of Saul

1. *Heliodorus (2 Maccabees 3)*

The following parallels between Heliodorus in 2 Maccabees 3 and Saul in Acts 9 may be observed:[113]

1. Both speak with authority (ἐξουσία), from the king (2 Macc. 3.6) // the High Priest (Acts 26.12).
2. Authority is communicated, in the form of commands (ἐντολάς, 2 Macc. 3.7) // letters (ἐπιστολάς, Acts 9.2; 22.5).
3. Both were travelling (ἐποιεῖτο τὴν πορείαν, 2 Macc. 3.8 // ἐν τῷ πορεύεσθαι, Acts 9.33; πορευομένῳ, 22.6; πορευόμενος, 26.12).
4. A High Priest, ἀρχιερεύς, is involved (2 Macc. 3.9 and *passim* // Acts 9.1; 22.5; 26.10).
5. A vision is perceived by Heliodorus (ὤφθη, 2 Macc. 3.25) // Saul (εἶδον, Acts 26.13; cf. 9.3).
6. The manner of the appearance of the vision is sudden (ἄφνω, 2 Macc. 3.27 // ἐξαίφνης, Acts 9.3; 22.6).
7. It causes them to fall to the ground (πεσόντα πρὸς τὴν γῆν, 2 Macc. 3.27 // καὶ πεσὼν ἐπὶ τὴν γῆν, Acts 9.4; ἔπεσά τε εἰς τὸ ἔδαφος, 22.7; πάντων τε καταπεσόντων ἡμῶν εἰς τὴν γῆν, 26.14).
8. Both are left blind (πολλῷ σκότει περιχυθέντα, 2 Macc. 3.27 // οὐδὲν ἔβλεπεν, Acts 9.8; οὐκ ἐνέβλεπον, 22.11).
9. They are carried (εἰς φορεῖον ἐνθέντες ... ἔφερον ἀβοήθετον, 2 Macc. 3.27-28) // led away in their helplessness χειραγωγοῦντες, Acts 9.8; χειραγωγούμενος, 22.11).

Further parallels may be observed in the account of Apollonius, the praetor of Syria, Phoenicia and Cilicia in *4 Maccabees* 4:

10. Threats are referred to (μετὰ ἀπειλῶν, *4 Macc.* 4.8 // ἀπειλῆς, Acts 9.1).
11. The verb 'flash around' is used to describe the light (περιαστρά-πτοντες τοῖς ὅπλοις, *4 Macc.* 4.10 // αὐτὸν περιήστραψεν, Acts 9.3;

---

113. Cf. H. Windisch, 'Die Christusepiphanie vor Damaskus (Acts 9:22 und 26) und ihre religionsgeschichtliche Parallelen', *ZNW* 31 (1932), pp. 1–23.

περιαστράψαι ... περὶ ἐμέ, 22.6), the only occurrences of this compound verb in the whole of Hellenistic literature.

The various verbal parallels are so strong that the similarities between the Maccabaean narratives and that of Acts are unlikely to have arisen merely from the similarity of theme but more probably indicate a certain deliberate modelling of Saul's experience on that of the foreign opponents of the Jews in the earlier history of Israel.

2. *Saul the King of Israel* (*1 Sam. 28.8-25*)

This passage tells of the final meeting between Saul the king of Israel and Samuel the prophet before Saul meets his death in a battle with the Philistines (1 Samuel 31). Samuel had died (25.1; 28.3), having not spoken to Saul since he had rebuked him for disobeying the Lord's command to fully exterminate the Amelekites (15.1-33) and warned him that the kingdom would be taken from him. Saul had been pursuing David, appointed by Samuel to replace him as king, in an attempt to kill him because he was jealous and saw that the Lord 'had departed from him' and was with David instead (18.12). David, aware of Saul's determination to kill him, had gone to live with the Philistines outside Israel to escape from Saul's pursuit of him. On an occasion when the Philistines were preparing to attack Israel, Saul discovered that the Lord had ceased all communication with him and, in desperation, decided to invoke the spirit of Samuel by consulting a medium in Endor.

There are a number of striking similarities between the account of the meeting between the spirit of Samuel and Saul king of Israel on the one hand and, on the other, the encounter between Jesus and Saul on the road to Damascus. The parallel operates despite the underlying difference in the situations, namely that Saul the king invoked Samuel whereas Jesus took the initiative in appearing to Saul/Paul.

1 Samuel (1 Kingdoms LXX)	*Acts 9*
Context: Saul is persecuting David (καταδιώκει, 26.20; 27.1)	Context: Saul is persecuting Jesus (διώκεις, 9.4)
Samuel, who had died, appears and speaks with Saul (28.13-15)	Jesus, who had died, appears to speak with Saul (9.4-6)
Samuel indicates to Saul his imminent death in battle, a path which the medium will encourage him to engage in (πορεύσῃ ἐν ὁδῷ, 28.22)	Jesus appeared to Saul when he had already embarked on his path (ἐν τῇ ὁδῷ ᾗ ἤρχου, 9.17)
Samuel represents God (θεοὺς ἑόρακα, 28.13: MT 'Elohim'; *TgJ* 'an angel of the Lord')[114]	Jesus is the Lord (κύριε, 9.5, 10, 13; ὁ κύριος, 9.11, 15, 17)
Saul is accompanied by two men (δύο ἄνδρας, 28.8)	Saul is accompanied by men (οἱ ἄνδρες, 9.7)

---

114. D.J. Harrington and A.J. Saldarim (Introduction, Translation and Notes), in K. Cathcart, M. Maher and M. McNamara (eds), *Targum Jonathan of the Former Prophets. The Aramaic Bible: The Targums* (Edinburgh: T&T Clark, 1987).

Saul asks Samuel, 'What shall I do?' (Τί ποιήσω; 28.15)

Saul asks Jesus, 'What do you want me to do?' (Τί με θέλεις ποιῆσαι; 9.6a WT)

Samuel foresees Saul's death (σὺ καὶ οἱ υἱοί σου μετὰ σοῦ πεσοῦνται, 28.19)

Saul will be baptized, signifying a death to the past (ἐβαπτίσθη, 9.18)

Saul fell to the ground, full of fear (ἔπεσεν ... ἐπὶ τὴν γῆν καὶ ἐφοβήθη σφόδρα, 28.20, cf. v. 21)

Saul fell to the ground (πεσὼν ἐπὶ τὴν γῆν, 9.4), in great bewilderment (ἐκστάσει μεγάλη, WT); he was trembling and terrified (τρέμων καὶ θαμβούμενος, 9.6a WT)

Saul had eaten nothing all day and all night (οὐ γὰρ ἔφαγεν ἄρτον ὅλην τὴν ἡμέραν καὶ ὅλην τὴν νύκτα, 28.20)

Saul neither ate nor drank for three days (οὐκ ἔφαγεν οὐδὲ ἔπιεν, 9.9)

Repetition of the idea of 'hear' (ἀκούω: 28.21 [× 2], 22, 23)

Repetition of the idea of 'hear' (ἀκούω: 9.4, 7, 13)

Saul had not listened to the voice of the Lord (διότι οὐκ ἤκουσας φωνῆς κυρίου, 28.18)

Saul heard the voice of the Lord (ἤκουσεν φωνήν, 9.4)

Traditionally, the medium sees the spirit but does not hear it; the one for whom the spirit appears hears the spirit but does not see it[115]

The men heard the voice (of Saul, WT) but did not see anyone (ἀκούοντες μὲν τῆς φωνῆς μηδένα δὲ θεωροῦντες, 9.7)

The woman feeds Saul to strengthen him (καὶ φάγε, καὶ ἔσται ἐν σοὶ ἰσχύς ... καὶ ἔφαγον, 28.22, 25)

Saul takes food and is strengthened (λαβὼν τροφὴν ἐνίσχυσεν, 9.19)

Saul arose from the ground (ἀνέστη ἀπὸ τῆς γῆς, 28.23)

Saul arose from the ground (ἠγέρθη ἀπὸ τῆς γῆς, 9.8a; ἐγείρατέ με ἀπὸ τῆς γῆς ... ἤγειρον αὐτόν, 9.8a, b WT)

Saul and his men go away at night (ἀπῆλθον τὴν νύκτα ἐκείνην, 28.25)

Saul's companions lead him by the hand because he cannot see (οὐδὲν ἔβλεπεν ... χειραγωγοῦντες, 9.8c)

A further similarity between the two Sauls is worth noting: despite his hostility against David and his disobedience to God's commands, King Saul was known after his death as 'the elect of God';[116] Saul of Tarsus is likewise described by Jesus in terms of election: σκεῦος ἐκλογῆς ἐστίν μοι, 'he is a chosen instrument for me' (Acts 9.15).

[BA′] 9.31–11.18 *Peter*

General Overview

The third sub-sequence [BA′] of the threefold sequence [B] is devoted to Peter. It corresponds to that of Philip, the Hellenist leader who was the topic of the first sub-sequence [BA]. Spanning over two chapters, it is as long as the other two sub-sequences together, an indication of the importance of the problem it treats for the whole of the book.

This is the first time in the book of Acts that Peter is presented on his own. He has been the spokesperson on earlier occasions (e.g. 1.15-26; 2.14-40) and has played an active, even leading, part in previous incidents of healing and

115. Ginzberg, *The Legends of the Jews*, IV, p. 70.
116. Ginzberg, *The Legends of the Jews*, IV, p. 72.

other miracles but always in the company of other apostles (5.12-16); even when he has appeared to be the sole protagonist, John has been there with him (3.1, 3, 11; 4.13, 19; 8.14, 25). Now, though, it is time for Peter's story, which will continue with intermittent diversions through to the end of chapter 12.

Structure and Themes
There are three episodes in this sub-sequence. The first divides into two scenes and the second into four:

[BA'-*A*]	9.31-43	Peter in Judaea
[*AA*]	9.31-35	Peter in Lydda
[*AA'*]	9.36-43	Peter in Joppa
[BA'-*B*]	10.1–11.1	Cornelius
[*BA*]	10.1-8	Cornelius in Caesarea
[*BB*]	10.9-16	Peter's vision in Joppa
[*BB'*]	10.17-23a	Cornelius' men find Peter in Joppa
[*BA'*]	10.23b–11.1	Peter meets Cornelius in Caesarea
[BA'-*A'*]	11.2-18	Peter's report to the apostles

[BA'-*A*] 9.31-43 *Peter in Judaea*

Overview

A summary statement (9.31) links this new sub-sequence to the previous one [BB] and brings the subject back to the topic of the first episode of the sequence overall [BA-*A*], namely, the development of the Jesus-believing groups, by describing the situation of the church (or churches, WT) in Judaea, Galilee and Samaria as peaceful and strong. The narrative then zooms in, so to speak, on two particular communities within Judaea where, despite the overall healthy state of the church, there were particular problems. In both, Peter exercises a ministry of healing but without dealing with the fundamental issue which he will have to confront in the remaining part of the narrative devoted to him (10.1–11.18), namely that of the entry of the Gentiles into the Church.

As Peter is brought back to the narrative, he is presented as travelling throughout the areas where churches had been established (διερχόμενον διὰ πάντων ... κατελθεῖν πρὸς τοὺς ἁγίους, 9.32). He will repeat at least part of this itinerary in the last scene of the sub-sequence that concerns him, revisiting these churches in order to strengthen the brethren (τοὺς ἀδελφοὺς ... διὰ τῶν χωρῶν, 11.2 D05). On his first visit, it will soon emerge that he still holds to a traditional Jewish way of thinking and that when he returns he will teach the believers what he has learnt from his experience with Cornelius in Antioch (see *Commentary*, 11.2).

Structure and Themes
The opening element of this episode looks back (οὖν) to summarize the situation at this point (μέν) as the same time as looking forward (δέ) to the account

concerning Peter which is about to follow.[117] The narrative then moves through two scenes, [AA] and [AA'], which, though closely connected, are structured independently and take place first in Lydda, and then in Joppa. The conclusion to the second scene prepares for the following episode of the sub-sequence [BA'-B] by specifying the house where Peter was staying, which will play a part in what happens next:

[AA]	9.31-35	Peter in Lydda
	Intro.	9.31	Summary and bridge
	[a]	9.32	Peter arrives in Lydda
	[b]	9.33	Aeneas' paralysis
	[c]	9.34a	Peter declares healing
	[b']	9.34b	Aeneas stands up
	[a']	9.35	The impact on the residents of Lydda and Sharon
[AA']	9.36-43	Peter in Joppa
	[a]	9.36	The disciple Tabitha
	[b]	9.37a	The death of Tabitha
	[c]	9.37b	The upper room
	[d]	9.38	The disciples send for Peter
	[e]	9.39a	Peter goes with them
	[f]	9.39b	The widows show him her handiwork
	[f']	9.40a	Peter heals Tabitha
	[e']	9.40b	Tabitha sits up
	[d']	9.41a	Tabitha is helped to stand
	[c']	9.41b	Peter presents her alive
	[b']	9.42	News of the healing is spread around Joppa
	[a']	9.43	Peter stays in Joppa

Translation

'Western' Text	Codex Vaticanus B03
[A] Intro.	**9.31** So the churches throughout all Judaea and Galilee and Samaria had peace as they were built up and walked in the fear of the Lord, and with the encouragement given by the Holy Spirit they were multiplied.	**9.31** So the Church throughout all Judaea and Galilee and Samaria had peace as it was built up and walked in the fear of the Lord, and with the encouragement given by the Holy Spirit it was multiplied.
[a]	**32** And it happened as Peter travelled around among them all that he came down to the saints who lived in Lydda.	**32** And it happened as Peter travelled around among them all that he came down to the saints who lived in Lydda.
[b]	**33** He found there a certain man named Aeneas who had been lying on his bed for eight years and who was paralysed.	**33** He found there a certain man named Aeneas who had been lying on his bed for eight years and who was paralysed.
[c]	**34a** And Peter said to him, 'Aeneas, the Lord Jesus Christ has healed you; get up and lay a table for yourself'.	**34a** And Peter said to him, 'Aeneas, Jesus Christ has healed you; get up and lay a table for yourself'.
[b']	**34b** And straightaway he got up.	**34b** And straightaway he got up.

---

117. On the force of μὲν οὖν as a connective looking back as well as forward, see Levinsohn, *Textual Connections*, pp. 137–50.

[a′]	**35** All the people living in Lydda and Sharon saw him, and they turned to the Lord.	**35** All the people living in Lydda and Sharon saw him, and they turned to the Lord.
[A′a]	**9.36** In Joppa there was a certain disciple named Tabitha, which in translation means Dorcas [Gazelle]. She was full of good works and acts of charity that she used to do.	**9.36** In Joppa there was a certain disciple named Tabitha, which in translation means Dorcas [Gazelle]. She was full of good works and acts of charity that she used to do.
[b]	**37a** It happened in those days that she fell sick and died.	**37a** It happened in those days that she fell sick and died.
[c]	**37b** When they had washed her, they placed her in the upper room.	**37b** When they had washed her, they placed her in an upper room.
[d]	**38** Since Lydda was near Joppa, when the disciples heard that Peter was there they sent two men to him begging him not to hesitate to travel on to them.	**38** Since Lydda was near Joppa, when the disciples heard that Peter was there they sent two men to him begging, 'Do not hesitate to travel on to us'.
[e]	**39a** Peter got up and went with them.	**39a** Peter got up and went with them.
[f]	**39b** When he arrived, they took him to the upper room and all the widows stood around him weeping and showing him coats and garments that Dorcas had made when she was with them.	**39b** When he arrived, they took him up to the upper room and all the widows stood beside him weeping and showing him coats and garments that Dorcas had made when she was with them.
[f′]	**40a** Peter put them all outside, knelt to pray and turned to the body and said, 'Tabitha, rise in the name of our Lord Jesus Christ'.	**40a** Peter put them all outside, knelt to pray and turned to the body and said, 'Tabitha, rise'.
[e′]	**40b** She opened her eyes, and when she saw Peter she sat up.	**40b** She opened her eyes, and when she saw Peter she sat up.
[d′]	**41a** He gave her his hand and made her stand.	**41a** He gave her his hand and made her stand.
[c′]	**41b** He called the saints and the widows and presented her alive.	**41b** He called the saints and the widows and presented her alive.
[b′]	**42** It became known throughout all of Joppa and many people believed in the Lord.	**42** It became known throughout all of Joppa and many people believed in the Lord.
[a′]	**43** It came about that Peter stayed for a considerable number of days in Joppa at the house of a certain Simon, a tanner.	**43** It came about that Peter stayed for a considerable number of days in Joppa at the house of a certain Simon, a tanner.

Critical Apparatus

9.31 Ἡ μὲν οὖν ἐκκλησία ... εἶχεν ... οἰκοδομουμένη καὶ πορευομένη ... ἐπληθύνετο B 𝔓⁷⁴ ℵ A C 36. 81. 88. 181. 242. 307. 323. 453. 610. 915. 945. 1175. 1646. 1678. 1739. 1877. 1891. 1898 *pc* c dem ph ro w vg (syᵖ co); PsDion Theoph ‖ Αἱ μὲν οὖν ἐκκλησίαι (+ πᾶσαι E) ... εἶχον ... οἰκοδομούμεναι καὶ πορευόμεναι (-οι καὶ -οι E Ψ) ... ἐπληθύνοντο E H L P [Ψ] 049. 056. 0142. 614 𝔐 e gig l p vgᴰ syʰ boᵐˢˢ (mae) aeth; Chr Aug.

That the variant reading of this verse is intentional is indicated by the fact that the singular noun in B03 is accompanied by verbs that are all in the singular, whereas the plural noun in the 'Western' text has all the corresponding verbs in the plural. On the one hand, the plural reading may have been influenced by the reference to 'churches' in the plural at 16.5. This later reference, however, is not a summary statement of the general situation in the same way that the description here at 9.31 is, but rather alludes to the various churches that Paul is said to have visited (cf. 15.41). The plural at 9.31 may, then, have been deemed too specific and a more general comment preferred, especially since there has been no mention in the narrative so far of churches outside Jerusalem (cf. 2.47 D05 Ierousalem; 8.1, 3 Hierosoluma), and Galilee has not been mentioned at all.

9.32 Λύδδα B ℵ² A Ψ 326 *pc* e gig l vg | ἐν Λ. ℵ* ‖ -δαν C E H L P 049. 056. 1739 𝔐 p vg^DO.

Both B03 and ℵ01 read the indeclinable form of the name of the town, Lydda, though ℵ01 prefaces it with the preposition which is not strictly necessary. The feminine form is found in other MSS. The same variant is found at 9.35, but at 9.38 the reading of the feminine form of the name Lydda is without variant. As D05 pays particular attention to the declension of names, the feminine may well reflect the Bezan reading.

9.34 ΕΙΑΤΑΙ B ‖ ΙΑΤΑΙ 𝔓⁷⁴ ℵ *rell*.

The form ΕΙΑΤΑΙ could have arisen because of phonetic confusion, ΕΙ not being distinguished from Ι in speech. Although strictly speaking ἴαται is the perfect (ΕΙΑΤΑΙ/ΙΑΤΑΙ in the MSS) of the verb and ἰᾶται is the present (normally written ΙΑΤΑΙ), there are instances in the MSS where the two spellings are interchangeable. The form with Ε is found in the present (Acts 10.38 D05), the perfect (Mk 5.29 B03, D05) and the imperfect (Acts 5.16 D05). Metzger's argument (*Commentary*, p. 322) that ΕΙΑΤΑΙ here in B03 must be a perfect because of the identical spelling in Mk 5.29 is therefore not valid. It is rather the sense of the proclamation in which the verb is found that shows that a perfect is intended (see *Commentary* below). Since most MSS read ΙΑΤΑΙ at Mk 5.29 where a perfect is clearly meant, the same could be said of the sentence in question here where ΙΑΤΑΙ is also read by most MSS. (See H.J. Cadbury, 'A Possible Perfect in Acts ix.34', *JTS* 49 [1948], pp. 57–58.)

Ἰησοῦς Χριστός B* 𝔓⁷⁴ ℵ C Ψ 048. 33^vid. 440 *pc;* Did^pt | Ἰ. ὁ Χρ. B² E H L P 049. 056. 1739 𝔐; Did^pt | ὁ Χρ. 614. 1241. 1505. 1611*. 1646. 2495 ‖ ὁ κύριος Ἰ. (+ ὁ A) Χρ. A 36. 94. 181. 307. 441. 1175 *pc* it vg^cl sa mae aeth.

In the original hand of B03 neither Ἰησοῦς nor Χριστός is preceded by the article. In this reading, both words could be understood as a simple name, but the corrected reading of B03 which is shared by other Greek MSS adds the article before Χριστός thereby giving it the value of 'the Messiah' rather than the name 'Christ'. The combination Ἰησοῦς Χριστός is found as a kind of theological formula in the context of healing at 8.12 and 16.18, preceded by 'in the name of'. There are no other instances in ℵ01, B03 or D05 of Ἰησοῦς ὁ Χριστός.

In the manuscripts of the 'Western' tradition that read ὁ κύριος before the name of Jesus, the whole phrase transmits an established formula: 'the Lord Jesus Christ'. This full expression is found twice at 11.17 and 15.26 in the text of Acts common to the AT and D05 but there are many more readings of it in the D05 text, always in a liturgical or formal context. For fuller information on the titles of Jesus, see Read-Heimerdinger, *The Bezan Text*, pp. 254–74, esp. 272–73.

9.35 Λύδδα B ℵ A H* Ψ 33^vid. 326. 618. 1837 *pc* gig vg ‖ -δαν 𝔓^53.74 C E H² L P 049. 056. 1739 𝔐 l p.

The attestation of the indeclinable or declinable form of the name of the town is much the same as for 9.32 (see above).

9.36 ἔργων ἀγαθῶν B 𝔓^45 C E 36. 69. 104. 453. 1175 *al* ‖ ἀγ. ἔργ. 𝔓^53.74 ℵ A H L P Ψ 049. 056. 1739 𝔐.

Both readings are attested by witnesses to the AT, with ℵ01 and B03 divided over the place of the adjective. The adjective before the noun is the more emphatic word order (Read-Heimerdinger, *The Bezan Text*, pp. 89–90).

9.37 (λούσαντες δὲ) ἔθηκαν B 36. 453. 1898 *pc*; Theoph ‖ ἔθ. αὐτήν 𝔓^74 ℵ* A 81. 181. 255. 1175. 1646. 1837. 2344 *pc* (p) t (vg) | αὐτὴν ἔθ. 𝔓^45.53 ℵ² C E H L P Ψ 33^vid. 1739 𝔐 c e gig l r t vg^U.

B03 omits the object pronoun; in the first and second hands of ℵ01 the order of the object pronoun and the verb varies.

ἐν ὑπερῴῳ B 𝔓^45 ℵ H L P Ψ 049. 056. 1739* 𝔐 mae ‖ ἐν τῷ ὑπ. 𝔓^53.74 A C E 33^vid. 36. 88. 181. 226^c. 323. 440. 453. 467. 522. 614. 945. 1175. 1646. 1739^c. 1891. 2344 *al* latt sy co; Chr Theoph.

The use of the article before a noun that has not been previously mentioned is generally an indication that the referent is known. In this case, it is not the actual room that the audience is expected to be familiar with but rather the upper room as a symbolic location that has already served as a setting in Luke's work at Acts 1.13 (see *The Message of Acts* I, pp. 100–101). The omission of the article could have one of two functions: either 1) in accordance with the symbolic significance of the upper room, it draws attention to it, or 2) since the room was not known, it causes it to be an indeterminate one.

9.38 Μὴ ὀκνήσῃς διελθεῖν ἕως ἡμῶν B 𝔓^74vid ℵ A C* E 81. 181. (1175). 1646. 1898. (2344) gig l p r vg mae^(+) ‖ μὴ ὀκνῆσαι διελ. ἕως αὐτῶν 𝔓^45 C² H L P Ψ (049). 056. 1739 𝔐 sy^p mae^(+) aeth.

B03 reports the words in direct speech whereas the form of indirect speech is found in many Western MSS among others. Elsewhere in Acts, the verb παρακαλέω is always followed by λέγων when it precedes direct speech (2.40; 8.19 D05; 16.9, 15, 39 D05; 27.33).

9.39 ἀνήγαγον B 𝔓⁷⁴ ℵ *rell* ‖ ἤγαγον 𝔓⁴⁵ latt syᵖ·ʰ sa mae aeth.
The prefix in B03 corresponds to the fact that Tabitha was lying in a room above ground level.

παρέστησαν αὐτῷ B 𝔓⁷⁴ ℵ *rell* ‖ περιέστ- αὐτόν 876. 913. 1518. 2138 latt aeth; Cyp Chr PsOec.
The verb of B03 is intransitive but some minuscules and versions, in accordance with the Greek of certain Fathers, read an equivalent transitive verb insisting on the fact that the widows stood around Peter (cf. 25.7).

9.40 (ἀνάστηθι) ἐν τῷ ὀνόματι τοῦ κυρίου ἡμῶν Ἰησοῦ Χριστοῦ it vgᴰᴼ syʰ** sa mae; (Cyp) Ambr Spec ‖ *om.* B 𝔓⁴⁵·⁷⁴ ℵ *rell*.
The inclusion of a liturgical formula at a healing or act of a formal character is typical of the text of Codex Bezae (see Read-Heimerdinger, *The Bezan Text*, pp. 260–61). In addition to 15.26 (a reading shared by B03 and D05), the full form of the reference to the name of Jesus is found at 18.8 D05.

9.42 (ὅλης) Ἰώππης B 𝔓⁵³ C* | τῆς Ἰ. 𝔓⁷⁴ᵛⁱᵈ ℵ A C² E H L P Ψ 049. 056. 33. 1739 𝔐.
According to Metzger (*Commentary,* p. 369), 'Luke always use the definite article after καθ' ὅλης (Lk. 4.14; 23.5; Acts 9.31; 10.37)'. This is not the case, however, at Acts 10.37 D05 and the use of the article in Greek should not be thought of as a matter of custom or style. Here the presence of the article is justified by this being an anaphoric reference to Joppa (cf. 9.36, 38). The omission of the article before the name of Joppa draws attention to the significance of the place that will later be important in the account of Peter's vision of the ritually unclean animals (Joppa will mentioned six times: 9.43; 10.5, 8, 23, 32; 11.5).

Commentary

[BA′-AA] 9.31-35 *Peter in Lydda*

Introduction 9.31 *Summary and Bridge*
9.31 This sentence is linked to the preceding narrative with the connective μέν οὖν, which looks both backwards and forwards as the narrative moves on to the next development. On the one hand, μέν presents a first element while anticipating a second, which will be introduced with δέ: this follows in the

next verse, 9.32. οὖν, meanwhile, indicates that what is said in both clauses is in accordance with what has gone before.

The first statement is a summary, providing an assessment of the general situation of the Church at this point, in the regions of Judaea, Galilee and Samaria. The WT makes reference to individual churches, which may be considered problematic in so far as no churches in Samaria have been mentioned specifically and Galilee has not been mentioned at all. The Church has spread to these areas through the various events narrated in the previous sections, principally the dispersion of the Hellenists from Hierosoluma (8.1, 4) which was brought about by the persecution of Saul. It was this that prompted Philip's preaching in a city of Samaria and, following the visit of Peter and John there, other towns in Samaria were also evangelized. Philip himself eventually settles in Caesarea (8.40; cf. 21.8-9). Other persecuted disciples must have settled elsewhere, though specific mention is not made of believers in other places except Damascus (9.2, 10, 19, 25). In the present section, however, communities of believers will be seen to have been established in both Lydda and Joppa in Judaea, which implies that Luke does not spell out the full extent of the spread of the Church but makes it plain in this summary statement.

Judaea is named first as the centre of Judaism, and Samaria last as a region where there was intense religious hostility with the Jewish people, which they reciprocated (see *Commentary*, 8.5). In the centre of the list stands Galilee, the only one of the three regions where no church is mentioned in Acts, either before or after this reference. Galilee was, of course, the focus of Jesus' ministry and the place where he first met with his disciples after his resurrection (13.31). The fact of omitting any reference to Jesus-believers in Galilee in no way means that Luke knew of no churches there or was not interested in them. On the contrary, it is when people or places have assimilated the gospel message without any difficulties that Luke makes only the briefest mention of them.[118] The importance of Galilee is confirmed by its position in the centre of the list here.

Three features characterize these churches, all of them young.[119] First, they enjoyed peace, a situation no doubt facilitated, if not brought about, by the conversion of Saul who had been a zealous persecutor. Secondly, they

---

118. This is particularly true of Barnabas as has been seen in earlier sections (see *The Message of Acts*, I, pp. 129–31; 308–10), and of John-Mark as will be seen in later passages (see *ibid.*, II, 12.25; III, 13.5).

119. The mention of 'eight years' in the story of Aeneas, by its symbolic force, gives some indication of the age of the churches. Some in Judaea may have been founded following the visit of people from the area around Ierousalem to see Peter (Acts 5.16) in the early thirties; others will have been the result of the scattering of the disciples after the death of Stephen (8.1, 3) in around 37 CE; and others still will not have emerged until Saul stopped his persecution, possibly three years earlier or more (Gal. 1.16) if the story concerning Peter is understood to have followed the events concerning Saul.

were strengthened and followed the Lord with a reverential awe.[120] Thirdly, they increased in number which, according to the plural reading 'churches' (see *Critical Apparatus*) means the number of communities, but according to the alternative reading in the singular, 'Church', it could equally mean the number of disciples overall. This expansion is associated with the encouragement of the Holy Spirit.[121] The combination 'the fear of the Lord' and 'the encouragement of the Holy Spirit' confers a particularly positive note on this summary statement describing the condition of the Church at this point.

[a] 9.32 *Peter Arrives in Lydda*
9.32 The focus of attention now switches to Peter who was last mentioned in the narrative in his role as representative of the apostles, together with John, in Samaria (8.14-25). The connection with the summary statement is that he is presented as visiting some of the churches mentioned in it, with Lydda in Judaea being named in particular. Lydda was a town some 25 miles to the north-west of Jerusalem on the road leading to the seaport at Joppa. In going there, Peter was exercising his apostolic function of 'overseer' (ἐπισκοπή).[122]

The term 'the saints' (τοὺς ἁγίους) has so far been applied only to the believers in Jerusalem (9.13; cf. 26.10); its use with reference to the believers in Lydda and later in Joppa is a positive comment which sets the tone for the following account of difficulties in both towns.

[b] 9.33 *Aeneas' Paralysis*
9.33 The manner of introducing Peter's meeting with Aeneas suggests that Peter was not already familiar with the community in Lydda. Aeneas is a representative character ('a certain', τινά),[123] symbolizing the state of the church he is part of, and a man (ἄνθρωπος), which establishes him as a universal character (as opposed to ἀνήρ, one with a specific function). His name is

---

120. The verb οἰκοδομέω, 'build up', is also used at 20.32 of the strengthening of the Church. The verb πορεύομαι, 'walk', expresses the typically Lukan concept of the walking in the paths of the Lord (cf. Lk. 8.14; 9.57; 10.38; 13.33 *et al.*; Acts 8.36, 39) as distinct from the ways of Judaism (21.21, cf. v. 24 D05) or the Gentiles (14.16). As for 'the fear of the Lord', ὁ φόβος τοῦ κυρίου, this expression is found only in 2 Cor. 5.11 but is reflected in the name given to people who faithfully followed God, οἱ φοβούμενοι τὸν θεόν, 'God-fearers' (cf. Lk. 1.50; 18.2, 4; 23.40; Acts 10.2, 22, 35; 13.16, 26).

121. In Acts, the noun παράκλησις, 'encouragement, comfort, consolation', and the corresponding verb παρακαλέω, is associated with the Holy Spirit only in this instance. The term is otherwise used in a personal sense with reference to Barnabas alone (4.36; 11.23, 26 D05; cf. 13.15; 15.31).

122. Cf. 1.20; see *The Message of Acts*, I, pp. 126–28.

123. The introduction of a new character with the adjective τις ('a certain') is a device Luke uses to indicate that the person is representative of the class of persons he belongs to, without in any way negating the historicity of the account; cf. 3.2; 8.9, 27 D05; 9.10.

Greek, indicating he was a Hellenist, possibly one of those who had had to flee from Hierosoluma (8.4).

Aeneas was paralyzed and had been unable to move from his bed for eight years. The information about his paralysis is emphatic, being given twice in different terms.[124] The paralysis is symbolic of a spiritual rigidity that is a hindrance to spiritual freedom.

'Eight years' would seem to refer to the length of time that the community had existed, implying that Aeneas had been paralyzed since its beginning, in the same way as the lame man in Acts 3 had been paralyzed 'since his mother's womb' (3.2). In other words, he and the part of the church that he represents have been restricted in their movement right from the start. Throughout Acts, Luke uses numbers to refer to underlying facts and thereby to express his evaluation of a situation. Here, 'eight' also serves as a positive comment, reflecting as it does the idea that Jesus was resurrected on the 'eighth' day, the first day of the week after the Sabbath:[125] the communities of those who believed in him participated in the new life of which his resurrection was a first fruit even though they were not perfect.

[c] 9.34a *Peter Declares Healing*

9.34a Once Peter arrives on the scene, things move rapidly forward. Addressing Aeneas by his name, the first word he pronounces is the verb 'has healed'[126] which he proclaims as the work of Jesus. The name of Jesus is given with his full title in the WT, as is typical of Codex Bezae in formal or liturgical situations (see *Critical Apparatus*). The verb is best understood as a perfect,[127] in line with similar healings where the perfect is clearly used (e.g. Lk. 7.50; 8.48; 17.19; 18.42, σέσωκεν; 8.2, τεθεραπευμέναι; 17.14 D05, τεθε−ραπεύεσθε; Acts 4.14, τεθεραπευμένον). In Greek, the force of the perfect is to express a change of state,[128] equivalent here of saying that Aeneas is a healed man and no longer a paralysed one.

The second part of Peter's declaration of healing is open to two possible interpretations according to the meaning given to the command

---

124. In the terms Luke uses to describe Aeneas there are echoes of the story of the healing of the paralytic in the Gospel: κατακείμενον, cf. Lk. 5.25 B03; ἦν παραλελυμένος, 5.18, 24 B03 (παραλυτικός D05, cf. 5.19 D05). ἐπὶ κραββάτου is found in the Bezan text of Luke's Gospel (Lk. 5.19 D05, 24 D05) and in Mark's parallel account (Mk 2.4, 9, 11, 12) whereas Luke according to B03 uses κλινίδιον (Lk. 5.19, 24).

125. Cf. Lk. 9.28; 24.1; Acts 20.7; Jn 20.1, 19, 26; and esp. Ignatius, *Mg* 9.1: μηκέτι σαββατίζοντες, ἀλλὰ κατὰ κυριακὴν ζῶντες, ἐν ἧ καὶ ἡ ζωὴ ἡμῶν ἀνέτειλεν δι' αὐτοῦ.

126. Luke uses the verb ἰάομαι more than all the other writers of the New Testament put together (Lk. × 11 [− 4 D05]; Acts × 4 [+ 1 D05]; × 11 by other writers).

127. See B-D-R, § 311,1: it is a passive of a transitive deponent verb, here ἰάομαι, equivalent to τεθεραπεύεσθαι.

128. S.E. Porter, *Verbal Aspect in the Greek of New Testament, with Reference to Sense and Mood* (Studies in Biblical Greek, I; New York: Peter Lang, 1989), p. 257.

στρῶσον, which means 'spread'. Some such noun as κλίνη, 'couch', has to be understood, which could be either for sleeping on or for reclining on at table.[129] On the first interpretation, Peter would be telling Aeneas to make his bed, corresponding to Jesus' command to the paralytic to 'pick up his bed (κλινίδιον B03 / κράβαττον D05) and walk' (cf. Lk. 5.24): the difficulty with this is that the point of making his bed would be to prepare it for use, which is contrary to the idea of his being healed and having no more need to lie in bed. The second interpretation would mean that Aeneas was to get ready to eat, preparing a couch to recline at table. This corresponds to the command of Jesus on healing the daughter of Jairus, the ruler of the synagogue, that she should be given something to eat (Lk. 8.55). It also is reminiscent of the setting of the last meal Jesus ate with his disciples, 'a room spread [with cushions and so on]', ἀνάγαιον μέγα (οἶκον D05) ἐστρωμένον (Lk. 22.12).

[b′] 9.34b *Aeneas Stands Up*
9.34b In fact, Aeneas only carries out the first part of Peter's command, since Luke only says that he stood up. The implication is that the community represented by Aeneas is made well again but without fully participating in the nourishment available in the teaching of Jesus.

[a′] 9.35 *The Impact on the Residents of Lydda and Sharon*
9.35 The healing of Aeneas made a considerable impression, not only on the people of his own town but also on the population of the Plain of Sharon which stretched along the coast between Joppa and Caesarea. The news of such a widespread turning 'to the Lord', that is to Jesus, echoes the report of the conversion of thousands in Jerusalem (cf. 2.41, 47; 4.4; 6.1, 7) but especially the mass movement in Samaria (cf. 8.6-8). In contrast to Jerusalem, however, there is no indication here of persecution on the part of fellow-Jews, confirming the suggestion that the opposition of the Hellenists to the Jesus-believers in Jerusalem arose from their desire to maintain the approval of the Temple authorities (see *Excursus* 1).

[BA′-AA′] 9.36-43 *Peter in Joppa*

[a] 9.36 *The Disciple Tabitha*
9.36 Joppa was the main sea-port that served Jerusalem, with a mainly Jewish population though it was a Greek city.[130] There was, in addition, a community of Jesus-believers, represented by the disciple, Tabitha. This is

---

129. Cf. 1 Kgdms 9.26 where Samuel 'spread out (a bed) for Saul on the roof': καὶ διέστρωσαν τῷ Σαοὺλ ἐπὶ τῷ δώματι, using a compound of the verb στρώννυμι.

130. E. Schürer, *The History of the Jewish people in the Age of Jesus Christ* (3 vols; rev. and ed. G. Vermes, F. Millar and M. Black; Edinburgh: T&T Clark, 1973), II, pp. 110–44.

the only time in the New Testament that the feminine form of the Greek word 'disciple' (μαθήτρια) is found. The fact that her name is given in Aramaic indicates that she was not of Hellenistic origin but the translation of her name and the use of it a second time (cf. 9.39) would imply that the community of believers included Greek as well as Aramaic speakers. In addition, the name is in itself important, for according to Jewish Law a 'gazelle' was a wild animal that was allowed to be eaten in the settlements of the people of Israel by both the ritually clean and unclean.[131] The reference to the gazelle in this context occurs three times in the course of the reformed laws in the book of Deuteronomy, and could be a way of indicating here that Tabitha represented a community of both Hebrews (clean) and Hellenists (unclean); the use of her name in Greek suggests as much. The church in Joppa is the first such mixed community to be mentioned since that of Jerusalem (6.1-7). It is also possible that the name 'gazelle' serves as a verbal 'hook' to link this incident with the death of Saul, king of Israel, who is referred to as a 'gazelle' in David's lamentation (2 Sam. 1.19; see *Excursus* 3).

In line with the significance Luke accords to the indefinite marker τις, 'a certain', its presence before the name of Tabitha here indicates that like Aeneas, she is a representative of a community of disciples (cf. v. 38, 'the disciples'; v. 41, 'the saints'). She is portrayed in particularly positive terms on account of her 'good works', which could refer to acts of piety such as prayer or fasting,[132] and her acts of charity.[133] It should be noted that when Cornelius is introduced in 10.2, he will be described in equivalent terms.

[b] 9.37a *The Death of Tabitha*

9.37a Tabitha's death is unexpected and all the more poignant for the exemplary life she lived among the disciples. It happens during the time of Peter's visits to the churches of the region (cf. 9.32), so that Peter's response to the death will be under scrutiny. There are parallels between this story and that of Jairus' daughter in Luke 8.41-42, 49-56 (cf. Mk 5.22-24, 35-43). Jairus was a leader of the synagogue and his daughter was dying when he came to ask Jesus to come to his house. By virtue of the positioning of the story of Jairus around the story of the healing of the woman who had had a haemorrhage for twelve years, it is given the same symbolical significance:

---

131. The gazelle is specified several times in the commandments God gives to Moses for the people when they arrive in the Promised Land. It is a 'clean' animal (Deut. 14.5): it is said three times that 'the unclean and the clean alike may eat it, just like the gazelle or a hart' (Deut. 12.15, 22; 15.22).

132. Haenchen, *Commentary*, p. 285.

133. The term ἐλεημοσύνη is used almost exclusively by Luke in the New Testament (Lk. × 2; Acts × 8 out of a total of 13 occurrences).

the woman with the flow of blood represents the Law separating the clean and the unclean, and the death of the girl, being twelve years old, is a sign of how this Law is being brought to an end. She dies, in fact, before Jesus reaches the house, while he is involved in healing the woman so that she is no longer affected by the law of separation. Once he arrives at Jairus' house, he heals the young girl, witnessed by Peter among other disciples so it is no surprise that the story of Peter's healing of Tabitha will be seen to be modelled in some ways on the Gospel paradigm. By virtue of the parallel with Jairus' daughter the community of Tabitha is identified as one that is faithful to the Law.

[c] 9.37b *The Upper Room*
9.37b According to Jewish custom,[134] 'they' (presumably members of her family or of the community) washed the body, and they then placed it in a room in the upper part of the house, ὑπερῷον. This word is exclusive to Luke's second volume where it occurs on four (five, D05) occasions.[135] The first is in the opening chapter, being the place to which the Eleven go when they return to Ierousalem to wait for the Holy Spirit (1.13). By virtue of the parallel scene at the end of the Gospel, where they are said to remain constantly in the Temple on their return (Lk. 24.53), the upper room becomes a way of referring to the official Jewish system. Clearly, here in Joppa the reference to the upper room is not to the Temple but it may be a way of referring to the Jewish mentality and attitudes. It further serves as an element linking this story with David's lament of the death of Saul (2 Sam. 1.19; see *Excursus* 3).

The upper room is where Peter will see the body of Tabitha and will heal her. There are further echoes in this scene of the healing of the widow's son in Zarephath (in Sidon; see 1 Kgs 17.17-24) by Elijah who takes the dead child into 'the upper room where he was staying' (17.19, cf. v. 23) and also the healing of the Shunamite woman's son by Elisha (2 Kgs 4.18-37, see 4 Kgdms 4.11 LXX, τὸ ὑπερῷον, cf. v. 10). The location of the upper room will set up a further parallel with the next episode as it is told in the text of Codex Bezae (Acts 10.9 d05, *in cenaculum*), for it is again in an 'upper room' that Peter receives his vision of the ritually unclean animals (cf. 'rooftop', AT).

[d] 9.38 *The Disciples Send for Peter*
9.38 The news that Peter was in Lydda would have been known from the healing of Aeneas, but the idea that Joppa was not far from Lydda (it was

---

134. *Mish. Sab.* 23.5
135. 1.13; 9.37, 39; 10.9 d05; 20.8. The negative connotations of the term distinguishes it from the synonym ἀνάγαιον (+ οἶκον D05) which Luke uses exclusively in a positive sense (Lk. 22.12).

about 10 miles) may express a closeness of fellowship, too, between the communities of Aeneas and Tabitha.

Two men were sent[136] to fetch Peter, to beg him to come to Joppa. Their opening words (in direct or indirect speech) imply that they are aware that he might have reason to hesitate to go to the community in Joppa, because of what would be expected of him there. The use of the same verb as at 9.32 describing Peter's travelling around (διερχόμενον/διελθεῖν), situates their plea for him to go to Joppa within the same setting, as if he had stopped his travels at Lydda (perhaps because of the problems in the church there) but the two men now urge him to carry on 'as far as', 'until' (ἕως) Joppa. The use of indirect speech in the 'Western' text, which may well have been what was intended (see *Critical Apparatus*), causes the words the men will speak to Peter to have been prepared by the disciples in Joppa, and their actual speaking of them is merely implied.

[e] 9.39a *Peter Goes with Them*
9.39a Peter does accept to go with the two men back to Joppa, 'rising up' (ἀναστάς) from the state of mind that had kept him in Lydda (see *Commentary*, 8.26).

[f] 9.39b *The Widows Show Him her Handiwork*
9.39b Once there, he is taken to the upper room where Tabitha is lying. The widows who stand beside (around WT) him weeping are portrayed as Hellenists since Luke re-uses the Greek name Dorcas in relation to them. It is also possible that the purpose of repeating the name at this point is to re-iterate the connection between Tabitha and Saul, king of Israel (cf. on 9.36). In any case, the widows represent the poor of the community, in contrast to 'the saints' (cf. v. 41), who have been cared for by Tabitha through her acts of charity and kindness. They show Peter garments, with the middle voice of the verb (ἐπιδεικνύμεναι) perhaps indicating ones that they themselves are wearing.

[f′] 9.40a *Peter Heals Tabitha*
9.40a Peter's movements are described in careful detail, with echoes of the scriptural paradigms of the healing of children by both Elijah and Elisha (for details see on 9.37b above), as well as the healing of Jairus' daughter by Jesus (see on 9.37a above). Peter puts everyone (the widows and the others)[137] outside the room[138] (cf. Jesus, Mk 5.40; Lk. 8.51), and prays (cf. Elijah, 1 Kgs 17.20-21; Elisha, 2 Kgs 4.33). The words Peter speaks, 'Tabitha, arise', are

---

136. H L P 049. 056 and the majority text (𝔐) omits 'two men'.

137. πάντας ('all') is masculine so must refer to members of the community other than the widows alone.

138. For the redundant use of ἐκβαλὼν ἔξω, cf. Lk. 4.29; 13.28; 20.15; Acts 7.58.

remarkably similar to those spoken by Jesus as recorded by Mark in Aramaic: '*Talitha cum*, meaning "Little girl, arise"' (Mk. 5.41).[139]

The WT includes in Peter's command the invocation of 'the name of our Lord Jesus', recalling the mention of his name to Aeneas (cf. 9.34) and also the repeated insistence on the power of the name of Jesus when he healed the lame man at the Temple (3.6, cf. 3.13, 16; 4.10, 12, 17, 18, 30).

[e'] 9.40b *Tabitha Sits Up*

9.40b In contrast to the healing of Jairus' daughter by Jesus, when the girl responded immediately to his command as her spirit returned and she got up, the account of Peter's healing of Tabitha unfolds almost in slow motion. The difference underlines Peter's hesitancy as he deals for the first time with a death as distinct from the simple healings he has undertaken so far. Taking into account the symbolical significance of Tabitha's death as the death of Jewish attitudes to Gentiles (cf. 9.37a above), Peter's uncertainty can be linked to the situation he finds himself confronted with concerning the Jewish Law – as he sees the old mentality being challenged, he struggles to explore new territory, feeling his way step by step.

So, first of all, Tabitha opens her eyes (see the Shunamite's son, 2 Kgs 4.35); next, on seeing Peter she sits up on her bed.

[d'] 9.41a *Tabitha is Helped to Stand*

9.41a The third step is for Peter to offer his hand to help her stand. It is at this point that Peter is bold enough to make physical contact with a body that hitherto he had been forbidden to touch because it was 'unclean'. Jesus, in contrast, took Jairus' daughter by the hand when she was still dead, before speaking to her (Lk. 8.54).

[c'] 9.41b *Peter Presents Her Alive*

9.41b The paradigms of Elijah and Elisha are invoked once more as Peter calls in the widows and the saints (cf. 1 Kgs 17.23; 2 Kgs 4.35). Tabitha is presented alive and, because she has a representative role, the community is restored. Something has died, however, in the attitudes of the disciples in Joppa in the same way that Saul of Tarsus 'died' to his previous life when he was baptized having been called by Jesus to leave his life of fanatical pursuit of the Law and take the gospel to the Gentiles (cf. 9.9, 18-19; see *Excursus* 3 on the parallel with the death of King Saul).

[b'] 9.42 *News of the Healing is Spread around Joppa*

9.42 The impact of the healing of Tabitha is as immediate as in the case of Aeneas (cf. 9.35) but it is less widespread both numerically and geograph-

---

139. D05 has a singular reading of Jesus' words: ΡΑΒΒΙ ΘΑΒΙΤΑ ΚΟΥΜΙ.

ically. It is only the people of the town this time who hear what has happened in the church and many, rather than all, believe in the Lord, that is in Jesus.

[a'] 9.43 *Peter Stays in Joppa*

9.43 Note is made that Peter stayed on for quite some time (ἡμέρας ἱκανάς) in Joppa, at the house of a tanner. His stay at this house is by no means casual, for all that Luke makes only a very brief statement about it. The indefinite pronoun once more (cf. on Ananias at 9.33 above), this time before the name of Simon, gives him the role of representing a class of people: because of his trade and the contact with dead animals it necessitated, Simon would be regarded as ritually unclean (cf. Lev. 11.39). For Luke's first audience, a great deal would be understood from this detail. Simon represents a community distinct from that of Tabitha: she had stood for those disciples, Hebrews and Hellenists, who continued to observe the Law while nevertheless faithfully looking after the people in need; like Saul of Tarsus, she dies and with her the observance of this Law. She is brought back to life but the ideology of the community has not yet changed (cf. *Commentary,* 11.2 D05). Peter has clearly learnt something from the practical experience of Tabitha's death, and yet has still to discover the full extent of the teaching that the distinction clean/unclean no longer has any force. This will follow while he is staying with Simon the Tanner, with whom Peter's affinity is indicated by the shared name. Meanwhile, he has interrupted his visits to the churches, perhaps taking time to reflect and pray about what he has witnessed in Joppa.

Excursus 3

Parallels between David's Lament for the Death of Saul (2 Sam. 1.17-27) and The Widows' Lament for the Death of Tabitha (Acts 9.36-43)

A parallel between Saul of Tarsus and King Saul of Israel was presented in *Excursus* 2.2. A further intriguing parallel may be noted between the two Sauls, to which the key is the name of Tabitha, meaning 'gazelle'[140] (in Aramaic, טביתא; in Greek, Δορκάς). This is the opening word found in the Hebrew text, צבי, of David's lament for the death of Saul and Jonathan, referring apparently to Saul in the singular. The similarities between the two passages are as follows:

2 Samuel (2 Kingdoms LXX)	Acts
Saul, 'the gazelle of Israel' (הצבי ישׂראל MT)[141]	Tabitha, 'the gazelle' (Ταβιθά ... Δορκάς)
has died (cf. τεθνηκότων, 1.19)	dies (ἀποθανεῖν, 9.36-37)

---

140. See translation by J.W. Welch, *Chiasmus in Antiquity* (Hildesheim: Gerstenberg, 1981), p. 138 and cf. *Commentary,* 9.36.

141. 2 Kgdms 1.19 LXX translates הצבי ישׂראל with Στήλωσον, 'Ισραήλ, taking the meaning of the verb נצב as 'be prominent' (B-D-B, 839–40).

Saul had a reputation for being a caring and generous king[142]	Tabitha was known for her good works and acts of charity (πλήρης ἔργων ἀγαθῶν καὶ ἐλεημοσυνῶν, 9.36)
He was killed on the high places (ἐπὶ τὰ ὕψη, 1.19)	She was placed in the upper room (ἐν τῷ ὑπερῴῳ, 9.37, 39)
The 'daughters of the uncircumcised' (Philistines) are not to be told of Saul's death lest they rejoice over it (1.20)	The news of Tabitha's healing becomes known to all Joppa (Gentile city) and many believe in the Lord (9.42)
The daughters of Israel are to weep (κλαύσατε, 1.24)	The widows of the church weep (κλαίουσαι, 9.39)
Saul clothed the women of Israel in beautiful garments (τὸν ἐνδιδύσκοντα ὑμᾶς ... ἐπὶ τὰ ἐνδύματα ὑμῶν, 1.24)	Dorcas, the 'gazelle' made coats and garments while she was with the women (χιτῶνας καὶ ἱμάτια ὅσα ἐποίει ... ἡ Δορκάς, 9.39)
Following his lament, David asks the Lord if he should go to any of the cities of Judah; he is told to go to Hebron (2.1)	Following the healing of Tabitha, Peter remains in Joppa (9.43)

The assimilation of characters is complex and works in several different ways. Tabitha is 'the gazelle' who is King Saul of Israel, who is Saul/Paul. In turning to Jesus and being baptized, Saul the Jew has died to his traditional Jewish mind-set with respect to Gentiles and the obligation on them to be circumcised (even though, as will be seen, he continues to hold firmly to other Jewish ways of thinking). The implications of the parallel are that Tabitha represents a traditional Jewish mentality which has died with the conversion of Saul and which is repeated in her own death. The church fetch Peter who is in the area; he, for his part, has yet to grasp the principle that uncircumcised Gentiles are equal in God's eyes and that there is no clean and unclean – that lesson is about to follow in the next episode (Acts 10). Nevertheless, in the name of Jesus, he brings Tabitha back to life and restores her to the church.

He restores the situation to exactly as it was before, which, on one level, is perceived as a positive action since it involves a miraculous healing and causes many people in the locality to believe in the Lord; on another level, it has negative connotations, which become apparent when Peter's way of thinking is revealed in his dialogue with God during his vision of the clean and unclean animals (10.14). Although he brings Tabitha back to life he fails to realize that it is the community's attitude to the Law that has caused her death. Working miracles, even in the name of Jesus, is no guarantee of doing the will of the Father (cf. Mt. 7.21-23).

---

142. Ginzberg, *The Legends of the Jews*, IV, p. 72: 'Mild and generous, Saul led the life of a saint in his own house.'

[BA'-B] 10.1–11.1 *Cornelius*

Overview

This is the second episode in the sub-sequence concerning Peter and is by far the most detailed, with the frequently repeated words and phrases reflecting the importance accorded by Luke to key aspects of the narrative. In the previous episode, the narrative focused on Peter's involvement with the churches in Judaea where the believers were Jewish. Now he is brought into direct contact with Gentiles, not by Peter's own design but by the intervention of God himself. This will be the first time that Gentiles as such are present in the narrative of Acts, at a point when the Church leaders other than Peter are noticeable by their absence. Indeed, the Gentiles have not been part of the apostles' plans and there have been no moves on their part to involve them in the sharing of the gospel message. What happens in the course of this episode is that Peter's understanding of the teaching of Jesus is caused to take on quite another dimension, and in the next episode he will be decisive in persuading the other apostles and Church leaders to adjust their thinking, too.

The progression in the spread of the gospel message so far apparent thus continues: having started with the Jews in Judaea (1.1–5.42; cf. 9.31-43), it was taken to the Samaritans (8.4-25), then to a eunuch representing those Jews excluded from full participation in Israel (8.25-40). Once introduced into the story of Acts, the Gentiles will continue to be present and their importance as recipients of the gospel will dominate the narrative from chapter 13 onwards.

Corresponding to the entry of the Gentiles in this episode, the scene of action shifts to Caesarea. For the first time, the action takes place in Gentile territory although the city has already been mentioned twice in this section of Acts from a distance, as it were – first, as the destination of Philip (8.26) and secondly, as a stopping place for Saul (9.30).

Structure and Themes

The episode opens by bringing the new character, Cornelius, on stage, surrounded by members of his family and household. In a series of four scenes, Cornelius is brought into contact with Peter who was staying in Joppa after the raising of Tabitha in the previous episode (9.43). In the first two scenes, divine participants intervene in order to prepare, first, Cornelius and secondly, Peter, for a meeting that takes both of them equally by surprise. The last two scenes portray Cornelius' men fetching Peter from Joppa and finally, Peter's arrival at Cornelius' house in Caesarea:

[*BA*]	10.1-8	Cornelius in Caesarea
[a]	10.1-3	Presentation of Cornelius and his vision
[b]	10.4a	Cornelius' response to the vision
[b']	10.4b-6	The angel's instructions
[a']	10.7-8	Cornelius' obedience

[BB]		10.9-16	Peter's vision in Joppa
	[a]	10.9	Peter goes to pray
	[b]	10.10a	Peter is hungry
	[c]	10.10b-12	Peter's vision
	[d]	10.13	A voice gives orders
	[d']	10.14	Peter's refusal to obey
	[c']	10.15	The voice speaks a second time
	[b']	10.16a	The dialogue is repeated for a third time
	[a']	10.16b	The vision ends
[BB']		10.17-23a	Cornelius' men find Peter in Joppa
	[a]	10.17a	Peter's perplexity over the vision
	[b]	10.17b-18	The arrival of Cornelius' men
	[c]	10.19-20	The Spirit's instructions to Peter
	[c']	10.21	Peter complies
	[b']	10.22	The men explain their purpose
	[a']	10.23a	Peter gives them lodging
[BA']		10.23b–11.1	Peter meets Cornelius in Caesarea
	[a]	10.23b	Peter's departure from Joppa
	[b]	10.24a	Peter's arrival in Caesarea
	[c]	10.24b	Cornelius' expectancy
	[d]	10.25a	The servant's announcement
	[e]	10.25b	Cornelius' welcome
	[f]	10.26	Peter's rebuke
	[g]	10.27-29	Peter's entry into the house of a Gentile
	[h]	10.30-33	Cornelius' explanation
	[g']	10.34-43	Peter's speech
	[f']	10.44	The Holy Spirit fell on the hearers
	[e']	10.45-46a	The amazement of the circumcision brethren
	[d']	10.46b-47	Peter's anticipation of baptism
	[c']	10.48a	Baptism of Cornelius' household
	[b']	10.48b	Peter's stay in Caesarea
	[a']	11.1	The brethren in Judaea

The main theme in this episode is Peter's discovery that the Gentiles are accepted by God on an equal basis with the Jews. Although this idea was evident in his speech at Pentecost (cf. 2.14b-21, 39), it becomes clear as these scenes unfold that he had not yet understood that the universal validity of Jesus' teaching was a present reality rather than one reserved for some future arrival of the Messiah at a later date (cf. 2.19-21).[143] He makes the discovery by means of a vision Jesus shows him of clean and unclean animals which, by analogy, enables him to understand what happens when he witnesses the Holy Spirit falling on Cornelius and his household. He is thus enabled to take the most significant step yet in his understanding of Jesus' teaching: the scene in Caesarea represents more accurately the conversion of Peter than the conversion of Cornelius.

---

143. The conflicting ideas in Peter's Pentecost speech are examined in *The Message of Acts*, I, pp. 179–84, 191–92.

It is important at this point that Cornelius, for his part, was not a Gentile who was hostile to Jews, for all that he was a member of the Roman army of occupation of their country, but one who had adopted Jewish ways and attitudes to a considerable degree. This factor casts the Jews' avoidance of contact with such people in a negative light, especially the disciples of Jesus who had seen their master refusing the traditional distinction between clean and unclean during his lifetime. Indeed, the hostile Jewish attitude that is seen in Acts to Gentiles living in Israel was contrary to the teaching of the Torah, which repeatedly urges the Jews to treat foreigners with kindness.

Translation

'Western Text'		*Codex Vaticanus B03*
[*A*a]	**10.1** A certain man in Caesarea named Cornelius, a centurion from the cohort called the Italian, **2** a pious and god-fearing person along with all his household, who used to do many charitable works for the Jewish people and pray to God regularly, **3** saw in a vision clearly (the time being about the ninth hour of the day) an angel of God coming in towards him and saying to him, 'Cornelius'.	**10.1** A certain man in Caesarea named Cornelius, a centurion from the cohort called the Italian, **2** a pious and god-fearing person along with all his household, who used to do many charitable works for the Jewish people and pray to God regularly, **3** saw in a vision clearly at round about the ninth hour of the day an angel of God coming in towards him and saying to him, 'Cornelius'.
[b]	**4a** He stared at him and becoming terrified he said, 'What is it, Lord'.	**4a** He stared at him and becoming terrified he said, 'What is it, Lord'.
[b']	**4b** He said to him, 'Your prayers and your acts of charity have gone up as a memorial before the face of God, **5** so now send men to Joppa and fetch Simon who is called Peter. **6** He is being lodged at the house of Simon, a tanner, who has a house near the sea.'	**4b** He said to him, 'Your prayers and your acts of charity have gone up as a memorial before God, **5** so now send men to Joppa and fetch a certain Simon who is called Peter. **6** He is lodged at the house of a certain Simon, a tanner, who has a house near the sea.'
[a']	**7** When the angel who spoke to him had left, he called two of his domestic slaves and a pious soldier from among those who faithfully served him **8** and, having explained the vision to them, he sent them to Joppa.	**7** When the angel who spoke to him had left, he called two of his domestic slaves and a pious soldier from among those who faithfully served him **8** and, having explained everything to them, he sent them to Joppa.
[*B*a]	**10.9** The next day, while they were on their journey and approaching the city, Peter had gone up to the upper room and was praying around the sixth hour.	**10.9** The next day, while they were on their journey and approaching the city, Peter went up to the rooftop to pray around the sixth hour.
[b]	**10a** And it happened that he was hungry and wanted to eat.	**10a** And it happened that he was hungry and wanted to eat.
[c]	**10b** While they were getting it ready, a trance fell upon him **11** and he sees heaven opened and some container, held by its four corners, a sheet of fine linen,	**10b** While they were getting it ready, a trance came upon him **11** and he sees heaven opened and some container coming down like a large sheet of fine

	lowered from heaven onto the earth, **12** in which were all kinds of four-footed creatures and reptiles and birds of the air.	linen lowered by its four corners onto the earth, **12** in which were all kinds of four-footed creatures and reptiles of the earth and birds of the air.
[d]	**13** And there came a voice to him: 'Peter, get up, kill and eat'.	**13** And there came a voice to him: 'Get up, Peter, and kill and eat'.
[d']	**14** But he said to him, 'By no means, Lord, because I have never eaten	**14** But Peter said, 'By no means, Lord, because I have never eaten
Codex Bezae D05		*Codex Vaticanus B03*
	anything common or unclean'.	anything common and unclean'.
[c']	**15** It called again a second time to him: 'What God has declared clean for you, do not continue to call common'.	**15** And a voice said again a second time to him: 'What God has declared clean, you must not continue to call common'.
[b']	**16a** This happened three times.	**16a** This happened three times.
[a']	**16b** And the container was taken up again towards heaven.	**16b** And straightaway the container was taken up towards heaven.
[*B'*a]	**10.17a** When he had come to his senses, Peter was at a loss as to what the vision he had seen was about.	**10.17a** While in his mind Peter was at a loss as to what the vision he had seen was about,
[b]	**17b** And suddenly, the men who had been sent by Cornelius, having made enquiries about the house of Simon, were standing in the porch, **18** and they called out and asked, 'Is Simon called Peter lodging here?'	**17b** suddenly, the men who had been sent by Cornelius, having found the house of Simon by making enquiries, were standing in the porch **18** and they called out to ask, 'Is Simon called Peter lodging here?'
[c]	**19** While Peter was pondering the vision, the Spirit said to him, **20** 'Look! some men are looking for you. Come on, get up, go down and go with them without any argument, because I myself have sent them.'	**19** While Peter was pondering the vision, the Spirit said, **20** Look! there are two men looking for you. Come on, get up and go down and go with them without any argument, because I myself have sent them.'
[c']	**21** So then Peter went down and said to the men, 'Here I am, the one you are looking for. What do you want? for what reason are you here?'	**21** Peter went down and said to the men, 'Here I am, the one you are looking for. For what reason are you here?'
[b']	**22** They said to him, 'A certain Cornelius, a centurion, a just and God-fearing man who is, moreover, well-spoken of by all the nation of the Jews, was warned by a holy angel to summon you to his house and to hear what you have to say'.	**22** They said, 'Cornelius, a centurion, a just and God-fearing man who is, moreover, well-spoken of by all the nation of the Jews, was warned by a holy angel to summon you to his house and to hear what you have to say'.
[a']	**23a** So then Peter took them inside and gave them lodging.	**23a** Therefore, calling them inside he gave them lodging.
[*A'*a]	**10.23b** The next day, he got up and went out with them, and some of the brethren from Joppa went with him.	**10.23b** The next day, he got up and went out with them, and some of the brethren who were from Joppa went with him.
[b]	**24a** The day after he entered Caesarea.	**24a** The day after he entered Caesarea.
[c]	**24b** Cornelius was looking forward to welcoming them, and having called together his relatives and close friends he was waiting.	**24b** Cornelius was waiting expectantly for them, having called together his relatives and close friends.

[d]   **25a** As Peter was approaching Caesarea,   **25a** As Peter was entering,
one of the slaves ran ahead and announced
that he had arrived.

[e]   **25b** Cornelius leapt up and when he met   **25b** Cornelius, when he met him, fell at
him, he fell before his feet and wor-   his feet and worshipped.
shipped him.

[f]   **26** But Peter lifted him up saying, 'What   **26** But Peter lifted him up saying, 'Get
are you doing? I am a man, too, just like   up. I am also a man myself.'
you.'

[g]   **27** And he actually went inside, and   **27** And talking with him, he entered in
moreover found many people gathered   and finds many people gathered together
together **28** and he said to them, 'You   **28** and he said to them, 'You yourselves
yourselves know very well that it is   know that it is forbidden for a Jewish
forbidden for a Jewish man to associate   man to associate with or approach a
with or approach a foreign man, but to   foreigner, but to me God has shown that
me God has revealed that I should not   I should not call any person common or
call any person common or unclean.   unclean. **29** That is why I came without
29 That is why I came without objection   objection when I was summoned. I ask
when I was summoned by you. I ask   then for what reason you summoned
then for what reason you summoned   me?'
me?'

[h]   **30** Cornelius said, 'For three days, up to   **30** Cornelius said, 'Three days ago
the present hour I had been fasting and,   exactly at this hour, I was praying during
praying during the ninth hour of prayer   the ninth hour of prayer in my house
in my house, suddenly there was a man   when suddenly there was a man standing
standing in front of me in a shining   in front of me in a shining garment
garment **31** and he says, "Cornelius,   **31** and he says, "Cornelius, your prayer
your prayer has been heard and your   has been heard and your alms have been
alms have been remembered before God.   remembered before God. **32** So send
32 So send someone to Joppa and sum-   someone to Joppa and summon Simon
mon Simon who is called Peter (this   who is called Peter; he is lodging in the
man is lodging in the house of Simon a   house of Simon a Tanner beside the
Tanner beside the sea) who will speak to   sea." **33** At once, therefore, I sent some-
you when he gets here." **33** At once,   one to you, and you did well to come. So
therefore, I sent someone to you, beg-   now we are all present before God to
ging you to come to us. You did well to   hear everything that has been com-
arrive speedily. Now here we all are   manded to you by the Lord.'
before you wanting to hear from you
what has been commanded to you from
God.'

[g']   **34** Peter, opening his mouth, said,   **34** Opening his mouth, Peter said,
[α]   'Truly, realising that God is not a   'Truly, I realise that God is not a
respecter of persons **35** but in every   respecter of persons **35** but rather in
nation the one fearing him and per-   every nation the one fearing him and
forming works of righteousness is   performing works of righteousness is
acceptable to him...   acceptable to him.

[β]   **36** For the message that he sent to the   **36** He sent the message to the sons of
sons of Israel announcing peace through   Israel announcing peace through Jesus
Jesus Christ (he is Lord of all), **37** you   Christ (he is Lord of all) – **37** you know
yourselves know, what happened through-   the things that happened throughout all
out the whole of Judaea – beginning   Judaea – beginning from Galilee after

especially in Galilee after the baptism that John preached; **38a** you know Jesus who was from Nazareth whom God anointed with the power of the Holy Spirit.

[γ]   **38b** He went about doing good and healing all those who had been oppressed by the devil because God was with him **39a** – and we are his witnesses, of what he did in both the country of the Jews and Jerusalem.

[δ]   **39b** The one they killed by hanging him on a tree **40** God raised after the third day **40b** – and granted him to become visible **41** not to all the people but to the witnesses who had previously been appointed by God, we who ate and drank with him and kept company with him after he rose from the dead, for forty days.

[ε]   **42** And he charged us to preach to the people and to affirm that he is the one who has been designated by God as judge of the living and the dead **43** – to this man all the prophets bear witness, that everyone believing in him will receive forgiveness of sins through his name…'

[f′]   **44** While Peter was still speaking these words, the Holy Spirit fell on all those listening to the message.

[e′]   **45** And the faithful from the circumcision party who had come with Peter were totally amazed that the gift of the Holy Spirit had also been poured out on the Gentiles, **46a** for they heard them speaking in new tongues and praising God.

[d′]   **46b** Peter said, **47** 'Surely no-one can forbid water to prevent them from being baptized, these people who have received the Holy Spirit in the same way as we did ourselves?'

[c′]   **48a** So he commanded that they should be baptized in the name of the Lord Jesus Christ.

[b′]   **48b** Then they begged him to remain with them for a few days.

[a′]   **11.1** It was heard by the apostles and the brethren who were in Judaea, that even the Gentiles had received the word of God.

the baptism that John preached; **38** you know Jesus who was from Nazareth, how God anointed him with the power of the Holy Spirit,

38b who went about doing good and healing all those who were being oppressed by the devil because God was with him **39a** – and we are witnesses of everything he did both in the country of the Jews and in Jerusalem.

39b The one they killed by hanging him on a tree **40** God raised on the third day **40b** – and granted that he should become visible **41** not to all the people but to the witnesses who had previously been appointed by God, we who ate and drank with him after he rose from the dead.

42 And he commanded us to preach to the people and to affirm that he is the one who has been designated by God as judge of the living and the dead **43** – to this man all the prophets bear witness, that everyone believing in him will receive forgiveness of sins through his name…'

44 While Peter was still speaking these words, the Holy Spirit fell upon all those listening to the message.

45 And the faithful from the circumcision party who had come with Peter were totally amazed that the gift of the Holy Spirit had also been poured out on the Gentiles, **46a** for they heard them speaking in tongues and praising God.

46b Then Peter said in response, **47** 'Surely no-one can forbid water to prevent these people from being baptized, these who have received the Holy Spirit just as we did ourselves?'

48a And he commanded that in the name of Jesus Christ they should be baptized.

48b Then they asked him to stay on for a few days.

11.1 The apostles and the brethren who were throughout Judaea heard that even the Gentiles had received the word of God.

Critical Apparatus

10.1 (τις) ἦν H⁴ P 056. 614 𝔐 gig l vg syᵖ co aeth ‖ *om.* B 𝔓⁵³·⁷⁴ ℵ A C E L Ψ 049. 33. 81. 104. 181. 226*. 255. 453. 629. 945. 1175. 1241. 1270. 1646. 1739. 1828. 1854. 1891. 1898. 2298. 2344. 2492 *al* p.

The verb ἦν which is present in some Greek MSS breaks up a long sentence, causing a new sentence to start without a connecting word when the main verb occurs at v. 3. The versions may reflect the presence of the verb in Greek or, alternatively, may have the verb because the sentence would be unacceptably long in translation (Boismard and Lamouille, II, p. 69: the verb 'est une leçon facilitante destinée à couper une phrase jugée trop longue').

10.3 ὡσεὶ περὶ (ὥραν) B 𝔓⁷⁴ ℵ² A C E Ψ 33. 104. 323. 440. 614. 927. 1175. 1270. 1611. 2412. 2344 sy; Ir^lat | ὡσεί H⁴ L P 049. 056 𝔐 latt | περί 1505. 2495 *pc* sa mae aeth; Ir^lat Cyp ‖ ὡς περί ℵ* 81. 88. 945. 1646. 1739. 1828. 1891 | ὡς 1241.

ὡσεί together with περί is pleonastic which probably explains the omission of one preposition or the other in many MSS. ὡσεί with a preposition is not found elsewhere in Luke's writings. In contrast, Winer (*Grammar*, p. 771) notes that the combination of ὡς and a preposition of direction (as in ℵ01*) occurs as a means of communicating a sense of definite intention. In this case, the narrative is drawing attention to the time of Cornelius' prayer, the ninth hour, which corresponded to the time of Jewish evening prayer (see Read-Heimerdinger, 'Luke's Use of ὡς and ὡσεί: Comparison and Correspondence as a Means to Convey His Message', in Pierri [ed.], *Grammatica Intellectio Scripturae: Saggi filologici di Greco biblico* [forthcoming]).

[From 10.4b (fol. 455a), the Latin text of Codex Bezae is available. The Greek page starts at 10.14b (fol. 455b).]

10.4 ἔμπροσθεν (τοῦ θεοῦ) B 𝔓⁷⁴ ℵ A 81. 88. 1175. 1646. 1739. 1891 ‖ ἐνώπιον C E H⁴ L P Ψ 049. 056. 33 𝔐 (d *coram [deo]*, D lac.).

The expression ἀνέβησαν εἰς μνημόσυνον ἔμπροσθεν τοῦ θεοῦ may be compared with 10.31, ἐμνήσθησαν ἐνώπιον τοῦ θεοῦ (d05, *in mente habitae sunt in conspectu dei*). ἔμπροσθεν usually has the sense of 'physically in front of someone' (but see Lk. 10.21, οὕτως εὐδοκία ἐγένετο ἔμπροσθέν σου). ἐνώπιον is more frequently found in Luke with a range of meanings, both literal and figurative. The Latin of d05, *coram* + ablative, is rare, being found only on one other occasion in Luke-Acts at Acts 7.46 where it corresponds to ἐναντίον, which, on the few occasions it is found in Luke's writings, always means 'in the presence of'.

10.5 (Σίμωνά) τινα B 𝔓⁷⁴ᵛⁱᵈ A C 0142. 36. 81. 88. 453. 630. 945. 1175. 1646. 1739. 1877. 1891 *al* ar vg sy^hmg bo ‖ *om.* d (D lac.) ℵ E H⁴ L P Ψ 049. 056. 33 𝔐 it sy^p.h sa mae aeth; Ir^lat Or Chr.

The omission of the indefinite particle after the name of Simon may be due to haplography (-να … -να). Metzger considers that it was deliberately omitted because copyists felt that it was 'belittling' and could 'lack proper respect for the chief of the apostles' (*Commentary*, p. 325). This evaluation ignores the function Luke assigns to τις of introducing a person as a representative of a type or a group (see *Commentary* on 9.33, 36 above) which would not be appropriate in this instance.

10.6 οὗτος ξενίζεται B 𝔓⁷⁴ ℵ *rell* ‖ καὶ αὐτός ἐστιν ξενιζόμενος, *hic est ospitans* d (D lac.) 614. 1108. 1518. 1611. 2138. 2412 syʰ; Chr Theoph.

The periphrastic present of the WT draws attention to the verb ξενίζω/ξε-νίζομαι which becomes a leitmotiv in these scenes, a symbol of the strangers Israel failed to love as their own people (see *Commentary*, 10.23a). Cf. 10.32 where all MSS read ξενίζεται.

παρά τινι Σίμωνι βυρσεῖ B 𝔓⁷⁴ ℵ *rell* | παρὰ Σ. τινι βυρσεῖ C 69 | πρὸς Σ-ά τινα βυρσέα Ψ 614. 1611. 2412, *apud Simonem quemdam* l vg ‖ *apud Simonem pellionem* d (retroversion: πρὸς Σίμωνα βυρσέα, D lac.).

The omission of the indefinite pronoun in d05 may well reflect the Greek of D05: while it is a marker Luke uses as the narrator to signal to his audience that a character is a representative of a type (as he did when first introducing Simon the Tanner, cf. 9.43), there is no reason for Jesus to use it when addressing Cornelius (cf. its absence in Cornelius' account, 10.32).

10.8 ἅπαντα αὐτοῖς B 𝔓⁷⁴ ℵ A E 81. 88. 1175. 1646. 2344 | αὐτοῖς ἅπαντα C H⁴ L P Ψ 049. 056 (33). 1739 𝔐 ‖ αὐτοῖς τὸ ὅραμα d (D lac.) gig syᵖ mae.

The versions, which frequently support D05, describe the nature of what Cornelius told his men specifically as 'the vision' rather than generally as 'everything'.

10.9 ἐπὶ τὸ δῶμα B 𝔓⁷⁴ ℵ A C E *rell* ‖ εἰς τ. ὑπερῷον, *in cenaculum* d (D lac.) gig l, *in superiora* e vg aeth; Or (Chr) CAp Tert (Cyp) Chromatius.

Instead of the roof, the Latin versions and several of the Latin Church fathers have Peter go to the 'upper room', connecting this incident with the time the apostles were waiting in Jerusalem for the promise of the Holy Spirit (cf. 1.13), and also the death of Tabitha in the church at Lydda (cf. 9.37, 39). On both these occasions, the participants shared an attitude of attachment to traditional Jewish beliefs and systems which the upper room symbolises (see *Commentary, ad loc.*)

(ἀνέβη …) προσεύξασθαι B 𝔓⁷⁴ ℵ A C E *rell* ‖ (*ascendit* …) *et oravit* d (retroversion: καὶ προσηύξατο, D lac.) gig p.

Attention is focused on the action of praying in d05, whereas in B03 it is on the intention of praying.

10.10 ἐγένετο (ἐπ᾽ αὐτὸν ἔκστασις) B 𝔓⁷⁴ ℵ A C P 36. 81. 88. 323. 945. 1175. 1646. 1739. 1891. 2344 *pm* | ἦλθεν 𝔓⁴⁵ || ἐπέπεσεν (ἔπεσ- 383. 610. 1243. 2492 *pc*; Cl), *cecidit* d (D lac.) E H⁴ L Ψ 049. 056. 33 𝔐 latt sy; (Cl) Cass.

The verb ἐπιπίπτω expresses the suddenness and the unexpected nature of Peter's altered mental state, and also the fact that it came from outside himself. ἐπέπεσεν has a more forceful connotation than the simple ἐγένετο. Cf. Gen. 15.12 LXX, referring to the ἔκστασις that fell on Abraham (see *Commentary*, 10.10, on the implications of this parallel). ἐπιπίπτω is found elsewhere in Acts to describe the falling of the Spirit (8.16, 39 [not AT]; 10.44 [not D05]; 11.15 [not D05]; 19.6 D05).

10.11 καταβαῖνον σκεῦός τι ὡς ὀθόνην μεγάλην τέσσαρσιν (τέτρασιν E) ἀρχαῖς καθιέμενον ἐπὶ τῆς γῆς B 𝔓⁷⁴ ℵ A C² E 88. 1175. 1646 *pc* ar e vg || καὶ (*ex* d) τέσ. ἀρ. δεδ. σκεῦός τι (+ *et linteum splendidum* d) καθιέμενον (+ *de caelo* d) ἐπὶ τ. γ. (+ *quasi velum lineum* l) d (D lac.) 𝔓⁴⁵ (Ψ l); Cl Didasc CAp | καταβαῖνον (+ ἐπ᾽ αὐτὸν 𝔐) σκ. τι ὡς ὀθ. μεγ. τέσ. ἀρ. δεδ. καὶ καθ. ἐπὶ τ. γ. C*ᵛⁱᵈ H⁴ L P (Ψ) 049. 056. (33). 1739 𝔐.

d05 describes the vision as a series of facts rather than metaphors (without ὡς; cf. 11.5, where Peter describes the sheet as an image because he is struggling to find words to convey to the brethren in Jerusalem what he had seen). There is a combination of variants in this sentence describing the descent of 'some container': 1) the word order varies, with the focus in the AT on the descent and in the WT (represented by d05 among others with further variants) on the fact of the container being held by its four corners; 2) the container is likened to a large sheet of fine linen (ὀθόνη) in the AT, whereas d05 simply states that it *is* a fine sheet and other witnesses omit the mention of the sheet altogether; 3) d05 repeats the mention of the sky. It should be noted that this description of the vision is given by the narrator; later, Peter will give his own account to the brethren in Jerusalem (11.5), where the wording is closer to the AT of 10.11 than the WT.

10.12 (τὰ τετράποδα) καὶ ἑρπετὰ τῆς γῆς B 𝔓⁴⁵ᵛⁱᵈ·⁷⁴ ℵ A C²ᵛⁱᵈ 81. (945). 1175. 1646. (1739. 1891) *pc* lat saᵖᵗ mae; (Cl) || κ. ἑρπ. 61. 630, *et serpentia* d (D lac.) saᵖᵗ; Aug Ambr Chromatius Cass Bar Sal | τ. γ. καὶ τὰ θηρία κ. τὰ ἑρπ. (E) H⁴ L P Ψ 049. 056. 614 𝔐 syʰ | κ. τ. θη. κ. τ. ἑρπ. τ. γ. C*ᵛⁱᵈ 33. (36). 104. 323. 440. 1270 *pc*.

Variation affects two features: 1) the number of types of creatures, with many witnesses including 'beasts', τὰ θηρία, among them (cf. 11.6; Gen. 1.24, 25; 9.2); 2) the position of τῆς γῆς, qualifying the quadrupeds and reptiles, the quadrupeds alone, or the beasts and reptiles; d05 omits the phrase altogether (see *Critical Apparatus,* 11.6).

10.13 Ἀναστάς, Πέτρε B 𝔓⁷⁴ ℵ *rell* | Ἀναστάς 𝔓⁴⁵ gig; Cl Ambr Epiph Ephr Cass LibGr || Π., ἀνάστα, *Petre, surge* d (D lac.) (104).

In d05, the voice gives a series of three commands ('get up, kill, eat') whereas most MSS express the first command as an aorist participle. The imperative confers greater importance on the order to 'get up' instead of considering it as simply preliminary to the other actions. The place of *Petre* before *surge* in d05 draws attention to this name given to him by Jesus.

10.14 ὁ δὲ Πέτρος εἶπεν B 𝔓⁷⁴ ℵ *rell* | εἶπεν δὲ ὁ Π. gig l t vg sa; Aug ‖ *at ille dixit* d (D lac.).

It is normal for Luke to omit the name of the speaker in a dialogue when it is clear who is meant. On the other hand, the repetition of Peter's name underlines his part in this scene as well as the symbolic significance of his name (cf. on 10.19 below).

[The Greek page of Codex Bezae is available from the middle of 10.14.]

(κοινὸν) καὶ ἀκάθαρτον B 𝔓⁴⁵·⁷⁴ ℵ A 88. 323. 945. 1175. 1646. 1739. 1891. 2344. 2495, *et inmundum* d ‖ ἤ ἀκ. D C E H⁴ L P Ψ 049. 056. 614 𝔐 e vgˢ co.

B03 assimilates 'common' and 'unclean' as two features of the same category of forbidden food. D05 distinguishes between them (cf. 11.8).

10.15 καὶ φωνή B 𝔓⁴⁵·⁷⁴ ℵ *rell, et vox* d ‖ φωνήσας δέ D.

Neither sentence has a finite verb, but whereas the subject is clearly started in B03 with a verb of speaking implied, D05 has an aorist participle with an implied impersonal subject.

10.16 (καὶ) εὐθὺς ἀνελήμφθη B 𝔓⁷⁴ ℵ A E 81 *pc* vg bo ‖ ἀν. πάλιν D p | πάλιν ἀν. H⁴ L P Ψ 049. 056. 33ᵛⁱᵈ. 1739 𝔐 p syʰ saᵐˢˢ mae | ἀν. 𝔓⁴⁵ 36. 453. 1175. 2344 *pc* (*adsumptum est ipsum* d) syᵖ saᵐˢˢ boᵐˢ aeth; CAp Cass Chromatius.

According to B03, the removal of the object is said to happen immediately after the third time the voice speaks, whereas in D05 it is simply said that it was taken up again.

10.17 (ὡς δὲ) ἐν αὐτῷ B 323. 330. 927. 2495 *pc* | ἐν ἑαυτῷ 𝔓⁷⁴ ℵ A E H⁴ L P Ψ 049. 056. 0142. 33. 1739 𝔐 ar e gig vg syᵖ sa bo; Chr ‖ ἐν ἑαυ. ἐγένετο D, *intra se factus est* d p syʰ.

The expression read by D05 is found again at 12.11 and a similar one at Lk. 15.17 (εἰς ἑαυτὸν δὲ ἐλθών). It refers back to the explanation that the previous scene happened while Peter was in ἔκστασις (Acts 10.10) – now he has come back to full consciousness. B03 does not read the verb ἐγένετο and has the contract form of the pronoun, αὐτῷ.

καὶ (ἰδού) D d C E H⁴ L P Ψ 049. 056. 614 𝔐 p vgᴹ syʰ aeth; Chromatius ‖ *om.* B 𝔓⁴⁵·⁷⁴ ℵ A 36. 81. 181. 242. 255. 453. 522. 945. 1175. 1739. 1891. 1898. 2298 *pc* lat syᵖ.

The omission of καί in B03 is explained by the absence of the previous verb ἐγένετο in that text.

ὑπὸ τοῦ Κορνηλίου B 𝔓⁷⁴ ℵ E 81. 226. 323. 440. 614. 1175. 1270. 1505. 1611. 1646. 1739. 1891. 2344. 2492. 2495 ‖ ἀπὸ Κ. D 547. 927* ‖ ἀπὸ τοῦ Κ. A C H⁴ L P Ψ 049. 056. 1. 33. 69. 330. 618. 927ᶜ. 1241. 1243. 1245. 1828. 1837. 1854. 2147. 2412.

After verbs of sending, it is usual for Luke to use the preposition ἀπό rather than ὑπό to introduce the agent of the passive verb, in line with other writers of the Hellenistic period (Read-Heimerdinger, *The Bezan Text*, pp. 183–87). The article before the name of Cornelius can be accounted for by the fact that he has already been introduced into the narrative (cf. first mention anarthrous, 10.1). However, the focus had since shifted to Peter who has been in the spotlight from 10.9 and continues to be so. The omission of the article views Cornelius as a character who is not yet established in the story, and as offstage at this point; he will be brought fully into the action when the men present him to Peter (10.22; cf. arthrous mention, 10.24, 25 D05, 30).

διερωτήσαντες B 𝔓⁷⁴ ℵ *rell* ‖ ἐπ- D, *inquirentes* d.

The verb διερωτάω of B03 is a hapax of the New Testament, meaning 'find by enquiry' (B-A-G). The alternative ἐπερωτάω is frequent in the New Testament and, like ἐρωτάω, means simply 'enquire' though the idea of 'persistently' is implied by the prefix.

10.18 ἐπύθοντο B C ‖ ἐπυνθάνοντο D, *interrogabant* d 𝔓⁴⁵·⁷⁴ ℵ *rell*.

While B03 reads the aorist of πυνθάνομαι, D05 has the imperfect with the result of underlining the concurrence of the enquiries of the men from Cornelius at the gate and the questioning of Peter at the top of the house.

10.19 (εἶπεν) τὸ πνεῦμα B ‖ αὐτῷ τ. πν. D d 𝔓⁴⁵ E H⁴ L P Ψ 049. 056. 33 1739 𝔐 it sy ‖ τ. πν. αὐ. 𝔓⁷⁴ ℵ A C 6. 36. 69. 81. 181. 431. 453. 1175. 1898 *pc* vg.

Within the book of Acts, Luke usually specifies the addressee (as a noun or pronoun) after verbs of speaking but there are times when the addressee is implied from the context; whether or not the addressee is specified varies 23 times between B03 and D05 (Read-Heimerdinger, *The Bezan Text*, pp. 176–82 [N.B. p. 182: 7.1 should be added to the first list of Bezan readings and 10.22 to the second]). In the non-variant text, when the addressee is specified by the narrator the preposition πρός + noun/pronoun in the accusative is most commonly used to signal the outset of a dialogue, as a means of establishing the relationship between speaker and hearer. When the dative case of the noun/pronoun is used instead, it is because the conversation is already under-way. At places where only one of B03 or D05 specifies the addressee, this pattern is maintained as clearly as in the common text. Here, it is D05 that specifies Peter as the addressee of the Spirit's words with the dative pronoun αὐτῷ, placing it in the emphatic position before the verb (ℵ01 reads the more usual order). The use of the dative rather than πρός + accusative pronoun suggests that Luke views the dialogue between Peter and the Spirit as already established – even though the Spirit has not been named as such, communication with the divine has been apparent throughout this scene in Peter's praying (10.9) and by means of 'the voice' (10.13, 15). The use of the verb ἐπιπίπτω in 10.10 in connection with ἔκστασις suggests that Luke viewed the Spirit as active in bringing about Peter's vision (Delebecque, *Les deux Actes*, p. 408; see *Commentary*, 10.10).

(ἄνδρες) δύο B | τρεῖς 𝔓⁷⁴ ℵ A C E 33. 81. 88. 104. 181. 323. 629. 630. 945. 1175. 1739. 1877ᶜ. 1891. 2344 ar e gig vg syᵖ·ʰᵐᵍ co aeth; Did ‖ *om.* D d H L P Ψ 049. 056. 0142. 614 𝔐 l m p* syʰ; CAp CyrJ Ambr Chr Aug Spec Theoph Cass.

Between the readings of B03 and ℵ01, the expected and therefore easier reading is τρεῖς, though Metzger adduces arguments to support both numbers, as well as the absence of any number as in D05 (*Commentary*, p. 328). A number could well have been introduced into the shorter reading because of τρεῖς at 11.11.

ζητοῦντες B 𝔓⁷⁴ ℵ 81 *pc* ‖ ζητοῦσιν D d 𝔓⁴⁵ A C E⁽*⁾ H L P Ψ 049. 056. 33. 1739 𝔐; CAp.

B03 reads the present participle with the verb understood, whereas D05 reads the present finite verb. The former, especially in combination with a number (see above), tends to bring the men sharply into focus.

10.20 (ἀλλὰ) ἀναστάς B 𝔓⁷⁴ ℵ Dᴰ *rell* ‖ ἀνάστα D* d 1838 l t vg mae; Ambr Cass.

The same variant between the aorist participle of ἀνίστημι in B03 and the imperative in D05 was seen at 10.13 d05 (D05 lac.; cf. 11.7 D05), with the imperative singling out the command to 'get up' as a distinct rather than an incidental action (cf. 11.7).

10.21 καταβὰς δὲ Πέτρος B 𝔓⁷⁴ ℵ *rell* ‖ τότε κατ. ὁ Π. D d E d syᵖ mae.

τότε in D05 presents Peter's action as a ready response to the Spirit's command (Read-Heimerdinger, *The Bezan Text*, pp. 211–25, esp. 214–15), with the article indicating that Peter has been the focus of attention throughout this episode (cf. anarthrous mention of Peter, 10.9, and note on 10.17 above; see *The Bezan Text*, pp. 116–35). δέ, in contrast, simply moves the narrative on to a new development (Levinsohn, *Textual Connections*, pp. 83–85), and since this development is a dialogue initiated by Peter it is typical of B03 to omit the article (*The Bezan Text*, pp. 134–35).

τίς ἡ (– B) αἰτία B 𝔓⁴⁵·⁷⁴ ℵ *rell* ‖ τί θέλετε ἢ τίς ἡ αἰτ. D, *quid vultis quae causa* d syʰ.

D05 prefaces the specific question with a more general one, using ἤ to separate the two in a construction that is typically Hellenistic (Delebecque, *Les deux Actes*, pp. 72, 189). B03 omits the article.

10.22 (εἶπαν) πρὸς αὐτόν D d syᵖ sa mae aeth ‖ *om.* B 𝔓⁷⁴ ℵ *rell*.

In the book of Acts, Luke more often than not specifies the addressee, with the use of πρός + accusative pronoun being the typical construction to intro-duce the opening of a dialogue as a means of establishing the relationship between the speakers (see on 10.19 above). At three places, B03 mentions the addressee where D05 does not, against 20 times when D05 mentions them and B03 does not. Although it is superfluous in this verse to specify the addressee from the point of view of sense, it serves to build up the relationship between Peter and the representatives of Cornelius, which is important for the overall tone of the story. Conversely, its omission makes the narrative more distant and detached (see Read-Heimerdinger, *The Bezan Text*, p. 182).

(Κορνήλιός) τις D (syᵖ) ‖ *om.* B 𝔓⁷⁴ ℵ *rell* d.

D05 underlines with τις that Cornelius is a representative of a type of people, not just an individual in his own right. This use of it by his servants shows that it is not a mark of disrespect (cf. Metzger *Commentary*, p. 325, on 10.5).

10.23 εἰσκαλεσάμενος οὖν αὐτοὺς ἐξένισεν B 𝔓⁷⁴ ℵ *rell* ‖ τότε εἰσαγαγὼν ὁ Πέτρος ἐξεν. αὐτούς D (p syᵖ·ʰ** sa mae) | *tunc ergo ingressus Petrus hospitio excepit eos* d.

The verb εἰσκαλέομαι is a hapax in the New Testament, meaning to 'invite to one's house' (B-A-G, εἰσκαλέομαι; cf. Delebecque, *Les deux Actes*, p. 257). It thus corresponds to the verb of D05. The connective τότε is used for the second time (cf. 10.21 above, and the notes given there), again stressing the readiness of Peter to act in accordance with what he observes God to be doing. The repetition of his name is superfluous from a sense point of view, but the mention of Πέτρος, now for the eighth time in either text of these last two scenes (10.5, 9, 13, 14 [*om.* d05], 17, 18, 19, 21, 23 [*om.* B03]), draws atten-tion to the symbolic meaning of his name and the measures that are taken to break down his resistance to change.

(τινὲς τῶν ἀδελφῶν) τῶν ἀπὸ Ἰόππης B 𝔓⁷⁴ ℵ *rell, qui ab Ioppen* (sic) d mae ‖ ἀπὸ Ἰ. (Ἰ-ν D*) D 88. 522. 915. 1838 *pc* gig l p vg sa bo.

With the repeated article, B03 stresses that the brethren who accompanied Peter to Caesarea were from Joppa.

10.24 (Τῇ δὲ ἐπαύριον) εἰσῆλθεν B D d Ψ 049. 81. 181. 330. 431. 467. 614. 1898. 2412 *pc* ar l p vg sy^{p.h} sa aeth^{pt} || -θον 𝔓^{74} ℵ A C E H L P 056. 0142. 1739 𝔐 e gig sy^{hmg} sa^{mss} mae bo aeth^{pt}; Chr | συνῆλθον 69. 1175 *pc*.

Both B03 and D05 read the singular verb referring to Peter, whereas ℵ01 reads the plural to refer to the whole group who are mentioned in the plural in the previous clause (συνῆλθον) as well as the following one (αὐτούς).

τὴν (Καισάρειαν) B 𝔓^{74} ℵ A C E H L P Ψ 049. 056. 1739 𝔐 || *om.* D 33. 69. 88. 104. 383. 614. 629. 913. 1175. 1505. 1838. 2138. 2412. 2495 *pc*; Theoph.

The article is present in B03 because the reference to Caesarea is anaphoric (cf. 10.1, anarthrous). Its omission in D05 draws attention to the city as a new place of action (cf. 10.25a D05, arthrous).

(ἦν) προσδοκῶν αὐτούς B 𝔓^{74} ℵ *rell* || προσδεχόμενος αὐ. καί D d p* sy^{hmg}.

The verb προσδοκάω read by B03 is a technical term used by Luke to refer to the messianic expectation of the Jews, often with the active sense of 'look for' (Lk. 3.15; 7.19, 20; 8.40; 12.46; Acts 3.5. Cf. προσδοκία, Lk. 21.26; Acts 12.11). προσδέχομαι likewise is used in the context of messianic hopes (Lk. 2.38; 23.51) but is also used neutrally and has the specific sense of 'waiting in order to welcome someone or something' (Lk. 2.25, 38; 12.36; 15.2; 23.51). There is one other place of *vl* between the two verbs at Lk. 1.21, where the sense is not messianic (the people are waiting for Zechariah): D05 reads προσδέχομαι in place of προσδοκάω in the AT. At Lk. 2.25, Simeon, who was waiting for (προσδεχόμενος) the consolation of Israel, is described as righteous (δίκαιος) and pious (εὐσεβής), two terms used of Cornelius in reverse order of occurrence (Acts 10.2, 22).

(φίλους) περιέμεινεν D d p* sy^{hmg} || *om.* B 𝔓^{74} ℵ *rell*.

περιμένω is only used on one other occasion in the New Testament, again by Luke at Acts 1.4. On both occasions, it expresses the sense of waiting for something for which preparation has been made and it only remains for the expected person to arrive. Both occurrences arise in the context of the gift of the Holy Spirit, although Cornelius is unaware that will be the precise outcome of his waiting.

10.25 ὡς δὲ ἐγένετο τοῦ εἰσελθεῖν τὸν Πέτρον B 𝔓^{74} ℵ *rell* || προσεγγίζοντος δὲ τοῦ Π-ου εἰς τὴν Καισάρειαν, προδραμὼν εἰς τῶν δούλων διεσάφησεν παραγεγονέναι αὐτόν D (d gig p) sy^{hmg} mae.

The phrasing of B03, which describes the moment at which Peter entered Caesarea, is 'certainly surprising to meet with in Luke' (Winer, *Grammar*, p. 412): the article τοῦ is not only redundant (Zerwick, *Biblical Greek*, §§ 386, 389), but is incorrect (Delebecque, *Les deux Actes*, p. 193). Luke uses τοῦ + infinitive frequently but never after ἐγένετο where the infinitive is the subject. The genitive of the article may express the idea of something about to happen, corresponding to προσεγγίζοντος τοῦ Πέτρου εἰς τὴν Καισάρειαν in D05. In fact D05, beginning in the previous verse (see above), describes in considerably more detail than B03 the moments leading up to Cornelius' meeting with Peter, seeing them from Cornelius' point of view. The narrative presents a flashback to the time just before Peter entered the city (cf. 10.24a), and shows a slave, either one of the two sent by Cornelius to Joppa or one posted by Cornelius as a lookout, who runs ahead to tell his master of Peter's arrival. Not only is the drama of Cornelius thus rendered more personal and immediate, but the parallel with the story of the centurion in Luke's Gospel is considerably strengthened (Lk. 7.1-10; see *Commentary*, 10.1). The function of the details is more to enhance the atmosphere of anticipation and welcome on the part of a Gentile than to simply iron out difficulties in the sequence of events (cf. Metzger, *Commentary*, p. 329).

συναντήσας αὐτῷ ὁ Κορνήλιος B 𝔓⁷⁴ ℵ *rell* || ὁ δὲ Κ. ἐκπηδήσας καὶ συν. αὐ. D (d gig p) sy^hmg mae.

Only Luke uses the verb ἐκπηδάω, here in D05 and at Acts 14.14, with the sense of a sudden dashing movement.

(πεσών) ἐπί B 𝔓⁷⁴ ℵ *rell* || πρός D.

ἐπί read by B03 is only found here in the New Testament to refer to someone falling at a person's feet; πρός is also found at Mk 5.22; Acts 5.10; Jn 11.32; Rev. 1.17.

(προσεκύνησεν) αὐτόν (-τῷ D^Avid) D* d Ψ || *om.* B 𝔓⁷⁴ ℵ *rell*.

Without the pronoun, the verb προσκυνέω on its own implies worship of God (cf. Acts 8.27; 24.11; Jn 4.20 [× 2]; 12.20); the text of D05 makes it clear that Cornelius worshipped Peter.

10.26 Ἀνάστηθι B 𝔓⁷⁴ ℵ *rell* || Τί ποιεῖς; D d | Τί ποιεῖς; ἀνάστηθι p (w) sy^hmg.

Peter's rebuke is expressed more strongly in the D05 reading (cf. 7.26 D05; 14.15; 21.13), corresponding to the more forceful correction in his following words (see next variant).

καὶ ἐγὼ αὐτὸς ἄνθρωπός εἰμι B 𝔓⁷⁴ ℵ *rell* || κἀγὼ ἄνθρ. εἰμι ὡς καὶ σύ D* d (E) it mae bo^mss.

According to B03, Peter makes the point that Cornelius should get up and not worship him because he is a man. In D05, he goes further, putting himself as a Jew on the same level as Cornelius, a Gentile.

10.27 καὶ συνομιλῶν αὐτῷ εἰσῆλθεν καὶ εὑρίσκει B 𝔓⁷⁴ ℵ D^F *rell* p vg || καὶ εἰσελθών γε καὶ εὗρεν D* d.

The MS of D05 in this verse has been heavily corrected with readings from the AT, and following the participle εἰσελθών, γε has been erased (for which

Scrivener reads τε). In the original hand, D05 omits the detail that Peter was talking with Cornelius as he went into his house. In contrast, γε underlines the fact of his entering the house of a Gentile, and the present tense of εὑρίσκει in B03, which expresses Peter's surprise at finding such a large gathering, is conveyed in D05 by an adverbial καί before the same verb in the aorist – the use of καί to introduce a finite verb after a participle is common in D05 and corresponds to a moment of particular drama (Read-Heimerdinger, *The Bezan Text*, pp. 206–10, esp. 209).

10.28 (Ὑμεῖς) ἐπίστασθε B 𝔓⁷⁴ ℵ *rell* ‖ βέλτιον ἐπ. D^{B?} (ἐφ- D*) d mae; Aug.

D05 qualifies the knowledge of his audience with a comparative adverb serving as an intensifier.

ἀνδρὶ (ἀλλοφύλῳ) D 𝔓⁵⁰ sy^p sa ‖ *om.* B 𝔓⁷⁴ ℵ *rell* d.

The presence of ἀνδρί in D05 (omitted by d05) balances the use of ἀνδρί with Ἰουδαίῳ at the beginning of the sentence and thereby confers emphasis (*contra* Parker, *Codex Bezae*, p. 235, who considers it may be an error caused by 10.1 and 17).

ὁ θεὸς ἔδειξεν (ἐπ- D 440) B D d 𝔓⁵⁰ A C Ψ 33^{vid} 𝔐; Ir^{lat} ‖ ἔδ. ὁ θ. 𝔓⁷⁴ ℵ A E 181. 242. 522. 945. 1739. 1891. 2298 *pc* p vg sy^M.

The word order of ℵ01 is the more usual order of verb–subject; the order subject–verb confers emphasis on ὁ θεός and also has the effect of juxtaposing ὁ θεός with κἀμοί. The compound verb of D05, ἐπιδείκνυμι, is more forceful than the simple verb with the sense of reveal, or give proof (B-A-G, ἐπιδείκνυμι, 2b).

10.29 (μεταπεμφθεὶς) ὑφ' ὑμῶν D d E 88. 915. 1270. 1837 p | ἀφ' ὑμῶν 2344 ‖ *om.* B 𝔓⁷⁴ ℵ *rell*.

By spelling out the agent of the passive verb, D05 reinforces, as it does so often, the relationship between Peter and audience (cf. 10.22 above, v. 33 below).

10.30 Ἀπὸ τετάρτης (D^{B?}) ἡμέρας μέχρι ταύτης τῆς ὥρας ἤμην B 𝔓⁷⁴ ℵ A* 81. 323. 945. 1739. 1891 | Ἀπὸ τετ. ἡμ. μέχ. ταύ. τ. ὥρ. ἤμ. νηστεύων A² P H Ψ 049. 056. 33 𝔐 ‖ Ἀπὸ τῆς τρίτης ἡμ. μέχ. τῆς ἄρτι ὥρας ἤμην νηστεύων D* (*a nustertiana* [?] *die usque in hunc diem eram ieiunans* d).— τὴν ἐνάτην προσευχόμενος B 𝔓⁷⁴ ℵ A* C 81. 323. 945. 1739. 1891 ‖ τὴν ἐν. τε πρ. D | καὶ τὴν ἐν. ὥραν (– 𝔓⁵⁰ A² *pc*) προσ. 𝔓⁵⁰ A² H Ψ 049. 056. 614 𝔐 d it sy sa mae | καὶ προσ. ἀπὸ ἕκτης ὥρας ἕως ἐνάτης E.

The indications given by Cornelius regarding the chronology vary in several ways in these two variants which function together (see diagram, *Commentary*). In D05: 1) Cornelius states that he was fasting; 2) the fasting extended over three days and ceased at the same time as he was talking with Peter; 3) this time was the ninth hour, at which time he began praying – a new clause begins with τὴν ἐνάτην which is highlighted by its position at the head of the clause; 4) the new clause is connected to the previous one by τε; the first verb is a present participle, προσευχόμενος, followed by the main verb ἔστη which is highlighted by καὶ ἰδού. B03 presents Cornelius account quite differently: 1) there is no mention of fasting; 2) the ninth hour is highlighted by its place between the two components of the periphrastic verb, ἤμην ... προσευχόμενος, but does not occupy the salient position of the head of the clause; 3) the absence of the mention of fasting causes the number of days to refer to the time between Cornelius' praying and his speaking with Peter; 4) in consequence, the number of days has to be four instead of three, so as to concord with the three mentions of τῇ ἐπαύριον since Cornelius' prayer (10.9, 23, 24). The result is that the Greek of the sentence in B03 reads oddly, especially the initial preposition ἀπό (Barrett, I, pp. 516–18; Metzger, *Commentary*, pp. 330–31).

10.32 (θάλασσαν) ὃς παραγενόμενος λαλήσει σοι D d C E H L P Ψ 049. 056. 0142. 1739 𝔐 it sy (sa mae) aeth^pt; Chr Beda^gr mss acc. to || *om.* B 𝔓^45.74 ℵ A 36. 81. 431. 453. 629. 1311 *pc* vg bo aeth^pt.

By the presence of this relative clause in D05, the previous clause becomes a parenthetical aside (Delebecque, *Les deux Actes*, p. 75; see *Translation*).

10.33 (πρός σε) παρακαλῶν ἐλθεῖν (+ σε D^C) πρὸς ἡμᾶς D* d p sy^M.h** mae || *om.* B 𝔓^74 ℵ *rell.*

The Syro-Palestinian fragment of Khirbet Mird (sy^M) gives support to this reading of D05 (C. Perrot, 'Un fragment christo-palestinien découvert à Khirbet-Mird [Actes des Apôtres, X, 28-29, 32-41]', *RB* 70 [1963], pp. 506–55) which, as often, is only supported by versional witnesses. Further support is given to the Bezan readings by sy^M in the following verses.

(σύ) τε B 𝔓^74 ℵ C E *rell* | γε A || δέ D d Ψ 323 e gig l t sy^M sa bo.

There is considerable confusion between τε and δέ in the MSS which is, in part at least, phonetic (Read-Heimerdinger, *The Bezan Text*, pp. 204–11). The additional phrase immediately preceding this clause in D05 (see above variant) as well as the adverbial qualification in the present clause (see following variant) accounts for δέ as a particle that highlights the agreement between Cornelius' action (ἔπεμψα πρός σε...) and Peter's response (σὺ δὲ καλῶς ἐποίησας...).

(ἐποίησας) ἐν τάχει D d sy^M || *om.* B 𝔓^74 ℵ *rell.*

According to D05, Peter had not only accepted Cornelius' request but had done so without delay.

(νῦν) οὖν B 𝔓⁷⁴ ℵ Dᶜ *rell, ergo* d ‖ <ἰ>δού D⁽*⁾·ᴬ syᴹ·ᵖ sa mae aeth.

This is the first of a series of variant readings in the conclusion to Cornelius' speech. In B03, he concludes his explanation of why he has summoned Peter by presenting the group assembled as the outcome (οὖν) of the preceding events. The focus in D05 will be maintained as Peter who was already established in the previous clause (especially with δέ, see above), with ἰδού presenting the group as seen with Peter's eyes.

(ἐνώπιον) τοῦ θεοῦ πάρεσμεν B 𝔓⁷⁴ ℵ Dᶜ *rell* ‖ σου D* d (629 *pc*) lat syᴹ·ᵖ sa mae aeth.

B03 has Cornelius present the group as assembled before God (as distinct from 'the Lord' at the end of the sentence, see below); as mentioned in the previous comment, D05 keeps the focus on Peter (cf. previous variant).

ἀκοῦσαι πάντα B 𝔓⁷⁴ ℵ *rell* ‖ (+ τοῦ Dᶜ) ἀκ. βουλόμενοι (– Dᶜ) παρά σου D* d (it syᴹ·ᵖ).

Once again, the effect of the D05 reading is to highlight the role of Peter.

ὑπό B 𝔓⁷⁴ ℵ* *rell* ‖ ἀπό D 𝔓⁴⁵·⁷⁴ ℵ² A C *pc*.

ὑπό is the usual preposition used by Luke to introduce the agent of a passive verb (cf. 10.17 above), but he also uses ἀπό when the verb implies movement away from the agent, in this case the commandments which come from God to Peter (Read-Heimerdinger, *The Bezan Text*, p. 185).

(τοῦ) κυρίου B 𝔓⁴⁵ ℵ A C E Ψ 81*. 181. 257. 323. 453. 467. 522. 614. 630. 945. 1108. 1175. 1611. 1175. 1518. 1739. 1891. 2138. 2298. 2344. 2412 *al* ar e gig l vg syʰ bo ‖ θεοῦ D d 𝔓⁷⁴ H L P 049. 056. 0142 𝔐 p syᴹ·ᵖ sa mae boᵐˢ aeth·

According to D05, κύριος is never used by a Gentile, only by Jews whether Jesus-believers or not (Read-Heimerdinger, *The Bezan Text*, pp. 286–87; see *Commentary*, 10.4).

10.34 (ἀνοίξας δέ) Πέτρος τὸ στόμα B 𝔓⁷⁴ ℵ *rell* ‖ τ. στ. Π. D d 𝔓⁴⁵ gig vgᴬ.

Emphasis is conferred on Peter as speaker by the word order of D05, his speech already signalled as of critical importance by the absence of the article before his name (cf. 11.4; see Heimerdinger and Levinsohn, 'The Use of the Article', p. 28).

καταλαμβάνομαι B 𝔓⁷⁴ ℵ A Dᴮ⁇ *rell, expedior* d | -νόμενος D* C E 2344.

D05 uses the present participle of the verb instead of the finite form. This could be interpreted as a periphrastic present, with elision of the verb 'to be' (cf. B-D-R, § 468, 2), or as a subordinate participle which Peter, in the rush of his ideas, omitted to complete with a finite verb. We have taken it as the latter in the translation of this verse.

10.36 τὸν λόγον B 𝔓⁷⁴ ℵ *rell, verbum suum* d ‖ τ. γὰρ λόγ. D C*ᵛⁱᵈ 614. 913. 1108. 1518. 1611. 2138. 2412 *pc* a l m p t vgᵐˢˢ syᴹᵛⁱᵈ·ᵖ·ʰ** sa mae; Spec.

γάρ occurs twice in Peter's speech in D05 (cf. 10.37 below), giving a structure to the words which come out in a confused state – this is very much Peter thinking aloud. Here, γάρ serves to expand on Peter's claim that the righteous from all nations are acceptable to God (Read-Heimerdinger, *The Bezan Text*, p. 242). At the same time, however, the particles also impose certain restrictions on the way the sentences are linked. Without them, the B03 has more freedom to link the clauses differently, which in turn gives rise to other variants (see below).

ὃν (ἀπέστειλεν) D 𝔓⁷⁴ ℵ* C E H L P Ψ 049. 056. 0142. 614 𝔐 syᴹᵛⁱᵈ·ᵖ·ʰ; CyrJᵖᵗ Chr | *om.* B ℵ² A 81. 467. (614). 1518. (1611). 1739. 2138. (2412) *pc, misit* d latt co aeth; Hipp Ath CyrJᵖᵗ.

B03 reads ἀπέστειλεν as the first main verb and the only one governing τὸν λόγον as the direct object. In D05, in contrast, ἀπέστειλεν is a subordinate verb, and τὸν λόγον is also governed by οἴδατε (v. 37).

10.37 ὑμεῖς (οἴδατε) D d 𝔓⁴⁵·⁷⁴ ℵ A C E Ψ *rell* ‖ *om.* B.

As Peter appeals to what is common knowledge among the Gentiles, he stresses that it is not only Jews who are aware of what God has been doing in Israel.

τὸ γενόμενον ῥῆμα B 𝔓⁴⁵ ℵ *rell* | τὸ ῥῆμα τὸ γεν. 36. 453. 431 *pc* ‖ τὸ γεν. D d.

Where participle forms of γίνεσθαι occur as a noun in Luke's writings, they are always absolute except at Lk. 2.15 (τὸ ῥῆμα τοῦτο τὸ γεγονός); τὸ γενόμενον, Lk. 23.47; τὰ γενόμενα, Lk. 23.48 (*om.* D05); 24.18; τὸ γεγονός, Lk. 8.34, 35 (*om.* D05), 56; Acts 4.21; 5.7; 13.12; τὸ γινόμενον, Acts 12.9; τὰ γινόμενα, Lk. 9.7.

τῆς (Ἰουδαίας) B 𝔓⁷⁴ ℵ Dᶜ *rell* ‖ *om.* D*.

The absence of the article may be due to Peter's speaking of Judaea to Gentiles in Caesarea – from their point of view, it is not their country nor are they associated with it. It is typical of the narrator in D05 to modify the point of view from which people and places are mentioned according to the (mental) position of the hearer (Read-Heimerdinger, *The Bezan Text*, p. 349).

ἀρξάμενος B ℵ C E H Ψ 88. 1739 | -νον 𝔓⁴⁵ L P 049. 056. 33. 𝔐; Did ‖ -νος γάρ D d 𝔓⁷⁴ A e l p t vg syᴹ; Irˡᵃᵗ.

For a second time, D05 uses γάρ to control the structure of Peter's discourse (cf. on 10.36 above), as the mention of Judaea leads on to describing the starting point for God's proclamation as Galilee.

10.38 ὡς ἔχρισεν αὐτόν B 𝔓⁷⁴ ℵ Dᶜ *rell* ‖ ὃν ἔχρ. D* d it syᴹ·ʰ·ᵖ mae aeth; Cyr Epiph Ambr.

B03 takes the statement about God anointing Jesus as the content of what Peter's audience know (οἴδατε, 10.37), whereas D05 take it as being related back to the mention of Jesus in the previous clause.

πνεύματι ἁγίῳ B 𝔓⁷⁴ ℵ *rell* ‖ ἁγ. πν. D d.

The various forms of the expression used by Luke to refer to the Holy Spirit are analysed in detail in Read-Heimerdinger, *The Bezan Text*, pp. 144–72. B03 reads the form that is something of a stereotyped expression in Luke's writings, generally used to signal a momentous event, as here. The adjective occurs after the noun when the focus is on the Spirit as such rather than on the holiness. The form attested by D05, in which the adjective is placed before the anarthrous noun, is found nowhere else in Luke's work. By disrupting the stereotypical formula, the expression draws attention to the Holy Spirit. This can be accounted for by the fact that although Peter is familiar with the Holy Spirit, he is talking to Gentiles who were not familiar in the same way. Once again, the account of D05 presents information from the point of view of the hearer (cf. on 10.37 above, Ἰουδαίας).

ὃς (διῆλθεν) B 𝔓⁷⁴ ℵ *rell* ‖ οὗτος D d it vgᶜᵀ syᴹ·ᵖ sa; Vig.

The demonstrative pronoun in D05 corresponds to the relative pronoun (ὅν) introducing the previous clause (see above). Since in place of D05's relative pronoun B03 read αὐτόν, a relative pronoun can be used here without difficulty.

(τοὺς) καταδυναστευομένους B 𝔓⁷⁴ ℵ *rell, qui obtenebantur* d ‖ -θέντας D syᴹ·ᵖ; Irˡᵃᵗ.

B03 views the oppressive action of the devil as being exercised at the time of Jesus' ministry, whereas D05 views it as an action previously accomplished.

10.39 (μάρτυρες) πάντων B 𝔓⁷⁴ ℵ *rell* ‖ αὐτοῦ D d syᴹ·ᵖ aeth | *om.* 383. 915. 2147.

It must be supposed that the reading of ΥΜΕΙΣ in D05 (*nos* d) at the beginning of the sentence instead of ΗΜΕΙΣ is due to itacism, especially in view of the reading 'his witnesses', since Cornelius and his household cannot be thought of as witnesses of Jesus.

ἐν (Ἰερουσαλήμ) 𝔓⁷⁴ ℵ A C E H L P 049. 056. 33. 1739 𝔐 syʰ; Irˡᵃᵗ ‖ *om.* B D d Ψ 330. 467. 1505. 2495 *pc* lat syᴹ·ᵖ sa mae.

Both B03 and D05 group as one the territory of the Jews and Jerusalem, which ℵ01 treats as distinct regions.

238   *The Message of Acts in Codex Bezae*

10.40 τῇ τρίτῃ ἡμέρᾳ Β 𝔓⁷⁴ ℵ² Α Dˢ·ᵐ Ε Ρ Ψ 049. 056. 0142. 33. 1739 𝔐; Irˡᵃᵗ Chr | ἐν τ. τρ. ἡμ. ℵ* C 6. 88. 181. 630 syʰ ‖ μετὰ τὴν τρίτην ἡμέραν D* d l t.

The reading of D05 is surprising, echoing as it does the expression μετὰ τρεῖς ἡμέρας found in Mk 8.31; 9.31 but not used by Luke in his Gospel. The time cited by Cornelius for the period of his fasting before the angel of God appeared to him may be intended to correspond to the three days Jesus was in the tomb (cf. 10.30 above).

(ἔδωκεν) αὐτόν Β 𝔓⁷⁴ ℵ Dᶜ *rell* ‖ αὐτῷ D* d 1311 *pc.*

The difference between the two constructions is slight and does not alter the sense – the verb δίδωμι is used with the meaning of 'grant' (B-A-G, δίδωμι, 1,b, β), with Jesus being the recipient in D05, who then becomes implied as the subject of the following verb, ἐμφανῆ γενέσθαι. In B03 meanwhile, ἔδωκεν is followed by an accusative–infinitive construction in which the subject is stated explicitly with the accusative pronoun.

10.41 (αὐτῷ) καὶ συν(-αν- Dᴮ)εστράφημεν D d gig l p t w syʰ mae; Didasc (CAp Vig) Cass ‖ *om.* Β 𝔓⁷⁴ ℵ *rell.*

This variant belongs with the next one at the end of the clause (see below). The verb συστρέφω is used by the AT at Acts 28.3 and by D05 at 11.28; 16.39; 17.5, meaning 'gather together'. It is only found otherwise at Mt. 17.22 B03.

(ἀναστῆναι) αὐτόν Β 𝔓⁷⁴ ℵ *rell* ‖ *om.* D d.

In B03, the verb is transitive with God as the subject of the verb, equivalent to τοῦτον ὁ θεὸς ἤγειρεν at 10.40; cf. 3.15; 4.10; 5.30; 13.30, 37. In D05, the verb is intransitive (cf. Lk. 9.22 D05 [ἐγερθῆναι B03]; 24.7), with Jesus himself as the subject, equivalent to those occurrences of ἠγέρθη which might be taken in a reflexive sense (cf. ἠγέρθη ὁ κύριος, Lk. 24.34; Acts 9.8, *Critical Apparatus*).

(ἐκ νεκρῶν) ἡμέρας ·μ· D d (E) it vgᴰᶿ (syʰ**) sa mae aeth; (CAp Vig) Aug Ephr ‖ *om.* Β 𝔓⁷⁴ ℵ *rell.*

In the D05 text, Peter makes particular mention of the time after Jesus' resurrection which he and the other apostles had spent with him (cf. 1.3).

10.42 παρήγγειλεν Β 𝔓⁷⁴ ℵ *rell* ‖ ἐνετείλατο D mae.

The verbs have a similar meaning, and both are used by Luke in the introduction to his second volume (cf. 1.2, ἐντειλάμενος; 1.4, παρήγγειλεν) which is being echoed throughout this episode.

(ὅτι) οὗτος B D C E 33. 242. 323. 522. 614. 876. 913. 945. 1108. 1611. 1739. 1765. 1891. 2298. 2402 *al* | αὐτός 𝔓⁷⁴ ℵ Α Η L Ρ Ψ 049. 056 𝔐 d lat aeth geo; Irˡᵃᵗ.

The demonstrative pronoun attested by both B03 and D05 causes the content of the witness to be seen as the words that the apostles were to report; in ℵ01, supported by d05, the third person pronoun presents the words more directly as those of Jesus himself.

10.44 ἐπέπεσεν B 𝔓⁷⁴ ℵ E H L P Ψ 049. 056. 1739 𝔐 ‖ ἔπεσεν D, *cecidit* d A 33. 36. 323. 431. 1241.

The compound verb is used by Codex Bezae when the Holy Spirit falls on people at 8.16 (Samaritans) and 19.6 (the Jewish Ephesian believers, cf. 8.39 *vl* [Ethiopian eunuch]), but the simple verb is preferred for the two occasions referring to Cornelius (here and at 11.15). In B03, in contrast, the compound verb is always used to refer to the Holy Spirit except at 19.6 (ἔρχομαι); the simple form is never used in this context in B03.

10.45 (πιστοὶ) οἵ B 1611 ‖ ὅσοι D 𝔓⁷⁴ ℵ *rell.*

The relative ὅσοι creates a stronger link than the simple οἵ, so identifying more precisely the people in question as the ones who had come from Joppa with Peter.

τοῦ πνεύματος τοῦ (– D*) ἁγίου B D⁽*⁾ᶜ d Ψ 6. 1175. 1611. 2412 *pc* | τοῦ ἁγ. πν. 𝔓⁷⁴ ℵ A E 33. 1739 𝔐.

The expression for the Holy Spirit in Luke's work takes various forms, depending on the presence or place of the article and/or the adjective (cf. on 10.38 above). The form attested by ℵ01, τὸ ἅγιον πνεῦμα, is normally used in the context of an existing personal relationship between the Spirit and the people in question – that is, in this case, the gift of the Spirit is being commented upon from the point of view of the Jewish believers who are onlookers. In contrast, the form attested here by B03, τὸ πνεῦμα τὸ ἅγιον, is that usually found in the context of a declaration, whether by the narrator or one of the characters – it may be the proximity of just such a declaration in the previous verse (10.44) and at 10.47 that causes the form to be repeated. Finally, the third form read by D05, τὸ πνεῦμα ἅγιον, is unique to Codex Bezae where it is found once more at 13.4. In both instances, the article before πνεῦμα can be accounted for by the previous reference to the Spirit (10.44; 13.2), the form πνεῦμα ἅγιον being the usual way of referring to receiving the Spirit, in particular at baptism (cf. 11.16; see *The Bezan Text*, pp. 160–61; 170–71).

10.46 γλώσσαις B Dᴰ?ᴬ? (D* lac.) 𝔓⁷⁴ ℵ *rell* ‖ ἑτέραις γλ. vgᴰ sa boᵖᵗ mae | καιναῖς Dᶜʲ·, *praevaricatis* d (as if reading ΚΕΝΑΙΣ).

For the reading of the versions, cf. Acts 2.4; Isa. 28.11; 1 Cor. 14.21.

Examination of f. 458b which contains this verse shows the first line of 10.46, line 21, to be intact and line 22 to be heavily corrected in such a way as to leave the reading of the original hand of D05 practically illegible. It seems that Corrector $D^{D?A?}$ wrote over the top of the original reading the B03 reading and crossed out the remaining letters that were not covered by his new entry:

line 21   ΗΚΟΥΟΝΓΑΡΑΥΤΩΝΛΑΛΟΥΝΤΩΝ
line 22 D^A ΓΛΩΣΣΑΙΣΚΑΙΜΕΓΑΛΥ~~ΝΟΝΤΩ~~ΝΤΟΝΘΝ

Elements of the original reading can be deduced, however, from the Latin d05 which has the strange reading of *praevaricatis*, 'empty, vain'. This is a rendering of the Greek ΚΕΝΑΙΣ which could have easily been written for ΚΑΙΝΑΙΣ ('new') because of the similar sounding vowel. But there is not room to add ΚΕΝΑΙΣ at the front of line 22 as it stands in the MS. It appears that a syllable at the end of the participle was omitted in the original. In the reconstruction below, the letters that are still visible at the end of line 22 are in italics, the second version showing the underlined syllable that could have been omitted by the scribe of D05$^{p.m.}$:

line 22 $D^{cj.}$ ΚΕΝΑΙΣΓΛΩΣΣΑΙΣΚΑΙΜΕΓΑΛΥΝΟΝΤΩ*ΝΤΟΝΘΝ*
line 22 D^* ΚΕΝΑΙΣΓΛΩΣΣΑΙΣΚΑΙΜΕΓΑΛΥΝΟ*ΝΤΩΝ ΤΟΝΘΝ*

The steps that are assumed in this explanation can be set out as follows:

1) $D^{p.m.}$ wrote ΚΕΝΑΙΣ for ΚΑΙΝΑΙΣ, through itacism; 2) $D^{p.m.}$, furthermore, omitted through haplography and homoioteleuton the sound ΤΩΝ (ΤΟΝ, in dictation) in the words ΜΕΓΑΛΥΝΟΝΤΩΝΤΟΝΘΝ (as indeed happens again in line 23 when ΥΣ is dropped from ΚΩΛΥΣΑΙ to produce ΚΩΛΑΙ) – the omission becomes obvious when line 21 (23 letters) is compared with the space that would be taken up if the whole sentence of line 22 were included (34 letters) which, as it stands, is already longer than the previous line (by 5.5 letters); 3) d05 read ΚΕΝΑΙΣ and translated it literally by *praevaricatis*; 4) D^A, realising that the reading 'empty languages' was nonsense, deleted ΚΕΝΑΙΣ in agreement with the AT reading and rewrote the sentence, ΓΛΩΣΣΑΙΣΚΑΙΜΕΓΑΛΥΝΟΝΤΩΝΤΟΝΘΝ; but this caused a space to be left of 2/3 letters (which is visible between the first legible letters ΓΛΩΣΣΑΙΣΚΑΙΜΕΓΑΛΥ, and the last ones that are only partially legible ΝΤΩΝΤΟΝΘΝ); 5) $D^{cj.}$, which is our reconstruction of how the original intended the line to read, reinserts the sound omitted through haplography, ΓΛΩΣΣΑΙΣΚΑΙΜΕΓΑΛΥΝΟΝ<ΤΩΝ>ΤΟΝΘΝ; 6) finally, the conjecture ΔΟΞΑΖΟΝΤΩΝ (Boismard and Lamouille, II, p. 76) proposed so as to overcome the problem of the length of ΜΕΓΑΛΥΝΟΝΤΩΝ (the available space is 23/24 letters rather than the necessary 29) overlooks the fact that d05 always translates δοξάζειν in Acts by *clarificare* (Acts 3.13; 4.21; 11.18; 21.20; in Luke's Gospel, the translator uses a variety of expressions: *honorificare* [Lk. 2.20; 5.20; 7.16; 13.13; 23.47], *honorare* [17.15], *gloriam accipere* [4.15]) while the translator of both Luke and Acts always renders μεγαλύνειν by *magnificare* (Lk. 1.46, 58; Acts 5.13; 10.46 d05; 19.17).

τότε ἀπεκρίθη (+ ὁ E Ψ 𝔐) Πέτρος B 𝔓⁷⁴ ℵ *rell* ‖ εἶπεν δὲ ὁ Π. D d syᵖ aeth.

The reading of τότε in B03 expresses a response to the situation (Read-Heimerdinger, *The Bezan Text*, p. 215), presenting Peter as taking a decisive and conclusive step as he initiates the act of baptizing Cornelius and his household with a rhetorical question. D05 reserves this decisive response until after he has considered the question (see final *vl* in 10.48 below).

The absence of the article before Peter's name in B03 is a typical practice in that MS when an apostle is named as he is about to speak (cf. on 10.21). D05 does not highlight the speaker in this way except twice, when Peter speaks for the first time to a Gentile audience (cf. 10.34) and then when he reports this incident to the brethren in Jerusalem (cf. 11.4). The presence of the article in D05 at this point tallies with the fact that Peter's words that follow are not viewed as a declaration in the Bezan text but are more of a discussion in an aside (see also below on τούτους/αὐτούς in this verse).

δύναται κωλῦσαί τις B 𝔓⁷⁴ ℵ A (E*) 81. 1837 ‖ κωλ. (ΚΩΛΑΙ D*) τις δύν. D⁽*⁾·E E² 323. 945. (1175). 1739. 1891 (d gig p l vg) | κωλ. δυν. τις Dˢ·ᵐ· H L P Ψ 049. 056. 1. 33. 88. 104. 226. 330. 440. 547. 614. 618. 927. 1241. 1243. 1245. 1270. 1505. 1611. 1646. 1828. 1854. 2147. 2344. 2412. 2492. 2495.

It is not certain what effect the different order of words might have. In both cases it is the direct object τὸ ὕδωρ that stands at the head of the sentence, causing it to be the focus of Peter's question. The placing of κωλῦσαι immediately after τὸ ὕδωρ in D05 causes this salient member of the sentence to be juxtaposed with the verb that is the other significant element of the question (see *Commentary, ad loc.*).

τούτους B 𝔓⁷⁴ ℵ *rell* // αὐτούς D 1175 *pc* e.

The use of the demonstrative in B03 is appropriate for the situation in which Peter is asking, in their presence, a question concerning the people in the room where he has been speaking. In D05, where it was already noted (cf. 10.46 above) that Peter's question at this point represents his thinking aloud rather than a decision to take action, Peter seems to be viewed as deliberating with his companions from Joppa in a discussion to which the Gentile audience are not party, as if he had turned aside to talk with his fellow-believers.

ὡς B 𝔓⁷⁴ ℵ A Ψ 33. 81. 226ᶜ. 323. 614. 927. 945. 1175. 1270. 1611. 1739. 1891. 2344. 2412 | καθὼς E H L P 049. 056. 1. 88. 104. 226*. 330. 440. 547. 618. 1241. 1243. 1245. 1505. 1646. 1828. 1837. 1854. 2147. 2492. 2495 ‖ ὥσπερ D.

In addition to this verse, ὥσπερ is read as an alternative to ὡς at Lk. 18.11 B03; Acts 11.15; 17.28 D05 (see Read-Heimerdinger, 'Luke's Use of ὡς and ὡσεί').

10.48 προσέταξεν δέ B ℵ E Ψ 33. 36. 81. 181. 431. 453. 614. 913. 1108. 1611. 1175. 1505. 1898. 2412 *al* | πρ. τε 𝔓⁷⁴ A 1739 𝔐; Amb ‖ τότε πρ. D d p syᵖ aeth; Cass.

According to the perspective of D05 which introduces the order for baptism with τότε, it is now that Peter takes decisive action rather than when he asked the question about baptism in the preceding sentence (cf. 10.46 above).

αὐτούς B D E H L P Ψ 049. 056. 33 𝕸 || αὐτοῖς 𝔓⁷⁴ ℵ A 1837.

Both B03 and D05 view Peter's order as being given to others, presumably to the believers from Joppa, that those gathered should be baptized (acc. + inf. construction), whereas with the dative of the pronoun in ℵ01 it is to the people themselves that Peter's command is addressed.

(προσέταξεν δὲ/τε αὐτοὺς/αὐτοῖς) ... βαπτισθῆναι B 𝔓⁷⁴ ℵ A 81. 1175. 1837 | (πρ. δὲ/τε αὐτοὺς) βαπτ. E H L P Ψ 049. 056. 33 𝕸 || (τότε πρ. αὐτοὺς) βαπτ. D d (p syᵖ aeth).

The infinitive verb βαπτισθῆναι is placed directly after the pronoun αὐτούς in D05, so keeping the idea of baptism as the foremost concern. Its position after the name of Jesus in B03 confers greater importance on the name in which the people are to be baptized.

(ἐν τῷ ὀνόματι) Ἰησοῦ Χριστοῦ B 𝔓⁷⁴ ℵ A E Ψ 33. 81ᶜ. 181. 323. 326. 614. 629. 630. 927. 945. 1739. 1837. 2344. 2412 *al* ar e gig l vgˢᵗ syʰ co aeth; Rebap CyrJ Chr || τοῦ κυρίου Ἰ. Χρ. D d 81* p vgᶜˡ (syᵖ) | τοῦ κυ. Ἰ. 436. 1241 | τ. κυ. H L P 049. 056. 0142 𝕸.

It is typical of Codex Bezae to use the full name and title of Jesus in a liturgical context (cf. 2.38 D05; 8.16 D05; 18.8 D05; 19.5 D05; Read-Heimerdinger, *The Bezan Text*, p. 267).

(τότε) ἠρώτησαν αὐτὸν ἐπιμεῖναι B 𝔓⁷⁴ ℵ (Dᴬ) *rell* || παρεκάλεσαν αὐτὸν πρὸς αὐτοὺς διαμεῖναι D* d (it vgᶜˡ sy).

Though both texts say essentially the same thing, the invitation extended to Peter in D05 is couched in stronger and more urgent terms than in B03 1) by virtue of the verb παρακαλέω rather than ἐρωτάω; 2) by the detail πρὸς αὐτούς; and 3) by the perfective compound διαμένω rather than ἐπιμένω. Luke frequently uses both ἐρωτάω (Lk. × 16 + Acts × 7) and παρακαλέω (Lk. × 7 + Acts × 23) with seven supplementary occurrences of the latter in D05. ἐπιμένω occurs again in Acts at 12.16; 15.34 D05; 21.4, 10; 28.12, 14, often with the sense of staying for a short time; διαμένω occurs only in the Gospel outside this occurrence in Acts, at Lk. 1.22 and 22.28, each time with the idea of persistence.

11.1 ἤκουσαν δὲ οἱ ἀπόστολοι καὶ οἱ ἀδελφοὶ οἱ ὄντες κατὰ τὴν Ἰουδαίαν B 𝔓⁷⁴ ℵ *rell* (*audito vero* [cf. D!] *apostoli et fratres qui erant in Iudaeam* d) || ἀκουστὸν δὲ ἐγένετο τοῖς ἀποστόλοις κ. τοῖς ἀδελφοῖς οἳ (τοῖς Dᴰ) ἐν τῇ Ἰουδαίᾳ D* syᵖ.

This is one of the rare units of variation that causes a substantial difference in the narrative structure. In the B03 text, the scene with Cornelius was brought to a close with 10.48 and the invitation to Peter to stay for a few days in Caesarea. This verse then opens a new scene with an active verb, ἤκουσαν, whose subject is 'the apostles and the brethren who were throughout Judaea' (cf. 8.14), thus re-introducing into the narrative new characters and transferring the action back to Judaea.

D05 views the closure of the Cornelius scene somewhat differently. Though giving the same information, that the apostles and the brethren in Judaea heard what had happened in Caesarea, it presents it only obliquely with an impersonal construction and the dative of the persons (cf. 9.42), leaving the focus of attention on Peter and the setting of the narrative remains for the moment in Caesarea. This is confirmed by the next verse, 11.2, with which the following scene opens in D05 (rather than continues as in B03), showing Peter's inner intentions and wishes as he takes the initiative in going to Jerusalem.

Judaea in the D05 text is more specifically a reference to the centre of Judaism, as it is elsewhere in Acts (10.37; 11.29; 12.1 D05, 19; 15.1; 21.10, 20 D05). The relative construction οἱ ἐν τῇ Ἰουδαίᾳ also causes the reference to Judaea to be rather more pointed in D05.

ἐδέξαντο B ℵ Dᴱ *rell* (*exceperunt* d) ‖ -ξατο D* 𝔓⁷⁴ᵛⁱᵈ 1243.

The B03 reading (sing.) considers the Gentiles, or nations, as having separate identities while D05 (pl.) views them collectively as representing one group of people.

Commentary

[BAʹ-BA] 10.1-8 *Cornelius in Caesarea*

[a] 10.1-3 *Presentation of Cornelius and his Vision*
[The Latin text of Codex Bezae is available from 10.4; the Greek only from 10.14b.]

The opening scene portrays Cornelius in Caesarea as a positive example of a foreigner living in Israel and sharing in the Jewish practices of worship and charity in an exemplary fashion. The portrayal is important for showing up the reaction of Peter when invited into his house, and especially the critical attitude of the Jewish brethren in Jerusalem displayed in the next episode after news of his contact with Gentiles in Caesarea reaches them.

10.1-2 Caesarea was a city that had recently been rebuilt by Herod the Great in honour of the Emperor Augustus Caesar, as a huge engineering project designed to establish a model city that would serve as Israel's main seaport connecting Jerusalem with Rome. It had a significant Gentile population though not a few Jews lived there, too. It is likely that there was a community of believers since Philip had gone there some time earlier (cf. 8.26) and will still be there when Paul stops off on his way to Jerusalem (21.8-14). It can be deduced, however, that the church in Caesarea had not had contact with

Gentiles since the conversion of Cornelius is presented in this scene as an entirely new happening.

The narrative presents Cornelius as a real-life figure, with a specific name, place of residence and military function. All three have a strongly Roman character: Cornelius is a Latin name, Caesarea contains the title of the Roman Emperor and his unit is the Italian cohort.[144] He is, at the same time a representative of a class of people, namely those Gentiles who sympathized with and were supportive of the Jewish religion. His representativity is signaled, as often in Luke's writing, with the indefinite pronoun τις, 'a certain'.[145] Thus the hearer is informed that Cornelius was not a unique example nor his case an unusual one.

He is portrayed as a person of exceptional qualities, which stand out all the more that Cornelius is a Gentile. The term 'pious', εὐσεβής, is repeated with reference to his trusted soldier in 10.7; the phrase 'fearing God', φοβούμενος τὸν θέον, is possibly a label, corresponding to σεβόμενος, given to a group of persons who sympathized with the synagogue without becoming proselytes, though how much this was true is a subject that continues to be debated.[146] His religious attitude extended to all his household, confirming that he was not an isolated case. Two criteria that justify the approval accorded to Cornelius are first, his generosity towards the Jews, referred to here with Luke's characteristic term, 'the people'; and secondly, his regular[147] worship of God.

It is necessary to recognize, at the same time, that as a Roman officer he would have also been obliged to participate in practices of Roman religion, in particular the cult of the Emperor. These obligations would have prevented Cornelius from becoming a Jewish proselyte.[148]

10.3 Having given evidence to demonstrate Cornelius' exemplary life, Luke has prepared for the intervention of God by which direct contact will be made between a Jew and a Gentile. Cornelius has a vision, an experience of

---

144. For a presentation of information about the Italian cohort, see Witherington, *Commentary*, pp. 346–47.

145. For other examples of representative characters, encountered so far, see e.g. Acts 7.58; 8.9; 9.10, 33, 36.

146. For comprehensive discussion of the topic of 'God-fearers' see I. Levinskaya, *The Book of Acts in its Diaspora Setting,* in B. Winter (series ed.), *The Book of Acts in its First Century Setting,* V (Grand Rapids: Eerdmans, 1996), esp. pp. 51–126.

147. The phrase διὰ παντός used to describe Cornelius' prayer is also found at Lk. 24.53 with reference to the apostles' presence in the Temple after the departure of Jesus. Literally meaning 'continually', it is used by the LXX (Numbers 28–29) to describe the twice-daily Temple sacrifices that had to be offered 'continually' in the sense of 'every day': ἡ ὁλοκαύτωσις ἡ διὰ παντός (see D. Hamm, 'Praying "Regularly" [not "Constantly"]: A Note on the Cultic Background of διὰ παντός at Luke 24.53; Acts 10.2, and Heb. 9.6; 13.15', *ExpT* 116 (2004), pp. 50–52. It is therefore quite plausible, especially in view of the insistence on the ninth hour in 10.3, 30, that Luke intends Cornelius' prayer to be seen as corresponding to Jewish official prayer – clearly not in the Temple and not sacrificial, but equal in its validity.

148. Levinskaya, *Diaspora Setting*, p. 121.

which he is entirely conscious, a mark of his spiritual perception. The time of the vision corresponds to the time of the Jewish afternoon prayer,[149] to which attention is drawn in some MSS but not Codex Vaticanus (see *Critical Apparatus*).[150] Further indirect references to the Jewish act of prayer will be made later in this episode. When Cornelius recounts his vision to Peter, he will make clear according to Codex Bezae that not only was he praying at this time but had been fasting for three days beforehand (10.30).[151] In both places, the importance of the hour is downplayed in Codex Vaticanus, and also Codex Sinaiticus at 10.30 (see *Critical Apparatus, ad loc.*).

The ninth hour was also, of course, the hour of the death of Jesus (Lk. 23.45) when another centurion recognized that: 'Certainly this man was righteous' (23.47).[152] And it is no coincidence that Cornelius should receive the visit of a messenger of God at precisely the hour at which Jesus' death opened the way for Gentiles to be counted as the people of God. It is the moment at which Jesus entrusted his spirit to the Father (23.46), the same spirit that is about to be given to the Gentiles for the first time according to the narrative of Acts.

This is, in fact, the third mention of a centurion in Luke's work, the remaining one being the centurion of Capernaum (Lk. 7.1-10). Although the two in the Gospel are presented favorably, the comparison between the person of Cornelius and that of the centurion of Capernaum, a parallel that is particularly striking, reveals that the narrator's evaluation of Cornelius is even more positive. Both men are centurions and display exemplary piety for all that they are not Jews; in addition, each has a servant to whom they are particularly attached. The incidents concerning both mark an initial step in the contact between Jesus or his apostles on the one hand, and a Gentile on the other. An important difference, however, is that whereas the centurion of the Gospel remains partially hidden by the figure of his sick slave who is the object of Jesus' healing, Cornelius is in the forefront and is the object of attention throughout. He has a name and a specific function, even though he is also a representative of a class of people. While the Capernaum centurion sends Jewish elders to Jesus to represent him, Cornelius sends his own servants to act on his behalf; this

---

149. D. Hamm, 'The Tamid Service in Luke-Acts: The Cultic Background behind Luke's Theology of Worship (Luke 1:5-25; 18:9-14; 24:50-53; Acts 3:1; 10:3, 30)', *CBQ* 65 (2003), pp. 215–31 (222–23).

150. For an analysis of Luke's highlighting of numbers, see Read-Heimerdinger, 'Luke's Use of ὡς and ὡσεί'.

151. Compare 10.30 B03: Ἀπὸ τετάρτης ἡμέρας μέχρι ταύτης τῆς ὥρας ἤμην τὴν ἐνάτην προσευχόμενος, with D05: Ἀπὸ τῆς τρίτης ἡμέρας μέχρι τῆς ἄρτι ὥρας ἤμην νηστεύων τὴν ἐνάτην τε προσευχόμενος.

152. The word order of Lk. 23.47 D05 emphasizes the word 'righteous' by placing it at the head of the clause: ὄντως δίκαιος ἦν ὁ ἄνθρωπος οὗτος (cf. ὄντως ὁ ἄνθρωπος οὗτος δίκαιος ἦν AT).

follows a vision in which an angel speaks to him directly. The contact between Gentiles and the power of God in the first case is, in other words, indirect; once Jesus has departed and his apostles continue his work, the spread of the gospel to the Gentiles becomes more definite and permanent, and God is seen to intervene to demonstrate the inclusion of the Gentiles in his people. Such a development, which leaves the ministry to the Gentiles to the book of Acts, is an important part of Luke's narrative intention.[153]

The angel, in the guise of a man (cf. 10.30), enters Cornelius' house, just as Gabriel entered Mary's,[154] and he addresses Cornelius by name.

[b] 10.4a *Cornelius' Response to the Vision*
10.4a Cornelius' reaction is to stare at the angel, for which Luke uses the same verb that he uses elsewhere to indicate a gazing at a divine representative.[155] He is also overcome with terror,[156] a normal response and typical in Luke's accounts of encounter with the divine.[157]

Cornelius addresses the angel as 'Lord' which at this stage is simply a term of respect (see *Commentary*, 9.5). From the point of view of Luke's hearers, however, it could be understood as a reference to the risen Jesus whom Cornelius does yet know as 'the Lord'.[158]

[b'] 10.4b-6 *The Angel's Instructions*
10.4b The angel continues by taking up in reverse order the qualities in Luke's initial portrayal of Cornelius, his prayers and his acts of charity. The

---

153. The organization of Luke's narrative overall ensures that the encounter of Gentiles with the power of Jesus does not occur until the book of Acts. In the story of the centurion from Capernaum in both Matthew (Mt. 8.5-13) and John (Jn 4.46b-54), it is the centurion himself who comes to ask Jesus to heal his servant whereas Luke is careful to have him send Jewish elders on his behalf. In a similar way, Luke omits the central section of Mark's narrative (Mk 7.24–8.10) dealing with the ministry of Jesus in Gentile territory. Furthermore, in the Bezan text of Simeon's hymn of praise in Luke's Gospel, the mention of the Gentiles is omitted from the allusion to Isaiah's prophecies (Lk. 2.32 D05, cf. Isa. 42.6; 49.6).

154. Compare Acts 10.3: ἄγγελον τοῦ θεοῦ εἰσελθόντα πρὸς αὐτὸν καὶ εἰπόντα αὐτῷ... with Lk. 1.28: εἰσελθὼν (+ ὁ ἄγγελος D05) πρὸς αὐτὴν εἶπεν....

155. Out of the 14 (16 D05) times that the verb ἀτενίζω occurs in the NT, it is used 12 (14 D05) times in Luke's work (see *The Message of Acts*, I, pp. 206, 212–13, on Acts 3.2-3). At Acts 10.4, it is found in the context of a vision as at 1.10; 7.55; 11.6.

156. The adjective ἔμφοβος is also almost exclusively used by Luke (× 5 in the NT: Lk × 2 + Acts × 2) and, except for Acts 24.25 (D05 lac.), always in the context of a vision (cf. Lk. 24.5, 37).

157. Cf. Lk. 24.5 (the women on seeing 'the two men' at the empty tomb), 37 (the disciples on seeing Jesus in Jerusalem).

158. κύριος is not used by Gentiles or with reference to them in the Bezan text of Acts, to mean either Yahweh or Jesus (cf. 10.33 D05 where Cornelius does not say κύριος but θεός; see Read-Heimerdinger, *The Bezan Text*, pp. 286–87).

chiastic structure (v. 2: ποιῶν ἐλεημοσύνας ... καὶ δεόμενος τοῦ θεοῦ // v. 4: αἱ προσευχαί σου καὶ αἱ ἐλεημοσύναι σου) reinforces their significance as characteristics of a Gentile. They have 'gone up' to God as a 'memorial', terms used with reference to sacrifices prescribed in the Torah.[159] In terms of Jewish mentality, it is indeed a bold statement to suggest that a Gentile's offerings were as acceptable to God as those given by the Jews in the Temple. The fact that his acts of charity were towards the Jewish people plays no doubt a significant part as a force behind the change, for this implies that as a Roman official he had gone out of his way to alleviate the situation created by the Roman occupation for the Jews in Israel. His sympathy for Jews and for their religion makes him a Gentile who is as close as possible to the Jews, and as such a suitable model for the first step in demonstrating how the gospel was intended for the nations as much as for Israel.

10.5-6 The dramatic consequence of God's acknowledgement of Cornelius' piety is about to unfold. The angel gives him quite specific orders, although at this point Cornelius does not know the significance of fetching Peter from Joppa. The way Peter is presented is not without irony from the audience's point of view, even though it is lost on Cornelius. He is named as Simon and qualified as the one 'who is called Peter', Πέτρος. The figurative meaning of this name, 'hardness', takes on its full significance here, in view of the resistance Peter is about to display with respect to God's acceptance of Gentiles (10.9-16), for it is this kind of 'hardness' that is meant by the Greek word rather than the firm stability that is generally understood to be behind the name Jesus gave him.[160]

Meanwhile, Cornelius will know what kind of a person he should tell his messengers to expect. He is distinguished from the other Simon, who has given him lodging, by the mention of the latter's trade. The repetition of 'a tanner' from 9.43 gives prominence to the juxtaposition of the two Simons: the one, a Jew who considers himself a 'sinner', ἁμαρτωλός (Lk. 5.8),

159. The 'memorial', μνημόσυνον, was that token part of the offering that was sacrificed rather than consumed by the priest (אזכרה, see Lev. 2.2, 9, 16; 5.12; 6.8) and burnt so that it 'went up' to God as smoke. It is usually interpreted as being a reminder to the Lord of the supplicant (see P. Harlé and D. Pralon, *Le Lévitique*, III, in M. Harl [ed.], *La Bible d'Alexandrie* [Paris: Cerf, 1988], p. 40; Zerwick and Grosvenor, *Analysis*, p. 382), and that is the sense explained by Cornelius when he relates his vision to Peter (10.31). It is therefore interesting to note a different interpretation given in the commentary on Lev. 2.1-16 in the *Jewish Study Bible*, p. 208: the 'memorial' served as a reminder to the people of God's lordship over them (cf. further examples of μνημόσυνον in LXX Exod. 3.15; 28.12).

160. Πέτρος is generally understood as meaning 'rock' but erroneously, for that is expressed by the Greek πέτρα (cf. Mt. 16.18); πέτρος has the sense of 'stone', something hard on which no impression is made (see Bailly, πέτρος, 1; L-S-J, πέτρος) and when Jesus assigns this name to Simon (cf. Lk. 6.14) he is making a negative rather than a positive evaluation (see Rius-Camps, *De Jerusalén a Antioquía*, p. 255, n. 436). Jesus himself will distinguish between the two aspects of Simon Peter's character when he warns him of future dangers before his crucifixion (Lk. 22.31-34; see *Commentary*, Acts 10.13 below).

known to be hard-headed and resistant to change, and the other, a Jew ritually unclean by reason of his contact with dead animals (see *Commentary*, 9.43). The fact that Peter has accepted to stay with the tanner is a hopeful sign that his openness to the reversal of Jewish laws of uncleanness is growing. The verb 'lodge', ξενίζω, will become a motif running through the scenes of this episode (cf. on 10.23a below), focusing attention on the association of a Jew with someone unclean or impure according to the Law. The use of the periphrastic form of the verb in the 'Western' text, including the Latin page of Codex Bezae, underlines the importance of the idea.

The fact that the house is beside the sea is a sign, in Luke's work, that the people occupying it are in the process of undertaking a departure ('exodus') from the Jewish religious system, as will be seen later (10.23b).

[a'] 10.7-8 *Cornelius' Obedience*
10.7-8 The departure of the angel signals the change from a spiritual experience to the carrying out of its message in practical terms. Cornelius' prompt obedience confirms the degree of his piety stated in the opening verses (vv. 1-4). He chooses messengers from among two groups of people: two from among his household servants and one soldier from among those who served him[161] – representatives, in other words, of his domestic and professional life whose faithfulness and loyalty to him is proved by the fact that he tells them about his vision or, more generally according to the AT (see *Critical Apparatus*), everything, which will obviously include directions on where to find Simon Peter in Joppa as well as the kind of person they are to meet. They have a journey of approximately 35 miles to undertake on a good road following the coast; it is not said how they travelled but the implication of 10.9 is that they arrived the following day (see *Commentary*, below).

[BA'-BB] 10.9-16 *Peter's Vision in Joppa*
The setting now transfers to Joppa. Peter, the leader of the apostles, is in the spotlight where, as Jesus speaks to him in a vision, he is seen to live up to the meaning of his name, Πέτρος, that is 'hard-headed', resistant and slow to learn. It is no accident that in the dialogue there should be echoes of the denial scene in Luke's Gospel. These verses present a finely drawn psychological portrait of someone who is torn between the restrictions of his traditional beliefs and the freedom he has learnt from his master, Jesus.

---

161. Barrett, I, pp. 503–504 suggests that the term τῶν προσκαρτερούντων refers to soldiers who had been kept on in Cornelius' service after his retirement. It could equally refer to soldiers who were faithfully attached to his service (B-A-G, προσκαρτερέω, 1).

[a] 10.9 *Peter Goes to Pray*
10.9 The timing of the vision is important: it was noted that the previous scene with Cornelius, the devout centurion, which took place at the ninth hour, echoed the scene in the Gospel when a centurion responded positively to Jesus' death, also at the ninth hour. Now, Peter is seen at the sixth hour, the time when Jesus was crucified. The timings are arranged in a chiastic pattern across the two accounts:

Gospel:	sixth hour: crucifixion	ninth hour: centurion
Acts:	ninth hour: centurion	sixth hour: Peter's vision

By presenting Peter as receiving his vision, in which the heavens open, at the same time as Jesus' crucifixion, Luke uses his narrative art to make clear the relationship between the death of Jesus and this critical moment in Peter's understanding of the implications of his death: it was by the death of Jesus that a way was opened for Gentiles to gain access to the kingdom of God, and that is what Peter will now at last come to accept.

The detail that it was the 'next day' that Peter had his vision may also be part of the narrative organization of events, rather than a literally accurate piece of information, serving to bring out how carefully planned these incidents appeared to be. The reading of several Latin witnesses (including the Latin side of Codex Bezae for which the Greek is still missing at this point – see *Critical Apparatus*) would seem to confirm the narrator's role with the mention of the 'upper room' where Peter is presented as going to pray. The upper room has been noted on three previous occasions[162] in Luke's writing as a place that symbolized the adherence to traditional Jewish customs and beliefs with regard to Israel: it was the room where the Eleven waited for the Holy Spirit, together with the family of Jesus and other disciples, holding firm to Jewish expectations and aspirations (1.13),[163] and it was the room where the church in Lydda placed the dead body of Tabitha, the representative of a community who continued in traditional Jewish ways of thinking (see *Commentary*, 9.37). Given the symbolism with which the upper room has been endowed by the narrator, the portrayal of Peter praying in a similar upper room functions as a device to represent his attitudes and thinking: as far as the Gentiles were concerned, he continued to hold to the idea that was so much a part of the Jewish self-definition, namely, that they were separate from Israel, that they were unclean.

From a literal point of view, the upper room is not a suitable setting for a vision in which heaven is opened and something comes down from the sky.

---

162. The word used here for the 'upper room' and also at 1.13 and 9.37, 39 is ὑπερῷον. It is not the same word that is found at Lk. 22.12 to refer to the room where Jesus met with his disciples for the Last Supper (ἀνάγαιον).

163. See *The Message of Acts* I, pp. 100–102.

The variant reading 'the rooftop' prepares better for the vision Peter sees but what it gains in realism it loses in symbolism.

The sixth hour was midday, and the hottest part of the day though that would only be relevant in the warmer months of the year. It was not one of the prescribed times for Jewish prayer and, although from the point of view of the narrative organization the correspondence with the time of the crucifixion is evident (see Lk. 23.44; cf. Mt. 27.45; Mk 15.33; Jn 19.14), the reason why Peter should have gone to pray at this point is not clearly stated. It can, however, be deduced from the context, especially in light of the account that follows.

[b] 10.10a *Peter is Hungry*

10.10a It is necessary to consider Peter's situation at the tanner's house in Joppa in order to understand something of what was going on in his mind at this point that would have motivated him to pray. He has been seen earlier visiting the churches in Judaea, where he performed acts of healing within communities of Jewish Jesus-believers who were paralysed or even without life because they continued in the ancient ways of thinking with regard to the status of Jews and Gentiles. Although they were restored by the power of Jesus, there is no indication that either Peter or the communities had grasped any better than before the radical effect of Jesus' death, namely, that of removing the barriers that separated the Jews from anyone else and in particular of bringing the Gentiles onto an equal footing with the Jews (see *Commentary*, 9.31-43).

Peter has, nonetheless, taken some steps forward in understanding the removal of old divisions that separated the clean from the unclean. He has witnessed the gift of the Holy Spirit to the Samaritans who had hitherto been considered to be outside Israel, a scene in which he played a key part (see *Commentary*, 8.14-25). In Joppa, he has accepted to stay with a tanner who was considered unclean by virtue of his trade (see *Commentary*, 9.43), and yet who displays none of the signs of paralysis or death that he had witnessed in the more 'orthodox' communities. As one of the twelve chosen disciples of Jesus, he had seen his master ignoring the regulations against outcasts and enjoying friendships with them in a similar way. He had seen much more, too – for, in the face of disapproval from the authorities, Jesus had eaten with people considered impure by the Jewish Law (Zaccheus, Lk. 19.2-10) and allowed himself to be touched by them (the woman with the jar of perfume, 7.36-50; cf. 7.34).

In the previous scene, it was observed that while the account of Peter's healing of Tabitha is modelled on Jesus' healing of Jairus' daughter (see *Commentary*, 9.36-42), there are notable differences that reveal Peter's hesitation in his dealings with a dead body. The scene illustrates Peter's desire to imitate Jesus and his empowering by God to do so at the same time as his diffidence in following the example of his master through to the end. A similar lack of confidence is seen in the present scene where Peter stays with a man considered to be impure but has not dared to go so far as Jesus in fully associating with this person. It is precisely his failure to live out Jesus' teaching completely, stopping short of its full consequences, that is the context of the vision that is about to follow.

Indeed, while Peter is praying, he is hungry, a fact that is doubly underlined ('he was hungry and wanted to eat').[164] The insistence on his hunger and the way that it disturbs his praying both suggest that Peter had not been freely participating in the meals of this household where he was staying. It was, from a Jewish point of view, an impure household and Peter's pressing hunger would indicate that he had so far not wanted to eat of their food. Peter's recent experiences can only have caused him considerable perplexity as he sought to match what he saw happening around him with, on the one hand, his deep-seated convictions that formed so much a part of Jewish beliefs about themselves as a people apart; and on the other, with his observation of Jesus during his lifetime and his recollection of his teaching. His urgent need for clarity and understanding concerning precisely this teaching accounts for his prayer at this unusual hour.[165]

[c] 10.10b-12 *Peter's Vision*

10.10b The mention of Peter's need of food is reinforced once more by the detail that it was now being prepared, meaning that he had overcome his reluctance to eat at the table of an impure household. It was precisely at that point that God intervened and taught him a further lesson concerning the removal of the barriers between the clean and the unclean.

His experience of the vision happened while he was in a trance-like state, expressed by the Greek ἔκστασις.[166] In the wording of the WT (ἐπέπεσεν, 'fell'),

---

164. The verb γεύομαι, usually used with an object, means to 'taste' and by extension has the sense of 'to partake of a meal' (cf. Acts 20.11). It is used in this way in Jesus' comparison of the kingdom of God to a banquet (Lk. 14.15-24) in which those outside the kingdom are welcomed in to partake of the king's meal (14.24) because those who had originally been invited had declined to come. By the use of the same verb, the parable anticipates Peter's thoughts at the point when he was struggling to come to terms with Jesus' teaching about the inclusiveness of the kingdom.

165. In Luke's Gospel, the partaking of food is presented as the equivalent of the sharing of teaching. See J. Rius-Camps, 'Lk 10,25–18,30: Una perfecta estructura concèntrica dins la Secció del Viatge (9,51–19,46)', *RCatT* 8 (1983), pp. 283–358, where the teaching episode of Lk. 13.10-30 is seen to correspond to the banquet scene of 14.1-24 [332–36].

166. ἔκστασις is used only by Mark (× 2) and Luke (× 1 Gospel; × 4 Acts) in the New Testament. At Mk 5.42 and 16.8, as also at Lk. 5.26 and Acts 3.10, it describes an extreme emotion in response to an extraordinary happening. With reference to the vision of both Peter (Acts 10.10; 11.5) and Paul (22.17), it describes an altered state of consciousness. The word is found in the two senses in the LXX, accompanied in places by the verb ἐπιπίπτω: in the second sense, it refers to the deep sleep brought about by God on Adam when he removed the rib from which to make Eve (Gen. 2.21), or on Abraham when God revealed to him the future of his descendants (15.12 [+ ἐπέπεσεν]).

it is more obvious than in the AT that this state was brought about by God, and that it happened suddenly; the verb itself is used elsewhere in Acts to refer to the Holy Spirit and the point being made here may be that the vision was given by the Spirit (cf. on the force of αὐτῷ in Codex Bezae, *Commentary*, 10.19).[167] The difference with the way in which Cornelius experienced his vision ('he saw in a vision clearly', φανερῶς, 10.3) is marked and suggests that there was considerable resistance to be overcome in the case of Peter in order for him to hear what God had to say to him. The same will be true of the one other use in Acts of ἔκστασις, 'trance', in relation to a vision: at 22.17, where Paul is confronted with Jesus' command to leave Jerusalem, he was still holding fast to the Temple traditions. Similarly, when God revealed to Abraham the fate that awaited his descendants, the ἔκστασις that fell on him was accompanied by a great and dark dread (Gen. 15.12). ἔκστασις does not, in other words, express a mystical experience in a positive sense but refers to the altered state of consciousness that is necessary for God to communicate with the person because of some inner resistance.[168]

10.11 The vision is described in some detail, with the order of the features varying according to the text followed. It starts with Peter seeing[169] 'heaven opened', not as if it were a new event but a pre-existent state that had, in fact, already been established[170] by virtue of the descent of the Holy Spirit at Jesus' baptism in the Jordan (Lk. 3.21-22) and that had been maintained ever since that time (cf. Stephen's vision, Acts 7.56). The opening of heaven always signifies communication between heaven and earth (typically, in Jacob's dream of the stairway set up between heaven and earth, Gen. 28.12; cf. Jn. 1.51; in the prophetic visions given to Ezekiel, Ezek. 1.1). What is new here is the receptacle that comes down onto the earth. The appearance of the object was a fine linen sheet ('like' a sheet in the AT, cf. 11.5) which was held by its four corners as it was lowered. The four corners are reminiscent of the 'four streams' (τέσσαρας ἀρχάς) into which divided the river that flowed out from

---

167. Cf. Delebecque, *Les deux Actes*, p. 408.

168. The negative connotations of ἔκστασις are apparent throughout the LXX where it expresses such emotions as fear, terror, horror. At Dan. 10.7, an interesting distinction is made between Daniel who had a vision (ὅρασις LXX; ὀπτασία Theodotion) and the men with him who saw nothing and ran away because ἔκστασις μεγάλη fell on them (in the Theodotion text only; the LXX speaks of φόβος ἰσχυρός).

169. The verb 'see' is in the present, θεωρεῖ. The use of the present tense in place of the expected past is rare in Luke's writing. It is more common in Matthew's Gospel where one of its functions has been analysed as presenting the 'preliminary event' of a section which is thereby detached 'from both the previous section and the foreground events that are to follow' (Levinsohn, *Discourse Features*, p. 141). In such situations, the purpose of 'the present in the past' is not to highlight the verb as is commonly assumed (because of the way it is used in English, for example), but rather to introduce a preliminary action that prepares for the main event. In this case, it is not what Peter saw that is the key feature of the scene but the instructions that he heard the voice commanding him to carry out.

170. The perfect ἀνεῳγμένον expresses a state that had already been acquired.

Eden and that, in mythical terms, watered the whole of the created earth (Gen. 2.10). In both instances, 'four' expresses the notion of the whole creation.

10.12 In the sheet was a variety of animals that represent the created species in their entirety. As such, they are a reminder of God's plan of creation (Gen. 1.20-25), renewed in the story of Noah (6.11–9.3) with the receptacle serving as a reminder of the ark in which every living creature was saved (6.19-20). The lowering of the container from heaven to earth thus stands as a physical representation of the transfer or communication of God's plan in creation, perfectly carried out in the heavenly sphere, to the domain of the earth where it is to be equally perfectly realized among and by people.

[d] 10.13 *A Voice Gives Orders*

10.13 The meaning of the vision, which was a preliminary to the main purpose of the heavenly communication with Peter at this point, is made clear in the words spoken by the voice: all the creatures of the earth are presented to him because all are to be taken as food. The commands are an echo of God's promise to Noah after saving every living creature from the flood: 'Every moving thing that lives shall be food for you' (Gen. 9.3). The voice, which can be presumed to be that of Jesus as will become clearer in the following dialogue, orders Peter to take action: to kill the animals and eat them. The opening imperative ('get up') is stronger in Codex Bezae (Latin page only still) than in the AT, setting it on a par with the other two commands and implying that Peter was literally lying prostrate in his trance-like state.

The use of the name 'Peter' (highlighted by the Latin Bezan text) by which the voice addresses him is particularly meaningful in the mouth of Jesus. For it was he who first gave him the name (Lk. 6.14) as a symbol of his hard-headedness (see *Commentary*, 10.5 above) and who reminded him of it as he warned him of his three-fold denial (22.34, 'I say to you, Peter…', in contrast to 22.31, 'Simon, Simon…', where Peter's frailty rather than his stubbornness is in view). That the echo of this latter scene is intentional on Luke's part is seen in the three-fold repetition of Peter's refusal to obey in the present instance (cf. Acts 10.16a; *Excursus* 5).[171]

The order given to Peter to kill and eat is made without any kind of qualification about selecting only certain animals, the implication being that all were to be eaten. This was, of course, in direct contradiction with the commands that would be so familiar to any Jew and so fundamental to his way of life (cf. Leviticus 7; 10–11; Deuteronomy 14). He would, however, have heard Jesus' teaching and observed his master's practice (cf. Mk 7.14-19) and so the idea of it being lawful to eat all food would not be new to Peter. Besides, Luke has just noted in the immediate context that Peter is waiting for

---

171. Further echoes of Peter's denial are heard in the repetition of ἡ φωνή in 10.13, 15, which tallies with ἐφώνησεν in Lk. 22.60 – the tally is even stronger in D05 which reads φωνήσας at Acts 10.15 (see *Critical Apparatus*).

food to be prepared by an impure household, so juxtaposing this vision and the orders with his present deliberations.

[d'] 10.14 *Peter's Refusal to Obey*
[From the second half of this verse, the Greek side of Codex Bezae is extant.]

10.14 In view of what has just been said about Peter's familiarity with Jesus' new teaching and practice concerning food laws, and the likelihood that he had already just asked for impure food to be prepared for him, his outright refusal to obey seems on the face of it unrealistic. However, the portrait Luke has been painting of Peter is precisely characterized by contradictions and inconsistency: the most flagrant example is his vow to accompany his master to death which was followed within hours by a three-fold denial that he ever knew him (Lk. 22.31-34, 54-62, see on 10.13 above). This had happened on the last occasion Jesus is recorded as speaking personally with Peter. Now, as he speaks again, Peter repeats his earlier pattern of denial. He knows Jesus' teaching about the eating of all foods, and has gone a certain way along that path by asking for food from Simon the Tanner, but is still held by the traditions and regulations of his ancestral religion. It is as if part of him cannot yet believe that the abolition of the food laws, upheld on the principle of holiness, is sanctioned by God himself. And so, when confronted by the divine command to do exactly what was in his mind to do (eat impure food), he protests – caught out, as it were, by his own boldness and trapped at the same time by his lack of daring. By refusing to eat what has previously been considered forbidden food, Peter is not only concealing his own openness but denying to Jesus (whom he addresses as Lord [κύριε]) the lessons he had learnt from him. The contradiction is not in the narrative but within Peter himself. Why is it so much easier to ascribe the confusion to Luke?[172] Is it not possible that even in the first century there was a clear psychological awareness of the inner tensions and conflicts caused by the upheaval as ancient Jewish customs, crucial facets of what it meant to be Jewish, were uprooted? And that Luke, knowing first hand what these tensions involved, would want to explain to Theophilus, a faithful Jew who was equally likely to face such difficulties (see *General Introduction*, § IV), how hard they were to resolve?

Peter expresses his refusal in words that recall those of Ezekiel when he was commanded to eat unclean food as a symbolic warning of the exile of the Jews among the nations: 'By no means, Lord God of Israel! See that from my birth until now my person was not defiled with uncleanness, and I have not eaten anything that dies of itself or that was killed by a wild beast, nor did any foul flesh enter my mouth' (Ezek. 4.14). This is the first in a series of clues

---

172. Barrett (I, pp. 507–508) finds Peter's refusal to obey highly problematic, concluding that the best explanation is that 'Luke (or Peter, if the narrative does in fact go back to him) failed to see the logical implication of what was said'. The real difficulty for Peter, however, is not one of logic at this stage, but rather one of psychological struggle.

that will appear in the Acts narrative to the assimilation of Peter with the prophet Ezekiel, here made by himself but later by the narrator (see *Commentary*, 12.10, 17; *Excursus* 8). Ezekiel's situation was that Israel was about to be punished by being sent out among the idolatrous Gentiles; for Peter, the situation is turned upside down, in that the lesson he is to learn is that the Gentiles have become accepted by God (cf. 10.28).

The terms Peter uses are 'common' and 'unclean' (Codex Bezae treating them as two different notions). The notions overlap, with both denoting that which was set aside for God (cf. Lev. 20.26), though they are not necessarily the same. 'Common' is the opposite of 'holy', whereas 'unclean' is the opposite of 'clean'.[173]

[c'] 10.15 *The Voice Speaks a Second Time*

10.15 The insistence on 'a second time' draws attention to the correspondence between this scene and that of Peter's denial (see on 10.13, 14 above). The declaration referring to 'God' in the third person is a further indication that it is Jesus who is speaking. It takes up the two terms Peter has just used, showing that there is a contradiction between God's intention and the interpretation of the Jewish food laws: he has pronounced everything clean, not as a recent revocation of the Law but as a general principle that is valid for all time;[174] Peter is to stop calling it common,[175] that is, not holy for God.

The force of the words is the same as that behind Jesus' teaching to the Pharisees recorded in Mark 7, where he makes it clear to them that the distinction between clean and unclean which they so zealously uphold is not the right one to make. Their laws are human constructions and cause them to go against the laws of God. There he states unequivocally that 'what goes into a man from outside cannot defile him...' (Mk 7.18) on which Mark comments 'In this way he declared all foods clean' (7.19). So the declaration Jesus makes now to Peter does not announce a new situation but rather a correct interpretation of God's creation: whatever God made is good (cf. Gen. 1.31).

[b'] 10.16a *The Dialogue is Repeated for a Third Time*

10.16a It has already been said that the voice spoke a second time; the comment 'this happened three times' supposes that the voice spoke a third time, making three times in all that Jesus attempted to persuade Peter to eat what he saw in his vision. After the vision disappears he is left still puzzling over its meaning but the insistence was sufficient to make sure Peter did not simply attribute the incident to a dream or imagination, as the rest of the story will demonstrate.

---

173. J. Klawans, 'Concepts of Purity in the Bible', *Jewish Study Bible*, pp. 2041–47.

174. The aorist ἐκαθάρισεν expresses this general (or gnomic) sense.

175. The present imperative in the negative, μὴ κοίνου, has the force here of ceasing to do something rather than not to start doing something.

[a'] 10.16b *The Vision Ends*
10.16b The removal of the container is related using the same term as that which Luke uses to describe the ascension of Jesus to heaven, not only by means of the resurrection (ἀναλαμβάνω, Acts 1.2, 11, 22) but even by his death (ἀνάλημψις, Lk. 9.51). Just as Jesus properly belongs to the divine sphere, so does the notion, symbolized by the contents of the sheet, that all of God's creation is equally pure.

[BA'-BB'] 10.17-23a *Cornelius' Men Find Peter in Joppa*

In this scene, the tension builds up as the first move towards the meeting of Jesus-believers and Gentiles is made. In keeping with the drama of the moment, the action unfolds slowly, step by step.

[a] 10.17a *Peter's Perplexity over the Vision*
10.17a In accordance with the way the Bezan text described the onset of Peter's trance (cf. 10.10b), so it makes special note of the end of that state when he came back to full consciousness. The same point is made after his miraculous deliverance from prison (12.11; see *Commentary, ad loc.*). It is then, following the vision and the voice he had heard that Peter is perplexed as to what it means.[176] As much is implied by the alternative reading of this verse, but less is made of the transition between Peter's two states of mind. Luke portrays Peter now reflecting by himself, but before long the Holy Spirit will intervene to give him further instructions (cf. 10.19 below).

[b] 10.17b-18 *The Arrival of Cornelius' Men*
10.17b-18 Peter's return to consciousness and his puzzlement over the vision coincides perfectly with the arrival in Joppa of the men whom Cornelius had sent (cf. 10.7-8). They had faithfully followed the angel's directions to Cornelius, having sought out the house of Simon the Tanner. This is the third and final time that this other Simon will be mentioned, drawing attention on each occasion to Peter's association with a Jew who was on the margins of society. It is noteworthy that Peter himself will omit this detail when relating the incident later to the brethren in Jerusalem (cf. 11.4-17). Simon the Tanner does not actually figure in the story other than as the owner of the house where Peter is lodged, confirming his figurative function.

The men have just arrived at the door of the house and are asking for Peter at the time that he is seeking the meaning of his vision. Their question again picks up the terms of the angel's instructions, and repeats the insistence on Peter's character as one who is hard-headed. Although they themselves may

176. The verb διαπορέω expresses strong puzzlement or questioning (cf. 2.12 D05 [AT reads mid.]; 5.24; Lk. 9.7 [ἀπορέω D05]).

be unaware of the significance of the name 'Peter' (see *Commentary*, 10.5), Luke's audience will understand the reference to his temperament that is the dominant theme of the whole of this episode.

[c] 10.19-20 *The Spirit's Instructions to Peter*

10.19-20 It is not, in fact, the owner of the house who calls Peter down to meet the men, but the Spirit who sends him. Although the Spirit is mentioned by name now for the first time in the episode, there are signs in the Bezan text that Luke has understood the presence or activity of the Spirit in the mani-festatations of the divine throughout the previous scene. First, the description of the trance as 'falling' on Peter uses the verb (ἐπιπίπτω) that is found else-where in Acts (though often with variants) in connection with the Spirit falling on people (cf. 10.10, *Critical Apparatus*). Secondly, the detail 'to him' (omit-ted by the AT) is expressed in two ways in Luke's writing, according to whether or not a relationship has already been established in the present scene between speaker and hearer (see *Critical Apparatus* for details); the form used here in Codex Bezae is rather the one that indicates that the Spirit has already been engaged in dialogue with Peter in this scene. The way in which the Spirit is introduced, simply as 'the Spirit' without the adjective 'holy', is typical of the form of the name that Luke uses when the Spirit speaks to guide dis-ciples.[177]

The extent to which the diverse aspects of the divine are assimilated in Luke's thought is seen in this passage through the words spoken by the Spirit to Peter while he is deep in reflection about the meaning of the vision. As the Spirit gives him further directions which will lead him on to the next step towards understanding its significance, reassurance is given that 'I have sent' the men who are looking for him: this may be compared with 10.3-7 where it was 'an angel of God' who appeared and spoke to Cornelius. Cornelius thus is seen again as totally in line with the plan of God – it is not he who needs con-verting but Peter, which is the purpose behind these scenes.

That Peter should need encouragement not to waver[178] but to go with the men even though they are Gentiles is indicative of his wariness to put into action the instructions Jesus gave the apostles when he told them that 'repen-tance and forgiveness of sins are to be preached, even to all nations' (Lk.

---

177. This observation is based on an exhaustive analysis of the terms used in Luke-Acts to refer to the Holy Spirit; see Read-Heimerdinger, *The Bezan Text*, pp. 145–72; esp. 158–60.

178. The verb διακρίνομαι in the middle can mean to 'doubt' or 'hesitate', though it can also have the sense of to 'dispute' from the active sense of 'discriminate' (as Peter uses it in his report of this incident according to the AT, 11.12 [μηδὲν διακρίναντα, *om.* D05]; and again at the Jeru-salem Council, 15.9 [οὐδὲν διέκρινεν]). The cognate noun διάκρισις is used at 4.32 D05 to describe the unity among the believers in Jerusalem who did not make any distinction among themselves. The idea here is that Peter should not refuse to go with them on the grounds that they are Gentiles – that is, he should allow no hesitation or objections arising from the Jewish regulations forbidding social contact with Gentiles to get in the way.

24.47) – or what he has known to be true since his speech at Pentecost when he proclaimed the universal nature of the salvation of Jesus.[179] This will be the first time that Peter himself is seen engaging directly with Gentiles, despite the awareness that he has earlier displayed of their inclusion in the kingdom.

[c'] 10.21 *Peter Complies*

10.21 Peter responds promptly to the Spirit's directions and 'goes down' from the roof/upper room. The verb chosen, καταβαίνω, has already been noted for its significance of abandoning the traditional Jewish mentality (see *Commentary,* 8.26). Hence, Peter's movement is not only a physical one but the beginning of an inner transformation as he starts his journey away from the hostile Jewish attitude towards non-Jews. He then identifies himself as the one they are looking for. His willingness to let himself be known contrasts directly with his denial of who he was when someone identified him as one of Jesus' followers after Jesus' arrest: 'Man, I am not' (ἄνθρωπε, οὐκ εἰμί, Lk. 22.58).

Peter is unaware of why the men have come to look for him, nor where he is to go with them – he must realize that there is some connection with his vision and wonder what it can be. If the soldier is in uniform (cf. 10.7) or carries any other sign of his military profession, he must have been even more intrigued. His question to the men, reiterated in Codex Bezae, is a genuine and open request for information to which they will readily respond.

[b'] 10.22 *The Men Explain their Purpose*

10.22 Codex Bezae spells out that the men's reply is directed to Peter, πρὸς αὐτόν. The detail is unnecessary but establishes, through the choice of phrasing, a relationship between the men and Peter. It is typical of Codex Bezae to be interested in relationships between characters, conferring on the narrative a tone that is more intimate and personal than in the AT (see *Critical Apparatus*).

They give Peter all the information that Luke has already supplied in his introduction to Cornelius (cf. 10.1-2), the repetition serving to underline his qualities:

1. He is, according to Codex Bezae, a representative of a class of people ('a certain', τις).
2. He is a centurion – an officer of the Roman army of occupation.
3. He is a just man (or 'righteous', δίκαιος) – a term of high approbation among Jews.
4. He fears God – another strong mark of approval.
5. The whole of the Jewish nation acknowledges his worth (cf. the centurion of Capernaum, Lk. 7.5; the same word μαρτυρούμενος, 'of good reputation, well-spoken of', is used of the Hellenist disciples in Acts 6.3).

---

179. See *The Message of Acts* I, pp. 143–47, 178–84.

6.   He has been directed by a holy angel – from whom Peter has just heard in the guise of the Holy Spirit (cf. 10.19-20).
7.   They have been sent to summon him to Cornelius' house – so making clear where Peter is to 'go with them' (cf. 10.20).
8.   Peter is to speak to Cornelius – what he is to talk about will not be made clear until Cornelius explains his side of the story (cf. 10.33).

The painstaking repetition of detail that Luke's audience have to hear for the second time has the purpose of showing how Peter was made aware, bit by bit, of what God was doing and how great a leap he had to make. Even as a believer in Jesus, even as one who had been in the privileged inner circle, hearing and observing Jesus from the beginning and throughout the time of his ministry, it was no easy matter for him and his fellow believers to change their ways of thinking and become open to the Gentiles. This is the conversion that Peter will need to make and persuade, in his turn, the other believers to make, too.

[a'] 10.23a *Peter Gives Them Lodging*
10.23a The deliberateness of Peter's gesture in taking the men into the house and giving them lodging for the night (which would, of course, involve eating with them) is brought out more clearly in the wording of Codex Bezae. That he was able to do this at the house of Simon the Tanner is a sign of the freedom exercised by his host and the absence of discrimination within the community that he represented (see *Commentary*, 9.43). The verb 'give lodging' is the same (ξενίζω) used of Peter staying with Simon on two occasions (10.6, the angel of God to Cornelius; 10.18, Cornelius' men at the door of the house), and will be repeated once more when Cornelius himself relates his experience to Peter (10.32). The cognate noun, ξένος, means 'stranger, alien'.[180] The terms are the equivalent of the Hebrew 'sojourn, dwell as a guest' (גּוּר) and 'sojourner, stranger' (גֵּר), although the verb ξενίζω is not used in the LXX and ξένος is only used in other contexts.[181] The Hebrew words are used frequently throughout the Torah to refer either to Israel dwelling temporarily in foreign lands or, more usually, to non-Jews living peaceably among the people of Israel.[182] The equivalence between the terms found in the Hebrew Scriptures and those used in Greek by Luke suggests that he is

---

180. B-A-G, ξένος, 2.
181. The LXX frequently translates the noun גֵּר as προσήλυτος, but the original sense of the Hebrew does not imply that the stranger had necessarily adopted the religion of the Jews, even though rabbinic tradition also understood it in this way (*Jewish Study Bible*, p. 246 on Lev. 16.29).
182. B-D-B, גּוּר, I, pp. 157–58, where the sense of 'give hospitality' or 'be a guest' is noted. See also *Jewish Study Bible*, on Lev. 16.29, pp. 246–47: 'The "ger" is not required to worship Israel's God but may do so voluntarily; thus the "ger" is not obligated to observe the performative commands, but must comply with all the prohibitions, and must observe the laws of fairness and justice (see 24.17-22)' [246].

deliberately calling to mind the ancient laws regarding the share in the privileges (e.g. Deut. 5.14; 16.11, 14) and rights (e.g. Deut. 1.16) that the non-Jews were to enjoy alongside the Jews when they lived in one another's countries. This is summed up most clearly in Lev. 19.33-34: 'When a stranger resides with you in your land, you shall not wrong him. The stranger who resides with you shall be to you as one of your citizens; you shall love him as yourself, for you were strangers in the land of Egypt.' This is a commandment that had been flouted by the rigid hostility that had grown up between Jews and Gentiles but that God is recalling loud and clear.

[BA′-BA′] 10.23b–11.1 *Peter Meets Cornelius in Caesarea*

The moment of drama is finally reached as Peter arrives in Caesarea and finds himself in a totally unexpected and unfamiliar situation, in which he discovers that God wants him to explain the message of Jesus to the gathering Cornelius has assembled in his house. As for Cornelius, he has been seen to be perfectly open to obey the instructions God gives him (cf. 10.1-8) and to be in tune with the Spirit (cf. 10.19). Before Peter will even have a chance to explain to him about repentance and believing in Jesus, the Holy Spirit will fall on the gathering, confirming their acceptance by God. It is Peter who is taken by surprise and who will need to change his way of thinking in order to bring it into line with the plan of God. That this is achieved is shown by the subsequent account he gives to the brethren in Jerusalem (11.4-17), although his complete break with old ways of thinking will not be achieved until he is delivered from prison by the angel of the Lord in 12.11.

The structure of the passage in Codex Bezae is somewhat different from that of the AT because of the absence in the latter of a complete sentence at 10.25 and significant rewording of 11.1-2. According to the wording of the AT, the scene could be considered to end at 10.48b with a change of location and characters at 11.1. In Codex Bezae, however, the first verse of chapter 11 belongs to this episode rather than the next one with the mention of the brethren in Judaea being made impersonally, and the focus of attention still in Caesarea and the spotlight on Peter who is not seen in Judaea until the end of 11.2 (see *Critical Apparatus*, 11.1).

[a] 10.23b *Peter's Departure from Joppa*
10.23b The new scene opens with a change of time, the 'next day', as often happens at the start of a new unit. It is at this point that Peter obeys the directive of the Spirit to 'get up' and 'go with them' (cf. 10.20). So far, it has been noted only that he obeyed the Spirit's central instruction, 'go down' (cf. 10.21), although it is obvious from a literal point of view that he had to 'get up' from where he was praying in order to go downstairs to meet Cornelius' men. However, in the coded style of writing Luke adopts, divine instructions usually have a deeper application at the level of inner thoughts and attitudes

and he carefully notes, by means of repeated terms, when such directives are fulfilled. It is only after spending time with the men that Peter is finally able to rise from his state of profound perplexity and to 'go out' (ἐξῆλθεν) with the Gentiles to Caesarea. At this point, the verb chosen by Luke again expresses a precise symbolic action that this time goes further than the instruction of the Spirit, πορεύου, 'go', for he uses ἐξέρχομαι to describe an 'exodus' in the sense of a release from enslavement or a state of being held prisoner (cf. Acts 7.3 [Gen. 12.1], 4, 7 [Gen. 15.14]; 12.9, 10, 17; 16.39-40; 22.18). In such instances, the sea is a symbol that marks the open way ahead, echoing the Red Sea which represented the way of escape for the Israelites when they fled Egypt. Peter's personal exodus from the restrictive and oppressive system of discrimination against the Gentiles has been anticipated by his stay in the house of a person considered impure, Simon the Tanner, whose house was by the sea.[183] Now that he leaves Joppa to accompany the Gentile messengers, his exodus is under way although it will not be completed until his release from prison in chapter 12 (see *Commentary*, 12.17).

In the parallel scene in the Gospel (Lk. 7.2-10, see *Commentary* on 10.1 above), it is also said that Jesus 'went (ἐπορεύετο) with them' (Lk. 7.6), that is, the Jewish elders whom the centurion had sent to Jesus on his behalf (7.3) but using the verb that does not have the symbolic sense of exodus.

Peter is accompanied by a group of brethren from Joppa: Luke will later draw attention to the fact that, for all that they were faithful believers (πιστοί), these men (of whom there were six, as Peter will later report in Jerusalem [11.12]) continued to uphold the practice of circumcision, in other words they were all Jewish. It seems it was they themselves who decided to go with Peter to Caesarea and not Peter who took them with him.

[b] 10.24a *Peter's Arrival in Caesarea*
10.24a Peter arrived in Caesarea the day after he left Joppa – the verb is in the singular, as it is for Peter's departure (cf. 10.23b), maintaining Peter as the centre of attention even though he is accompanied by a group of people. The point of noting the chronology is not so much to establish the historicity of the account as to allow a pattern of times, based on the sixth and the ninth hours, to be set up (see *Commentary*, 10.9), for when Cornelius talks with Peter and when the Holy Spirit will be given it will be 'the ninth hour', the same time as when Cornelius had the vision two days earlier (cf. 10.3). As for Peter's vision, it had happened on the day in between, at the sixth hour (cf. 10.30).

---

183. Cf. 10.6: ᾧ [Σίμωνί] ἐστιν οἰκία παρὰ θάλασσαν and 10.32: ἐν οἰκίᾳ Σίμωνος βυρσέως παρὰ θάλασσαν, information given to Cornelius by the angel, which is an indication of its importance.

[c] 10.24b *Cornelius' Expectancy*

10.24b Attention now turns to Cornelius who had gathered his friends and family and was waiting for Peter in Caesarea even before he entered the city (cf. 10.25). The AT uses the verb of waiting (προσδοκάω) that is found elsewhere referring to Jewish messianic expectation, which may be a deliberate choice to show how in this case a Gentile shared in the Jewish hope and how he had understood that Peter would in some way fulfil it. Codex Bezae uses two other verbs to express Cornelius' expectancy, each with its own associations. The first, προσδέχομαι, is used by Luke to mean waiting in order to welcome someone but, in particular, is used with reference to Simeon who was waiting for the consolation of Israel (Lk. 2.25): it can hardly be a coincidence that the two adjectives used to describe Simeon, righteous (δίκαιος) and pious (εὐσηβής), are also terms applied to Cornelius, though in the reverse order (10.1, 22).

The second verb, περιμένω, is only found on one other occasion in the New Testament, at Acts 1.4 in the reported words of Jesus as he instructed the apostles 'to wait for the promise of the Father' in Hierosoluma. The drama, of course, was that the apostles neither went to Hierosoluma nor did they 'wait' for the Father's promise but instead went back to Ierousalem (cf. 1.12) where they took the decision to get on with electing a replacement for Judas.[184] So what the apostles failed to do, Cornelius did, without knowing that the outcome will be the gift of the Holy Spirit as promised through the words of Jesus.

Cornelius is not, in fact, alone but has with him a group of people who it may be presumed shared his expectation – he is not an isolated case but represents a whole community which has been assembled to listen to the man whom they had been instructed to fetch by an angel of God. Unlike the centurion in the Gospel who sent his friends (φίλους) to tell Jesus not to come to his house because he was not worthy, Cornelius and his friends (φίλους) and family were only too happy to receive Peter. Luke draws a contrasting parallel to show that during the ministry of Jesus the time had not yet come for Gentiles to become part of the people of God but now, through the ministry of the apostles, the time has finally arrived.[185]

[d] 10.25a *The Servant's Announcement*

10.25a For a second time, the AT uses the verb 'enter' of Peter to refer to his entry of Caesarea, thus underlining the drama of his arrival (a third occurrence will arise in the following verse referring to his entry into Cornelius' house). Between the first two occurrences, Luke has given a glimpse of the prepara-

---

184. See *The Message of Acts*, I, pp. 68–69; 107–39.

185. In the Bezan text of Luke's Gospel, the words pronounced by Simeon with reference to the child Jesus (Lk. 2.32) omit any mention of the Gentiles but restrict the benefits of the Messiah to Israel (cf. Isa. 42.6; 49.6).

tions Cornelius had made in anticipation of Peter's arrival. The point is that he is presenting a scene in which a Jew 'enters' into the domain of a Gentile and is highlighting it as a gesture of the highest significance and solemnity.

Codex Bezae places the emphasis elsewhere, on the eagerness of Cornelius to meet Peter (cf. the repetition of his name in 10.25b). He was informed of Peter's approach to the city (before he actually entered) by 'one of the slaves' who obviously was aware how pleased Cornelius' would be to hear the news. This slave may have been posted as a lookout by Cornelius, but it is equally possible that he was one of the servants who had been sent to fetch Peter and who ran ahead to tell his master when Peter was about to arrive. There are echoes in this detail of the parallel scene in the Gospel, at the moment that Jesus was approaching the centurion's house (ἤδη δὲ αὐτοῦ οὐ μακρὰν ἀπέχοντος, Lk. 7.6), with the difference that on that occasion the centurion sent friends to tell Jesus not to come any further.[186] As was already pointed out with reference to the previous verse, the situation of Cornelius displays a marked progression compared with the situation of Gentiles in the Gospel.

[e] 10.25b *Cornelius' Welcome*

10.25b The Bezan text continues to focus on Cornelius' eager anticipation of Peter's arrival with the repetition of his name and the detail that he leapt up to go to welcome him: the sense of expectancy and hope on the part of Gentiles is yet again intensified (cf. 10.24 above). His prostration before Peter is perhaps an expression of the religious inferiority pious Gentiles felt towards Jews (as did the centurion of Capernaum with the respect to Jesus, Lk. 7.6, 7). At the same time, however, this detail adds to the picture of Cornelius performing the actions of the Jewish afternoon prayer, which had already been intimated at 10.3 (see *Commentary*).

[f] 10.26 *Peter's Rebuke*

10.26 Peter's indignation at Cornelius' gesture is more strongly conveyed in the Bezan text – he not only tells him to get up, insisting that he is a man (and therefore not to be worshipped), but expresses some alarm at what he is doing and underlines the fact that he is not different from Cornelius (cf. Herod who accepted being hailed as a god, 12.22; Paul and Barnabas who refused, 14.15). A declaration that parallels and yet contrasts with Peter's is found in the story of the centurion of Capernaum: there, is it the centurion who insists to Jesus that 'I also am a man under authority', καὶ γὰρ ἐγὼ ἄνθρωπός εἰμι ὑπ' ἐξου- σίαν τασσόμενος (Lk. 7.8), that is, not like Jesus but like those who obey his orders.

---

186. A further echo, this time one that concords with the Acts story, is found in the story of the prodigal son at the point that the father runs out to meet his son: ἔτι δὲ αὐτοῦ μακρὰν ἀπέχοντος ... δραμών ..., Lk. 15.20.

[g] 10.27-29 *Peter's Entry into the House of a Gentile*

10.27 The dramatic moment has arrived when Peter will actually go into Cornelius' house, underlined by the construction of the Greek in Codex Bezae (see *Critical Apparatus*). For the first time in Acts, there will be social contact between the apostles and the Gentiles, taking the teaching of Jesus about the universal nature of his kingdom further even than he did in his lifetime when, according to the Gospel of Luke, he did not actually enter the house of a Gentile (see *Commentary*, 10.24 above). Once inside, Peter discovers that this is far from a private moment between himself and Cornelius for he finds a large crowd of people assembled – his surprise is indicated with the present tense in the AT and by the underlining of the verb 'found' in the Bezan text.

10.28 Peter immediately points out his precarious position by drawing attention to the prohibition that forbade Jews to have any dealings with 'foreigners', a rule only too familiar to the Gentiles who were discriminated against in this way. It is important to understand just what Peter is claiming here. He specifically does not say that his entering into Cornelius' house was contrary to the Law (νόμος) and indeed there is nothing in the Torah that forbids Jews to have social contact with foreigners – on the contrary, foreigners who had settled in Israel and who wished to observe Jewish customs and festivals were to be treated with kindness and respect (see *Commentary*, 10.23a). The word Peter uses is ἀθέμιτος,[187] 'wrong', in the sense that it is contrary to the divine ordering of things and not specifically the Torah, though there is no doubt that within Jewish discussion it was also a term that was applied to the Law[188] and Peter may well have hitherto accepted that the avoidance of contact with Gentiles was integral to the Torah.

Peter then goes on to explain why he has accepted to come into Cornelius' house and talk with him and his assembled guests: God has shown him that no person is to be regarded as common or unclean. In the word order of the Greek is reflected the idea that Peter has received a special revelation: '(lit.) to me God showed…'. Interestingly, because Peter is talking with a Gentile he uses the word θεός, 'God', not κύριος, 'Lord', even though in his vision he addresses the speaker as 'Lord' (see *Commentary*, 10.14 above). This is in keeping with the usage throughout Codex Bezae, where all references to God that are made by non-Jews or in addressing them before they know Jesus avoid the term 'Lord'.[189] It will not be used to refer to the divine from the point of view of Cornelius until his baptism at the end of this scene, and then only in the Bezan text (10.48 D05; cf. 10.33 D05).

---

187. D05 uses the older spelling ἀθέμιστος (B-A-G). The sense of 'lawless, unlawful' is a general one.

188. S.G. Wilson, 'Law and Judaism in Acts' (*SBL Seminar Papers*, 1976, pp. 251–65), 257–58.

189. Read-Heimerdinger, *The Bezan Text*, pp. 278–93.

Peter had previously distinguished between clean and unclean, common and holy, because he believed that was the correct Jewish way. That is why he had refused to obey the order he heard when he saw the sheet full of all kinds of animals (cf. 10.9-16). What he now understands and accepts as God's view is that all people are equal in his sight and that it is permissible for him to enter into the house of a Gentile. It is not, however, that God has changed his mind or that the Law has been abrogated, but rather an interpretation of the Law that has been corrected so as to bring the behaviour of the believers into line with God's way of thinking, so to speak.

10.29 Thus, Peter appeals to his vision as the justification for accepting to come to Cornelius' house without further ado, as the Spirit instructed him (cf. 10.20). His words make it clear that the invitation has come from Cornelius – he has not gone to Caesarea on his own initiative or because he received a divine order to do so, but because Cornelius sent for him (in obedience to a divine order to Cornelius, as he will soon discover). Peter will make much of this factor when reporting the events to the brethren in Jerusalem, in order to underline the fact that he did not deliberately seek to associate with a Gentile. Nor, from Cornelius' point of view, did Peter force himself on his household to present the gospel but spoke at his invitation.

Accordingly, Peter asks why he has been sent for, reiterating the question (or questions in D05) he put to Cornelius' men when they came to fetch Peter from Simon's house (10.21). Luke thus prepares his own hearers to pay attention to Cornelius' speech that is about to follow.

[h] 10.30-33 *Cornelius' Explanation*

10.30 Cornelius' vision while he was praying is placed at the very centre of the episode for it is on God's action and his view of Cornelius that the whole incident turns. It is related for the third time, on this occasion by Cornelius himself (cf. 10.4-6, told by the narrator; 10.22, by Cornelius' envoys). The sequence of events differs according to the MSS.[190] According to the AT, he refers to a time four days ago (counting inclusively, as was normal) when he was praying in his house during the ninth hour, the same hour now as he speaks with Peter, and a man appeared. In Codex Bezae he presents things

---

190. The time schedule expressed by Cornelius in Codex Bezae, where he mentions 3 days of fasting before his vision, can be represented in the following schema. The 4 days mentioned by the AT are counted backwards from the day of the meeting with Peter (in brackets):

Day 3	Day 2	Day 1 (Day 4)	(Day 3)	(Day 2)	(Day 1)
Cornelius was fasting	Fasting	Cornelius was fasting until the ninth hour His vision	Cornelius sends men to Joppa Peter's vision, sixth hour	Peter sets off for Caesarea	Cornelius explains to Peter, ninth hour

somewhat differently: he had been fasting for three days up to the time it is now as he speaks with Peter, and then, as he was praying during the ninth hour, a man appeared. The form of the Greek expression 'the ninth', τὴν ἐνάτην, refers to not so much to the time of day as the time of Jewish prayer when the afternoon sacrifice was offered in the Temple,[191] suggesting that Cornelius was performing a ritual act of Jewish prayer (cf. *Commentary*, 10.3 above). It is because the AT does not mention the fasting that the number of days comes to refer to the time between his vision and Peter's arrival instead of the days preceding his vision, which amounts to four instead of three days.

The mention of Cornelius fasting for three days is full of significance on various levels. On the one hand, it echoes the discussion between Jesus and the Pharisees about the lifestyle of his disciples (Lk. 7.33-35), when he assimilates the days of fasting[192] with the time when he will have gone away, when the 'bridegroom' is no longer with the wedding guests. John the Baptist, in particular, was characterized by his fasting and praying (7.24-35), as he awaited and prepared for the coming of the Messiah. Here, it is Cornelius who is fasting, before praying in accordance with Jewish practice: his actions can thus be seen as reflecting an awareness of the absence of the Messiah, for whom he is preparing and waiting (see *Commentary*, 10.24b).

In summary, the various details included in Cornelius introduction compress a great deal of information, explicit and implicit:

1. *Three days* corresponds to the length of time between the crucifixion and resurrection of Jesus, to which Luke often draws attention (Lk. 9.22; 18.33; 24.7, 21; Acts 10.40).
2. *Fasting* is a sign of mourning and also of preparation for the Messiah.
3. *The present hour*, which was 'the ninth', was the time of Jesus death and the time at which his death will become effective for the Gentiles as they hear the good news and receive the Holy Spirit.
4. *The ninth hour* was the time of the Jewish afternoon sacrifice and prayer which coincided not only with Jesus' death (see above) but also with the healing of the lame man symbolizing the release of Israel from the crippling effects of the Law (Acts 3.1); the vision of Cornelius (10.3); the entry of Peter into Cornelius' house (10.27, 30).
5. *Praying* during the ninth hour is an act of ritual prayer.
6. *In his house* insists in a somewhat surprising way that Cornelius had been performing the ritual prayer not in the Temple but in his house. This indication tallies with the declaration he is about to make concerning the presence of God in his house (10.33), though only in its form in the AT.[193]

---

191. The hour is given in the accusative, τὴν ἐνάτην, which is not normally used to express 'time at which'; but because the ninth hour corresponds to the time of the afternoon Tamid service (cf. 10.3) the accusative can be construed as expressing the duration of the ninth hour of prayer.

192. τότε νηστεύσουσιν ἐν ἐκείναις ταῖς ἡμέραις; it should be noted that Luke modifies the phrase found in Mark (2.20): καὶ τότε νηστεύσουσιν ἐν ἐκείνῃ τῇ ἡμέρᾳ.

193. Hamm, 'Tamid Service', pp. 222–23.

The man who appeared to Cornelius was originally described by the narrator as 'an angel of God' (10.3) and by the men Cornelius sent to Peter as 'a holy angel' (10.22). The description Cornelius gives himself to Peter, 'a man in shining garment', finally makes it clear that this was none other than Jesus himself even though Cornelius did not recognize him as such – on one other occasion only in the New Testament is the adjective λαμπρός, 'bright', used, again by Luke and again referring to clothing: when he describes how Herod clothed Jesus 'in bright clothing' in order to mock him (Lk. 23.11).[194] Here, by taking up the identical phrase, Luke underlines once more the connection between Jesus' death and the entry of the Gentiles into the people of God.

10.31 Cornelius repeats the words he heard, which make clear the basis on which he had been granted the vision and led to send for Peter. This is the third mention of his prayers and acts of charity (cf. 10.2, 4), and the second time it is said that God has paid attention to them (cf. 10.4).

10.32 The instructions Cornelius received (10.5-6) are repeated once more, as they have already been repeated before. The repeated elements are:

1. To send for Peter in Joppa: cf. 10.22, in the explanation given to Peter in Joppa by the men sent by Cornelius; 10.29, especially D05, for the idea that it was in response to Cornelius' request that Peter went to Caesarea, and again 10.33 D05.
2. Peter's name in addition to his name of Simon, as a reminder of his hard-headedness (cf. Lk. 6.14; Mt. 16.18): cf. 10.18, called out by the men looking for him in Joppa.
3. His lodging with another person named Simon: cf. 9.43, at the end of the previous episode; 10.17b, in indirect speech when Cornelius' men were looking for him.
4. A tanner: cf. 9.43, at the end of the previous episode; with a house beside the sea: 10.6.
5. A message Peter has to give to Cornelius: cf. 10.22, Cornelius' men to Peter in Joppa. This not only creates a dramatic tension in preparation for Peter's speech but it also contributes to firmly establishing Peter's decisive role in setting the scene for the manifestation of the gift of God among the Roman army of occupation, a particular kind of Gentile who had hitherto been regarded as enemies of the Jewish people.

In Peter's own account to the brethren in Jerusalem, all of this information will be repeated once more, except the detail that he had been staying with Simon the Tanner in his house by the sea (cf. 11.5-14). The reason for this omission will be examined in due course (see *Commentary*, 11.11).

194. Shining or bright clothing is a characteristic of the divine sphere: cf. δύο ἄνδρες (δύο ἄνδρες B03) … ἐν ἐσθῆτι ἀστραπτούσῃ, Lk. 24.4 (the two men who speak to the women at the tomb); ἄνδρες δύο … ἐν ἐσθῆτι λευκῇ (pl. B03), Acts 1.10 (the two men who speak to the apostles on the Mt of Olives). The noun from which λαμπρός in Lk. 23.11 and Acts 10.31 is derived is always used of celestial or divine light in the LXX (cf. Pss. 89.17; 109.3; Isa. 60.3) and in Theodotion (cf. Dan. 12.3).

10.33 In the conclusion to Cornelius' explanation he spells out his prompt response to the divine instructions and his eagerness to listen to Peter. He begins by stating that he acted by sending for Peter without delay, (lit.) 'at the very same hour', ἐξαυτῆς, underlining yet again the significance of the ninth hour. The text thereon varies on a number of points. According to Codex Bezae, Cornelius insists on the fact that he begged Peter to come to them, a detail that the AT does not note. Apart from repeating the insistence that the initiative for Peter's visit came from Cornelius and not Peter (cf. 10.32), his comment adds another echo of the centurion's story in the Gospel, for he also sent men to ask Jesus to come (cf. Lk. 7.3, 4).[195] He then acknowledges Peter's compliance with his request, noting in the Bezan text his speediness to respond. Finally, he invites Peter to address the gathering. In the AT, Cornelius sets the scene by invoking the presence of God (see *Commentary*, 10.30 above) with all who have come to hear everything the Lord has commanded Peter to say. In the Bezan text, there is a greater emphasis on the role of Peter in the gathering: they are assembled in *his* presence, and are *wanting* to hear *from him* what *God* has commanded him to say. The avoidance of the term 'Lord' in the mouth of a Gentile in the Bezan text is typical (see *Critical Apparatus*), this being a designation of God that is reserved either for Yahweh when referred to by Jews or for Jesus when referred to by believers.

[g′] 10.34-43 *Peter's Speech*

Peter's speech to the gathering in Cornelius' house is interrupted brusquely by the unexpected arrival of the Holy Spirit while he was still speaking (10.44), with the result that it does not have the usual parenesis but stops short some way into the exposition.

The development of Peter's thought is far from clear as he moves from one idea to the next without finishing his sentences and bringing in new points as they occur to him. It would seem that Luke has written the speech in this way so as to represent Peter's unpreparedness to explain the gospel to a gathering of Gentiles and the tumbling out of his thoughts in consequence. Nevertheless, a certain thread can be identified that holds the successive points together. The connections are a little different in the AT from the Bezan text whose structure is given here:

α	10.34b-35	Introduction
β	10.36-38a	God's message to Israel
γ	10.38b	Presentation of Jesus' ministry
	10.39a	Corresponding witnesses
δ	10.39b-40a	Jesus' death and resurrection
	10.40b-41	Corresponding witnesses

---

195. παρακαλῶν ἐλθεῖν (+ σε D^C) πρὸς ἡμᾶς: cf. Lk. 7.3, ἐρωτῶν αὐτὸν ὅπως ἐλθών; 7.4, ἠρώτων (D05; παρεκάλουν B03) αὐτόν. In the Bezan text of Luke, the centurion does not ask Jesus to come with the same degree of confidence as does Cornelius when he sends for Peter.

ε   10.42   Jesus as judge
         10.43   Corresponding witnesses

10.34a Luke's presentation of Peter's speech, pronounced in response to Cornelius' account of what had caused him to send for him, is couched in solemn language which is found elsewhere to introduce a speech of proclamation.[196] There is no doubt that the occasion for the speech that is about to follow is a momentous one, the first declaration of the Gospel to a soldier of the army of occupation, together with his household. In view of this, it may have been expected that Peter's speech would be a paradigm for the presentation of the gospel message to Gentiles. And yet it will not be so for, as will be seen, Peter presents Israel as the primary beneficiaries of God's action in sending Jesus and angles the message of Jesus in such a way as to privilege the Jews. It is not for nothing that his speech is cut short as the Holy Spirit falls on his listeners.

It must be concluded that Luke does not portray Peter as speaking under the inspiration of the Holy Spirit but guided by his own understanding and response to the situation in which he finds himself. Although he has begun to grasp something of the meaning of his vision in Joppa, which has given him the confidence to enter a Gentile's house and allowed him to take the step of addressing the assembled crowd of people, at the same time he still retains the idea that Jesus was first and foremost the Messiah of the Jews. As usual, Luke constructs the speech so as to reflect the mentality of the speaker at the time (see *General Introduction,* § VI). That he should be in any doubt as to its inspired natured is shown by the fact that no mention is made of the Holy Spirit being with Peter as he sets out to speak (cf. 2.4; 4.8, 31; 13.9; 15.7 D05). The underlying contrast is greatest with Stephen who was singled out as being full of the Holy Spirit (6.8, 10; 7.55) and whose speech is therefore to be understood as in line with the plan of God (see *Commentary,* 7.2). Barnabas is another character who is presented positively by virtue of his being full of the Holy Spirit (11.24), although he does not contribute a speech to the story of Acts.

[α] 10.34b-35 *Introduction*
10.34b-35 As Peter begins to respond, he takes stock of the situation in which he finds himself. He proclaims a summary of what he perceives to be the mind of God – this is expressed in the Bezan text as a realization that is dawning on

---

196. ἀνοίξας ... τὸ στόμα: similar formulae are found at 8.32 (in the negative, of Jesus); 8.35 (of Philip); 18.14 (of Paul). Cf. Mt. 5.2; 17.27 (literal sense); 2 Cor. 6.11; Rev. 13.6. The expression 'he opened his mouth' occurs in the LXX (× 41). The absence of article with the name of Peter is typical of the AT as a means to draw attention to Peter or Paul as the speaker of a key speech (cf. 11.4; 17.22; 19.4; see Heimerdinger-Levinsohn, 'The Use of the Article', p. 28); the device is used only here in the Bezan text and for the parallel speech at 11.4; it is not used for the speeches of Paul.

Peter as the scene unfolds,[197] which corresponds to the fact that although Peter already knew in theory the universal scope of the gospel message he had so far not properly, 'truly',[198] come to terms with its implications. It is the recent events – the vision in Joppa and the urgent call to Caesarea – that have caused a major shift in his thinking and understanding. The qualities he now recognizes as being the sole conditions for a person to be accepted by God are fearing God and practising righteousness, precisely as he has heard from Cornelius' account (10.22; cf. 10.2). In other words, he acknowledges that the privilege of being Jewish counts for nothing. Specifically, Peter declares that God is not a 'respecter of persons',[199] to which the adjective 'acceptable'[200] corresponds as a positive expression of the same idea.

Peter does not present this as a new situation, as representing a change from an earlier order, in accordance with the fact that it was never intended that Jews should be considered (or consider themselves) as intrinsically better than Gentiles. Indeed, the view that the people of Israel were more deserving of God's love and favour was a distortion of the message given to Israel as recorded in the Jewish Scriptures. It is not God who has now changed his mind but rather Peter who, despite having been a close companion of Jesus during the time of his ministry and despite the last orders of his master ('repentance and forgiveness of sins should be preached to all nations', Lk. 24.47), has only now understood the truth of the matter. Yet the message was already clearly taught in the Gospel. It was urged on Jesus by the Jewish elders when they asked Jesus to help the centurion of Capernaum by healing his slave: 'He is worthy that you do this for him, for he loves our nation and it was he who built our synagogue' (Lk. 7.4-5), an entreaty that he responded to without question. Jesus himself insisted on the way of life necessary to inherit eternal life, which had nothing at all to do with being Jewish but everything to do with just social relationships: in the parable of the Good Samaritan spoken in response to the lawyer's question, 'Teacher, what must I do to inherit eternal life?' (10.25); and in his teaching on wealth in response to the identical question posed by a rich ruler (18.18).[201]

197. Whether καταλαμβανόμενος in D05 be read as a periphrastic present (with the elision of εἰμί) or as a subordinate participle, Peter's new understanding of God's attitude towards the Gentiles is an awareness that is growing as he speaks.

198. ἐπ' ἀληθείας: cf. Lk. 4.25; 20.21; 22.59; Acts 4.27; Mk 12.14, 32.

199. The term προσωπολήμπτης ('show favour') is a *hapax* in the New Testament but equivalent expressions occur: Lk. 20.21: οὐ λαμβάνεις πρόσωπον, of Jesus, cf. Mk 12.14; Mt. 22.16: οὐ γὰρ βλέπεις εἰς πρόσωπον ἀνθρώπων. Cf. Gal. 2.6; Jude 16. προσωπολημπτέω: Jas. 2.9; προσωπολημψία: Rom. 2.11; Eph. 6.9; Col. 3.25; Jas. 2.1.

200. δεκτός is a term used elsewhere by Luke (cf. Lk. 4.19, 24), and otherwise only at 2 Cor. 6.2 *vl* and Phil. 4.18.

201. The two Gospel passages, 10.25-37 and 18.18-30, constitute parallel components at the beginning and the end of a structural unit (see Rius-Camps, 'Lk 10,25–18,30: Una perfecta estructura concèntrica', pp. 311–12).

[β] 10.36-38a *God's Message to Israel*

10.36-38a The syntax of these verses is confused with a series of disjointed sentences, asides and unfinished ideas. The muddled language is unlikely to be a sign of Luke's ineptitude.[202] Rather it should be seen as part of the typical narrative skill he applies to his work, here deliberately writing a speech for Peter that reflects the rush of his thoughts – as he hurriedly tries to work out in his own mind the meaning of all that is happening while putting together at the same time an adequate explanation about Jesus for Cornelius. He has to take account of what his audience is bound to already know about this man from Nazareth and decide what needs to be added so that they understand how salvation is through him. There is, in point of fact, a thread running through the series of clauses and although it is tangled, the very tangle expresses Peter's state of mind. Is it more realistic that he would have had a well constructed, flowing speech ready to deliver at this point?

The main subject throughout the verses in question is God – the subject of the finite verb 'sent' at the beginning (v. 36) and of 'anointed' at the end (v. 38a); and also of the present participles 'announcing' (v. 36) and 'beginning' (v. 37). The 'message' in the opening clause may be the object of 'you yourselves know', or the familiarity of Cornelius with the Jesus story may only be suggested to Peter once he mentions his name. If the former, then it is justified to take the second reference to Jesus in v. 38a as a repetition of the notion that he was already a familiar figure. In either case, Peter does actually conclude this long, disjointed sentence with the idea he started with, namely Jesus as sent by God. He was sent, it should be noted, as the Messiah to the Jews according to Peter, who also sets his ministry in Judaea, recalling that things went on in Galilee especially,[203] with John the Baptist (Lk. 3.3) and Jesus' origin in Nazareth. Both the names of Galilee and Nazareth would, of course, be synonymous with rebellion and trouble for a Roman officer, contrasting with the peace that was Jesus' purpose. It may be the idea that Jesus was sent to the Jews that causes Peter to use the name of Judaea here though he seems to mean by it the whole of the Jewish territory and not just the southern province around Jerusalem (cf. 'the land of the Jews', 10.39a).[204] This is a limita-

---

202. The ungrammatical nature of 10.36-38 has been highlighted by a number of commentators and grammarians (see Barrett, I, p. 522–24 and his conclusion: 'It remains probable that we have a piece of careless and uncorrected writing').

203. ἀρξάμενος ἀπό could mean 'beginning in Galilee', but the explanation given by Delebecque (*Actes*, p. 53), that it singles out a noun from within a general group, is an attractive one: 'Luc emploie encore une expression très attique ἀρξάμενος ἀπό, dans laquelle la personne, ou la chose, dépendant de la préposition, est la première ou la plus importante par opposition à d'autres, ou à une totalité, ici ὅλης. De là l'emploie du nominatif absolu, et le sens "avant tout", "essentiellement", "principalement", "à commencer par".'

204. Judaea was the name originally given to the area corresponding to the southern kingdom of Israel and was distinct from Samaria (in which lay Caesarea) to the north, Galilee in the far north, Idumaea to the south-west and Peraea to the east of the Jordan, though all but Samaria were

tion that Peter puts on the scope of Jesus' ministry, for in the Gospel Luke presents him as teaching and healing in the region of Samaria (Lk. 9.51-56; 17.11), though not in Gentile districts.[205] Nevertheless, Peter's train of thought does also contain an awareness of the universal purpose of Jesus – he was to announce peace, and he is 'Lord of all'. The parenthesis supports Peter's declaration that God accepts righteous Gentiles (cf. 10.35). Here, for the first time in Luke's work, Jesus is identified for the benefit of a Gentile as κύριος, the 'Lord'. The juxtaposition of the notion of peace and the declaration of Jesus as Lord of all reflects Peter's main concern as he starts to talk with Cornelius, the abolition of the division between Jew and Gentile which Paul also expresses in terms of peace being announced in Jesus: 'He is our peace (εἰρήνη) ... he came and announced (εὐηγγελίσατο) peace to you who were far off and peace to those who were near ... you are no longer strangers (ξένοι) and sojourners...' (Eph. 2.14-19).

From Cornelius' point of view, the term κύριος, 'lord', was familiar as a designation of the Emperor. Peter may even be deliberately introducing the phrase 'Lord of all' to identify Jesus as the one who should rightly have this title rather than the emperor of the time, Nero, with whom it had otherwise been associated.[206]

The transition from the mention of John's baptism back to Jesus and the detail that God anointed him with 'the Holy Spirit and power' tallies with Luke's account of the baptism in the Gospel (Lk. 3.22), especially the form in the Bezan text where the words heard by Jesus vary from those recorded in other MSS: 'You are my beloved son, today I have begotten you (with you I am well pleased', AT).

Jewish territories. However, the precise definition of Judaea was constantly shifting after its conquest by Pompey in 64 BCE: according to the extent of the rule of the current king or governor, 'Judaea' could mean just the southern region or could include any or all of the territories between Galilee in the north and Idumaea in the south (Safrai and Stern, I, pp. 78–104, 308; Pritchard, *Atlas of the Bible*, pp. 151–52, 154–55).

Luke does use the term ἡ Ἰουδαία to refer to the land of Israel in general (cf. Lk. 1.5; 4.44 [not D05]; 6.17; 7.17; 21.21; Acts 2.9; 26.20; 28.21) rather than the region of Judaea in particular, but he also uses it in the narrow sense when Galilee is mentioned in the same context (Lk. 2.4 [εἰς γῆν Ἰούδα D05]; 3.1; 5.17; Acts 9.31) or Samaria (Acts 1.8; 8.1), and on other occasions, too (Lk. 1.65; Acts 11.1, 29; 12.1 D05, 19; 15.1; 21.10, 20 D05). At Lk. 23.5 where the chief priests accuse Jesus before Pilate, most MSS except D05 read a sentence similar to one at Acts 10.37: διδάσκων καθ᾽ ὅλης τῆς Ἰουδαίας καὶ ἀρξάμενος ἀπὸ τῆς Γαλιλαίας (D05 reads γῆς for Ἰουδαίας and omits καί).

205. Luke omits the sections in Mark's Gospel that portray Jesus ministering in Gentile territory (Mk 7.24–8.10).

206. Nero was referred to as ὁ τοῦ παντὸς κόσμου κύριος Νέρων; see C.K. Rowe, 'Luke-Acts and the Imperial Cult: A Way through the Conundrum?', *JSNT* 27 (2005), pp. 279–300 (292–93).

[γ] 10.38b-39a *Presentation of Jesus' Ministry*
10.38b The subject of Peter's speech changes at this point to Jesus, who is represented by the first word in the sentence in Greek (οὗτος D05; ὅς AT). However, just as God was the one whom Peter showed to be responsible for sending Jesus, so now he also presents his work as being possible because God was with him. This comment corresponds to the previous statement that Jesus was anointed by God with the Holy Spirit (cf. Lk. 4.18; Isa. 61.1-2). The salient points of Jesus' ministry that Peter selects are: a) he travelled around; b) he did good; and c) he healed those oppressed by the devil. The state of the people healed by Jesus is thus summarized in terms of oppression by the devil, and his work as liberation from that state. This view of Jesus' ministry tallies with the account of the confrontation between Jesus and the devil immediately after his baptism (Lk. 4.1-13), in which the devil figures as the opponent of the divine plan.

10.39a Peter supports his description of Jesus' ministry by presenting the witnesses, 'we' being probably the disciples who were eye-witnesses though it is not clear if a wider group than that described at 10.41 is intended. In the Bezan text, they are Jesus' witnesses in particular.[207] He again refers to the area in which Jesus operated as being 'the land of the Jews' (τῶν Ἰουδαίων, cf. comments on 10.37 above) and more narrowly as Ierousalem (Ἰερουσαλήμ) with the two names grouped closely together in Greek (see *Critical Apparatus*). His insistence on limiting the area of Jesus' ministry to the territory of the Jews and to the holy city of Ierousalem (rather than the geographical location, Hierosoluma) is emphatic.

This is the first appeal Peter makes to a witness which, on this occasion and the next (cf. 10.40b-41), accounts for his own knowledge and justifies the authority with which he speaks.

[δ] 10.39b-41 *Jesus' Death and Resurrection*
10.39b-40a The account moves rapidly on to Jesus' death on the cross. The expression 'hanging on a tree' (cf. 5.30; 13.29) conveys the sense of shame attached to the manner of death since the body is exposed to public view; in the Torah, a hanging body is specifically named as coming under God's curse (Deut. 21.22-23). The subject of the verb 'killed' (ἀνεῖλαν) is not spelt out but is understood as the people 'in the country of the Jews and Jerusalem'. Peter thereby attributes responsibility for the death of Jesus to the Jews, omitting any mention of the part played by the Roman officials though Cornelius cannot have been ignorant of their role.

---

207. The phrase here is μάρτυρες αὐτοῦ, where the adjective after the noun is a possessive adjective: the disciples are witnesses belonging to, or selected by, Jesus. What they are witnesses of is 'what he did'. Cf. 1.8: ἔσεσθέ μου μάρτυρες, which should be translated 'You will be witnesses of me', where the position of the adjective μου before the noun causes it to be an objective not a subjective genitive (see *The Message of Acts*, I, p. 78).

Although the sentence starts with the death of Jesus, once again Peter focuses on God's action in raising him, as he has done in earlier speeches (cf. 2.24, 32; 3.15; 4.10). The Bezan reading of 'after three days' is surprising, echoing as it does Mark's 'to rise again after three days' (μετὰ τρεῖς ἡμέρας ἀναστῆναι, Mk 8.31; 9.31; 10.34; cf. Mt. 27.63).[208]

10.40b-41 It is a crucial piece of evidence for the resurrection that Jesus was seen by many people, an event again planned by God.[209] In Peter's mind, the Jewish context of the coming of Jesus continues to be the only one as he specifies that the appearances of Jesus were not to 'all the people', using the term λαός that Luke reserves for the Jews.[210] The witnesses were selected from among the Jews, disciples who shared their lives with him after his resurrection. According to the qualifications of the Bezan text, the group was limited to the apostles for not only did they eat and drink but also kept company with him for the forty-day period between his resurrection and ascension. There are obvious allusions in these details to the opening verses of the book, Acts 1.2-3, where the forty-day interval is mentioned by Luke and where the apostles are described as being 'chosen' by Jesus, ἐξελέξατο. The information also tallies with the Gospel accounts of Jesus' life after his resurrection (cf. Lk. 24.30, 35, 36-43).

The details included in Peter's brief description of the forty days between Jesus' resurrection and ascension may have been intended to counter any claims that Jesus only 'seemed' to come back to life. The very emphasis on the resurrection serves to correct the idea that Jesus did not really die, as was claimed by some, since if he came back to life then he must have died first.[211] In the AT, it is God who is portrayed as raising Jesus, repeating the idea of 10.40 though with a different verb.[212] In Codex Bezae, in contrast, Jesus himself is the subject of the intransitive verb, expressing the idea that he himself was the agent of the resurrection.[213]

208. It may be that in the Bezan text Luke is using Peter's words to set up a parallel between Jesus' resurrection after three days in the tomb and Cornelius' experience of the resurrected Jesus after his three days' fast (cf. 10.30 D05).

209. For the use of the AT construction δίδωμι + accusative + infinitive, cf. 2.27; 13.35 (= Ps. 15.10 LXX); 14.3. The D05 form, δίδωμι + dative + infinitive, is found at Lk. 1.74; 8.10, 55; 9.13, 16; Acts 2.4; 4.29.

210. The expression ἔδωκεν αὐτῷ (αὐτὸν B03) ἐμφανῆ γενέσθαι οὐ παντὶ τῷ λαῷ echoes the lament of Yahweh to Isaiah about the rebelliousness of the people of Israel, ἐμφανὴς ἐγενόμην τοῖς ἐμὲ μὴ ζητοῦσιν, Isa. 65.1 LXX.

211. Anti-docetic teaching first appears in the New Testament and is an indication that docetic claims were already rife in the earliest Christian communities (cf. Jn 20.17, 27; 21.12-13; Lk. 24.30, 39-43; Acts 1.3-4). See also Ignatius, *Smyrn.* 3.3; see Rius-Camps, 'Ignacio de Antioquía, ¿testigo ocular de la muerte y resurrección de Jesús?', *Bib.* 70 (1989), pp. 449–72 [463–64].

212. The verb for the resurrection in Acts is sometimes ἐγείρω (3.15; 4.10; 5.30; 10.40; 13.30, 37) and at others ἀνίστημι (2.24, 30 D05, 32; 3.22, 26 [= Deut. 18.15]; 13.33-34; 17.31).

213. The idea that Jesus had the power over his own life is typically Johannine (Jn 2.19-22; 10.17-18; 21.14). It is also found in Ignatius (ὡς καὶ ἀληθῶς ἀνέστησεν ἑαυτόν, *Smyrn.* 2c; 7.1;

[ε] 10.42-43 *Jesus as Judge*
10.42 Peter moves on to describe the exact nature of the witness they were to bear, namely that it is Jesus whom God had ordained to be the judge. God still remains the one whose plan is being accomplished and at whose initiative events unfold. However, Peter returns to the idea that the people of Israel are the ones concerned by this declaration: 'he charged us to preach to the people…' (λαός is once again the term used, cf. 10.41 above). This limiting of the beneficiaries of Jesus' command to the Jews is in contradiction with the words Luke records Jesus as speaking to the apostles before he left them, when he specifically charged them to preach not a message of judgment but of repentance and forgiveness, and not to Israel but to 'all the nations' (εἰς [ὡς ἐπὶ D05] πάντα τὰ ἔθνη, Lk. 24.47-48; cf. Acts 1.8). In the opening account in Acts of the forty days Jesus spent instructing the apostles, Codex Bezae makes quite clear what it was that Jesus commanded the apostles to preach: 'to whom he had ordered to preach the gospel' (1.2 D05 = Lk. 9.2).[214]

Peter's defective understanding on this point is precisely an example of the way in which Luke considers his speech not to be inspired (cf. on 10.34a above). The absence of any mention of Peter being full of the Holy Spirit as he opened his mouth to address Cornelius is an indication that Peter is speaking here his own thoughts and not accurately transmitting the message of Jesus.

The restricted scope of Jesus' message was already noted in Peter's speech in Solomon's Porch (Acts 3.20-21).[215] The notion that Jesus ordered the apostles to proclaim him as judge, a portrayal of Jesus that is repeated in Paul's speech in Athens (17.30-31; cf. 24.25), does not appear as such in the Gospel and is foreign to Luke's theology.[216] What Luke is conveying here is the confusion of Peter's thought, as later that of Paul, when he finds himself confronted with a new situation that leaves him perplexed and causes him to fall back on traditional Jewish ideas of salvation and judgment.[217] His attachment

---

Rom. 6.1). When ἠγέρθη is used to refer to the resurrection, the sense could also be reflexive (Lk. 24.6 [not D05], 34).

214. See *The Message of Acts*, I, pp. 49–50.

215. See *The Message of Acts*, I, pp. 224–26 on Acts 3.20-21.

216. The only mention of judgment in Luke's Gospel is in the scene of Jesus' last meal with the Twelve where he declares to them that, in the kingdom, they (not he) will judge the twelve tribes of Israel (Lk. 22.30). The idea that the apostles had any relationship to the tribes of Israel is, however, done away with by the death of Judas which leaves the group as a diminished group of eleven who no longer have the function of representing Israel (see *The Message of Acts*, I, *Excursus* 1, pp. 79–87; J. Rius-Camps and J. Read-Heimerdinger, 'After the Death of Judas: A Reconsideration of the Status of the Twelve Apostles', *RCatT* 29 [2004], pp. 305–34).

217. Although eschatological judgment is a theme proclaimed by Paul (Rom. 2.16; 14.10; 2 Tim. 4.1; cf. 1 Pet. 4.5; 2 Cl. 1.1; Pol., *Phil.* 2.1; *Acts Thomas* 30), in the Gospel of John it becomes a present reality through the coming of the Son (Jn 3.17-18; 5.25-29, 30; 12.47-48) and the Spirit (16.8, 11), though the idea of future judgment is not altogether absent (5.28-29). In Luke's Gospel, whereas John the Baptist proclaimed a baptism 'with the Holy Spirit and fire' in

to his own people in this sense prevents him from being properly open to the Gentiles.

10.43 The witnesses whom Peter appeals to in this case are the prophets of the Jewish Scriptures whose collective purpose, he affirms, is to testify that the name of Jesus is the means for everyone who believes in him to receive forgiveness of sins – the connection between this and the previous statement, that Jesus is the divinely appointed judge, is implicit, so that judgment does not incur punishment for those who believe in Jesus.

At this point, Peter returns to the idea of universal salvation he began with (cf. 10.34-35), salvation accessible to all (πάντα), Gentiles as well as Jews. This idea in itself is not new in Peter's proclamations, indeed he concluded his first speech at Pentecost with a similar declaration, though the universal application was more veiled in the Bezan text (in brackets): 'the promise belongs to you (us) and to your (our) children and to any of those who are far off whom the Lord our God will call' (2.39), where the expression 'those who are far off' (οἱ εἰς μακράν) is a phrase designating the Gentiles. What is new is that Peter is now becoming aware (as he says – even as the scene unfolds according to Codex Bezae, see on 10.34b above) that the time for 'those who are far off' to be accepted by God is now, there is nothing else that needs to happen, the tense of God's call is not future (as at 2.39) but present or even past.[218] This scene, as was suggested in the introduction to this episode (see *Overview* above), is fundamentally about Peter's conversion much more than about that of Cornelius who, for his part, has always had an attitude that was acceptable to God.[219] It is difficult to speak of the conversion of a person whose prayer and piety has been described as exemplary, who experiences clearly a vision of the risen Jesus and who follows the instructions given to him promptly and with eagerness, who acts on behalf of the Holy Spirit (though without knowing it), who indicates to Peter the way he is to take and who finally receives the Holy Spirit without any preliminary process.

Forgiveness of sins in the speeches in Luke's writings has hitherto been a possibility open only to Israel (Lk. 1.77; 3.3; Acts 2.38; 5.31), except in Jesus' own words on the day he left his apostles with his command to preach to all nations (Lk. 24.47-48). Even once Peter has recognized that it was in fact available to all, he continues to take the Jewish people and the Jewish prophets as the point of reference. It is apparent now that he is about to move on to

the context of future judgment (Lk. 3.16-17), Jesus speaks only of 'baptism with the Holy Spirit' (Acts 1.5).

218. Joel 3.5 which Peter cites in his Pentecost speech (Acts 2.39) has the past tense, '(those whom God) has called προσκέκληται', and it is Peter who changes it to the future, προσκαλέσηται.

219. The term 'Peter's conversion' was used as early as the beginning of the twentieth century (E.C. Selwyn, 'The Carefulness of Luke. 2. Peter's Conversion', *The Expositor* 7/10 [1910], pp. 449–63) but few commentators have paid attention to Luke's focus on Peter's changing attitude in Acts 10.

an exhortation, similar to that seen in his earlier speeches (cf. 2.38-39); in the explanation he will give later in Jerusalem, he will say that he was only 'beginning to speak' (cf. 11.15). Although there can be no certainty about how Peter was going to continue his discourse, what happens next to stop him talking prevents any possibility of his continuing to make the forgiveness of Gentiles related to the Jewish issue.

[f'] 10.44 *The Holy Spirit Fell on the Hearers*
Corresponding to Peter's rebuke of Cornelius for mistaking him for a divine being ([f] 10.26) is the sudden and unexpected arrival of the Holy Spirit on the scene.

10.44 Normally at this point in the speech a final exhortation would be expected,[220] but the Spirit falls on (upon, AT) those listening to Peter while he is in the middle of speaking.[221] 'Those listening' includes Cornelius and all those he had gathered together in his house (cf. 10.24, 27), but not the six men from Joppa who had accompanied Peter and whose response is noted separately. They were listening to Peter's declaration of 'the message' (τὸν λόγον) which he had begun by explaining was sent by God to 'the sons of Israel' (10.36) and which has been extended to the Gentiles only indirectly. It is the Holy Spirit who, in contrast, takes the initiative in opening up the good news to the Gentiles without any further ado. That Peter was not expecting this to happen is shown by his response as he describes it to the brethren in Jerusalem (cf. 11.15-16) – he evidently thought there was quite a bit more for him to explain to the Gentiles before they could be in the same position as the Jewish believers when they received the Holy Spirit.

The gift of the Holy Spirit to all the nations has been anticipated since Pentecost when Luke presented the gathering of 'every nation' in Jerusalem as

---

220. All the speeches in Acts apart from this one of Peter's and the three Pauline apologies conclude with a parenesis which is introduced by a variety of means: καὶ (τὰ) νῦν (3.17; 4.29; 5.38; 20.32), νῦν οὖν (10.33b AT; 15.10), νῦν ἰδού (10.33b D05), οὖν (1.21; 11.17; 13.38; 17.30), τί οὖν ἐστιν; (6.3 D05; 21.22), διό (15.19), the imperative (2.38-40), or direct invective (7.51). None of Paul's apologies comes to a proper conclusion (22.1-21, cut short, cf. v. 22; 24.10-21, adjourned, cf. v. 22; 26.2-23, interrupted, cf. v. 24).

221. The actions of speaking and listening are expressed by present participles, with the action of the Holy Spirit, ἐπέπεσεν/ἔπεσεν, taking the form of an aorist that cuts across the durative actions. Luke often uses the present participle of the verbs λαλέω // ἀκούω to indicate: 1) those in the process of speaking with such expressions as ὁ/οἱ λαλῶν/-οῦντες // listening/hearing with the expression πάντες οἱ ἀκούοντες: Lk. 7.1 D05; Acts 2.6, 7, 11; 6.11, 13 (explicit: οὐ παύεται λαλῶν); 7.38, 44; 10.7, 46; 11.19; 14.9; 16.14 (pass. part.); 17.19 B03 (pass. part.); 20.30; 22.9 // Lk. 20.45 (gen. abs.); Acts 5.5 B03, 11; 10.44; 26.29; 2) a close connection between two concurrent actions: Lk. 8.49 (par. Mk 5.35); 22.47 (par. Mk 14.43); Acts 2.11; 10.46; 13.45 B03 (pass. part.) // Lk. 2.47; 19.11, 48 B03; Acts 7.54 AT (see *Commentary, ad loc.*); 9.7 (εἱστήκεισαν with imperf. meaning); 9.21; 10.44; 13.48; 18.8; 3) an interruption: Lk. 5.4 (explicit: ὡς [ὅτε D05] δὲ ἐπαύσατο λαλῶν); 22.60; 24.36; Acts 4.1; 10.44; 23.7 AT // Lk. 4.28; Acts 5.5, 11; 17.8.

a reality already achieved on the spiritual level (2.1, 5-11).[222] On the historical level, because the apostles had not understood that the gift was a universal one from the start, the only people who received the Spirit in actual fact were Jews. Peter himself had preached on that occasion that God's promise of the Spirit is for everyone (2.14b-21, cf. v. 39) before going on to restrict the promise to his Jewish hearers (2.22-40). In other words, he had known in theory that access to God had been opened through Jesus for all people, including Gentiles but, because his understanding was imperfect, he had not known that nothing more needed to be waited for before this became a present reality.

[e'] 10.45-46a *The Amazement of the Circumcision Brethren*
10.45 The people who accompanied Peter were mentioned by the narrator as he left Joppa for Caesarea (10.23b). They are described here as 'the faithful' (οἱ πιστοί), so Jesus-believers, and 'of the circumcision' (ἐκ περιτομῆς) which would seem to be an allusion to the strength of their characteristic Jewish belief about who was acceptable to God;[223] the same expression will be used of disciples at 11.2 where they are referred to as 'brethren' by Codex Bezae (see *Critical Apparatus*, 11.2 below).

Their reaction at seeing the manifestation of the Holy Spirit among the Gentiles was no slight surprise but utter astonishment. The term 'the gift' (ἡ δωρεά) is used with reference to the Spirit on other occasions: at Pentecost, by Peter who promises his Jewish audience that they will receive 'the gift of the Spirit' if they submit to water baptism for the forgiveness of their sins (2.38); and again by Simon Magus who wanted to buy the 'gift of God' with money (8.20; cf. Jn 4.10) after first being baptized (8.13). Peter will relate this giving of the Spirit back to the same gift that the Jewish believers received on the day of Pentecost (11.17). He himself, though far from expecting the arrival of the Spirit as he was talking, is apparently not so surprised when he sees what is happening, having being prepared through the events of the last three days and remembering as he does words of Jesus (cf. 11.16).

The verb 'pour out' (ἐκχέω) is likewise typically used of the Spirit in Luke's work: it was prophesied by Joel (Joel 3.1-2) as a future event for all humanity, and cited by Peter (Acts 2.17-18)[224] at Pentecost as an event real-

222. It is important to discern in Luke's account of the coming of the Spirit at Pentecost two distinct registers: the historical register expressing a literal reality and the narrative register expressing a spiritual reality. According to this duality with which Luke plays, the Spirit was only actually received on that day by the gathering of believers in Jerusalem but was in fact given to all of humankind. A similar interplay of registers is apparent in the Jewish interpretations of the giving of the Torah on Mt Sinai, an event mirrored in the giving of the Spirit at Pentecost (see *The Message of Acts*, I, pp. 146–47; 152, 158–64; 178–92).

223. Outside Acts, the label οἱ ἐκ περιτομῆς is only found in Paul's letters (Rom. 4.12; Gal. 2.12; Col. 4.11; Tit. 1.10).

224. *The Message of Acts*, I, pp. 181–82.

ized through the glorified Jesus (2.33). At that time, however, there was no expectation that the Gentiles would be the beneficiaries of the pouring out of the Spirit there and then. It is only now that the resistance of the Jewish Jesus-believers to the idea of uncircumcised Gentiles being equally acceptable to God is overcome as God himself takes the initiative and the Holy Spirit is given to them.

What the Jewish onlookers observed was a similar phenomenon to that which occurred on the day of Pentecost, namely, the expression of the Spirit in other languages.[225] They understand the contents of the speaking, however, even though the languages are described as 'new' in Codex Bezae (see *Critical Apparatus*), for they hear the people 'praising God' (cf. 2.11). 'New (κεναῖς) tongues' is particularly appropriate to describe the way the Jews heard the Gentiles praising God, which was quite new (more than simply 'different' as in the AT, ἑτέραις) compared to what they were used to.

[d'] 10.46b-47 *Peter's Anticipation of Baptism*
10.46b-47 It is Peter who brings up the matter of baptism. The AT expresses his response as decisive and conclusive but Codex Bezae reserves this step until after he has considered the possible objections to baptism (see *Critical Apparatus*); furthermore, his questioning about the possibility of going ahead with baptism is not so much a proclamation preceding the act of baptism, as it could be read in the AT, but a deliberation that he holds with the believers who had come with him from Joppa. They are the only other believers on the scene and it is normal that he should turn to them to discuss the next step in what is more of an aside than a public declaration.

Normally, in the case of a Gentile who wished to become a proselyte the rites of circumcision and baptism were indispensable prerequisites, to be completed with a sacrifice offering in the Temple.[226] It does not seem to have crossed his mind before now (confirmed by his report in Jerusalem, cf. 11.15-17) that circumcision could be unnecessary for Cornelius and his household to be accepted into the community of Jesus-believers, so much does he continue to think in terms of Jewish Law.

It was noted in the case of the Ethiopian eunuch, who had been barred from full acceptance as a Jew because of his condition as a eunuch, that the question about baptism that he put to Philip ('What is to prevent me being baptized?', τί κωλύει με βαπτισθῆναι, 8.36) was not merely a rhetorical question but reflected a standard procedure followed at baptism, that of asking for

---

225. *The Message of Acts,* I, pp. 150–51, 161, on 2.4, 6.

226. The exact requirements in the first century for foreigners who wished to become Jews are a matter of some debate, and were already disputed between the schools of Shammai and Hillel at the time. There is, however, fair evidence to show that up to 70 CE three conditions had to be fulfilled: circumcision, baptism and Temple sacrifice (see W. Flemington, *The New Testament Doctrine of Baptism*, London: SPCK, 1957, pp. 3–11).

information about any reason why the baptism could not go ahead. Peter pronounces a similar formula here: 'Surely no-one can forbid water...?', with 'water' placed first in the sentence in Greek and, in Codex Bezae, juxtaposed with the verb 'forbid' to highlight the question. The evidence for Jewish rites of baptism in the first century is scanty, but it would seem from the emphatic formulation of Peter's question, so closely resembling the question put by the eunuch to Philip, that before Christian baptism was established it was already a familiar practice within Judaism to investigate the legal grounds on which a baptism may or may not proceed.

Peter's grounds for proceeding with baptism, which had become the usual step to take to confirm a person's belief in Jesus, are that God had already shown by pouring out the Holy Spirit on the people who had gathered in Cornelius' house that they were accepted by him in the same way as they, the Jewish believers had been, and the decision about baptizing them has therefore been taken out of his hands. As he will explain to the disciples in Jerusalem when he defends his action in baptizing the Gentiles (11.17), who was he to stop God?

On the other hand, why does Peter insist on baptism with water since these people had already received the baptism in the Spirit promised by Jesus? Baptism in water was normally a sign of repentance (cf. Lk. 3.3; Acts 2.38; 13.24; 19.4) for the forgiveness of sins, and takes place before, not after, baptism in the Spirit. If the Spirit had been poured out, it was an indication that the people did not need to repent in order to be accepted by God. Water baptism in these circumstances would appear to be a rite that served as a procedure to admit the believers into the Jesus-believing community, preventing anyone from insisting on the need for circumcision in order for them to be part of the Church.

[c'] 10.48a *Baptism of Cornelius' Household*

10.48a It is at this point that Codex Bezae presents Peter as moving on to the decisive step that brings this scene to a close when he orders that Cornelius and the audience he had gathered to listen to Peter are to be baptized. According to the AT, the decisive step was already taken when Peter declared the possibility of baptism (cf. 10.46b above). It is noteworthy that as he orders baptism, he makes no mention of its purpose as being 'for the forgiveness of sins', since the gift of the Holy Spirit has already been a sign that forgiveness has been granted (see above). This is in contrast to the invitation he had given to the Jews to be baptized on the day of Pentecost (2.38), when both forgiveness of sins and the subsequent gift of the Holy Spirit are mentioned as consequences of baptism.

The act of baptism in the name of (the Lord, D05) Jesus Christ is an external affirmation of the belief in him the participants have already demonstrated – not by name, certainly, but by their readiness to carry out the commands of the resurrected Jesus who appeared to Cornelius (see *Commentary*, 10.30) and their openness to hear Peter's message from God (cf. 10.33, 44).

A number of similarities exist between the baptism of Cornelius and his guests by Peter and that of the Ethiopian eunuch by Philip:

1. Each is situated on either side of the central episodes concerning Saul who will become the champion of the uncircumcised and their entry into the Church.

2. Both characters correspond to a person in the Gospel: the eunuch // the man on the road to Jericho (Lk. 10.30-37); Cornelius // the centurion of Capernaum (7.2-10), but those in Acts are identified by a name and place of origin: the eunuch is from Ethiopia, the treasurer of Queen Candace (Acts 8.27), and Cornelius is a Roman centurion of the Italian cohort (10.1).

3. Both are excluded from being fully integrated into the people of God: the eunuch by reason of his physical condition, and Cornelius because of his profession as a Roman soldier.

4. Despite these obstacles, they both display an exemplary piety and their conduct is irreproachable, so that they are accepted by God: the eunuch had been on a journey to the Temple in Jerusalem and was wanting to understand the prophecies of Isaiah (8.27-33), while Cornelius was devout and generous in his almsgiving to the Jewish people (10.2-4, 22, 31, 35).

5. The baptism of each is preceded by a question concerning a possible obstacle to the administration of water: 'Here is water; what is to prevent me from being baptized?' (8.36); 'Surely no-one can forbid water so as to prevent them (these people, AT) from being baptized?' (10.47).

6. While both are baptized (8.36, 37, 38; 10.47), no mention is made in either case of repentance or forgiveness of sins which are normally associated with water baptism (cf. Lk. 3.3; Acts 2.38), even though in the case of Cornelius Peter had started to allude to the subject (10.43).

7. On the other hand, the question of their faith in Jesus is ascertained/ supposed in each case: the eunuch, according to the long text of 8.37 states his belief in Jesus as the Son of God, and Cornelius is said to have believed in Jesus before he was baptized (11.17; 15.7-9).

8. The Holy Spirit is given spontaneously, without any prior warning, to both the eunuch (again according to the long text, 8.39) and to Cornelius (10.44) .

The lesson Luke gives from these parallel situations is that it is God who takes the initiative at each new step in the spread of the gospel away from and out of the Jewish community in Ierousalem – first to a Jew from Ethiopia, despised by the people of God because of his condition as a eunuch, and secondly to a Gentile, a member of the army of occupation. Philip as a representative of the Hellenist believers and then Peter as a representative of the apostles each witness God in action, despite their own hesitations or shortcomings.

[b'] 10.48b *Peter's Stay in Caesarea*

10.48b The invitation for Peter to stay in Caesarea came from Cornelius and his guests, expressed more forcefully in the Bezan text (see *Critical Apparatus*). The suggestion is that he would otherwise have left straight away, which might have lessened the strength of the accusations he faced in Jerusalem but would not have avoided the problems they raised altogether (cf. 11.3). His stay of several days no doubt gave Peter the opportunity to take stock of what had happened and to consider his next move. The outcome will be made clear at the beginning of the next scene.

[a′] 11.1 *The Brethren in Judaea*

11.1 The present scene comes to a close in different ways according to the text followed. In the AT, the scene ended with Peter's stay in Caesarea and a new scene now begins with a transfer of the action to Judaea and the reappearance of 'the apostles and the brethren, who were throughout Judaea'. The Bezan text, however, maintains the focus on Peter for this verse (and indeed throughout the opening of the next scene that starts in 11.2 in this text), by presenting these new characters only obliquely, using an impersonal verb. Furthermore, the location is more specifically 'in Judaea' rather than 'throughout' the region, with the name standing for Jerusalem;[227] the significance of the location is apparent in the careful situating of the apostles and the brethren there in Codex Bezae, οἱ ἐν τῇ ᾿Ιουδαίᾳ.

Judaea is still regarded as the centre of the Church at this point, at least by the Jesus-believing Jews who live there. So when the news about what had happened in Caesarea reached the ears of the apostles and the other brethren, they were not expecting it. The same words, 'even the Gentiles' (ὡς καὶ ... τὰ ἔθνη), are used as were spoken by the circumcision brethren in Caesarea when they witnessed the manifestation of the Holy Spirit in Cornelius' house (cf. 10.45). But here the event is summed up not in terms of the gift of the Holy Spirit but in terms of the Gentiles receiving 'the word of God', just as when 'the apostles in Ierousalem' heard 'that Samaria had received the word of God' (8.14). In the text of Codex Bezae, the expression ὁ λόγος τοῦ θεοῦ ('the word of God') stands for something quite precise: it represents the general notion of God communicating with people, as distinct from ὁ λόγος τοῦ κυρίου, 'the word of the Lord', where 'the Lord' refers to Jesus meaning the teaching of or about Jesus (see *General Introduction,* § VIII). In other words, what the people in Judaea conclude about the happenings in Caesarea is that God's revelation, which had for so long been the privilege of Israel, the mark of God's love for the Jews,[228] has been given to the other nations, the faithless and the rebellious peoples who oppressed the Jews and worshipped foreign gods. This event marks such a dramatic shift in the self-identity of the Jewish people that it is hard to sense, some 2000 years later, just how momentous and difficult it would have been for Jews, even those who believed in Jesus as the Lord and the Messiah, to accept that the change they were hearing about really

227. Cf. 11.29; 12.1 D05; 21.20 D05. Judaea also represents the centre of Jerusalem when people are said to 'go down from Judaea': 12.19; 15.1; 21.10.

228. The notion of the privilege of Israel consisting in their possessing God's revelation, the Torah, is discussed with reference to Pentecost in *The Message of Acts,* I, pp. 145, 152, 158–59.

had taken place, and had been allowed to take place. Some notion of their perplexity and shock, however, must be borne in mind when considering the
scene that follows where Peter is challenged about his conduct in Caesarea.

[BA′-A′] 11.2-18 *Peter's Report to the Apostles*

Overview

Section II of Acts (8.1b–11.30) consists of a central sequence [B] (8.4–11.18)
made up of portraits of the three great leaders in successive sub-sequences,
Philip [BA], Saul [BB] and Peter [BA′]; this is now the final episode in the
Peter sub-sequence. It is an episode of key significance in Luke's narrative
scheme as it emerges in the text of Codex Bezae, for it is here that is finally
found the fulfilment of Jesus' command to Peter to 'strengthen the brethren'
when he has turned after denying his master (cf. Lk. 22.32 // Acts 11.2 D05;
Excursus 5).

Peter has just been observed in two episodes that took place each in a different location: in Judaea [BA′-A] (9.31-43) and in Joppa/Caesarea [BA′-B]
(10.1–11.1). Now, in this final episode [BA′-A′], the setting is Jerusalem
where Peter's progress can be measured against his position in the corresponding episode in Judaea when he was seen to be maintaining the validity of
the Jewish Law that distinguished between Jew and Gentile. Among the
Jewish Jesus-believers, he was popular and was successful in working
miracles but when he healed and restored to life it was without causing the
believers to move forward in their understanding of the good new of Jesus,
since Peter's own grasp was still imperfect. However, by God's intervention
in Caesarea in the central episode, he had come recognize that both Gentiles
and Jews were accepted by God and that circumcision was not an essential
step to being incorporated into his people. His new understanding is now
shared with the brethren and tested as he relates what he had learnt to the
other apostles and brethren in Jerusalem, preparing for the ultimate section of
this part of Acts (Section IV, 12.1-25) when Peter's liberation will be finally
complete.

Structure and Themes

The AT, which does not include any account of Peter's movements between
Caesarea and Jerusalem, starts this new section already at 11.1 (see *Critical
Apparatus*, 11.1, 2). According to the text of Codex Bezae, the final episode
of the sub-sequence concerning Peter opens now, with the same construction
μὲν οὖν as the first episode (cf. 9.31) just as μὲν οὖν also opened the first and
last episodes of the corresponding sub-sequence concerning Philip [BA] (8.4,
25). As often happens with a μὲν οὖν clause, it presents a first incident arising
from the preceding narrative that is followed by a second incident, in a clause
introduced with δέ that takes the story on further. The first incident is prepara-

tory to the events of the new episode which starts properly at the δέ clause, 11.2b [a].[229] This describes the reaction of those 'of the circumcision' to Peter's actions in Caesarea and is followed by Peter's explanation in 11.4-17 [b]. That his account satisfied his opponents is made clear by their changed response, 11.18 [a'], with which the episode ends. These three elements make up a three-part concentric arrangement as follows:

Intro.	11.2a	Peter's journey to Hierosoluma
[a]	11.2b-3	The negative reaction of the circumcision brethren
[b]	11.4-17	Peter's explanation
[a']	11.18	The brethren's positive reaction

Translation

Codex Bezae D05		*Codex Vaticanus B03*
Intro.	**11.2a** Now Peter after some time wished to journey to Hierosoluma and after calling the brethren to him and having strengthened them by holding long talks as he taught them going through the villages, he finally arrived there and he announced to them the grace of God.	**11.2a** When Peter went up to Ierousalem,
[a]	**2b** But the brethren of the circumcision raised objections against him **3** saying, 'Why did you go into the houses of men who are uncircumcised and eat with them?'	**2b** those of the circumcision raised objections against him **3** saying that he went into the houses of men who are uncircumcised and he ate with them.
[b]	**4** Starting at the beginning, Peter explained things to them step by step, saying,	**4** Starting at the beginning, Peter explained to them step by step, saying,
[α]	**5** 'I was in the city of Joppa praying, and I saw in a trance a vision, some kind of container coming down like a huge linen sheet, lowered out of heaven by its four corners, and it came right down to me; **6** staring into it, I examined it and I saw four-footed animals of the earth, including wild beasts, and reptiles and birds of the air. **7** And I heard a voice saying to me, "Get up, Peter, sacrifice and eat". **8** I said, "By no means, Lord, because something unclean or common never entered my mouth". **9** There came a voice from heaven addressed to me, "What God has cleansed, stop making common".	**5** 'I was in the city of Joppa praying, and I saw in a trance a vision, some kind of container coming down like a huge linen sheet, lowered out of heaven by its four corners, and it came right down to me; **6** staring into it, I examined it and I saw the four-footed animals of the earth, the wild beasts, and the reptiles and the birds of the air. **7** And I heard a voice saying to me, "Get up, Peter, and sacrifice and eat". **8** I said, "By no means, Lord, because something unclean or common never entered my mouth". **9** But the voice answered a second time from heaven, "What God has cleansed, stop making common". **10** This hap-

229. Levinsohn, *Textual Connections*, pp. 141–50.

10 This happened three times and everything was pulled up again to heaven.

[β]　11 And then at that very moment three men stood by the house in which I was, having been sent to me from Caesarea. 12 The Spirit told me to go with them. These six brethren came with me, too, and we went into the house of the man. 13 He reported to us how he saw an angel standing in his house and saying to him, "Send to Joppa and summon Simon, the one named Peter, 14 who will speak words to you by which you may be saved, you and all your household". 15 As I was starting to speak to them, the Holy Spirit fell on them just as he did on us in the beginning. 16 And I remembered the word of the Lord, how he used to say, "John baptized with water but you will be baptized in the Holy Spirit".

[γ]　17 If then, he gave the same gift to them as to us when we believed in the Lord Jesus Christ, who was I to be able to hinder God from giving them the Holy Spirit when they believed in him?'

[α']　18 When they heard this they were silent and they started glorifying God saying, 'Then to the Gentiles also God has given repentance leading to life'.

pened three times and everything was pulled up again to heaven.

11 And then at that very moment three men stood by the house in which I was, having been sent to me from Caesarea. 12 The Spirit told me to go with them without discriminating. So these six brethren came with me, too, and we went into the house of the man. 13 He reported to us how he saw the angel standing in his house and saying, "Send to Joppa and summon Simon, the one named Peter, who will speak words to you 14 by which you may be saved, you and all your household". 15 As I was starting to speak, the Holy Spirit fell upon them just as he did on us in the beginning. 16 And I remembered the word of the Lord, how he used to say, "John baptized with water but you will be baptized in the Holy Spirit".

17 If then, God gave the same gift to them as to us after believing in the Lord Jesus Christ, who was I to be able to hinder God?'

18 When they heard this they were silent and they glorified God saying, 'Then to the Gentiles also God has given the repentance leading to life'.

Critical Apparatus

11.2 ὅτε δὲ ἀνέβη Πέτρος εἰς Ἰερουσαλήμ B 𝔓⁴⁵·⁷⁴ ℵ A 81 *pc* | ὅτε δὲ ἀν. Π. εἰς Ἰεροσόλυμα E H L P Ψ 049. 056. 33. 1739 𝔐 lat ‖ Ὁ μὲν οὖν Π. διὰ ἱκανοῦ χρόνου ἠθέλησε (-εν Dᴱ) πορευθῆναι εἰς Ἰεροσόλυμα· καὶ προσφωνήσας τοὺς ἀδελφοὺς καὶ ἐπιστηρίξας αὐτούς, πολὺν λόγον ποιούμενος διὰ τῶν χωρῶν διδάσκων αὐτούς· ὃς καὶ κατήντησεν αὐτοῦ (Dᶜʲ·, αὐτοῖς D*, *eis* d) καὶ ἀπήγγειλεν αὐτοῖς τὴν χάριν τοῦ θεοῦ D d (p w vgᵐˢˢ syʰ** mae).

On the reading of D05, see M.-É. Boismard, 'The Texts of Acts: A Problem of Literary Criticism?', in E.J. Epp and G.D. Fee (eds), *New Testament Textual Criticism* (Oxford: Clarendon, 1981), pp. 147–57 [149]; Boismard and Lamouille, II, p. 77.

The conjecture of (κατήντησεν) αὐτοῦ as the original reading of D05 in place of the present reading αὐτοῖς, is made on the grounds that 1) κατανταάω is always followed by εἰς/ἐπί + accusative and never the dative; 2) Luke is the only evangelist to use the verb καταντάω, and only in Acts (× 9 + × 3 D05), where he always uses εἰς + accusative except at 20.15 (ἄντικρυς); 3) a similar confusion of pronouns is found in the additional material of Acts 15.34 D05: αὐτούς D C 33 | αὐτοῦ 88. 614. 1739 *al.*; B03 uses adverbial αὐτοῦ at Lk. 9.27 (ὧδε D05); Acts 18.19 (ἐκεῖ D05); 21.4 (D05 lac., *apud eos* d); 4) the adverb αὐτοῦ here at 11.2 picks up the mention of εἰς Ἱεροσόλυμα in the first clause of the sentence.

Supported by a variety of early versions, D05 expands on Peter's inner thoughts and plans as he goes from Caesarea to Jerusalem. The language is complex and the relationship between the various propositions is not entirely certain. One way to deal with it is to break it down into chunks that cluster around the finite verbs. The sentence, of which the subject is Peter throughout, has a first main finite verb with a dependent infinitive – ἠθέλησε πορευθῆναι – then continues with a series of two aorist participles – προσφωνήσας, ἐπιστηρίξας – followed by two present participles, the first of which qualifies the means of ἐπιστηρίξας – ποιούμενος – and the second – διδάσκων – standing in a temporal relation to the first; a second finite verb is then reached, with the subject repeated by means of a relative pronoun and the action emphasized with an adverbial καί; this is linked straightforwardly to the concluding verb with a conjunctive καί. The relationships between the various propositions can be expressed in the following diagram:

> ἠθέλησε πορευθῆναι
>   καὶ προσφωνήσας
>   καὶ ἐπιστηρίξας
>   ποιούμενος,
>   διδάσκων
> ὃς καὶ κατήντησεν
>   καὶ ἀπήγγειλεν

Summarizing the sentence by tracking the three finite verbs, the line of thought is: 'Peter wanted to go to Hierosoluma … he arrived there and announced the grace of God.' On this analysis, the calling and strengthening of the brethren by teaching them took place in the course of the journey, as they went through the villages on the way to Hierosoluma. The following points are made: 1) Peter spent a considerable time in Caesarea first – διὰ ἱκανοῦ χρόνου, cf. 10.48b; 2) it was his decision to leave – ἠθέλησε; 3) it was to Hierosoluma that he wanted to go, not Ierousalem as in B03; 4) he called the brethren – προσφωνήσας τοὺς ἀδελφούς, and he made their faith firm – ἐπιστηρίξας; 5) he did this by teaching them – διδάσκων αὐτούς – through long conversations – πολὺν λόγον – in the villages between Caesarea and Hierosoluma – διὰ τῶν χωρῶν; 6) when he arrived in Hierosoluma – κατήντησεν αὐτοῦ (where the genitive case expresses a locative referring to the city) – he is responsible for telling the brethren there – ἀπήγγειλεν αὐτοῖς – about what God had done, about his grace – τὴν χάριν τοῦ θεοῦ.

B03 has none of these details, except the information that Peter arrived in the city, referred to as Ierousalem, that is, the holy city as opposed to the geographical location (see *General Introduction*, § VII).

διεκρίνοντο πρὸς αὐτὸν οἱ ἐκ περιτομῆς B 𝔓⁴⁵·⁷⁴ ℵ A E H L P Ψ 049. 056. 33. 1739 𝔐 lat ‖ οἱ δὲ ἐκ’ περ. ἀδελφοὶ διεκ. πρ. αυτόν D (d p w vgᵐˢˢ mae).

The word order variation is explained by the fact that in D05 this is the opening clause, but not so in B03. D05 qualifies the people of the circumcision with the term 'brethren' (cf. 10.45: οἱ ἐκ περιτομῆς πιστοί), making it clear that they were believers, not Jews who were opposed to the Jesus-believers.

11.3 εἰσῆλθεν … καὶ συνέφαγεν B 𝔓⁴⁵ 36. 81. 453. 1175 *al* syᵖ·ʰ | -θεν κ. -γεν L 33. 614. 1611. 2412. 2492 ‖ Εἰσῆλθες … κ. -γες D 𝔓⁷⁴ ℵ A 242. 945. 1739. 1891. 2298 *pc* d latt syʰᵐᵍ co aeth; Chr | -θες κ. -γες E H P Ψ 049. 056. 𝔐.

B03 reports the accusations of the brethren in indirect speech, whereas D05 uses direct speech where it is likely that the introductory ὅτι stands for the interrogative τί (Metzger, *Commentary*, p. 338).

σὺν (αὐτοῖς) D d ‖ *om.* B 𝔓⁷⁴ ℵ (Dˢ·ᵐ·) *rell.*

D05 reinforces the prefix of the compound verb συνέφαγες by repeating the preposition.

11.4 τὰ (καθεξῆς) D ‖ *om.* B 𝔓⁷⁴ ℵ *rell.*

The verb ἐκτίθημι normally requires an object (Delebecque, *Les deux Actes*, p. 77).

11.5 ἐν πόλει ’Ιόππῃ B 𝔓⁷⁴ ℵ *rell.* ‖ ἐν ’Ι. πόλ. D d bo geo; Chr.

The position of the name of Joppa before the noun in apposition in D05 has the effect of underlining it (Read-Heimerdinger, *The Bezan Text*, p. 84). It is as if Peter wished to insist that he had gone to Joppa not Caesarea – he only went on to the other city because of the divine revelation in Joppa. The word order of B03 is the neutral one, cf. πόλις Λασαία, 27.8 (D05 lac.).

ἐν (ἐκστάσει) B 𝔓⁷⁴ ℵ *rell* ‖ *om.* D.

D05 omits the preposition, with the dative case alone expressing the means by which Peter saw his vision (cf. 10.10: ἐγένετο [*cecidit* d] ἐπ’ αὐτὸν ἔκστασις [D05 lac.]).

τέσσαρσιν (ἀρχαῖς) B 𝔓⁷⁴ ℵ *rell* ‖ τέτρασιν D.

D05 uses the form of the number that is more generally, though not necessarily, the cardinal form (B-A-G, τετράς).

ἄχρι (ἐμοῦ) B* 𝔓⁷⁴ ℵ *rell* | ἕως D 241.

ἕως is used in place of ἄχρι at 13.11 D05 (and in place of μέχρι at Mt. 28.15; Mk 13.30; Lk. 16.16). ἄχρι, however, is by no means avoided by D05; it is read in common with B03 at Lk. 1.20; 4.13; 17.27; 21.24; Acts 1.2; 2.29; 3.21; 7.18; 13.6; 20.11; 22.22; and as a *vl* at 13.31 D05 (in an additional clause); 20.26 D05.

11.6 τὰ τετράποδα τῆς γῆς καὶ τὰ θηρία καὶ τὰ ἑρπετὰ καὶ τὰ πετεινά B 𝔓⁷⁴ ℵ Dᶜ *rell* || τετρ. τ. γ. κ. τὰ θηρ. κ. ἑρπ. κ. πετ. D*.

The description of the contents of the sheet in Peter's vision already varied in the narrator's account at 10.12 according to the MS read (cf. 10.12 and *Critical Apparatus, ad loc.*). Here, the list of animals is the same, but D05 omits the article except before θηρία. Accordingly, in Peter's account in D05, he refers to all the animals generally but qualifies the four-footed animals in an appositional phrase, 'including the wild beasts'. Since wild animals are a type of four-footed animal, the D05 reading makes more sense, though the reason for singling them out is only apparent in terms of the Jewish regulations concerning consumption of meat – the restrictions on the types of land animals imposed in Lev. 11.2-8 (they must have cloven hooves and ruminate) limit consumption to domestic animals or those resembling them (cf. Deut. 14.5). Most wild animals were therefore ruled out as unclean.

11.7 ἤκουσα δὲ καὶ φωνῆς λεγούσης μοι B 𝔓⁷⁴ ℵ *rell* || καὶ ἤκ. φωνὴν λέγουσάν μοι D d (𝔓⁴⁵ 1175).

The mention of the voice is introduced as a new element (δέ) and with an emphatic adverb (καί) in B03 where D05 uses a more neutral construction. In contrast, the second mention of the voice at 11.9 will be more emphatic in D05 (see below). The genitive of φωνή after ἀκούω is found elsewhere where it is the sound rather than the message communicated that is in focus (Lk. 15.25; Acts 9.7 [see *Commentary, ad loc.*; cf. 9.4, acc.]; cf. Heb. 4.7 = Ps. 94.7 LXX).

Ἀναστάς B 𝔓⁷⁴ ℵ Dᴱ *rell, surgens* d || Ἀνάστα D* gig l p vg.

The same *vl*, between the aorist participle (B03) and the present imperative (D05) is found at 10.13 (between B03 and the Latin text d: *surge* [D05 lac.]) and 10.20 (see *Critical Apparatus, ad loc.*).

11.8 εἶπον B 𝔓⁷⁴ ℵ *rell* || εἶπα D.

The first aorist form of D05 instead of the second aorist of B03 is a rare form though known in Attic Greek, and is found again at 26.15, ἐγὼ δὲ εἶπα (D05 lac.; see Winer, *Grammar*, p. 183). The third plural εἶπαν is very common.

11.9 ἀπεκρίθη δὲ ἐκ δευτέρου φωνὴ ἐκ τοῦ οὐρανοῦ B 36. 453 *pc* | ἀπ. δέ μοι ἐκ δευ. φ. ἐκ τ. οὐρ. E Ψ | ἀπ. δέ μοι φ. ἐκ δευ. ἐκ τ. οὐρ. H L P 049. (056. 33) 𝔐 | ἀπ. δὲ φ. ἐκ δευ. ἐκ τ. οὐρ. 𝔓⁴⁵·⁷⁴ ℵ A 81. 945. 1739 *pc* ‖ ἐγένετο (+ δὲ Dᴬ) φ. ἐκ τ. οὐρ. πρός με D* (*respondit vero vox de caelo ad me* d) sa mae.

The reading of B03 repeats the expression ἐκ δευτέρου found in the narrator's account of 10.15 and records the second occurrence of the voice as a continuation of the dialogue. The D05 reading mentions the voice as if it were simply the vehicle for the words that were spoken rather than of interest for its own sake – no connective, no ἐκ δευτέρου – but underlines the fact that the voice was addressed to Peter personally: πρός με (cf. 10.15; see Read-Heimerdinger, *The Bezan Text*, pp. 176–82, esp. 182). The reading of d05 is a conflation of the readings of B03 and D05.

11.12 (αὐτοῖς) μηδὲν διακρίναντα (-νοντα ℵ* E Ψ) B ℵ² A (E Ψ) 33. 81. 945. (1175). 1739. 1891 *al* | μηδ. -νόμενον (-νόμενος 1241. 1837) H L P 049. 056 𝔐 | μηδ. ἀνακρίναντα 𝔓⁷⁴ ‖ *om.* D d 𝔓⁴⁵ᵛⁱᵈ 1 p* syʰ.

The Spirit's instruction to Peter to go to Caesarea without any kind of prevarication was noted at 10.20, using the middle voice of the verb διακρίνομαι. The sense of the middle can be either 'hesitate' or 'dispute' (cf. 11.2b), whereas the active, used here by B03, has more the sense of 'discriminate'. It will be used again in this sense at the Jerusalem Council at 15.9. According to D05, Peter omits to mention this instruction when he reports to brethren in Jerusalem what the Holy Spirit said to him in Caesarea.

(ἦλθον) δὲ B 𝔓⁷⁴ ℵ *rell* ‖ *om.* D (d) 1838.

D05 has another sentence (cf. 11.9 above) that has no connecting word linking it to the previous one.

11.13 (εἶδεν) τὸν ἄγγελον B 𝔓⁷⁴ ℵ A E 33. 1739 𝔐 co ‖ ἄγγ. D 𝔓⁴⁵ Ψ.

The article in B03 is anomalous since the angel has not been mentioned before by Peter.

(εἰπόντα) αὐτῷ D d E H L P Ψ 049. 056. 33. 1739 𝔐 latt sy ‖ *om.* B 𝔓⁷⁴ ℵ A 6. 81 *pc*.

It happens with some frequency that D05 specifies the addressee of a speech where the AT does not; it is typical for the dative case to be used rather than πρός + accusative when a conversation is related by a third party (Read-Heimerdinger, *The Bezan Text*, pp. 176–78; 181–82).

11.15 (λαλεῖν) αὐτοῖς D d p vgˢ aeth; Aug ‖ *om.* B 𝔓⁷⁴ ℵ *rell*.
The comment on the previous *vl* is equally valid here, too.

ἐπέπεσεν B 𝔓⁷⁴ ℵ *rell* ‖ ἔπεσεν D, *cecidit* d.

This same variant was found in the parallel verse in the narrator's account, 10.44 (see *Critical Apparatus*). On both these occasions in D05, but on no others, the simple verb is used rather than the compound to express the coming of the Spirit.

ἐπ᾽ αὐτούς B 𝔓⁷⁴ ℵ Dᴮ *rell, super eos* d ‖ ἐπ᾽ αὐτοῖς D.

The accusative of B03 matches the accusative in the following clause, ἐφ᾽ ἡμᾶς, and corresponds to the parallel account of 10.44 (ἐπὶ πάντας). The dative of D05 would not normally be used with ἐπί after a verb of movement but there is another occurrence of πίπτω with ἐπί + dative at 20.10 D05.

ὥσπερ (καὶ ἐφ᾽ ἡμᾶς) B 𝔓⁷⁴ ℵ *rell* ‖ ὡς D.

The variant was also noted at 10.47, the parallel verse of the previous scene though there the situation was the reverse, for D05 was the sole witness to read ὥσπερ and all other MSS read ὡς. According to B03, Peter would have used the stronger term of comparison in speaking with Cornelius but the weaker one when speaking with the brethren in Jerusalem, as if he wanted to insist to Cornelius as a Gentile on his equality with the Jews; D05, on the other hand, has Peter use the stronger term in Jerusalem, emphasizing to his Jewish brethren how similar was the Gentiles' experience of the Holy Spirit to their own, whereas it was not necessary for him to stress this point to Cornelius.

11.17 (αὐτοῖς) ὁ θεός B 𝔓⁷⁴ ℵ *rell* ‖ *om.* D d vgᵂ; Aug Rebap.

The subject of the verb ἔδωκεν is held over to the end of Peter's question in D05, while it is made explicit in the first part of the sentence in B03.

(τὸν θεὸν) τοῦ μὴ δοῦναι αὐτοῖς πνεῦμα ἅγιον πιστεύσασιν ἐπ᾽ αὐτῷ D d 467 (p) w (vgᴰᴼᴼ syʰ** mae) ‖ *om.* B 𝔓⁷⁴ ℵ *rell*.

The reading of D05 is not empty repetition but reiterates the critical element of his argument to make it quite clear to those he is speaking to. It has the effect of making the participle πιστεύσασιν in the first part of Peter's sentence refer to the Jewish believers, in parallel to the second occurrence of the participle where it is a reference to the Gentile believers.

The expression used for the Holy Spirit in the D05 reading is the usual one when the Spirit is referred to in a general way as God's gift, for example, rather than for any precise activity (such as prophesying; Read-Heimerdinger, *The Bezan Text*, pp. 160–61, 162). Just before, in contrast, Peter had used the form that is the one typically used when explaining an incident concerning the Holy Spirit, τὸ πνεῦμα τὸ ἅγιον (*The Bezan Text*, pp. 163–64). The same duality of language can be seen in the narrator's account, 10.44, 45 D05*.

11.18 ἐδόξασαν B 𝔓⁷⁴ ℵ Dᴮ 056. 81. 104. 440. 547. 614. 945. 1175. 1241. 1611. 1739. 1854. 1891. 2147. 2344. 2412. 2492 *al*, *clarificaverunt* d ‖ -ζον A E H L P Ψ 049. 33. 88 𝔐 | ΕΔΟΞΑΝ D*.

A syllable has clearly dropped out of the D05* verb – this could either be -σα- of the aorist (= B03) or -ζο- of the imperfect (= 𝔐). The most likely explanation is that D05 read the imperfect and the syllable ΖΟ dropped through homoioteleuton: ΕΔΟΞΑ<ΖΟ>Ν ΤΟΝ ΘΝ.

τὴν (μετάνοιαν) B 𝔓⁷⁴ ℵ *rell* ‖ *om.* D 2147 sa mae.

The article in B03 causes the reference to repentance take on a specific character, i.e. the repentance that Peter has already so often talked about as being the condition for his Jewish audiences to receive forgiveness of sins and the Holy Spirit (cf. 2.38; 3.26; 8.28).

Commentary

Introduction 11.2a *Peter's Journey to Hierosoluma*
The first part of 11.2 in Codex Bezae prepares the way for the episode that follows, showing something of Peter's inner thoughts and intentions after the events in Caesarea and confirming the critical significance of the experience in his own life as well as that of his fellow-disciples.

11.2a Having shifted the scene of the action to Judaea in the previous verse (see *Commentary*, 11.1 above), the AT simply presents Peter as having arrived in Ierousalem in a subsidiary clause before moving into the account of the accusations brought against him (see 11.2b below). He appears to go to Ierousalem without any delay, as if in response to the news reaching the apostles and brethren in Judaea (cf. the apostles' rapid response when they heard the news about Samaria, 8.14; or their response later when they hear about Antioch, 11.22).

Note must be made in the AT of the Hebrew-derived form of the name for Jerusalem, which differs from the Hellenistic form in the Bezan text. It is not certain that the AT accords a theological importance to the spelling of the name, unlike the Bezan text which maintains a clear distinction with the Hebrew-derived spelling signifying the religious centre of Judaism and the alternative form designating the city as a neutral location (see *General Introduction*, § VII). In the AT, the last mention of the apostles had situated them in Hierosoluma (8.14, cf. 'Peter and John returned to Hierosoluma', 8.25 AT and D05); and when mention is next made of news about the Gentiles reaching Jerusalem, it is the Ierousalem church that is specified (11.22, 'the church that was in Ierousalem' underlined by AT). The fluctuation between the two spellings in the AT suggests that a pattern is not being observed. That said, the placing of the apostles in Ierousalem here in 11.2a, when they challenge Peter's openness to the Gentiles, does concord with the conservative view-point characterized by the Jewish institution located in Ierousalem, just as it does at 11.22 when the Ierousalem church sent Barnabas to see what was happening in Antioch.

The Bezan reading of Hierosoluma is entirely in accordance with the pattern of spellings that can be observed in Codex Bezae where Hierosoluma is a name with positive connotations, meaning that Peter has detached himself from the religious authority of Ierousalem and, moreover, had acquired a measure of understanding concerning the spread of the gospel beyond the confines of Judaism. This was seen after his experience in Samaria in the company of John for, although he had gone to Samaria from Ierousalem (8.14 D05, cf. 8.1d D05), he returned to Hierosoluma once he had seen for himself how the Holy Spirit was given to the Samaritans even though they were considered to be outside Judaism (8.25). It is therefore to Hierosoluma that he wished to go after his experience in Caesarea, with no intention of returning to the Jewish institution represented by Ierousalem.

The whole of the account of Peter's movements between Caesarea and Hierosoluma is presented from Peter's point of view, providing glimpses into his intentions and plans in preparation for his visit, insights that are absent from the AT.[230] The sentence in Greek is a complex one, made up a series of participles whose relationship to each other is not always obvious. According to our analysis (see *Critical Apparatus*), it is made clear from the outset that it is Peter's decision to go to see the brethren in Hierosoluma and that he goes when he is ready, after spending quite some time in Caesarea.[231] He took with him the six Jesus-believers who had gone with from Joppa (cf. 11.12) and these may be included in the ones whom he called,[232] though the brethren from the villages he had previously visited (cf. 9.31-43) are likely to be the ones principally intended. He strengthened[233] them and taught them at length[234] as he travelled through the villages[235] on the way to his destination. As far as the six Jewish believers who accompanied him are concerned, it may be surmised that the reason why Peter would take such special care to consolidate their understanding was to prepare them for the opposition that was

---

230. A similar interest in inner thoughts can be observed in relation to Paul, cf. 19.1 D05; 20.3-4; 21.13.

231. For διά + genitive with the sense of 'after', cf. Mk 2.1; Acts 24.17; 27.5 (*vl*); Gal. 2.1 (cf. B-D-R, § 223.2b); for ἱκανὸς χρόνος, cf. Lk. 8.27; 20.9; 23.8; Acts 8.11; 14.3; 27.9.

232. προσφωνέω is only used by Luke in the New Testament apart from a parallel passage of Matthew. It has the sense of 'call/shout out loud' (Lk. 7.32 [par. Mt. 11.16]; 13.12, not D05; 23.20; Acts 21.40; 22.2) except once where it means 'call to oneself' as here but where D05 has the simple instead of the compound verb (ἐφώνησεν, Lk. 6.13 D05 [Jesus calls his disciples]).

233. ἐπιστηρίξας: the verb ἐπιστηρίζω is used of Barnabas and Paul, 14.22; Judas and Silas, 15.32; Paul, 15.41; 18.23 D05 (στηρίζω AT).

234. πολὺν λόγον ποιούμενος, cf. 2.40; 13.44 D05; 15.32, not D05; 18.6 D05; 20.2 (with παρακαλέσας AT; χρησάμενος D05).

235. διὰ τῶν χωρῶν: διά + genitive is used here in a local sense (B-D-R, § 223.1), cf. Lk. 6.1; Acts 9.32; 20.3 and *passim*.

bound to arise from the Jewish Jesus-believers who did not accept that the Gentiles could be brethren.

To explain the extensive Bezan reading as arising from a desire to avoid the negative impression that Peter was subjected to the control of the Jerusalem brethren, or to create a positive parallel between Peter and Paul[236], or to play down the Gentile problem,[237] is to miss the immense significance of this paragraph in Luke's portrait of Peter. Its importance lies in the connection it makes with the warning Jesus gave to Peter before his death. It will be recalled that during the evening of the Passover meal Jesus shared with the apostles (Lk. 22.14-38), Jesus warned Peter that he would deny knowing him three times (v. 34). But first, addressing him by his original name, Simon, he had told him that Satan had demanded to 'sift you [pl., the apostles] like wheat' (v. 31) but that he had prayed for Peter that his faith would not fail; he also had given him a command: 'And you (sing.), when you have turned (As for you, you must turn and, D05), strengthen your brethren' (στήρισον τοὺς ἀδελφούς σου, v. 32). Now, nowhere in Luke's writings is the fulfilment of this order recorded, nor is it followed up in any way – except, that is, here in the text of Codex Bezae where the very word 'strengthen' reappears with the 'brethren', following the echo of Peter's denial that was heard in the previous episode (10.13-16, see *Commentary*) and his grasp at last of the fact that Jesus had come for all the Gentiles without demanding that they first become Jews, and once he had turned from his restricted understanding of Jesus' message that he had been preaching (see *Excursus* 5).

The fulfilment of Jesus' prophecy concerning Peter is generally situated by exegetes at the time of his bitter remorse when he heard the cock crow after his threefold denial of Jesus (Lk. 22.61-62). However, tears of regret are by no means a sign of conversion (cf. Simon Magus who 'did not cease weeping copiously', Acts 8.24 D05) and furthermore, the portrait of Peter in Codex Bezae is one of a disciple who does not faithfully or consistently follow his master's teaching from the beginning[238] but rather learns and understands as he sees God intervening in people's lives.

Once in Hierosoluma, Peter maintains the initiative in speaking to the disciples there,[239] presented as 'the apostles and the brethren in Judaea' at 11.1.

---

236. Metzger presents both the negative and the positive reasons for the 'expansion in the Western text', citing J. Crehan, 'Peter According to the D-text of Acts', *Theological Studies* 18 (1957), pp. 596–603 (*Commentary*, pp. 337–38).

237. E.J. Epp (*The Theological Tendency of Codex Bezae Cantabrigiensis in Acts* [Cambridge: Cambridge University Press, 1966], pp. 105–107) interprets the Bezan reading as an indication that Peter's visit to Jerusalem was not prompted by the Gentile problem, a problem that is 'a sort of excuse for Peter to go there' since he was planning on going sometime anyway.

238. See *The Message of Acts*, I, pp. 107–39, esp. 115–21.

239. See Boismard, *The Texts of Acts*, p. 152 on the use of the personal pronoun after mentioning a locality: 'the personal pronoun "them" refers to the inhabitants of the country just mentioned ("there" = Jerusalem); such an anomaly in style is also found in Acts 8.5, 14; 16.4, 10

At 8.1b Luke noted that all the disciples had to leave Jerusalem (Hierosoluma) following the death of Stephen and that they had been scattered throughout Judaea and Samaria. Only the apostles had remained behind, in Ierousalem according to Codex Bezae. It would seem that by this time there was once more a group of believers present in the city, in addition to the apostles.

Peter began by telling them what had happened in Caesarea. In contrast to their initial opposition to him, they will be persuaded of the divine sanction of his behaviour among the Gentiles by the end of his speech; in this way, Jesus' order given to Peter to 'strengthen your brethren' (Lk. 22.32) is also fulfilled with respect to the apostles and it can be assumed that they, too, make the same steps forward in their understanding of Jesus' mission, following the example of Peter as the leader of the apostles (cf. 1.13, 15).[240]

[a] 11.2b-3 *The Negative Reaction of the Circumcision Brethren*
11.2b-3 In contrast to the joyous reception Peter may have been expecting, his news was met with objections on the part of 'those of the circumcision'. Codex Bezae makes it clear with the word 'brethren' that they were disciples, not opponents to the Jesus-believers as on previous occasions of hostility (e.g. 4.1-2). The description of them as 'of the circumcision', the characteristic definition of a Jewish person, categorizes them as Jewish and refers to the Jewish Jesus-believers generally whom Peter was talking with. It is contrary to the story Luke has been telling so far to interpret, as commentators do, his reference to 'those of the circumcision' as meaning that there was at this stage a group among the Jewish believers who were particularly attached to the rite of circumcision (in contrast to the situation Paul was addressing in Galatia, cf. Gal. 2.12, τοὺς ἐκ περιτομῆς). Circumcision was held as essential by all Jews, and it is only with the events in Caesarea that the believers who were present there had altered their view. There are, as yet, no other disciples who do not consider circumcision to be a *sine qua non* of purity. The reference to the Jewish believers as 'of the circumcision' thus implicitly contrasts them with the Gentile believers whom Peter had left in Caesarea. A similar contrast was introduced in the previous scene in Caesarea where the Joppa disciples witnessing the pouring out of the Spirit on the Gentiles are also referred to as 'the faithful from the circumcision party' – they, too, were Jewish believers (see *Commentary*, 10.45). For the first time in his work, Luke thus sets up the matter of circumcision as an issue dividing the believers and distinguishing the Jews from the Gentiles.

The Jewish believers, then, objected to Peter and argued with him – they did precisely what Peter was instructed by the Spirit not to do (cf. 10.20; 11.12 AT). Their objection reflects the understanding that Jews were forbid-

[AT]; 20.2 [AT]; and in Luke 4.31 where Luke adds the pronoun αὐτούς to Mark's text'. To Boismard's list may be added Acts 17.15 D05 and 18.11 D05.
    240. See *The Message of Acts,* I, pp. 102, 116.

den to have any contact with Gentiles and especially not to eat with them (cf. 10.28). This precise objection was raised against Jesus in Luke's account of Jesus' ministry (by the Pharisees and scribes: Lk. 5.30; 15.2; by 'everyone': 19.7). Luke thereby encapsulates the essence of the Jews' problem with Jesus, and their problem now with this latest manifestation of God's plan: the mixing of the pure with the impure, Jews with outcasts in the Gospel, Jews with Gentiles in Acts. The Jews' reference to eating recalls Peter's vision of the food he was commanded to kill and eat (10.11-16) and confirms that this was the heart of the problem.[241] It is, however, a legalistic concern – the Jews appear not to be interested in what Peter has told them about 'God's grace' in Caesarea but are bothered about his socializing with the Gentiles there. The inappropriateness of their reaction is sufficient comment in itself on what was most important to them.

[b'] 11.4-17 *Peter's Explanation*
Peter's reaction was to set out the facts and let them speak for themselves. For all that his explanation seems to repeat the account of the previous episode, it is not a simple repetition of what has already been said. Certain details are left out, others are summarized, and yet others settle questions that were not raised, let alone answered, in the first account. The speech is structured in three parts that follow the events from Peter's point of view: [α] 11.5-10, his vision in Joppa, which sets out the basis for what follows; [β] 11.11-16, the subsequent events: the arrival of the men from Caesarea, the Spirit's instructions, the journey to Caesarea, information about the task assigned to him, the arrival of the Holy Spirit, Peter's recollection of Jesus' words; [γ] 11.17, his conclusion, that God accepts the Gentiles as equals with the Jews.

11.4 Peter takes care to explain the events in Caesarea exactly as he had experienced them, going back to how things had started.[242] He relates them 'step by step',[243] showing the connection between them both in time as well as in the divine plan.

---

241. Cf. the conclusion that sharing food with Gentiles was the most frequently cited indication of apostasy in the Diaspora in J.M.G. Barclay, 'Who was Considered an Apostate?', in Stanton and Stroumsa (eds), *Tolerance and Intolerance*, pp. 80–98.

242. The introduction to Peter's speech, ἀρξάμενος, is similar to the introduction to the exposition of Scripture by both Jesus (Lk. 24.27) and Philip (Acts 8.35). The sense is not so much chronological but theological, whereby explanation is given about a spiritual event by means of tracing a historical story.

243. The word is καθεξῆς, meaning lit. 'in order'; it is a term exclusive to Luke: in the Prologue to his work (Lk. 1.3) and again at 8.1, it denotes an order that is more theological than chronological since in neither case is Luke's concern with the strict time sequence of events but the theological connections between them (see J. Rius-Camps, 'Estructura i funció significativa del tercer cicle o Secció de les Recognicions (Lc 6,12–9,50)', *RCatT* 9 [1984], pp. 269–329). Elsewhere, though (Acts 3.24 and 18.23), the sense is a time or geographical sequence.

[α] 11.5-10 *Peter's Vision in Joppa*

11.5 Peter starts with himself, ἐγώ, not because he is going to try to defend himself but because he wants to insist on his inactive role in the events that took place in Caesarea. For a start, he was in Joppa, a city with a large Jewish population[244], though the term πόλις, 'city', indicates that there was probably at least some element of Greek inhabitants.[245] In other words, he had been working within Jewish circles; he had not intended to go to Caesarea nor did he go there on his own initiative. What Peter omits to say, however, is that he was staying in the house of a person considered unclean, that of Simon the Tanner. His silence about this person is in striking contrast to the underlining of Simon's role in the previous account (cf. 9.43; 10.6, 17b-18, 32). It avoids any chance that his listeners may interrupt him or find grounds for invalidating what happened while he was praying. Likewise, Peter makes no mention of the fact that he had asked for a meal, which would have caused even further outrage and diversion at this point (cf. 10.10).

He states that he was praying and though he leaves out the time detail, as he will throughout his account, he does include the detail that he was in a trance when he saw a vision, an indication that he had no responsibility for what he saw since he was not in charge of his mental faculties as he would have been had his state been one of normal consciousness. The description of the vision is similar to that given by the narrator in 10.11-12 except that Peter focuses on the appearance of the container – it was *like* a linen sheet[246] – whereas Luke had paid more attention to the theological significance of the communication between heaven and earth. He also describes how it came right up to him – there was no way he could have escaped it.

11.6 Peter is emphatic that he looked very carefully at what was in the container: there can be no question that he ignored its contents or made any kind of mistake about what was there. The list he gives is an inclusive summary of the animal kingdom, as on the original occasion except that here Peter makes particular mention of the wild beasts, animals that were almost all considered to be unclean.[247] In Codex Bezae, these animals are singled out from

---

244. S. Applebaum, *Judaea in Hellenistic and Roman Times* (Leiden: E.J. Brill, 1989), p. 20; Schürer, *History of the Jewish People,* II, pp. 110–14.

245. Schürer disagrees (*History of the Jewish People,* II, pp. 196–97); see Applebaum, *Judaea,* pp. 83, 165 on the use of Greek by the Jewish population.

246. In the Bezan (d05) text, Luke as narrator had simply said that the vessel was a sheet (cf. 10.11); see Read-Heimerdinger, 'Luke's Use of ὡς and ὡσεί'.

247. In the early chapters of Genesis, the word θηρία, 'wild beasts', is frequently employed in LXX as a generic term rather than as a reference to a specific type of animal (Gen. 2.19; 3.1, 14; 8.17; 9.5; cf. Lev. 11.27). On occasions, it also refers to specifically to harmful, wild animals (e.g. Gen. 37.20, 33; Exod. 23.11, 29; Lev. 26.6, 22). At times, θηρία are distinguished as a class of animal separate from domestic animals (cf. Gen. 7.14, 21; 9.10; Lev. 25.7), or separate from birds and reptiles (Gen. 8.19; 9.2) but are not categorized as forbidden meat. Nevertheless, among the laws regulating the consumption of flesh (Lev. 11.1-47), a distinction is made among the animals

among the four-footed creatures, giving special emphasis to the surprising fact that he even saw forbidden non-domestic animals in the receptacle. Peter is at pains to convey to his Jerusalem interrogators that at every stage he noted what was happening in accurate detail.

11.7 Peter moves on to describe the voice, repeating the words exactly as given in 10.13. The report of the words would have a particular impact on the apostles who, realizing that it was Jesus who spoke to Peter, would recognize his attitude to the impurity regulations that had become so familiar to them during their time with him. The calling of Peter by the name Jesus himself had given to Simon would also have resonated with them, knowing as they did how hard-headed and slow to learn their fellow-disciple could be (see *Commentary*, 10.13). The apostles will register not just that Peter heard a divine voice commanding him to ignore the most fundamental of Jewish regulations but that Jesus their master had told him to do so, Jesus whom they knew and had learnt to trust.

11.8 Peter's answer is reported in much the same way as by the narrator (cf. 10.14) but is expressed in even stronger terms: impure food has never entered his mouth. What this means is often overlooked by modern readers, but if Peter's attitude of mind is to be properly understood at this point it is essential to pay attention to what he is saying: it is now some time since Jesus had died, come back to life and ascended to heaven; since the apostles have been responsible for announcing the message of Jesus to people in Jerusalem, Judaea and Samaria; since they have been opposed by the Temple authorities; and since they set up their own communities under their authority having ceased to worship in the Temple. Yet Peter (so he claimed) at the time of his vision, and all the other disciples of the circumcision now as he addresses them, still maintained strict observation of purity laws. Peter is careful to tell his audience what his answer to Jesus was so that they know that he was continuing to comply with the regulations they all believed were still in force – though he chooses not to tell them that just before his vision he had asked an unclean household to prepare him a meal (see *Commentary*, 10.10). For all the apostles' training by Jesus, and their filling with the Holy Spirit and their freedom from traditional thinking about the Temple, they continued to believe that the food laws were essential to please God. This insistence on the part of Peter, and of Luke, will of course be important for Theophilus if he is indeed a member of the high priestly family who would know better than anyone the inviolable nature of the Jewish food purity laws (see *General Introduction*, § IV).

---

of the land between the clean animals and the unclean – the ones permitted for food were characterized by their cloven hooves and the fact that they chew the cud. Such features are absent from most wild animals (a list of seven exceptions is given in Deut. 14.5) and in consequence they were necessarily impure (see *Jewish Study Bible*, pp. 228–29).

11.9 Peter goes on to explain what the voice said when he refused to obey the initial commands, with the Bezan text making clear that the voice was addressed in personal terms to him: he is not to impose human regulations where God makes none. And of course, as is implied, if Peter accepts all creation as pure, then the rest of the disciples can expect to do nothing less.

11.10 That the dialogue between Jesus and Peter happened three times was necessary because of Peter's refusal. At the same time, the repetition can leave no doubt in the disciples' mind that Peter heard the words correctly. It further gives him the justification he needs for having complied with the directions that were given to him. He could do no other, unless he were to maintain the attitude of denial he had adopted after Jesus' arrest (Lk. 22.34, 56-62) but which he had already bitterly regretted (22.62; see *Commentary*, 10.16). It is worth making the point again here that when Jesus warned Peter of his impending denial, he had addressed him as 'Peter' (Πέτρε, Lk. 22.34), even though moments before he had talked with him as 'Simon' (cf. 22.31), just as when he spoke to him in the vision he addressed him as 'Peter' as if to remind him that he, Jesus, knew Peter's hard-headed character and the difficulty he had in modifying his ways of thinking (cf. on 11.7 above).

[β] 11.11-16 *Subsequent Events*

The events following Peter's vision involve a series of six characters whose actions or words will serve as 'witnesses for the defence' to justify Peter's behaviour to which objection has been raised by the Jerusalem brethren. He makes it perfectly plain that he did nothing on his own initiative but only acted as he did because it had become impossible to do otherwise.

11.11 The first 'witnesses for the defence' are the three men sent from Caesarea to Peter at the house where he was staying. At no point does Peter mention that he was staying with a person considered unclean, nor does he explain that the three men were sent by a Roman centurion, nor does he even mention the name of Cornelius – all are details that would have obvious negative implications from a Jewish point of view. The care Luke portrays Peter as taking in order to avoid any risk of alienating his hearers before he has reached the end of his story is exceptional. This is a man who knows his audience very well indeed. The fact that there were three men (not specified in the narrator's account, cf. 10.17, 19 D05) validates their testimony (cf. Deut. 19.15, alluded to by Jesus, Mt. 18.16) and confers on it the traditional value of completeness by virtue of the number three.[248]

---

248. In Judaism, the number three expresses in particular the idea of 'completeness' (see E. Frankel, and B.P. Teutsch (eds), *The Encylopaedia of Jewish Symbols* (Northvale, N.J.: Jason Aronson Inc., 1995).

11.12 The second witness is none less than the Holy Spirit, referred to here without the adjective as is customary when talking among disciples.[249] Peter reports that the Spirit instructed him to go with the three men from Caesarea, omitting (according to Codex Bezae) to say how the Spirit had intervened to settle his doubts about the vision and to drive away any hesitations he had in accompanying the men (cf. 10.19-20). In seeking to convince his brethren of the truth of what he has experienced, it is important that he gives them no indication that there was ever anything less than certainty about what was happening, so giving no cause for doubting on their part.

Next to be named are the six men who had been travelling with Peter since they left Joppa for Caesarea and who had come to Jerusalem with him. They are important witnesses, for they are Jewish (cf. 10.45), they are Jesus-believers (cf. 10.23, 45), and had known Peter since the time of his stay in Joppa when he had brought Tabitha back to life (9.38-42). Above all, they saw and heard everything that happened in Caesarea. This is the first time that their number is specified (cf. 10.23b). The number is significant for it means that, together with Peter, there were seven believers who witnessed the entry of the Gentiles into the people of God. It parallels the number of Hellenist leaders (cf. 6.1-7), both occurrences being associated with the universal dimension of the gospel message.

Peter's narrative now moves into the plural as he recounts how all seven of them 'went into the house of the man' – there is still no mention of Cornelius' name or profession.

11.13-14 'The man' continues to be anonymous as he in turn is invoked as a new witness. His explanation of why he had sent for Peter is reported in direct speech, but certain details are once more omitted – that Cornelius had been praying, and fasting (cf. 10.30 D05); the time of his vision (cf. 10.3, 30); the appearance of the angel in bright clothing (cf. 10.30); the eager preparations made for Peter's visit (10.23-24 D05, 33 esp. D05); the name of the owner of the house where Peter was staying (cf. 10. 6, 17, 32). He does, however, include the double name of the person he is to send for: Simon named Peter, which would be a reminder to the apostles hearing this account of the warnings they had heard Jesus give him (cf. on 11.7, 10 above). This name, if nothing else, would let them know that it was Jesus speaking (see *Commentary*, 10.30). Peter also has 'the man' include some further information about the words spoken to him by 'an/the angel', namely the mandate for Peter to speak words[250] 'by which you will be saved', an echo of the prophecy of Joel cited by Peter at Pentecost (Acts 2.21).[251] It is only at this point that it becomes clear to the audience of Acts that Peter knew from Cornelius exactly

---

249. See Read-Heimerdinger, *The Bezan Text*, pp. 158–59.

250. ῥήματα, as at 10.22, 44.

251. σωθήσῃ, future passive, cf. Joel 3.5 LXX. Jesus proclaimed his mission as the Son of Man 'to seek and to save (σῶσαι) the lost' (Lk. 19.10).

why he had been called to Caesarea: to tell the Gentiles that salvation was not confined to Jews but was for them, too.[252]

Just as Jesus validated in a supreme way Stephen's testimony when he was on trial before the Sanhedrin (see *Commentary*, 7.55), so Jesus is a 'witness for the defence' on behalf of Peter, giving divine sanction to the words that he spoke in the house of a Gentile and that produced such a dramatic and unexpected effect. All the time, Peter is making sure that it is quite clear to his hearers that he did nothing more than Jesus told him to.

11.15 In the narrator's account, it was noted that the Holy Spirit fell upon Peter's hearers while he was still speaking, and his speech was interrupted by the manifestation of the Spirit (cf. 10.44). From Peter's point of view, he had hardly started to explain his message to Cornelius and the people assembled in his house. Certainly, he had not had time to develop his point about sin, repentance and forgiveness (cf. 10.43) before the Spirit came. What struck Peter (he mentions it three times, 10.47; 11.15, 17) is that the way the Spirit fell on the Gentile listeners was identical to the way they, Peter and the other Jewish believers, had received the Spirit at Pentecost (cf. 2.3-4). On that occasion, they had been sure that the Spirit had been poured out in fulfilment of the promise given to Israel and awaited by Israel for so long (cf. 1.4; 2.33).[253] Peter had been aware that all the nations would be eventually included in the promise[254] but, judging from his reaction of surprise now when the Spirit has been poured out on the Gentiles, he had not expected it to be a present reality nor to occur without any further messianic developments (cf. 3.21). In view of what he has witnessed, he has had to revise his understanding, at last bringing it into line with Jesus' way of thinking (see *Commentary*, 11.1 above).

11.16 The change in Peter's understanding of the Gentiles' position in the divine plan is brought about by his reflection on the words of Jesus, invoked,

---

252. Salvation (σωτηρία) was traditionally associated with the Jews (cf. Jn 4.22), and was intended for the 'people' of the Jews (cf. Lk. 1.69, 71, 77; Acts 4.12; 7.25; 13.26), and Jesus extended the possibility of salvation to those on the margins of Jewish society (cf. Lk. 19.9: he [Zaccheus] also is a son of Abraham). It was his disciples, however, who were given the task of extending salvation to non-Jews (cf. Acts 13.47; 16.17); although the idea of Gentiles having access to God's means of salvation (σωτήριον) had been hinted at in the Gospel (cf. Lk. 3.6), it is not until the end of Acts (28.28) that it becomes fully realized. The theme of salvation is particularly strong in Luke's writing compared with the other evangelists: σωτήρ, Jn ×1; Lk. × 2 + Acts × 2; σωτηρία, Jn × 1; Lk. × 4 + Acts × 6; σωτήριον, Lk. × 2 + Acts × 1; σώζω, Mt. × 14 (+ 2 D05); Mk × 13; Jn × 6; Lk. × 16 (+ 3 D05) + Acts × 13.

253. The promise of the Holy Spirit is most clearly apparent in Joel 2.28-29 (3.1-2 LXX), but cf. *Targ. Isa.* 42.1b; 44.3b.

254. Peter's interpretation of Joel's prophecy in the Bezan text of Acts 2.16-21 is even more universalistic in tone than the AT but he does not recognize that the universal application is already valid (see *The Message of Acts*, I, pp. 165–201, esp. 181–84).

as it were, as his final witness. His 'remembrance' of them at this point is not just a matter of calling them to mind but a comprehension of them, as is frequently the sense of this expression in the Gospels.[255] The words pronounced by Jesus ('John baptized with water but you will be baptized with the Holy Spirit', Acts 1.5) were originally spoken by John the Baptist but with the additional words 'and fire' after the mention of the Holy Spirit (cf. Lk. 3.16). Jesus, omitting the mention of fire so as not to present the coming of the Spirit as a matter of vengeance and punishment (cf. Lk. 3.17), had apparently spoken of the baptism in the Spirit on several occasions (ὡς ἔλεγεν, 'he used to say', imperfect), which is also suggested by the Bezan text of Acts 1.5. What Peter appears to have understood with the falling of the Spirit on the Gentiles is that the time of the pouring out of the Spirit has arrived in all its fullness and that the promise is already complete.

[γ] 11.17 *Peter's Conclusion*

11.17 Peter's re-consideration of Jesus' promise as signalling the introduction of a new universal dimension to the people of God, leads him to the conclusion that the gift of the Spirit to the Gentiles can be nothing else than the work of God which he has no power to oppose or resist. Since the gift of the Holy Spirit fulfils the Father's promise (cf. Lk. 24.49; Acts 1.4-5, 8), then from the moment that the Gentiles receive the gift they have to be considered as equals to the Jews.

The question Peter asks has two elements: 1) who was he to hinder God? (cf. Exod. 3.11 LXX); 2) was he able to hinder God?

It is interesting that he uses the word κωλύω meaning 'hinder' or 'prevent', precisely the verb that the Ethiopian eunuch uses when he asks 'what is to prevent me from being baptized?' (8.36, see *Commentary*). This word has a formal, almost legal connotation of 'impediment', an obstacle that might stand in the way of some act being performed, and may well have formed part of the Jewish baptismal liturgy that Peter is echoing in his question.

Both parts of the question are, of course, rhetorical, implying the answer that he, Peter, was not someone with the power to stop God from giving the Spirit to the Gentiles. His reasoning seems inappropriate since he could not stop what had already happened[256] but the idea is that the gift of the Spirit was entirely God's action which Peter was in no position to object to, or refuse to acknowledge. In consequence, he could impose no further condition – that is, circumcision – before proceeding with water baptism of Cornelius and his guests and thereby confirming their place within the community of Jesus-believers, on an equal footing with the Jewish disciples.

---

255. With the verb μιμνήσκομαι: Mt. 26.75; Jn 2.17, 22; 12.16; Lk. 24.6, 8; Acts 7.18 D05 (as a neg.); 11.16; with the compounds ἀναμιμνήσκω: Mk 11.21; 14.72; Acts 16.35 D05, and ὑπομιμνήσκω: Jn 14.26; Lk. 22.61.

256. Bruce, *Text*, p. 233.

[a′] 11.18 *The Brethren's Positive Reaction*

11.18 The silence with which the brethren greeted Peter's account is an indication of their acceptance of his testimony.[257] When they did speak, it was to praise God which may be understood as expressed in the words reported in direct speech (especially if the Bezan reading is taken as the imperfect, see *Critical Apparatus*) or as followed by the reported words.

As may be observed, although the reaction is positive the Jerusalem brethren stop short of acknowledging that the Gentiles have been given the Holy Spirit without any prior act or confession of faith. On the contrary, their interpretation of the events in Caesarea is that the Gentiles have been granted the possibility of repentance that leads to life, a conclusion they draw with a degree of admiring surprise. The expression may be compared first, with the instruction of the angel to the apostles in the Temple prison (5.20) to 'speak to the people all the words of this life' where the life in question is a matter of salvation. Secondly, repentance was a theme addressed several times by Peter in his initial discourses (cf. 2.38; 3.26; 5.31)[258] and at 2.38 was presented specifically as a prior condition for the gift of the Holy Spirit. However, nowhere in the scene in Caesarea does repentance appear as a prerequisite – on the contrary, just as Peter begins to speak about repentance to Cornelius, the Spirit interrupts him and falls on the gathering without warning (cf. 10.44). So although the Jewish believers in Jerusalem have recognized that God has accepted the Gentiles, Luke does not present them as having grasped at this point the terms on which the Gentiles were accepted as equals with the Jews, or whether observance of the Mosaic Law or of circumcision were necessary. And it would seem that these remain unresolved questions for the time being, for they are brought up by certain disciples from Judaea at a later date. Luke leaves them on one side for now to concentrate on the 'conversion' of Peter which is his main concern at this stage in the narrative.

Meanwhile, the positive reaction on the part of the apostles and the brethren in Jerusalem brings to a close not only the episode in Jerusalem but also the sub-sequence concerning Peter and, indeed, the whole of the sequence relating the stories of the three characters, Philip (a Hellenist), Saul (a Hellenist and a zealous Pharisee) and Peter (a Hebrew). In this way, the various obstacles to the progress of the Gospel are cleared out of the way and the admission of the Gentiles into the community of Jesus-believers is assured. The stage is set for the ministry of Saul/Paul among the Gentiles in the second half of the book of Acts, but first, the story of the inclusion of the Gentiles in

257. The verb ἡσυχάζω is almost exclusive to Luke (Lk. 14.4; 23.56; Acts 11.18; 21.14; 22.2 D05; cf. ἡσυχία, Acts 21.40 D05; 22.2 AT). It has the general sense of 'rest', at times meaning to 'cease protesting' as here (cf. 21.14).

258. Compare δοῦναι μετάνοιαν τῷ Ἰσραὴλ καὶ ἄφεσιν ἁμαρτιῶν (5.31) with Ἄρα καὶ τοῖς ἔθνεσιν ὁ θεὸς [τὴν] μετάνοιαν εἰς ζωὴν ἔδωκεν (11.18). The D05 reading without the article before μετάνοιαν reinforces the parallel.

the Church is consolidated (11.19-26, 27-30) and the story of Peter's conversion brought to a final close (12.1-25).

[A'] 11.19-26b *Jews and Gentiles in Antioch*

General Overview

Having completed the sequence [B] that deals with the three key characters and the lessons they needed to learn, the narrator now returns to those disciples who had been scattered after the death of Stephen, picking up the story from where he had left it at 8.3 (Sequence [A]). This final sequence brings to a close the section overall (Section II). The steps taken by each of the three key characters in the previous sequence prepared the way for the break with the synagogue, which is noted in the final colophon that brings the section to a close at 11.26c.

Structure and Themes

The sequence consists of three episodes, essentially set in Antioch though brief glimpses are seen of both Ierousalem and Tarsus, and the overall theme is the establishment of a church that is made up of both Gentile and Jewish believers.

The opening episode brings back the Hellenist disciples, picking up the narrative from where it broke off at 8.3 with the dispersion of the Hellenist disciples following the death of Stephen; they are the first to arrive in Antioch. The second episode brings back into the story Barnabas who, last seen assisting Saul in Ierousalem, still has associations with the Ierousalem church and is sent by them to Antioch when they hear about the Hellenists' activity there. Barnabas, in turn, gets Saul to come to Antioch when he hears he is in the vicinity of Tarsus, so creating a third episode. To each fresh arrival in Antioch corresponds a large number of disciples whom the leader(s) evangelize (the Hellenists) or exhort (Barnabas) or bring together ([D05; teach, AT] Barnabas and Saul). The omission in the Bezan text of the mention of teaching is almost certainly intentional (see *Critical Apparatus*).

The three parallel episodes are as follows:

> [A'-A] 11.19-21   The Hellenists in Antioch
> [A'-B] 11.22-24   Barnabas is sent to Antioch
> [A'-A'] 11.25-26b Barnabas and Saul in Antioch

A distinction between two groups of disciples in Jerusalem, such as was already noted in the corresponding sequence [A] 8.1b-3, reappears here: there is the church in Hierosoluma to which the Hellenists belong, characterized by their freedom with regard to the holy city, the Temple and the Jewish authorities; and there is the church of Ierousalem, represented by the apostles who are eventually to be replaced by James (see *Commentary*, 12.17), and who are characterized by their exclusivist Jewish attitudes and attachment to Jewish nationalistic ways of thinking.

[A'-A] 11.19-21 *The Hellenists in Antioch*

Overview

This is the opening episode in the final sequence of Section II, in which the narrative returns to the subject of the disciples who had to flee from Jerusalem at the time of the persecution that affected the church in Hierosoluma generally. The setting transfers to Antioch for the first time in Acts.

Structures and Themes

The first clause introduces the Hellenists, Jews whose origins were in the Diaspora (see *Excursus* 1), and then the second clause moves on to focus on a particular group who were active in preaching the gospel in Antioch. The important, new theme that is brought into the narrative of Acts for the first time here is the sharing of the good news with non-Jews. Since their initiative is part of God's plan for the Church, it meets with a favourable response. The linear structure of the three elements that make up this episode will be reflected in a similar structure in the following two episodes:

[a] 11.19 The Hellenists speak to Jews alone
[b] 11.20 Some speak to Greeks in Antioch
[c] 11.21 A large number turn to the Lord

Translation

Codex Bezae D05	*Codex Vaticanus B03*
[a] **11.19** Those who had been scattered because of the oppression that had arisen on account of Stephen, made their way to Phoenicia and Cyprus and Antioch, speaking the word to no-one except to Jews alone.	**11.19** Those who had been scattered because of the oppression that had arisen on account of Stephen, made their way to Phoenicia and Cyprus and Antioch, to no-one speaking the word other than Jews.
[b] **20** Some of them were men from Cyprus and Cyrene who, on arriving in Antioch, began speaking to the Greeks, announcing the good news that the Lord was Jesus Christ.	**20** Some of them were men from Cyprus and Cyrene who, on arriving in Antioch, began speaking to the Hellenists, too, announcing the good news of the Lord Jesus;
[c] **21** The hand of God was with them and a large number believed and turned to the Lord.	**21** and the hand of God was with them, and a large number who believed turned to the Lord.

Critical Apparatus

11.19 ἐπὶ Στεφάνῳ B ℵ H L P 049. 056. 1739 𝔐 | ἐπὶ Σ-ου 𝔓⁷⁴ A E Ψ 6. 33. 181. 945. 1898. 2344 *pc*; Theoph | *sub Stephano* d ‖ ἀπὸ τοῦ (– Dˢ·ᵐ·) Σ-ου D* p vg^Rmg.

The preposition ἐπί + dative read by B03 has the sense of 'over', i.e. 'on account of', whereas ἐπί + genitive means 'in the time of'. The causal sense of B03 can also be conveyed by the D05 reading ἀπό + genitive ('arising out of', cf. Delebecque, *Les deux Actes*, p. 78), but the preposition ἀπό could equally be taken to signify 'from the time of'.

The absence of the article before Stephen in B03 can be explained by the fact that no mention has been made of Stephen since 8.2. By maintaining the article, D05 ties the two parts of the story of the scattered disciples closely together (Read-Heimerdinger, *The Bezan Text*, pp. 123–25).

(μηδενὶ) λαλοῦντες τὸν λόγον B 𝔓⁷⁴ ℵ *rell* ‖ τ. λόγ. λαλ. D d.

The word order variation causes no difference in meaning but the order of D05 confers a certain emphasis on the activity of the travelling disciples; in the order of B03, speaking the word is presented as if it could be taken for granted that this would be their expected activity.

('Ιουδαίοις) μόνον B 𝔓⁷⁴ ℵ *rell* ‖ μόνοις D d 33. 614. 913. 945. 1518. 1611. 1739. 2412 *pc* lat; Chr^pt Cass.

B03 reads the adverb, where D05 reads the adjective qualifying 'Ιουδαίοις. The latter draws more attention to the Jews as the only beneficiaries of the disciples' evangelizing.

11.20 (ἐλάλουν) καὶ (– 𝔐) πρὸς τοὺς Ἑλληνιστάς B D^F E H L P Ψ 049. 056. 0142. 614. 1739 𝔐 | πρ. τ. εὐαγγελιστάς ℵ* ‖ (ἐλάλουν + καὶ 𝔓⁷⁴ A) πρ. τ. Ἕλληνας D* (𝔓⁷⁴) ℵ² (A) 383. 1518. 1611. 2138 *pc* (*cum Graecos* d [*sic*]); Eus Chr^pt Ps-Oec Theoph.

B03 mentions the 'Hellenists', which is otherwise used by Luke to mean the Jews of Greek-speaking origin (6.1; 9.29; see *Excursus* 1). Here, it is clearly Gentiles who are meant, as indicated by the D05 reading. Barrett (I, pp. 550–51) suggests that the term Ἑλληνιστάς could apply to Greek-speaking Gentiles but there is no evidence for this application outside Acts. The reading of ℵ01* is strange but seems to have arisen under the influence of the following word εὐαγγελιζόμενοι.

(τὸν κύριον Ἰησοῦν) Χριστόν D d 618 *pc* w mae ‖ *om.* B 𝔓⁷⁴ ℵ *rell*.

Contrary to popular perception, D05 does not add Χριστός indiscriminately in Acts (see Read-Heimerdinger, *The Bezan Text*, pp. 264–67; cf. Metzger, *Commentary*, pp. 225–26; Barrett, I, 551). When Χριστός is present in D05 but not in B03, it always follows ὁ κύριος Ἰησοῦς, never the name Ἰησοῦς alone (cf. 1.21; 4.33; 8.16; 11.20; 15.11; 16.31; 19.5; 20.21; 21.13) except for once when it follows ὁ παῖς Ἰησοῦς (3.13). Several of these occurrences arise in the context of the message of salvation (11.20; 15.11; 16.31; 20.21). At 11.20, its use picks up Peter's reference to the full title of Jesus at 11.17 in the context of the believing Gentiles, and it therefore contributes to the literary and theological cohesion of the narrative. It is also possible to interpret the clause in D05 as meaning 'they announced that the Lord was Jesus Christ', where 'the lord' would be a concept familiar to the Greek audience as usually referring to the Emperor (cf. 5.42 D05, where exactly the same reading is found and where the same interpretation could be given, except that there the concept of the Lord among Jews would obviously be associated with Yahweh).

11.21 καὶ ἦν (χείρ) B 𝔓⁷⁴ ℵ d *rell* || ἦν δέ D (τε p²).

The conjunction δέ in D05 brings the new sentence into sharper focus, causing the narrator's comment to stand out more than in the B03 text.

ὁ (πιστεύσας) B 𝔓⁷⁴ ℵ A 36. 81. 431. 453. 1175 *pc* || *om.* D E H L P Ψ 049. 056. 33. 614 𝔐.

The article before the participle has the effect of giving it an adjectival force, rendered in the English translation with the relative pronoun, and according slightly less prominence to the act of believing.

Commentary

[a] 11.19 *The Hellenists Speak to Jews Alone*

The first clause brings the Hellenists (cf. 8.1b) back into the narrative, as an introduction to the sequence overall. It is connected to the previous sequence with the connective μέν which, in turn, anticipates a second clause connected with δέ that moves the story on to the action proper.

11.19 The scattered disciples were believers from the church in Hierosoluma who had had to flee from the city when the persecution to which Stephen had been subjected spread to the disciples generally. 'Scattered', διασπαρέντες, picks up the Greek verb from 8.4 (cf. 8.1b), while 'oppression', θλῖψις, was also mentioned in the same context but only by D05 (8.1b).

By associating these disciples with Hierosoluma rather than Ierousalem (cf. 8.1b), Luke had already indicated their open-mindedness and the distance they had put between themselves and the Jewish Temple authorities (in contrast to the apostles; cf. 11.22 below, and see *Commentary*, 8.1b). They are to be understood as predominantly of Jewish-Hellenistic origin, just as Stephen had been and also Philip who, as the second-named in the list of Hellenist leaders (cf. 6.5), acquires the role of their representative within the narrative perspective. 'Some of them' were originally from Cyrene and Cyprus according to the following verse, 11.20 (see *Excursus* 1).

So far, the gospel has been seen to be announced in various places outside Jerusalem: in Samaria (8.5, by Philip; 8.14, 25, by Peter and John); between Jerusalem and Gaza (8.26, by Philip); between Azotus and Caesarea (8.40, by Philip); in Judaea (9.32-43, by Peter). Furthermore, mention is made of disciples or churches in other places, too: in Galilee (as well as Judaea and Samaria, 9.31); in Damascus (Ananias, 9.10; Judas, 9.11; generally, 9.19b); in Tarsus (Saul, 9.30). Now, for the first time, localities outside Israel are mentioned as places where the gospel was announced: Phoenicia, in the far north bordering on Galilee, with its coastal towns that served as ports for Jerusalem – the relationship between Jerusalem on the one hand, and Tyre and Sidon in Phoenicia on the other, will be important in the story of Herod in Acts 12; Cyprus, the nearest island to mainland Israel, a vital trade link between Israel and Alexandria and home of many Diaspora Jews, including Barnabas (cf. 1.23 D05; 4.36) – Cyprus will become the starting point of the mission of Barnabas and Saul in Acts 13; and Antioch, the capital of Syria and seat of the Roman governor – though it was a Roman city of considerable importance, again a large proportion of its population was Jewish. Antioch will become a focus of the narrative for subsequent chapters of Acts, its significance already hinted in this sequence with the repeated occurrence of the name (11.19, 20, 22b, 26a, 26b). The city has already been introduced into the narrative of Acts, but only in an oblique way, qualifying Nicolaus, the last of the seven Hellenists who, as 'a proselyte from Antioch' (6.5), represents the bridge between Gentiles and Jews in anticipation of the direction that the mission of the Hellenists will take. It is noteworthy that the name of Antioch first arises in this context of Gentile–Jewish relations since the church there will become the centre where the two peoples are equally accepted.

Initially, however, the disciples did not take the step of announcing the gospel to Gentiles, the wording of the Bezan text accentuating this point (see *Critical Apparatus*). It is unusual in Luke's writings for 'the word' that they spoke to be qualified neither by 'of God' nor by 'of the Lord', especially when referring to the gospel message as presumably it is here. A similar use of 'the word' on its own is found at 8.4 where Philip is said to have announced 'the word' to the Samaritans. At both places, since the listeners had already received the 'word of God' in the past, as the Torah, it may be assumed that 'the word' here is the gospel message.[259]

[b] 11.20 *Some Speak to Greeks in Antioch*

11.20 Having brought the narrative back to the topic of the dispersed Hellenists, Luke now moves the story on with an exception to what he had stated in the introductory summary. From among those who had been announcing the gospel in places outside Israel, he selects some whose origin was far away from the centre of Judaism: in Cyrene, at the edge of the Jewish world, in the extreme south-west (cf. 2.10) which, to some extent, had negative connotations from a Jewish point of view.[260] It is remarkable that this group of dis-

---

259. The term 'word of God' would have been unsuitable at both 8.4 and here at 11.19 (see *General Introduction*, § VIII).

260. It is 'a certain passer-by, Simon of Cyrene' (παράγοντά τινα Σίμωνα Κυρηναῖον) who is forced to carry the cross of Jesus (Mk 15.21 [cf. τὸν Σίμωνα παράγοντα τὸν Κυρηναῖον D05]; cf. Lk. 23.26, Σίμωνά τινα Κυρηναῖον [τινὰ Σίμωνα Κυρηναῖον D05]). Mark presents him as 'the father of Alexander [Greek name] and Rufus [Latin name]', symbolizing (τις confers on him the status of a representative) his openness to other nations.

ciples began to speak to non-Jews about Jesus on their own initiative, without any kind of vision or special instruction, in contrast to Peter who had required a great deal of persuasion by various means before he was even able to accept that it was permitted to share the gospel with Gentiles. The identification of their listeners as 'the Greeks' makes more sense than 'the Hellenists' a term which elsewhere in Luke's writings always refers to Greek-speaking Jews (see *Critical Apparatus*) whereas here it is clearly non-Jews who are meant.

What exactly these disciples announced varies not only according to the text followed but also the way the Greek is construed (see *Critical Apparatus*). The variant is that the Bezan text reads 'Christ' after 'the Lord Jesus' but not so the AT; in either case, the sentence could be translated: 'they announced the good news of the Lord Jesus (Christ)'. However, it is also possible in constructions that use a verb of speaking followed by the contents of the message spoken that the verb 'to be' is implied so as to give the sense: 'they announced the good news that the Lord was Jesus (Christ)'.[261] This would be relevant in a situation where 'the Lord' would be an existing concept, either as the Roman emperor[262] or, indeed, in so far as the Greeks would have had contact with the synagogue (as Nicolaus apparently had), as Yahweh. The wording of the Bezan text is identical to that used of the preaching of the apostles at 5.42, at the end of the first part of Acts which focused on their role, so establishing an implicit positive parallel between the independent Hellenist disciples and the first disciples chosen by Jesus. The designation of Jesus as the Christ, which was originally a title with quite specific Jewish connotations, may already be becoming a proper name but it is more likely that this happened later when the 'Christians', as they will now be called (cf. 11.26b), had completely separated from Judaism.

[c] 11.21 *A Large Number Turn to the Lord*
11.21 Luke typically refers to 'the hand of the Lord' to indicate divine approbation of an ongoing activity or situation (cf. Lk. 1.66, John the Baptist as a child), or comparable expressions: 'God was with him' (Acts 7.9, Joseph son of Jacob ; 10.38, Jesus his anointed); 'the grace of God was with him' (Lk. 2.40, Jesus as a child). Although in earlier references to 'the hand of the Lord', 'the Lord' would have been understood as Yahweh (cf. 3 Kgdms 18.46, χεὶρ κυρίου ἐπὶ τὸν Ἠλίου), the title has now been transferred to Jesus who has just been identified as the Lord (cf. 11.20) and who will be referred to three more times in the following clauses (vv. 21b, 23, 24b).[263] In this way, through their master's endorsement, the Hellen-

261. In the Bezan text, linguistically the interpretation could also be 'they announced the good news that the Lord Jesus was the Christ', but this would have little sense in a Gentile context where the Lord Jesus is not yet known as such.

262. See Rowe, 'Luke-Acts and the Imperial Cult', pp. 292–93.

263. For an analysis of the use of the term κύριος in Acts, see Read-Heimerdinger, *The Bezan Text*, pp. 275–93.

ists' activity in Antioch is validated; the comment is brought into sharp focus in Codex Bezae with the conjunction δέ in place of καί in the AT. The result is closely connected with it (reinforced by the Greek conjunction τε), namely, the large number[264] of Gentiles who believed and turned to 'the Lord'. The mention of a large number of believers will be repeated twice in this sequence with the phrase 'a large crowd' (ὄχλος ἱκανός), once with reference to Barnabas (11.24b) and once with reference to Barnabas and Saul (11.26a).

[A'-B] 11.22-24 *Barnabas is Sent to Antioch*

Overview

The importance of this episode is to hint at the attitude of the church in Ierousalem towards the events in Antioch. Although the narrator simply notes here that they heard the news and sent Barnabas to Antioch, the difficulty the disciples in Ierousalem have with the acceptance of Gentiles into the Church because of their traditional Jewish attitude towards Gentiles as unclean will re-surface later in Acts 15.

Barnabas has already been established in the narrative as a character of exemplary generosity and with the gift of encouragement or exhortation (cf. 1.23 D05; 4.36; 9.27). His appearances so far have been brief, an indication in itself of the approval with which Luke views him and intends him to be viewed by his audience. He is a Hellenist from Cyprus but since the beginning he has been close to the apostles in his role as encourager (especially in the light of 1.23 D05) and in his ability to be a bridge between the apostles and those outside the apostolic circle (9.27). That the church in Ierousalem trust him at this point to investigate the happenings in Antioch is a mark of the high esteem in which he is held by them.

Structures and Themes

The structural pattern of this episode is similar to that of the first [A'-A], and will be repeated again in the third [A'-A']. This time, it is Barnabas who is reintroduced into the story and who arrives in Antioch where he has a positive effect on the gathering of disciples, composed of Gentiles and Jews:

[a]	11.22	The Ierousalem church send Barnabas to Antioch
[b]	11.23-24a	Barnabas exhorts the disciples in Antioch
[c]	11.24b	A large crowd is added to the Lord

---

264. The term 'number' is used repeatedly in Acts to designate those who became believers (cf. 4.4; 6.7; 16.5). There may be an allusion to the command given in Eden to 'be fruitful (αὐξάνεσθε), multiply (πληθύνεσθε) and fill (πληρώσατε) the earth' (Gen. 1.28 LXX), from where the verbs are also taken up in several places by Luke (Acts 6.1, 7; 7.17; 9.31 [D05 lac.]; 12.24; 19.20); the implication is that the Jesus-believers are fulfilling the commands of the Torah just as the Jews had done beforehand (cf. B. Barc, *Les arpenteurs du temps: Essai sur l'histoire religieuse de la Judée à la période héllenistique* [Lausanne: Éditions du Zèbre, 2000], p. 174).

Translation

Codex Bezae D05	*Codex Vaticanus B03*
[a] **11.22** The news concerning them came to be heard by the church in Ierousalem, and they sent out Barnabas to make his way to Antioch.	**11.22** The news concerning them came to be heard by the church that was in Ierousalem, and they sent out Barnabas to Antioch.
[b] **23** When he finally arrived there and saw the grace of God, he rejoiced and he exhorted them all to continue with the Lord by the determination of their hearts **24a** (for he was a good man and full of the Holy Spirit and faith);	**23** When he arrived there and saw the grace, that of God, he rejoiced and he exhorted them all to continue in the Lord by the determination of their hearts **24a** (for he was a good man and full of the Holy Spirit and faith);
[c] **24b** and a large crowd was added to the Lord.	**24b** and a large crowd was added.

Critical Apparatus

11.22 τῆς οὔσης (ἐν Ἰερουσαλήμ) B 𝔓⁷⁴ ℵ E Ψ 33. 36. 81. 88. 181. 431. 453. 467. 614. 915. 1108. 1175. 1518. 1611. 1852. 1898. 2138. 2344. 2412 *pc* d sy^h || τῆς D A H L P 049. 056. 1739 𝔐.

The present participle of εἰμί is found elsewhere in Luke's writing giving the sense of 'local' (Bruce, *Text*, p. 140; cf. 5.17; 13.1; 14.13; 28.17 [D05 lac.]). The reason for underlining the presence of the church in Ierousalem is theological – it is in Ierousalem not Hierosoluma (cf. 8.1b; *General Introduction*, § VII). In D05, the significance of the Hebrew-derived spelling is maintained throughout the book of Acts, whereas in B03 it is not always apparent; the participle οὔσης in this instance would seem to be an indication that the significance is recognized and the participle is necessary to make sure the significance does not go unnoticed.

ἕως Ἀντιοχείας B 𝔓⁷⁴ ℵ A 81. 629. 1175. 1642. 1739. 1891 *pc* vg sy^p bo aeth || διελθεῖν ἕως τῆς Ἀ. D* d (– τῆς E H L P Ψ 33 𝔐.) gig p sy^h sa mae.

The verb διελθεῖν in D05 picks up the reference to the travelling of the Hellenists from 11.19, with the article before Antioch echoing the previous mention at v. 20 in a similar fashion. That Barnabas should be sent to go over the route travelled by those who have been speaking with Gentiles in Antioch suggests that his mandate is to check the situation along the route as well as in the city itself. For further examples of the expression διελθεῖν ἕως, cf. Lk. 2.15; Acts 9.38.

11.23 (ὃς) καί D (gig) sy^p || *om.* B 𝔓⁷⁴ ℵ d *rell.*

καί in D05 has an adverbial force and ties in with the previous sentence in D05 which had Barnabas 'make his way' to Antioch, causing the city to be the final goal rather than the sole one. καί now brings the narrative to the point when he arrived in Antioch itself at the end of his journey.

(τὴν χάριν) τὴν τοῦ θεοῦ B ℵ A *pc* ‖ τοῦ θ. D d 𝔓⁷⁴ E H L P Ψ 049. 056. 614. 1739 𝔐.

The repeated article in B03 underlines the fact that it was God whose grace was displayed in the situation Barnabas found in Antioch. The expression is elsewhere read without the second article as in D05 (cf. 13.43; 14.26; 20.24). Metzger (*Commentary*, p. 343) assigns the presence of the article to the wrong MSS.

ἐν (τῷ κυρίῳ) B Ψ 181. 326 *pc* lat ‖ *om.* D 𝔓⁷⁴ ℵ A *rell* (*ad dominum* d) sy^{p.h} sa^{ms}.

B03 makes the relationship explicit with the preposition ἐν, thereby creating an expression used frequently by Paul, whereas D05 uses the dative case alone.

11.24 (ὅτι) ἦν ἀνὴρ ἀγαθός B D d 𝔓⁷⁴ A *rell* ‖ ἀν. ἦν ἀγ. ℵ 1175.

The reading of ℵ01, while giving particular emphasis to ἀγαθός, disrupts the word order of the phrase as it is found applied to the patriarch Joseph (*T. Sim.* 4.4; see *Commentary, ad loc.*).

(προσετέθη …) τῷ κυρίῳ D d 𝔓⁴⁵·⁷⁴ ℵ *rell* ‖ *om.* B*.

B03 is alone among the MSS in omitting τῷ κυρίῳ which would seem to be an accidental error.

Commentary

[a] 11.22 *The Ierousalem Church Send Barnabas to Antioch*

11.22 A passive expression is used to describe how the news of the activity of the Cypriots and Cyrenians[265] came to the attention of the church in Ierousalem, reminiscent of the impersonal construction read by the Bezan text of 11.1 where it was used to relate how the news of the conversion of the Gentiles had likewise been heard by the apostles and the brethren in Judaea (see *Commentary, ad loc.*; cf. 9.42, γνωστόν … ἐγένετο). Literally, the clause reads: 'the news was heard into (εἰς) the ears of the church', where the preposition εἰς expresses the idea that the news travelled until it reached Ierousalem.[266] The AT makes particular note of the fact that the locality of the church was Ierousalem,[267] as if conscious of the disturbance the news would create there above all places, at the centre of Jewish authority; the Bezan text of Acts, employing more systematically as it does the dual spelling of Jerusalem to distinguish the

---

265. περὶ αὐτῶν could be understood as a neuter, meaning the events in Antioch, but the series of pronouns referring to the Cypriots and Cyrenians (τινὲς ἐξ αὐτῶν … οἵτινες … μετ' αὐτῶν) makes it more likely that it refers to the ἄνδρες Κύπριοι καὶ Κυρηναῖοι personally.

266. For the pregnant use of εἰς in Acts, see Read-Heimerdinger, *The Bezan Text*, pp. 192–97.

267. For the participial use of εἶναι to express the idea of a local group, cf. 5.17; 13.1; 14.13.

spiritual centre of Judaism from the geographical location, does not need to draw special attention to the spelling of Ἰηρουσαλήμ here. In both cases, it is clear that it is the church that is still associated with the Jewish authorities that is in question, that presided over by the apostles as distinct from the church in Hierosoluma (ἐν Ἱεροσολύμοις) which was persecuted and from which the Hellenist disciples, present now in Antioch, were scattered (cf. 8.1b; see *Commentary, ad loc.*).

What would have been particularly disconcerting for the Ierousalem church is the fact that some Hellenist believers had taken a radically new step without instruction from or consultation with the apostolic authorities. There had been concern enough over the activity of Philip in Samaria (cf. 8.14a) which Peter and John had gone down to oversee. Then, it was the behaviour in Caesarea of Peter himself, the leader of the apostles, that had caused disquiet and that had only been settled when he explained in careful detail how he had taken no initiative in what had happened there (cf. 11.2-18); now, disciples without any authority at all were going against the beliefs and principles to which the Church had so far adhered, and worst of all, were doing so outside Jewish territory. There is here the germ of a problem that will beset Jewish Jesus-believers for some time afterwards and be a major cause of persecution by other Jews: the acceptance of Gentiles into the Jesus-believing communities. At this stage, while the Church is still continuing to function within the Jewish faith, as a type of Judaism, this development would amount to making proselytes, an activity that was carried on by other Jews, too, in the Diaspora especially.[268] While the matter of circumcision is not yet raised explicitly, it was bound to be an issue that would concern the Ierousalem leaders and that would be raised sooner or later (cf. 15.1), even if for the time being no demands for circumcision are being made.

The act of sending out Barnabas to Antioch is reminiscent, and probably deliberately so, of the periodic practice among the Jewish authorities of sending out from Ierousalem envoys, also known as 'apostles', to check up on the Jewish communities in the Diaspora (see *Excursus* 1). The Ierousalem church seemingly continue to see themselves as responsible for what is happening beyond the borders of Jewish territory (cf. 8.14; 11.2) and send one of their trusted members to Antioch. According to the Bezan text which takes up the same verb διελθεῖν, 'to make one's way', used of the scattered disciples in 11.19, he, in fact, has the task of finding out what had been happening along the way too, as if there was the possibility of other Gentiles who had 'turned to the Lord' elsewhere.

---

268. The topic of Jewish proselytism in the first century CE is much debated but it is likely that there was some deliberate activity in the Diaspora at least designed to convert people to Judaism; see J.C. Paget, 'Jewish Proselytism at the Time of Christian Origins: Chimera or Reality', *JSNT* 62 (1996), pp. 65–103.

Barnabas has already figured in the narrative of Acts as a disciple with a particular gift of encouragement or exhortation (cf. the meaning of his name given at 4.36; his support of Saul, 9.27a).[269] In Codex Bezae, an additional mention of him was made as one of the two candidates put forward by Peter to replace Judas (1.23 D05). At that point, according to the Bezan readings, the disciples had rejected him but it would seem from the mission entrusted to him now that his value was later recognized.

[b] 11.23-24a *Barnabas Exhorts the Disciples in Antioch*
11.23 Barnabas is not reported as finding anything to report before he actually arrived in Antioch at the end of his journey. His reaction, once there, was almost certainly unexpected for, far from being alarmed by the situation he found of Jews rubbing shoulders with Gentiles, he rejoiced at what he discerned to be 'the grace of God'. A play on words in Greek between χάριν, 'grace', and ἐχάρη, 'he rejoiced', brings out how well Barnabas was in harmony with the mind of God. Furthermore, he exercised his special gift by encouraging the believers – all of them, Jews and Greeks – to continue firm in the steps they had taken. In the circumstances, this is more than an exhortation to hold fast to a new-found faith in Jesus. True, some of the disciples in Antioch were new converts but others were already believers, including Cypriots like Barnabas himself, and had been responsible for announcing the good news of Jesus to the people of Antioch. The situation they all found themselves in was particularly precarious because of the unheard of co-existence of Jews and Gentiles, and it required their determination not to abandon what had been created in Antioch. Barnabas would be well aware of the likelihood of attempts that would be undertaken by other Jews to break up the mixed community but, realizing that it had come about through the work of God, persuaded them to stand firm in what they had discovered to be God's plan.

11.24a The positive endorsement given to Barnabas, that he 'was a good man and full of the Holy Spirit and faith', is forceful: not only is no such evaluation ever made of any of the apostles, it echoes that given to the leader of the Hellenists, Stephen ('full of faith and Holy Spirit', 6.5; 'full of grace and power', 6.8; 'the wisdom [that was in him, D05] and the [Holy, D05] Spirit with which he spoke', 6.10). Few people in Luke's work are said to be filled with the Spirit as a general, rather than punctual, state: it is said first of Jesus (Lk. 4.1), and then of the seven Hellenists (Acts 6.3), and of Stephen in particular as was noted above (cf. also 7.55). It will not be said of anyone else in Acts, least of all Saul/Paul whose trial appearances especially are characterized by the absence of the Spirit.[270]

---

269. For a detailed study of the role of Barnabas in Acts, see J. Read-Heimerdinger, 'Barnabas in Acts: A Study of his Role in the Text of Codex Bezae', *JSNT* 72 (1998), pp. 23–66.
270. See Rius-Camps, 'Gradual Awakening'.

Barnabas was not one of the Hellenists but had been a disciple of Jesus according to Peter's account in Codex Bezae (1.21-23 D05). In Acts 1 (as at 4.36), his real name is given as Joseph and it is apparent from a series of indications that Luke is aligning his character with that of Joseph the son of Jacob, the great hero of Diaspora Judaism who had kept the faith pure even when in exile in Egypt.[271] Among these is the narrator's comment here which is strikingly similar to the description of Joseph attributed to his brother Simeon in the *Testament of Simeon*:

> ἦν ἀνὴρ ἀγαθὸς καὶ πλήρης πνεύματος ἁγίου, Acts 11.24a
> ἦν ἀνὴρ ἀγαθὸς καὶ ἔχων πνεῦμα θεοῦ ἐν ἑαυτῷ, *T. Sim.* 4.4

Yet another Joseph introduced by Luke into his Gospel narrative is the only other person to be called 'good' in his work:

> καὶ ἰδοὺ ἀνὴρ ὀνόματι Ἰωσὴφ ... ἀγαθὸς [+ καὶ D05] δίκαιος, Lk. 23.50

It was a man like this who was needed, to be fully open to the universal nature of the gospel message in the here and now, and to dare to insist on its being acknowledged and maintained when it was manifested among the people of Antioch.[272]

[c] 11.24b *A Large Crowd is Added to the Lord*

11.24b The result, the same as was already noted following the preaching of the Hellenists in Antioch (see *Commentary*, 11.21 above), is that again the number of disciples increased, another sign of the presence of God with them. The process of the growth of the Church is now well underway and will be confirmed with a third increase in numbers at the end of this account.

[A'-A'] 11.25-26b *Barnabas and Saul in Antioch*

Overview

The third episode in the sequence brings back a third character, this time Saul who was last heard of heading for Tarsus when he had to flee from the Hellenists who were plotting against him in Jerusalem (9.29). Part of the significance of his return to the story is that he is seen working for the first time alongside Barnabas, the pair having previously been acquainted when Saul arrived in Ierousalem (9.26-27). In this episode, their association with the church in Antioch is established, and Saul's concern with Gentiles (also previously mentioned, by Jesus himself, 9.15) is given a specific object.

---

271. See *The Message of Acts*, I, *Excursus* 5, pp. 308–10.

272. Paul's criticism of Barnabas in Gal.2.13 is all the more surprising, although that of Peter is more expected (2.11-12).

Structures and Themes
The now familiar pattern of the episodes in this sequence is repeated for a final time, with first, the introduction of a new character, then his arrival in Antioch and finally, the gathering of a large crowd:

[a] 11.25   Barnabas looks for Saul in Tarsus
[b] 11.26a Barnabas exhorts Saul to come to Antioch
[c] 11.26b They were mingled as a large crowd

Translation

Codex Bezae D05

[a]   **11.25** On hearing that Saul was some-where near Tarsus, he went searching for him;

[b]   **26a** and, appearing to meet him by chance, he exhorted him to come to Antioch;

[c]   **26b** and when they arrived, for a whole year they were mingled together as a large crowd.

Codex Vaticanus B03

11.25 He went to Tarsus to search for Saul,

26a and having found him he brought him to Antioch.

26b It came about that they were assem-bled in the church for a whole year and taught a large crowd.

Critical Apparatus

11.25 ἐξῆλθεν δὲ εἰς Ταρσόν B 𝔓⁴⁵·⁷⁴ ℵ A 945. 1175. 1739. 1891 | ἐξ. δὲ εἰς Τ. ὁ Βαρναβᾶς E H L P Ψ 049. 056. 33 𝔐 ‖ ἀκούσας δὲ ὅτι Σαῦλός ἐστιν εἰς Θαρσόν (Ταρ- Dˢ·ᵐ·) ἐξῆλθεν D d gig p vgᴿᵐᵍ syʰᵐᵍ mae; Cass.— ἀναζητῆσαι Σαῦλον B 𝔓⁴⁵·⁷⁴ ℵ *rell* ‖ ἀναζητῶν αὐτόν D d gig p vgᴿᵐᵍ syʰᵐᵍ mae; Cass.

First, D05 makes explicit that the reason for Barnabas' going to Tarsus was that he heard that Saul was there and that he went there looking for him.

11.26a-b καὶ εὑρὼν ἤγαγεν (εἰς Ἀντιόχειαν) B 𝔓⁴⁵·⁷⁴ ℵ A 056. 81. 226ᶜ. 945. 1175. 1270ᶜ. 1739. 1837. 1891 | κ. εὑρ. αὐτὸν ἤγ. 88. 323. 440. 547. 927. 1241. 1505. 2147. 2344. 2495 | κ. εὑρ. ἤγ. αὐτόν E Ψ 614. 1611. 2412 | κ. εὑρ. αὐτὸν ἤγ. αὐτόν H L P 049. 1. 104. 226*. 330. 618. 1243. 1245. 1270*. 1646. 1828. 1854. 2492 ‖ καὶ ὡς (– Dˢ·ᵐ·) συντυχὼν παρεκάλεσεν (+ αὐτὸν Dᶠ) ἐλθεῖν D* (d gig p*, syʰᵐᵍ) mae.

D05 describes Barnabas' action overall in relation to Saul in more detail: the verb παρακαλέω has already been used of Barnabas, and is even given as the meaning of his name (cf. 4.36; 11.23); the participle συντυχών (from συν-τυγχάνω, 'meet', used only here and at Lk. 8.19 in the whole of the New Testament) preceded by the adverb ὡς has the sense of 'as if Barnabas just happened to meet Saul…'.

ἐγένετο δὲ αὐτοῖς καὶ ἐνιαυτὸν ὅλον B 𝔓⁷⁴ ℵ A (Ψ) 33. 614. 1611. 2344. 2412 | ἐγ. δὲ αὐτοῖς ἐν. ὅλ. 𝔓⁴⁵ E H L P 049. 056. 1739 𝔐, *contitigit vero eis annum totum* d ‖ οἵτινες παραγενόμενοι ἐν. ὅλ. D (gig p, syʰᵐᵍ mae).— συναχθῆναι (συναναχυθῆναι D^E Ψ, συναναχθῆναι 𝔓^74) ἐν τῇ ἐκκλησίᾳ καὶ διδάξαι ὄχλον ἱκανόν B (D^E 𝔓^74) ℵ A (Ψ) *rell* ‖ συνεχύθησαν ὄχλ. ἱκ. D* | *commiscere ecclesiam* d, *congregati sunt* sy^hmg | *commiscuerunt se ecclesiae et docebant turbam multam* p vg^Rmg (retroversion: συνεχύθησαν τῇ ἐκκλησίᾳ καὶ ἐδίδασκον ὄχλ. ἱκ.).

The passive of συνάγω in B03 is regularly used to express a reflexive sense, 'they assembled'. But since two people could hardly be said to 'assemble' (E. Delebecque, 'Saul et Luc avant le premier voyage missionaire', *Rev. Sc. ph. th.* 66 [1982], pp. 551–59 [552]) it could equally be a true passive here, with the meaning 'they were received as guests' (Lake and Cadbury, *Translation and Commentary,* p. 130). The infinitive is dependent on ἐγένετο at the start of the sentence with the dative αὐτοῖς as the subject of the infinitive συναχθῆναι following.

A different verb, συγχέω, is read by D05 meaning literally to 'pour together'. It is possible that the words ἐν τῇ ἐκκλησίᾳ καὶ διδάξαι have accidentally been omitted (cf. Delebecque, *Les deux Actes*, p. 80; and 'Saul et Luc avant le premier voyage missionaire', p. 552, where he does not recognize the original reading of D05*). Alternatively, the reading of D05 may be understood as it stands by taking 1) the pronominal phrase οἵτινες παραγενόμενοι referring to Barnabas and Saul as a 'nominative absolute' (cf. B-D-R, § 466.4, n. 5: 'etwas wie ein absoluter nominativ [statt gen. abs.] nach Klass. Art'); 2) the subject of the verb συνεχύθησαν, meaning to 'blur, mingle' (L-S-J, συγχέω), as the unspecified disciples in Antioch; and 3) the accusative ὄχλον ἱκανόν as an adverbial accusative of manner (B-D-R, § 160; Mayser, II/2, p. 328). In this way, the entire sentence describes the way in which the Jewish and Gentile disciples were brought together without discrimination as one large gathering for a whole year once Barnabas and Saul arrived in Antioch.

The infinitive in D^E turns the original construction into an accusative infinitive of which the 'great crowd' is the subject. In the MS, where the original is ΣΥΝΕΧΥΘΗΣΑΝ, Corrector E has made several modifications: erased slightly the E and written A over the top of it, then added the syllable NA above the X so as to obtain: ΣΥΝΑΝΑΧΥΘΗ-; at the end, D^E has further changed the second Σ into N, and used the first stroke of the final N for I and the second stroke for T, and finally completed the sentence above the line with ΗΕΚΚΛΗΣΙΑΚΑΙΔΙΔΑΞΑΙ; the result is practically the reading of the AT: ΣΥΝΑΝΑΧΥΘΗΝΑΙ ΤΗ ΕΚΚΛΗΣΙΑ ΚΑΙ ΔΙΔΑΞΑΙ.

Commentary

[a] 11.25 *Barnabas Looks for Saul in Tarsus*
11.25 The final elements of this sequence contain notable variants – although the content is roughly identical, the exact meaning is different. In the AT, without any preamble Barnabas goes to Tarsus in search of Saul. That he knew he would find him there is presumed from the last mention of Saul at the

end of the narrative concerning him (9.30), when it was said that the brethren in Ierousalem (9.28) helped him to escape from the hostility of the Hellenists by taking him to Caesarea from where they sent him out (ἐξαπέστειλαν) to Tarsus, his native city (cf. 9.11; 22.3). Since Barnabas had been present in Jerusalem at the time (cf. 9.27), it is reasonable to suppose that he knew where Saul had gone and that he would therefore think of going to Tarsus to search him out[273] when he was in Antioch.

It must be asked why Barnabas thought of fetching Saul to bring him to Antioch. As has already been learned through the story so far, Saul was a Hellenist with first-hand experience of persecution of the Jesus-believing disciples, both as persecutor and persecuted. This would have equipped him particularly well to help with the problems that were foreseeable in Antioch. In addition, it will be learned later, once the narrative turns to focus on Saul's ministry in particular, that he was a teacher (13.1), educated in the school of Gamaliel (22.3), and thus able to complement Barnabas' prophetic gifts.[274]

The Bezan text presents Barnabas's search for Saul with some subtle nuances. First, it is explained that he goes to Tarsus in search of him because he hears that he is there. The comment seems superfluous since, as noted above, Barnabas could be presumed to know that that was where he had gone after leaving the Jerusalem brethren. On the other hand, it could be supposed that Saul had not stayed there ever since and indeed, the preposition εἰς before Tarsus suggests movement towards, or in the vicinity of, the place (ἀκούσας δὲ ὅτι Σαῦλός ἐστιν εἰς Θαρσόν).[275] What Barnabas heard then was not just what he already knew, that Saul was in Tarsus, but that he was somewhere near Tarsus, as if he had been away from the city. The Bezan presentation of the search for Saul has a corresponding consequence in the following verse. The association of Saul with Tarsus reinforces his status as a Hellenist Jew which he himself seemed to want to ignore (see *Excursus* 1).

[b] 11.26a *Barnabas Exhorts Saul to Come to Antioch*
11.26a The AT continues with the bare elements of the story, relating that Barnabas found Saul and brought him to Antioch. Once there, they spent a year, 'assembled' or, more probably, being 'received as guests' (see *Critical Apparatus*) in the church. The 'large crowd' is mentioned again, the third

---

273. The verb ἀναζητέω refers to a search involving some difficulty (cf. Bruce, *Text*, p. 237).

274. Acts 13.1 speaks of there being in the church of Antioch 'prophets and teachers among whom Barnabas ... and Saul'. Barnabas' gift of prophetic exhortation and encouragement has already been seen on numerous previous occasions and will continue to be evident as he and Saul work together in various places. Saul, in contrast, is the one who is seen explaining the gospel and discussing the Scriptures (see, e.g., 13.16, 44).

275. In both the AT and the Bezan text of Acts, the distinction between εἰς and ἐν is generally maintained, εἰς in D05 always denoting movement even if it is implicit (cf. on 11.22 above).

time that reference is made to the considerable impact made on people in Antioch, whether by evangelizing (v. 21) or exhorting (v. 24) or, as now, teaching (v. 26).

The Bezan text continues with a second, nuanced description of events (cf. 11.25 above): instead of baldly stating that Barnabas found Saul, it uses the present participle συντυχών, 'meeting up with'[276] coupled with the adverb ὡς, suggesting that Barnabas wanted to avoid giving Saul the impression that he had deliberately sought him out with the intention of making him go to Antioch. The idea is that, from Saul's point of view, Barnabas seemingly just happened to come across him and then applied his gift of exhortation to per-suade him to go back with him to Antioch.

[c] 11.26b *They were Mingled as a Large Crowd*
11.26b The text of Codex Bezae raises a difficulty in the next clause. It is possible that a line has dropped out and that the sentence should read: 'when they arrived, for a whole year they were mingled [with the church and taught] a large crowd', the words in square brackets being accidentally omitted (see *Critical Apparatus* for full discussion of the verse). However, the text as it stands makes perfect sense: the verb translated 'mingled', συνεχύθησαν, literally means 'pour together' (συγχέω),[277] and is an entirely appropriate choice to describe the first time that Jews and Gentiles joined together within the same gathering, forming 'a large crowd'. On this interpretation, the subject of the verb 'mingled' is the believers of Antioch in general.

In the AT, on the other hand, Barnabas and Saul are the subject of the alternative verb 'assembled' and they are portrayed as teaching in the church in Antioch. Later (13.1), it will be seen that Barnabas was a prophet more than a teacher, which contradicts the AT picture of him here, teaching alongside Saul.

Colophon: 11.26c *A 'Christian' Identity*

Overview

A concluding comment for the whole section, standing outside the main structure, explains that the name of Christians was given to the disciples at this time, an indication that they were clearly distinguished from other Jews by their attachment to the 'Christ', Jesus the Messiah.

In Codex Bezae, the sentence stands as an independent clause, introduced with καί and with a finite verb. However, in Codex Vaticanus, the verb is an

---

276. The verb συντυγχάνω is only found here and at Lk. 8.19 in the whole of the New Testament.
277. B-A-G, συγχέω; cf. L-S-J, συγχέω.

infinitive followed by τε, dependent on the impersonal ἐγένετο of the previous clause and so cannot stand alone.

Translation

Codex Bezae D05
Col.   **11.26c** And it was then in Antioch that for the first time the disciples were called Christians.

Codex Vaticanus B03
11.26c … and that it was in Antioch that the disciples were called Christians for the first time.

Critical Apparatus

11.26c χρηματίσαι τε πρώτως Β 𝔓⁴⁵ ℵ 323. 1739. 1891 | χρ. τε πρῶτον 𝔓⁷⁴ A *rell* | πρώτως χρηματίσ[τ]αι Dᶠ ‖ καὶ τότε πρῶτον ἐχρημάτισεν D* (gig p, sy^hmg).— (ἐν Ἀντιοχείᾳ) τοὺς μαθητὰς Χριστιανούς Β Dᶠ 𝔓^(45).74 ℵ *rell* d ‖ οἱ μαθηταὶ Χ-οί D* (gig p, sy^hmg).

The infinitive in B03 is the third verb (following συναχθῆναι … καὶ διδά-ξαι) dependent on the initial impersonal ἐγένετο. D05 begins a new sentence with καί and the finite form of the same verb, conferring greater importance on the information. The difference in the case of μαθηταί arises from the differences in the preceding words.

Commentary

11.26c *The Disciples Were Called Christians*
11.26c The verb form is active in both texts (χρηματίσαι/ἐχρημάτισεν) but since it often has a passive force,[278] the meaning is ambiguous. If it taken in its active sense, Luke's observation means that it was in Antioch that the disciples began to call themselves Christians, adherents of Christ, for the first time. Their purpose would be presumably to distinguish them-selves from the Jews who did not believe in Jesus as the Messiah because their community included Gentiles with equal status to Jews. It is questionable, however, whether the disciples would have felt the need to self-consciously identify themselves in this way in a city like Antioch. On the other hand, the distinguishing features of the church in Antioch where, for the first time, Gentiles were admitted freely could have caused other Jews (in Antioch or elsewhere) who wished to dissociate themselves from such a heresy to label the Jesus-believers as a distinct group, using their insistence on Jesus as the Messiah (the 'Christ' in Greek) as a mocking term.

---

278. L-S-J, χρηματίζω, III.: 'in later writers, from Plb. [Polybius] downwards, the Act. χρη-ματίζω takes some special senses: 1. *to take and bear a title* or *name, to be called* or *styled* so and so … 2. generally, *to be called*'.

A third possibility is that it was the Gentiles of Antioch who labelled the group 'Christians' because of their proclamation of Jesus as the Christ – to a Gentile audience, the term would not necessarily mean anything since the concept of Messiah to which it refers was a Jewish one and so Χριστός, 'Christ', became a proper name with which to identify them.[279] Whatever its origins, the name 'Christians' was being used in Roman circles as early as the time of Nero, according to Tacitus,[280] the word sometimes being confused with the similar sounding χρηστός, meaning 'kindly'.[281]

The introduction of the name 'Christians' suggests that Luke's observation coincided in time with the entry of the Gentiles into the Church around the early 40's. This means that within 10 years, or even less, of the death of Jesus his disciples were no longer considered as simply Jews. Now that they have spread beyond the borders of Judaea and Samaria, the name of the Messiah, for all that it was a uniquely Jewish concept, has become the identifying mark of a group of people who stand apart, and 'Christians' will become the name that is handed down throughout the centuries.

The use of the adverb 'then' (τότε) in Codex Bezae serves to tie this moment when the disciples were identified as a group apart closely to the events in the church of Antioch.

279. A similar use of a proper name to identify a group is found in the 'Herodians' (Mt. 22.16; Mk 3.6; 12.13); see Barrett, I, pp. 556–57 for other examples.

280. Tacitus, *Annals*, 15.44; cf. Pliny, *Letters*, 10.96. For details of the Roman use of 'Christians', see H.B. Mattingly, 'The Origin of the Name Christiani', *JTS* NS 9 (1958), pp. 26–37. Ignatius uses it as a self-identifying label (*Eph.* 11.2; 14.2; *Rom.* 3.2; *Magn.* 4; *Pol.* 7.3), as early as the 90s CE according to the analysis of Rius-Camps, 'Ignacio de Antioquía'.

281. Bruce, *Text*, p. 238.

III. THE PUBLIC MANIFESTATION OF THE ANTIOCH CHURCH
TO JERUSALEM
11.27-30

Overview

The third section of the second part of Acts (Section III) is exceptionally short. It corresponds to the manifestation of the church in Jerusalem to Israel in 3.1–4.35 when the first Jesus-believers became recognizable as a group distinct from other groups within Israel. Now, it is a matter of the church in Antioch, the first to include Gentile believers on an equal basis with Jewish ones, which becomes identifiable as a distinct group within the Church in general, distinguished in particular from the church in Ierousalem. There was a long period of gestation (8.1b–11.18), starting with the first steps to take the gospel outside Jerusalem and culminating in the birth of the Antiochene church (11.19-26). Now, there follows a section that is brief and succinct in the extreme but that is of critical importance because it displays the church in Antioch as a self-sufficient and well-functioning community. Its very brevity is a typically Lukan procedure that indicates that everything was in order (cf. the presentation at 1.23 D05 or 4.36 of Barnabas whom Luke spends little time on but endorses as an exemplary model of discipleship). By the positive portrayal of the Antioch church, formed by the grace of God (11.23) and in tune with the Holy Spirit (11.28), Luke makes clear in one short account that the situation of the Church in general is developing according to the plan of God and that, in contrast, the church in Ierousalem (cf. 11.22), where the members are concerned about the entry of the Gentiles and insisting, as will be seen in time, on observance of the Jewish Law by the disciples of Jesus, is out of step with the truth of the gospel. Both those who initiated the preaching of the gospel in Antioch, disciples from Cyprus and Cyrene, and those who built the church up, Barnabas and Saul, were Hellenist Jews who were not dependent on the authority or the approval of the Ierousalem apostles and elders for their actions. The former had been acting independently since they fled Hierosoluma under the persecution (8.1b); Saul had left Ierousalem for the same reason (9.29-30); and Barnabas, although initially sent as an envoy by the Ierousalem church (11.22), had not referred back to them since arriving in Antioch.

Structure and Themes

Section III is made up of just one sequence composed of six elements, arranged in pairs so as to form three double elements made up of a main statement followed by a parenthetical comment (though the parenthesis is absent after the first statement in the AT):

[a₁]	11.27a	The arrival of prophets from Hierosoluma
[a₂]	11.27b	The exultation of the 'we'-group
[b₁]	11.28a	Agabus' prophecy
[b₂]	11.28b	The realization of the prophecy
[a′₁]	11.29	The decision to send aid to Judaea
[a′₂]	11.30	The carrying out of the decision

The overall theme of these few verses is the mutual exchange of spiritual gifts between the church of Antioch and the church in Judaea. The first double element relates the arrival in Antioch of a group of prophets from Hierosoluma (not Ierousalem, cf. 11.22) who put their prophetic gifts at the disposal of the church; an aside in Codex Bezae notes the positive impact their visit had. The central element consists of a prophetic warning concerning a famine which, again in an aside, the narrator confirms actually took place. The section is brought to a close with a report of the response of the disciples in Antioch to the warning, namely, to send relief to the brethren in Judaea; a final aside states that this did indeed take place, mentioning as bearers of the gifts the names of Barnabas and Saul whose visit will serve as a frame for the forthcoming section concerning the church in Judaea. The sending of help from Antioch to Judaea is the first indication in Acts of the theme of financial support given by the Gentile disciples to their Jewish brethren, a theme that will become prominent in the narrative concerning Saul/Paul.

Translation

Codex Bezae D05	Codex Vaticanus B03
[a₁] **11.27a** It was in these days that prophets came down from Hierosoluma to Antioch.	**11.27** It was in these same days that prophets came down from Hierosoluma to Antioch.
[a₂] **27b** (There was much exultation.)	
[b₁] **28** When we were gathered together, one from among them called Agabus spoke, indicating through the Spirit that there was about to be a great famine over all the inhabited earth.	**28** One from among them called Agabus stood up and indicated through the Spirit that there was about to be a great famine over all the inhabited earth.
[b₂] (This happened in the time of Claudius.)	(This happened in the time of Claudius.)
[a′₁] **29** So the disciples, depending on how they prospered, determined each one of them to send something as a service to the brethren living in Judaea.	**29** So according to how any of the disciples prospered, they determined each one of them to send something as a service to the brethren living in Judaea.
[a′₂] **30** (They did indeed do this, sending it to the elders by the hand of Barnabas and Saul.)	**30** (They did indeed do this, sending it to the elders by the hand of Barnabas and Saul.)

Critical Apparatus

11. 27 (᾽ Ἐν) αὐταῖς B 323. 614. 1611. 2412 ‖ ταύταις D d ℵ *rell.*

B03 gives particular emphasis to the idea that the visit of the prophets took place during the very time just mentioned, that is, the year Barnabas and Saul spent in Antioch (cf. Barrett, I, p. 561 who wrongly ascribes the reading of αὐταῖς to D05).

ἦν δὲ πολλὴ ἀγαλλίασις D d (p w vg^R mae); Aug BarS ‖ *om.* B 𝔓^{45.74} ℵ *rell.*

The joyful impact made on the church in Antioch by the visit of the prophets from Hierosoluma is noted by D05 but not by B03. ἀγαλλίασις is a noun that occurs on three other occasions in Luke's writings: Lk. 1.14, anticipating the response to John the Baptist; 1.44, the response of John in his mother's womb to the greeting of Mary, mother of Jesus; Acts 2.46, the attitude shared by the first community of believers. Otherwise it is found in the New Testament at Heb. 1.9 and Jude 24. Heb. 1.9 cites Ps. 44.8 LXX (45.8 MT) referring to 'the oil of gladness' (ἔλαιον ἀγαλλιάσεως) with which David was anointed by God as king ('the central ritual of kingship', *Jewish Study Bible*, p. 1332, cf. 1285). The joy that is expressed by ἀγαλλίασις is especially associated with experiencing something of the divine.

The following variant makes it clear that the observation is made from a first-hand point of view, as if the narrator were actually present at the time.

11.28 συνεστραμμένων δὲ ἡμῶν D d p w vg^R mae; Aug ‖ *om.* B 𝔓^{45.74} ℵ *rell.*

This is the second of two lines present in D05 but absent in B03. With the verb in the first person plural, this is the earliest evidence of the 'we'-group in the book of Acts, preceding the first occurrence in the AT at 16.10. The verb itself is συστρέφω 'bring/gather together' (B-A-G, συστρέφω, 1 and 2). Outside Acts, it is only found at one other place in the New Testament at Mt. 17.22, but not in D05. Within Acts, there is one other firm occurrence in the active at 28.3 referring to Paul gathering sticks, but nowhere else in Luke's writing except three times more in Acts D05, always in the active: 10.41 D05 (of the disciples who gathered together with Jesus after his resurrection); 16.39b D05 (of the mob who might assemble in Philippi); 17.5 D05 (of the Jews who gathered men in Thessalonica). Here the verb is in the middle and the perfect tense, describing the setting for Agabus' prophecy that follows as one in which the disciples in Antioch were gathered together.

ἀναστὰς δέ B 𝔓^{45.74} ℵ *rell* | καὶ ἀν. gig vg | ἀν. p; Aug ‖ ἔφη D d.

The setting for the prophetic warning given by Agabus has already been established in the previous clause in D05 with a genitive absolute (see above variant). This being absent from B03, a new clause is introduced here, connected with δέ and using the participle ἀναστάς to set the scene for the prophecy.

("Αγαβος) ἐσήμαινεν B (Ψ) d vg; Aug | -μανεν 𝔓⁷⁴ ℵ A E 33. 1739 𝔐 ‖ σημαίνων D p vgᴿ.

The participle in D05 is necessary to concord with the finite verb in the previous clause (see variant above); since B03 had a participle in the previous clause, a finite verb is required now.

μεγάλην B Dᶜ 𝔓⁴⁵·⁷⁴ ℵ A 81. 88. 323. 1175. 1270. 1739 ‖ (λιμὸν) μέγαν D* d E H L P Ψ 049. 056. 1. 104. 226. 330. 440. 547. 614. 618. 927. 945. 1241. 1243. 1245. 1505. 1611. 1646. 1828. 1891. 1837. 1854. 2147. 2412. 2492. 2495; Chr.

B03 uses a feminine adjective to describe the famine (cf. Lk. 15.14, λιμὸς ἰσχυρά), in accordance with the feminine relative pronoun following (ἥτις). D05, however, treats the noun as masculine, an occurrence that is also found within Luke's Gospel (cf. λιμὸς μέγας, Lk. 4.25).

11.29 τῶν δὲ μαθητῶν B 𝔓⁴⁵·⁷⁴ ℵ *rell*; Eus Aug ‖ οἱ δὲ μαθηταί D d e gig p vg syᵖ (sa mae aeth).— (καθὼς) εὐπορεῖτό τις B 𝔓⁷⁴ ℵ *rell*; Eus Aug ‖ εὐποροῦν-το D d p vgᴿ.

The two variants function in combination with each other. The construction of B03 tends to view the disciples as separate individuals whereas the D05 text considers them as a collective whole, operating as a single community.

Commentary

[a₁] 11.27a *The Arrival of Prophets from Hierosoluma*
11.27a The section is linked to the previous events by a strong time connection, setting the new incident within the time framework ('In these days', Ἐν ταύταις [αὐταῖς B03] ταῖς ἡμέραις) of the year Barnabas and Saul spent with the church in Antioch. The particular order of words in Greek (demonstrative before the noun) carefully underlines that the visit of the prophets occurred in that first year of the church in Antioch.[1]

The prophets came from Hierosoluma, not from Ierousalem where the church that sent out Barnabas was situated (see *Commentary*, 11.22 above). The juxtaposition of the two forms of the name of Jerusalem highlights the difference between them, in the same way as the juxtaposition of Hierosoluma in Jesus' command in 1.4 and Ierousalem (twice!) referring to the non-compliance of the apostles in 1.12 (see *General Introduction,* § VII). Luke thereby contrasts the community of Jewish Jesus-believers that remain attached to the importance of Ierousalem, with their conservative religious attitude, and that of the prophets who are more open and prepared to share fully with the mixed

---

1. When the demonstrative is in the pre-noun position in expressions of time, the link between the new event and the previous one seems to be particularly close; see Read-Heimerdinger, *The Bezan Text*, pp. 103–107, esp. 104.

group of believers in Antioch. The freedom the prophets enjoy with respect to Ierousalem and the centre of Judaism is apparent even in the choice of the verb 'go down', for which Luke uses κατέρχομαι instead of καταβαίνω which he always selects when it is a question of going down from the religious centre.[2] It may well have been precisely for the purpose of encouraging and building up the believers that the prophets went to Antioch for the gift of prophecy, while including the foretelling of the future (as here in v. 28), is to do with communicating the mind of God in a more general way – in the Scriptures, exhorting, rebuking and giving hope are all part of prophetic activity, with the Spirit of God acting through the prophet as the means for communicating the divine word with the people.[3]

It is to be noted that the people who come to share in the community life of Antioch (made clear by 11.27b D05) are prophets from Hierosoluma and not the apostles. They, for their part, have put in no appearance in Antioch, unlike the presence of Peter and John in Samaria (8.14) and despite Peter's explanation of what God had done for the Gentiles in Caesarea which appeared to have silenced the objectors (11.18). Just how much the apostles (including Peter) are still attached to Ierousalem, or who else may be imposing their point of view there, is not entirely clear at this stage in the narrative. At 4.31, following the attack on the apostles by the Jewish High Priests (4.5-22), a move away from the Temple authorities was initiated by the apostles as they recognized clearly for the first time the enmity of the Jewish leaders to the Messiah – symbolized and divinely endorsed in the shaking of the Temple and the filling of the disciples with the Holy Spirit. Nevertheless, despite the apostles taking over the leadership function of the Temple leaders,[4] part of the believing community continued to cling to the traditional ways (represented by Ananias and Sapphira, 5.1-11).[5] From chapter 6, a division among the Jewish Jesus-believers became even more apparent, with the Hellenists displaying a clearer understanding and acceptance of the universal aspects of the message of Jesus which, in turn, caused

---

2.   Luke is the only evangelist to use the verb κατέρχομαι which is not found in the LXX (Lk. × 2; Acts × 13; × 1 in the rest of the New Testament). D05 does not read it at Acts 18.5 or 19.1, but has additional readings at 17.1 and 20.13. The point of departure or arrival is always indicated (ἀπό × 6; εἰς × 10; πρός × 1) or both at once (× 2). Unlike καταβαίνω, it does not have the idea of 'descent' (Lk. 3.22; 10.15; 19.5, 6; Acts 7.34; 8.38; 10.11, 20, 21; 11.5; 14.11) or 'leaving the holy city/land' (Lk. 10.30, 31; Acts 7.15; 8.26), but rather expresses a direction taken to or from a place.

3.   For an examination of the role of the Spirit in prophecy, see R.P. Menzies, *The Development of Early Christian Pneumatology with Special Reference to Luke-Acts* (JSNTSup, 54; Sheffield: JSOT Press, 1991); M.M.B. Turner, *Power from on High: The Spirit in Israel's Restoration and Witness in Luke-Acts* (Journal of Pentecostal Theology Supplement, 9; Sheffield: JSOT Press, 1996). On the particular role of the Holy Spirit in the Isaiah Targum, see B. Chilton, *The Aramaic Bible*, vol. II: *The Isaiah Targum: Introduction, Translation, Apparatus, Notes* (Edinburgh: T&T Clark, 1987), p. 49.

4.   See *The Message of Acts*, I, pp. 267–81.

5.   See *The Message of Acts*, I, pp. 290–308.

them to be persecuted by their fellow Diaspora Jews (6.9; 8.1b; see *Excursus* 1). In contrast, it is noted that the apostles were still holding to a more exclusive understanding, represented by Ierousalem (8.1b). It is not until his encounter with Cornelius that Peter will be able to freely embrace the entry of the Gentiles into the community of believers and so take steps to distance himself from Ierousalem (11.2 D05, see *Commentary, ad loc.*), but even as the leader of the apostles he meets with opposition from disciples who are not happy with his contact with Gentiles (11.3). Although he calms their disquiet with his account (11.4-17, 18), a church continues to exist in 'Ierousalem' which seeks to keep at least a watchful eye on the happenings in Antioch when they hear about Hellenist disciples successfully persuading Gentiles to believe in Jesus (11.22). More will be learnt about this church in due course (see *Commentary,* 12.17b); for the moment, it is sufficient to bear in mind that it still exists and that Luke has distinguished it from the church in Hierosoluma.

[a₂] 11.27b *The Exultation of the 'We'-Group*
11.27b The Bezan text notes that the arrival of the prophets is an occasion for great joy. The word used for this is not the usual one, χαρά, but ἀγαλλίασις, a word that is almost exclusive to Luke in the New Testament[6] but one found in the Jewish Scriptures to express the emotion of exultation that is especially associated with experiencing something of the divine (see *Critical Apparatus*). It is linked in the Gospel with the birth of both John the Baptist (Lk. 1.14) and Jesus (1.44). In Acts, ἀγαλλίασις was already experienced by the first community of disciples in Jerusalem (2.46), a positive parallel that endorses the mixed Gentile and Jewish community in Antioch.[7]

There are number of other parallels between the birth of the church in Antioch and the birth of Jesus, which are explored in *Excursus* 4. There is a good reason for this: from a Messiah who was rejected by his own people, misunderstood and treated as an outsider because he did not fulfil their expectations there could only come communities that were also marginalized and persecuted because they lived by a scale of values that turned on its head the accepted way of life.

[b₁] 11.28a *Agabus' Prophecy*
11.28a The setting for Agabus' prophecy is described by Luke according to Codex Bezae as if he were present on this occasion. This then becomes the first instance in Acts when Luke writes in the first person, as one of a group of people who were with Saul/Paul not just on his journeys but from the start,

---

6.   Lk. × 2; Acts × 1 + 1 D05.
7.   In addition to the references to the noun ἀγαλλίασις in Luke's work, the verb ἀγαλλιάω is also found: Lk. 1.47 and 10.21, in connection with the prophetic Spirit; Acts 2.26, of David inspired by the Holy Spirit; 16.34, of the Philippian gaoler as he received the disciples at his table following his belief in God.

here in Antioch.[8] A full discussion of the identity and function of the 'we'-group will be presented at their next appearance at 16.10[9] but meanwhile it may be noted that this first appearance establishes the group's association with Antioch and their positive attitude towards the church there. Nothing is said about their relationship with Saul in particular, but they enjoy an intimate relationship with the Antioch church in general. They also are positive towards the activity of the prophets from Hierosoluma, and in tune with their prophesying. This endorsement of the Jewish-Gentile church and the Spirit-led activity of the Hierosoluma disciples in itself are entirely in keeping with the views of the narrator as they have been revealed so far and will continue to be so.

[b₂] 11.28b *The Realization of the Prophecy*
11.28b Since Luke mentions several prophets as coming to Antioch it is probable that there were other exchanges and prophecies given to the church than the one recorded. Agabus is named as 'one from among them' and will be mentioned again for his unsuccessful warning to Paul in Caesarea not to go to Jerusalem (21.10). It was seemingly the far-reaching significance of his prophecy on this occasion that caused it be specially noted. He warns of an impending famine, which Luke associates with the time of the Emperor Claudius whose reign lasted from 41–54 CE. There are, indeed, records of a widespread food shortage during his time, through all after the time of Herod Agrippa whose death (44 CE) is recorded in the following section (12.23).[10]

[a′₁] 11.29 *The Decision to Send Aid to Judaea*
11.29 The prophecy of the famine has a significance that goes far beyond simply demonstrating the Spirit-inspired gift of foreseeing the future. Most importantly, it provides an opportunity for the believers in Antioch to demonstrate their generosity towards their brethren in Judaea. The way in which they do this reveals notable differences between the organization of the Antioch church and the church in Jerusalem that was portrayed earlier (4.32–5.11). Here, the decision is taken collectively by the disciples that each person (ὥρισαν ἕκαστος αὐτῶν) will give what they can, whereas in Jerusalem all material goods were handed over to the community as shared possessions under the administration of the apostles (4.32, 34-35, 37). The earlier arrangement had initially been blessed by God (χάρις τε μεγάλη ἦν ἐπὶ πάντας αὐτούς,

---

8.   The next appearance of the 'we'-group is at 16.10 when Paul received the call from the Macedonian in a vision. Another additional occurrence in Codex Bezae of the first person plural, not generally recognized, is at 21.29 D05 when the people of Jerusalem accuse Paul of having taken Greeks into the Temple (ἐνομίσαμεν; cf. ἐνόμιζον, AT).

9.   The question has been examined in an article by J. Rius-Camps, 'L'aparició/desaparició del "nosaltres" en el llibre dels Fets: un simple procediment teològico-literari?', *RCatT* 6 (1981), pp. 35–75.

10.   Josephus (*Ant.* 20, 101) speaks of τὸν μέγαν λιμὸν κατὰ τὴν Ἰουδαίαν between 44–48 CE; cf. 3, 320.

'great grace was on them all', 4.33b), but it led to both dissimulation (in the case of Ananias and Saphhira, 5.1-11) and injustice (in the case of the Hellenist widows, 6.1).

The fact that the Antioch community acts upon Agabus' prophecy forthwith, as it would seem, implies that there was already some shortage among the disciples in Judaea. What exactly is meant by 'Judaea' is a moot point (see *Commentary*, 9.31), but Luke generally seems to use the name in Acts to refer to the region where the church was made up of Jewish Jesus-believers; in this case and as it turns out (cf. 12.25), it means specifically Ierousalem. So even though the warning of the famine applies to 'the whole earth', the situation in Antioch is such that the disciples there are prepared to give to their fellow disciples who are in need. And if there is no longer prosperity in Judaea, it is a sign that the 'grace of God' is no longer being shown to them, a reflection of the erroneous position they have adopted with respect to the Gentiles (cf. 7.11-12, where the situation of Joseph in Egypt who is favoured by God [7.9] is contrasted with that of Jacob in Canaan). Luke has noted, on the other hand, that God looked favourably on the disciples in Antioch (11.21, 23).

The gifts are donated by the Antioch disciples 'as a service'.[11] The thought may well be that their contributions are seen as fulfilling scriptural prophecies (notably Isaiah 60, especially vv. 5-9) concerning the Gentiles who are portrayed in the end-times as bringing their wealth for the benefit of the Jews in Jerusalem.[12] Saul, as Paul, will be particularly eager to ensure that this prophetic vision is also carried out by the churches he founds, though in his case Luke portrays his zeal as misplaced and, in the end, failing to achieve its goal.[13] As far as Antioch is concerned, the tone of the narrative is wholly approving – it seems that Paul's error was to seek to continue to enact the fulfilment of the prophecy when it had, in fact, already been achieved in a token way by the Antiochene disciples (cf. 12.25).

Agabus' prophecy of the famine is further important because it creates a context for the following section in which the narrative turns to focus on the

---

11. The word διακονία is used only by Luke among the evangelists and is applied on other occasions to practical aid: Acts 6.1; 12.25. Elsewhere, it refers to service in a more general sense (cf. Lk. 10.40; Acts 1.17, 25; 21.29) or in relation to preaching (Acts 6.4; 20.24 D05). διακονία in the LXX is rare. It translates either the Hebrew עֲבֹד referring to ordinary domestic service, but also שְׁרֵת which refers to a higher order of service, notably gifts for the Temple (B-D-B).

12. An important point of comparison is Rom. 15.31 where Paul speaks of his handing over of the Gentiles' collection to the believers in Ierousalem as his 'service' (ἡ διακονία μου) according to most MSS (but not B03 among others). On this notion, see B. Chilton, 'Aramaic and Targumic Antecedents of Pauline Justification' in D.R.G. Beattie and M.J. McNamara (eds), *The Aramaic Bible: Targums in their Historical Context* (JSOTSup, 166; Sheffield: Sheffield Academic Press, 1994), pp. 379–97.

13. See J. Rius-Camps, 'The Gradual Awakening of Paul's Awareness of his Mission to the Gentiles', in T. Nicklas and M. Tilly (eds), *Apostelgeschichte als Kirchengeschichte: Text, Traditionen und antike Auslegungen* (BZNW, 22; Berlin: Walter de Gruyter, 2000), pp. 281–96 [294–95].

situation in Judaea and the role played by Herod Agrippa in the increasing separation of the Jesus-believers from the Jewish institution.

[a′₂] 11.30 *The Carrying out of the Decision*
11.30 As with the two (one, AT) preceding elements, this final one concludes, too, with a parenthetical comment from the narrator. The gifts are to be taken to the 'elders' (of the 'brethren in Judaea', cf. v. 29), the first time that this term is used of a community of believers. Previous references have been limited to the Jewish leadership, usually viewed as hostile (2.17; 4.5, 8, 23; 6.12; cf. 23.14; 24.1; 25.15), but the same pattern of oversight was apparently adopted in the churches as they developed (cf. 14.23; 20.17). In the Ierousalem church, the elders exercised a position of authority together with the apostles (15.2, 4, 6, 22, 23; 16.4), though eventually the apostles are no longer mentioned as the elders are named as leaders alongside James (21.18, especially D05). When they were introduced is not explained nor when the apostles ceased to be leaders, but it may well be relevant that their first appearance here follows the dispute that the Jewish Jesus-believers in Jerusalem had had with Peter, leader of the apostles (11.3). The elders would have been instated in order to exercise some kind of control over their progressive attitude which explains why they are repeatedly in evidence in chapter 15, especially in the Bezan text, during the meeting to discuss the position concerning circumcision in which James, and not any of the apostles, took the leading role (cf. 15.2, 4, 5 D05, 6, 11 D05, 22, 23, 41 D05).

Barnabas and Saul (in that order, which Luke will maintain until Paul takes over as the dominant member of the pair, cf. 13.43) are entrusted with the gifts as representatives of the Antioch community, an indication of the esteem in which they were held from the beginning (cf. 13.1). Thus Barnabas, who had been originally sent out from the Ierousalem church to inspect the situation in Antioch, returns; but far from coming back to report to his superiors, he will serve as a delegate on behalf of the new community.

Excursus 4

Parallels between the Public Appearance of the Antioch Church and the Birth of Jesus

There are a number of echoes, both verbal and thematic, of the birth of Jesus in the account concerning the public manifestation of the Antioch church. In both cases, something comes to life that is contrary to the expectations of how things would be according to the religious teachings and regulations in place within Judaism. In the case of Jesus, he was conceived while his mother was not yet married and his birth was humble and without any public acclamation or acknowledgment by the religious authorities. In a similar way, the church in Antioch came into being in a discreet manner, bringing together Jews and Gentiles in a manner that was contrary to the Jewish Law and in a way that was unplanned by the leaders in Ierousalem and was without their endorsement. The following specific parallels, often clearer in the Bezan text, may be noted:

1. An initial time framework is given to each account, relating it to the immediately preceding narrative:᾽Εν ταύταις δὲ ταῖς ἡμέραις... (Acts 11.27a) //᾽Εγένετο δὲ ἐν ταῖς ἡμέραις ἐκείναις... (Lk. 2.1).

2. A declaration prepares the scene for the manifestation of the church/ the birth: διὰ τοῦ πνεύματος (Acts 11.28) // ἐξῆλθεν δόγμα παρὰ Καίσαρος Αὐγούστου (Lk. 2.1).

3. A community is formed in each case: in Antioch, the church is gathered together: συνεστραμμένων δὲ ἡμῶν (Acts 11.28 D05) // Mary is betrothed to Joseph: σὺν Μαρίᾳ τῇ ἐμνηστευμένῃ αὐτῷ (Lk. 2.5 D05).

4. A universal scope is given to Agabus' prophecy: ἐφ᾽ ὅλην τὴν οἰκουμένην (Acts 11.28a) // Caesar's decree: πᾶσαν τὴν οἰκουμένην (Lk. 2.1).

5. The narrator confirms the anticipated event in a parenthetical aside and links it to the Roman Emperor: ἥτις ἐγένετο ἐπὶ Κλαυδίου (Acts 11.28b) // αὕτη ἐγένετο ... Κυρηνίου (Lk. 2.2 D05).

6. People are mobilized to take action: each of the disciples: καθὼς εὐποροῦντο, ὥρισαν ἕκαστος αὐτῶν εἰς διακονίαν (Acts 11.29 D05) // each citizen: ἐπορεύοντο πάντες ... ἕκαστος εἰς τὴν ἑαυτοῦ πατρίδα (Lk. 2.3 D05).

7. Both events bear fruit: the gifts from the Antioch disciples: εἰς διακονίαν πέμψαι (Acts 11.29) // the conception of a child: οὔσῃ ἐγκύῳ (Lk. 2.5).

8. A response of joy: ἦν δὲ πολλὴ ἀγαλλίασις (Acts 11.27 D05) // ἐσκίρτησεν ἐν ἀγαλλιάσει (Lk. 1.44).

9. Judaea is the end goal of both accounts: ἐν τῇ ᾽Ιουδαίᾳ (Acts 11.29) // εἰς τὴν ᾽Ιουδαίαν AT, εἰς γῆν ᾽Ιούδα D05 (Lk. 2.4).

10. Two people are named as responsible for taking care of the fruit: διὰ χειρὸς Βαρναβᾶ καὶ Σαύλου (Acts 11.30) // ᾽Ιωσὴφ ... σὺν Μαρίᾳ (Lk. 2.4-5D05).

IV. THE RELEASE OF THE CHURCH FROM ISRAEL
12.1-25

General Overview

It is without exaggeration to say that, in certain key respects, this chapter is the most important of the book of Acts because of the symbolic significance of the events it narrates. The theological message underlying the account of Herod's attack on the Church, in particular his imprisonment of Peter, is not immediately clear in the AT but in Codex Bezae the narrator leaves ample clues to make it quite clear to the audience that the real purpose of the chapter is to use the story it tells to illustrate how the Jews, represented here by Herod, have become enemies of the people of God and how Peter is finally freed from his traditional Jewish expectations of the restoration of Israel.

The two main characters in the episode are Herod Agrippa I who, as king of Judaea, oppresses the Jewish Jesus-believers; in other words, he turns on his own people and is therefore destroyed by the angel of the Lord, so that his death is also a comment on Jews who rejected Jesus and attacked his followers. Meanwhile, Peter is back in focus (cf. 9.31–11.18) after two passages (11.19-26; 11.27-30) that looked at the entry of Gentiles into the church in Antioch. Not only is he freed from the prison where Herod shuts him up but he leaves Ierousalem definitively.

Two scriptural paradigms form the historical background to the narrative in Acts 12 which need to be recognized in order to understand Luke's theological message. The first is an event, that of the Exodus as recorded in Exodus 12 (see *Excursus* 6), whereby Peter's deliverance from prison is likened to the liberation of Israel from Egypt; the second is a set of prophecies, those of Ezekiel from which a number of themes are developed (see *Excursus* 8), notably the punishment of the Prince of Tyre with whom Herod is assimilated (see *Excursus* 9). The allusions to the models are skilfully woven together in an intricate network of cross-references that is more fully developed in Codex Bezae, as is often observed to be the case when it is a question of adopting a Jewish perspective on an incident (see *General Introduction*, § I). Some of the allusions may seem tenuous to a modern reader who is accustomed to thinking within a framework of western logic and literalness, and who has only the canonical text of Exodus to refer to. Addressees of Acts who were of a Jewish background, especially if he were Theophilus the High Priest as we propose for the Bezan text (see *General Introduction*, § III), would have had a great deal more in terms of oral and written tradition on which to draw. They would furthermore be accustomed to the use of analogy to communicate teaching that depended for its interpretation on a linking of scriptural passages.

In terms of the development of the Church, this section shows the Antioch church as a community independent of Jerusalem, the visit of Barnabas and Saul serving as the framework for the events it relates (11.30, cf. 12.25). It is, indeed, the decision of the Antioch church, where there are Gentiles as well as Jews, to send gifts to help the brethren in Judaea that provokes the wave of attacks. The fact that it is the apostles who come under attack, having been left in peace since the intervention of Gamaliel on their behalf (cf. 5.34-39), is indicative of something new having happened that was unacceptable in Jewish eyes.

No direct reference will made to Barnabas and Saul until the colophon at the end of the section, but even though they are not mentioned by name they were probably present among the believers praying for Peter in the house of Mary (12.12). The portrayal of the church in Mary's house in this section as separate from 'James and the brethren' who are mentioned in a passing reference, brings the distinction between the disciples who were still attached to the Jewish ideology and those who were free of it into sharper focus (cf. 8.1b, c; see *Commentary, ad loc.*).

Structure and Themes

The structure of the section is unusual for it is unified by a single story, which is made up of three sequences followed by a colophon: the second sequence is longer than any other in Acts and represents a change in the way the story is told compared to earlier chapters because of the amount of detail that is provided. The three sequences are given cohesion by the presence of Herod in the first and third, and the presence of Peter in the first and second; the colophon gives further cohesion to the narrative by the mention of Saul and Barnabas' mission to Ierousalem, so linking chapter 12 back to the end of chapter 11.

The first sequence (12.1-4) serves as an introduction to set the scene and bring king Herod Agrippa I into the book of Acts for first time.[1] The second sequence (12.5-17) describes Herod's attack on Peter and his miraculous escape; the third (12.18-23) shows the events leading up to Herod's death. The colophon (12.24-25) brings Section IV as well as this second part of Acts to a close, with a backwards look at Section III (11.30) that causes an overlap between sections by the mention of Barnabas and Saul. A similar overlap was seen in the link between the end of the first part of Acts (1.1–5.42) and the beginning of the second (6.1–12.25), in the colophon to the first part that was held over to 6.7 (see *Commentary, ad loc.*). The structure of Acts, through carefully constructed, does not always form neat, self-contained boxes in a way that contemporary analysts may expect it to (see *General Introduction*, § VIII):

---

1.   J. Dupont ('Pierre délivré de prison [Acts 12.1-11]', in *idem, Nouvelles études sur les Actes des Apôtres* [Lectio Divina, 118; Paris: Cerf, 1984], pp. 329–42) considers the introduction to continue through to v. 5. The connective μὲν οὖν at v. 5, however, indicates the start of a new unit of development rather than the conclusion of the previous one.

[A]	12.1-4	Herod's persecution of the church in Judaea
[B]	12.5-17	Peter's escape from prison
[A′]	12.18-23	The death of Herod
Colophon	12.24-25	Conclusion

The first sequence sets the scene in Judaea, implicitly in the AT but explicitly in the Bezan text. In the second sequence, the scene goes from the prison where Peter is kept, to the city and finally to the house of Mary. The third and final sequence starts in Jerusalem but quickly moves to Caesarea.

[A] 12.1-4 *Herod's Persecution of the Church in Judaea*

Overview

The opening sequence of this fourth and final section of the second part of the book of Acts serves as an introduction to the section overall. First, a new character is introduced, Herod Agrippa I. His appearance in Acts will be brief since his death is recorded at the end of chapter 12. He belongs, however, to a family which has already played a significant part in the life of John the Baptist and of Jesus in the Gospel (Herod the Great; his son, Herod Antipas; Herodias, the wife of Philip), and his son, Agrippa I, will continue to influence the trial of Paul in the latter chapters of Acts. Agrippa's role in this section as oppressor of the Church will cause him to be assimilated a) with Pharaoh and b) with the Prince of Tyre. The oppression is directed against the apostles who had been left in peace since Gamaliel's intervention (5.35-39); James (brother of John) and Peter in particular are named in this sequence.

In addition to introducing a new character, this first sequence also serves to establish the setting of the section in Judaea; and crucially, the time, which coincides with the visit of Barnabas and Saul from Antioch (cf. 11.30), during the week of Passover.

Structure and Themes

Once the narrative framework is established by relating the new action to the previous section, the first sequence brings on stage without further ado the new character, Herod, and focuses immediately on his attacks on the church in Judaea. His killing of James is simply stated before moving on to present in greater detail his arrest of Peter who will become the principal character of the second, central sequence [B] of this section. As for Herod, he will be returned to in the final sequence [A′]. The time of year, the Feast of Unleavened Bread, is stated in an aside which the narrator makes in order to provide the first of several clues concerning the theological significance of the incidents in this section:

[a]	12.1	Herod's oppression of the Judaean church
[b]	12.2	The killing of James
[c]	12.3a	The arrest of Peter
[b′]	12.3b	The days of Unleavened Bread
[a′]	12.4	The imprisonment of Peter

Translation

<table>
<tr><td></td><td>*Codex Bezae D05*</td><td>*Codex Vaticanus B03*</td></tr>
<tr><td>[a]</td><td>12.1 It was on that particular occasion that Herod the king laid hands violently on some of the people from the church in Judaea in order to ill-treat them;</td><td>12.1 It was on that particular occasion that Herod the king laid hands violently on some of the people from the church in order to ill-treat them.</td></tr>
<tr><td>[b]</td><td>2 and he killed James the brother of John with the sword;</td><td>2 He killed James the brother of John with the sword.</td></tr>
<tr><td>[c]</td><td>3a and seeing that it was pleasing to the Jews – his attack on the faithful – he went on to arrest even Peter.</td><td>3a Seeing that it was pleasing to the Jews, he went on to arrest even Peter</td></tr>
<tr><td>[b′]</td><td>3b (It was the Days of Unleavened Bread.)</td><td>3b (it was the Days of Unleavened Bread),</td></tr>
<tr><td>[a′]</td><td>4 This man he seized and put in prison, having handed him over to four quaternions of soldiers to guard, intending to bring him before the people after Passover.</td><td>4 whom he indeed seized and put in prison, having handed him over to four quaternions of soldiers to guard him, intending to bring him before the people after Passover.</td></tr>
</table>

Critical Apparatus

12.1 (ἐπέβαλεν) Ἡρῴδης ὁ βασιλεὺς τὰς χεῖρας B 𝔓⁴⁵·⁷⁴ A H L P 049. 056. 33 𝔐 | ὁ βασ. Ἡ. τ. χεῖρας ℵ Ψ 81. 255. 614. 1108. 1241. 1518. 1611. 2138. 2298. 2412 *pc* syʰ; Chr ‖ τ. χεῖρ. Ἡ. ὁ βασ. D d syᵖ sa mae (aeth).

The variant here involves the order of words in the presentation of King Herod. Both B03 and D05, unlike ℵ01, mention his name before his title, an indication that it is chiefly the person who is important rather than his role as king. B03, however, inserts the reference to Herod within the phrase ἐπέβαλεν τὰς χεῖρας whereas D05 places it after the phrase – the difference is lost in an English translation. Both word orders could be said to draw attention to the king, for the purpose of introducing a new character and also to highlight his importance for the story that follows: in B03, by its position in the middle of the phrase, and in D05 by its position at the end. Since the usual order in Luke's narrative is for the verb to be followed immediately by the subject, it may be D05 that has the more emphatic order of words but the effect of breaking up the phrase in B03 may be even more forceful. An analysis of word order in Acts that includes the place of the verb would need to be carried out to be more specific about the significance of this particular variant (cf. Read-Heimerdinger, *The Bezan Text*, pp. 82–85).

(ἐκκλησίας) ἐν τῇ Ἰουδαίᾳ D d 614. 2412 p w vgᴿ syʰ** mae; cf. 11.29 ‖ *om.* B 𝔓⁴⁵·⁷⁴ ℵ *rell*; Eus Lcf.

The detail that the church attacked by Herod was in Judaea is not superfluous nor even simply explanatory information (*contra* Barrett, I, p. 574). On the one hand, it reinforces the connection between this incident with the previous one (cf. 11.29; Metzger, *Commentary*, p. 345); and on the other, it situates Herod clearly within the territory of which he was king, symbolizing the land of the Jews whom he represents in this chapter of Acts (see *Commentary*).

12.2-3 ἀνεῖλεν δέ B 𝔓⁴⁵·⁷⁴ ℵ *rell* | ἀν. 460. 462. 1838 sa mae || καὶ ἀν. D d bo. —
ἰδών δέ B 𝔓⁴⁵·⁷⁴ ℵ A E 33. 81. 945. 1739. 1891. 2344 || καὶ ἰδ. D d H L P Ψ 049.
056 𝔐 gig; Lcf.

With δέ in B03, the killing of James and the arrest of Peter are treated as
separate developments that move the story on (Levinsohn, *Textual Connections*,
pp. 86–120). In D05, however, καί groups together the two examples of Herod's
mistreatment of the Jesus-believers in a series of clauses that prepare for the main
action in v. 5.

12.3 ἡ ἐπιχείρησις αὐτοῦ ἐπὶ τοὺς πιστούς D d p* sy^hmg (mae); Lcf || *om.* B 𝔓⁷⁴ ℵ
rell; Lcf.

D05 spells out just what it was that pleased the Jews, in keeping with the
overall insistence in this chapter in the Bezan text on the oppression of the Jesus-
believers by the Jews, their own people.

αἱ (ἡμέραι) D A E Ψ 049. 33 𝔐 || *om.* B 𝔓⁴⁵·⁷⁴ᵛⁱᵈ ℵ H L P 056. 0244. 1. 6. 88. 330.
440. 1175. 1241. 1739 *al.*

With the article, D05 treats the Festival of Unleavenen Bread as a known and
familiar celebration, in keeping with the Jewish perspective that is apparent
throughout this chapter of Acts in particular. The omission of the article may suggest
a lesser familiarity or, alternatively, it may draw attention to the time that was critical
for the theological interpretation Luke places on the incidents of this chapter.

12.4 ὃν καὶ (πιάσας) B 𝔓⁷⁴ ℵ *rell* || τοῦτον D d gig; Lcf.

B03 continues the account of Peter's arrest with a relative clause, and καί
drawing attention to Peter's plight. With the demonstrative pronoun, D05
switches the focus of the narrative at this point from Herod to Peter who from
now until v. 19 will be centre stage under the spotlight, so to speak.

φυλάσσειν D lat; Lcf || φυλ. αὐτόν B ℵ *rell, custodire eum* d | *om.* 𝔓⁷⁴ 1311 *pc.*

The absence of the accusative pronoun in D05 is accounted for by the use of
the demonstrative at the head of the beginning of the sentence (see previous
variant). That said, in B03 the pronoun is not strictly necessary but it happens
that in places both texts of Acts read a redundant object pronoun (Read-
Heimerdinger, 'Tracking of Participants: The Use of the Third Person Pronoun in
Acts', *RCatT* 31 [2006] forthcoming).

Commentary

[a] 12.1 *Herod's Oppression of the Judaean Church*

12.1 The persecution of the Judaean church by Herod appears at first sight to
be a completely new development but the Greek word order of the time

expression[2] shows how his hostility is closely connected to the visit of Barnabas and Saul who have come from Antioch to bring aid to the disciples of Judaea in response to the prophetic warning (11.27-30). The sequence of events from the founding of the church in Antioch, through Herod's persecution and Peter's liberation, and eventually to the death of Herod is being shown by Luke to be more than coincidental: it happened when the occasion was right.[3] The exact timing is not necessarily historically accurate: Luke's concern is not to situate the events in 'real' time but to show how events in the development of the early Church were linked from a theological perspective.[4]

Herod is brought on stage simply as 'king', though with a particular focus on his name in the text of both Codex Bezae and Codex Vaticanus (see *Critical Apparatus*), with Luke thus making much of his family relationship with other Herods who figure in the Gospel, even though he was not referred to by the name of 'Herod' outside Acts. He is, in fact, Agrippa I, grandson of Herod the Great (cf. Lk.1.5) and nephew of Herod Antipas, tetrarch of Galilee (Lk. 3.1, 19; 8.3; 9.7, 9; 13.31; 23.7-12, 15; Acts 4.27). He was made king over areas in north-east Palestine, Galilee and Perea by the Roman Emperor Caligula in 37–38 CE. In 41 CE, Caligula's successor, Claudius, added to his kingdom Judaea and Samaria which had previously been Roman provinces. Herod died three years later in 44 CE.[5] After an intervening period his son, Agrippa II (cf. Acts 25.13–26.32), took over at least part of his kingdom; his two daughters are also mentioned in Acts, Drusilla (24.24) and Bernice (25.13).

Herod Agrippa I was the fourth or fifth generation to have descended from the Edomites who were forced to convert to Judaism in the second century BCE. In addition, his ancestors on his mother's side were of the ancient high-priestly and royal Hasmonean family. At the same time, he had grown up in Rome where he had been close to Caligula and especially to Claudius. Consequently, he was well-placed to represent the Roman Emperor among the Jews, having an understanding of the values, beliefs and customs of both peoples. The fact that it was he who, on coming to the throne, removed Theophilus (son of Annas, brother-in-law of Caiaphas) from the office of High Priest (he had been appointed by the legate Vitellus in *c*.38 CE) is of no little significance for Luke who addresses his work to this same Theophilus, at least in so far as Codex Bezae is concerned (see *General Introduction*, § III).

---

2.   The placing of the demonstrative adjective before the noun (ἐκεῖνον ... τὸν καιρόν) intensifies the link not just between the time of the two sections but also the events (Read-Heimerdinger, *The Bezan Text*, pp. 103–108).

3.   Luke uses a word for 'time' that can mean the 'favourable time', especially preceded by κατά (B-A-G, καιρός, 1, cf. 2); cf. 19.23.

4.   Read-Heimerdinger, *The Bezan Text*, p.104, n. 60.

5.   For detailed information about Agrippa I, see L.H. Feldman, 'Palestinian and Diaspora Judaism in the First Century', in H. Shanks (ed.), *Christianity and Rabbinic Judaism* (London: SPCK, 1993), pp. 1–40; M. Grant, *The Jews in the Roman World* (London: Weidenfeld and Nicolson, 1973), pp. 120–25; 133–41; Schürer, *History of the Jewish People in the Age of Jesus Christ* (3 vols; rev. and ed. G. Vermes, F. Millar and M. Black; Edinburgh: T&T Clark, 1973), I, pp. 442–54.

The opportunity presented itself with the arrival of Barnabas and Saul from Antioch for him to win favour with his Jewish subjects by attacking the Jesus-believers, the 'faithful' (cf. v. 3 D05): that Jewish disciples is meant is implicit in the insistence in Codex Bezae on the locality, 'in Judaea'.[6] Besides, both James and Peter who are mentioned by name were Jewish believers. Agrippa I was, by all accounts, often attempting to please his fellow-Jews, possibly to strengthen his Jewish identity.[7] The problem created by Barnabas and Saul lay in the money they brought with them from Antioch – this was money that, in part at least, had been given by uncircumcised Gentiles and it was brought to the believers in Jerusalem who were Jews (cf. 'to the brethren living in Judaea', 11.29) 'as a service'. The use of the term διακονία, 'service', corresponds to the Hebrew שׁרת meaning a service for the Temple (see *Commentary*, 11.30). The situation would be quite unacceptable to the non-believing Jews who, placed in a position of inferiority by evidence of Gentile wealth, would regard the gift as impure and an offence.

The people Herod attacked were 'some from the church [in Judaea, D05]',[8] suggesting that there were more people involved than the two apostles named in the next sentences. Luke describes two aspects of his attack: he 'laid hands on them' (ἐπέβαλεν τὰς χεῖρας),[9] which is an expression peculiar to Luke, 'to ill-treat them' (κακῶσαι), a verb that is reminiscent of the language Stephen uses to refer to the oppression of the Israelites by Pharaoh (cf. 7.6, 19: cf. κάκωσις, 7.34), it being found frequently in the LXX with reference to the Exodus event (Exod. 1.11; 5.22-23; Num. 20.15; Deut. 26.6; Josh. 24.4). This is the first clue that Luke intends Herod to be understood as a kind of 'new Pharaoh', and that a situation equal to the Exodus in drama and significance is about to be enacted (see *Excursus* 6 for a full discussion).

[b] 12.2 *The Killing of James*
12.2 The first person to be singled out by name is an apostle. The apostles had been protected from persecution from the Jews since Gamaliel had spoken on their behalf in the Sanhedrin some years earlier (cf. 5.35-39). That a new cause

---

6.   See *Commentary*, 9.31, for discussion of the identity of 'Judaea' in Acts.

7.   A story in the Mishnah (*Sot.* 7.8) tells how Agrippa I was publicly received as a brother during his reading from the Torah at the Feast of Tabernacles in Jerusalem in 41 CE (Schürer, *History of the Jewish People*, I, p. 447). L.H. Schiffman (*Who Was a Jew?* [Hoboken, NJ: KTAV, 1985] pp. 13.14) contests the application of this reference to Agrippa I, but cf. D. Daube, *Ancient Jewish Law* (Leiden: Brill, 1981), pp. 23–25. What may have been the legal position the rabbis defined was still a matter of contention and discussion in the first century, a situation that would have been to Agrippa's advantage should there have been any real doubt as to his Jewish identity.

8.   τινὰς τῶν ἀπὸ τῆς ἐκκλησίας ἐν τῇ Ἰουδαίᾳ: the preposition ἀπό is unusual in Luke's writings, a simple partitive genitive generally expressing the idea of 'belonging to'. The purpose of ἀπό may either (according to the text of D05) be to underline the distinction between the church in Judaea and that in Antioch, from where Barnabas and Saul, present in Jerusalem, had come at this time; or to suggest the idea that Herod took them from the church in order to persecute them.

9.   Luke uses this same expression of hostility 6 times in all (with ἐπί + acc.: Lk. 20.19; 21.12; Acts 5.18; 21.27; with the dat.: Acts 4.3; without any object: Acts 12.1).

for silencing them has now arisen may be presumed from the situation created when the Jewish believers in Judaea received the aid brought from the church in Antioch (see on 12.1 above): as leaders of the church, the apostles would naturally have been the ones held responsible for accepting the gifts.

James, the brother of John, was the third in the list of the apostles at 1.13 (cf. Lk. 8.51; 9.28 B03 [the second, D05]).[10] By identifying his relationship with John, Luke distinguishes him from the other apostle James (the son of Alphaeus, Lk. 6.15) and also, more significantly as will be seen, from James the brother of Jesus (cf. 12.17b). Herod moved swiftly to kill him by beheading him with the sword.[11] James thus becomes the first apostle to die a martyr's death, as had Stephen, leader of the Hellenists, before him (cf. 7.54-60; 8.2).

[c] 12.3a *The Arrest of Peter*

12.3a Herod was encouraged to continue[12] with his attack by the reaction of the Jews. His concern to please the Jews in no way means that the narrative presents him as a Gentile[13] – on the contrary, the historical information available on Agrippa I suggests precisely that he was keen to preserve his good standing with Jews because he wanted to be accepted as one of them;[14] but he had to work hard to maintain the Jews' approval because of his compromising position as ruler on behalf of the Romans (see *Commentary*, 12.1). Codex Bezae summarizes that what in particular pleased the Jews about Herod was 'his attack (lit. 'laying hands')[15] on the faithful': it is not just his killing of James that won approval but his campaign of hostility against the Jewish Jesus-believers in general who are

---

10. The order of the disciples listed when they were first chosen by Jesus (Lk. 6.14) is different: 'Simon ... Peter and Andrew his brother and James and John' (where καί between each one has the effect of linking them as equals). In fact, it will be Peter and John who will become the foremost leaders of the group (cf. Lk. 22.8; Acts 3.1, 3, 4, 11; 4.13, 19; 8.14). It is not clear why John is not directly mentioned here unless it is that he had left Judaea by this time, having seemingly detached himself from the church in Ierousalem after his visit to Samaria (Hierosoluma, 8.25, cf. Ierousalem, 8.14 D05) – unlike Peter (cf. 10.11-17, and *Commentary, ad loc.*), there is nothing to indicate that he may have later had doubts about the message of Jesus that prevented him from remaining free from the traditional Jewish ways of thinking. Alternatively, Herod may have begun his attack on the apostles cautiously with the least of the three leaders and then, seeing how successful that was (cf. 12.3 D05), may have become bold enough to go directly to the most prominent, Peter.

11. It is possible that the beheading of James meant that his offence was viewed as a political one (Grant, *The Jews in the Roman World*, p. 138). Some caution, however, is required with this interpretation (see Barrett, I, pp. 574–75).

12. The verb προσέθετο in the middle has the sense of 'proceed, continue to do sthg [something]', especially with the idea of repeating a previous action (B-A-G, προστίθημι, 1, c). It may be relevant that it is twice used of Pharaoh, whom Herod comes to represent in this sequence, hardening his heart against the Israelites (Exod. 8.25; 9.34 LXX).

13. Barrett, I, p. 575–76, assumes that Luke thought of Herod as a Gentile because of the reference to 'the Jews' in 12.3.

14. His building projects in Jerusalem may be cited in this respect (Grant, *The Jews in the Roman World*, pp. 139–41), but also his observance of Jewish Temple rites (Schürer, *History of the Jewish People*, I, p. 446).

15. ἡ ἐπιχείρησις αὐτοῦ corresponds to the expression ἐπέβαλεν ... τὰς χεῖρας in 12.1.

distinguished from the rest of the Jews by the adjective 'faithful'. It is important for an appreciation of the theological 'story' being enacted through the literal events to bear in mind throughout this narrative that the Jesus-believers are themselves Jews. The effect of the comment in Codex Bezae is that it makes quite clear what Herod's goal was and establishes his role as the 'killer of the faithful', a point that will be important in the final sequence (see *Commentary*, 12.18-23 below).

Peter was the next to whom he turned his attention, 'even Peter', who would have been well-known among the Jews as the leader of the apostles.

[b'] 12.3b *The Days of Unleavened Bread*

12.3b An important narrative aside is inserted at this point, interrupting the account of Herod's mistreatment of Peter. It informs the audience, precisely at the moment when Peter is about to be put in prison, that this was taking place during the Festival of Unleavened Bread, another name by which Passover (cf. 12.4) was known (cf. Lk. 22.1, 7 AT).[16] The festival began at sunset of 14 Nisan when the actual Passover was celebrated, and lasted for a week (cf. Exod. 12.18). Luke provides the information so that it might serve as essential background for what is about to follow, that is, Peter's deliverance from prison by the angel of the Lord during the night.[17]

[a'] 12.4 *The Imprisonment of Peter*

12.4 Luke takes great care to underline the precautions Herod took when he put Peter in prison: he put him under the guard of four quaternions of soldiers, that is four groups of four, who would probably have taken it in turns to be on guard. The place of imprisonment is not specified: the details given in 12.10 are not particularly of help in determining the locality in so far as they serve as clues to the theological symbolism rather than the physical reality of the prison (see *Commentary*, 12.10).

Peter's reaction to his imprisonment is not noted and, indeed, throughout this episode until he realizes that he has been released by the angel of the Lord (12.11), he remains a silent participant. The very silence enhances the echo in this incident of the declaration Peter boldly made to Jesus at his last meal with the disciples: 'I am ready to go with you to prison and even death' (Lk. 22.33).[18] This same scene has already been evoked in the previous section and will be again alluded to in Acts 12.13-17 (see *Excursus* 5).

16. The association of the Festival of Unleavened Bread with Passover is discussed in *Jewish Study Bible*, pp. 126–27.

17. When δέ is used to introduce an aside, it is generally relevant to the narrative that is to follow, p. 91).

18. The parallel is pointed out by D.T.N. Parry, 'Release of the Captives: Reflections on Acts 12', in C.M. Tuckett (ed.), *Luke's Literary Achievement: Collected Essays* (JSNTSup, 116; Sheffield: Sheffield Academic Press, 1995), pp. 156–64 [159], where other parallels with the Gospel of Luke are also noted.

From a human perspective, Peter's situation is hopeless, it only being a matter of time now before he is executed in the same way as James. The reason that he was put in prison rather than being executed there and then is implied in the statement that is was 'the Festival of Unleavened Bread'. This was a time of Sabbath for the Jews when it would have been inconceivable for any of them, let alone Herod, to participate in any kind of trial or execution (cf. Exod. 12.16). Herod deliberately intends therefore to wait until the end of Passover week. The mention of Passover strengthens the allusions that have been building up to the theme of the Israelites' deliverance from the oppression of Pharaoh (see *Excursus* 6), clearly establishing the theological context for Peter's deliverance from prison. The force of the parallel at this stage is to demonstrate that just as the Jews were oppressed and mistreated by the Egyptians under their ruler, Pharaoh, so the faithful of the people of God are oppressed and mistreated by the Jews under their king, Herod. The tragedy is that the oppressors of the faithful have become the Jews themselves.

After the Passover, then, which would be a matter of days away (see above on the Festival of Unleavened Bread, v. 3b), Herod intends to bring Peter before 'the people', ὁ λαός, the term Luke uses to designate the Jews, implying that it is they who will decide his fate. The responsibility for Peter's death will not be Herod's alone: ruler and people are of one mind on this matter.

[B] 12.5-17 *Peter's Escape from Prison*

Overview

The paradigm of the Exodus that was already hinted at in the opening sequence is now reinforced and developed, notably in the Bezan text (see *Excursus* 6). In this central sequence, it will emerge that just as Yahweh delivered his people from the oppression of Egypt, so now, in this night of messianic expectation,[19] he will deliver Peter from the oppression of the Jews, indeed from the system of Jewish regulations and expectations that held him prisoner. The application of the paradigm is nothing less than shocking for, with the message that the Jews have become the enemy of the people of God, the original roles in the Exodus event have been turned upside down.

The details provided by the text of Codex Bezae to describe the path taken by the angel as he leads Peter out of the prison make clear that the prison at one level is a metaphor for the restored Temple seen by Ezekiel in his vision of the new Jerusalem to which Israel will return and where the Messiah is expected to appear (Ezekiel 40–46: see *Excursus* 8 for further discussion). The clue to the metaphor is the well-known reading in Codex Bezae of the 'seven steps' at Acts 12.10b, but other aspects of the exit route in 12.10a of both texts anticipate and confirm the clue. Peter himself sums up his release from prison as nothing less

---

19. On the subject of the night of Passover being time when the Messiah was expected, especially among the Pharisees, see Le Déaut, *La nuit pascale* (Rome: Biblical Institute Press, 1965), pp. 279–83.

than deliverance from 'all the expectations of the Jews' (12.11) which, in addition to echoing the Exodus event and emphasizing the treachery of the Jewish people against him, also allude to the future expectations of his own people which he now acknowledges have been overturned by Jesus, the Messiah who has already arrived once and for all. The force of Luke's use of Ezekiel's Temple as a metaphor is to indicate, in a tragic reversal of what was foreseen by Ezekiel as Israel's future hope, that the Messiah will not enter a restored Temple but has rather led his people out of it.

It may seem strange that Peter should need any further assistance to distance himself from his traditional attitudes and ways of thinking since he had already recognized them as contrary to the thoughts of God when he acknowledged that the Gentiles were as acceptable to God as the Jews (cf. 10.34; 11.16-17). Yet, in so many respects, Luke portrays Peter as a disciple who, though quick to seize on new ideas, does not readily stick to with them or easily give up the old ones (cf. Jesus' warning to him, Lk. 22.31-34; or his wavering over the question of unclean food while at Simon the Tanner's house, Acts 10.9-16 [see *Commentary, ad loc.*]). A similar picture of Peter is painted by Paul in his letter to the Galatians (Gal. 1.11-14), though Paul is not without his own problems, too!

Once Peter is freed from prison he goes to the community of disciples praying for him at the house of Mary, mother of John-Mark. This group of believers is distinguished explicitly from another group of brethren under the leadership of James. This is the first time in Acts that James, silently present at the meeting of the 120 after Jesus had left the apostles (cf. 1.14), is openly named, but he will emerge in the later chapters of Acts as the leader of the community of disciples who remained attached to traditional Jewish practices and systems of belief.

As for Peter, after relating the story of his miraculous deliverance, he will disappear altogether from the scene in Acts, except for a brief appearance at the meeting in Jerusalem, 15.7-11.

Structure and Themes
The sequence is organized in two parts which consist of parallel sets of elements that are repeated in the same order the second time: the first [a–m] portrays Peter shut up in prison and released by the intervention of the angel of the Lord (12.5-10); the second [a′–m′] continues with the portrait of Peter now freed from prison and entering, thanks to the intervention of the servant Rhoda, into the community that was praying for him:

[a]	12.5a	Peter in prison
[b]	12.5b	The church at prayer for Peter
[c]	12.6	Peter is asleep with guards at the door
[d]	12.7a	The angel of the Lord appears
[e]	12.7b	The angel orders Peter to get up
[f]	12.7c	Peter's chains fall off
[g]	12.8a	The angel orders Peter to get dressed
[h]	12.8b	Peter obeys
[i]	12.8c	The angel's further orders
[j]	12.9	Peter's compliance

[k]	12.10a	The angel and Peter make their way out of the prison
[l]	12.10b	They go down the seven steps
[m]	12.10c	The angel leaves Peter alone
[a′]	12.11	Peter's realization of his deliverance
[b′]	12.12	His arrival at the house of the praying church
[c′]	12.13	Peter knocks at the porch door
[d′]	12.14a	Rhoda in her joy does not open the porch
[e′]	12.14b	Rhoda's announcement that Peter is standing at the porch
[f′]	12.15a	The disciples' response that she is mad
[g′]	12.15b	Rhoda's insistence that Peter is there
[h′]	12.15c	The disciples' supposition that it was his angel
[i′]	12.16a	Peter's persistence in knocking at the porch
[j′]	12.16b	The disciples' amazement at seeing him
[k′]	12.17a	Peter's account of his escape
[l′]	12.17b	His command concerning James
[m′]	12.17c	Peter's departure from Ierousalem

The correspondences between the two sets of elements are striking:

1. The first element [a // a′] presents Peter's situation.
2. The second [b // b′] mentions the church praying for his freedom.
3. The third [c // c′] mentions the door – the guards guarding the prison door and the servant Rhoda listening at the door of the community.
4. The fourth [d // d′] shows the angel appearing to Peter and Rhoda responding with joy to recognizing Peter's voice.
5. The fifth [e // e′] through to the tenth [j // j′] constitute a series of three exchanges between the angel and Peter, and between Rhoda as Peter's representative and the disciples of the community.
6. The eleventh [k // k′] refers to the escape from the prison.
7. The penultimate [l // l′] shows first, Peter's definitive departure from Ierousalem symbolised by the seven steps and then, in the corresponding element, makes reference to James as the leader of the church in Ierousalem.
8. Finally [m // m′], the angel departs once Peter is out of the prison and Peter departs, too, once he has related his deliverance.

In each case, the first three elements introduce the scene, preparing for the entrance of the character who comes to Peter's aid; the next six elements consist of alternating exchanges with Peter carrying out the angel's orders but the disciples not daring to trust Peter's knocking; the last three bring the scene to a conclusion with the escape from prison, that is Ierousalem, finally accomplished.

This sequence has more elements than any other so far in Acts, the account of Peter's liberation being given in careful detail and each point being important for its contribution to the overall comparison of Peter's release with the Exodus of Israel.

Translation

	Codex Bezae D05	Codex Vaticanus B03
[a]	**12.5a** So Peter was being kept in the prison.	**12.5a** So Peter was being kept in the prison.
[b]	**5b** Meanwhile, there was much prayer in earnestness concerning him, from the church to God concerning him.	**5b** Meanwhile, there was prayer taking place earnestly by the church concerning him.

[c]   **6** When Herod was about to bring him forward, in that night Peter was sleeping between two soldiers, bound with two chains and, additionally, two guards in front of the door were guarding the prison.

[d]   **7a** Then suddenly, the angel of the Lord came and stood by Peter and a light shone out in the chamber.

[e]   **7b** Nudging Peter's side, he woke him up saying, 'Get up quickly!'

[f]   **7c** And the chains peeled off from his hands.

[g]   **8a** The angel said to him, 'Fasten your belt and put on your sandals'.

[h]   **8b** He did so.

[i]   **8c** And he says to him, 'Put your cloak around you and keep following me!'

[j]   **9** And he went out and he started to follow, and he did not know that what was happening with the angel was true for he thought he was seeing a vision.

[k]   **10a** When they had gone through the first and the second prisons, they came to the Iron gate leading to the city which of its own accord was opened for them;

[l]   **10b** and having gone out they went down the seven steps and went on one street nearer.

[m]   **10c** And immediately the angel went away from him.

[a′]   **11** Peter, having come to his senses, said, 'Now I know that the Lord truly sent his angel and delivered me out of the hand of Herod and all the expectation of the people of the Jews'.

[b′]   **12** And when he realized this he went up to the house of Mary, the mother of John, called Mark, where many people had gathered and were praying.

[c′]   **13** When he knocked at the door of the porch, a servant named Rhoda approached to answer;

[d′]   **14a** and having recognized the voice of Peter, in her joy she did not open the porch.

[e′]   **14b** Instead, she ran in and announced that Peter was standing at the porch.

[f′]   **15a** But they said to her, 'You're mad!'

[g′]   **15b** However, she insisted that it really was so.

[h′]   **15c** So they said to her, 'Maybe it is his angel?'

6 When Herod was about to bring him forward, in that night Peter was sleeping between two soldiers, bound with two chains and, additionally, two guards in front of the door were guarding the prison.

7a Then suddenly, the angel of the Lord came and stood by and a light shone in the chamber.

7b Striking Peter's side, he woke him up saying, 'Get up quickly!'

7c And his chains peeled off from his hands,

8a and the angel said to him, 'Fasten your belt and put on your sandals'.

8b He did so.

8c And he says to him, 'Put your cloak around you and keep following me!'

9 And he went out and he started to follow, and he did not know that what was happening with the angel was true (he thought he was seeing a vision).

10a When they had gone through the first prison and the second one, they came to the Iron gate leading to the city which of its own accord was opened for them;

10b and having gone out they went on one street.

10c And immediately the angel went away from him.

11 Peter, having come to his senses, said, 'Now I know truly that the Lord sent his angel and delivered me out of the hand of Herod and all the expectation of the people of the Jews',

12 and when he realized this he went up to the house of Mary, the mother of John, called Mark, where many people had gathered and were praying.

13 When he knocked at the door of the porch, a servant approached to answer, named Rhoda;

14a and having recognized the voice of Peter, in her joy she did not open the porch,

14b but she ran in and announced that Peter was standing at the porch.

15a But they said to her, 'You're mad!'

15b However, she insisted that it really was so.

15c But they said, 'It's his angel'.

[i′]	**16a** But he continued knocking.	**16a** But he continued knocking.
[j′]	**16b** When they opened up and saw him, they were quite stupefied.	**16b** When they opened, they saw him and were stupefied.
[k′]	**17a** Having signalled to them with his hand that they should be quiet, he came in and related to them how the Lord had brought him out of the prison.	**17a** He signalled to them with his hand to be quiet and related to them how the Lord had brought him out of the prison,
[l′]	**17b** Then he said, 'Report these things to James and the brethren!'	**17b** and he also said, 'Report these things to James and the brethren!'
[m′]	**17c** And after going out he went to another place.	**17c** And after going out he went to another place.

Critical Apparatus

12.5 προσευχὴ δὲ (ἦν) B 𝔓⁷⁴ ℵ *rell* ‖ πολλὴ δὲ προσ. D d sa mae.

D05 reinforces the notion of the church praying for Peter during the night before he was due to be brought out to the people (in combination with the other two variants in this verse, see below).

(ἦν) ἐκτενῶς γινομένη ὑπὸ τῆς ἐκκλησίας B 𝔓⁷⁴ ℵ A* 33. 181. 216. 440. 453. 1898 e vg; Lcf | ἐκτενὴς γιν. ὑπὸ τ. ἐκκλ. A² E Ψ 1739 𝔐 p syᵖ·ʰ ‖ ἐν ἐκτενείᾳ περὶ αὐτοῦ (– Dˢ·ᵐ·) ἀπὸ τ. ἐκκλ. D* (*instantissime pro eo ab ecclesia* d p).

B03 completes the verb ἦν with a present participle, γινομένη.

ἐκτενῶς and ἐν ἐκτενείᾳ are equivalent adverbial forms, but the latter in D05 is a phrase used elsewhere only in association with the prayers of Israel for salvation or deliverance (i.e. Acts 26.7 [D05 lac.] and Judith 4.9 LXX). ἐκτενῶς is not found elsewhere in Luke's writings (though the comparative form is read by Lk. 22.44 D05 [*om.* B03]); in the LXX, the context is one of repentance (Jon. 3.8; *3 Macc.* 5.9).

The phrase περὶ αὐτοῦ (= Peter) in D05 is in an emphatic position following the adverbial phrase. That it is repeated at the end of the verse may be intentional, to insist that it was Peter that the church was praying for or it may reflect a conflation of two readings (Boismard and Lamouille, II, p. 82).

The difference in preposition ὑπό/ἀπό makes little difference to the sense but rather arises out of seeing either prayer being made by the church to God (B03), or prayer emanating from the church (D05), the latter corresponding to the phrase πρὸς τὸν θεόν which is omitted by B03 (see next variant).

πρὸς τὸν θεόν D d 𝔓⁷⁴ ℵ *rell* ‖ *om.* B 𝔓⁴⁵ᵛⁱᵈ; Cass?

The prepositional phrase may have been omitted because it was thought to be obvious that the church's prayer would be made to God. The idea of prayer as communication is reinforced with the preposition ἀπό in the immediately preceding prepositional phrase in D05 (see previous variant).

12.6 προσαγαγεῖν B 33. 254. 467 *pc* | προσάγειν ℵ Ψ 6. 323. 436. 440. 450. 1611. 2180. 2344. 2412 *pc* aeth ‖ προάγειν D d E H L P 1739 𝔐 gig p vg syʰ |

προαγαγεῖν 𝔓⁷⁴ A 8. 36. 51. 81. 242. 307. 337. 453. 460. 467. 522. 915. 945. 1874. 1891 *al.*

There are two differences here between B03 and D05: first, the choice of verb and secondly the aspect of the verb. προσάγω 'bring forward', echoes the statement of Herod's intention in v. 4, 'to bring him before the people'. προάγω has a similar meaning but is found elsewhere in the context of a trial (B-A-G, προάγω, 1), as at 17.5 (not D05); 25.26 (D05 lac.). As for the aspect, the aorist of B03 presents the action in a global sense whereas with the continuous aspect of the present in D05 the narrator takes the audience into the detail of the action as it unfolds.

ὁ (Ἡρῴδης) B 𝔓⁷⁴ ℵ *rell* || *om.* D; Chr.

The presence of the article is expected, given that Herod has already been introduced into the narrative at 12.1. Its absence therefore draws attention to him, first because Peter has become the focus of attention and secondly, as a means of marking his plan to kill Peter as particularly salient. Compare 12.19, where Herod's name will be anarthrous as he re-enters the story as the principal character (Heimerdinger and Levinsohn, 'The Use of the Article', pp. 25–26).

(φύλακές) τε B 𝔓⁷⁴ᵛⁱᵈ ℵ *rell* || δέ D d e.

It is possible here that τε was the intended connective, the clause adding a supplementary detail to the description of Peter's prison. Although δέ would mark the clause as a particularly significant parenthetical detail, stressing the circumstances in which Peter was imprisoned, this information adds nothing to the narrative at this point and therefore was probably not intended.

12.7 (ἐπέστη) τῷ Πέτρῳ D 1243. 2344 d p vgᴿ sy⁽ᵖ⁾·ʰ** sa mae aeth || *om.* B 𝔓⁷⁴ℵ *rell*; Lcf.

Peter is kept clearly in focus with the repetition of his name in D05.

(φῶς) ἔλαμψεν ἐν τῷ οἰκήματι B 𝔓⁷⁴ᵛⁱᵈ ℵ *rell* (*refulgens in illo loco* d gig p) || ἐπέλαμψεν τ. οἰκ. D 1243. 2344 syʰᵐᵍ mae.

The verb ἐπιλάμπω in D05 suggests that the light emanated from the angel (as is spelt out in some versions which add in varying positions ἀπ᾿ αὐτοῦ [retroversion] (gig p r syʰᵐᵍ; Lcf), see Boismard and Lamouille, II, p. 83). Furthermore, the verb is rare, being found only once in the LXX at Isa. 4.2 to refer to God shining forth in the last days (cf. Isa. 2.2) from the sanctified city of Jerusalem. The prepositional prefix allows the dative of the following noun to be used without a further preposition. The simple verb λάμπω read by B03 is more common but on the four occasions it is used by the LXX it is never associated with light from God.

πατάξας B 𝔓⁷⁴ᵛⁱᵈ ℵ *rell* || νύξας D 1243. 2344, *pungens* d gig syᵖ·ʰ mae; Lcf Chr.

πατάσσω, the reading of B03, is shared by all Greek MSS and, while it can mean to give a light push, it also has a stronger meaning and is the verb used to describe the killing of Herod (12.23), as indeed the killing of the first-born at the Passover, the paradigm for the present incident. D05 avoids any ambiguous echo of that scene by using νύσσω instead.

αὐτοῦ αἱ ἁλύσεις ἐκ τῶν χειρῶν B 𝔓⁷⁴ ℵ *rell, eius catenae de manibus* d ‖ αἱ ἁλ. ἐκ τ. χειρ. αὐτοῦ D gig p r vg syᵖ sa mae aeth; Lcf Ephr.

B03 associates 'the chains' with Peter, whereas D05 reads the possessive pronoun with 'the hands'.

12.8 (εἶπεν) δέ B D d E H Ψ 049. 36. 81*. 88. 453. 614. 618. 945. 1175. 1270. 1611. 1739. 1891. 2412 *al* lat syʰ ‖ τε 𝔓⁷⁴ ℵ A L P 056. 33 𝔐.

ℵ01 with τε considers the continuation of the angel's words as complementing what had already been said. Both B03 and D05 view it as a new development.

12.9 (ἐδόκει) δέ B 𝔓⁷⁴ ℵ² *rell* | *om.* ℵ* a aeth ‖ γάρ D d 36. 453. 431. 1828 *pc* gig p r vg^{DOT} syᵖ sa mae.

In both B03 and D05, the narrator makes a parenthetical comment but whereas B03 makes a descriptive comment with δέ looking forward to the following narrative (cf. v. 11 when he becomes sure that he was not just seeing things), D05 looks back with γάρ to explain what he has just said, i.e. that Peter did not know that what was happening was really true (Levinsohn, *Textual Connections*, p. 91; Read-Heimerdinger, *The Bezan Text*, pp. 244–45).

12.10 (πρώτην) φυλακὴν καὶ δευτέραν B 𝔓⁷⁴ ℵ *rell* ‖ κ. δευτ. φυλ. D d 2401 gig p r vg syᵖ·ʰ; Lcf Chr.

The word order of the two cardinal adjectives and the noun varies: B03 separates the two adjectives and thereby treats the two prisons as separate and as unexpected to some extent; D03, in contrast, keeps the adjectives together, thus linking the prisons together and regarding their dual existence as something to be expected. The difference probably reflects two different ways of reading the account of Peter's escape from prison, either as a literal escape (B03) or as a metaphorical one (D05; see *Commentary*).

(ἐξελθόντες) κατέβησαν τοὺς ·ζ· βαθμοὺς D d (p mae) ‖ *om.* B 𝔓⁷⁴ ℵ *rell*.

The seven steps mentioned by D05 are commonly supposed to reflect the scribe's local knowledge of the Jerusalem prison in the first century (cf. Bruce, *Text*, p. 246; Clark, *Acts*, pp. 348–49; Metzger, *Commentary*, pp. 347–48), despite the fact that for most of the text the Bezan scribe is assumed to be a Gentile from a later century! The detail is more likely to have a theological purpose, echoing the description of the eschatological Temple seen in Ezekiel's vision (cf. Ezek. 40.22, 26) which the Lord is causing Peter to leave (see *Commentary*). Ropes (*Text*, p. 111) claims that the reference to seven steps in Ezekiel's Temple 'furnishes no satisfactory explanation' for their mention in Acts 12 D05. The explanation becomes satisfactory once the other pointers to Ezekiel in Acts 12 are taken into account and once the symbolic nature of the episode is recognized.

προῆλθον Β 𝔓⁷⁴ ℵ A E H P Ψ 049. 056. 33. 1739 𝔐 | προσ- L 104*. 209. 618 ‖ καὶ προσῆλθαν D d.

The connective in D05 is necessary because of the supplementary verb in the previous clause (see variant above). προέρχομαι in B03 is the easier reading, meaning that 'they carried on, went further' (B-A-G, προέρχομαι, 1), with the accusative ῥύμην μίαν expressing the distance covered, 'for one street'. προσέρχομαι in D05 means 'approach' (B-A-G, προσέρχομαι, 1), where again the accusative following can express the distance (the dative would be used to express the object approached). What is odd is the use of the verb in an absolute sense – what or whom did Peter and the angel approach? The explanation will become apparent as Peter's story continues when it emerges that the angel of the Lord had in mind the house of Mary, the church that was free from Ierousalem, as the goal of Peter's journey out of his spiritual prison (see *Commentary*).

12.11 αὐτῷ Β* ‖ ἐν ἑαυτῷ D d Β² 𝔓⁷⁴ ℵ *rell* sy; Chr.

B03 is alone in reading the weaker reflexive form of the pronoun in the simple dative without a preposition. The variant is comparable to that found at 10.17 where B03 again reads the weaker pronoun and D05 has the strong reflexive, except that there the verb on which the pronoun depends varies according to the text followed. A truer comparison can be made with Lk. 15.17 where the reflexive pronoun is read by both texts (εἰς ἑαυτὸν δὲ ἐλθών).

(οἶδα) ἀληθῶς ὅτι Β 𝔓⁷⁴ ℵ A H L P 049. 056. 33 𝔐 ‖ ὅτι ἀλ. D d E Ψ 913. 1108. 1611. 2138 e p r aeth; Lcf Chr.

The word order gives a somewhat different sense to the comment. The context is that Peter was not sure if what was happening to him through the angel was true (cf. 12.9a). Now, according to B03, he becomes sure, 'I know truly', as if before he thought he must have been dreaming. D05 puts it differently: he now realizes that God had truly sent his angel, whereas before he thought quite literally that he was having a vision (cf. 12.9b). D05, in other words, indicates that Peter's belief that God was showing him a vision (such as he had had before, cf. 10.10-16) is corrected; B03, on the other hand, simply portrays Peter as becoming certain in his knowledge that what was happening was real.

(ἐξαπέστειλεν) ὁ κύριος Β 𝔓⁷⁴ᵛⁱᵈ Ψ 614. 1611. 1837. 2344. 2412 | ὁ θεός 36. 242. 323. 431. 453. 522. 945. (1241). 1739. 1891. 2298 p ‖ κύριος D ℵ A E H L P 049. 056. 33 𝔐.

The omission of the article before κύριος can be explained partly by the fact that Peter's words echo those of Jethro, Moses' father-in-law, on learning of the deliverance of the Israelites from Pharaoh (Exod. 18.8-11) and that κύριος is anarthrous in the LXX of that passage. However, in both instances, the omission of the article may well arise on the grounds of salience: this is the first time that

Peter has become aware of the presence of the Lord throughout his escape from prison, and that Jethro learns of the Lord's action in freeing his people. Their reference to 'the Lord' is consequently, from their point of view, a first mention. The presence of the article takes account of neither of these factors, both of them typically more usually observed in the D05 text than that of B03 (see Read-Heimerdinger, *The Bezan Text*, pp. 139–43; 294, 296).

12.12 συνιδών τε B 𝔓⁷⁴ ℵ E H L P Ψ 049. 056. 1739 𝔐 | συν. δέ A 33. 36. 81. 242. 257. 330. 431. 440. 453. 522. 927. 945. 1245. 1270. 1505. 1837. 2344. 2401. 2495 e gig p r sa; Theoph || καὶ συν. D d | συνιδών mae aeth.

The variants τε and δέ could be dependent one on the other by reason of phonetic confusion whereas καί in D05 is distinct, introducing as it does a step that is linked to the Peter's new-found awareness (12.11) but not as closely as with τε.

12.13 προσῆλθεν B* D 𝔓⁷⁴ *rell* || προ- B² ℵ 3 *pc* lat.

The same variant was noted in v. 10 above. Here, both B03* and D05 share προσέρχομαι.

(παιδίσκη) ὑπακοῦσαι (-ούουσα ℵ*) ὀνόματι Ῥόδη B ℵ² *rell* c syᵖ·ʰ | ὑπαντῆσαι ὀν. Ῥ. 𝔓⁷⁴ || ὀν. Ῥ. ὑπακοῦσαι D d r.

The order of words in ℵ01*, where a participle follows the noun it relates to, is perhaps easier than that in B03 (or 𝔓⁷⁴) where the name of the servant is separated from the noun by an infinitive, as if her task of answering the door was of foremost importance. The order of D05, where the name of the servant follows the noun, accords more importance to her identity.

12.14 καὶ (εἰσδραμοῦσα δέ) D* d p || *om.* B Dˢ·ᵐ· 𝔓⁷⁴ ℵ *rell*.

The particle before the participle could be considered to be adverbial, reinforcing Rhoda's action of running back into the house; but it is also possible to view καί as the connecting word and δέ as underlining the contrast between Rhoda's action and what she would have been expected to do, namely, open the door to Peter. There is no need to consider the initial καί as an error, for καί ... δέ is found elsewhere in the New Testament, especially with the force of the second explanation above (cf. e.g. Mt. 16.18; Jn 6.51 B03; Acts 6.15 D05; 13.6 D05; 22.29 [D05 lac.]; 1 Jn 1.3; see Moule, *Idiom Book*, p. 165; Winer, *Grammar*, p. 553).

τὸν (Πέτρον) B Dᶜ 𝔓⁷⁴ ℵ *rell* || *om.* D*.

The absence of the article in D05 is explained by the fact that the observation is made from the point of view of Rhoda speaking to the assembled disciples – the mention of Peter is totally unexpected and is signalled as such by the omission of the article. It is typical of D05 to respect the point of view of the speaker rather than the narrator or the hearer (cf. comments on the absence of the article before κύριος in 12.11 above).

12.15 (οἱ δὲ) πρὸς αὐτὴν εἶπαν B (D^C) 𝔓^74 ℵ A E H L P Ψ 1739 𝔐 d | εἶπον πρ. αὐτήν 𝔓^45vid 33. 2344 gig p r vg; Chr ‖ ἔλεγον αὐτῇ D* gig p vg sy^p.

The two constructions (πρός + acc. or the dat. alone) used by Luke to introduce the addressee after a verb of speaking give rise to a number of variants (for an analysis of the question, see Read-Heimerdinger, *The Bezan Text*, pp. 176–82, esp. 178). Typically, πρός + accusative is used at the onset of a conversation, and the dative alone when the conversation is already underway. Here in B03, the use of the preposition can be explained by the fact that this is the first time that the disciples address Rhoda. It is unusual, however, for a preposition to be used for a conversation between two speakers that does not continue (see next variant below). In D05, in contrast, the dative case is an indication that the disciples were not intending to engage with Rhoda in the conversation she had initiated, as their disparaging comment implies. When her insistence forces them to take notice of her, they then address her in a more direct manner (see next variant below).

(οἱ δὲ) ἔλεγον 𝔓^45.74 ℵ A H L P 049. 056. 33. 1739 𝔐 | ἐλ. ὅτι Ψ | εἶπαν B ‖ ἐλ. πρὸς αὐτήν· Τυχόν D (*dixerunt ad eam: Forsitan* d) sy^p (mae).

D05 specifies the addressee of the disciples' comment about the person knocking at the door as Rhoda. On the use of the preposition, see variant above. In B03, where the disciples have previously engaged in conversation with Rhoda, their comment would now seem to be addressed to no-one in particular but is made as a suggestion among themselves.

τυχόν is read only here and as a variant at Lk. 20.13 D05 in the whole of the New Testament.

ὁ ἄγγελός ἐστιν αὐτοῦ B 𝔓^74 A | ἄγγ. ἐστ. αὐ. ℵ 𝔓^45vid ‖ ὁ ἄγγ. αὐ. ἐστ. D d ℵ^2 E H L P Ψ 049. 056. 33. 1739 𝔐.

The word order of D05 may well have arisen because of the presence of τυχόν at the beginning of the disciples' sentence according to that text (see previous variant above).

12.16 (ὁ δὲ) Πέτρος B 𝔓^45.74 ℵ *rell* ‖ *om.* D d 2344 p r aeth; Chr.

Peter is mentioned by name in B03. The reference to him by the simple pronoun in D05 is an indication that the spotlight has been on Peter throughout this incident.

ἀνοίξαντες B D^s.m. 𝔓^45.74 ℵ *rell* (*cum aperuisset* d) ‖ ἐξ- D*.

D05 uses the compound verb which is the more difficult reading (there is no other use of it in the New Testament), but it may be translated 'opened up' as if the house were securely locked up as, indeed, it may well have been in the middle of the night.

εἶδον (-αν B A) B 𝔓^74 ℵ *rell, viderunt* d ‖ καὶ (– D^s.m.) ἰδόντες D* bo (aeth); Chr (BarS).

B03, having started the sentence with a participle (see previous variant), continues with two finite verbs conjoined with καί. D05, in contrast, has a series of two participles conjoined with καί and followed by a finite verb (ἐξέστησαν) preceded by an adverbial καί. The main notion of the sentence is thus clearly signalled as being the disciples' amazement, because it is expressed by the only finite verb and is preceded by an adverbial καί in a manner that is typical of D05 at points of particular drama in a story (Read-Heimerdinger, *The Bezan Text*, pp. 206–10; J. Rius-Camps, 'Le substrat grec de la version latine des Actes dans le Codex de Bèze', in D.C. Parker and C.-B. Amphoux [eds], *Codex Bezae: Studies from the Lunel Colloquium June 1994* [Leiden: Brill, 1996], pp. 271–295 [283]).

12.17 (τῇ χειρὶ) σιγᾶν B D[s.m.] 𝔓[45.74] ℵ *rell* ‖ ἵνα σιγῶσιν D*, *ut silerent* d p vg[ms] sy[p.h**] mae.

D05* spells out with a subjunctive clause what is implied in the infinitive of B03.

εἰσῆλθεν καί D, *introiens et* d p sy[p.h**] mae ‖ *om*. B 𝔓[45vid.74] ℵ *rell*.

D05 further makes explicit that Peter came into the house to talk with the disciples who had gathered there.

(διηγήσατο) αὐτοῖς B D d E H L P Ψ 049. 056. 614. 𝔐 gig (r) sy mae ‖ *om*. 𝔓[45vid.74vid] ℵ A 33. 81. 945. 1739. 1837. 1891. 2344 *pc* p vg.

Both B03 and D05 use the dative pronoun to make explicit Peter's addressees, but it is not unusual for it to be omitted by the AT (Read-Heimerdinger, *The Bezan Text*, pp. 181–82).

(εἶπεν) δέ D d H L P Ψ 049. 056. 1. 33*. 614. 1739 𝔐; Chr ‖ τε B 𝔓[45.74] ℵ A E 33[c]. 81. 1175. 1837.

While B03 views Peter's request for his account to be passed on to other brethren (not present at Mary's house) as closely linked to his telling of the story, D05 presents it in a separate sentence, thereby conferring on it a certain importance.

Commentary

[a] 12.5a *Peter in Prison*

12.5a The conjunction μὲν οὖν in Greek introduces the first event of the new sequence as arising from the previous statement, and anticipates a second (see 12.5b).[20] The opening picture, accordingly, is of Peter kept in his cell. The imperfect passive, ἐτερεῖτο, 'was being kept' expresses Peter's helplessness.

[b] 12.5b *The Church at Prayer for Peter*

12.5b In contrast, and as the more significant action at this point, the church was engaged in praying for Peter, with the imperfect again placing special emphasis

20. Levinsohn, *Textual Connections*, pp. 141–50.

on the continuous persistence of the church. In Codex Bezae there are a number of variants that function together to heighten the sense of urgency in the praying and confirm the awareness of the people praying of the real purpose of their prayer (see *Critical Apparatus* for details): the adjective πολλή, 'much' describes the prayer; it is made ἐν ἐκτενείᾳ, 'earnestly', using a rare word that is only used in the Scriptures of the prayers of Israel for deliverance or salvation; περὶ αὐτοῦ, 'about him (Peter)', is repeated twice which, if not accidental, underlines the focus of their praying as Peter; the prayer goes from the church and is directed to God – the last point is obvious but making the addressee of the prayers explicit has the effect of drawing attention to their reliance on God to rescue Peter from the extreme danger of his situation (both literally and metaphorically).

The community praying for him are portrayed, unlike Peter himself as will be seen (v. 6 below), as conscious of the importance of what is at stake in his imprisonment and what his deliverance will mean. The attitude of the church further tallies with the attitude that the Israelites were to adopt on the night of Passover: it was to be 'night of watching' (Exod. 12.42), a theme that was extensively developed in Jewish tradition.[21]

According to the portrait of the church in 12.12, they were indeed praying during the night of his release, although it becomes apparent at that point that the church (ἐκκλησία) referred to here in v. 5b as praying for Peter may mean only a section of the church in Jerusalem (unlike v. 1), since it is doubtful whether the church led by James would have appreciated what was at stake in terms of Peter's liberation from the Jewish ways of thinking.

[c] 12.6 *Peter is Asleep with Guards at the Door*
12.6 The time is now specified as 'that night', the one before Herod was intending to bring Peter before the people. Although logically, within the chronology of the account this night would be at the end of the Passover week (the end of the twenty-first day, cf. Exod. 12.17) whereas the Passover itself would have been celebrated on the fifteenth day (cf. on v. 3. above), Luke applies another logic to his narrative which causes this night now to be the night of Passover. This is not an author who was careless about detail and who adjusted the facts to suit his purpose; rather, it was an author who was fully in tune with a way of thinking that considered 'spiritual' facts to be more real than 'historical' facts, and time to be irrelevant to the former.[22] The evocation of the Passover night, the night when the Lord freed the Israelites from Egypt by striking dead all the first born of the Egyptians, is achieved here by use of the phrase 'in that night' (τῇ νυκτὶ ἐκείνῃ) which echoes the phrase used repeatedly in the Exodus account (τῇ νυκτὶ ταύτῃ, Exod. 12.8, 12, 42 LXX *passim*).

---

21. The idea of 'watching' was invested with special importance in the second century Quartodeciman community of Jewish Christians, for whom the whole period of Unleavened Bread appeared to be time of watching (Le Déaut, *La nuit pascale*, pp. 292–93; cf. p. 296, n. 116).

22. On the Jewish view of history and time, see D. Patte, *Early Jewish Hermeneutic in Palestine* (Dissertation Series, 22; Richmond, VA: SBL, 1975), p. 69; J. Sacks, *Crisis and Covenant* (Manchester: Manchester University Press, 1992), pp. 208–46.

In direct contrast with the church 'watching' in prayer, Peter is portrayed as 'sleeping'. The imperfect periphrastic construction ἦν ... κοιμώμενος, 'was sleeping', emphatically underlines his lack of awareness of what was really happening, just as the disciples who accompanied Jesus both on the mountain at his transfiguration (Lk. 9.32)[23] and in the garden before his crucifixion (22.45)[24] were equally unaware of what was happening because they were sleeping. In all three cases, the state of sleep reflects Peter's inner state of mind which caused him to be unaware of the significance of what was going on, or prevented him from being engaged in any way with it.[25]

Not only is Peter sound asleep, making any kind of escape unlikely, but he is tied up with two chains and closely guarded, with two guards on either side of him and another two at the door of the prison, making the notion of escape hopelessly unrealistic. All the more striking, then, is the fact that the praying community, aware of the significance of Peter's imprisonment and of the night of Passover, are prepared to invest their efforts in asking God for his release.

In addition to the Exodus parallel running through this scene (see *Excursus* 6), another model serves as a point of reference for it. It is one created by Luke himself in his Gospel, the shepherds on the night of Jesus' birth:[26] by their positive attitude and behaviour they show up the weaknesses of Peter in contrast. The shepherds, like Peter, were ordinary people and not the religious powers; but during the night when the Messiah arrived, they were keeping watch, unlike Peter who was asleep.[27] They were prepared and watching for the Messiah to arrive (it is not important from the spiritual point of view that they did not know he was going to arrive that night), whereas Peter was unprepared and sleeping while the church 'watched' on his behalf. The paradigm of the shepherds continues as the story of Peter unfolds (see *Excursus* 7).

[d] 12.7a *The Angel of the Lord Appears*
12.7a A new participant is brought on stage to interrupt the scene in the prison just described. The appearance of the angel of the Lord, unexpected from a human point of view in so far as Herod had made every effort to ensure the security of the prison, is introduced with the formula (literally): 'And behold!',

---

23. Lk. 9.32: 'Peter and those with him were overcome by sleep', ἦσαν βεβαρημένοι ὕπνῳ, another periphrastic construction.

24. Lk. 22.45: Jesus found the disciples 'sleeping', κοιμωμένους αὐτούς, for sorrow; cf. 22.46, where he encouraged them to pray instead: Τί [*om.* D05] καθεύδετε; ἀναστάντες προσεύχεσθε.

25. Cf. Jesus who fell asleep (ἀφύπνωσεν) in the boat during the storm, quite unaffected by the problems the disciples were facing (Lk. 8.23).

26. The paradigm of the shepherds at the nativity was first identified by J. Rius-Camps, in 'Qui és Joan, l'anomenat "Marc"?', *RCatT* 5 (1980), pp. 303–309.

27. The shepherds were said to be literally 'keeping the watches of the night', ἦσαν ... φυλάσσοντες (+ τὰς D05) φυλακὰς τῆς νυκτός (Lk. 2.8); Peter, on the other hand, was sleeping during the 'night of watching' while being himself heavily guarded by four guards in prison. In Greek, 'keep', 'watch', 'guard', 'prison' all derive from the same root, φυλακ-: in Acts 12.4, the verb φυλάσσω is used, the noun φυλακή 5 times in 12.4, 5, 6, 10, 17, and the noun φύλαξ twice in 12.6, 19.

translated as 'Then suddenly'.[28] Another resonance is set up with the story of the shepherds to whom the angel of the Lord also appeared: 'Then suddenly the angel of the Lord appeared to them.'[29] In the Exodus scene, although according to the initial declaration it is the Lord himself who frees Israel from slavery to Pharaoh when he passes through the land of Egypt during the night (Exod. 12.12-13, 23, 29), in later tradition it is 'the angel of the Lord' who is mentioned (cf. Num. 20.16).

A further parallel with the Exodus scene is evoked by the mention of the light. In the Bezan text, the choice of verb (ἐπιλάμπω, 'shine out') implies that the light emanated from the angel, as indeed several versions spell out (see *Critical Apparatus*). The verb is rare, being found only occasionally in the LXX, and only in a figurative sense as at Isa. 4.2[30] where it refers to God shining forth from the sanctified city of Jerusalem in the last days (cf. Isa 2.2) when, as a clear reminder of the Exodus event, there will also be a cloud by day and the light of fire by night. In the targums to Exodus, the theme of light associated with the Passover is considerably expanded with the light standing for the actual presence of God. Codex Bezae, by using the rare verb to describe the light that shone in Peter's cell as the angel appeared, echoes the Isaiah passage and thereby enables the light to be understood as an allusion to the light of God's presence with his people during the Exodus. At the same time, the light recalls the shepherds' scene where glory (of the Lord, not D05) shone around them (Lk. 2.9).[31] The shepherds reacted to the light, albeit with fear, unlike Peter who continues sleeping, unaware of the presence of the angel or of the light in his chamber.

The word Luke uses (οἴκημα) to refer to the room where Peter was a prisoner and which was lit up by the light, is a rare one and with associations that at this point in the narrative may appear as odd, even misplaced. At Ezek. 16.24 LXX it refers to the chamber of prostitution the Jews had built in Jerusalem in their faithlessness and rebellion against God. At the only two other references in the Bible, it designates a room to set up for an idol (Wisd. 13.15), and a room to store a dead body (Tob. 2.4). The implication here is that Peter's prison represents the summit of Israel's wickedness and desertion of their God. This notion will be developed in the following verses as it becomes clear that the underlying significance Luke seeks to communicate through this incident overall is that the Jews have rebelled against Yahweh and become faithless to him.

---

28. καὶ ἰδού introduces an unexpected new element into a narrative, frequently from the point of view of the character already on stage (cf. 2.2 D05; 8.27; 10.30); that is clearly not the case here as Peter is asleep and the guards do not see the angel.

29. The two sentences are particularly similar in the D05 text: καὶ [+ ἰδού D05] ἄγγελος κυρίου ἐπέστη αὐτοῖς (Lk. 2.9) // καὶ ἰδού ἄγγελος κυρίου ἐπέστη [+ τῷ Πέτρῳ D05] (Acts 12.7).

30. Isa. 4.2 LXX: τῇ δὲ ἡμέρᾳ ἐκείνῃ ἐπιλάμψει ὁ θεὸς ἐν βουλῇ μετὰ δόξης ἐπὶ τῆς γῆς τοῦ ὑψῶσαι καὶ δοξάσαι τὸ καταλειφθὲν τοῦ Ἰσραήλ, 'In that day, God will shine out in his purpose with glory on the land to exalt and glorify the remnant of Israel'.

31. Lk. 2.9: δόξα κυρίου [*om.* D05] περιέλαμψεν αὐτούς.

[e] 12.7b *The Angel Orders Peter to Get Up*

12.7b The first task of the angel is to wake Peter up in order to get him to move. The verb used by all Greek manuscripts except Codex Bezae and two minuscules is πατάσσω which can mean to 'give a light push', as presumably here, but also has a stronger sense of 'strike a blow' and even 'kill'. It is used repeatedly in the Exodus narrative with the meaning of 'kill' to refer to the slaying of the first-born of Egypt on the night of Passover; it will also be used of the killing of Herod by the angel of the Lord (cf. Acts 12.23). These associations, inappropriate in the context of Peter being awoken, are avoided by the more neutral verb in Codex Bezae, νύσσω, meaning here to 'nudge'. The fact that they seem not to cause a difficulty for the AT suggests either that they were not recognized or that, if they were, the verb had a sufficiently general meaning for it to be used without creating ambiguity.

The angel will give Peter three orders which he will obey without question but (as will be seen in v. 9) without understanding what was going on or even knowing whether it was real. The first order is to 'Get up quickly', reminiscent both of the order to the Israelites to eat the lamb quickly on the night of Passover (Exod. 12.11) and of the speed with which the Egyptians told the Israelites to 'get up' and leave their land (12.33).[32]

[f] 12.7c *Peter's Chains Fall off*

12.7c The reaction to the first order of the angel happens without Peter's involvement, as the chains fall off his hands. The first step in his deliverance has thus been achieved and from now on he will begin to respond himself.

[g] 12.8a *The Angel Orders Peter to Get Dressed*

12.8a The angel's second order follows immediately, with clear echoes of the Lord's commands to the people of Israel on the night of Passover: 'Fasten your belt (lit. 'gird, clothe yourself') and put on your shoes', two procedures necessary for walking quickly, just as the Israelites had to be prepared to move quickly out of Egypt and so were to eat the Passover meal in a state of preparedness: 'clothed and your sandals on your feet' (Exod. 12.11).[33]

[h] 12.8b *Peter Obeys*

12.8b Now Peter responds of his own accord without any deliberation or hesitation. He is about to undertake his exodus from the oppression of the religious system of values and attitudes that were preventing him from fully realizing the freedom of Jesus' teaching.

---

32. In this instance, the language of Acts, ἐν τάχει, does not use the same terms as the Greek of Exodus 12 LXX which reads μετὰ σπουδῆς (12.11); Ἀνάστητε ... σπουδῇ (12.31-33). On the other hand, the parallel scene of the shepherds in Luke's Gospel does use the Exodus language (cf. σπεύσαντες [-δοντες D05], Lk. 2.16).

33. Acts 12.8: ζῶσαι καὶ ὑπόδησαι τὰ σανδάλιά σου; Exod 12.11 LXX: αἱ ὀσφύες ὑμῶν περιεζωσμέναι, καὶ τὰ ὑποδήματα ἐν τοῖς ποσὶν ὑμῶν.

[i] 12.8c *The Angel's Further Orders*
12.8c The third order of the angel is the final order that completes the preparations for the escape from the prison. The use of the present tense, λέγει, 'he says' (cf. aor. v. 8a), anticipates the importance of the action about to follow,[34] that is, the last order Peter has to carry out means that the departure is imminent. Putting his cloak on signifies readiness for a journey, just as it did for the Israelites who were instructed to wrap their kneading bowls in their cloaks as they travelled (Exod. 12.34). In the second part of the command, ἀκολούθει μοι, 'follow me', it becomes evident that the angel is no less than Jesus the Lord himself who has come to free Peter, for the verb ἀκολουθέω is only used in Luke's Gospel as a technical term with reference to Jesus, and the command ἀκολούθει μοι is always spoken by Jesus (Lk. 5.27; 9.23, 59; 18.22). It is Jesus who invites Peter to follow him out of the prison.

[j] 12.9 *Peter's Compliance*
12.9 Peter began his journey as he 'went out', presumably out of his cell, this being the first of a series of compounds of the verb, ἔρχομαι, 'go', that mark the progressive steps the angel causes him to take to get out of the prison.[35] As he left, Peter 'started to follow'[36] the angel. The use of the imperfect expresses his uncertainty at this point, which the narrator explains in an aside: although he was awake, Peter was not fully aware of what was going on. In the AT, the comment reads as if he thought he was dreaming, anticipating his declaration as he comes fully to his senses, 'Now I know truly…' (12.11). In Codex Bezae, however, there are some slight differences which, combined, have the effect of portraying Peter literally believing that he was experiencing a vision (ὅραμα) – he has, of course, had a vision not so long ago (cf. 10.9-17) and now he thinks that what is happening is another one (see *Critical Apparatus*): first, the narrator's comment about seeing a vision is intended to justify the observation that Peter did not know what was happening, whereas in the AT the comment is added as if making another point; secondly, at 12.11, the word order of Codex Bezae makes it clear that Peter had known that he was witnessing the Lord acting but he had not realized it was happening literally, unlike the AT which shows Peter as being uncertain as whether anything was happening at all (see *Commentary,* 12.11).

[k] 12.10a *The Angel and Peter Make their Way out of the Prison*
12.10a The next three elements comprise the successive steps taken to get out of the prison itself, described in exact detail (especially in Codex Bezae) not

---

34. The rhetorical effect of the historic present in the New Testament when it occurs in sentences introducing direct speech has been observed to be to detach the speech in order to highlight it. When the historical present is used to introduce the concluding speech of an incident, the reason for highlighting it is often because it prepares the way for the action that follows (see Levinsohn, *Discourse Features*, pp. 141, 144–45).

35. Other occurrences of the verb ἔρχομαι or one of its compounds arise in 12.10a: διελθόντες, ἦλθαν; 12.10b: ἐξελθόντες; 12.10c: προῆλθον (προσῆλθαν D05).

36. The imperfect ἠκολούθει following an aorist participle has the force of the inceptive aspect.

because Luke had an interest in the topography of the prison in Jerusalem but rather because each element represents a distinct step in Peter's spiritual journey to freedom.

First, the angel and Peter go through two prisons. The existence of two prisons is often commented on as puzzling and causes some to interpret, quite legitimately, the word φυλακή as the soldiers guarding the prison because it is easier to think of the route out of the prison going past two guards than through two buildings. It will be seen, however, that in the Bezan text the prison in which Peter has been kept by Herod, on behalf of the Jewish people, is a metaphor for the eschatological expectations of the Jews from which the Lord is delivering him by means of his angel (cf. on vv. 10b, 10c, 11 below). According to this metaphor, the prison represents the restored Temple seen by Ezekiel in his vision of Jerusalem when Israel has returned there from exile (Ezekiel 40–46; see *Overview* and *Excursus* 8). The 'first and the second prison' can thus be seen to represent the two courts that are an integral part of the restored Temple, the outer and the inner one, repeatedly referred to throughout Ezekiel's vision. In order to leave the sanctuary where the presence of Yahweh was found, and reach the gate leading out to the city, the two courts would have to be crossed. The order of the phrase in the Bezan text (see *Critical Apparatus*) reflects better than the AT the understanding of the two prisons/courts as closely related to each other and as an expected feature of the place out of which Peter was, figuratively, being led.

The metaphor continues with the reference to 'the Iron gate (τὴν πύλην τὴν σιδηρᾶν) ... that of its own accord was opened for them'. The gates or doors of the Temple (also referred to with the noun πύλη, cf. Acts 3.10) generally are an important and recurring idea in scriptural traditions where mention is made of the opening or closing of the doors in order either to protect the holiness of the Temple or in order for God to enter into his house (cf. e.g. Mal. 1.10; Acts 21.30). The door of the Temple is specifically mentioned as an element of the Passover observance by Josephus who records that it was left open on the night of Passover for the return of the Messiah.[37] In Ezekiel's vision, the eastern outer 'porch' (ἡ πύλη) of the new Temple by which 'the Lord the God of Israel' had entered had to remain locked: no-one else was allowed to open it or go through it (Ezek. 44.2). In the case of Peter, the outer door of the Temple by which he left the metaphorical Temple was the eastern one, as is about to be made clear; it was shut but now opens of its own accord as the Lord leaves the Temple prepared for him in the restored city of Jerusalem taking his people with him.[38]

37. *Ant.* 18, 29, cited by Le Déaut, *La nuit pascale*, p. 288; cf. p. 294 on the significance of the door for the Quartodeciman community.
38. A further tradition, recorded by the Artapanus, a Hellenistic Jew of the third/second century BCE, has Moses escaping from the prison where Pharaoh had locked him up by a gate that opened of its own accord (αὐτομάτη): according to Artapanus, Pharaoh had imprisoned Moses because he was jealous of him (cited by Eusebius, *Praeparatio Evangelica*, 9.27); cf. the High Priests and the Sadducees who were 'jealous' of the apostles, Acts 5.17.

[I] 12.10b *They Go down the Seven Steps*
12.10b It is with the detail that as the angel and Peter went out of the Temple 'they went down the seven steps', that Codex Bezae leaves the clearest clue that Ezekiel's vision of the restored Temple for the end-times is the figurative paradigm on which the release of Peter from prison is constructed. The description of the construction of the Temple given to Ezekiel in his vision is very detailed and includes precise measurements and quantities. Among many other things, the number of steps between the levels of the different courts is specified; in particular, at the gates leading from outside the wall of the Temple up into the outer court, and only there, there were seven steps (Ezek. 40. 22, 26, cf. vv. 5-6). In Luke's account of Peter's route out of the 'prison' he has already shown him going through the inner and the outer courts, through the Iron gate (cf. 12.10a above) and now, he goes down the seven steps leading from the outer court into the city.

The interpretation given to the seven steps is supported by the verb Luke uses to 'go down', καταβαίνω. This verb has specific connotations in the work of Luke who uses it when he means to 'go down' from the holy city (cf. Lk. 10.30, 31), as opposed to 'go down' in a neutral, geographical sense for which he uses κατέρχομαι (cf. the prophets who 'went down', κατῆλθον, from Judaea, 11.27, and see *Commentary, ad loc.*). The fact that he selected the religious term here is in accord with his use of 'the seven steps' to refer to the eschatological Temple as a symbol of the Jewish hopes of restoration and messianic deliverance from which Peter is being freed by the angel of the Lord.

The theological purpose of alluding to Ezekiel means that the mention of the seven steps in Codex Bezae has nothing to do with Luke or his sources or the Bezan scribe having access to first-hand knowledge about the prison in Jerusalem where Peter was kept, as is frequently supposed (see *Critical Apparatus*), but everything to do with the figurative sense of Peter's imprisonment and his liberation from the prison by the angel of the Lord. That the AT omits the mention, just as it omits here in Acts 12 and elsewhere many other expressions and words that express a theological message, is yet one more instance of the tendency of this text to turn the narrative into more of a historical, chronological account. The omission of 'the seven steps', which could actually have made the account seem more realistic and historically accurate, suggests that the allusion to Ezekiel's vision has been recognized and deliberately removed. The same will happen to the assimilation of Herod with the Prince of Tyre, which is also derived from the prophecy of Ezekiel and which, though evident in Codex Bezae, is all but absent from the AT (see *Excursus* 9).

The final part of the journey out of the prison which the angel makes with Peter is along one street in the town: just one, enough to make sure that Peter is really out of prison and is safely in the freedom of the city. Exactly the same point was made in the account of the flight of the Israelites from Egypt: 'God did not lead them by the way of the land of the Philistines, although that was near, for God said: "Lest the people repent when they see war, and return to Egypt"' (Exod. 13.17).

The Bezan text gives a hint here of there being a particular destination intended for Peter, for instead of saying that they 'went on one street' it says they 'went one street nearer'. 'Nearer' to what? It will become clear in v. 12 that the goal of the journey on which the angel took Peter was the community of disciples that met in the house of Mary, a community that was itself free of the restrictions of the Jewish expectations since they were 'earnestly praying' for Peter with a view to his release (see *Commentary*, 12.6, 12). These disciples are distinct from those under the leadership of James (cf. 12.17b) who, as will be seen in chapter 15, continued to live within the traditional boundaries of Judaism in Ierousalem.

[m] 12.10c *The Angel Leaves Peter Alone*

12.10c Once there is no risk that Peter will turn back to stay within the familiar security of the traditional religious system he knows so well, the angel leaves him to continue the journey on his own. In the parallel situation in the Gospel, the angels who had appeared to the shepherds also left them (Lk. 2.15)[39] but whereas the shepherds had joyfully received the news that was announced to them (cf. 2.10), Peter has yet to become aware of what has happened to him.

[a'] 12.11 *Peter's Realization of his Deliverance*

12.11 Once Peter has been brought out of the prison by the angel of the Lord, he makes another journey, this time towards a positive goal, a community of disciples where once again there will be someone to help him, but to enter rather than to leave. The first thing is that he must become aware of what had happened in order to act as a free person.

Accordingly, Peter 'came to his senses', just as he had done after his vision in Joppa according to the Bezan text (cf. 10.17 D05). The observation here that Peter now becomes aware of what had gone on takes up the idea of a vision, mentioned in an aside as Peter started to leave the prison (cf. 12.9), but with a slight difference according to the text followed. In the AT, Peter now is quite sure that his deliverance was real, as if before he had thought he was dreaming. In the Bezan text, however, he now realizes that what he had thought was a vision (such as he had seen in Joppa, for example) was not a vision at all but had happened in reality and he truly had been brought out of the prison.

In fact, the words of Peter's declaration at this point reveal that he understood only too well that it was not (or not only) a literal prison from which he had been freed. For they are reminiscent of the words of Jethro, on hearing from his son-in-law Moses about the deliverance of the Israelites from Egypt:

> Exod. 18.10-11 LXX: Εὐλογητὸς κύριος, ὅτι ἐξείλατο τὸν λαὸν αὐτοῦ ἐκ χειρὸς Αἰγυπτίων καὶ ἐκ χειρὸς Φαραώ· νῦν ἔγνων ὅτι μέγας κύριος παρὰ πάντας τοὺς θεούς...

---

39. ἀπῆλθον, cf. Lk. 1.38 AT (ἀπέστη D05: the angel left Mary); 7.24 (the messengers from John left Jesus); Acts 10.7 (the angel left Cornelius). In the case of Peter, the angel 'separated' (ἀπέστη) from him, cf. Lk. 1.38 D05; 4.13 (the devil separated from Jesus); 24.51 D05 (Jesus separated from the disciples); Acts 15.38 (Mark separated from Paul and Barnabas).

Acts 12.11 D05: Νῦν οἶδα ὅτι ἀληθῶς ἐξαπέστειλεν κύριος τὸν ἄγγελον αὐτοῦ καὶ ἐξείλατό με ἐκ χειρὸς Ἡρῴδου καὶ πάσης τῆς προσδοκίας τοῦ λαοῦ τῶν Ἰουδαίων.

Comparison may also be made with Exod. 3.8: καὶ κατέβην ἐξελέσθαι αὐτοὺς ἐκ χειρὸς Αἰγυπτίων, 'I went down and delivered them from the hand of the Egyptians'. Reference is also made by Stephen in his account of the history of Israel to the Lord who 'delivered' (ἐξείλατο/ἐξελέσθαι: Acts 7.10 [Joseph], 34 [the people]).

The echoes are an additional element that contributes to the Exodus paradigm on which the liberation of Peter is freed. The combination of the Exodus parallels and the allusions to Ezekiel's vision of the eschatological Temple in the previous verse causes his declaration at this point to take on a specific meaning: that he has not only been rescued from an attempt on his life[40] but from a whole set of hopes and aspirations that he had hitherto been holding to, 'all the expectations'[41] of the Jewish people that after the punishment of their enemies the Jews would be brought back to Jerusalem and that the Lord would appear in the new Temple there. It has been observed on several occasions, especially in his early speeches, that Peter seemed to be still waiting for the messianic times to be fulfilled (cf. 3.19-21),[42] which explains his surprise when he witnessed the Gentiles in Caesarea receiving the Holy Spirit because he had understood that the universal application of Jesus' promise was for some future time (see *Commentary*, 10.34). Now, finally, Peter realizes that the hopes of a future restoration of Israel when the Jewish people[43] would welcome the Messiah and the Gentiles would be brought into the kingdom have been totally turned upside down. With this final display of opposition by the Jews to the 'faithful', the Jesus-believers from among the Jewish people, the ancient prophecies which promised the gathering in of the Jews in Jerusalem, the construction of a new Temple and the appearance of the Lord there, have been reversed and the Lord has been seen leaving the Temple of Ezekiel's vision, taking his people with him. Further evidence of this interpretation of Peter's release will be seen in subsequent verses (see 12.17; 18-23 below). In particular, he will be seen to dissociate himself from the church under the leadership of James the brother of Jesus which continued to view itself as Jewish – as distinct from that in Antioch, for example, where the disciples were known as 'Christians' (cf. 11.26).

---

40. The adjective 'all' scarcely allows the 'expectations' to be limited to the anticipation of Peter's execution; cf. W. Dietrich, *Das Petrusbild in der lukanischen Schriften* (Stuttgart: W. Kohlhammer, 1972), p. 311: 'Lukas will vielmehr zum Ausdruck bringen, daß Petrus jetzt jedweder προσδοκία durch das jüdische Volk enthoben ist …, daß von nun an eine Trennung zwischen Petrus und dem "Volk der Juden" sich vollzieht.'

41. The noun προσδοκία (cf. Lk. 21.26; Acts 12.11), like the verb προσδοκάω (cf. Mt. 11.3; 24.50; Lk. 1.21 AT [προσδέχομαι D05]; 3.15; 7.19, 20; 8.40; 12.46; Acts 3.5; 10.24 AT [προσδέχομαι D05]; 27.33; 2 Pet. 3.12, 13, 14), are favourite terms of Luke who often uses them in a technical sense to allude to the messianic expectations of the people of Israel.

42. See *The Message of Acts*, I, pp. 233–36.

43. It may be noticed how Peter gives special prominence to his reference here to the Jews with the expression 'the people of the Jews'. The phrase will be used again at 13.5; 14.1; 17.1, 10 in a critical way. Cf. Lk. 23.51, where it may already have negative overtones. John uses a similar procedure (cf. Jn 2.13; 5.1; 6.4; 7.2; 11.55; 19.42).

[b′] 12.12 *His Arrival at the House of the Praying Church*
12.12 Peter's identification with other believers who had already made the step of separating from the Jewish expectations is made concrete in his arrival at the church that was praying for him in the house of Mary. Both the noun 'house' and the name 'Mary' have the article, an indication that they were known to Peter and probably also to Luke's audience.[44] The nature of the community is clearly defined by the second named person, 'John, called Mark'. John-Mark is, indeed, a character for whom Luke has the highest esteem and who is to be identified as Mark the author of the second Gospel.[45] Luke re-uses two thirds of Mark's Gospel in his own Gospel and makes frequent indirect allusion to it in the book of Acts. John-Mark, presented here for the first time, is a discreet but important character in the narrative of Acts because he is a positive model who quietly goes about his business despite disagreeing with Paul and later being rejected by him (13.13b, cf. 15.36-40). He appears three times with both names (12.12, 25; 15.37), twice with the name of John alone (13.5, 13) and once, at the final mention, simply as Mark (15.39). When Luke includes the name of Mark in referring to him as he does here, his function as writer of the Gospel and 'minister' of the word is relevant. It is significant that Peter should go to John-Mark's mother's house now, to a place where teaching and attitudes approved of by Luke will be found, because he considers them to mirror authentically those of Jesus. The mention of John-Mark also suggests that Barnabas may have been there at Mary's house if reference to them in the Letter to the Colossians as cousins is to be accepted (Col. 4.10). The family connection of John-Mark with Barnabas would also confirm his identity as a Hellenistic Jew and his association with those believers whom Luke so far in Acts has portrayed as most free from the traditions and aspirations of the Jews in Israel (see *Commentary*, 6.1-7; *Excursus* 1). It is precisely this group of disciples who were 'praying in earnestness' for Peter (cf. 12.5),[46] longing for him to share with them in the freedom Jesus had given them as his followers. Their presence in Jerusalem is not associated with Ierousalem but Hierosoluma where, despite the general fleeing recorded at 8.1b, Luke later mentions disciples who must have continued or were able to return (cf. 8.25; 11.2 D05, 27).

Following on from what has already been observed about parallels between Peter and the shepherds in Luke's Gospel (see on 12.6, 7, 10 and *Excursus* 7),

---

44. Other communities in Luke's writings are presided over by women: cf. Lk. 8.2 (Mary Magdalena, cf. 24.10); 10.38-39 (Martha, who had a sister called Mary); Acts 9.36 (Tabitha in Joppa).

45. For further detail on the identification of John-Mark as the author of Mark's Gospel, see Rius-Camps, 'Qui és Joan, l'anomenat "Marc"?'. One of the keys to his identity is Luke's description of him as a 'minister' (ὑπηρέτην, AT) or 'ministering' (ὑπηρετοῦντα D05) to Barnabas and Saul (13.5), taking up a term he uses at the very beginning when he refers to his predecessors as 'ministers' (ὑπηρέται) of the word (Lk. 1.2).

46. As often, Luke expresses the same idea twice by means of two different but corresponding constructions: The first clause (following D05): πολλὴ (1) δὲ προσευχὴ ἦν (2) ... ἀπὸ τῆς ἐκκλησίας (3), has the same three themes as the second: οὗ ἦσαν ἱκανοὶ (1) συνηθροισμένοι (3) καὶ προσευχόμενοι (2).

further allusions can be seen in Peter's arrival at Mary's house. The shepherds had 'made haste' (σπεύδοντες D05/σπεύσαντες AT, Lk. 2.16; cf. ἐν τάχει, Acts 12.7; μετὰ σπουδῆς, Exod. 12.11; σπουδῇ, 12.31-33) to go to Bethlehem where they, too, found a gathering with another mother called Mary, together with Joseph and 'a new-born baby'. In the case of both Peter and the shepherds, the place they went to was not one officially recognized by the religious authorities as a place of meeting, but was rather a place where people who were outside the boundaries of the religious system of Ierousalem had gathered. Apart from the disciples gathered in Mary's house, there was another group of disciples under the leadership of James (cf. 12.17b) who will become the official church of Ierousalem, if they are not already so.

That the name of Mary should figure in both communities has a purpose, for as the mother of Jesus she comes to represent those who obey the Lord faithfully and as the mother of John-Mark she represents the disciples who are faithful to the teachings of Jesus.

[c'] 12.13 *Peter Knocks at the Porch Door*

12.13 Peter is now a free man, released from any kind of religious or nationalistic constraints and ready to enter the community of believers who are likewise detached from the legal obligations and limitations of the Jewish Law. But he does not gain entry easily: three times his knocking at the door of the porch (the outer entrance to the house) will not be answered (cf. vv. 14a, 15a, 15b), re-enacting his three-fold denial of Jesus recorded in a parallel scene in Luke's Gospel (cf. Lk. 22.34, 54-62). This is a community of which Peter has not yet been a part and, having learnt from past experience to be wary of him, they do not yet know they can trust him. In both scenes there is a 'servant' (παιδίσκη) whose task is to test Peter: in the Gospel, she does not have a name but serves to provoke Peter's initial denial (Lk. 22.56); in Acts, she is called Rhoda and has the role of door-keeper (Acts 12.13).[47] Her name is the feminine form of the Greek word for a 'rose' (ῥόδον), always a positive image of joy and contentment in the Jewish Scriptures (cf. Est. 1.6; Wisd. 2.8; Sir. 24.14; 39.13; 50.8). She will represent Peter to the disciples inside the house by announcing and insisting on his arrival (see vv. 14-15).

[d'] 12.14a *Rhoda in her Joy does not Open the Porch*

12.14a Rhoda recognizes Peter's voice, just as the servant in the Gospel recognized Peter as one of Jesus's disciples (cf. Lk. 22.56), but because of her joy at realizing he has been released, she does not open the porch straightaway. Rhoda's reaction shows that she evidently belongs to the community of disciples; her not letting Peter in corresponds to his first denial of Jesus (cf. Lk. 22.57).

---

47. The verb is a technical term used to refer to the activity of the person whose duty it is to listen out for people at the door (B-A-G, ὑπακούω, 3).

[e´] 12.14b *Rhoda's Announcement that Peter is Standing at the Porch*
12.14b The tension of the scene is increased at this point, first with Rhoda's running back into the house being highlighted as an action that was not the expected one; there will then follow in both texts a series of three rapid exchanges between Rhoda and the disciples (see *Overview* to this sequence, above). In her announcement to the disciples, she states that Peter is 'standing' (ἑστάναι) at the porch, corresponding to the angel's command to him in 12.7b ([e]) to 'get up' (ἀνάστα). This is the third of three repetitions of the word 'porch' (πυλών, cf. vv. 13, 14a), echoing the 'porch'-gate (πύλη) at the exit of the prison/Temple which opened of its own accord and through which Peter and the angel had to pass to come out into the city (12.10a). Just as Peter had to go through a gateway to leave his Jewish way of thinking, so he will have to go through a gateway to enter into the community of disciples who have freely adopted Jesus' way of thinking.

[f´] 12.15a *The Disciples' Response that She is Mad*
12.15a The disciples, however, far from rushing to welcome Peter, cannot believe what they hear, and can only think that Rhoda is imagining things. Their incredulity reproduces Peter's second denial of Jesus.

[g´] 12.15b *Rhoda's Insistence that Peter is There*
12.15b In the Gospel, after Peter refuses for a second time to admit to any knowledge of Jesus, a third person insisted that he had been with Jesus (διϊσχυ-ρίζετο, Lk. 22.59). Now Luke, the only writer in the New Testament to use this verb, repeats it as he applies it to Rhoda insisting that it was indeed Peter standing outside the house.[48]

[h´] 12.15c *The Disciples' Supposition that it was his Angel*
12.15c For a third time, Peter's knocking goes unanswered as the disciples continue not to believe that he can possibly have taken the step of detaching himself from the hopes of Israel, of renouncing the traditional expectations of a glorious and successful Messiah which no doubt led him to deny Jesus in the first place (see *Excursus* 5).

[i´] 12.16a *Peter's Persistence in Knocking at the Porch*
12.16a Peter proves, however, that his faith is real and that his liberation is definitive by persisting in trying to gain entry to the community where disciples like John-Mark and his mother Mary, probably John-Mark's cousin Barnabas and even Barnabas' companion Saul were gathered. The AT repeats his name at this point, whereas the Bezan text simply uses the pronoun as a means of indicating that Peter continues to be the focus of the scene.

---

48. διϊσχυρίζομαι is not found in the LXX or elsewhere in the New Testament but will be used once more at Acts 15.2 D05.

[j'] 12.16b *The Disciples' Amazement at Seeing Him*
12.16b Finally, the disciples open up but when they do so and when they see
Peter, they are utterly amazed, they are totally bowled over at the sight of him.
The Bezan text uses a construction that underlines their amazement as a moment
of particular drama (see *Critical Apparatus*). In both texts, the verb Luke
chooses is a technical term in his writing that literally means the loss of one's
senses such as might occur when faced with a piece of unexpected news or a
happening that is humanly inexplicable.[49] So familiar were they with Peter as
someone who remained attached at least to some aspects of the traditional
Jewish view of the Messiah and the future of Israel that when he appears at
their door wanting to be let into their community which had detached itself
from such a perspective, they are stupefied.

[k'] 12.17a *Peter's Account of his Escape*
12.17a There must have followed a moment of considerable confusion and
noise as the disciples wanted to know what was happening, for Peter had first
to get them to be quiet,[50] while he was still at the door of the house according
to Codex Bezae. Once inside, he describes to them what had happened. The
terms Luke ascribes to him as he relates his deliverance continue to evoke the
Exodus parallel: the Lord had brought him out (ἐξήγαγεν) of prison. In just
the same way in ancient times, by means of the Exodus that was to be the
basis of Israel's existence in the Promised Land, the Lord had brought his
people out of Egypt.[51] The association of the prison with the Exodus of Israel
from Egypt is not, in itself, an idea unique to Peter, or Luke: it is found in a
rabbinic midrash which is unlikely to be related to Luke's account of Peter's
experience.[52]

---

49.   The imperfect ἐξίστα(ν)το is used at Acts 2.7, 12 of the people who had gathered in
Jerusalem immediately following the 'confusion' that had been created when they heard the
Galileans speaking their own languages (see *The Message of Acts*, I, pp. 161–62, 164); at 8.13,
it expresses the reaction of Simon Magus to the signs and wonders performed by Philip; at 9.21,
it describes the surprise felt by the Jews of the synagogue of Damascus when they heard Saul
talk about Jesus in a way that contradicted his persecution of his followers. The aorist ἐξέστησαν
is used twice, at 10.45 to describe the effect on the Jewish Jesus-believers from Joppa when
they saw the effects of the Holy Spirit on Cornelius' household in Caesarea; and finally here at
12.16 it is used of the community of Mary. The noun ἔκστασις expresses the same idea of
surprise so strong that it causes loss of the power of thought, cf. Lk. 5.26 AT; Acts 3.10;
10.10b; 11.5; 22.17.
50.   The expression κατασείσας τῇ χειρί is used only by Luke, here and at 13.16; 19.33b (τὴν
χεῖρα, AT); 21.40 (σείσας D05).
51.   The verb ἐξάγω is already established as a technical term that recurs frequently in the book of
Exodus (cf. e.g. LXX Exod. 3.8, 10, 11, 12; 6.6; 12.17, 42, 51 *et al.*). Of the 12 occurrences of the verb
in the New Testament, nine are to be found in Luke (Lk. × 1 + Acts × 8), of which three refer to the
Exodus event directly (Acts 7.36, 40; 13.17) and three others in a figurative sense (Lk. 24.50a; Acts
5.19; 12.17). For the importance of the equivalent Hebrew verb in diverse contexts, see D. Daube,
The Exodus Pattern in the Bible (London: Faber and Faber, 1963), pp. 32–33.
52.   See *Exod. R.* 12.42, cited by Le Déaut (*La nuit pascale*, p. 235) who notes that the tradition is
likely to date from a much earlier time than the rabbinic period.

[ľ] 12.17b *His Command Concerning James*

12.17b Peter goes on to instruct the disciples to tell James and the brethren what he has told them. His instructions have an importance far greater than a simple request to pass on his news to some people who happened to be absent, as indicated by the construction that introduces the second part of Peter's discourse.[53]

The James in question is the brother of Jesus (cf. Gal. 1.19), mentioned once so far in Acts and then only indirectly as one of 'his [Jesus'] brothers' (1.14), in the first section of the book which presented Peter's attempts to restore the number of apostles back to Twelve by choosing a replacement for Judas (1.15-26). On that occasion, James' presence was seen to be the probable motive that prompted Peter to propose this action because, as Jesus' brother, he would have had a claim to take over his work or, at least, his role as representing Israel. Only if the apostles are brought back to their complete number, so that as a group of Twelve they can themselves claim to represent the Messiah of Israel, do they have a chance of warding off the threat posed by James to their leadership.[54] It seems that the plan worked but only for a time and only to some extent: in the end, James did take over the leadership of the church but only in Ierousalem, that is, the part of the Church that still remained firmly attached to traditional Jewish practices and systems of authority.

James is now named for the first time, with an implicit contrast set up between him and the other James, brother of John who, because of his openness to receive the gifts from Antioch (see *General Overview* to this section and the *Overview* to the first sequence), insulted the Jews and was put to death by King Herod (cf. 12.1-2). James the brother of Jesus is apparently not under threat, implying that he was keeping himself and the disciples in his care on good terms with 'the Jews'. That he is absent from the gathering praying for Peter's release is no accident, but precisely an expression of the distance between the community he was presiding over and the one that met in Mary's house. Peter has no intention of going to James or making contact himself with the brethren (τοῖς ἀδελφοῖς) from whom he now dissociates himself (cf. Gal. 2.9, 12 where Paul implies James's connection with and influence on Peter at some point). He nevertheless wants them to be informed about his release.

[μ'] 12.17c *Peter's Departure from Ierousalem*

12.17c In the briefest of sentences Luke makes the boldest of statements: (lit.) 'Having gone out, he went to another place'. To start with, the verb 'go out' (ἐξελθών) takes up a verb found numerous times in the story of the Exodus and repeated now for the third time in the story of Peter's escape from prison (cf. 12.9, 10b). It is followed by a comment whose vagueness is uncharacteristic of Luke, containing an enigmatic phrase that is found nowhere else in the New Testament: 'he went to another place'. Various suggestions are made as to what

---

53. Within a single discourse, the transition from indirect to direct speech occurs at points of particular significance, cf. e.g. Lk. 9.21-22; Acts 5.34-35; 19.21; 21.20.

54. See *The Message of Acts*, I, pp. 104–106;119–21.

Luke meant by this, all more or less based on the assumption that Luke had in mind a geographical location, whether precise or indeterminate.[55]

However, the meaning of the phrase is likely, given the tenor of this section of Acts overall, to be symbolical. Indeed, the strangeness of its wording leaps out at the one other occurrence of the phrase in the LXX, at Ezek. 12.3, where its use sheds light on the sense Luke gives to it in Acts 12. In the course of the early part of the book of Ezekiel, the prophet records how he is instructed to perform a series of prophetic actions to illustrate to the people of Israel that, because of their wickedness in Jerusalem, they are going to be brought out of the city and scattered among the nations. He is to equip himself like an exile who had to leave his city and dig through the walls of Jerusalem and 'go like an exile from your place to another place'.

The implication of taking up this phrase with regard to Peter is that he left Jerusalem at this point. Whether he went immediately, or whether he went in the literal sense, are questions that are of no relevance to Luke's narrative intention. Just as Ezekiel was to go from Jerusalem, the city that was the centre of Israel's life and worship, because the people had rebelled against the Lord (Ezek. 12.1-3a), so Peter leaves Jerusalem – Ierousalem as Luke calls it when he refers to the religious centre – because the people have oppressed those who are faithful to the Lord (cf. Acts 12.3 D05). His departure confirms the exit in the first part of this sequence of the Lord from the 'Temple' of Ezekiel, the ideal of the restored Jerusalem that Ezekiel portrays as the final state to which the Jews will be brought back once their rebellion has been dealt with. The Lord has brought Peter out of this vision of the future and as Peter leaves Ierousalem his move signals the shift of the Church's activity away from the Jewish centre, a shift that prepares the ground for the future missionary activity of Barnabas and Saul/Paul in Acts 13. A preliminary confirmation of this will be seen in the colophon to this part of Acts in 12.25 (see *Commentary*, below).

Excursus 5

Peter's Denial of Jesus (Lk. 22.34, 56-62): Allusions in Acts 12.13-17

It was Jesus who first warned Peter that he would deny him three times before the cock crowed (Lk. 22.34). It is interesting to trace the steps which led up to Jesus' warning:

1. Lk. 22.31: Jesus says to Simon: Satan has demanded to sift you (plural) like wheat –
   ὁ Σατανᾶς ἐξῃτήσατο ὑμᾶς τοῦ σινιάσαι ὡς τὸν σῖτον.
2. 22.32a: he, Jesus, has prayed concerning him that his faith would not fail – ἵνα μὴ ἐκλίπῃ ἡ πίστις σου.
3. 22.32b: and that, when he 'turns again', he must strengthen the brethren – καὶ σύ ποτε ἐπιστρέψας στήρισον (σὺ δὲ ἐπίστρεψον καὶ στήριξον D05) τοὺς ἀδελφούς σου.

---

55. Both Antioch and Rome have been suggested as specific places where Peter may have gone (cf. Barrett, I, p. 587; Bruce, *Text*, p. 248).

4. 22.33: Simon says he is ready to go to prison or to die with Jesus – Μετὰ σοῦ ἕτοιμός εἰμι καὶ εἰς φυλακὴν καὶ εἰς θάνατον πορεύεσθαι.
5. 22.34: Jesus warns Peter than he will deny him three times before the cock crows – ἕως (+ ὅτου D05) τρίς με ἀπαρνήσῃ εἰδέναι (μὴ εἰδέναι με D05).

The first appeal Luke makes to this exchange in his second volume is when, according to Codex Bezae along with other witnesses, he shows Peter 'strengthening the brethren' (ἐπιστηρίξας αὐτούς [τοὺς ἀδελφούς]) after his experience in Caesarea where he had witnessed the Gentiles who worshipped God receiving the Holy Spirit (Acts 11.2 D05). What he had seen was contrary to all his expectations that the acceptance of the Gentiles by God was reserved for some future time when the Messiah would return in glory to Israel: this belief was part of the traditional Jewish teaching with which he was familiar, based on the notion that the Jews were a privileged people and leading to the idea that all the Gentiles were unclean and separate nations who had been rejected by God.[56] At this stage, Peter had not understood that Jesus had rejected this teaching by already making it possible for Gentiles to be accepted by God without any further ado, by removing the privilege of the Jews. It is only when God intervenes, despite Peter's holding firm to the traditional view of the Jews as the people of God and the time of the inclusion of the Gentiles as a future event, that he begins to realize that the perspective of the Jewish Law with its view of the Gentiles as unclean is no longer valid.

It is precisely at this point that Luke describes him as 'strengthening the brethren' (point 3 in the list above). The undeniable allusion back to Jesus' command during the Last Supper means, in turn, that Jesus' prayer for Simon not to fail (point 2), itself in response to Satan's demand to sift the disciples like wheat (point 1), was to do with Simon Peter clinging to the old Jewish ways of thinking and not grasping the new teaching of Jesus about the status of the Jews and the Gentiles in his kingdom. It is striking to realize that, accordingly, Satan's plan was to do with keeping the disciples from understanding what Jesus was really about. In Peter's case, his resistance (the meaning of the name Jesus gave to him, cf. Mt. 16.18) to change his religious traditions and beliefs of his upbringing was apparently so strong that it can be believed that without Jesus' prayer on his behalf Satan may easily have succeeded.

Peter's confident assertion that he was ready to go to prison and even die with Jesus (point 4) was put to the test when Herod Agrippa I had him shut up, ready to bring him out to the Jewish people, his own people, after Passover some 10 years after Peter's conversation with Jesus. The imprisonment was part of Herod's attempt to please the Jewish people as a whole by being hard on those Jews who were believers in Jesus, an opportunity being given to him when they accepted gifts from other believers in Antioch who had admitted Gentiles into their community. That Peter was one of those arrested suggests that he had been party to accepting the gifts, a clear demonstration that he had renounced his traditional avoidance of contact with Gentiles, and again tying in with what

56. See *The Message of Acts*, I, *Excursus* 1, pp. 79–87.

appears to have been the basis of Satan's demand and Jesus' prayer (points 1+2). Once again God intervened and brought Peter out of prison, not just the physical prison in Jerusalem but the prison of the ancient ways of thinking about the Jewish people and their future.

When Peter is released from prison, he knows that the ancient Jewish way of thinking with its view of the Gentiles and its hopes for a gloriously restored Israel, is no longer valid and he therefore leaves what Luke calls figuratively Ierousalem (Acts 12.17c), the holy city with its Temple as the centre of Jewish worship and seat of authority among the Jewish people to which, incidentally, some disciples do continue to be attached under the leadership of James (12.17b, cf. 15.2c D05, 2d, 4 D05). In doing so, he becomes part of the community of Jesus' followers who had already understood the freedom of his message and who had been praying for his release. When he first attempts to enter, however, the disciples themselves clearly have a view of Peter that is conditioned by his denial of Jesus shortly after their last meal together (point 2).

What had happened was this: as Jesus was arrested that evening and taken to the house of the High Priest Caiaphas (the brother-in-law of Theophilus who would be High Priest himself for the four years prior to Herod's attack on the Jewish Jesus-believers and to whom the Bezan text of Luke's writings was addressed – see *General Introduction,* § III), Peter followed him from a distance and sat in the courtyard warming himself (θερμαινόμενος D05) at the fire that had been kindled (Lk. 22.54-55). It was then that Peter had three times denied that he knew this Jesus who he could see inside the house being mocked and ill-treated (cf. 22.61, 63-65). In view of the change that took place in Peter and that led to his 'strengthening of the brethren' (Acts 11.2 D05), namely his realization that the Gentiles were accepted by God as equals to Jews (10.34, 47; 11.17), his denial can now be seen to have everything to do with denying Jesus as a Messiah with a new message that turned upside down the Jewish system of belief in the glorious Messiah who would defeat the Gentiles and restore the fortunes of Israel. In other words, his denial of Jesus meant that he still clung to the hopes and expectations that Jesus himself had revoked by being a Messiah who was a failure in terms of the traditional aspirations and whose kingdom was more to do with a way of life than the exercise of political power.

Peter's denial of Jesus must have made a strong impression on other believers for, at the point when he tries to join those who had truly understood the message of Jesus, his denial is reproduced as three times these disciples fail to believe that he has really come out of prison and is a free person:

1. Acts 12.14a, first denial: Rhoda does not open the porch when he first knocks – ἐπιγνοῦσα τὴν φωνὴν τοῦ Πέτρου ... οὐκ ἤνοιξεν τὸν πυλῶνα.
2. 12.15a, second denial: the disciples say she is mad when she announces that Peter is standing at the porch – ἀπήγγειλεν ἑστάναι τὸν (– D05) Πέτρον πρὸ τοῦ πυλῶνος. οἱ δὲ ... Μαίνῃ.
3. 12.15c, third denial: they suppose it is his angel when she insists he is there – ἡ δὲ διϊσχυρίζετο οὕτως ἔχειν. οἱ δὲ ... Ὁ ἄγγελός ἐστιν αὐτοῦ (Τυχὸν ὁ ἄγγελος αὐτοῦ ἐστιν D05).

When they do finally open the door and see Peter standing there, they are utterly amazed and still do not let him in (12.16b). He first has to quieten them and then step inside himself and tell them how the Lord, this Jesus who had prayed that his faith would not fail (point 2), had led him out of a prison that was every bit as real and dramatic as the slavery of Israel in Egypt (12.17a) – Jesus' prayer, reinforced as it was by the prayer of the church for him (cf. 12.5b), has been answered. The shadow over Peter's miraculous deliverance is that there are still other disciples who remain in a condition of bondage and who are not recorded, as far as Luke's writings go, as ever being delivered (cf. James' insistence on Paul's observance of the Law, Acts 21.18-26, esp. D05).

Excursus 6

The Exodus Theme in Acts 12

The account of Peter's imprisonment by Herod and his miraculous deliverance by the angel of the Lord has a number of similarities with the account of Jesus' death and resurrection in the Gospels, as a number of exegetes have noted.[57] At the same time, Peter's story provides the second occasion in Acts for the paradigm of the Exodus of Israel to be evoked as a model for the release of the Jesus-believers from the oppression and limitations of the Jewish religious system and the authorities that governed it. The first was in 5.12-40, the miraculous deliverance of the apostles from the hostility of the High Priest and the Sadducees which culminated in their imprisonment.[58] Exegetes sometimes draw attention to isolated allusions to the Exodus theme in Acts 12 but are not on the whole convinced that Luke intended his audience to make much of them.[59] If the addressee of the Alexandrian text was a Greek or Roman official without any first-hand knowledge of Judaism, it is perhaps possible that the narrator did not expect him to draw any particular conclusions from similarities between Peter's fate and that of the Israelites who were enslaved by Egypt and then freed by divine intervention.[60] The situation is rather different in the Bezan text where first, the

57. See e.g. Parry, 'Release of the Captives', pp. 159–61, where he also discusses further similarities with other scriptural stories of imprisonment and salvation without accepting, however, any interdependence between texts (p. 164); see also Witherington, *Commentary*, pp. 381–82.

58. See *The Message of Acts*, I, *Excursus* 8, pp. 358–63. The two passages, 5.12-40 and 12.1-17, are compared for the use they make of the Exodus story by J. Read-Heimerdinger, 'The Re-Enactment of the History of Israel: Exodus Traditions in the Bezan Text of Acts', in R. Pope (ed.), *Honouring the Past and Shaping the Future: Religious and Biblical Studies in Wales* (Leominster: Gracewing, 2003), pp. 81–96.

59. Commentators are generally reluctant to accept that Luke drew purposeful parallels with the Exodus (see e.g. Barrett, I, pp. 577–78), although the idea is tentatively welcomed in some separate studies; see Dupont, *Nouvelles études*, pp. 336–41. The parallel is explored more fully for its typological value by I.H. Marshall, 'Apg 12 – ein Schlüssel zum Verständnis der Apostelgeschichte', in C.H. Thiede, *Das Petrusbild in der neueren Forschung* (Wuppertal: Brockhaus, 1987), pp. 192–220.

60. See e.g. Witherington (*Commentary*, p. 382) who believes that the parallels with the death of Jesus would have been more accessible and obvious to Theophilus.

allusions to the Jewish Scriptures generally are more forceful and complex, and secondly, the addressee was most probably a Jew who could not have failed to see what Luke meant by comparing the release of Peter from prison with the deliverance of the Israelites from Egypt, so dominant a theme was the Exodus throughout the Jewish Scriptures and so extensively developed was it in Jewish tradition.[61] Luke in Codex Bezae uses the ancient event in a way that was, in itself, typically Jewish, as a paradigm to interpret the recent developments in the history of Israel.

Underlying the message of the Bezan text is a basic principle concerning the Jewish understanding of life in Israel, namely that all of history is contained in the Torah. The work of the contemporary historian consists in bringing to light the ancient models that lie behind present events and that give them coherence and meaning. Since, in the case of a Jewish audience, the writer could suppose that they knew the biblical stories already, it was sufficient to make isolated references to the model for the allusion to be clear. While such a reference could be by explicit quotation it was more frequent in early Jewish literature to slip in a simple word or phrase from the text the historian wished to allude to as a means of identifying it. Such words or phrases, which could be taken from the scriptural form of the story as well as from a form it had acquired in later tradition, served as keys to the biblical paradigm.[62]

The targumic and rabbinic literature shows that some time before the first century CE the Passover night was incorporated into a number of stories as being the time *par excellence* of deliverance;[63] it was already anticipated by some as the time of the arrival of the Messiah before the crucifixion and subsequent resurrection of Jesus;[64] furthermore, a rabbinic midrash on Exodus 12 speaks of the celebration of the Passover as comparable to a reminder of the day on which 'a king set free his son from prison', because when the people of Israel escaped from Egypt 'God brought Israel out of prison'.[65] Concerning the theme of light, the targums (to Exodus, but also to the prophets such as Isaiah) illustrate how the theme is expanded and becomes synonymous with the presence of God and

---

61. The evidence of the Quartodecimans, the second-century community of Asia Minor, demonstrates that when the story of Peter was read within a Jewish framework, the parallels were understood. *Epistula Apostolorum*, a writing dating from around 150–160 CE and belonging to this community, makes specific mention of Peter's escape from prison in Passover terminology.

62. On oral tradition, see B. Barc, 'Le texte de la Torah a-t-il été récrit?', in M. Tardieu (ed.), *Les règles de l'interprétation* (Paris; Cerf, 1987), pp. 69–88; see also M. Fishbane, *Biblical Interpretation in Ancient Israel* (Oxford: Clarendon Press, 1987), pp. 281–91, where he discusses in some detail the interconnectedness of biblical texts in Jewish exegesis and sets out useful guidelines for recognizing intended exegetical links. J.L. Kugel presents detailed information on how scriptural traditions developed in different ways, see *Traditions of the Bible. A Guide to the Bible as it was at the Start of the Common Era* (Cambridge, MA.: Harvard University Press, 1998).

63. The development of the Exodus theme in Jewish tradition is explored in detail by Le Déaut, *La nuit pascale*, pp. 279–92.

64. Notably in *Exod. R.* 18.81a.

65. Cited by Le Déaut, *La nuit pascale*, p. 235.

ultimately with salvation. Similarly, in a cycle of synagogue readings,[66] the text of Exodus 12 is set as a parallel to the creation story of Genesis 1, so enhancing the theme of light (God, freedom, purity) and underlining the contrast with the darkness (Egypt, sin, bondage).

The development of the scriptural account of the Exodus must be taken into account when discerning allusions in Acts. It was seen already at 5.12-40 that reference was made there to elements of the Exodus story that are not present in the biblical tradition but are evident in later traditional versions.

The following allusions to the Exodus have been pointed out in the commentary on Acts 12.1-11 and are gathered here to show the consistency of the theme running through the sequence:[67]

1. Peter is arrested during the Festival of Unleavened Bread (ἦσαν [+ αἱ D05] ἡμέραι τῶν ἀζύμων, Acts 12.3b; ἑπτὰ ἡμέρας ἄζυμα ἔδεσθε, Exod. 12.15), and he was to be brought before the people after Passover (μετὰ τὸ πάσχα, Acts 12.4; Θυσία τὸ πάσχα τοῦτο κυρίῳ, Exod. 12.27).

2. The release happens at night (τῇ νυκτὶ ἐκείνῃ, Acts 12.6; ἐν τῇ νυκτὶ ταύτῃ, Exod. 12.12).

3. The church was praying (προσευχὴ ἦν ἐκτενῶς γινομένη, 12.5b AT / πολλὴ προσευχὴ ἦν ἐν ἐκτενείᾳ περὶ αὐτοῦ D05, cf. v. 12) just as the Israelites were told to 'watch' during the night of Passover (νυκτὸς προφυλακή ἐστιν τῷ κυρίῳ, Exod. 12.42). The Bezan text of Acts 12.5b underlines the importance of the praying with a) the adjective πολλή and b) the adverbial phrase ἐν ἐκτενείᾳ.

4. The angel of the Lord delivers Peter (ἄγγελος κυρίου ἐπέστη τῷ Πέτρῳ, Acts 12.7a). Initially, it is the Lord himself who effected the deliverance of the people of Israel (Exod. 12.23, 29, 50) but in subsequent accounts the angel of the Lord is mentioned (ἀποστείλας ἄγγελον ἐξήγαγεν ἡμᾶς ἐξ Αἰγύπτου, Num. 20.16; cf. Exod. 14.19).[68]

5. A light shines (φῶς ἔλαμψεν ἐν τῷ οἰκήματι, Acts 12.7a AT / φῶς ἐπέλαμψεν τῷ οἰκήματι D05) in the building, corresponding to the pillar of fire that gave the Israelites light at night (τὴν δὲ νύκτα ἐν στύλῳ πυρός, Exod. 13.21). The verb of D05 is a rare compound, used at Isa. 4.2 LXX (ἐπιλάμψει ὁ θεός) to refer to God shining forth in the restored city of Jerusalem like the fire of the Exodus.

6. The angel wakes Peter by 'striking' (πατάξας, Acts 12.7b AT / νύξας D05) his side, the AT using the same verb πατάσσω as is found repeatedly in Exodus to describe the killing of the first-born (e.g. Exod. 12.12, 23 [× 2], 27) as it will be used later of the angel killing Herod (ἐπάταξεν, Acts 12.23), whereas D05 avoids the misplaced connection between waking Peter and killing the Egyptians by using the verb νύσσω.

7. Peter is told to act in haste (ἐν τάχει, Acts 12.7b). In the same way, but with a different expression, the Israelites were instructed to eat the Passover (μετὰ σπουδῆς, Exod. 12.11) or the Egyptians sent them out of their land (σπουδῇ, Exod. 12.33).

---

66. Le Déaut, *La nuit pascale*, pp. 218–21; cf. J. Mann, *The Bible as Read and Preached in the Old Synagogue*, I (New York: KTAV, 1940; 2nd edn 1971).

67. Some of these elements are noted by A. Strobel, 'Passa-Symbolik und Passa-Wunder in Act. XII.3ff', *NTS* 4 (1957–58), pp. 210–15 (esp. 213) who does not, however, recognize the theologizing intentions of Luke.

68. For further examples of the tradition concerning the angel, see Kugel, *Traditions of the Bible*, pp. 584–85. Daube (*Exodus Pattern*) draws attention to the tradition, evident in Exod. 33.2-6, that the presence of an angel in place of God himself was viewed as a consequence of the people's sinfulness (pp. 40–41).

8. He is also to gird himself and put on his sandals (Ζῶσαι καὶ ὑπόδησαι τὰ σανδάλιά σου, Acts 12.8a), instructions given to the Israelites for the eating of the Passover (αἱ ὀσφύες ὑμῶν περιεζωσμέναι, καὶ τὰ ὑποδήματα ἐν τοῖς ποσὶν ὑμῶν, Exod. 12.11; cf. also Lk. 12.35).

9. He is to wrap his cloak (Περιβαλοῦ τὸ ἱμάτιόν σου, Acts 12.8c) around himself, reflecting the gesture of the Israelites who carried their kneading bowls wrapped up in their cloaks (τὰ φυράματα αὐτῶν ἐνδεδεμένα ἐν τοῖς ἱματίοις αὐτῶν, Exod. 12,34).

10. The door to the prison opens of its own accord, echoing a tradition recorded by Artapanus that Moses witnessed a similar happening when he escaped from the prison in which Pharaoh had shut him up.[69]

11. The angel makes sure Peter is safely away from the prison before leaving him (Acts 12.10b, c), just as God sure the Israelites would not return to Egypt (Exod. 13.17).

12. Peter's words on finding himself outside the prison and realizing that what had happened was real (Νῦν οἶδα ὅτι ... κύριος ... ἐξείλατό με ἐκ χειρὸς Ἡρῴδου, Acts 12.11) are reminiscent of those of Moses' father-in-law, Jethro, on learning how the Lord had freed his people from Pharaoh's harsh oppression of them (Εὐλογητὸς κύριος, ὅτι ἐξείλατο τὸν λαὸν αὐτοῦ ἐκ χειρὸς Αἰγυπτίων καὶ ἐκ χειρὸς Φαραώ· νῦν ἔγνων..., Exod. 18.10-11).

13. Peter relates to the church gathering in Mary's house how the Lord had 'brought him out' (ἐξήγαγεν, Acts 12.17a) of prison, using the same verb that describes the Exodus on several occasions (ἐξάξω, Exod. 12.17 and *passim*).

By activating the Exodus model, the narrative of Acts accords the story of the Church a layer of meaning that goes deeper than a merely historical one: it is a theological meaning, derived from the place the Church is seen as occupying in the history of Israel.

In describing the release of Peter in Passover terminology, a powerful comparison is drawn between the past liberation of the Israelites from the oppression of the Egyptians under Pharaoh and the present deliverance of Peter from the oppression of the Jews under Herod. As one of the 'faithful' (Acts 12.3a D05), he has been the leader of the emerging Church representing the people of God, with Herod, king of the Jews, representing Pharaoh. His assimilation with the Prince of Tyre brings in another model on which the story of Peter's escape from prison is based (see *Excursus* 9), confirming the notion that the enemies of the people of God are identified as those Jews who have turned against their own people. This is the tragic new element that Luke introduces in the application of the Passover theme to the unfolding history of Israel: it is from the hostility and persecution of their own people that the Jesus-believers are set free.

Excursus 7

Parallels between the Shepherds in Luke's Infancy Narrative (Lk. 2.8-20) and Peter

In the course of Acts 12, a series of close verbal and thematic resemblances occurs between the appearance of the angel to the shepherds in Luke's Gospel

---

69. Artapanus, *De Judaeis*, is cited by Eusebius, *Praep. Evang.* 9. 27.23; Josephus, *Ant.* 2, 254–55.

and the appearance of the angel to Peter. They are given below in the order of the Acts narrative:

Luke 2

Shepherds were keeping watch (Ποιμένες ἦσαν ... φυλάσσοντες τὰς [– ΑΤ] φυλακάς, 2.8)

It was night (τῆς νυκτός, 2.8)

The shepherds were awake, watching over their sheep (φυλάσσοντες ... ἐπὶ τὴν ποίμνην αὐτῶν, 2.8)

The angel of the Lord appeared to the shepherds (καὶ ἰδοὺ [– ΑΤ] ἄγγελος κυρίου ἐπέστη αὐτοῖς, 2.9a)

The glory of the Lord shone around the shepherds (καὶ δόξα κυρίου [– D05] περιέλαμψεν αὐτούς, 2.9b)

The shepherds went with haste (ἦλθαν σπεύσαντες, 2.16a)

The shepherds made their way to Bethlehem (Διέλθωμεν δὴ ἕως Βηθλέεμ, 2.15c)

The angels left the shepherds (ὡς ἀπῆλθον ἀπ' αὐτῶν εἰς τὸν οὐρανὸν οἱ ἄγγελοι ΑΤ / οἱ ἄγγελοι ἀπ' αὐτῶν εἰς τὸν οὐρανόν D05, 2.15a)

The shepherds spoke to each other (Οἱ ποιμένες ἐλάλουν πρὸς ἀλλήλους, 2.15b)

The shepherds found three people, the first of whom was called Mary and the third was a child (καὶ ἀνεῦραν τήν τε Μαριὰμ [εὖρον τὴν Μαρίαν D05] καὶ τὸν Ἰωσὴφ καὶ τὸ βρέφος κείμενον ἐν τῇ φάτνῃ , 2.16b)

The shepherds marveled (ἐθαύμασαν, 2.18)

The shepherds went back to their fields (ὑπέστρεψαν οἱ ποιμένες, 2.20)

Acts 12

Peter was being kept in the prison (Ὁ μὲν οὖν Πέτρος ἐτηρεῖτο ἐν τῇ φυλακῇ, 12.5a)

It was night (τῇ νυκτὶ ἐκείνῃ, 12.6a)

Peter was sleeping (ἦν ὁ Πέτρος κοιμώμενος, 12.6b)

The angel of the Lord appeared to Peter (καὶ ἰδοὺ ἄγγελος κυρίου ἐπέστη τῷ Πέτρῳ [– ΑΤ], 12.7a)

A light shone (out D05) in Peter's 'chamber' (καὶ φῶς ἔλαμψεν ἐν τῷ οἰκήματι ΤΑ / ἐπέλαμψεν τῷ οἰκήματι D05, 12.7b)

Peter was ordered to get up quickly (Ἀνάστα ἐν τάχει, 12.7c)

The angel and Peter made their way through two prisons (διελθόντες δὲ πρώτην φυλακὴν καὶ δευτέραν, 12.10a)

The angel left Peter (εὐθέως ἀπέστη ὁ ἄγγελος ἀπ' αὐτοῦ, 12.10c)

Peter spoke to himself (Ὁ Πέτρος ἐν ἑαυτῷ γενόμενος εἶπεν, 12.11)

Peter went to the house of Mary, mother of John-Mark, where Rhoda was the servant-girl (καὶ συνιδὼν ἦλθεν ἐπὶ τὴν οἰκίαν τῆς Μαρίας τῆς μητρὸς Ἰωάννου ... παιδίσκη ὀνόματι Ῥόδη, 12.12-13)

The disciples were amazed (ἐξέστησαν, 12.16)

Peter went to another place (ἐπορεύθη εἰς ἕτερον τόπον, 12.17c)

The similarities between the text of the two narratives set up a parallel between the shepherds and Peter. In the case of the shepherds, the portrait is entirely positive: they were watching as Israel should have been in the night that the Messiah arrived. They, despite their lowly status and unlike the religious authorities, went and found Jesus, the Messiah who is expected to bring freedom to Israel. As the Gospel of Luke shows, however, Israel did not respond to the Messiah in the way that had been foreseen in the scriptural prophecies and the divine plan was modified in response to the rejection of the Messiah by Israel as a nation.[70] Peter was the leader of the disciples who were taught by Jesus about the changes he was bringing about, whereby the Messiah was no longer a nationalistic hope but a universal one that viewed Israel and the other nations on an equal footing. But Peter was resistant to change and struggled to absorb the lessons he was being taught. His difficulty is expressed here as elsewhere in his sleeping position. On this occasion, however, through the angel of the Lord he

70. See *The Message of Acts*, I, *Excursus* 1, pp. 79–87.

makes a startling discovery concerning the Messiah: at last he becomes fully aware of the freedom given by Jesus from the religious aspirations of Israel.

[A'] 12.18-23 *The Death of Herod*

Overview

King Herod (Agrippa I, cf. 12.1) is now back in focus in this concluding sequence of Section IV which takes up his story from 12.5. There, he was intending to bring Peter out of prison the next day to appear before the people, most probably with the intention of having him executed. In the course of the actions he takes when he discovers Peter's escape, he becomes assimilated with the Prince of Tyre, the most powerful and most hated enemy of the people of Israel in Jewish scriptural as well as legendary tradition. The assimilation is made most clearly in the Bezan text, though it is not altogether absent from the AT.

Structure and Themes

As the action moves on to the next day when Peter's escape is discovered, the setting shifts to Caesarea where people from Tyre and Sidon will come to meet the king. These steps form the first part of the sequence. The crowd's acclamation of him as a god sets in motion Herod's downfall which comes as he is struck by an angel of the Lord and dies a gruesome death:

[a]	12.18	The discovery of Peter's escape
[b]	12.19a	Herod orders the death of the guards
[c]	12.19b	Herod's stay in Caesarea
[d]	12.20a	Herod's anger with the Tyrians and the Sidonians
[e]	12.20b	The Tyrians and the Sidonians seek peace
[e']	12.21a	Herod addresses them from his throne
[d']	12.21b	His reconciliation with the Tyrians
[c']	12.22	The mob acclaim Herod as a god
[b']	12.23a	The angel of the Lord strikes him dead
[a']	12.23b	Herod dies, eaten by worms

Translation

Codex Bezae D05	*Codex Vaticanus B03*
[a] **12.18** When day came, there was a commotion among the soldiers over what had become of Peter.	**12.18** When day came, there was no small commotion among the soldiers over what had become of Peter.
[b] **19a** Herod, having searched for him but not having found him, after interrogating the guards ordered them to be killed;	**19a** Herod, having searched for him but not having found him, after interrogating the guards ordered them to be led away;
[c] **19b** and he went down from Judaea and stayed in Caesarea,	**19b** and he went down from Judaea and stayed in Caesarea.
[d] **20a** (for he was in a rage with the Tyrians and Sidonians).	**20a** Now he was in a rage with the Tyrians and Sidonians.

[e]	**20b** People from both cities came as one body to the king and, having gained the favour of Blastus who was over his bed-chamber, they sought to ask for peace since their countries were provided for from the king's.	**20b** They came to him in one body and, having gained the favour of Blastus who was over the king's bed-chamber, they sought to ask for peace since their country was provided for by the king's.
[e']	**21a** On the appointed day, Herod, arrayed in regal vestments and seated on the tribunal, formally addressed them.	**21** On the appointed day, Herod, arrayed in regal vestments, seated on the tribunal, formally addressed them.
[d']	**21b** (Note that he had been reconciled with the Tyrians.)	
[c']	**22** The mob cried out, 'The proclamations of a god and not a man!'	**22** The mob cried out, 'The proclamation of a god and not a man!'
[b']	**23a** Immediately the angel of the Lord struck him because he did not give the glory to God;	**23a** Immediately the angel of the Lord struck him because he did not give the glory to God;
[a']	**23b** and as he came down from the tribunal, he was eaten by worms while still alive and in this way he died.	**23b** and he was eaten by worms and died.

Critical Apparatus

12.18 (τάραχος) οὐκ ὀλίγος B 𝔓⁴⁵.⁷⁴ ℵ *rell* ar e vg syʰ bo | μέγας 36. 94. 307. 431. 453. 1175 *pc* (syᵖ) sa mae boᵐˢˢ || *om.* D d gig p; Lcf.

B03 emphasizes by means of an understatement the importance of the disturbance among the soldiers on discovering Peter's absence from the prison, using a literary device that is typical of Luke.

12.19 (ἐκέλευσεν) ἀπαχθῆναι B Dᴬ·ᴮ 𝔓⁷⁴ ℵ *rell, obduci* d || ἀποκτανθῆναι D* syᵖ·ʰ (sa) mae bo aeth; Ephr.

The verb used by B03, ἀπαχθῆναι, literally means 'led away' and is sometimes used in the sense of 'led to execution' (cf. Lk. 23.26). ἀποκτανθῆναι in D05 is more explicit and is found frequently in the active in Luke-Acts as throughout the New Testament (though only once in the passive, cf. Lk. 9.22).

12.20 (ἦν) δέ B 𝔓⁷⁴ ℵ *rell* || γάρ D d syᵖ aeth; Cass.

D05 links Herod's visit to Caesarea to his dispute with the Tyrians and the Sidonians. B03, on the other hand, makes the comment in anticipation of what is to follow (cf. notes on 12.9 above).

ὁμοθυμαδόν δέ B 𝔓⁷⁴ ℵ *rell, unanimiter autem* d | καὶ ὁμ. 𝔓⁴⁵; Lcf | ὁμ. τε Ψ 226ᶜ | ὁμ. H* 945* || οἱ δὲ ὁμ. D 1828 gig p vg syʰᵐᵍ sa mae. — ἐξ ἀμφοτέρων τῶν πόλεων (μερῶν 614. 2412) D d (614). 808. (2412 syʰᵐᵍ) mae || *om.* B 𝔓⁷⁴ ℵ *rell*.

D05 makes a particular point of the fact that people came to Herod from both Tyre and Sidon. This will be important for the next part of the story in D05 when the Tyrians are mentioned alone (see *Commentary*).

(παρῆσαν) πρὸς αὐτόν B 𝔓⁷⁴ ℵ *rell*; Lcf ‖ πρ. τὸν βασιλέα D d mae.

At the point at which the people come to him, the function of Herod as king is underlined in D05 by the mention of his role rather than obliquely, as in the next clause of B03 (see next variant below).

(ἐπὶ τοῦ κοιτῶνος) τοῦ βασιλέως B 𝔓⁷⁴ ℵ *rell* mae ‖ αὐτοῦ D (d) 440. 1758.

Unlike D05, B03 has not already mentioned the role of Herod as king (see previous variant).

(τρέφεσθαι) αὐτῶν τὴν χώραν B 𝔓⁷⁴ ℵ *rell* ‖ τὰς χώρας αὐ- D d 242. (1270) gig p vg sa mae; Lcf.

D05 continues to treat the Tyrians and the Sidonians as two separate identities (cf. the first variant of this verse above).

ἀπὸ (τῆς βασιλικῆς) B 𝔓⁷⁴ ℵ *rell* ‖ ἐκ D 𝔓⁷⁴ 181. 242. 1898.

The preposition ἀπό in B03 could be construed either as introducing the agent of the passive verb τρέφεσθαι (which is possible in Koine Greek after a verb implying movement away from the agent, see Read-Heimerdinger, *The Bezan Text*, pp. 183–84), or it may simply indicate the source of the food supply. ἐκ in D05 can only have this second meaning.

12.21 ὁ (Ἡρῴδης) D 𝔓⁷⁴ᵛⁱᵈ ℵ A E H L P Ψ 049. 056. 33 𝔐 ‖ *om.* B 𝔓⁴⁵ᵛⁱᵈ 88. 945. 1175. 1739 *pc*.

The article with Herod in D05 is in keeping with the fact that, once brought back on stage without the article at 12.19, he is the main character in this part of the narrative and that the others are introduced in relation to him. The omission of the article in B03 gives Herod special prominence (cf. 12.6).

καὶ (καθίσας) D d 𝔓⁷⁴ A E H L P Ψ 049. 056. 33. 1739 𝔐 gig syʰ ‖ *om.* B ℵ 81. 1175 *pc* p vg; Lcf.

B03 leaves unconnected two participles (ἐνδυσάμενος – καθίσας) which D05 conjoins with καί, thereby conferring a certain note of drama on the description of the scene.

καταλλαγέντος δὲ αὐτοῦ τοῖς Τυρίοις D, *cum ingratiasset cum Tyrios* d (pᶜ w) vg^Θ (syʰ**) mae ; Ephr ‖ *om.* B 𝔓⁷⁴ ℵ *rell*.

The importance of the Tyrians is crucial for the symbolical significance of this scene according to its articulation in D05, that is, the assimilation of Herod with the Prince of Tyre as the arch enemy of the Jewish people (see *Commentary*). The genitive absolute clause may, however, be thought to create a grammatical problem for the finite clause that follows it is also connected with δέ (the Latin of d05 has no connective in the participial clause, which is thereby connected with the previous finite verb rather than the following one). It may be that a sentence has dropped out of D05 after the genitive clause, but as it stands the text can be taken as a particularly strong aside on the part of the narrator who wishes his audience to take careful note of the fact that Herod was now at peace with the Tyrians, before going on with the story. The reason for this aside is purely theological, to establish Herod's role as the Prince of Tyre (see *Commentary*).

12.22 θεοῦ φωνή B D^H 𝔓^74 ℵ A E Ψ 33. 81. 614. 927. 945. 1175. 1270. 1611. 1739. 1891. 344 mae | φ. θ. H L P 049. 056 𝔐 || θ. φωναί D* d gig p vg sy^p; Lcf.

The singular φωνή in B03 could mean 'the voice' but also the 'proclamation' (i.e. what the voice utters). The plural in D05 tends to suggest this meaning (cf. B-A-G, φωνή, 2c).

ἀνθρώπου B D d 𝔓^74 ℵ^2 A E H L P Ψ 049. 056. 1739 𝔐 mae || ἀνθρώπων ℵ* sy^p.

B03 and D05 read the singular, establishing a balanced comparison with θεοῦ at the beginning of the phrase; the balance is absent in ℵ01* which reads the plural.

12.23 ἐπάταξεν αὐτόν B 𝔓^74 ℵ *rell*; Lcf || αὐ. ἐπ. D Ψ 36. 431. 453. 467. 614. 616. 945. 1108. 1270. 1518. 1611. 1739. 1891. 2138. 2298. 2412 *pc* d gig; Chr Theoph.

The placing of the pronoun before the verb highlights the ironic application of the verb πατάσσω to Herod, it being the verb used of the angel of the Lord smiting the first-born on the night of Passover in Egypt. The text of B03 does not appear to identify the irony, having already selected this verb for the angel awaking Peter at 12.7 (see v. 7 above).

τὴν (δόξαν) B 𝔓^74 ℵ A 33. 81. 323. 945. 1175. 1739. 1891. 2344 || *om.* D E H L P Ψ 049. 056. 614 𝔐.

'To give glory/honour to God' is a common expression in the Jewish Scriptures or liturgy (B-A-G, δοξα, 3), without the article in the LXX (see e.g. Jos. 7.19; 1 Kgdms 6.5; 1 Chron. 16.28, 29; cf. Num 27.20, δώσεις τῆς δόξης σου) as in Lk. 17.18. Thus, D05 follows the Jewish pattern here.

(καὶ) καταβὰς ἀπὸ τοῦ βήματος D d mae; Ephr || *om.* B 𝔓^74 ℵ *rell*.— (σκωλη-κόβρωτος) ἔτι ζῶν D d mae || *om.* B 𝔓^74 ℵ *rell*.— καὶ οὕτως (ἐξέψυξεν) D d mae; Ephr || *om.* B 𝔓^74 ℵ *rell*.

The text of D05 gives a more graphic account of Herod's death, highlighting two details, namely, that he came down from the tribunal and that it was while he was still alive that he was eaten by worms and thus died. The first detail makes explicit his dethronement, in parallel with that of the Prince of Tyre as described in Ezek. 28.8, 17; cf. 26.15-18. Being eaten alive by worms was a typical punishment in Jewish tradition for blasphemers and slanderers (cf. 2 Macc. 9.9; Ginzberg, *Legends*, VI, p. 213, n. 136).

Commentary

[a] 12.18 *The Discovery of Peter's Escape*

12.18 As the focus of the narrative switches back to Herod, the story is picked up from 12.6 with the picture of Peter under heavy guard in prison, the night before Herod was intending to bring him before the people. As daytime arrives and the soldiers discover Peter's disappearance, there is understandably something of a commotion. With the care Herod had taken to ensure the strength of the guard (cf. 12.4, 6), the soldiers are obviously aware of the value of their prisoner and will know what his escape will mean to Herod. A similar scene occurs when the apostles are found to be missing from the Temple prison in Acts 5, though the discovery of their escape in that instance is described in fuller detail (cf. 5.22-23).

Peter's name is mentioned here for the last time in this sequence, and indeed in Acts apart from when he makes a brief appearance in Acts 15 at the meeting in Jerusalem. His presence throughout this sequence up till now has been the focus of attention because the main theme has been his personal liberation. The number of times his name is repeated within the space of 23 verses hammers this home: cf. 12.3, 5, 6, 7a D05, 7b, 11, 14a, 14b, 16a AT, 18). His disappearance has nothing to do, however, with the fact that Luke had run out of source material.[71]

[b] 12.19a *Herod Orders the Death of the Guards*

12.19a The switch of attention to Herod is signalled as he is brought back on stage with the mention of his name without the article in Greek.[72] Herod will now be the topic for the rest of the sequence. The piling up of participles that follows his name expressively describe his frenzy as he starts off by looking for Peter and, when he does not find him, he moves on to interrogating the guards. Since they presumably are unable to give any satisfactory account of what happened during the night, Herod attributes to them the blame for their prisoner's disappearance and has them killed. The army of the Egyptians had not met with a better fate after Pharaoh learnt that the Israelites had fled during the night since they drowned when they were sent to pursue them (Exod. 14.5-31).

[c] 12.19b *Herod's Stay in Caesarea*

12.19b The setting changes from Judaea as Herod went to stay in Caesarea.[73] Judaea in this context means not the Roman province of which Caesarea was the capital, but the 'territory of the Jews' as has been observed on previous occasions (cf. 9.31; 12.1 D05). Agrippa I's visit to Caesarea is documented by Josephus.[74]

---

71. Cf. Barrett, I, p. 587; Witherington, *Commentary*, p. 376.

72. When a character who was already established in the narrative reappears after being off stage for some time, the name is typically mentioned without the article (see Heimerdinger and Levinsohn, 'The Use of the Article', pp. 25–26).

73. Note that the verb describing Herod's departure from Judaea is the neutral κατέρχομαι and not the technical term καταβαίνω which Luke reserves for departure from Jerusalem or Judaea as the religious centre (see *Commentary*, 11.27).

74. Josephus, *Ant.* 19, 343–46. Cf. Bruce, *Acts*, pp. 254–56.

The change of setting causes Herod to be now viewed within the narrative perspective as no longer a Jewish king but a foreign one. Of course, nothing has changed in reality but it is important for Luke's theological purpose that in this sequence Herod acts in his role as a Roman king and no longer as a Jewish king as he did in the first sequence (see *Commentary*, 12.1-3a above). The presence in Caesarea of Philip (cf. 8.40), Cornelius (cf. 10.1) and other believers (cf. 21.8-12) is not relevant to Luke's story at this point.

[d] 12.20a *Herod's Anger with the Tyrians and the Sidonians*
12.20a The Bezan text explains the motive for his journey in a narrative aside, linking his departure for Caesarea with his anger against the Tyrians and Sidonians in a relationship of cause and effect. The psychological observation is typical of the Bezan narrator: Herod diverts his anger over Peter's escape to another problem, one he has with the people of Tyre and Sidon, countries in the province of Syria which bordered on the Roman province of Judaea. He went to Caesarea on the rebound of his fury over Peter – he had another quarrel to settle. The AT, in contrast, views the comment about Herod's anger as the preparation for the start of a new incident that continues in the next verse.

[e] 12.20b *The Tyrians and the Sidonians Seek Peace*
12.20b A new group of participants enter on stage at this point, the people from Tyre and Sidon just mentioned. What happens next is clear enough from the account in the AT: from their point of view, it is important to calm the anger of the king of Judaea for they depend on his province for provisions of food; they therefore present themselves as one body in Caesarea and first approach Blastus who is the royal 'chamberlain', that is, a close and trusted person in charge of the king's household.[75] The articulation of the events varies in the Bezan text, with several effects: 1) Codex Bezae treats Tyre and Sidon as two separate places, represented by two separate groups of people (they came from both cities, their two countries were dependent on the king's, ἐξ ἀμφοτέρων τῶν πόλεων ... διὰ τὸ τρέφεσθαι τὰς χώρας αὐτῶν ἐκ τῆς βασιλικῆς); 2) the relationship between the people and the king is reinforced by the use of the noun in the first clause ('they came to the king', πρὸς τὸν βασιλέα D05), rather than as a dependent genitive in the second ('the bed-chamber of the king', ἐπὶ τοῦ κοιτῶνος τοῦ βασιλέως AT).

The reason for separating the people of Tyre and those of Sidon will become apparent in the next verse (see. 12.21 below). The way attention is drawn to the relationship of the people with the king in the Bezan text keeps Herod clearly in focus. The role of Blastus seems to have been to serve as intermediary in order for the people to gain access to the king so that they could ask for peace. Like other people who are named by Luke as associated with the household of Agrippa I or of other Herods, he may well have been known to Theophilus the High Priest.[76]

---

75. Louw and Nida, 7.29.
76. The following references are relevant (taken from the Bezan text of the Gospel and Acts):
   1. Ἰωάννα γυνὴ Χουζᾶ ἐπιτρόπου Ἡρῴδου, Lk. 8.3;

The dependence of Tyre and Sidon on Judaea for food has a historical precedence, for Hiram of Tyre, who was also king over the neighbouring city of Sidon, had supplied Solomon with cedar wood for the Temple in exchange for food for his household (1 Kgs [3 Kgdms LXX] 5.1-12, esp. vv. 9, 11 [5.15-26, esp. vv. 23, 25 MT]; cf. Ezek. 27.17). By referring here to the economic dependence of Tyre and Sidon on the country of Herod, Luke is continuing to prepare for the moment when Herod will be assimilated with the Prince of Tyre in 12.22 below. Whether or not it was a historical fact that Tyre and Sidon really were supplied with food from Herod's territory in 44 CE, the year of his death, is more or less irrelevant, at least in the Bezan text where Luke is constructing a theological narrative, not a historical one.

[e′] 12.21a *Herod Addresses Them from his Throne*
12.21a It would appear that a day was fixed for the people to meet with the king. Luke describes the pomp with which Herod took his position on the raised platform, which served as a throne even though it may not have been one literally, and from there he addressed them in a grand and formal speech.[77] The description of the splendour agrees with Josephus' account of Herod's visit to Caesarea[78] and with reports elsewhere of Herod's love of ceremony and display of wealth.[79]

[d′] 12.21b *His Reconciliation with the Tyrians*
12.21b A narrative aside (corresponding from a structural point of view to the aside of 12.20a) is inserted in the Bezan text in a form that is grammatically unusual, to insist that the audience take careful note of the information it supplies. Luke uses the device to provide the crucial piece of information that Herod had been reconciled with the Tyrians. He does not say when this happened, or how, or why the Sidonians were not included in whatever arrangement Herod had come to with the Tyrians. It is now becoming clear, however, why the Bezan text made such a point in v. 20 of distinguishing the Tyrians from the Sidonians. The point is that there is no longer hostility between Herod and the people of Tyre: this prepares the way for their exaggerated praise of him in the next sentence.

2. (Jesus) ἐκ τῆς ἐξουσίας Ἡρῴδου ἐστίν ... ἦν γὰρ θέλων ἰδεῖν αὐτὸν ἐξ ἱκανῶν χρόνων, 23.7-8;

3. ὄντες δὲ ἐν ἀηδίᾳ ὁ Πιλᾶτος καὶ ὁ Ἡρῴδης ἐγένοντο φίλοι ἐν ἀτῇ τῇ ἡμέρᾳ, Lk. 23,12; cf. Acts 4.27;

4. Μαναήν τε Ἡρῴδου καὶ τετράρχου σύντροφος, Acts 13.1;

5. Ἀγρίππας ὁ βασιλεὺς καὶ Βερνίκη κατήντησαν εἰς Καισάρειαν ἀσπασάμενοι τὸν Φῆστον, Acts 25.13;

6. ἐβουλόμην καὶ αὐτὸς (Agrippa II) τοῦ ἀνθρώπου (Paul) ἀκοῦσαι, Acts 25.22.

77. The verb δημηγορέω has connotations of a formal oration (Louw and Nida, 33.26). It is found here only in the New Testament but occurs in the LXX at Prov. 30.31 and *4 Macc.* 5.15.

78. Josephus (*Ant.* 19, 344) describes the king's garment as woven with silver thread, glinting in the sun; the setting is the city theatre.

79. See E.M. Smallwood, *The Jews under Roman Rule from Pompey to Diocletian* (Leiden: E. J. Brill, 1976), pp. 187–200.

[c'] 12.22 *The Mob Acclaim Herod as a God*

12.22 There being no enmity now between Herod and the Tyrians, the scene is prepared for the crowd to respond to his magnificent speech with a great shout of adulation,[80] hailing the king as divine rather than human.

It is at this point that not only does the comparison of Herod with the Prince of Tyre become most evident but also its relevance is finally made apparent. The words with which the crowd, including or representing the Tyrians according to the Bezan text with whom the king had been reconciled, acclaim Herod, replicate almost exactly the rebuke that Ezekiel is instructed to issue to the Prince of Tyre:

> Say to the Prince of Tyre, Thus says the Lord God: 'Because your heart is proud and you have said, "I am a god, I sit in the seat of the gods in the heart of the seas", whereas you are not a god but a man…' (Ezek. 28.2, cf. vv. 6, 9).

In the prophecies of Ezekiel against the enemies of Israel, the Prince of Tyre is portrayed as one of the fiercest (Ezek. 26.1–28.19; a 'postscript' concerning Sidon follows in 28.20-23) with the most severe of punishments pronounced against him. His greatest fault was to have become arrogant and boastful about his fabulous wealth and his wisdom. Although the prophecy relates to a historical situation, especially in the beginning, it moves on to portray Tyre and its ruler in an eschatological context, so that the Prince of Tyre becomes a symbolic and timeless representation of a ruler who harshly oppresses Israel and whose rebellion against God culminates in the sin of setting himself up as a god.

In view of the allusions to Ezekiel already noted in Acts 12, it is no surprise to see that Luke draws on the book again in order to comment on the king who figures in the narrative, Herod Agrippa I.[81] The theological significance, however, of the assimilation he makes between Herod and the Prince of Tyre is remarkable in its daring: Herod king of Judaea, himself a Jew and with the support of his Jewish subjects, has oppressed those Jews who are faithful to God by following Jesus as the Messiah; in his arrogance, he allows himself to be acclaimed as a god; he thus imitates the ruler of Tyre, in his oppression of God's people and in his hubris, and his punishment will follow without delay. In taking on the features of the eschatological ruler of Tyre, Herod, on behalf of the Jewish people, has turned against the people of God. The Jews have become the enemies of the people of God. The response of God to their rebellion has been to lead his faithful people out of the eschatological hopes of Israel, to take them out of Jerusalem like an exile. This experience has been embodied in the deliverance of Peter from prison and his departure 'to another place' (Acts 12.17c).

---

80. δῆμος is exclusive to Luke and is only ever used of a pagan crowd (cf. Acts 17.5 [Thessalonica]; 19.30, 33 [Ephesus]). ἐπιφωνέω is likewise exclusive to Luke (cf. Lk. 23.21 AT; Acts 21.34; 22.24 AT).

81. The parallel between Acts 12.22 and Ezek. 28.1-9 has been discussed briefly by M.R. Strom, 'An Old Testament Background to Acts 12.20-23', *NTS* 32, (1986), pp. 289–92. It is rarely mentioned by commentators except to point out the similarities of language.

[b′] 12.23a *The Angel of the Lord Strikes Him Dead*
12.23a In Ezekiel's prophecy, the Prince of Tyre is destroyed by a cherub who is appointed by God to carry out his judgment (Ezek. 28.14, 16). In Acts, it is again the angel of the Lord who led Peter out of prison who acts now by striking Herod dead. The verb Luke uses is the same that is used to describe the angel of the Lord striking the first-born of the Egyptians on the night of the Passover (πατάσσω, Exod. 12.29).[82] The reason for Herod's punishment is spelt out as his failure to give God the glory, just as the reason for Prince of Tyre's punishment was that he said 'I am a god' (Ezek. 28.2).[83]

[a′] 12.23b *Herod Dies, Eaten by Worms*
12.23b The end of Herod is gruesome, as he dies[84] by being eaten by worms. Codex Bezae adds two details that make the account even more graphic: he comes down from the tribunal (where he was sitting as if on a throne), and is consumed by worms while still alive. At the same time, they reinforce the parallel with the Prince of Tyre who, likewise, is brought down (to the pit, Ezek. 26.20; 28.8; to the ground, 28.17; cf. 27.16), and who dies a horrible death ('I made a fire issue from you, and it has devoured you; I have reduced you to ashes on the ground', 28.18). Moreover, eaten alive by worms is an especially ignoble death, being reserved as it was in Jewish tradition for blasphemers and slanderers.[85]

The death of Herod thus brings to an end a long series of kings who, though ruling on behalf of the Romans as client kings, were of Jewish birth and were notable for their hostility and cruelty against Jesus and his followers. The son of Herod Agrippa I, Agrippa II, will appear later in the narrative of Acts, but without the name of Herod as an indication that the tradition of oppression and ruthlessness has been broken.

Excursus 8

The Prophecy of Ezekiel in Acts 12

The number of allusions to the book of Ezekiel that occur in Acts 12 is remarkable, and surprising because of the concentration and the variety of the allusions. References to the Jewish Scriptures observed in earlier chapters of Acts have

---

82. The verb πατάσσω was already used of the angel of the Lord waking Peter at 12.7 AT, where D05 chose νύσσω, a verb without the Passover associations.
83. The conjunction ἀνθ᾽ ὧν introducing the reason for the angel's punishment is unusual (Lk. × 3; otherwise only at 2 Thess. 2.10 in the New Testament) but is exactly the same as the one introducing the punishment of the Prince of Tyre in Ezekiel's prophecy, Ezek. 28.2 LXX et *passim*. Barrett (I, p. 592) discusses the conjunction from a grammatical point of view.
84. Lit. 'he expired', ἐξέψυξεν, the same word used of the deaths of Ananias and Sapphira (5.5, 10) but only there in the New Testament.
85. Cf. 2 Macc. 9.9; L. Ginzberg, *The Legends of the Jews* (7 vols; Philadelphia: The Jewish Publication Society of America, 11th edn, 1982), VI, p. 213, n. 136.

taken a range of forms: some have been individual references that served as hooks to connect the narrative of Acts with a scriptural model (such as the linking of the meeting of the 120 in Acts 1.15 with the census in Numbers 1);[86] others have been a series of references to one particular episode (for example, to the Exodus event in the deliverance of the apostles from prison in Acts 5.12-40),[87] and yet others have been seen in the intermittent drawing on the stories of Elijah and Elisha (as in the hostility to Stephen in 6.8-15; 7.54-59, which echoes that of Naboth's vineyard in 1 Kgs 21.1-14).[88] This is the first time, however, that allusions are found throughout a whole section of Acts to different themes within a single book of the Jewish Scriptures. A striking parallel with a prophetic gesture of Ezekiel was already noted in Acts 10.14 where just as Ezekiel had protested against the order to eat unclean food: Μηδαμῶς, κύριε ... οὐδὲ εἰσῆλθεν εἰς τὸ στόμα μου πᾶν κρέας ἕωλον (Ezek. 4.14), so Peter protested against the order to eat unclean food: Μηδαμῶς, κύριε, ὅτι οὐδέποτε ἔφαγον πᾶν κοινὸν καὶ/ἢ ἀκάθαρτον (Acts 10.14). The fact that Luke has made such extensive use of the prophecy of Ezekiel is an indication of the importance he accorded to its contents for his interpretation of the events in the Church at the time of Herod's persecution. The allusions relating to Herod are discussed in detail in *Excursus* 9 but are summarised here along with the others to provide a complete picture.

Ezekiel	*Acts*
The Jews had built a chamber (οἴκημα, 16.24) of prostitution in Jerusalem	Herod shut Peter up in a prison chamber (οἴκημα, 12.7a) where the angel of the Lord appeared to him
Ezekiel's Temple had an outer court (τῇ αὐλῇ τῇ ἐξωτέρᾳ, 40.20 *et passim*) and an inner one (τῇ αὐλῇ τῇ ἐσωτέρᾳ, 40.23 *et passim*)	The angel of the Lord and Peter went through a first and a second prison (πρώτην φυλακὴν καὶ δευτέραν AT / πρ. κ. δευ. φυλ. D05, 12.10a)
The gate by which the Lord had entered the Temple was to remain shut and not be opened (αὕτη ἦν κεκλεισμένη ... οὐκ ἀνοιχθήσεται, 44.1-2)	The Iron Gate was closed but opened to let the angel of the Lord bring Peter out (ἐπὶ τὴν πύλην τὴν Σιδηρᾶν ... ἥτις αὐτομάτη ἠνοίγη αὐτοῖς, 12.10a)
There were to be seven steps (ἑπτὰ κλιμακτῆρες, 40.22, 26) between the outer court of the new Temple and the city	They went down the seven steps (κατέβησαν τοὺς ἑπτὰ βαθμούς, 12.10b D05) that took them into the streets of the city
Ezekiel was to go like an exile from his place to another place (αἰχμαλωτευθήσῃ ἐκ τοῦ τόπου σου εἰς ἕτερον τόπον, 12.3)	Peter went to another place (ἐπορεύθη εἰς ἕτερον τόπον, 12.17c)
Tyre had a Prince (τῷ ἄρχοντι Τύρου, 28.2), with a seal and a crown as symbols of royalty (ἀποσφράγισμα ὁμοιώσεως καὶ στέφανος κάλλους, 28.12)	The people of Tyre came to the king (πρὸς αὐτόν AT / τὸν βασιλέα D05, 12.20)
Judah and Israel provided Tyre with food (ἔμποροί σου ἐν σίτου πράσει..., 27.17)	Tyre received food from Herod's country (τρέφεσθαι αὐτῶν τὴν χώραν ἀπὸ τῆς βασιλικῆς AT / τρ. τὰς χώρας αὐ. ἐκ τ. βασ., 12.20)

86. See *The Message of Acts*, I, pp. 117–18.
87. See *The Message of Acts*, I, *Excursus* 8, pp. 358–63.
88. See *Commentary, ad loc.*

The King of Tyre was dressed with every precious stone (πᾶν λίθον χρηστὸν ἐνδέδεσαι…, 28.13)

Herod was dressed in regal clothing (ἐνδυσάμενος ἐσθῆτα βασιλικήν, 12.21a)

The Prince of Tyre said, 'I am a god' (θεός εἰμι ἐγώ, 28.2a, 9a), but God said 'You are a man and not a god' (σὺ δὲ εἶ ἄνθρωπος καὶ οὐ θεός, 28.2b, 9b)

The crowd acclaimed his speech as of a god and not a man (θεοῦ φωναὶ [φωνὴ D05] καὶ οὐκ ἀνθρώπου, 12.22)

The Prince of Tyre was driven out of Eden by the guardian cherub (ἤγαγέν σε τὸ χερούβ ἐκ μέσου λίθων πυρίνων, 28.16) because (ἀνθ' ὧν) he has been so haughty (28.1)

Herod was struck down by the angel of the Lord (ἐπάταξεν αὐτὸν ἄγγελος κυρίου) because (ἀνθ' ὧν) he did not give glory to God (12.23a)

The Prince of Tyre was thrown down into the sea (καταβιβάσουσίν σε, καὶ ἀποθανῇ θανάτῳ τραυματιῶν ἐν καρδίᾳ θαλάσσης, 28.8)

Herod came down from the tribunal (καταβὰς ἀπὸ τοῦ βήματος, 12.23b D05)

God brought Tyre to a dreadful end (ἀπώλειάν σε δώσω, καὶ οὐχ ὑπάρξεις ἔτι εἰς τὸν αἰῶνα, 26.21)

Herod died a gruesome death (γενόμενος σκωληκόβρωτος ἐξέψυξεν ΤΑ / καὶ γενόμενος σκωληκόβρωτος ἔτι ζῶν καὶ οὕτως ἐξέψυξεν D05, 12.23b)

The allusions to Ezekiel start at the point the angel and Peter begin to leave the prison, when the prison takes on the aspect of the restored Temple of Ezekiel's vision. The details of the two prisons/courts, the closed gate and the seven steps are all features of the Temple that Luke mentions. Ezekiel's prophetic actions provide the context for Peter's departure after his release from prison 'to another place' which is likened to Ezekiel's departure from Jerusalem like an exile because of the rebellion of the Jewish people. Finally, Ezekiel's prophecy against the Prince of Tyre, the city which rejoiced at the misfortunes of Jerusalem (Ezek. 26.2), is realized in the person of Herod who is assimilated with the ruler of Tyre and who is punished by God for his arrogance and violence.

The realization of Ezekiel's prophetic vision of a restored Jerusalem with a new Temple was conditional on Israel repenting of their rebellion against God (Ezek. 43.11). By his identification of Herod, king of Judaea, as the Prince of Tyre, Luke conveys the message that Israel has not repented and therefore portrays the vision of the new Temple, the dwelling place of the Lord, as being reversed: the Lord leaves the anticipated restored Temple and brings his faithful people out with him. The non-fulfilment of the vision is summarized in Peter's action of going 'to another place' and so leaving Ierousalem, the religious system of Israel, like an exile because of its faithlessness (Ezek. 12.1-6).

Excursus 9

Herod and the Prince of Tyre

A clear correspondence between the first sequence of Acts 12 (vv. 1-5) and the last (vv. 18-23) is established by the three-part structure of the passage which presents Herod's determination to persecute the church and his subsequent death in a relationship of cause and effect on either side of the central episode of Peter's deliverance. It is God's intervention with regard to Peter that, in fact, allows the end of Herod to be interpreted as divine punishment for his treatment of the Church. And not just this Herod, Agrippa I, but all the Herods who have figured in the Gospel and Acts (see *Commentary*, 12.20b), for even though Agrippa I's son, Agrippa II, will play a role in the trial of Paul, he will never be mentioned as a 'Herod', as if the wickedness of the family was well and truly brought to an end with the judgment of God on Agrippa I. From the point of view of the narrative of Acts 12, the reason this can be so is because Herod Agrippa I is assimilated with the Prince of Tyre, the worst of Israel's enemies who had to be punished before Israel could be restored.

It was seen in *Excursus* 7 that through the re-enactment of the Exodus in which Peter is presented as taking part, Herod takes on the role of Pharaoh because of his oppression of Peter and the Jewish Jesus-believers in general. The use that is made of the model of the Prince of Tyre, however, takes the process of analogy one step further and portrays the situation facing the Church in Acts 12 as even more dire than that with which the Israelites in Egypt were confronted. The difference is that whereas the oppressor of Israel in Egypt was a foreign ruler, the oppressor of the Church in Judaea is a Jewish king who acts with the encouragement of his Jewish subjects.

The allusions to the Prince of Tyre in the AT are relatively sparse compared with those that can be discerned in the Bezan text. The first mention of Tyre is at 12.20a where Herod is said to have been furious with the Tyrians and the Sidonians, expressing the ancient hostility between these people and the Jews. According to the articulation of Codex Bezae, Herod's reason for going to Caesarea was his anger with them, so giving an outlet for his fury over Peter's escape. In other words, from their first mention these people are linked to Herod's actions regarding Peter.

In almost all the MSS, Tyre and Sidon are treated collectively as one country (12.20b AT) but Codex Bezae regards them as separate places represented by two separate groups of people who go to Caesarea to meet Herod (see *Critical Apparatus*). Their relationship with the king is also emphasized in the Bezan text. This comes out in the following three readings of 12.20b D05:

1. The people are from both places: οἱ δὲ ὁμοθυμαδὸν ἐξ ἀμφοτέρων τῶν πόλεων.
2. They go to the king: πρὸς τὸν βασιλέα.
3. Their separate countries are dependent on Herod's kingdom: τὰς χώρας αὐτῶν ἐκ τῆς βασιλικῆς.

A fourth reading at the end of 12.21b D05 confirms the separate identity of the people of Tyre as being the ones with whom Herod was reconciled:

4. καταλλαγέντος δὲ αὐτοῦ τοῖς Τυρίοις.

The reason for distinguishing between the Tyrians and the Sidonians, and especially for underlining that Herod was reconciled with the Tyrians, is that it alerts the audience to recognize the linking of Herod with the ruler of Tyre in the crowd's acclamation of him as divine in a fifth reading common to both texts of 12.22:

5. θεοῦ φωνὴ [φωναὶ D05] καὶ οὐκ ἀνθρώπου.

This cry is a striking echo of a section of the prophecy of Ezekiel concerning the Prince of Tyre because above all else, in his arrogance the ruler had set himself up as a god (28.2; cf. vv. 6, 9):

᾽Ανθ᾽ ὧν ὑψώθη σου ἡ καρδία, καὶ εἶπας θεός εἰμι ἐγώ, ... σὺ δὲ εἰ ἄνθρωπος καὶ οὐ θεός...

A number of sources indicate that the story of the Prince of Tyre and of his fate was well-known in first-century Judaism and was regarded as an example of what happens to those who set themselves up as gods.[89] In the rabbinic writings, legends are transmitted from earlier times in which the ruler of Tyre is embodied in the person of Hiram, the first king of Tyre to be mentioned in the Scriptures, who supplied Solomon with cedar wood for the building of the first Temple (1 Kgs 5.1-12). One story has it that Hiram became so proud because of his contribution that God destroyed the Temple in order to humble him.[90] In the Targum to Ezekiel, too, the already lengthy description of the ruler of Tyre is embellished and expanded: although the Targum is thought to have been written after 70 CE, it is likely that it incorporates material from existing traditions.[91] Two comments are of particular interest: in *Targ. Ezek.* 28.13, the account of the beauty of the Prince of Tyre is contrasted with a comment that was traditionally interpreted as a statement of his mortality:

> However, you did not reflect wisely on your body which consists of orifices and organs, of which you have need for it is impossible to survive without them.[92]

In the following verse 14, the description of the ruler of Tyre is amplified in the following terms:

> You are a king anointed for the kingdom and I have given you greatness, but you looked with contempt on the holy mountain of the Lord, and planned to exercise dominion over the holy people.

Herod was not to escape unpunished, no more than did the Prince of Tyre. Similarities can be seen between the accounts of the judgment of God on both of them, especially if the more graphic accounts of *Targum Ezekiel* on the one hand, and Codex Bezae on the other, are considered. In the case of both rulers, it is God himself who brings about the death of the proud oppressor of his people (Acts 12.23; cf. Ezek. 28.17-18). Two supplementary details describing how Herod died are read in Codex Bezae of Acts 12.23: first, after being struck by the angel, 'he came down from tribunal', and secondly, when he is eaten by worms he is 'still alive, and it is in this way' that he dies:

---

89. See L. Ginzberg, *The Legends of the Jews*, IV, pp. 335–56.

90. Midrash in *Yalkut* II, 367, cited by Ginzberg, *The Legends of the Jews*, IV, p. 336; cf. S.H. Levey, *The Aramaic Bible*, vol. XIII: The *Ezekiel Targum: Introduction, Translation, Apparatus, Notes* (Edinburgh: T&T Clark, 1987), p. 83, n. 12.

91. Levey, *The Ezekiel Targum*, pp. 2, 4.

92. This quotation and the following one from *Targ. Ezek.* 28.14 are taken from the English translation by Levey, *The Ezekiel Targum*. On the significance of the expansion in v. 14, cf. p. 85, n. 14.

1.   καταβὰς ἀπὸ τοῦ βήματος
2.   γενόμενος σκωληκόβρωτος ἔτι ζῶν καὶ οὕτως ἐξέψυξεν

These comments take their force from the context of Ezekiel 28 with its several references to the Prince of Tyre being dethroned (Ezek. 28.8, 17; cf. 26.15-18). The inevitable consequence of the death of a king is that he is removed from the throne; by spelling out that implication, the Bezan text points to the symbolic meaning of Herod's dethronement which is a humiliating punishment more than it is a natural result of his death.

The humiliation of Herod's death is apparent in the way he died. In Ezekiel, the death of the Prince of Tyre is equally related in horrific terms: 'I brought fire from the midst of you, it consumed you ... all who know you among the peoples are appalled at you, you have come to a dreadful end' (Ezek. 28.18-19). Attention has already been drawn to the emphasis in the Targum on the mortality of the ruler of Tyre. The detail in the Bezan text that Herod was eaten alive by worms contributes to the graphic picture of Herod's ignoble death, which was that reserved in Jewish tradition for blasphemers and slanderers (see *Commentary*, 12.23).

In considering the points of similarity between the Prince of Tyre and King Herod, the legend concerning Hiram and the destruction of the first Temple (see above) is strangely relevant in that it was Herod's own family, from the time of his grandfather Herod the Great, who had been responsible for the building of the second Temple in Jerusalem. This Temple will be destroyed in 70 CE during the time that his son Agrippa II is tetrarch of the northern territory of Israel. In this sense, the idea is confirmed that in his death Herod Agrippa I represents the family of Herods and that he bears in his punishment a family responsibility.

Colophon: 12.24-25 *Conclusion*

Overview

The final two verses of Acts 12 draw together the results of all that has gone on throughout Part Two, from 6.1 to 12.23, showing both the positive and negative outcomes of the growth of the Church beyond Jerusalem. At the same time, the colophon prepares for the next chapters of Acts by presenting a 'List of Contents' so to speak of what Part Three will contain. It parallels the colophon of Part One of Acts which, placed at 6.7, serves the additional purpose of summarizing the opening sequence of Part Two.

Structure and Themes

The two verses appear, at first sight, to be of a contrasting nature, the one a general comment on the spread of the word, and the other a piece of particular information relating to the visit of Barnabas and Saul to Jerusalem. In actual fact, both are comments that describe the consequences of the punishment of Herod for his oppression of the Church: first, the expansion of the Church continued, though in what sense will be seen in the *Commentary* for it varies according to the text followed; and secondly, the nature of the relationship of Barnabas and Saul, as delegates from the church in Antioch, with the church in Ierousalem was determined, again in different ways according to the text adopted. The two verses mirror each other in their positive and negative aspects, according to the articulation of Codex Bezae:

[a]	12.24	The expansion of the word of God
[a′]	12.25	The separation of Barnabas and Saul from Ierousalem

Translation

Codex Bezae D05	*Codex Vaticanus B03*
[a] **12.24** The word of God was fruitful and multiplied.	**12.24** The word of the Lord was fruitful and multiplied.
[a′] **25** Barnabas and Saul turned away from Ierousalem, having completed the service and they took with them John who had been called Mark.	**25** Barnabas and Saul returned having completed the service in Ierousalem, and they took with them John who had been called Mark.

Critical Apparatus

12.24 (λόγος) τοῦ κυρίου B 1837 vg bo^mss ‖ τ. θεοῦ D d 𝔓⁷⁴ ℵ A E H L P Ψ 049. 056. 33. 1739 𝔐 gig p sy co.

D05 makes a clear distinction between the word of God, meaning communication between God and humanity in general (originally through the Torah), and the word of the Lord, meaning the message of Jesus in particular (*General Introduction,* § VIII). The AT does not appear to distinguish between the two terms. The variation on this occasion affects the interpretation of the verse (see *Commentary*).

12.25 ὑπέστρεψαν B Dᴴ 𝔓⁷⁴ ℵ *rell, reversi sunt* d | ὑπέστρεψεν 38. 2412 sy^hmg ‖ ἀπέστρεψεν D*.

B03 reads the verb ὑποστρέφω, to 'return', and in the plural to concord with Barnabas and Saul as the subject. D05 has the verb ἀποστρέφω meaning to 'separate', which reflects the theological separation from Ierousalem, a motif not apparent in the B03 text of Acts in general but a dominant theme in that of D05. The singular considers Barnabas and Saul to be acting in unison. This variant should be considered in combination with the following one.

εἰς ('Ιερουσαλήμ) B ℵ² H P L 049. 056. 0142 𝔐 sy^hmg sa^ms aeth^pt; Chr^pt Theoph ‖ ἀπό D d E Ψ 36. 181. 226^c. 323. 431. 436. 440. 453. 614. 1108. 1175. 1270. 1518. 1611. 1799. 1898. 2138. 2412 *al* ar e gig vg sy^h?; Chr^pt | ἐξ 𝔓⁷⁴ ℵ* A 33. 242. 383. 522. 547. 630. 876. 913. 945. 1739. 1765. 1838. 1891. 2127. 2298 *al* sy^h? bo aeth^pt; Chr^pt.

The same intention as was noted in the above variant is seen to continue in this one, with B03 having Barnabas and Saul continuing their journey towards Ierousalem and D05 leaving it. The B03 reading makes little sense at first sight and has been extensively discussed (see Barrett, I, pp. 595–96; Metzger, *Commentary*, pp. 350–52) but without taking account of the theological significance underlying the D05 text. It is possible that εἰς Ἰερουσαλήμ should be read with the participle πληρώσαντες, and that the previous verb ὑπέστρεψαν is used in an absolute sense, meaning 'they returned to Antioch' (see *Commentary*).

τὸν (Ἰωάνην [-νν- B ℵ A]) D* | καί Dᴴ E H L P Ψ 049. 056. 614 𝔐 || *om.* B 𝔓⁷⁴ ℵ 1739. 1891.

The article in D05 is anaphoric, referring back to the mention of John-Mark at 12.12 and viewing his presence from the point of view of Barnabas and Saul who already know him; its omission in B03 treats the mention of John-Mark at this point as not necessarily expected as far as the audience of Acts is concerned (cf. Read-Heimerdinger, *The Bezan Text*, pp. 139–43, where the variant of 12.25 could be added to the discussion).

(τὸν) ἐπικληθέντα B D E H L P Ψ 049. 056. 614. 1739 𝔐 || ἐπικαλούμενον 𝔓⁷⁴ ℵ A 33. 81. 88. 927. 1175. 1270. 1505. 1646. 1828. 1837. 2344. 2495 *al, qui cognominatur* d gig sa.

The aorist participle in both B03 and D05 refers back to the time when John was first recognized as having the function of communicating the gospel (12.12, present participle, see *Commentary, ad loc.*). The use of the aorist aspect signifies that his function here had been recognized in the past although he was not currently exercising it (cf. present tense at 15.37). The present tense of ℵ01 suggests that the function is being exercised at this point, if indeed the difference in the two aspects of the expression is recognized by that text.

Commentary

[a] 12.24 *The Expansion of the Word of God*
12.24 The first element of this colophon echoes the wording of the first colophon at 6.7:

> And the word of the Lord (God, B03) was fruitful and the number of disciples in Jerusalem was multiplied greatly and, moreover, a great crowd of priests obeyed the faith.

It was seen (*Commentary, ad loc.*) that as a conclusion to the first part of Acts the colophon summarized the situation in the church of Jerusalem which, at that point, was still united even if separate groups of disciples were beginning to emerge. The word of the Lord referred to the message of Jesus which, following the selection of the seven Hellenist leaders, was preached clearly and openly for the first time, as something new and distinct from the exposition of the Torah (see *Critical Apparatus*, 6.7) for, hitherto, only the word of God had been announced. In the AT, however, which continues to read 'the word of God' at 6.7 this progression was not made apparent.

Now, the readings of the two texts are inversed, with the AT reading 'the word of the Lord' and the Bezan text reading 'the word of God'. It is not clear that the AT attributes any difference in significance to the two expressions,[93] but may use both interchangeably to mean the message of the gospel. In Codex Bezae, on the contrary, the reference here is to the word of God as the principle of God communicating with humanity which, in the Bezan text, always precedes the word of the Lord. It is a gift, equivalent to the Torah, which the various nations receive before they receive the word of the Lord, the specific message about Jesus (see *General Introduction,* § VIII). Each time the disciples of Jesus have contact with a new people, it is the word of God that they present first.

In describing the word, whether of God or the Lord, as fruitful and multiplying, Luke picks up the vocabulary of the first Creation account in Gen. 1.28, when God told the people he had created: 'Be fruitful and multiply' ('Αυξάνεσθε καὶ πληθύνεσθε). The order was fulfilled in the second account of the Creation when God made all the living animals to be with Adam, all the types of creatures that Peter was presented with in his vision in Joppa (Gen. 2.18-19; cf. Acts 10.12; 11.6). Peter came to realize that the animals in his vision represented people of every kind, both Jews and Gentiles, whom God accepted without any distinction (Acts 10.34-35). The order to bear fruit and multiply is thus now seen to apply to the Church to which new disciples are added from all nations. The Bezan text makes clearer than the AT the subtle point that the word of God, communication between God and humanity that had for so long been the preserve of Israel, now reached other nations, in preparation for receiving the message about Jesus. This was a step of a fundamental order, changing the whole balance of relationships between God and the nations and also between Israel and the nations.

[b] 12.25 *The Separation of Barnabas and Saul from Ierousalem*

12.25 The final verse takes up the mention of Barnabas and Saul from 11.30 at the end of Section III, where they were named as the delegates to bring the offerings of the Antioch church to the brethren in Judaea. They are re-introduced without the article in Greek because they had not been active in the intervening sequences but were waiting, as it were, in the wings ready to re-enter at the appropriate time.

There is variation between the two texts here that once again signals a difference in the message communicated. In both cases, Barnabas and Saul take an action with regard to Ierousalem, after first completing the service – the taking of gifts to the brethren of Judaea (11.29) – and they took with them John-Mark. Since the significance of these three elements is interdependent, they are best considered together, looking at first the Bezan text and then the AT.

In Codex Bezae, Barnabas and Saul, acting of one accord as indicated in Greek by the singular verb (see *Critical Apparatus*), go away from Ierousalem. That this is much more than a simple geographical note is obvious from the use of the term Luke reserves in the Bezan text for the religious centre of Judaism

---

93. See the conclusion of the analysis of the expressions and their variants in Read-Heimerdinger, *The Bezan Text*, p. 309–10.

(see *General Introduction,* § VII). Now, it has just been seen in the previous section (12.1-23) that because of the attack of the Jews on the Jewish Jesus-believers, especially their leaders, the apostles, a powerful and dramatic change has been brought about in the concept of Israel as the people of God and in their hopes for a restored kingdom with its centre in Ierousalem where the Lord would dwell in a glorious new Temple (see *Excursus* 7, 8 and 9). God has delivered the Jesus-believers, 'the faithful', from the oppression of the Jews and has led them out from the expectations of a renewed Israel. This was the first time in Acts that the split of the Church away from the religious authority and concepts and hopes of Judaism has been so clearly spelt out, though there have been hints of it at various points. Peter himself only became fully conscious of the separation from the Jewish expectations that had to be made if he were to follow Jesus when he was miraculously delivered from the prison where Herod had shut him up. After relating his realization to the church praying for him in the house of Mary, the mother of John-Mark who is about to mentioned for a second time, he left Ierousalem, like an exile because of the sins of his people (12.17c). He did not visit James and the brethren who from now on will represent Ierousalem among the Jesus-believers because of their continued attachment to the Jewish system, but asked for his news to be passed on to them.

What had provoked the ferocious attack on the apostles was precisely the gift that Barnabas and Saul had brought from the Antioch church 'as a service' (εἰς διακονίαν, 11.29). This aid, coming as it did not only from the Diaspora but also from a community that included Gentiles, would have been a shocking cause of offence to the Jews who were not Jesus-believers and would have provided the motive for Herod to persecute them (see *Commentary,* 12.1-3). Barnabas and Saul would have observed first-hand the effect of their 'service', and may well have been in the house of Mary when Peter came to tell them of his miraculous deliverance, his 'exodus' from the Jewish hopes of restoration. Now they, in their turn, leave Ierousalem where they would have left their gifts and carry out a similar move to Peter, making a break with the church led by James who will be seen later (cf. 15.13-21; 21.18-25) to take a hardened position with respect to the status of the Gentiles in the Church.[94]

When they go, they take with them John-Mark, the son of Mary. When he was first mentioned at 12.12, he was noted for his function as the faithful transmitter of the gospel, a function that was recognized by the church and that he was exercising there and then. Here, the participle is aorist,[95] indicating that although his function had been recognized he was not exercising it at that point. Barnabas and Saul took John-Mark with them to Antioch, knowing what his gifts were and probably because of that. The article in Greek before the name of John expresses

---

94. The verb ἀποστρέφω is not common in the New Testament but in addition to the one occurrence in each of Luke's Gospel and Acts, D05 has another four readings. On every occasion, the sense is strongly negative, implying a sense of rupture or harmful separation.

95. The present participle (τοῦ ἐπικαλουμένου Μάρκου) at 12.12, indicating the activity John-Mark was carrying out at that time, contrasts with the aorist participle here (τὸν ἐπικληθέντα Μᾶρκον) (see *Critical Apparatus*).

the relationship that they had already established with him as well as referring back to the previous mention of his name as the son of Mary (see *Critical Apparatus*).

In the AT, the relationships between the various parties and their motives are less clear but perhaps also less complex. Barnabas and Saul are seen as acting as two people (the verb is plural, see *Critical Apparatus*), but it is less common in the AT generally compared with the Bezan text to see them presented as one unit.[96] On a straightforward reading, they do not go away from Ierousalem but, on the contrary, go back there after they have delivered the gifts, and they take John-Mark with them. It is not at all sure that the AT recognizes the significance of the spelling of Jerusalem at this point, if anywhere in Luke-Acts. Commentators generally assume that no difference is intended and it is certainly difficult to discern a logic that might give rise to a pattern of usage (see *General Introduction*, § VII). For this reason, the AT reading is usually considered to be so difficult as to be impossible.[97]

However, what may have happened, if the Bezan text can be considered to have been written first, is that the idea of Barnabas and Saul turning their backs on Ierousalem, or even Jerusalem if the theological significance were not recognized, was viewed as too harsh. It has been noted that the AT of Acts elsewhere tends to tone down the conflict between the different groups of disciples (cf. e.g. 6.1-7; 8.1b, and *Commentary, ad loc.*),[98] and that could have been the motive here for adjusting the text so as to present Barnabas and Saul returning (to Antioch) after delivering the gifts to Jerusalem, leaving an unusual word order reflected in the English translation, but avoiding any hint of tension between the church of Antioch and the church under James of Jerusalem.

96. See Read-Heimerdinger, *The Bezan Text*, pp. 135–37.

97. In order to make sense of the AT, a comma could be placed after ὑπέστρεψαν with the goal understood as Antioch; εἰς taken as having the stationary force of ἐν (which does happen in the AT, see Read-Heimerdinger, *The Bezan Text*, pp. 192–95); and the participle πληρώσαντες attached retrospectively to the prepositional phrase, to read thus: 'Barnabas and Saul returned, having fulfilled their service in Jerusalem, taking with them John who had been called Mark.' The word order in this case is somewhat forced.

98. The disagreement between Paul and the 'we'-group will be notably less marked in the AT; see J. Rius-Camps, 'The Gradual Awakening of Paul's Awareness of his Mission to the Gentiles', in T. Nicklas and M. Tilly (eds), *Apostelgeschichte als Kirchengeschichte. Text, Traditionen und antike Auslegungen* (BZNW, 122: Berlin-New York: Walter de Gruyter, 2003), pp. 281–96.

BIBLIOGRAPHY

I. *Works of Reference and Frequently Cited Works*

The following works are referred to either by an abbreviation or, in the case of commentaries on Acts, by the name of the author.

Abécassis A., and G. Nataf, *Encyclopédie de la mystique juive* (Paris: Berg, 1977).

Aland, B. and K., *et al.* (eds), *Novum Testamentum Graece* (Stuttgart: Deutsche Bibelgesellschaft, 27th edn, 1993).

— *The Greek New Testament* (Stuttgart: Deutsche Bibelgesellschaft/United Bible Societies, 4th edn, 1993).

The American and British Committees of the International Greek New Testament Project (eds), *The Gospel According to St. Luke.* Part I, Chapters 1–12; Part II, Chapters 13–28 (Oxford: Clarendon Press, 1984, 1987).

Bailly, A., *Dictionnaire grec-français* (Paris: Hachette, 16th edn, 1950).

Balz, H., and G. Schneider (eds), *Exegetisches Wörterbuch zum Neuen Testament* (3 vols; Stuttgart: Verlag W. Kohlhammer GmbH, 1980–83).

Barrett, C.K., *A Critical and Exegetical Commentary on the Acts of the Apostles* (2 vols; Edinburgh: T&T Clark, 1994, 1998).

Bauer, W., *A Greek English Lexicon of the New Testament and Other Early Christian Literature* (ed. and trans. W.F. Arndt and F.W. Gingrich; Chicago: Chicago University Press, 1957).

Berlin, A., and M.Z. Brettler (eds), *The Jewish Study Bible* (Jewish Publication Society; TANAKH Translation; Oxford: Oxford University Press, 2004).

Blass, F., A. Debrunner and F. Rehkopf, *Grammatik des neutestamentlichen Griechisch* (Göttingen: Vandenhoeck & Ruprecht, 15th edn, 1979).

Boismard, M.-É., and A. Lamouille, *Le texte occidental des Actes des Apôtres: Reconstitution et réhabilitation.* I. *Introduction et textes*; II. *Apparat critique* (Paris: Éditions Recherche sur les Civilisations, 1984).

Brown, F., S. Driver and C. Briggs, *Hebrew and English Lexicon* (Peabody, MA: Hendrickson Publishers Inc., repr. 2003).

Bruce, F.F., *The Acts of the Apostles. The Greek Text with Introduction and Commentary* (London: The Tyndale Press, 1951).

— *Commentary on the Book of Acts. The English Text with Introduction, Exposition and Notes* (London: Marshall, Morgan and Scott, 1954).

Cadbury H., and K. Lake (eds), *Additional Notes to the Commentary*, in Foakes-Jackson and Lake (eds), *The Beginnings of Christianity*, V (1933).

Clark, A.C., *The Acts of the Apostles* (Oxford: Clarendon Press, 1933; repr. 1970).

Conzelmann, H., *Acts of the Apostles* (trans. J. Limburg, A.T. Kraabel and D.H. Juel; ed. E.J. Epp; Philadelphia: Fortress Press, 1987).

Delebecque, É., *Les Actes des Apôtres* (Paris: Belles Lettres, 1982).

— *Les deux Actes des Apôtres* (ÉBib, NS, 6; Paris: J. Gabalda, 1986).

Dunn J.D.G., *The Acts of the Apostles* (Peterborough: Epworth Press, 1996).

Foakes-Jackson, F.J., and K. Lake (eds), *The Beginnings of Christianity.* I. *The Acts of the Apostles* (5 vols; London: Macmillan, 1920–33).

Freedman, D.N. (ed.), *Anchor Bible Dictionary* (6 vols; New York: Doubleday, 1992).

Goodenough, E.R. *Jewish Symbols in the Greco-Roman Period* (13 vols; New York: Pantheon Books, 1953–65).

Gryson, R. (dir. Vetus Latina Institut, Beuron), *Vetus Latina Database* (Brepols: Turnhout, 2002).

Haenchen, E., *The Acts of the Apostles: A Commentary* (trans. B. Noble, G. Shinn and R. McL. Wilson; Oxford: B. Blackwells, 1981).

Hatch E., and Redpath H.A., *A Concordance to the Septuagint and Other Greek Versions of the Old Testament* (2 vols; Graz: Akademische Druck- und Verlagsanstalt, 1954).

Heimerdinger, J., and S.H. Levinsohn, 'The Use of the Definite Article before Names of People in the Greek Text of Acts with Particular Reference to Codex Bezae', *FN* 5 (1992), pp. 15–44.

Johnson, L.T., *The Acts of the Apostles* (Sacra Pagina, 5: Collegeville, MN: The Liturgical Press, 1992).

Levinsohn, S.H., *Textual Connections in Acts* (Atlanta: Scholars Press, 1987).

— *Discourse Features of New Testament Greek* (Dallas: Summer Institute of Linguistics, 1992).

Liddell, H.G., R.J. Scott and H.S. Jones, *A Greek-English Lexicon: A New Edition* (Oxford: Clarendon Press, 1940).

Louw, J.P., and E.A. Nida, *Greek-English Lexicon of the New Testament Based on Semantic Domains* (2 vols; New York: United Bible Societies, 2nd edn, 1989).

Marshall, I.H., *The Acts of the Apostles* (Tyndale New Testament Commentaries; Leicester: IVP, 1980).

Mayser, E., *Grammatik der Griechischen Papyri aus Ptolemäerzeit* (2 vols; Berlin: Walter de Gruyter, 2nd edn, 1970).

Metzger, B.M., *A Textual Commentary on the Greek New Testament* (Stuttgart: Deutsche Bibelgesellschaft, 2nd edn, 1994).

Moule, C.F.D., *An Idiom-Book of New Testament Greek* (Cambridge: Cambridge University Press, 2nd edn, 1959).

Moulton, J.H., *A Grammar of New Testament Greek.* I. *Prolegomena* (Edinburgh: T&T Clark, 1908).

Moulton, J.H., and W.F. Howard, *A Grammar of New Testament Greek.* II. *Accidence and Word-Formation* (Edinburgh: T&T Clark, 1929).

Nestle, E., *Novi Testamenti Graeci: Supplementum editionibus de Gebhardt Tischendorfianis; Codex Cantabrigiensis Collatio* (Leipzig: Tauchnitz, 1896).

Neusner J., and Green W.S. (eds), *Dictionary of Judaism in the Biblical Period 450 BCE to 600 CE* (New York: Macmillan Reference Library, 1996).

Parker, D.C., *Codex Bezae. An Early Christian Manuscript and Its Text* (Cambridge: Cambridge University Press, 1994).

Parsons, M.M., and M.M. Culy, *Acts: A Handbook on the Greek Text* (Waco, TX: Baylor University Press, 2003).

Porter, S.E., *Idioms of New Testament Greek* (Biblical Languages: Greek, 2; Sheffield: JSOT Press, 1992).

Pritchard J. (ed.), *Atlas of the Bible* (London: HarperCollins, 2nd edn, 1989).

Rahlfs, A. (ed.), *Septuaginta* (Stuttgart: Deutsche Bibelstiftung 1985).

Read-Heimerdinger, J., *The Bezan Text of Acts. A Contribution of Discourse Analysis to Textual Criticism* (JSNTSup, 236; Sheffield: Sheffield Academic Press, 2002).

Rius-Camps, J., *Comentari als Fets dels Apòstols* (4 vols; Barcelona: Facultat de Teologia de Catalunya–Herder, 1991–2000).

Rius-Camps, J., and J. Read-Heimerdinger, *The Message of Acts in Codex Bezae: A Comparison with the Alexandrian Text*. I. *Acts 1.1-5.42: Jerusalem* (JSNTSup, 257; London: T&T Clark International, 2004).

Robertson, A.T., *A Grammar of the Greek New Testament in the Light of Historical Research* (Nasville, TN: Broadman, 4th edn, 1934).

Ropes, J.H., *The Text of Acts*, in Foakes-Jackson and Lake (eds), *The Beginnings of Christianity*, III (1926).

Roth C. (ed.), *Encyclopaedia Judaica* (16 vols; 3rd edn; Jerusalem: Ketev Publishing House, 1974).

Safrai, S., and M. Stern (eds), *The Jewish People in the First Century* (2 vols; I, Philadelphia: Fortress Press, 1974; II, Assen – Amsterdam: Van Gorcum, 1976).

Schneider, G., *Die Apostelgeschichte* (2 vols; Herders Theologische Kommentar zum Neuen Testament; Freiburg: Herder, 1980, 1982).

Scrivener, F.H., *Bezae Codex Cantabrigiensis* (repr.; Pittsburgh, PA: Pickwick Press, 1978).

Singer, I. (ed.), *The Jewish Encyclopaedia* (12 vols; New York: KTAV Publishing House, 1901).

Spencer, F.S., *Acts* (Readings: A New Biblical Commentary; Sheffield: Sheffield Academic Press, 1997).

Strack, H.L., and P. Billerbeck, *Kommentar zum Neuen Testament aus Talmud und Midrasch* (6 vols; München: C.H. Beck, 6th edn, 1974–75).

Swanson, R., *New Testament Greek Manuscripts: Variant Readings Arranged in Horizontal Lines against Codex Vaticanus. The Acts of the Apostles* (Sheffield: Sheffield Academic Press, 1998).

Turner, N., *A Grammar of New Testament Greek*. III. *Syntax*; IV. *Style* (Edinburgh: T&T Clark, 1963, 1976).

Wallace, D.B., *Greek Grammar beyond the Basics* (Grand Rapids: Zondervan Publishing House, 1996).

Winer, G.B., *A Treatise on the Grammar of New Testament Greek* (trans. W.F. Moulton; Edinburgh: T&T Clark, 1882).

Witherington, B., *The Acts of the Apostles: A Socio-Rhetorical Commentary* (Grand Rapids: Eerdmans/Carlisle: Paternoster, 1998).

Zerwick, M., *Biblical Greek* (trans., rev. and ed. J. Smith; Rome: Biblical Institute Press, 1963).

Zerwick, M., and M. Grosvenor, *A Grammatical Analysis of the Greek New Testament* (Rome: Biblical Institute Press, 1981).

II. *Other Works Referred to*

Aland, K., 'Der neutestamentliche Text in der vorkonstantinischen Epoche', in Romero-Pose (ed.), *PLÉROMA. Salus carnis*, pp. 53–79.

Applebaum, S., *Judaea in Hellenistic and Roman Times* (Leiden: E.J. Brill, 1989).

Anderson, R., 'À la recherche de Théophile', in *Saint Luc, évangéliste et historien* (*Dossiers d'Archéologie* 279 [2002–3]), pp. 64–71.

Attridge, H.W., and G. Hata (eds), *Eusebius, Christianity and Judaism* (Leiden: E.J. Brill, 1992).

Avery-Peck, A.J., and J. Neusner (eds), *Judaism in Late Antiquity*. Part 3, *Where We Stand: Issues and Debates in Ancient Judaism*. IV. *The Special Problem of the Synagogue* (Leiden: E.J. Brill, 2001).

Bammel, E, 'Erwägungen zur Eschatologie Jesu', *SE* 3 (1964), pp. 3–32.

Bar-Efrat, S., *Narrative Art in the Bible* (Sheffield: Sheffield Academic Press, 1989; repr. T&T Clark International, 2004).

Barc, B., 'Le texte de la Torah a-t-il été récrit?', in Tardieu (ed.), *Les règles de l'interprétation*, pp. 69–88.

— *Les arpenteurs du temps: Essai sur l'histoire religieuse de la Judée à la période héllenistique* (Lausanne: Éditions du Zèbre, 2000).

Barclay, J.M.G., *Jews in the Mediterranean Diaspora: From Alexander to Trajan (323 BCE – 117 CE)* (Edinburgh: T&T Clark, 1996).

— 'Who was Considered an Apostate?', in Stanton and Stroumsa (eds), *Tolerance and Intolerance in Early Judaism and Christianity*, pp. 80–98.

Beattie, D.R.G., and M.J. McNamara (eds), *The Aramaic Bible: Targums in their Historical Context* (JSOTSup, 166; Sheffield: Sheffield Academic Press, 1994).

Black, M., 'The Holy Spirit in the Western Text of Acts', in Epp and Fee (eds), *New Testament Textual Criticism*, pp. 166–67.

Black, D., and S.H. Levinsohn (eds), *Linguistics and New Testament Interpretation* (Nashville, TN: Broadman Press, 1992).

Boismard, M.-É., 'The Texts of Acts: A Problem of Literary Criticism?', in Epp and Fee (eds), *New Testament Textual Criticism*, pp. 147–57.

Bremer, J. N. (ed.), *The Apocryphal Acts of Paul and Thecla* (Kampen: Kok Pharos, 1996).

Brodie, T.L., 'The Accusing and Stoning of Naboth (I Kgs 21:8-13) as One Component of the Stephen Text (Acts 6:9-14; 7.58a)', *CBQ* 45 (1983), pp. 417–32.

Cadbury, H.J., 'A Possible Perfect in Acts ix.34', *JTS* 49 (1948), 57–58.

Callow, J, 'Constituent Order in Copula Clauses: A Partial Study', in Black and Levinsohn (eds), *Linguistics and New Testament Interpretation*, pp. 68–89.

Carleton Paget, J., 'Jewish Proselytism at the Time of Christian Origins: Chimera or Reality?', *JSNT* 62 (1996), pp. 65–103.

Chilton, B., *The Aramaic Bible*, vol. II: *The Isaiah Targum: Introduction, Translation, Apparatus, Notes* (Edinburgh: T&T Clark, 1987).

— 'Aramaic and Targumic Antecedents of Pauline Justification', in Beattie and McNamara (eds), *The Aramaic Bible*, pp. 379–97.

Collins, J.J., *Jewish Identity in the Hellenistic Diaspora* (Grand Rapids: Eerdmans, 2nd edn, 2000).

Conybeare, F., 'The Commentary of Ephrem on Acts', in Ropes, *Text*, pp. 373–453.

Crehan, J., 'Peter According to the D-text of Acts', *Theological Studies* 18 (1957), pp. 596–603.

Crown, A.D. (ed.), *The Samaritans* (Tübingen: J.C.B. Mohr [Paul Siebeck], 1989).

Czachesz, I., 'The Acts of Paul and the Western Text of Luke's Acts: Paul between Canon and Apocrypha', in Bremer (ed.), *The Apocryphal Acts of Paul and Thecla*, pp. 106–25.

Daube, D., *The Exodus Pattern in the Bible* (London: Faber and Faber, 1963).

— *Ancient Jewish Law* (Leiden: E.J. Brill, 1981).

De Boer, M.C., 'The Nazoreans: Living at the Boundary of Judaism and Christianity', in Stanton and Stroumsa (eds), *Tolerance and Intolerance in Early Judaism and Christianity*, pp. 239–62.

Delebecque, É., 'Saul et Luc avant le premier voyage missionaire', *Rev. Sc. ph. th.* 66 (1982), pp. 551–59.

Dexinger, F., 'Samaritan Eschatology', in Crown (ed.), *The Samaritans*, pp. 266–92.

Dietrich, W., *Das Petrusbild in der lukanischen Schriften* (Stuttgart: W. Kohlhammer, 1972).

Dunn, J.D.G., *The Partings of the Ways Between Christianity and Judaism and their Significance for the Character of Christianity* (London: SCM Press, 1991, repr. 1996).

Dupont, J., 'Pierre délivré de prison (Acts 12.1-11)', in *idem*, *Nouvelles études sur les Actes des Apôtres* (Lectio Divina, 118; Paris: Cerf, 1984), pp. 329–42.

Enns, P., *Exodus Retold: Ancient Exegesis of the Departure from Egypt in Wis 10:15-21 and 19:1-9* (Harvard Semitic Museum Monographs, 57; Atlanta: Scholars Press, 1997).

Epp, E.J., *The Theological Tendency of Codex Bezae Cantabrigiensis in Acts* (Cambridge: Cambridge University Press, 1966).

Epp, E.J., and G. D. Fee, (eds), *New Testament Textual Criticism* (Oxford: Clarendon, 1981).

Feldman, L.H., 'Palestinian and Diaspora Judaism in the First Century', in Shanks (ed.), *Christianity and Rabbinic Judaism*, pp. 1–40.

Fishbane, M., *Biblical Interpretation in Ancient Israel* (Oxford: Clarendon Press, 1987).

Flemington, W., *The New Testament Doctrine of Baptism* (London: SPCK, 1957).

Flesher, P.V.M., 'Prolegomenon to a Theory of Early Synagogue Development', in Avery-Peck and Neusner (eds), IV, *The Special Problem of the Synagogue*, pp. 121–53.

Frankel E., and B.P. Teutsch (eds), *The Encylopaedia of Jewish Symbols* (Northvale, N.J.: Jason Aronson Inc., 1995).

Garrard, A., *The Splendour of the Temple* (Eye, Suffolk: Moat Farm Publications, 1997).

Ginzberg, L., *The Legends of the Jews* (7 vols; Philadelphia: The Jewish Publication Society of America, 11th edn, 1982).

González Echegaray, J., *Arqueología y evangelios* (Estella, Navarra: Verbo Divino, 2nd edn, 1999).

Goodman, M., *The Ruling Class of Judaea. The Origins of the Jewish Revolt against Rome AD 66-70* (Cambridge: Cambridge University Press, 1987).

Grant, M., *The Jews in the Roman World* (London: Weidenfeld and Nicolson, 1973).

Hamm, D., 'The Tamid Service in Luke-Acts: The Cultic Background behind Luke's Theology of Worship (Luke 1:5-25; 18:9, 14; 24:50-53; Acts 3:1; 10:3, 30), *CBQ* 65 (2003), pp. 215–31.

— 'Praying "Regularly" (not "Constantly"): A Note on the Cultic Background of διά παντός at Luke 24.53; Acts 10.2, and Heb. 9.6; 13.15', *ExpT* 116 (2004), pp. 50–52.

Harl M. (ed.), *La Bible d'Alexandrie* (5 vols; Paris: Cerf, 1986–94).

—*La Genèse*, in *idem* (ed.), *La Bible d'Alexandrie*, I (Paris: Cerf, 1986).

Harlé, P., and D. Pralon, *Le Lévitique*, in Harl (ed.) *La Bible d'Alexandrie*, III (Paris: Cerf, 1988).

Harrington, D.J., and A.J. Saldarim (Introduction, Translation and Notes), in K. Cathcart, M. Maher and M. McNamara (eds), *Targum Jonathan of the Former Prophets. The Aramaic Bible: The Targums* (Edinburgh: T&T Clark, 1987).

Hengel, M., *The 'Hellenization' of Judaea in the First Century after Christ* (London: SCM, 1989).

Hill, C.C., *Hellenists and Hebrews: Reappraising Division within the Earliest Church* (Minneapolis: Augsburg, 1992).

Hur, J., *A Dynamic Reading of the Holy Spirit in Luke-Acts* (JSNTSup, 211; Sheffield: Sheffield Academic Press, 2001).

Kilgallen, J., *The Stephen Speech: A Literary and Redactional Study of Acts 7.2-53* (Rome: Biblical Institute Press, 1976).

Klawans, J., 'Concepts of Purity in the Bible', *Jewish Study Bible*, pp. 2041–47

Kugel, J.L., *Traditions of the Bible. A Guide to the Bible as it was at the Start of the Common Era* (Cambridge, MA.: Harvard University Press, 1998).

Kuhli, H., 'Ναζωραῖος', in *EWNT*, II, cols. 1117–21.

Lake, K., and H.J. Cadbury, *English Translation and Commentary*, in Foakes-Jackson and Lake (eds), *Beginnings of Christianity*, IV.

Le Boulluec, A., and P. Sandevoir, *L'Exode* in Harl (ed.) *La Bible d'Alexandrie*. II (Paris: Cerf, 1989).

Le Déaut, R., *La nuit pascale* (Rome: Biblical Institute Press, 1963).

Levey, S.H., *The Aramaic* Bible. XIII. The *Ezekiel Targum: Introduction, Translation, Apparatus, Notes* (Edinburgh: T&T Clark, 1987).

Levinskaya I., *The Book of Acts in Its Diaspora Setting*, in Winter (series ed.), *The Book of Acts in its First Century Setting*, V (1996), pp. 51–126.

Levinsohn, S.H., 'Towards a Unified Linguistic Description of οὗτος and ἐκεῖνος' (*SBL Seminar Papers 2003*; K.H. Richards [ed.]; Atlanta: Scholars Press, 2003).

Mann, J., *The Bible as Read and Preached in the Old Synagogue*, I (New York: KTAV, 1940; 2nd edn, 1971).

Marshall, I.H., 'Apg 12 – ein Schlüssel zum Verstandnis der Apostelgeschichte', in Thiede (ed.), *Das Petrusbild in der neueren Forschung*, pp. 192–220.

Mattingly, H.B., 'The Origin of the Name Christiani', *JTS* NS 9 (1958), pp. 26–37.

Menoud, P.H., 'The Western Text and the Theology of Acts', *SNTS Bulletin* 2 (1951), pp. 19–32.

Menzies, R.P., *The Development of Early Christian Pneumatology with Special Reference to Luke-Acts* (JSNTSup, 54; Sheffield: JSOT Press, 1991).

Nicklas, T., and M. Tilly (eds), *Apostelgeschichte als Kirchengeschichte. Text, Traditionen und antike Auslegungen* (BZNW, 122: Berlin-New York: Walter de Gruyter, 2003).

Overman, J.A., and R.S. MacLennan (eds), *Diaspora Jews and Judaism* (Atlanta: Scholars Press, 1992).

Paget, J.C., 'Jewish Proselytism at the Time of Christian Origins: Chimera or Reality', *JSNT* 62 (1996), pp. 65–103.

Parker, D.C., and C.-B. Amphoux (eds), *Codex Bezae: Studies from the Lunel Colloquium June 1994* (Leiden: Brill, 1996).

Parry, D.T.N., 'Release of the Captives: Reflections on Acts 12', in Tuckett (ed.), *Luke's Literary Achievement*, pp. 156–64.

Patte, D., *Early Jewish Hermeneutic* (Dissertation Series, 22; Richmond, VA: SBL, 1975).

Perowne, S., *The Life and Times of Herod the Great* (London: Arrow Books, 1960).

Perrot, C., 'Un fragment christo-palestinien découvert à Khirbet-Mird (Actes des Apôtres, X, 28-29, 32-41)', *RB* 70 (1963), pp. 506–55.

Petersen, W.L., 'Eusebius and the Paschal Controversy', in Attridge and Hata (eds), *Eusebius, Christianity and Judaism*, pp. 313–17.

Pierri, R. (ed.), *Grammatica Intellectio Scripturae: Saggi filologici di Greco biblico* (forthcoming).

Pope, R. (ed.), *Honouring the Past and Shaping the Future: Religious and Biblical Studies in Wales* (Leominster: Gracewing, 2003).

Porter, S.E., *Verbal Aspect in the Greek of New Testament, with Reference to Sense and Mood* (Studies in Biblical Greek, I; New York: Peter Lang, 1989).

Puigdollers i Noblom, R., 'Els grans sacerdots jueus des de l'època d'Herodes el Gran fins a la guerra jueva', *RCatT* 30 (2005), pp. 49–89.

Radday, Y.T., 'Chiasmus in Biblical Hebrew Poetry', in Welch (ed.), *Chiasmus in Antiquity*, pp. 50–117.

Read-Heimerdinger, J., 'La foi de l'eunuque éthiopien: le problème textuel de Actes 8:37', *Etudes Théologiques et Religieuses* 4 (1988), pp. 521–28.

— 'Acts 8:37: A Textual and Exegetical Study', *The Bulletin of the Institute for Reformation Biblical Studies* 2 (1991), pp. 8–13.

— 'Barnabas in Acts: A Study of his Role in the Text of Codex Bezae', *JSNT* 72 (1998), pp. 23–66.

— 'Les Actes des Apôtres dans le Codex de Bèze: leur intérêt et leur valeur', in *Saint Luc, évangéliste et historien* (*Dossiers d'Archéologie* 279 [2002–3]), pp. 44–55.

— 'The Re-Enactment of the History of Israel: Exodus Traditions in the Bezan Text of Acts', in Pope (ed.), *Remembering the Past and Shaping the Future*, pp. 81–96.

— 'Luke's Use of ὡς and ὡσεί: Comparison and Correspondence as a Means to Convey His Message', in Pierri (ed.), *Grammatica Intellectio Scripturae (*forthcoming).

— 'Tracking of Participants: The Use of the Third Person Pronoun in Acts', *RCatT* 31 (2006).

Read-Heimerdinger, J., and J. Rius-Camps, 'Emmaous or Oulammaous? Luke's Use of the Jewish Scriptures in the Text of Luke in Codex Bezae', *RCatT* 27 (2002), pp. 23–42.

Richard, E., 'The Polemical Character of the Joseph Episode in Acts 7', *JBL* 98 (1979), pp. 255–67.

Rius-Camps, J., 'Qui és Joan, l'anomenat "Marc"?', *RCatT* 5 (1980), pp. 297–329.

— 'L'aparició/desaparició del "nosaltres" en el llibre dels Fets: un simple procediment teològico-literari?', *RCatT* 6 (1981), pp. 35–75.

— 'Lk 10,25–18,30: Una perfecta estructura concèntrica dins la Secció del Viatge (9,51–19,46)', *RCatT* 8 (1983), pp. 283–358.

— 'Estructura i funció significativa del tercer cicle o Secció de les Recognicions (Lc 6,12–9,50)', *RCatT* 9 (1984), pp. 269–329.

— *El camino de Pablo a la misión de los paganos. Comentario lingüístico y exegético a Hch 13–28* (Madrid: Cristiandad, 1984).

— 'Ignacio de Antioquía, ¿testigo ocular de la muerte y resurrección de Jesús?', *Bib.* 70 (1989), pp. 449–72.

— 'El καὶ αὐτός en los encabezamientos lucanos, ¿una fórmula anafórica?, *FN* 2 (1989), pp. 187–92.

— *De Jerusalén a Antioquía: Génesis de la iglesia cristiana. Comentario lingüístico y exegético a Hch 1–12* (Córdoba: El Almendro, 1989).

— 'Le substrat grec de la version latine des Actes dans le Codex de Bèze', in Parker and Amphoux (eds), *Codex Bezae*, pp. 271–95.

— 'Une lecture différente de l'œuvre de Luc', in *Saint Luc, évangéliste et historien* (*Dossiers d'Archéologie* 279 [2002–3]), pp. 56–63.

— 'The Gradual Awakening of Paul's Awareness of his Mission to the Gentiles', in Nicklas and Tilly (eds), *Apostelgeschichte als Kirchengeschichte*, pp. 281–96.

— '"Nazareno" y "Nazoreo", con especial atención al Códice Bezae', in Pierri (ed.), *Grammatica Intellectio Scripturae* (forthcoming).

Rius-Camps, J., and J. Read-Heimerdinger, 'After the Death of Judas: A Reconsideration of the Status of the Twelve Apostles', *RCatT* 29 (2004), pp. 305–34.

Romero-Pose, E. (ed.), *PLÉROMA. Salus carnis* (Santiago de Compostela: Publicaciones Compostellanum, 1990).

Rowe C.K., 'Luke-Acts and the Imperial Cult: A Way through the Conundrum?', *JSNT* 27 (2005), pp. 279–300.

Sacks, J., *Crisis and Covenant* (Manchester: Manchester University Press, 1992).

Schiffman, L.H., *Who Was a Jew?* (Hoboken, NJ: KTAV, 1985).

Schmidt, F., *How the Temple Thinks. Identity and Social Cohesion in Ancient Judaism* (E.T.: J.E. Crowley; The Biblical Seminar 78; Sheffield: Sheffield Academic Press, 2001).

Schürer, E., *The History of the Jewish people in the Age of Jesus Christ* (3 vols; rev. and ed. G. Vermes, F. Millar and M. Black; Edinburgh: T&T Clark, 1973).

Selwyn E.C., 'The Carefulness of Luke. 2. Peter's Conversion', *The Expositor* 7/10 (1910), pp. 449–63.

Shanks. H., (ed.), *Christianity and Rabbinic Judaism* (London: SPCK, 1993).

Simon, M., and A. Benoit, *Le Judaisme et le Christianisme antique d'Antiochus à Constantin* (Nouvelle Clio, l'histoire et ses problèmes, 10; Paris: PUF, 1968).

Smallwood, E.M., *The Jews under Roman Rule: From Pompey to Diocletian* (Leiden: E.J. Brill, 1976).

Spencer, F.S., *The Portrait of Philip in Acts: A Study of Roles and Relations* (Sheffield: JSOT Press, 1992).

— 'Neglected Widows in Acts 6.1-7', *CBQ* 56 (1994), pp. 715–33.

Stamford, T., 'The Neglected Widows: Were They Stinted or Snubbed? An Examination of the Literary Evidence' (paper presented to the British New Testament Conference, 2001).

Stanton, G.N., and G.G. Stroumsa (eds), *Tolerance and Intolerance in Early Judaism and Christianity* (Cambridge: Cambridge University Press, 1998).

Strobel, A., 'Passa-Symbolik und Passa-Wunder in Act. XII.3ff', *NTS* 4 (1957–58), pp. 210–15.

Strom, M.R., 'An Old Testament Background to Acts 12.20-23', *NTS* 32 (1986), pp. 289–92.

Tardieu, M., (ed.), *Les règles de l'interprétation* (Paris; Cerf, 1987).

Taylor, J., 'Why Did Paul Persecute the Church?', in Stanton and Stroumsa (eds), *Tolerance and Intolerance in Early Judaism and Christianity*, pp. 99–120.

Thiede, C.P., *Das Petrusbild in der neueren Forschung* (Wuppertal: Brockhaus, 1987).

Thrall, M.E., 'Paul of Tarsus: a Hellenistic Jew', in Pope (ed.), *Honouring the Past and Shaping the Future*, pp. 97–111.

Tuckett, C.M. (ed.), *Luke's Literary Achievement: Collected Essays* (JSNTSup, 116; Sheffield: Sheffield Academic Press, 1995).

Turner, M.M.B., *Power from on High: The Spirit in Israel's Restoration and Witness in Luke-Acts* (JPTSup, 9; Sheffield: JSOT Press, 1996).

Vermes, G., *Jesus the Jew* (London: SCM, 1973).

Welch, J. W., *Chiasmus in Antiquity* (Hildesheim: Gerstenberg, 1981).

Wilcox, M., 'The Promise of the "Seed" in the New Testament and the Targumim', *JSNT* 5 (1979), pp. 275–93.

Wilson, S.G., 'Law and Judaism in Acts' (*SBL Seminar Papers*, 1976), pp. 251-65.

Windisch, H., 'Die Christusepiphanie vor Damaskus (Acts 9:22 und 26) und ihre religionsge-schichtliche Parallelen', *ZNW* 31 (1932), pp. 1–23.

Winter, B., (series ed.), *The Book of Acts in its First Century Setting* (6 vols; Grand Rapids: Eerdmans, 1994–98).

Wright, N.T., *What Saint Paul Really Said: Was Paul of Tarsus the Real Founder of Christianity?* (Oxford: Lion, 1997).